The University of Law

This book must be returned to the library on or before the last date
stamped below. Failure to do so will result in a fine.

Bloomsbury Library
T: 01483 216387
library-bloomsbury@law.ac.uk

Moorgate Library
T: 01483 216371
library-moorgate@law.ac.uk

PARLIAMENT AND THE LAW

Parliament and the Law (Second Edition) is an edited collection of essays, supported by the UK's Study of Parliament Group, including contributions by leading constitutional lawyers, political scientists and parliamentary officials. It provides a wide-ranging overview of the ways in which the law applies to, and impacts upon, the UK Parliament, and it considers how recent changes to the UK's constitutional arrangements have affected Parliament as an institution. It includes authoritative discussion of a number of issues of topical concern, such as: the operation of parliamentary privilege, the powers of Parliament's select committees, parliamentary scrutiny, devolution, English Votes for English Laws, Members' conduct and the governance of both Houses. It also contains chapters on financial scrutiny, parliamentary sovereignty, Parliament and human rights, and the administration of justice. Aimed mainly at legal academics, practitioners, and political scientists, it will also be of interest to anyone who is curious about the many fascinating ways in which the law interacts with and influences the work, the constitutional status and the procedural arrangements of the Westminster Parliament.

Volume 8 in the series Hart Studies in Constitutional Law

Hart Studies in Constitutional Law

Parliament and the Law

Second Edition

Edited by
Alexander Horne and Gavin Drewry

·H A R T·
PUBLISHING
OXFORD AND PORTLAND, OREGON
2018

Hart Publishing

An imprint of Bloomsbury Publishing Plc

Hart Publishing Ltd	Bloomsbury Publishing Plc
Kemp House	50 Bedford Square
Chawley Park	London
Cumnor Hill	WC1B 3DP
Oxford OX2 9PH	UK
UK	

www.hartpub.co.uk
www.bloomsbury.com

Published in North America (US and Canada) by
Hart Publishing
c/o International Specialized Book Services
920 NE 58th Avenue, Suite 300
Portland, OR 97213-3786
USA

www.isbs.com

HART PUBLISHING, the Hart/Stag logo, BLOOMSBURY and the
Diana logo are trademarks of Bloomsbury Publishing Plc

This edition published 2018

First edition 2013

British Library Cataloguing-in-Publication Data

A catalogue record for this book is available from the British Library.

ISBN:	HB:	978-1-50990-871-4
	ePDF:	978-1-50990-873-8
	ePub:	978-1-50990-872-1

Library of Congress Cataloging-in-Publication Data

Names: Horne, Alexander, editor. | Drewry, Gavin, editor.

Title: Parliament and the law / edited by Alexander Horne and Gavin Drewry

Description: [Second edition]. | Oxford ; Portland, Oregon : Hart Publishing, 2018. |
Series: Hart studies in constitutional law | Includes bibliographical references and index.

Identifiers: LCCN 2017050496 (print) | LCCN 2017051675 (ebook) |
ISBN 9781509908721 (Epub) | ISBN 9781509908714 (hardback : alk. paper)

Subjects: LCSH: Great Britain. Parliament—Powers and duties. | Great Britain. Parliament—Privileges
and immunities. | Legislative power—Great Britain.

Classification: LCC KD4210 (ebook) | LCC KD4210 .P369 2018 (print) | DDC 342.41/052—dc23

LC record available at https://lccn.loc.gov/2017050496

Typeset by Compuscript Ltd, Shannon
Printed and bound in Great Britain by CPI Group (UK) Ltd, Croydon CR0 4YY

To find out more about our authors and books visit www.hartpublishing.co.uk. Here you will find extracts,
author information, details of forthcoming events and the option to sign up for our newsletters.

Foreword

I'm delighted to have been asked to write this foreword to the new edition of *Parliament and the Law*. Its publication is particularly timely, as there is an unusual degree of public interest in, and focus on, Parliament's law-making powers at present.

The previous edition of this work came out in the wake of the members' expenses scandal and the resulting legislation. If the times seemed difficult then, they were nothing to the difficulties Parliament is facing now. The *Miller*[1] litigation, heard in the autumn of 2016, focused attention on the role of Parliament in the UK constitution, and individual parliamentarians were to be found vehemently expressing views both in favour and against requiring legislation before notice of withdrawal could be given under Article 50 of the Treaty.

At the time of writing, there are 18 months remaining until the expiry of the notice given under Article 50 in March 2017, and the House of Commons has just begun to debate the European Union (Withdrawal) Bill. It would take a braver writer than I to predict the eventual form that the Bill will take when it reaches Royal Assent.

We are promised a wide range of legislation relating to the UK's departure from the European Union. In addition to the Withdrawal Bill, the Government will be bringing forward major pieces of legislation on immigration, customs and international sanctions. This legislative programme is to be carried out by a minority government, supported by a confidence and supply agreement with the Democratic Unionist Party. That adds an unusual degree of unpredictability to proceedings in Parliament.

There is also a high level of interest in the secondary legislation that is likely to be made in exercise of the powers conferred by the Withdrawal Bill. This is likely to focus unwonted attention on the work of the Joint Committee on Statutory Instruments, an area which has historically had relatively little attention from the public or the media. It is not that it is unusual for significant changes to the law to be made by statutory instrument, but the process has tended to take place below the radar. It remains to be seen whether parliamentarians will consider that the technical scrutiny carried out by the Committee is sufficient for the Brexit legislation, or whether the Bill will be amended to provide for additional or alternative scrutiny.

Leaving Brexit aside, Parliament faces challenges closer to home over the next few years. The parlous state of the Palace of Westminster—riddled with asbestos,

---

[1] *R (on the application of Miller and another) v Secretary of State for Exiting the European Union* [2017] UKSC 5.

at risk of a second catastrophic fire on the scale of the one which devastated the old Palace in 1834, and supplied with services that are wholly inadequate to the twenty-first century—is well-documented, and a decision has yet to be taken on the repair works. The way forward may be somewhat clearer by the time the next edition of this work is published.

In this uncertain context, the essays in this volume will be an invaluable resource for academics and practitioners. Knowledge of the law relating to Parliament, and the way in which its procedures operate, is less widespread even among lawyers than it deserves to be. I hope that this work is widely read.

Saira Salimi
Speaker's Counsel
September 2017

Summary Contents

Detailed Contents

Part 4: Rights, Justice and Scrutiny

List of Contributors

Megan Conway has worked for the House of Lords in a variety of legislative and committee roles, having previously studied Social and Political Sciences at the University of Cambridge. She was the Lords Clerk to the Joint Committee on Human Rights from 2013 to 16.

Gavin Drewry is Emeritus Professor of Public Administration at Royal Holloway, University of London and an Honorary Professor in the Faculty of Laws at UCL. He is a Fellow of the Academy of Social Sciences and a former Chair of the Study of Parliament Group. He has written extensively on many aspects of politics and public administration, particularly on Parliament and the legislative process and on legal institutions.

Paul Evans is the Clerk of Committees in the House of Commons. Previously he has been Clerk of the Journals and Principal Clerk of the Table Office, and has worked in the House service since 1981. The eighth edition of his *Handbook of House of Commons Procedure* was published in 2012 (Dod's Parliamentary Publishing), and he has contributed chapters to a number of books published under the auspices of the Study of Parliament Group and elsewhere. He has edited *A History of Parliamentary Procedure: Essays in honour of Thomas Erskine May*, which will be published by Hart in 2017.

Oonagh Gay is a retired member of the House of Commons service. She was co-editor of the Study of Parliament volume *Conduct Unbecoming: The Regulation of Parliamentary Behaviour* (Politico's, 2004), and a contributor to *Parliament: Legislation and Accountability* (Hart, 2016). She is a former Chair of the Study of Parliament Group, and former head of the Parliament and Constitution Centre, House of Commons Library. She received an OBE for services to Parliament in 2014.

Matthew Hamlyn is Principal Clerk of the Overseas Office, House of Commons, and was previously Head of the Office of the Chief Executive and Clerk of Bills. In 2009–10 he managed the project to transfer responsibility for Members' expenses and salaries from the House to the Independent Parliamentary Standards Authority.

Alexander Horne was called to the Bar by Lincoln's Inn in 1999. He has worked as an employed barrister in Parliament since 2003 and is currently Legal Adviser to the House of Lords European Union Committee. In the 2015–17 Parliament he was Deputy Legal Adviser to the Joint Committee on Human Rights. Alexander is also an honorary lecturer at UCL. He is co-editor of *Parliament: Legislation and Accountability* (Hart, 2016).

Dr Christopher Johnson has worked for the House of Lords since 1999, having previously taught English literature at St Catherine's College, Oxford, and St Stephen's College, Delhi. He was Clerk of the Journals in the House of Lords from 2007 to 2013, and since 2014 has been Principal Clerk of the European Union Committee.

Richard Kelly is a Senior Researcher at the Parliament and Constitution Centre in the House of Commons Library.

Dr Phil Larkin is Adjunct Associate Professor of Public Policy in the Institute for Governance and Policy Analysis at the University of Canberra. He has published on legislatures, political parties and British and Australian politics. He has also worked on committees in both the House of Commons and the Australian Senate.

Liam Laurence Smyth has been a House of Commons Clerk since 1977. He is now Clerk of Legislation.

Colin Lee is a Principal Clerk in the House of Commons, and has served as a Clerk for more than 28 years. He is the author of various articles and contributions to books on the historical development of parliamentary procedure and on financial procedure. He is Chair of the Study of Parliament Group.

Lucinda Maer is Head of the Parliament and Constitution Centre in the House of Commons Library and a member of the Executive Committee of the Study of Parliament Group.

Philip Norton (Lord Norton of Louth) is Professor of Government and Director of the Centre for Legislative Studies at the University of Hull. He was elevated to the peerage in 1998. He is a member of the House of Lords Select Committee on the Constitution and served as the first Chairman of the Committee when it was appointed in 2001.

Dawn Oliver, FBA QC (Hon) is Emeritus Professor of Constitutional Law, UCL. She was President of the Study of Parliament Group from 2010 to 2015.

Sir Paul Silk was Chair of the Commission on Devolution to Wales between 2011 and 2014. He spent most of his career as a Clerk in the House of Commons, but was Clerk of the National Assembly for Wales from 2001 to 2006, He is currently President of the Study of Parliament Group. He was appointed KCB in 2015 and is a Fellow of the Learned Society of Wales.

Dr Jack Simson Caird is a constitutional law specialist in the Parliament and Constitution Centre in the House of Commons Library. Jack is a research fellow at the University of Bristol. Prior to joining the House of Commons in 2015 Jack was a lecturer in public law at the University of Sussex.

Dr Adam Tucker is Senior Lecturer in the School of Law and Social Justice, University of Liverpool.

Dr Ben Yong is a lecturer in law at the University of Hull.

1

Introduction

ALEXANDER HORNE AND GAVIN DREWRY

THE GENESIS OF the *Parliament and the Law* project was a discussion between Dawn Oliver and the two current editors at the Study of Parliament Group's (SPG) annual conference at Worcester College, University of Oxford, in January 2011.

For those unfamiliar with the work of the SPG, it was originally founded in 1964 by the distinguished political scientist, Bernard Crick, and the senior House of Commons Clerk, Michael Ryle, as a forum in which scholars and officers of the two Houses of Parliament could meet to discuss (under the Chatham House rule) matters of mutual interest to do with parliamentary practice and reform. The SPG is a registered charity: as its name suggests, its core remit is the study of parliaments and parliamentary assemblies, though in practice its interests range much more widely than this, encompassing the broad agenda of government and politics and constitutional reform. It has, over more than 50 years since it was first established, published extensively in books, articles, its own series of papers, and in evidence by its academic members to parliamentary select committees. In 2017, the SPG is still going strong, with over 200 members and a website (www. studyofparliament.org.uk) where various lectures and papers are published. In addition to political scientists and parliamentary officials, the SPG also includes a number of prominent constitutional lawyers. Contributors to this book include members from each of these categories.

How did the present project begin? In 1998, the SPG had commissioned the publication of a collection of essays, entitled *The Law and Parliament* from Dawn Oliver and Gavin Drewry. This book formed part of Butterworth's *Law in Context* series. By 2011, the time seemed ripe to revisit the subject. Matters had moved on significantly—in particular, the parliamentary expenses scandal of 2009 had resulted in a new interest in issues relating to parliamentary privilege, freedom of information and Members' conduct. Accordingly, the first edition of *Parliament and the Law*, edited by Alexander Horne, Gavin Drewry and Dawn Oliver, was published by Hart as part of its *Studies in Constitutional Law* series in 2013. Both books also considered many other thought-provoking issues of the day, including devolution, human rights, sovereignty and wider issues around accountability and modernisation of Parliament. As noted below, events have continued to move, and are still moving—to an extent and in directions that could not realistically have been foreseen when the first edition was commissioned.

What kind of book is this? As with the previous editions, it is important to note at the outset that it is neither a textbook, nor a comprehensive guide to Parliament, nor indeed is it a treatise on the law-making process. The book's title, containing the usefully versatile conjunction 'and', was carefully chosen to facilitate both flexibility and eclecticism—in approach and in content. Had we, for instance, used a form of words suggestive of a focus on the law 'of' Parliament, we would inevitably have found ourselves trespassing on the well-established territory of the hugely authoritative *Erskine May on Parliamentary Practice* (London, Lexis Nexis, 2011), now in its 24th edition and frequently cited in this volume. Two well-regarded textbooks on Parliament and the legislative process that may also be of particular interest to our readers are Robert Rogers and Rhodri Walters, *How Parliament Works*[1] and Michael Zander, *The Law Making Process*.[2] The present collection of essays offers expert commentary, on a range of subjects pertaining to Parliament and the law, written from a variety of different perspectives. It is designed as a collaborative and multi-disciplinary work, containing contributions from insiders including lawyers, Clerks and researchers from the House of Commons Parliament and Constitution Centre (based in the House of Commons Library) and critical academic perspectives.

Our book is therefore quite different from and is intended to be complementary to other works like those mentioned above. Like its predecessors, it examines issues that are at the heart of concerns and debates about constitutional reform. It provides a wide-ranging overview of the ways in which the law applies to Parliament and considers how changes to our constitutional arrangements have impacted on Parliament as an institution.

This new edition of our book also follows on swiftly from a complementary title in Hart's *Studies in Constitutional Law* series: Alexander Horne and Andrew Le Sueur, *Parliament: Legislation and Accountability* (2016). That title contained two chapters on the relationship between the UK Parliament and European Union law and a significant amount of material on legislative scrutiny. This explains the omission from the present volume of specific chapters on these important and topical subjects.

The law in this field is fast-moving. Much changed between 1998 and 2013. And the editors of this new edition have again faced the challenge of accounting for further, significant, constitutional change, including: the Scottish referendum of 2014; 'Brexit'; and the unexpected election of 2017. As a consequence, while seven of the chapters in this volume essentially update chapters in the original work (namely the chapters on parliamentary privilege; Members' conduct; select committee powers; Devolution; Parliament and human rights; parliamentary

---

[1] 7th edn (London, Routledge, 2015).
[2] 7th edn (Oxford, Hart, 2015).

sovereignty; and, Parliament and the administration of justice); there are also six substantively new chapters on issues of current concern: the governance of Parliament; the relationships between the Houses; English Votes for English Laws (EVEL); Parliament and public legal information; financial control; and parliamentary scrutiny of delegated legislation.

We faced a particular editorial dilemma about what to do about the implications of Brexit, the dauntingly complex and rapidly shifting ramifications of which remain unresolved even as we are writing this Introduction. After much reflection, we came reluctantly to the conclusion that it would be imprudent and impracticable to commission a chapter, or chapters, on Brexit that would, perforce, be shooting at a constantly moving target—and that would inevitably have been overtaken by events by the time that the book went to press. But, at the same time, we could hardly ignore such a high-profile subject that raises so many key constitutional issues about parliamentary sovereignty and the legislative process. So we have encouraged all our contributors to refer in their chapters to any particularly pertinent Brexit-related events and issues, including matters relevantly pertaining to it (such as the *Miller* litigation). As can be seen from the index, there are many such references, scattered throughout the book. The editors of a third edition, a few years hence, may be in a position to tackle the subject more directly, but for the time being we must refer our readers to the continuing flow of blogs, articles and books about Brexit—of which there has been a super-abundance.

Although the chapters should be seen as self-standing essays, they have been cross-referenced where the editors thought that this would be of assistance to readers. The book has been divided into four substantive parts. The first part: 'Privilege, Exclusive Cognisance and Conduct' considers how the law (and other rules) apply to both Houses and contains chapters on the operation of parliamentary privilege and the conduct of Members (including electoral offences, lobbying, expenses, and parliamentary standards).

The second part of the book 'Select Committees and Internal Arrangements' also focuses on internal issues relating to Parliament. It includes chapters on the governance of the Houses; select committee powers and functions; relations between the two Houses; and, public legal information and law making in Parliament.

Part three of the book, 'Devolution and the English Question', contains two chapters looking at complementary matters: how devolution impacts on the UK Parliament and the introduction of a process for EVEL which was utilised in the 2015–17 Parliament. The former has become increasingly important following the referendum on Scottish independence in September 2014. It is rather too early to say what the consequences of Brexit and the 2017 election will be on these two subjects; but we envisage that (as both John McEldowney and Sir Paul Silk have dryly observed) 'the devolution settlement will inevitably continue to evolve'.

The final part of the book 'Rights, Justice and Scrutiny' is wide-ranging and encompasses essays on Parliament and human rights (which focuses on the effectiveness of one of Parliament's watchdog committees, the Joint Committee on Human Rights); parliamentary sovereignty, Parliament's responsibility for the administration of justice (at a time where we have seen three Lord Chancellors in three years); the difficult question of the effectiveness of Parliament's financial scrutiny of the Government; and, Parliament's role in scrutinising delegated legislation (a subject which is likely to prove particularly challenging following Brexit).

The editors have benefited from the kind and invaluable assistance of many members of the SPG—both as contributors and when editing the various chapters. We offer our thanks to all the colleagues who helped us with this task. Particular thanks is owed to Dawn Oliver, who was a previous editor of the original SPG volumes, and Jeff King, both of whom offered invaluable help in getting the project off the ground. We would also like to thank the UK Constitutional Law Group which assisted in organising a joint round table event with the SPG in February 2017, where a number of our authors presented draft papers which eventually became chapters in this volume. Finally, we would like to thank Bill Asquith, Francesca Sancarlo, Anne Flegel and Vicki Hillyard at Hart Publishing for their assistance and support throughout this project.

As with the previous edition, all the royalties from this book will be donated to the SPG to help fund further study of and research into methods of government through Parliament.

Part 1

Privilege, Exclusive Cognisance and Conduct

2

Privilege, Exclusive Cognisance and the Law

PAUL EVANS[1]

I. INTRODUCTION: ROOTS AND PURPOSES

A WEIGHTY BUT populist guide to Parliament, undated but clearly published around the turn of the nineteenth and twentieth centuries, had this to say about parliamentary privilege:

> What exactly constitutes parliamentary privilege it would be difficult to say. For centuries, controversy has raged over the question without a definite understanding being reached as to the limits to which the strong arm of the House may extend in cases where it considers that offence has been given. As we shall show, at different periods a singularly wide range has been given to this doctrine … The House has elected to be its own interpreter of its prerogatives, and naturally in such circumstances they have varied with the changing conditions and sentiments of the times. Selden, the great Parliamentarian of the Civil War period, once said: 'Parliament men are as great princes as any in the world. Whatsoever they please is privilege of Parliament; whatsoever they dislike is breach of privilege'. That shrewd description aptly describes the position in his day, and it still to a certain extent applies. In these broad outlines the rights and powers of the House are understood; but he would be a clever constitutionalist who could say absolutely where they begin and where they end.[2]

This state of puzzlement has a long pedigree: the seventeenth-century jurist, Sir Edward Coke, in his survey of the English common law first published in 1628, referred to the law and custom of Parliament as 'ab omnibus quaeranda, a multis ignoranda, a paucis cognita'.[3]

---

[1] This chapter draws extensively on the chapter written by Liam Laurence Smyth for the first edition of this work (Oxford, Hart, 2013), and also on Eve Samson's chapter in P Evans (ed) *A History of Parliamentary Procedure: Essays in honour of Thomas Erskine May* (Oxford, Hart, 2017).

[2] A Wright and P Smith, *Parliament Past and Present* (London, Hutchinson & Co). According to the British Library catalogue it was deposited in 1902–03.

[3] Asked after by everyone, unknown to many, understood by few. E Coke, *The first part of the Institutes of the lawes of England. Or, A commentarie vpon Littleton, not the name of a lawyer onely, but of the law it selfe* (London, 1629), fo 11v (book 1, ch 1, s 3). Coke uses a similar phrase at fo 110, book 2, ch 10, s 164 where it is apparently attributed to the Parliament Rolls. Coke's main discussion of Parliament is in the fourth part of the Institutes, published in 1644, where he devotes the first 52 pages to it, much more attention than is given to any other 'court'.

The concept of privilege, that is some collection of immunities and privileges attaching both to the legislature and to its individual members,[4] is one that would be readily recognised in most parliamentary systems. The purpose, broadly, is to protect the legislature from threat and coercion by other arms of the state, in particular the executive. As Blackstone's Commentaries put it:

> The dignity and independence of the two Houses are in great measure preserved by keeping their privileges indefinite. If all the privileges of Parliament were set down and ascertained, and no privilege to be allowed but what was so defined and determined, it were easy for the executive power to devise some new case, not within the line of privilege, and under pretence thereof to harass any refractory Member and violate the freedom of Parliament.[5]

But to a greater degree in the modern circumstances of the UK, the arguments about privilege and the courts is not about any fear of arbitrary trial and punishment but anxiety about misinterpretation of or disobedience to the clear will of Parliament, or interference in its internal self-regulation.[6]

The greatest confounding factor in establishing the scope and meaning of Westminster's claims to certain rights and immunities is, therefore, that these immunities and privileges have never been fully codified and many have no statutory form. They have been argued to form part of the common law, and they have been asserted to be entirely outside it. As Coke put it, the law of Parliament 'is so transcendent and absolute, that it cannot be confined, either for causes or persons, within any bounds'.[7] There was in his time no recognised external check apart from the appeal to precedent and antiquity. A seventeenth-century commentator claimed that the law of Parliament 'cannot be meant or intended to signify any Prescription or Application of Laws to that power, which in itself is boundless … The Parliament itself is, no doubt, properly to be stiled, *The Fundamental Law and Constitution of this Kingdom, as it comprehends all* Legal Powers *whatsoever*'.[8]

This theoretical boundlessness can be argued to be derived from the doctrine of the sovereignty of Queen-in-Parliament. But the argument over where and how to

---

[4] See, for example, Resolution 2127 (2016) of the Parliamentary Assembly of the Council of Europe and the associated Report (Doc. 14076) (www.coe.int).

[5] William Blackstone's *Commentaries on the Laws of England* (1765–1769) quoted by the Prime Minister (Rt Hon Neville Chamberlain) in the final debate on the Sandys affair (HC Deb 21 November 1939, col 1071) cited by the Campbell Committee (the Select Committee on an Issue of Privilege) in its Report, 'Police Searches on the Parliamentary Estate', Session 2009–10, HC 62, at para 168.

[6] A good example of this anxiety is the fate of a provision in the Parliamentary Standards Act 2009. As originally enacted, s 8 handed over the duty of devising and regulating the code of conduct relating to MPs' financial interests to the new authority, reflecting a dramatic loss of self-confidence in the regulatory competence of MPs themselves. This would have shifted the burden of regulation of what MPs did in proceedings of the House to the IPSA. But before the provision was commenced, after the House realised what the full implications were for its exclusive cognisance and the Committee on Standards in Public Life had reported, it was repealed by s 32 of the Constitutional Reform and Governance Act 2010.

[7] Coke's *Institutes* (n 3), fourth part, s 36.

[8] George Petyt, *Lex Parliamentaria: or, a Treatise of the Law and custom of Parliaments*, 2nd edn (1734), preface.

place some kind of boundaries around the prerogatives of each branch has moved, since the seventeenth century, from being an argument principally between Parliament and the King to one principally between Parliament and the courts, and the tide of assertiveness has ebbed and flowed over the last two or three centuries between these two arms of the state. A constant theme of that debate has been whether or not placing privilege on a statutory footing would strengthen the hand of Parliament or make it subservient to that of the courts. As long ago as 1844, in the first edition of his *Treatise upon the Law, Privilege, Proceedings and Usage of Parliament*, Thomas Erskine May rehearsed this debate:

> The present position of privilege is, in the highest degree, unsatisfactory. Assertions of privilege are made in Parliament and denied in the courts; the officers who execute the orders of Parliament are liable to vexatious actions, and if verdicts are obtained against them, the damages and costs are paid by the Treasury ... It is not expected that Parliament should surrender any privilege that is essential to its dignity, and of the proper exercise of its authority; but the privileges of both houses should be secured by a legislative definition; and a mode of enforcing them should be adopted which would be binding on the courts.[9]

In the course of exchanges over the Aylesbury election case in 1704/1705, the two Houses of Parliament agreed that 'neither House of Parliament have power, by any vote or declaration, to create for themselves new privileges, not warranted by the known laws and customs of Parliament'.[10] So any tinkering with the extent of privilege can only be done by legislation, not by mere assertion. Once legislated, the extent and application of any claim of privilege is justiciable. Parliament may pass legislation to abridge or define its traditional privileges, but to do so places Parliament at the mercy of the courts.[11] This dilemma has been a neuralgic point for Parliament for at least two centuries.

II. THE FOUR ANCIENT PRIVILEGES

At the start of each Parliament, when the Speaker-Elect goes up to the House of Lords to receive the royal approbation on his or her election, they make the following rather archaic petition:

> It is now my duty, in the name of and on behalf of the Commons of the United Kingdom, to lay claim, by humble petition to Her Majesty, to all their ancient and undoubted rights and privileges, especially to freedom of speech in debate, to freedom from arrest, and to free access to Her Majesty whenever occasion shall arise, and that the most favourable construction shall be put upon all their proceedings.

---

[9] T Erskine May, *A Treatise upon the Law, Privileges, Proceedings and Usage of Parliament*, 1st edn, (London, Charles Knight & Co, 1844) 129–30.

[10] House of Commons Journals vol 14, 1702–04, 555, 559, 569, 569, 570 and 572. The Conferences between the Houses were held in February 1704 (1705 New Style).

[11] In the case of jury service (discussed in this chapter below), a long-standing parliamentary privilege of exemption was first incorporated in statute and then later repealed.

To which one of Her Majesty's Commissioners responds:

> [W]e have it further in Command to inform you that Her Majesty does most readily confirm all the rights and privileges which have ever been granted to or conferred upon the Commons by Her Majesty or any of her Royal predecessors.

The claims of access to the sovereign and for a 'favourable construction' can be dismissed fairly briefly so far as modern considerations are concerned. The claim of freedom from arrest is exiguous, though not wholly insignificant, and will be dealt with below. The claim of freedom of speech is fundamental, and remains highly relevant. This chapter will therefore deal more extensively with that, and with a more slippery notion known as 'exclusive cognisance', which is essentially the claim of each House to be the sole determiner of the validity of its own proceedings. An important extension of the two House's privileges is their further claim (arguably based in their original claims to be courts themselves—the famous 'High Court of Parliament') to have powers to compel evidence and the attendance of witnesses, and this is discussed below. Finally, the questions of contempts, and of enforcement or penal powers without which other powers may be rendered meaningless, are considered.

One of the more enduring constants of the debate over privilege between the courts and Parliament is the general acceptance by Parliament that the boundaries of privilege are set by the judges—Parliament and its committees can assert whatever they wish, but nonetheless the question of whether privilege applies in a particular case is for the courts to decide. The most recent and illuminating rehearsal of these arguments is to be found in the judgment of the Supreme Court in the case of *R v Chaytor*.[12] The issues raised there are further considered below. But the reasoning in that judgment draws attention to the confusion between the claims of statutory privilege (mostly pursuant to Article IX of the Bill of Rights of 1688/89) and the non-statutory assertions of the concept of exclusive cognisance which are also in play.

III. TO LEGISLATE OR NOT TO LEGISLATE

Parliament has generally legislated on matters of its own privileges mostly reluctantly (and occasionally carelessly) only when it needs to solve a specific problem or where it feels the courts have failed to respect the boundaries of the extra-judicial domain of privilege. The result is an uneven and sometimes confusing overlap between statutory and non-statutory claims.

The immediate cause of Thomas Erskine May's exasperation, cited above, was the case of *Stockdale v Hansard*.[13] The essence of the matter at issue was whether a report, published under the authority of the Commons, was immune from civil action.

---

[12] *R v Chaytor and others* [2010] UKSC 52, at paras 14ff.
[13] *Stockdale v Hansard* (1839) 9 Ad & El 96.

Mr Stockdale claimed that Luke Hansard, the Commons' printer, had defamed him by publishing a report under the authority of the Commons alleging that he was a pornographer. In a series of robust exchanges between the Commons and the judges the courts refused to accept that Parliament could define the scope of its own privileges by virtue of passing resolutions telling the courts what to think. The upshot was the Parliamentary Papers Act 1840, which protects a report of a speech in Hansard, and all other proceedings published on the authority of either House.

Later in the nineteenth century, Parliament made a number of less noticed moves to put privileges on a statutory footing. The Parliamentary Witnesses Act 1858 enabled committees of the House of Lords to put witnesses on oath. The Parliamentary Witnesses Oaths Act 1871 extended this to committees of the Commons. Section 3 of the latter made a nod to the doctrine of not extending privileges, stating: 'Nothing in this Act contained shall be held to confer any additional or further power or privilege on the Commons House of Parliament with reference to impeachment or other criminal jurisdiction or otherwise howsoever than is herein expressly enacted'. The punishment for false witness was to be the same as that for perjury: the Perjury Act 1911 consolidated these provisions.[14] The Witnesses (Public Inquiries) Protection Act 1892, which made it an offence, in section 2, to intimidate or punish witnesses at inquiries included committees of both Houses in its definition of inquiries in section 1. The implication, in each of these cases, can only be that Article IX was impliedly repealed insofar as it would be necessary to use the proceedings before any committee as evidence in any prosecution—otherwise the Acts would be meaningless—and that Parliament was handing over its power to punish for certain contempts to the courts.[15]

In 1938, a complaint from Duncan Sandys MP that the Attorney-General had asked him about the 'highly secret' sources of information Mr Sandys had evidently used in a draft of a parliamentary question (about shortages of anti-aircraft guns) which he had enclosed in a letter to the Secretary of State for War was referred a Select Committee on the Official Secrets Act.[16] In due course the House agreed with the Committee in its report that the definition of parliamentary proceedings should be extended to communications between one MP and another, or between

---

[14] In fact a similar provision, criminalising perjury under oath before an Election Committee of the House of Commons (which was technically a court) had been made in the Election Act 1778 and subsequently.

[15] See also A Horne, 'Evidence under oath, perjury and parliamentary privilege' UK Const L blog (29 January 2015) (available at: http://ukconstitutionallaw.org)). In the 2016–17 Session the Home Affairs Committee referred an allegation of perjury under oath before a committee in the previous Parliament to the police for investigation; see Formal Minutes of the Committee for 15 November 2016, item 1. This is believed to be the first occasion on which the provisions of the Parliamentary Witnesses Oaths Act have been invoked in this way. Although the doctrine of implied repeal has been doubted (see for example the 'Metric Martyrs' case—*Thoburn v Sunderland City Council* [2002] EWHC 195 (Admin)—and also *R (HS2 Action Alliance Ltd) v Secretary of State for Transport* [2014] UKSC 3) it would seem a very extensive interpretation of the notion of a requirement of express repeal for 'constitutional statutes' to suggest that it might apply in these cases.

[16] Reports from the Select Committee on the Official Secrets Act, HC 146 and HC 173 of Session 1937–38, and HC 101 of 1938–39.

an MP and a minister, so closely related to some matter pending in or expected to be brought before the House that they formed part of the business of the House, and that to that extent a Member of the House when engaged in parliamentary proceedings was beyond the reach of the criminal law.[17] Some 20 years later the House of Commons Committee of Privileges concluded that a letter written by George Strauss MP to the Paymaster General about the London Electricity Board was a 'proceeding in Parliament' and that accordingly the MP could not be prosecuted for allegedly defamatory comments contained in the letter. The Committee also found that, in threatening a libel action against the Member, both the Board and its solicitors had committed a breach of privilege. But by 218 votes to 213, the House of Commons rejected a motion to agree with the Committee's report, and an amendment declaring that Strauss's letter was not a proceeding in Parliament and that no breach of privilege had been committed was carried.[18] With hindsight, it might be argued that, in the 20 years between the Sandys and the Strauss cases, the House had turned away from the advanced claims for parliamentary privilege made in the former.[19]

This state of uncertainty led to a Select Committee on Parliamentary Privilege being appointed in July 1966 to carry out a comprehensive review of parliamentary privilege. It recommended that the decision of the House in the Strauss case should be reversed by legislation, but that call for legislation went unheeded and its other recommendations, which took an extensive view of the scope of privilege, languished for a decade. The Committee itself seemed ambivalent about the case for codification:

> [T]he claim of the courts to interpret and to define the rights and immunities of the House and of its members, insofar as they form part of the common law of the land and are consequently possible in the courts, has led to a history of fruitless, and, in the past, often undignified conflicts between the courts and the House.[20]

Nonetheless, the Committee was of the opinion 'that this power of the House cannot be surrendered since it is essential to the exercise by the House of its control over its own procedure and to the protection which its penal jurisdiction provides'.[21]

In a 1976 report the Committee of Privileges concluded that neither of two press releases issued by Iain Sproat MP and the Social Democratic Alliance alleging that some Labour MPs held Communist or Trotskyite views amounted to a contempt. The Committee took the opportunity to express its opinion that that the recommendations of the 1966–67 Committee should be referred to the Committee of Privileges for review.[22]

---

[17] HC Deb 21 November 1939, vol 353, cols 1071–84.

[18] HC Deb 8 July 1958, vol 591, cols 208–345.

[19] For a discussion of the impact of the Strauss case, see DCM Yardley, 'The House for Commons and its privileges since the Strauss affair', *Parliamentary Affairs* XV (1962) 4, 500–10.

[20] Select Committee on Parliamentary Privilege, Report of Session 1967–68, HC 34, para 71.

[21] ibid.

[22] The Committee of Privileges can consider only specific matters referred to it by the House.

The House having taken the hint in January 1977, the Committee of Privileges reported in June of that year. Among its other recommendations, the Committee of Privileges followed the Joint Committee on Publication of Proceedings in Parliament in recommending legislation to define 'proceedings in Parliament'.[23]

In 1994, the *Guardian* newspaper made certain allegations in what came to be known as the 'cash-for-questions' case. Neil Hamilton MP began an action for defamation, but the *Guardian* successfully argued that the case could not proceed without examining certain proceedings in Parliament (the parliamentary questions at the very least), and that Article IX of the Bill of Rights prevented this. The case was stayed. Subsequently, a last-minute amendment was made to the Defamation Bill in the House of Lords in 1996, enabling an individual MP unilaterally to waive the protection of Article IX in defamation proceedings. Hamilton restarted his action against the *Guardian*, but withdrew almost immediately when new evidence was lodged.[24] In 1998 Hamilton began a separate libel action against Mohamed Al Fayed on the basis of allegations made in a TV documentary. An attempt to stay the case again on Article IX grounds was disallowed. The House of Lords held unanimously that the claimant's waiver under section 13 of the Defamation Act 1996 was a complete answer to the application for a stay. Such a waiver had the effect of allowing the questioning of parliamentary proceedings for the purpose of the defamation action without it being an infringement of the exclusive cognisance of Parliament or the provisions of Article IX.[25] The trial of the action proceeded, and Neil Hamilton lost.[26]

The decision to appoint a Joint Committee on Parliamentary Privilege in July 1997 followed a growing sense of discomfort with section 13. When it reported in March 1999, the Joint Committee took the view that the apparent mischief dealt with by section 13 ought to be addressed in a different way, and suggested that it should be replaced by a statutory provision empowering each House to waive Article IX for the purpose of any court proceedings, whether relating to defamation or to any other matter, where the words spoken or the acts done in proceedings in Parliament would not expose the speaker of the words or the doer of the acts to any legal liability.[27]

---

[23] Joint Committee on the Publication of Proceedings in Parliament, Second Report of Session 1969–70, HC 251, paras 25 to 28.

[24] Section 13(1) of the Defamation Act 1996 read as follows: 'Where the conduct of a person in or in relation to proceedings in Parliament is in issue in defamation proceedings, he may waive for the purposes of those proceedings, so far as concerns him, the protection of any enactment or rule of law which prevents proceedings in Parliament being impeached or questioned in any court or place out of Parliament'. It was repealed by para 44 of Sch 23 of the Deregulation Act 2015.

[25] *Hamilton v Fayed* [2001] AC 395.

[26] See also A Horne and O Gay, 'Ending the Hamilton Affair?' *UK Const L* blog (21 May 2014) (available at https://ukconstitutionallaw.org).

[27] The Defamation Bill as introduced in the 2012–13 Session left untouched s 13 of the 1996 Act. The Joint Committee on the draft Defamation Bill in Session 2010–12 had made no comment on s 13 of the 1996 Act, which was not raised in evidence to the Joint Committee; see Joint Committee on the Draft Defamation Bill, Report of Session 2010–12, HL Paper 203, HC 930-I and Cm 8318, para 191.

The recommendations of the Joint Committee's 1999 report, however, covered a much broader canvas than the specific point on defamation. It recommended legislation on a number of topics, including the definition of 'proceedings in Parliament' and contempt of Parliament, legislation to confirm that both Houses had the power to levy fines but not to imprison, and a concurrent jurisdiction with the courts to punish non-Members for contempts such as failing to attend proceedings or to answer questions. Each House debated the recommendations, but its proposals for legislation never attained sufficient priority to be included in any government's legislative programme. Despite this lack of statutory implementation, the comprehensiveness of the Joint Committee's recommendations remained influential over the next dozen or so years in persuading other committees not to endorse proposals for legislative tinkering with particular aspects of privilege. For example, in 2003 the Joint Committee on the draft Corruption Bill considered that 'it would be better if the Joint Committee [on Parliamentary Privilege] recommendations were followed and a Parliamentary Privilege Bill dealing with all these matters [affecting parliamentary privilege] were brought forward'.[28] In 2009 the House of Commons Justice Committee, considering the impact of the proposed clause 10 of the Parliamentary Standards Act, offered the view that it was an appropriate time for another look at statutory codification of privilege.[29] The Joint Committee on the draft Bribery Bill in 2008–09 reached a similar view, after having also weighed in to clause 10 of the Parliamentary Standards Bill which had been deleted in committee that year. It concluded:

> The issue of parliamentary privilege has arisen in relation to several pieces of legislation and draft legislation in recent years. Legislating in a piecemeal fashion risks undermining the important constitutional principles of parliamentary privilege without conscious-ness of the overall impact of doing so. This issue was examined in considerable detail by the 1999 Joint Committee on Parliamentary Privilege, which concluded that a Par-liamentary Privileges Act was required. We believe that, should the Government deem it necessary, such an act would be the most appropriate place to address the potential evidential problems in relation to bribery offences.[30]

Subsequently, however, the tide seems to have shifted against statutory codifica-tion. In 2010 a select committee was appointed to look at the question of whether the privileges and immunities of the House had been breached by a police search conducted of an MP's office on the parliamentary estate. The Committee, although critical of the police's conduct, concluded that no breach of privilege had occurred.[31] It went on to ruminate on the admissibility of any evidence that might

---

[28] Joint Committee on the draft Corruption Bill, Report of Session 2002–03, HL Paper 157, HC 705, para 114.

[29] Clause 10 was another form of waiver of Article IX designed to allow the IPSA to investigate and adjudicate on matters relating to MPs' financial conduct (see ch 1 of the first edition of this book (n 1) for further details).

[30] Joint Committee on the draft Bribery Bill, Report of Session 2008–09, HL Paper 115-I, HC 430-I, para 228.

[31] The case is discussed at length in ch 3 of the first edition of this work (n 1) 74–80.

have been gathered by the police. It recognised that the situation was uncertain but expressed the view that:

> It would ... be a mistake for Parliament to legislate in haste or to address only one aspect of the multi-faceted relationship between liberty, Parliament and the law. While we have no unanimous conclusion on the wisdom or necessity of legislating on parliamentary privilege, we agree in recommending that before any Government Bill on the subject was introduced it would be highly desirable for the whole question to be addressed in the round by a special joint committee drawn from both Houses. Before setting out to define and limit parliamentary privilege in statute, there needs to be a comprehensive review of how that privilege affects the work and responsibilities of an MP in the twenty-first century.[32]

The Committee on the Damian Green case was pursuing another argument about the boundaries of exclusive cognisance that had occasionally reared its head—the extent of the jurisdiction of the House over its own estate. This had been at issue in the Zircon case in 1986, where the Government sought and obtained an injunction against the disclosure of information about a defence project which had allegedly been concealed from the Public Accounts Committee. Robin Cook MP obtained a copy of the documentary and arranged for it to be shown in a room on the House of Commons estate. After ministerial intervention, the Speaker ruled that the film should not be shown and asked for the advice of the Committee of Privileges. The Committee concluded in its report that private arrangements to show a film within the precincts did not amount to a proceeding in Parliament and were therefore not privileged, although by this time the film had been publicly shown elsewhere and the matter was taken no further.[33]

The eventual establishment of another Joint Committee on Parliamentary Privilege was provoked more proximately than by the Damian Green affair when, in the wake of the 'expenses scandal' of 2008–09, three MPs sought to prevent their criminal trial for offences of false accounting by claiming the protection of privilege, citing both Article IX of the Bill of Rights and the principle of exclusive cognisance. The Conservative party had promised in its 2010 manifesto that, if the courts concluded that MPs accused of criminal offences relating to expenses claims were to be found to be protected from trial by virtue of parliamentary privilege, they would bring forward proposals to remove any such immunity. In the event, the attempt to claim privilege failed in the courts, and the heat went out of the question.[34] Nonetheless, the coalition Government brought forward a Green Paper in April 2012.[35] It asked the rather leading question whether those it was

---

[32] Committee on an Issue of Privilege, Report of Session 2009–10, 'Police Searches on the Parliamentary Estate' HC Paper 62, para 169.

[33] Committee of Privileges, First Report of Session 1986–87, 'Speaker's Order of 22 January 1987 on a Matter of National Security', HC Paper 365.

[34] However, in September 2016 similar outrage was briefly stirred up when the trial of Lord Hanningfield on charges of false accounting relating to a claim for expenses as a member of the House of Lords was stayed on the apparent grounds that the court could not determine what was and was not 'parliamentary work'.

[35] Cm 8318.

consulting agreed that 'the case has not been made for a comprehensive codification of parliamentary privilege'.[36] A Joint Committee was established to examine the Green Paper (although it ended up taking a more extensive view of its remit). After considering the experiences of both Australia and New Zealand in codifying privilege, the 2013 report of the Joint Committee came down on the other side of the fence from the 1999 Joint Committee:

> We do not consider that comprehensive codification is needed at this time. This does not mean that we reject all legislation; but legislation should only be used when absolutely necessary, to resolve uncertainty or in the unlikely event of Parliament's exclusive cognisance being materially diminished by the courts.[37]

The Committee, however, took a more adventurous line on the question of Parliament's penal powers, as will be discussed below. But the net result of all these examinations is that the case for codification remains as contested now as it was at the time of Thomas Erskine May's outburst in 1844.

Another rather oblique question relating to privilege and legislation was considered by the 2013 Joint Committee. In its response to the expenses scandal, the Committee on Standards in Public Life, had recommended that there should be at least two lay members who had never been parliamentarians on the Standards and Privileges Committee of the House of Commons.[38] The Committee on Standards in Public Life's proposals were swiftly endorsed by the Committee on Standards and Privileges,[39] and on 2 December 2010 the House resolved to agree with the principle and invited the Procedure Committee to bring forward proposals for its implementation.[40]

In its Report, the Procedure Committee drew attention to the risk that the addition of lay members with full voting rights to a committee might call into question whether the activities of such a committee would still be 'proceedings in Parliament' and so covered by parliamentary privilege.[41] The Committee made several practical proposals, for the process of appointing lay members and for splitting of the Committee on Standards and Privileges into separate Committees.[42] The House amended its Standing Orders on 12 March 2012 and three lay members nominated by the House of Commons Commission were approved by the House

---

[36]   ibid, paras 38 and 39.

[37]   Joint Committee on Parliamentary Privilege, Report of Session 2013–14, 'Parliamentary Privilege', HL 30, HC100, para 47.

[38]   Twelfth Report from the Committee on Standards in Public Life, *MPs' expenses and allowances*, Cm 7724, November 2009.

[39]   Committee on Standards and Privileges, Second Report of Session 2009–10, 'Implementing the Twelfth Report from the Committee on Standards in Public Life', HC 67.

[40]   HC Deb 2 December 2010, cols 995 to 1017.

[41]   Procedure Committee (Commons), Sixth Report of Session 2010–12, HC 1606.

[42]   HC 1606, para 53. The Procedure Committee noted that it would of course be open to the House to reject both options. For more on lay members see ch 4.

on 13 December 2012.[43] The Government's undertaking to consider the case for legislating to place beyond doubt the position of a Committee on Standards with lay members who did have full voting rights was fulfilled in its Parliamentary Privilege Green Paper.[44] The 2013 Joint Committee on Parliamentary Privilege concluded that:

> There are procedural rules in place to ensure lay members can play a full part in the House of Commons Committee on Standards, and it would be inappropriate to legislate to confer the protection of parliamentary privilege upon certain classes of individuals sitting on specified committees. Moreover, such legislation would cast doubt on the position of the House of Lords Committee for Privileges and Conduct, which would include non-Members when deciding a peerage claim. We therefore oppose legislating to confer voting rights on lay members of the House of Commons Committee on Standards.[45]

IV. FREEDOM OF SPEECH

Article IX of the Bill of Rights is the most striking and fundamental statutory expression of parliamentary privilege. In modern English it declares 'That the Freedom of Speech and Debates or Proceedings in Parliament ought not to be impeached or questioned in any Court or Place out of Parliament'. Although the other articles contain statements which undoubtedly form the continuing basis of the constitutional settlement arrived at after half a century of civil war, Article IX is the only one to have any great currency in in present day debates.[46] Article IX could be read principally as a general political assertion about the need to respect Parliament (especially in that mysterious 'any ... place'),[47] but has instead been

---

[43] See Report from the House of Commons Commission, 'Lay members of the new Standards Committee: Nomination of Candidates', HC 709. The Committee on Standards subsequently recommended that there should be an equality of elected and lay members (seven of each) on the Committee (Committee on Standards, Sixth Report of Session 2014–15, 'The Standards System in the House of Commons', HC Paper 383, para 90) and this proposal was approved by the House on 17 March 2015 and put into effect in the 2015–17 Parliament.

[44] Cm 8318, paras 232 to 244, with a draft clause on p 59.

[45] Joint Committee on Parliamentary Privilege, Report of Session 2013–14 (n 37), para 111.

[46] For example, it is rare to hear concern expressed about the requirement of Article V that the Crown may not maintain a standing army in time of peace without the consent of Parliament; and Art VI on the right of Protestants to bear arms might be considered a dead letter in most parts of the UK.

[47] The *sub judice* resolution, for example, refers to proceedings 'in United Kingdom courts'. The lack of explicit reference to tribunals leaves it unclear whether there are any circumstances in which tribunals should be considered 'courts' for the purposes of the resolution. Section 19 of the Contempt of Court Act 1981 defines 'court' as including 'any tribunal or body exercising the judicial power of the State'. The 2004–05 Procedure Committee noted this definition, but also cited the Bar Council which described this as a 'very uncertain area: for example valuation courts have been held not to be included, but employment tribunals are'. The status of bodies such as the Independent Police Complaints Commission or the General Medical Council, for example, is more constestable. Generally, the legal advisers of the two Houses have appeared to apply principally the test of whether the 'place' in question has penal powers which it can exercise against an individual under statute. See also pp 43–4 of the first edition of this work (n 1).

justified, particularly in the last 30 years or so, into the cornerstone of the present constitutional settlement between Parliament and the courts.[48] The Bill of Rights has come itself to be argued to belong to the class of 'constitutional' statutes which cannot be repealed or amended except by new legislation expressed in clear and unambiguous terms.[49] But Article IX was not a new departure; it was, rather, a recapitulation of the traditional parliamentary privilege of freedom of speech: in 1563, the Speaker's claim for freedom of speech in debate was already justified as 'according to the old antient order'.[50]

Of the four privileges claimed by the Speaker, the freedom of speech in debate is undoubtedly the 'most valuable and most essential'.[51] But the House of Commons has become self-conscious about its exercise, as it has about its other powers and privileges. Since 2004 it has been the custom of the House of Commons for the Speaker to make some general remarks on the opening day of a Session, prior to the opening of the debate on the Queen's Speech.[52] In 2012, for example, Mr Speaker Bercow's address to the House included this passage:

> Our ancient privileges allow us to conduct our debate without fear of outside interference. Parliamentary privilege underpins proper democratic debate and scrutiny. It will be under renewed scrutiny over the next few months, with the Government's consultation on the subject. In particular, we enjoy freedom of speech in Committee proceedings and in debate. Freedom of speech in debate is at the very heart of what we do here for our constituents, and it allows us to conduct our business without fear of outside interference. But it is a freedom that we need to exercise responsibly in the public interest and taking into account the interests of others outside this House.[53]

Josef Redlich, the great Austrian scholar of parliamentary procedure, asserted at the turn of the nineteenth and twentieth centuries that there were:

> [T]wo features which give to debate in Parliament its unique legal nature: first its being under the protection of the great constitutional principle of unrestricted *freedom of speech*, and secondly its being subjected by parliamentary law to definite rules and standards indicating how to apply the principle of freedom and partially limiting its operation.[54]

---

[48] See for example the judgment in *Chaytor* (n 12) paras 47 and 61.

[49] The notion of constitutional statutes as expounded by Laws LJ in *Thoburn v Sunderland City Council* [2003] QB 151, is described in D Greenberg (ed) *Craies on Legislation*, 8th edn (Hebden Bridge, Sweet and Maxwell, 2004) at 14.4.6. See also *R (HS2 Action Alliance Ltd) v Secretary of State for Transport* [2014] UKSC 3. It has been argued (though it has not been accepted) that the Bill of Rights was impliedly repealed by the Act of Union of 1707.

[50] *Journals of all the Parliament during the Reign of Queen Elizabeth*, Sir Symonds D'Ewes vol 66 (full text available at www.british-history.ac.uk).

[51] J Hatsell, *Precedents of Proceedings in the House of Commons*, in four volumes 1776–1818 (reprinted in facsimile, Shannon, Irish University Press, 1971) vol I, 85.

[52] Procedure Committee, Third Report of Session 2002–03, 'Sessional Orders and Resolutions', HC 855, and 'The Government's Response to the Committee's Third Report of Session 2003–04', HC 613. The Sessional Resolutions covered motions relating to Elections, Witnesses, Commissioner of Police of the Metropolis, Votes and Proceedings and the Journal of the House of Commons.

[53] HC Deb 9 May 2012, col 1.

[54] J Redlich, *The Procedure of the House of Commons: A Study of its History and Present Form* (London, Archibald Constable & Co, 1908) vol III, 45.

The House of Commons committees which have considered this matter have consistently urged responsibility and moderation in the use of the privilege of freedom of speech, and occasionally examined the need for stricter rules to prevent or punish irresponsibility. To be effective, however, rulings from the Chair need to be peremptory. In a May 2016 judgment of the Grand Chamber of the European Court of Human Rights in the case of *Karácsony and Others v Hungary*[55] the Court held, unanimously, that there had been a violation of Article 10 (freedom of expression) of the ECHR. The case concerned fines imposed by the Presiding Officer on Hungarian MPs from two opposition parties who had disrupted parliamentary proceedings. The UK intervened to argue (cautiously) that two complementary principles applied and both were essential to the proper functioning of a representative democracy. First, free speech, protected from any fear of litigation or external sanction, was essential if MPs were to represent the people and debate matters of importance. Otherwise, there would be a powerful chilling effect on debate within the legislature. Parliament had to be free to organise and determine its own procedure and to hear robust debate on any subject, without fear of external interference. Second, as a counterbalance, there had to be a system of parliamentary discipline, under which the conduct of MPs was controlled by Parliament itself, to ensure that the right to freedom of speech of its members was not abused, and that the work of the legislature proceeded effectively. The Court found nonetheless that the interference with the applicants' freedom of expression had not been proportionate to the legitimate aims pursued because it had not been accompanied by adequate procedural guarantees, although it noted that subsequently an amendment to the law had been made which allowed an MP to seek a remedy and submit his or her arguments before a parliamentary commission. The Court suggested that the necessary minimum procedural guarantees therefore appeared to have been put in place, but that those changes had been too late to affect the applicants' situation. In trying to steer between the Scylla of reputation-damaging freedom and the Charybdis of the threat of judicial oversight, committees of the UK Parliament have often come to conflicting conclusions.[56]

In practice, Article IX has been presumed to accord absolute privilege to things said or done in the course of parliamentary proceedings—the difficult point has been to define the precise extent of 'proceedings'. This was considered by the 2013 Joint Committee in the context of claims of 'effective repetition' in actions for defamation. The Committee in particular considered the case of Lord Triesman, who was being sued on the grounds that he had told an inquiry of the Football Association that 'my evidence in respect of this issue is set out in the transcript of the statement that I made to the Culture, Media and Sport Committee'. Although the court found that Lord Triesman enjoyed qualified privilege, and that there was

---

[55] (2016) 64 EHRR 595.

[56] For example, Committee of Privileges, Second Report of Session 1978–79; Select Committee on Procedure, First Report of Session 1988–99, *Conduct of Members in the Chamber and the Alleged Abuse of Parliamentary Privilege*, HC 290; Joint Committee on Parliamentary Privilege, Report of Session 1998–99, HL Paper 43-I, HC 214-I, paras 224–25; Joint Committee on Privacy and Injunctions, Report of Session 2010–12, HL Paper 273, HC 1443, para 221.

no case of malice that could be tried, the Committee found this unsatisfactory. It concluded that 'These cases appear to have left Members of both Houses unsure of the extent to which they can subsequently repeat or refer to statements made by them in Parliament (statements which, as proceedings in Parliament, are themselves protected by absolute privilege)'. They argued:

> It is right that absolute privilege should be reserved to proceedings in Parliament; but Members do not work only in the Chamber—their public duties extend to their relationships with constituents, to speeches, and to interactions with the media, and it is not right that they should be inhibited in performing these duties by fear of court proceedings. It is essential that the same qualified privilege that we have outlined above, in our recommendations regarding the replacement of the Parliamentary Papers Act 1840, should apply to parliamentarians themselves, in repeating or commenting on speeches made in Parliament.[57]

The Committee went on to recommend legislation to 'confirm, for the avoidance of doubt, that Members of either House enjoy the same protection as non-Members in repeating or broadcasting extracts or abstracts of proceedings in Parliament'.[58]

The 2013 Joint Committee on Parliamentary Privilege also considered the extent of protection given to wider publication of parliamentary proceedings under the Parliamentary Papers Act 1840, as had the 1999 Joint Committee. It concurred with the 1999 report of its predecessor that the 1840 Act needed replacement in order to:

— confirm that publications and broadcasts made under the authority of either House enjoy absolute privilege, and that any proceedings initiated in respect of such publications or broadcasts shall be stayed upon production of a certificate signed by the Speaker or Clerk of either House;

— establish that qualified privilege applies to all fair and accurate reports of parliamentary proceedings in the same way as to abstracts and extracts of those proceedings;

— provide that in all court proceedings in respect of such fair and accurate reports, extracts or abstracts, the claimant or prosecution shall be required to prove that the defendant acted maliciously; confirm that the term 'broadcast' includes dissemination of images, text or sounds, or any combination of them, by any electronic means;

— provide for a delegated power, subject to affirmative procedure, allowing the Secretary of State to update the definition of 'broadcast' in light of further technological change, without the need for primary legislation.[59]

Freedom of speech, therefore, is limited to a certain extent by self-regulation within Parliament. Rules limiting freedom of speech are imposed on their Members by the two Houses themselves, either by practice and usage (the written and

---

[57] Joint Committee on Parliamentary Privilege, Report of Session 2013–14 (n 37) para 203.
[58] ibid, para 207.
[59] Joint Committee on Parliamentary Privilege, Report of Session 2013–14 (n 37) para 196.

unwritten rules of procedure), standing orders, and constitutional convention (such as the rules forbidding criticism of judges, Members of the other House, members of the royal family, etc) or by specific rules, such as the *sub judice* rule. The limitations provided for in the general procedural rules and conventions of the two Houses are too extensive to be discussed here. The *sub judice* rule is, however, one of the most elaborate and complex and picked-over of these limitations on free speech, and is examined in some detail in the next section.[60]

A preoccupation of the various committees which have examined the scope of Article IX in the last 20 years or so has been the use of parliamentary proceedings in courts or other places. On a strict reading, Article IX could be held to prevent any use of words spoken in debate or evidence before or conclusions of select committees. In 1980, the Commons resolved:

> That this House, while re-affirming the status of proceedings in Parliament confirmed by Article 9 of the Bill of Rights, gives leave for reference to be made in future Court proceedings to the Official Report of Debates and to the published Reports and evidence of Committees in any case in which, under the practice of the House, it is required that a petition for leave should be presented and that the practice of presenting petitions for leave to refer to parliamentary papers be discontinued.[61]

In 1992, for the first time a court used the record of proceedings in a legislative committee of the Commons as an aid to interpretation, in the case of *Pepper v Hart*, in contradiction to the argument of the Attorney-General. The court held, however, that use of proceedings in this way was only permitted when legislation is ambiguous or obscure, or leads to an absurdity; when the material relied upon consists of one or more statements by a Minister or other promoter of the Bill together if necessary with such other parliamentary material as is necessary to understand such statements and their effect; and when the statements relied upon are clear.[62] The ruling caused considerable controversy at the time and has continued to resonate. Geoffrey Marshall, for example, argued strongly against the blurring of lines implied by the decision.[63] The 1999 Joint Committee considered the development and showed itself relatively relaxed.[64] Subsequently, the concern began to centre on the use of select committee findings in judicial review, particularly the findings of the Joint Committee on Human Rights.[65] In its 2012

---

[60] There are also limitations placed by the Code of Conduct on the extent to which Members may raise issues where they have a direct pecuniary interest. For example, 'No Member shall act as a paid advocate in any proceeding of the House' and 'The acceptance by a Member of a bribe to influence his or her conduct as a Member, including any fee, compensation or reward in connection with the promotion of, or opposition to, any Bill, Motion, or other matter submitted, or intended to be submitted to the House, or to any Committee of the House, is contrary to the law of Parliament'.

[61] Commons Journals (1979–80) 823.

[62] *Pepper (Inspector of Taxes) v Hart* [1993] AC 593, Lord Browne-Wilkinson, [1992] UKHL3.

[63] See G Marshall, 'Hansard and the Interpretation of Statutes' in D Oliver and G Drewry (eds), *The Law and Parliament* (London, Butterworths, 1998).

[64] Joint Committee on Parliamentary Privilege, Report of Session 1998–99 (n 56) para 51.

[65] See the discussion by Oonagh Gay and Hugh Tomlinson in ch 2 of the first edition of this work (n 1) 59–62.

Green Paper, the Government had seemed as relaxed as the 1999 Joint Committee, concluding that:

> Recent developments have seen proceedings in Parliament used in court more regularly than in the past without encroaching upon the protections provided by parliamentary privilege.

And that:

> [T]he current situation, whereby the courts can use proceedings in Parliament as long as they are not questioned or impeached, is perfectly satisfactory.[66]

The 2013 Committee, having yet again reviewed the state of play,[67] typically took a less relaxed view than its 1999 predecessor (many of the positions of which it seemed often to find uncongenial to its temper) or the Government and warned against this more open-minded view, while at the same time maintaining its opposition to any statutory clarification except as a last resort, concluding:

— We welcome the clarification by the Lord Chief Justice as to the extent of the *Pepper v. Hart* principle, namely, that those instances in which proceedings, including Committee reports, are questioned, are best 'treated as … mistakes'.

— We consider that the comments of Mr Justice Stanley Burnton, in *OGC v. Information Commissioner*, represent an accurate statement of the legal limitations upon the admissibility of Select Committee reports in court proceedings, including judicial review cases. Such reliance by the courts upon Select Committee reports is not only constitutionally inappropriate, but risks having a chilling effect upon parliamentary debate.

— We do not at this stage believe that the problem of judicial questioning is sufficiently acute to justify either legislation prohibiting use of privileged material by the courts, along the lines of section 16(3) of the Australian Parliamentary Privileges Act 1987, or the introduction of a formal and binding system of notification when reference to privileged material is contemplated.

— We trust that less formal means than those above, building on the current good relations between the judiciary and the parliamentary authorities, will address recent problems. But in this matter, as in others covered in our Report, Parliament should be prepared to legislate if it becomes necessary to do so in order to protect freedom of speech in Parliament from judicial questioning.[68]

The ebb and flow on the use of parliamentary proceedings seems set to continue, the tide being as much affected by the communications between the judges and Parliament at a relatively informal level as by the formal interventions of the Attorney-General or the conflicting conclusions of parliamentary committees.

---

[66] Cm 8318, paras 48 and 88.
[67] Joint Committee on Parliamentary Privilege, Report of Session 2013–14 (n 37) ch 5.
[68] Joint Committee on Parliamentary Privilege, Report of Session 2013–14 (n 37) para 136.

A. Comity and the *sub judice* Rule

The House of Common's *sub judice* rule is a self-denying ordinance limiting the freedom of speech of its Members, in order to preserve the relationship between the House and the courts. In its present form it is set out in a resolution agreed to in 2001.[69] This version superseded two previous resolutions, from 1963 (the first formal codification of the rule) and 1972, both agreed to following reports by the Procedure Committee.[70] These resolutions in turn built upon practice of the House which had developed through Speakers' rulings since the 1880s.[71] The history of the *sub judice* rule shows that it was originally developed in relation to criminal proceedings and only later, and with some difficulty, adapted to civil proceedings. The rule applies when proceedings are 'active' in both criminal and civil cases. It is much easier to determine the former than the latter. In criminal cases, the period in which proceedings are active runs from when a charge has been made or a summons to appear has been issued, until they are concluded by verdict and sentence or discontinuance. Civil proceedings, however, are deemed by the resolution to be active 'when arrangements for the hearing, such as setting down a case for trial, have been made, until the proceedings are ended by judgement or discontinuance', a much vaguer and harder to apply measure. The most recent general inquiry into the operation of the rule by the Procedure Committee was in 2005.[72] This was followed by an inquiry in 2006 into the specific issue of the application of the rule to proceedings in coroners' courts.[73] The rule as it presently stands, reads as follows:

> That, subject to the discretion of the Chair, and to the right of the House to legislate on any matter or to discuss any delegated legislation, the House in all its proceedings (including proceedings of committees of the House) shall apply the following rules on matters sub judice:
>
> (1) Cases in which proceedings are active in United Kingdom courts shall not be referred to in any motion, debate or question.
>
>   (a)(i) Criminal proceedings are active when a charge has been made or a summons to appear has been issued, or, in Scotland, a warrant to cite has been granted.
>
>   (ii) Criminal proceedings cease to be active when they are concluded by verdict and sentence or discontinuance, or, in cases dealt with by courts martial, after the conclusion of the mandatory post-trial review.

---

[69] Resolution of 15 November 2001, CJ (2001–02) 194–95. The Resolution of the House of Lords of 11 May 2000 is slightly differently worded; it can be found in the *Companion to the Standing Orders and Guide to the Proceedings of the House of Lords*, 2017 edn, para 4.6.3. The author is indebted to Robin James for his research in this area.

[70] Resolution of 23 July 1963, CJ (1962–63), 297; First Report of Session 1962–63, 'The Rule relating to Reference in the House of Commons to Matters considered as Sub Judice', HC 156; Resolution of 28 June 1972, CJ (1971–72), 408; Fourth Report of Session 1971–72, 'Matters Sub Judice', HC 298.

[71] See HC (1962–63) 156, Appendix 1 (memorandum from the Clerk of the House) 47–52.

[72] First Report of Session 2004–05, 'The Sub Judice Rule of the House of Commons', HC 125.

[73] Second Report of Session 2005–06, 'Application of the sub judice rule to proceedings in coroners' courts', HC 714.

(b)(i)   Civil proceedings are active when arrangements for the hearing, such as setting down a case for trial, have been made, until the proceedings are ended by judgment or discontinuance.

(ii)   Any application made in or for the purposes of any civil proceedings shall be treated as a distinct proceeding.

(c) Appellate proceedings, whether criminal or civil, are active from the time when they are commenced by application for leave to appeal or by notice of appeal until ended by judgment or discontinuance.

But where a ministerial decision is in question, or in the opinion of the Chair a case concerns issues of national importance such as the economy, public order or the essential services, reference to the issues or the case may be made in motions, debates or questions.

(2)   Specific matters which the House has expressly referred to any judicial body for decision and report shall not be referred to in any motion, debate or question, from the time when the Resolution of the House is passed until the report is laid before the House ...[74]

At the heart of the discussions of the various committees which have considered the rule are two conflicting views of its purpose. The 1962 Procedure Committee report which first formulated it as a rule was concerned in its deliberations almost exclusively with the question of prejudice. In other words, the purpose of the rule appeared to that committee to be to prevent Members from appearing to try and influence the decisions of the courts in active cases. In this respect, the main reference point was the concept of contempt of court, and it was perhaps because such a concept extended to civil proceedings that the rule was explicitly so extended in later formulations.

The notion of contempt of court has been subject to more change since 1962 than has been seen in the *sub judice* resolution. Following the Phillimore Committee's 1974 recommendations, that 'a publication should give rise to strict liability in the law of contempt only if it creates a risk that the course of justice will be seriously impeded',[75] the Contempt of Court Act 1981 restricted criminal contempt to this notion of strict liability. The Phillimore Committee had also observed that 'if our recommendations are accepted, there will be very little difference between the restrictions in Parliament and those which apply outside it'.[76] However, the practice in the interpretation of the House's rule has tended to be far more restrictive than as it is applied to the media.

Reflecting the increasing preoccupation with judicial activism as evidenced by judicial review, and the increasing salience of Article IX, by the time of the 1999 Joint Committee on Privilege, the concept of 'comity' between Parliament and the courts had come much more to the fore, and largely displaced the notion of 'prejudice':

It is important that a debate, a committee hearing, or any other parliamentary proceeding should not prejudice a fair trial, especially a criminal trial. But it is not only a question

---

[74] Resolution of the House of Commons of 15 November 2001. The House of Lords equivalent is for all practical purposes identical.

[75] Report of the Committee on Contempt of Court, 1974, Cmnd. 5794, para 113.

[76] ibid, para 120.

of prejudicing a fair trial. Parliament is in a particularly authoritative position and its proceedings attract much publicity. The proper relationship between Parliament and the courts requires that the courts should be left to get on with their work. No matter how great the pressure at times from interest groups or constituents, Parliament should not permit itself to appear as an alternative forum for canvassing the rights and wrongs of issues being considered by the judicial arm of the state on evidence yet to be presented and tested. Although the risk of actual prejudice is greater in a jury trial, it would not be right to remove appeal cases or other cases tried without a jury from the operation of the rule. Restrictions on media comment are limited to not prejudicing the trial, but Parliament needs to be especially careful: it is important constitutionally, and essential for public confidence, that the judiciary should be seen to be independent of political pressures. Thus, restrictions on parliamentary debate should sometimes exceed those on media comment.[77]

The resolution as it now stands contains specified exemptions. It does not restrict debate on legislation (primary or secondary); nor does it extend to proceedings in foreign and international courts (including the European Court of Justice and the European Court of Human Rights). In addition, it specifies that 'where a ministerial decision is in question, … reference to the issues or the case may be made in motions, debates or questions'.

This last exemption was not found in the original 1963 resolution. It was added in 1972 in a separate, free-standing, resolution, which stated (in a demonstration of the by then common difficulty in steering a course between privilege and responsibility) that 'reference may be made in Questions, Motions or debate to matters awaiting or under adjudication in all civil courts, including the National Industrial Relations Court, in so far as such matters relate to a Ministerial decision which cannot be challenged in court except on grounds of misdirection or bad faith, or concern issues of national importance such as the national economy', unless, in the opinion of the Speaker, 'there is a real and substantial danger of prejudice to the proceedings'.[78]

The Procedure Committee report which recommended this relaxation of the rule makes clear that the driver of the change was a desire to allow parliamentary debate on the role of the Secretary of State for Employment in proceedings of the newly created National Industrial Relations Court (NIRC).[79] Industrial relations in this period were a major issue of political contention, and the NIRC, unusually for a British court, was a politically controversial institution, brought into being by the Conservative administration of Edward Heath, and abolished shortly after the transfer of power to Harold Wilson's Labour administration in 1974. The Act which created the court empowered the Secretary of State to apply for the power to impose a 'cooling-off period' in an industrial dispute. The normal operation of the rule, when applied to such proceedings before the NIRC, would have had

---

[77] Joint Committee on Parliamentary Privilege, Report of Session 1998–99 (n 56) para 192.

[78] CJ (1971–72), 408.

[79] House of Commons Procedure Committee, 'Matters Sub Judice', Fourth Report of Session 1971–72, HC 298.

the effect of stifling parliamentary debate on issues of major public and political importance. In these circumstances there was a feeling on both sides of the House that a relaxation of the rule was needed; this led to the Committee's report and the 1972 resolution.

The exemption in respect of ministerial decisions remained in force despite the demise of the NIRC. The 1999 Joint Committee on Parliamentary Privilege recommended that it should be extended to apply to any judicial review of a ministerial decision rather than being limited to reviews on grounds of misdirection or bad faith; subject as before to the absolute discretion of the Chair.[80] The reason given was that 'it seems questionable how far there are any ministerial decisions that can be challenged only on these limited grounds'.[81] This recommendation was put into effect in the 2001 revision of the resolution.

There can be no doubt that this further relaxation of the *sub judice* rule was intended by the House as a means of ensuring effective scrutiny of ministerial decision-making. The Minister who opened the debate on the motion which became the 2001 resolution commented: 'The purpose of the *sub judice* rule is to protect the courts from parliamentary interference; it is not to provide Ministers with a convenient protection against questioning in the House'.[82]

However, in interpreting the resolution in particular cases, it is by no means clear what the phrase 'where a ministerial decision is in question' means in practice. It seems obvious that some decisions are in fact those of a Minister—in some circumstances a decision to deport or not to deport may be of this nature and may be subject to judicial review. But it could be argued under the Haldane doctrine that, for example, a social security decision which is being contested at tribunal is a ministerial decision.[83] Many tribunals are concerned with the actions of officials, and if the exemption were to be applied strictly, such proceedings would appear to fall outside the scope of the resolution. It does not appear to have been the intention of the House either in 1972 or 2001 to except such proceedings involving one private party and officials acting under the authority of a Secretary of State.

The rule was revisited by a Joint Committee of the two Houses appointed in 2011 to look at the question of the disclosure of details of cases covered by court

---

[80] Joint Committee on Parliamentary Privilege of Session 1998–99 (n 56).

[81] HC (1998–99) 214-I, para 198.

[82] HC Deb 15 November 2001, col 1014 (speech by the Parliamentary Secretary, Privy Council Office (Mr Stephen Twigg).

[83] The Haldane doctrine is that Ministers are accountable to Parliament for the actions of their officials, so called after the 1918 Report of the Machinery of Government Committee (Co 9230), chaired by Viscount Haldane, para 33 of which states: 'We are so far from thinking that the importance of a service to the community is prima facie a reason for making those who administer it immune from ordinary Parliamentary criticism, that we feel that all such proposals should be most carefully scrutinised, and that there should be no omission, in the case of any particular service, of those safeguards which Ministerial responsibility to Parliament alone provides'. It is sometimes confused with the largely mythical 'Haldane principle' applied to government funding of scientific research, supposedly derived from the same document.

injunctions (so-called anonymised injunctions and super-injunctions). The Committee followed a committee set up by the Master of the Rolls to look at the issue, which had concluded that Article IX meant that:

> No super-injunction, or any other court order, could conceivably restrict or prohibit parliamentary debate or proceedings.[84]

The Joint Committee reported in March 2012.[85] The Committee broadly concluded that in revealing the names of those individuals or organisations covered by injunctions the *sub judice* rule had not been breached (as the Speaker of the House of Commons had ruled) and that the scale of the problem was not sufficient to warrant amendment of the rule, although it did recommend legislation to clarify the application of qualified privilege to reports of parliamentary proceedings—an issue subsequently taken up by the 2012–13 Joint Committee. The brief fashion for MPs revealing information behind injunctions appears to have been a flash in the pan, and no further action has seemed to be required to deal with a problem which has largely gone away.[86]

As a result of the 1972 revision, the current *sub judice* resolution also contains two references to the right of the Speaker to waive the rule. It is not altogether clear how they relate to each other. The rule as a whole is 'subject always to the discretion of the Chair' (wording which has been in place since 1963). In addition, and more specifically, 'where … in the opinion of the Chair a case concerns issues of national importance such as the economy, public order or the essential services, reference to the issues or the case may be made in motions, debates or questions'. As noted above, this latter proviso had its origin in the political circumstances of the early 1970s. The presence of two separate references to the discretion of the Chair probably reflects the fact that the 2001 resolution is a composite, comprising elements from both previous resolutions (those of 1963 and 1972), but also representing the constant and unresolved tension within Parliament between the desire to exercise its freedom of speech as fully as possible and its recognition of an only half-articulated bargain with the courts over how to effectively patrol the boundaries between the two. It might be argued that the terms of the resolution could usefully be broadened to allow the Speaker to waive the rule in any circumstances where he considers that it is in the public interest to do so, perhaps by removing the proviso altogether, on the grounds that the opening clause of the resolution confers on the Speaker a blanket discretion to waive the

---

[84] Master of the Rolls, 'Report of the Committee on Super-Injunctions: Super-Injunctions, Anonymised Injunctions and Open Justice' (20 May 2011), available at www.judiciary.gov.uk/publications/committee-reports-super-injunctions, p vii.

[85] Joint Committee on Privacy and Injunctions, Report of Session 2010–12, HC Paper 1443, HL Paper 273.

[86] The super-injunctions issue was discussed at greater length by Oonagh Gay and Hugh Tomlinson in ch 2 of the first edition of this work (n 1) 52–55.

rule. But the history of the emergence of the rule is another indicator of the ebb and flow between Parliament and the courts, and the still unresolved tensions in that relationship.[87]

V. FREEDOM FROM ARREST

Freedom from arrest, trial and imprisonment is an immunity typically claimed to different degrees by legislators (and elected executives) throughout the world on the basis that it frees them from the risk of intimidation by the agents of the state (or other states). The UK Parliament has never seriously claimed such extensive immunity, and the claim to the privilege of freedom from arrest is now obsolete. John Hatsell observed in his *Precedents*, that the 'principal view, which the House of Commons seem always to have had in the several declarations of their Privileges was of securing to themselves … their personal presence in the House, not to be withdrawn, either by the summons of inferior Courts; by the arrest of their bodies in civil causes; or, which was of more importance, by commitment of orders from the Crown for any supposed offences'. He went on to note that:

> [T]here is not a single instance of a Member's claiming the privilege of Parliament to withdraw himself from the criminal law of the land: for offences against the public peace they always thought themselves amenable to the laws of their country; they were contented with being substantially secured from any violence from the Crown, or its ministers, but readily submitted themselves to the judicature of the King's Bench.[88]

The 1967 Select Committee on Parliamentary Privilege had recommended the abandonment of this claim.[89] The Joint Committee on Parliamentary Privilege in 1999 had agreed with its conclusion,[90] and the 2013 Joint Committee had concurred.[91] Nothing has been done, since the committees appeared to agree that legislation would be required to extinguish the claim (which on the face of it seems a rather pedantic view of the mechanics of dropping it from the Speaker Elect's petition). All these committees concurred in the conclusion that MPs are subject to the normal course of criminal justice. Each also noted that with the abolition of imprisonment for civil debt in 1870, the last vestige of a requirement for this privilege had evaporated. *Erskine May* considers whether the privilege might apply in the case of a contempt of court of a 'civil' rather than 'criminal' nature, but

---

[87] It is worth noting, in the context of the debate over whether to place privilege on a statutory basis, that the Scottish Parliament, the National Assembly for Wales and the Northern Ireland Assembly have all have in place their own versions of the *sub judice* rule, which differ markedly not only from Westminster's but from each other's, but they all rely on reference to the definitions in the Contempt of Court Act 1981.

[88] Hatsell, *Precedents of Proceedings* (n 51) vol 1, 205–06.

[89] Select Committee on Parliamentary Privilege, Report of Session 1967–68, HC Paper 34, para 98.

[90] Joint Committee on Parliamentary Privilege, Report of Session 1998–99 (n 56) para 327.

[91] Joint Committee on Parliamentary Privilege, Report of Session 2013–14 (n 37) para 257.

the House has in the past generally declined to intervene in favour of a Member imprisoned for contempt of court.[92]

The privilege of freedom from arrest has been most recently discussed in a House of Commons Procedure Committee report of 2015.[93] The immediate cause of the inquiry was a complaint made by an MP that the publication of another Member's name in the Votes and Proceedings, when read alongside a news release from the Metropolitan Police, revealed the nature of an alleged offence for which he had been briefly arrested and interviewed (no charges were ever brought). This, it was claimed, violated his right to privacy. The Speaker when writing to the Committee asking it to look at the matter expressed his own opinion:

> I personally rather doubt that a regime designed some centuries ago for the protection of Members from arbitrary arrest by the executive is necessary now, although some form of informal notification might be retained, which preserved the privacy of the Member concerned.[94]

The Committee's inquiry revealed that the claim in *Erskine May* that 'in all cases in which Members of either House are arrested on criminal charges, the House must be informed of the cause for which they are detained from their service in Parliament',[95] had been disregarded for some 30 years between the arrest of Jeremy Thorpe on charges of conspiracy to murder in 1978 (he was acquitted) to the arrest of Damian Green (discussed above) in 2008 on suspicion of conspiracy to commit misconduct in public office (no charges were brought), when the requirement had been somewhat mysteriously revived. Nonetheless, the Committee went on to assert the continuing significance of the requirement:

> We have therefore asked ourselves, as invited by the Speaker, to consider whether the requirement of notification should simply be renounced. We have concluded that it should not. It seems to us that the ancient claim to freedom from arrest was founded on the House's determination to protect its Members from harassment by the agents of the Crown or of other authorities claiming jurisdiction, or by other individuals. Although this threat is no longer present, the House's assertion of its right to the attendance and participation of its Members in its proceedings should not be lightly abandoned, as it could not readily be reclaimed. The House must be in a position where it can ensure the attendance of its Members should this be required. The formal notification of an arrest is one means by which the House asserts the right to be kept informed by agents of the Crown of actions taken against Members which may impair their ability to attend the House. The formal notification of imprisonment or other detention of a Member is another.[96]

---

[92] See also the *Chaytor* judgment (n 12) which discusses at paras 117, 118 and 122 the concept of 'ordinary crimes' from prosecution for which MPs and peers are not immune.

[93] Procedure Committee, Second Report of Session 2015–16, 'Notification of the arrest of Members', HC Paper 649.

[94] ibid, app 1.

[95] *Erskine May* (n 50), 243.

[96] Procedure Committee, Second Report of Session 2015–16 (n 93) para 23.

The Committee, however, concluded that the arrangements by which the name of an arrested MP was published, with no apparent discretion for the Speaker to withhold it, failed to strike an appropriate balance between the rights enjoyed by MPs under Article 8 of the European Convention on Human Rights (ECHR) and the right of the House to know what was happening to its Members if they were prevented from attending.[97] However, the Committee also recognised a conflict between the House's assertion of its privilege and the law:

> In continuing this requirement, the House needs to recognise the dilemma which police forces face in complying with it. They are required both to respect the privileges of the House and to obey the law. There is a potential conflict between the duty to notify and the obligation to respect the privacy of individuals.[98]

It therefore proposed a new resolution of the House which would (it was implicitly hoped) enable the police to avoid any legal action for breach of privacy in obeying the order of the House. A resolution in the terms proposed by the Committee was agreed by the House as follows:

> That Members of the House shall be under no undue restraint from being able to attend the House, and that this principle has been, and continues to be, encompassed in the privileges of the House claimed at the beginning of each Parliament;
>
> *Ordered*, That this House accordingly:
>
> (1)   endorses the Second Report of the Procedure Committee, Session 2015–16, Notification of the arrest of Members, HC 649;
> (2)   directs the Clerk of the House and the Speaker to follow the protocol on notification of arrest of Members set out in Annex 2 to that Report; and
> (3)   directs each chief officer of police in the United Kingdom, immediately upon the arrest of any Member by the police force under that officer's command, to notify the Clerk of the House in accordance with the provisions of that protocol.[99]

There are other examples of assertions of the House's right to expect the attendance of its Members (and its officials) which have been softened or abandoned. The privilege of exemption of an MP from attending court as a witness, in criminal as well as civil proceedings, has been asserted on these grounds.[100] An MP may, however, choose to attend court in response to a subpoena even on a day on which the House sits.[101] Schedule 33 to the Criminal Justice Act 2003 repealed section 9(1) of and Part III of Schedule 1 to the Juries Act 1974, which had restated in statutory form the ancient parliamentary privilege of exemption from jury

---

[97]   ibid, para 25.
[98]   ibid, para 26.
[99]   Votes and Proceedings of the House of Commons, 10 February 2016, item 13.
[100]   *Erskine May* (n 50) 248.
[101]   On 23 May 2005, Mrs Sylvia Heal, one of the Deputy Speakers, voluntarily gave evidence at the Bow Street magistrates' court about the incursion of pro-hunting demonstrators into the Chamber during a sitting of the House on 15 September 2004.

service, applicable to Members and officers of either House of Parliament.[102] MPs and parliamentary staff are now as liable to be summoned to perform jury service as other citizens.[103]

VI. EXCLUSIVE COGNISANCE

Exclusive cognisance (sometimes known as autonomous jurisdiction) is defined in *Erskine May* as 'the right [of both Houses] to be the sole judge of the lawfulness of their own proceedings, and to settle—or depart from—their own codes of procedure'.[104] It goes on to assert that the 'principle holds good even where the procedure of a House or the rights of its Members or officers depends on statute'.[105]

Article IX of the Bill of Rights is one assertion, in compressed form, of exclusive cognisance, but the concept pre-dates that and has wider application than the wording of Article IX immediately suggests.[106]

The 2013 Joint Committee considered the meaning of exclusive cognisance at some length in chapter 2 of its report. It noted that the 'principle of exclusive cognisance underpins all privilege, including those aspects of privilege which are now based in statute' and that 'It is, in effect, an exception to the general principle of the rule of law'. It accepted that 'The tension between parliamentary privilege and the general rule of law can be uncomfortable' and concluded that 'The possibility of tension between parliamentary privilege and the rule of law means that Parliament's claim to exclusive cognisance should be strictly limited to those areas where immunity from normal legal oversight is necessary in order to safeguard the effective functioning of Parliament'. Despite this, the Joint Committee opined that 'It is ... neither possible nor desirable to identify and specify every single element

---

[102] Although the term 'officers' of either House was not defined in statute, in the context of exemption from jury service the term 'officer' had come to embrace all employees of the House of Commons Commission. A comparably broad definition covered all House of Lords staff.

[103] The risk of jury service disrupting the work of Parliament is mitigated by administrative practice: MPs who seek excusal on the grounds of parliamentary duties are to be offered deferral in the first instance. If an MP feels that it would be inappropriate to do jury service in their own constituency, then they should be allowed to do it elsewhere. The Speaker of the House of Commons and his deputies should in the first instance be deferred to a time when Parliament is not sitting, because of the difficulties their absence from the House would cause.

[104] For example, in the case of *British Railways Board v Pickin*, the House of Lords (acting in its judicial capacity) decided that it was not lawful to impugn the validity of a statute by seeking to establish that Parliament, in passing it, had been misled. *Erskine May* (n 50) 295; [1974] All ER 609. For a contrary view, expressed by Lord Denning MR, see [1973] QB 219 at 230.

[105] *Erskine May* (n 50) 227.

[106] In *Attorney General v Leigh* [2011] NZSC 106, exclusive cognisance is described as 'largely the opposite side of the Article IX coin'; and the judgment in the case of *Baron Mereworth v Ministry of Justice* [2012] 2 WLR 192, applies *Chaytor* but comes to the conclusion that the right to receive a writ of summons to the House of Lords is a matter squarely within exclusive cognisance of the House of Lords (it also cites the *Viscountess Rhondda* case). *Mereworth* asserts that 'Where a matter falls within the internal affairs of Parliament, it is within the area of Parliament's exclusive cognisance except where legislation provides to the contrary'. On what matters exactly constitute 'internal affairs' it is less helpful, but it seems on the face of it quite a narrow formulation.

of parliamentary privilege', which led it to the conclusion that the best test of the limits of any claim by Parliament to be outside the general law was the 'doctrine of necessity': that a privilege should only be asserted to the extent that it was essential to protect the core functions of Parliament. The Committee persuaded itself to disagree with the 1999 Joint Committee and concluded that seeking to define the scope of privilege (and therefore the limits of exclusive cognisance) in law was too risky:

> Absolute privilege attaches to those matters which, either because they are part of proceedings in Parliament or because they are necessarily connected to those proceedings, are subject to Parliament's sole jurisdiction or 'exclusive cognisance'.

> The extent of Parliament's exclusive cognisance changes over time, as the work of Parliament evolves: it would be impracticable and undesirable to attempt to draw up an exhaustive list of those matters subject to exclusive cognisance.[107]

The Committee therefore saw the future as a continuation of the approach of reactive and piecemeal legislation which had characterised Parliament's approach to the question in the past.

A. Control of Membership

Perhaps the most fundamental expression of exclusive cognisance is the right each House asserts to determine who may or may not be a Member and on what terms. Even the assertion by the Commons of the Speaker's powers to suspend its own Members for unruly behaviour has been an anxious point of debate in the past (hence the inclusion in Standing Order No 44 of that House the picturesque proviso that 'Nothing in this order shall be taken to deprive the House of the power of proceeding against any Member according to its ancient usages').[108] It is for this reason that questions relating to its membership (for example the moving of writs for by-elections) have priority over all other business in the Commons. Parliament has long since abandoned the attempt to deal with this issue without legislation.

The House of Commons began to determine the outcome of disputed elections in the 1580s. It did this mostly through the Committee of Privileges, but the exclusive right of the Commons to determine the outcome of disputed elections was not recognised by the courts until the late seventeenth century. Over the course of the eighteenth century, the first session of almost every Parliament was usually greatly preoccupied with the determination of election petitions, and there was much unseemly politicking in defiance of any pretence of due process and natural justice. At the end of the century a curious compromise was reached in which a quasi-judicial statutory committee of the House was established (with most of the

---

[107] Joint Committee on Parliamentary Privilege, Report of Session 2013–14 (n 37) para 47.
[108] See for example the discussion of the Irish obstruction crisis of the 1880s in Redlich, *The Procedure of the House of Commons* (n 54) 133–85.

powers of a court), selected by lot, to deal with election petitions. It failed to solve the problem, and in 1868 the House handed over to the courts entirely the trial of 'controverted elections' by the Parliamentary Elections Act.[109]

Evidently, for both Houses, the question of membership is now largely determined by statute. But once elected (if not disqualified by law) the House of Commons itself may in theory determine whether a Member may take their seat.[110] It is notable, however, that in 2016 an Act was required to establish beyond doubt the right of the House of Lords to expel a Peer.[111]

A *locus classicus* of the dispute between Parliament and the courts is the case of Charles Bradlaugh, an atheist who refused to swear an oath of allegiance (though he was quite willing to make a non-theistic solemn declaration or affirmation) and was expelled by the House, not being allowed to take his seat. He stood repeatedly for the seat which had been vacated by the House and was returned each time with an increased majority. When the House (at Gladstone's urging) eventually resolved to allow him to make the affirmation and take his seat, a certain Mr Clarke petitioned the courts for him to be expelled from the House as being in breach of the requirements of the Parliamentary Oaths Act 1866. The courts found for the plaintiff, and the House once again passed a motion for a new writ. The toing-and-froing continued until the House of Lords upheld Bradlaugh's argument that Clarke was not competent to bring the action.[112] Bradlaugh subsequently began an action against the Serjeant-at-Arms in which the courts ruled decisively in favour of exclusive cognisance.[113] In his judgment upholding the right of the House to expel and detain Bradlaugh, Lord Coleridge CJ made his famous statement which may still mark the high-water mark of judicial deference to exclusive cognisance:

> What is said or done within the walls of Parliament cannot be inquired into in a court of law … The jurisdiction of the Houses over their own members, their right to impose discipline within their walls, is absolute and exclusive.[114]

Eventually Bradlaugh, who also has the distinction of being the *last* person to be imprisoned on an order of the House of Commons, did take his seat, in curious circumstances.[115]

Although the House of Commons has seldom resorted to expulsion, three Members were expelled in the last century. In August 1922, Horatio Bottomley

[109] Sometimes known as the Election Petitions and Corrupt Practices at Elections Act, or simply the Corrupt Practices Act. This topic is explored by Richard Kelly and Matthew Hamlyn in ch 4 of the first edition of this work (n 1) 92–95.

[110] It is notable that when the Australian Parliament came to clarify parliamentary privilege in its Parliamentary Privileges Act 1987, it removed the right of either House to expel its own Members.

[111] House of Lords (Expulsion and Suspension) Act 2016. The Bill was introduced as a Private Member's Bill in the Lords. It experienced some opposition in the Commons on the grounds that it afforded too wide a discretion to the other House.

[112] *Bradlaugh v Clarke* [1883] 8 App Cas 354.

[113] *Bradlaugh v Gosset* [1884] 12 QBD 271.

[114] ibid 275.

[115] For a sympathetic but very full account of the Bradlaugh saga see B Niblett, *Dare to Stand Alone: The Story of Charles Bradlaugh, Atheist and Republican* (Oxford, Kramedart Press, 2010).

(Independent, South Hackney) was expelled following his conviction for fraud which resulted in a sentence of seven years' imprisonment. In October 1947, Garry Allighan (Labour, Gravesend) was expelled for gross contempt of the House after lying to a Committee following the publication of an article accusing MPs of insobriety and of taking bribes for the supply of information. And in December 1954, Peter Baker (Conservative, South Norfolk) was expelled after receiving a custodial sentence of seven years following a conviction for forgery.[116] The Representation of the People Act 1981 provided for the automatic disqualification from the House of Commons.[117] So while the House has the right to expel any of its Members, it cannot simply by Resolution prevent the return of a Member at any election.[118]

B. Recall

The House's power of expulsion was not deployed at any point throughout the 2008–09 expenses scandal. The exposures resulted in a handful of criminal prosecutions and it contributed to several political careers coming to an end at the 2010 general election, either as a result of Members standing down, being deselected or being defeated.[119] One strand in the parties' response to public dismay over the expenses scandal was to hold out the possibility of voter-led dismissal of MPs between general elections.[120]

In December 2011, the coalition Government published a White Paper including a draft Bill on the recall of MPs, which was then subjected to pre-legislative scrutiny by the Political and Constitutional Reform Select Committee.[121]

---

[116] Horatio Bottomley's offences were not felonies, so at the time he would not have been automatically disqualified. In the case of Mr Baker, the motion for expulsion need not have been moved: under the provisions of the Forfeiture Act 1870 then still in force, he would have been automatically disqualified by reason of his conviction for a felony.

[117] All distinctions between felony and misdemeanour were abolished by s 1 of the Criminal Law Act 1967. An apparently inadvertent consequence of treating almost all offences as misdemeanours was the lack of an automatic disqualification from membership of the House of Commons following a criminal conviction for a serious offence. This was not restored until the Representation of People Act 1981, passed in the wake of the death of Bobby Sands (Anti-H Block, Fermanagh and South Tyrone) on hunger strike in the Maze prison in Northern Ireland.

[118] Tony Benn (Labour) was returned for Bristol South East at a by-election on 4 May 1961, after he had been disqualified from membership of the House of Commons on inheriting his late father's peerage, but an election court found that he had not been duly returned because as a Peer he was ineligible and that Malcolm St Clair (Conservative), the candidate who came second at the poll, was duly elected. The House accordingly voted, by 235 to 145, that the return from the by-election should be amended and Mr St Clair took his seat in the House.

[119] Dr Ian Gibson (Labour, Norwich North) left Parliament by taking the Chiltern Hundreds in June 2009 after being deselected in the wake of the expenses scandal. By doing so, he precipitated a by-election, which was won by Chloe Smith (Conservative).

[120] Conservative Party manifesto, 'Invitation to join the Government of Britain' (2010) 65–66; Liberal Democrat Party manifesto (2010) 89; Labour Party manifesto (2010) 9; *The Coalition: our programme for government* (May 2010) 27.

[121] The *Recall of MPs* White Paper was published as Cm 8241.

The Government's draft Bill set out how a petition from constituents might result in a by-election where a Member had been sentenced to a custodial sentence of 12 months or less (the first recall condition). The draft Bill also left it open to the House itself to decide how, when and why to trigger a recall petition (the second recall condition), as in effect an extension of the House's existing disciplinary powers. The White Paper, and the memorandum submitted by the Clerk of the House to the Select Committee, set out how the new power might be exercised, after a reasonable and fair process involving the Committee on Standards and Privileges, in relation to serious wrongdoing by a Member. The absence of explicit safeguards in the text of the Bill on the use of the second recall condition was intended to avoid making any part of the House's self-disciplinary machinery subject to legal challenge in the courts. The Political and Constitutional Reform Committee agreed that it would be undesirable to define 'serious wrongdoing' in the Bill.[122] Noting that expulsion would not prevent the person concerned standing in the resulting by-election, the Committee was not, however, persuaded there was a gap in the House's disciplinary procedures which needed to be filled by the introduction of a statutory power of recall, as the House already had the power to expel Members who were guilty of serious wrongdoing. Eventually, in the Bill as presented, the trigger was a suspension from the House for 21 or more sitting days.

The Bill was introduced in September 2014. During its passage, it was amended in two significant respects. The period of suspension of a Member required to trigger the conditions for a recall petition was reduced from 21 to 10 days (with the slightly perverse effect of introducing a much more precipitate cliff edge when the Committee of Standards and the House were considering the proportionality of a punishment); and a third condition was introduced, which was conviction of an offence under section 10 of the Parliamentary Standards Act 2009 (in other words, being found guilty of fiddling your expenses). The Act appears to some observers as a rather half-hearted gesture towards allowing the electorate to hold their MPs to account between general elections, and to others as further evidence of the Commons' loss of self-confidence in its ability to regulate its own proceedings. Its provisions have not yet been used.

C. Mental Health

More recently, the House of Commons has legislated in a slightly contrary direction to the general drift of handing decisions about its membership to the courts or other places out of Parliament. The 2010 report of the Speaker's Conference on Parliamentary Representation had perceived a danger that section 141 of the Mental Health Act 1983 (which re-enacted earlier provisions in an amended form)

---

[122] Political and Constitutional Reform Select Committee, 'Recall of MPs', First Report of Session 2012–13, HC 373, para 30.

might deter Members from admitting mental health problems and seeking suitable treatment, and that, from a purely medical point of view, the section might not operate in the best interests of Members.[123] Under the 1983 Act, MPs could lose their seats if they were detained under the Act for more than six months. Under section 1 of the Mental Health Discrimination Act 2013, section 141 was repealed. The Act (which started as a Private Member's Bill) also abolishes any rule of the common law which disqualifies a person from membership of the House of Commons on grounds of mental illness.

D. The Application of Statutes to Parliament

Following the approach confirmed in *R v Graham Campbell, ex parte Herbert* the courts presumed that, in the absence of express provision or necessary implication, an Act does not apply to the internal workings of the Houses of Parliament.[124] It is probable that nowadays the courts would take a stricter view over a matter such as the applicability of the ordinary law of the land on licensing hours to the Palace of Westminster.[125] In the *Chaytor* judgment the Supreme Court observed:

> In summary, extensive inroads have been made into areas that previously fell within the exclusive cognisance of Parliament. Following *Ex p Herbert* there appears to have been a presumption in Parliament that statutes do not apply to activities within the Palace of Westminster unless they expressly provide to the contrary. That presumption is open to question. In 1984 three Law Lords, Lord Diplock, Lord Scarman and Lord Bridge of Harwich, on the Committee for Privileges expressed the view that sections 2–6 of the Mental Health Act 1983 applied to members of the House of Lords, although the Act did not expressly so state.[126]

Increasingly, however, the authorities in both Houses pledge themselves to comply fully with relevant legislation in fields such as employment law or health and safety as if it were binding on them. This policy of voluntary application has been gradually supplanted by provisions expressly applying statutes to Parliament and parliamentary staff.[127]

---

[123] Speaker's Conference on Parliamentary Representation, Final Report of Session 2009–10, HC Paper 239, paras 316–29.

[124] [1935] KB 594.

[125] The influence of *R v Graham Campbell ex p Herbert* [1935] KB 594 is discussed by Geoffrey Lock in his chapter, 'Statute law and case law applicable to Parliament' in Oliver and Drewry, *The Law and Parliament* (n 63) and is also discussed at pp 72–73 of the first edition of this work (n 1).

[126] *R v Chaytor* (n 12) para 78.

[127] This paragraph follows D Greenberg (ed), *Craies on Legislation*, 8th edn (London, Sweet and Maxwell, 2004) para 11.6.1. Examples of express application include s 65 of the Disability Discrimination Act 1995 and s 36 of the Apprenticeships, Skills, Children and Learning Act 2009.

Express provision in statute may include a reference to 'proceedings in Parliament'. In the absence of a generally applicable statutory definition of proceedings, it would presumably fall to a court what actually constitutes proceedings if the point required decision in a litigated case. For example, the requirements placed by section 29 of the Equalities Act 2010 on service-providers not to discriminate, harass or victimise persons requiring the service do not apply, under paragraph 1 of Schedule 3 to the Act, to a function of Parliament or a function exercisable in connection with proceedings in Parliament, provided that what is done is in pursuance of a resolution or other deliberation of either House or a Committee of either House. The public sector equality duty under section 149 of the Act does not apply to the House of Commons or the House of Lords, or to the exercise of functions in connection with proceedings in either House.

An example of legislating to protect privilege without defining it is section 34 of the Freedom of Information Act 2000. It states that 'Information is exempt information if exemption … is required for the purpose of avoiding an infringement of the privileges of either House of Parliament' and that 'The duty to confirm or deny does not apply if, or to the extent that, exemption … is required for the purpose of avoiding an infringement of the privileges of either House of Parliament'. In a more extensive assertion of this exemption, it provides that certificate signed by the Speaker of the House of Commons (or, in the Lords, the Clerk of the Parliaments) stating that an exemption is required for the purpose of avoiding an infringement of the privileges of either House of Parliament, that 'shall be conclusive evidence of that fact'. The implication is that a certificate of this nature is non-justiciable before the Information Commissioner of the courts. So far, no attempt to challenge a certificate has been made.[128]

The 2013 Joint Committee briefly considered the applicability of statute to Parliament. It recommended that:

> [T]he two Houses be invited to adopt resolutions stating that the House of Commons and the House of Lords should in future be expressly bound by legislation creating individual rights which could impinge on parliamentary activities, and that in the absence of such express provision such legislation is not binding upon Parliament.

And that:

> [T]he Government take steps to ensure that all Departments comply with the official guidance issued by the Treasury Solicitor in 2002, which asked them to consult the House authorities on whether any proposed legislation that is to apply to the Crown, or its servants, should apply also to the two Houses.[129]

---

[128] Section 34 did not, of course, protect Parliament from the freedom of information request which ultimately triggered the 2008–09 expenses débâcle. Section 36 of the Act ('Prejudice to effective conduct of public affairs') has similar certification provisions applying only to Parliament, but it includes a 'reasonable opinion' test which is, on the face of it, justiciable.

[129] Paras 226–27.

VII. PUNISHMENT FOR CONTEMPT OF PARLIAMENT

Erskine May sets out the history of the conflict between Parliament and the courts over limits of the claim of the 'High Court of Parliament'.[130] The lack of enforceable sanctions has called into question Parliament's power to punish contempts effectively. It has become the practice of the both Houses to pursue alleged contempts only rarely: recent examples of references of alleged contempts to the Committee of Privileges include the treatment of a witness (in 2003), a firm of solicitors attempting to dissuade a Member from making allegations by threatening action against third parties (in 2009), the hacking of Members' mobile phones, and witnesses misleading a select committee (between 2010 and 2016) and the serving of an Information Notice on an MP by the police (in 2014—which also raised interesting side issues about qualified privilege and the distribution of Hansard).[131]

The existence and extent of the penal powers of the two Houses has been a matter of debate for centuries. In the *Chaytor* judgment, Lord Phillips noted:

> Parliament has no criminal jurisdiction. It has limited penal powers to treat criminal conduct as contempt. These once included imprisonment for a limited period ... Imprisonment has not been imposed in recent times and the same is true of the theoretical power to fine. Nor is it clear that Parliament is in a position to satisfy all the requirements of article 6 [of the ECHR] which apply when imposing penal sanctions—see *Demicoli v Malta* (1991) 14 EHRR 47.[132]

Among the principal recommendations of the 1966–67 Committee Select Committee which secured the approval of the House of Commons in 1978 was that the penal jurisdiction of that House ought to be exercised in any event as sparingly as possible only where it was essential to do so.[133] The importance of respecting the principles enshrined in the European Convention on Human Rights looms over Parliament, though its exemption from being treated as a public authority under the Human Rights Act 1998 and the wide margin of appreciation afforded by the European Court of Human Rights preserve the legislature still from excessive judicial intervention.[134]

---

[130] *Erskine May* (n 50), ch 17.

[131] Committee on Standards and Privileges, 'Privilege: Protection of a Witness', Fifth Report of Session 2003–04, HC 447 (the *Weleminsky* case); Committee on Standards and Privileges, 'Privilege: John Hemming and Withers LLP', Report of Session 2009–10, HC 373. The report on the cases relating to the hacking of mobile phones was eventually published in 2016 (Committee of Privileges, 'Conduct of witnesses before a select committee: Mr Colin Myler, Mr Tom Crone, Mr Les Hinton, and News International', First Report of Session 2015–16, HC Paper 662). There have been several other Reports by the Committee on Standards and Privileges about leaks of Committee proceedings, which could constitute contempts.

[132] *R v Chaytor* (n 12) para 61.

[133] Select Committee on Parliamentary Privilege, Report, 1967–68, HC 34, para 15; Committee of Privileges, 'Recommendations of the Select Committee on Parliamentary Privilege', Third Report of Session 1976–77, HC 417, para 5.

[134] *Erskine May* (n 50) 301, deals with the case of *A v the United Kingdom* (Application 35373/97) in the European Court of Human Rights [2003] EHRR 917. See also article by Malcolm Jack on the case in (2003) 73 *The Table* 31–36.

Early in the 2012–13 Session, the House of Commons referred to its Committee on Standards and Privileges the conclusions of the Culture, Media and Sport Select Committee in its Report on *News International and the hacking of mobile phones*, that certain witnesses had misled the select committee (the matter had been referred back to the CMS Committee by the Committee of Privileges after an earlier referral in 2010).[135] The debate on 22 May 2012 on referring the matter traversed some of the territory covered in Chapter 7 of the Green Paper on Parliamentary Privilege, in connection with the powers of select committees and the penal jurisdiction of the House.[136] Christopher Johnson, in Chapter 5, discusses the eventual and much delayed outcome of this referral on which the Committee of Privileges finally reported in 2016.[137]

In approaching its task, the Standards and Privileges Committee (subsequently the Privileges Committee) announced how it would conduct its inquiry.[138] The Committee noted that the House of Commons had decided that

> its penal jurisdiction should be exercised (a) as sparingly as possible and (b) only when the House is satisfied that to exercise it is essential in order to provide reasonable protection for the House, its Members or its officers, from such improper obstruction or attempt at or threat of obstruction as is causing, or is likely to cause, substantial interference with the performance of their respective functions.[139]

Bearing this in mind, the Committee had decided that it would not recommend that the House should exercise any power of committal to prison in the matter referred to it, and that if it found any of the allegations to be proved, the maximum penalty it would recommend the House to impose would be admonishment. The Committee set out the procedure for its inquiry, to include taking oral evidence on oath, and affording any subjects of its inquiry whom the Committee intended to criticise opportunity to receive and comment on warning letters before the Committee made its report to the House.[140] All this suggested that the Committee had taken on board the recommendations of the 1999 Joint Committee and recognised the need to demonstrate more respect for the principles of due process than had perhaps characterised proceedings of the Committee of Privileges in earlier times.

Meanwhile, the issue of the Houses' penal jurisdictions had been thoroughly considered by the 2013 Joint Committee. In line with the general tone throughout,

---

[135] Culture, Media and Sport Select Committee, 'News International and Phone-hacking', Eleventh Report of Session 2010–12 HC 903-I, para 275.

[136] HC Deb 22 May 2012, cols 990 to 1014.

[137] See n 113.

[138] Formal Minutes of the House of Commons Standards and Privileges Committee, 3 July 2012.

[139] *Erskine May* (n 50) 218; Committee of Privileges, 'Recommendations of the Select Committee on Parliamentary Privilege', Third Report of Session 1976–77, HC 417; and the Resolution of the House of 6 February 1978.

[140] In July 2012, the Liaison Committee concluded that 'we are persuaded that the disadvantages of enshrining parliamentary privilege in statute would outweigh the benefits', House of Commons Liaison Committee, 'Select committee effectiveness, resources and powers', Second Report of Session 2012–13, HC Paper 697, para 133.

when the Committee reported it combined a robustness of assertion with a dislike of legislative solutions, concluding that 'We consider that the disadvantages of legislating to confirm Parliament's penal powers outweigh the advantages. We accordingly recommend against such legislation'.[141] The main preoccupation throughout was the need to reinforce the powers of select committees to send for persons, papers and records and the power of the House to punish those who disregarded the orders of committees or deliberately sought to mislead them in evidence. The Joint Committee rejected the option of doing nothing to clarify Parliament's penal powers. Having rejected the legislative solution, it proposed two draft resolutions for each House, and even took the bold step of beginning to codify what constituted a contempt. The first proposed resolution was as follows:

> The House notes the need to ensure that its penal powers should be exercised in accordance with modern standards of fairness, and that those standards include the need for clear guidance. It therefore affirms the House's continuing powers to punish contemnors.

> Without derogating from its power to determine that acts constitute contempts, the House declares, as a matter of general guidance, that the following conduct is likely to amount to an improper interference with the free exercise by a House or committee of its authority or functions, or with the free performance by a member of the member's duties as a member and consequently may be treated as contempts:

> (i)   Disrupting the proceedings of the House or a committee or inciting others to do so;
> (ii)   Refusing to produce documents or give evidence to a committee when ordered to do so;
> (iii)   misleading the House or a committee;
> (iv)   disclosure of confidential proceedings or documents without leave of the House or of the relevant committee;
> (v)   obstructing or intimidating a Member in relation to his or her parliamentary duties;
> (vi)   obstructing or intimidating a member of the House's staff carrying out the House's orders;
> (vii)   obstructing or intimidating a witness, or penalising a witness for evidence given to the House or a committee;
> (viii) improperly influencing, or attempting to improperly influence, a Member, member of staff or witness;
> (ix)   attempting to bring legal proceedings in respect of proceedings in Parliament.

The second proposed resolution, on the exercise of penal jurisdiction, was as follows:

> In exercising its penal jurisdiction the House will have regard to:

> (a)   the principle that its penal jurisdiction should be exercised:
>   (i)   as sparingly as possible; and
>   (ii)   only when the House is satisfied that to exercise it is essential in order to provide reasonable protection for the House, its Members or its officers, or

---

[141] Para 75.

others involved in Parliamentary proceedings, from such improper obstruction or attempt at or threat of obstruction as is causing, or is likely to cause,
substantial interference with the performance of their respective functions;

(b)   the existence of any other remedy for any act which may be held to be a contempt; and

(c)   whether any such act was committed knowingly or without reasonable excuse.[142]

Neither House has implemented any of these recommendations. When the Privileges Committee eventually reported on the Culture, Media and Sport Committee's case, the House at the conclusion of its debate on 27 October 2016, having
admonished two of the witnesses concerned in the events of 2009, passed a further
resolution referring the matter of the exercise and enforcement of the powers of
the House in relation to select committees and contempts to the Committee of
Privileges once again, with a general encouragement to revisit the recommendations in Chapter 8 of the 2013 Joint Committee's report. The question of whether
legislation is needed to make credible the Houses' penal powers will no doubt once
again be ventilated. Given the variety of opinions on the matter that have been
expressed by committees in the last 50 years, it would be unwise to predict their
conclusions.

VIII. CONCLUSION

Writing in 1776, in the preface to his *Precedents*, John Hatsell warned:

> The Reader will not suppose, that the OBSERVATIONS upon the several Cases, are made
> with a view of declaring what the Law of Privilege is, in the instances to which those
> Observations refer: they are designed merely to draw the attention of the Reader to par-
> ticular points, and, in some degree, assist him in forming his own opinion upon that
> question.[143]

The author of this chapter feels he must probably attach a similar disclaimer. The
state of uncertainty surrounding privilege identified more than a century ago in
the quotation that opened this chapter still persists. He would indeed be a clever
constitutionalist who could say absolutely where privilege begins and where it
ends. Despite a century of cogitation and occasional attempts at obviation, neither
House has been able to come to any very definite conclusions. To some scholars
of the matter this is its glory, displaying the same flexibility and adaptability as the
British Constitution of which the law of Parliament is itself a part. To others, this
uncertainty is simply a mess. Surely, they might demand, the electorate in this age
of transparency and accountability, has a right easily to discover under what laws
their elected representatives operate, and what those representatives' immunities
and rights are and why are they needed?

---

[142]   Joint Committee on Parliamentary Privilege, Report of Session 2013–14 (n 37) Annex 2.
[143]   Hatsell, *Precedents of Proceedings* (n 51) vii–viii.

The answer, if there is one, lies with the two Houses themselves. The lack of definite action in response to the (admittedly conflicting) recommendations of the 1999 and 2013 Joint Committee reports seems to stem not so much from any definite view of their merits as from a lack of attention on the part of successive government and opposition business managers. And despite the era of backbench business inaugurated in 2010, no determined committee, or backbench coalition of either House, seems to have been able to create any momentum around a belief that something must be done. The long running tension between the urge to codification and the desire for mystery seems unlikely to be resolved unless the accumulation of piecemeal legislation and resolutions finally collapses under the weight of its own complexity, or a crisis (perhaps an epic conflict with the courts) occurs which makes it a political priority to do something decisive.

3

The Law and the Conduct of Members of Parliament

RICHARD KELLY, MATTHEW HAMLYN AND OONAGH GAY[*]

I. INTRODUCTION

PARLIAMENT AND ITS Members have long protected their right to regulate their own conduct, in line with the principle of exclusive cognisance: 'Parliament must have sole control over all aspects of its own affairs: to determine for itself what the procedures shall be, whether there has been a breach of its procedures and what then should happen'.[1] Statute law therefore has played little part in the regulation of Members' conduct, despite mounting criticism of self-regulation.

The Parliamentary Standards Act 2009 appeared to mark a watershed in the move from self-regulation to external regulation. Under the Act members of the House of Commons ceded the regulation of their expenses (and subsequently the determination of their salaries and pensions) to an independent statutory body, the Independent Parliamentary Standards Authority (IPSA), and created a specific offence of 'providing false or misleading information for allowance claims'.[2] The circumstances leading to its creation are covered in more detail below.

The establishment of IPSA was not the first time that Members had reduced the extent of self-regulation over their own affairs and put that regulation on a statutory footing. In 1868, the existing parliamentary procedure for dealing with contested elections was replaced with a system in which judges tried such cases.[3] But this too was the result of a specific crisis and was the subject of criticism from a minority of Members that the Commons was abdicating its ancient rights.

---

[*] Richard Kelly is a senior researcher in the House of Commons Library; Matthew Hamlyn is Clerk of the Overseas Office, House of Commons; and Oonagh Gay is the retired head of the Parliament and Constitution Centre, House of Commons Library.

[1] Joint Committee on Parliamentary Privilege, First Report of Session 1998–99, HC 214-I, para 37.

[2] Parliamentary Standards Act 2009, s 10.

[3] Parliamentary Elections Act 1868. Similar provisions to those it introduced were used in 2010, when Phil Woolas was found guilty of an illegal election practice under the Representation of the People Act 1983 and his seat was declared vacant. See below for further consideration of this case.

Previous responses to concerns in the 1990s (discussed below) about the inability of Members to regulate themselves led to more formalised but still non-statutory procedures and the appointment of an independent (but non-statutory) Parliamentary Commissioner for Standards (PCS) in the House of Commons. The Commissioner is appointed by the House, investigates complaints about Members' conduct and reports his or her findings to the Committee on Standards and Privileges (the Committee on Standards from 7 January 2013),[4] but the Committee, not the Commissioner, makes recommendations to the House about punishments; and the House, not the courts, takes the final decision.

As discussed in chapter two, parliamentary privilege has never been held to extend to criminal matters, as was clearly shown by the successful prosecution under the Theft Act 1968 of a number of Members (in both Houses) over fraudulent expense claims following the expenses scandal of 2009 (see section VII below for further consideration of this case).

Unlike MPs, the House of Lords has largely retained control over its internal affairs. The House of Lords inserted a provision into the Parliamentary Standards Bill 2008–09 that ensured that 'Nothing in this Act shall affect the House of Lords'.[5] In 2009, after allegations were made that four members of the House of Lords had been prepared to accept fees to propose amendments to bills, the Lords Privileges Committee resisted the advice of the then Attorney-General that the Lords had no power to suspend its members, in favour of advice from a former Lord Chancellor, Lord Mackay of Clashfern, that the House did possess such a power.[6] The House of Lords used the powers to suspend members who had breached the code (see section VIII below).[7] Legislation in 2015 has subsequently clarified and extended this power of suspension and added a power of expulsion.

The Lords also followed the Commons in appointing a Commissioner for Standards in 2010, responsible for the independent and impartial investigation of alleged breaches of the House of Lords Code of Conduct. The PCS (in the Commons) and the House of Lords Commissioner for Standards are both officers of Parliament. Both positions are non-statutory; they are appointed by resolution of the respective Houses of Parliament.

---

[4] See the section on lay members of the Committee on Standards in ch 7 of A Horne, G Drewry and D Oliver (eds), *Parliament and the Law* (Oxford, Hart Publishing, 2013) 180.

[5] Parliamentary Standards Act 2009, s 2(1). The amendment was moved by the Leader of the House of Lords, Baroness Royall of Blaisdon, at report stage, HL Deb 20 July 2009, cols 1415–17; see also debate at Committee Stage, HL Deb 14 July 2009, cols 1046–61.

[6] House of Lords Privileges Committee, 'The Powers of the House in Respect of its Members', HL 2008–09, 87.

[7] HL Deb 20 May 2009, cols 1394–1418.

II. ELECTORAL MATTERS

A. Determination of Election Disputes by the House of Commons

Until 1770 disputed elections were determined on the floor of the House of Commons, in accordance with party strengths.[8] From 1770 to 1839 Members' names were chosen by lot to take part in a Commons committee to try election petitions.[9] Further scandals led to reform in 1868 when the jurisdiction of the House in controverted elections passed by law to the courts.[10] *Erskine May* states that 'This in no way supersedes the jurisdiction of the House, in determining questions affecting the seats of its own Members, not arising out of controverted elections'.[11]

Cornelius O'Leary reviewed the background to the 1868 legislation, noting the scale of fraud in the 1865 election. Fifty petitions were lodged, 35 came up for trial, 13 Members were unseated, and four of the successful cases led to Royal Commissions.[12] After two unsuccessful attempts, in 1868 the Parliamentary Elections Bill was introduced by Prime Minister Disraeli. During its passage some Members raised concerns about the loss of the House's rights. Disraeli faced a backbench revolt of 'modest proportions', comprising 'backbenchers who objected in principle to the Commons abdicating their rights and allowing an outside body to "brand with infamy" their members'.[13] The legislation, combined with the Ballot Act 1872 and the Corrupt and Illegal Practices Prevention Act 1883, led to a considerable reduction in electoral fraud cases.

i. Criminal Offences in Election Campaigns

In 1999, Fiona Jones MP was convicted in a *criminal* court of election expenses fraud during the 1997 election. Her conviction was overturned on appeal, and it was subsequently ruled that she could resume her seat, which had remained vacant. Following that case, the Political Parties, Elections and Referendums Act 2000 (PPERA 2000) amended the Representation of the People Act 1983 (RPA 1983) so that if an MP is found guilty of electoral offences through a criminal prosecution (ie not as a result of an electoral petition) there is a three-month suspension before the seat is vacated to allow for an appeal.[14]

---

[8] *Erskine May: Parliamentary Practice,* 24th edn (London, Butterworths, 2011) 29 fn.

[9] P Seaward, The *History Of Parliament: Director's blog: Ballots,* https://historyofparliamentblog.wordpress.com/2017/02/05/ballots (accessed 24 April 2017).

[10] *Erskine May* (n 8) 29 fn.

[11] *Erskine May* (n 8) 30.

[12] O'Leary, *The Elimination of Corrupt Practices in British Elections 1868–1911* (Oxford, Clarendon Press, 1962) 28.

[13] ibid 32–40; HC Deb 16 March 1868, cols 296–321.

[14] For further background, see House of Commons Library Standard Note, 'Election Petition: Oldham East and Saddleworth', SN/PC/5751, December 2010.

ii. Election Court: The Phil Woolas Case

Phil Woolas was returned as the Member for Oldham East and Saddleworth at the 2010 general election. However, his Liberal Democrat opponent, Elwyn Watkins, presented an election petition alleging that Mr Woolas had made a number of false statements about him in election pamphlets.

In accordance with section 123 of the RPA 1983, the case was held before an election court consisting of two judges, Mr Justice Teare and Mr Justice Griffith Williams. They handed down a joint judgment of the court and found Mr Woolas guilty of some of the allegations; their judgment was given on 5 November 2010.[15]

The judgment considered the burden and standard of proof to be applied. They held that the petitioner

> has the burden of proving the respondent is guilty of the alleged illegal practice and that, although these proceedings are civil in their nature, the standard of proof is not on the balance of probabilities but is the criminal law standard of proof beyond reasonable doubt.[16]

They concluded that Mr Woolas had made 'statements of fact in relation to the personal character or conduct of the Petitioner which he had no reasonable grounds for believing were true and did not believe were true'. Accordingly, they ruled that his election was void pursuant to section 159 of the RPA 1983 because Mr Woolas was personally guilty of an illegal practice.

On 8 November 2010, the Speaker informed the House of Commons of the court's decision. The Speaker confirmed that 'In accordance with section 160(4) of Act, Mr Phil Woolas has been reported personally guilty of an illegal practice and must vacate his seat from the date of the report, 5 November 2010'.[17]

The changes to the RPA 1983, following the Fiona Jones case, introduced a three-month suspension before the seat is vacated to allow for an appeal, following a *criminal* conviction. But it was not clear whether the decision of an election court hearing a parliamentary election petition could be subject to judicial review. Mr Woolas's first application for a judicial review was rejected by a single judge at the High Court on 8 November 2010. But he said Mr Woolas could apply to the Court of Appeal.[18]

The renewed application for permission for judicial review was held before the High Court on 16–17 November 2010. The Court concluded that it could hear a judicial review because the judges who heard the election petition, although High Court judges, were not sitting in that capacity; and also that 'it would not be right that an error of law could not be corrected by the High Court'.[19] They also concluded

---

[15] *Watkins v Woolas* [2010] EWHC 2702 (QB).

[16] ibid [48].

[17] HC Deb 8 November 2010, col 1.

[18] BBC News, 'Woolas makes fresh effort to overturn ban from politics' (8 November 2010), www.bbc.co.uk/news/uk-politics-11708723.

[19] *R (Woolas) v The Parliamentary Election Court and others* [2010] EWHC 3169 (Admin) [55]–[56].

that Woolas was entitled to have one of the findings made against him set aside but that this did not affect the other two matters which were deemed to be 'not of a trivial nature', since they amounted to 'a serious personal attack on a candidate by saying he condoned violence by extremists and refused to condemn those who advocated violence'.[20] Following this judgment and Mr Woolas's decision not to appeal, the Speaker confirmed that the seat had been vacated since 5 November 2010.[21]

Following the judgment, there was speculation that future candidates might be more wary about making inaccurate personal allegations against opponents in the knowledge that even if they won the election, their victory could be taken from them.[22] An election petition against Alastair Carmichael MP was unsuccessful in 2015 but the court found that a false statement by a candidate about his own personal character or conduct made before or during an election for the purpose of affecting his return at the election also has the effect of engaging section 106.[23] There is no equivalent to section 160 in respect of false statements during the course of a referendum campaign, an omission which was the subject of some discussion after the Brexit referendum of June 2016.

III. THE DECLARATION AND REGISTRATION OF MEMBERS' INTERESTS

The House of Commons' formal requirement for Members to register their interests dates from 1974, replacing earlier conventions on declaration of pecuniary interests by Members in both Houses in debate.[24] The motions were tabled by the incoming Labour Government, anxious to disassociate itself from the Poulson corruption scandal, and the involvement therein of the former Conservative Home Secretary Reginald Maudling.[25] In 1974, the House agreed:

> That, in any debate or proceeding of the House or its committees or transactions or communications which a Member may have with other Members or with Ministers or servants of the Crown, he shall disclose any relevant pecuniary interest or benefit of whatever nature, whether direct or indirect, that he may have had, may have or may be expecting to have.[26]

---

[20] [2010] EWHC 3169 (Admin) [125]–[126].

[21] HC Deb 6 December 2010, col 1.

[22] BBC Online, 'Phil Woolas Says Legal Fight has Hit "End of the Road"' (3 December 2010), www.bbc.co.uk/news/uk-politics-11904630.

[23] *Timothy Morrison and Others v Alistair Carmichael MP and Alistair Buchan* [2015] ECIH 90.

[24] In the Commons, there was a rule that 'no Member who has a direct pecuniary interest in a question shall be allowed to vote upon it: but in order to operate as a disqualification, this interest must be immediate and personal, and not merely of a remote or general character'. The 1971 edition of *Erskine May* stated that 'In addition to the arrangements governing the votes of Members with a personal pecuniary interest, there is a convention in both Houses that peers and Members should declare such an interest in debate. This is a custom of comparatively recent origin, being more in the nature of courtesy, or prudent precaution, in case the peer or Member concerned should be suspected of unavowed motives' (*Erskine May, Parliamentary Practice*, 18th ed (London, Butterworths, 1971) 398, 402–03).

[25] O Gay and P Leopold (eds), *Conduct Unbecoming* (London, Study of Parliament Group/Politicos, 2004, 96.

[26] HC Deb 22 May 1974, cols 537–38.

And:

> That every Member of the House of Commons shall furnish to a Registrar of Members'
> Interests such particulars of his registrable interests as shall be required, and shall notify
> to the Registrar any alterations which may occur therein, and the Registrar shall cause
> these particulars to be entered in a Register of Members' Interests which shall be available
> for inspection by the public.[27]

The House broadly accepted the conclusions and recommendations of the Select
Committee on Members' Interests (Declaration).[28] A minority of Members,
notably Enoch Powell, never accepted the principle of a register and effective
enforcement action was rarely taken.[29]

IV. THE COMMITTEE ON STANDARDS IN PUBLIC LIFE AND A CODE OF CONDUCT FOR MEMBERS OF PARLIAMENT

The regulation of Members' conduct became contentious in the 1990s. 'Cash for
questions',[30] allegations of impropriety, former ministers acquiring private sector
jobs after leaving office and the 'arms to Iraq affair'[31] all 'contributed to a general
atmosphere of what became known as "sleaze"—that corruption and questionable behaviour generally had become increasingly common in British political
life'.[32] Parliamentary self-regulation was seen to have failed, as the Committee on
Members' Interests could not enforce the parliamentary resolutions on interests or
effectively investigate when allegations of breaches were made.

In October 1994, the then Prime Minister, John Major, responded by asking a
senior judge, Lord Nolan, to chair the newly created, and independent of Parliament and Government, Committee on Standards in Public Life (CSPL):

> To examine current concerns about standards of conduct of all holders of public office,
> including arrangements relating to financial and commercial activities, and make rec-
> ommendations as to any changes in present arrangements which might be required to
> ensure the highest standards of propriety in public life.[33]

Unusually, it was established as a standing body, with an ongoing remit to make
recommendations to improve the conduct of public life. It has been very influential across the whole public sector in the first two decades of its existence.

---

[27] ibid, cols 538–43.
[28] *Erskine May* (n 8) 421; HC Deb 12 June 1975, cols 735–804.
[29] See Gay and Leopold, *Conduct Unbecoming* (n 25).
[30] Committee of Privileges, Complaint Concerning an Article in the 'Sunday Times' of 10 July 1994 relating to the Conduct of Members HC 1994–95, 351.
[31] Report of the Inquiry into the Export of Defence Equipment and Dual-Use Goods to Iraq and Related Prosecutions HC 1995–96, 115.
[32] M Rush, 'The Law Relating to Members' Conduct' in D Oliver and G Drewry (eds), *The Law and Parliament* (London, Butterworths, 1998) 106.
[33] HC Deb 25 October 1994, col 757.

The Committee reported in May 1995 and identified seven principles of public life: selflessness; integrity; objectivity; accountability; openness; honesty; and leadership. It also recommended that all public bodies should draw up codes of conduct incorporating these principles; and that internal systems for maintaining standards should be supported by independent scrutiny. It addressed specific recommendations to Members of Parliament on holding paid outside interests; it set out a draft Code of Conduct for Members; it recommended that the Commons should continue to be responsible for enforcing its own rules but that the House 'should appoint as Parliamentary Commissioner for Standards, a person of independent standing who will take over responsibility for maintaining the Register of Members' Interests; for advice and guidance to MPs on matters of conduct; for advising on the Code of Conduct and for investigating allegations of misconduct'.[34] In June 1995, the House appointed a Select Committee on Standards in Public Life to recommend specific resolutions for decision by the House. The Select Committee's two Reports were debated on 19 July and 6 November 1995, respectively, and resolutions were approved to implement Nolan recommendations.[35]

The House agreed to appoint a Parliamentary Commissioner for Standards to establish a Committee of Standards and Privileges in place of the Committee on Privileges and the Committee on Members' Interests; and to the drawing up of a Code of Conduct for Members. The Code of Conduct and Guide to the Rules relating to the Conduct of Members were originally published as the third report of the Committee on Standards and Privileges and approved by the House in July 1996.[36]

The Code of Conduct and Guide to the Rules are regularly reviewed by the PCS and then the Committee on Standards to put to the Commons. If the House agrees to any revisions, the amended Code and Rules are republished. The Code and Rules were reviewed during the 2010 Parliament, with the new Code being approved by the House on 12 March 2012 and the new Rules approved on 17 March 2015. The Rules now make clear that the Commissioner may investigate the conduct of a Member in respect of private or personal life, only with the express consent of the Committee. A new review of the Code and Rules was launched in the 2015 Parliament, but the unexpected 2017 general election has meant that the review was temporarily suspended.

The Register of Members' Interests remained in place. In 2009, it became the Register of Members' *Financial* Interests, after the House agreed with government proposals to require Members to provide more details on directorships, remunerated employment and clients.[37] Currently, there are 10 categories of registrable interests.

---

[34] Committee on Standards in Public Life, *Standards in Public Life* Cm 2850 (1995) ch 2 and Summary, para 104.

[35] *Erskine May's Parliamentary Practice*, 22nd edn (London, Butterworths, 1997) 419.

[36] Committee on Standards and Privileges, 'The Code of Conduct and the Guide to the Rules Relating to the Conduct of Members' HC 1995–96, 604; HC Deb 24 July 1996, cols 392–407.

[37] HC Deb 30 April 2009, cols 1063–132.

The position of Registrar of Members' Financial Interest is held by a member of Commons staff, reporting to the PCS. They offer informal guidance to Members on registrable interests and compile the Register, which is posted online and updated to reflect the requirement on Members to declare new interests within 28 days. The Register has been criticised as the format in which it is presented does not allow for complex data searches. Nor is there any external audit of the accuracy of the information presented by each MP.[38]

A. The Parliamentary Commissioner for Standards

The first PCS, Sir Gordon Downey, was appointed by the House following an appointment procedure approved by the Speaker on the advice of the House of Commons Commission, as recommended by the Committee.[39] His status as a former Comptroller and Auditor General (C&AG) and the designation of the PCS as an Officer of Parliament helped to make this post a prestigious office. However, unlike the C&AG, the Commissioner's role is non-statutory.

The main responsibilities of the PCS have changed over time. They are set out in Standing Order No 150 of the House of Commons:

(a)   to maintain the Register of Members' Financial Interests and any other registers of interest established by the House, and to make such arrangements for the compilation, maintenance and accessibility of those registers as are approved by the Committee on Standards or an appropriate sub-committee thereof;

(b)   to provide advice confidentially to Members and other persons or bodies subject to registration on matters relating to the registration of individual interests;

(c)   to advise the Committee on Standards, its sub-committees and individual Members on the interpretation of any code of conduct to which the House has agreed and on questions of propriety;

(d)   to monitor the operation of such code and registers, and to make recommendations thereon to the Committee on Standards or an appropriate sub-committee thereof; and

(e)   to investigate, if he thinks fit, specific matters which have come to his attention relating to the conduct of Members and to report to the Committee on Standards or to an appropriate sub-committee thereof, unless the provisions of paragraph (4) apply.[40]

A list of the Parliamentary Commissioners for Standards appointed by the House of Commons is given in Table 3.1.

---

[38]   Committee on Standards, 'Oral Evidence by Martin Williams' [freelance journalist], 13 December 2016, Q59.

[39]   HC Deb 6 November 1995, cols 683–99.

[40]   House of Commons, 'Standing Orders of the House of Commons—Public Business 2016' HC 2015–16, 2, February 2016, Standing Order No 150(2).

Table 3.1: Parliamentary Commissioners for Standards

	Period of office	Date of appointment by the House
Sir Gordon Downey	15 November 1998 for three years	6 November 1995[41]
Elizabeth Filkin	February 1999–14 February 2002	17 November 1998[42]
Sir Philip Mawer	March 2002–31 December 2007	13 February 2002[43]
John Lyon	1 January 2008–31 December 2012	15 November 2007[44]
Kathryn Hudson	1 January 2013–31 December 2017	12 September 2012[45]
Kathryn Stone	1 January 2018–31 December 2022	20 July 2017[46]

The eighth report from the (Wicks) Committee on Standards in Public Life in 2002 commented on the ambiguous nature of the office in terms of its operational independence.[47] It recommended a longer fixed-length, non-renewable term of office. Responses to Wicks from the Committee on Standards and Privileges and the House of Commons Commission argued that statute would be necessary to ensure the model of an independent office-holder in the manner described by Wicks.[48]

The House did accept significant changes to the appointment and dismissal process for the PCS in amendments to Standing Order No 150 on 26 June 2003. The main changes were:

— all future appointments of Commissioners would be for a term of five years, non-renewable;

— the term of the current Commissioner would be extended for a five-year period until June 2008;

[41] HC Deb 6 November 1995, cols 683–99.

[42] HC Deb 17 November 1998, cols 808–24.

[43] Sir Philip Mawer was originally appointed for three years from March 2002 (HC Deb 13 February 2002, cols 224–69). His appointment was extended to 25 June 2008 (HC Deb 26 June 2003, col 1258). However, on 28 June 2007, the Speaker announced that Sir Philip wished to step down on 31 December 2007 (HC Deb 28 June 2007, col 473).

[44] HC Deb 15 November 2007, cols 861–68.

[45] HC Deb 12 September 2012, cols 382–87. Details of the appointment process for Kathryn Hudson are set out in House of Commons Commission, 'Parliamentary Commissioner for Standards: Nomination of Candidate' HC 2012–13, 539.

[46] HC Deb 20 July 2017, cols 1036–37. Details of the appointment process for Kathryn Stone are set out in House of Commons Commission, *Parliamentary Commissioner for Standards: Nomination of Candidate* HC 2017–19, 294.

[47] Committee on Standards in Public Life, 'Standards of Conduct in the House of Commons' Cm 5663, 2002.

[48] House of Commons Commission, 'Response to the Eighth Report of the Committee on Standards in Public Life: Standards of Conduct in the House of Commons' HC 2002–03, 422; Committee on Standards and Privileges, 'Eighth Report of the Committee on Standards in Public Life: "Standards of Conduct in the House of Commons"' HC 2002–03, 403 paras 79–82.

—   the Commissioner may only be dismissed following a resolution of the House, where the Committee of Standards and Privileges has reported (with reasons) that he cannot carry out his functions or is unfit for the office;

—   the Standards and Privileges Committee would no longer have a government majority, but would consist of five government and five opposition members, chaired by an opposition spokesman (selection will remain with the whips);

—   no Parliamentary Private Secretary would be appointed to the Committee; and the Commissioner would publish an annual report giving details of the budget for the office.[49]

The Commissioner's independence is limited by his or her relationship with the Standards Committee. He or she makes recommendations, but it is for the Committee to specify the penalty, which the House endorses. The model means the disciplinary machinery is still 'owned' by the Commons, rather than being entirely external. This model has come increasingly under strain.

B.   Standards Committee—Addition of Lay Members

The CSPL report into Members' allowances in 2009 argued that to enhance public credibility of the standards system there should be three lay (non-MPs) added to the Commons Standards Committee, following an open recruitment process.[50] This was agreed by the Commons. The lay members cannot vote, but if they disagree with the conclusions of the Standards Committee, they may add their own comments in the report of the Committee.[51] They work with Members on disciplinary cases and general reviews of standards issues.[52] Four more lay members were recruited, following recommendations from the Standards Committee in 2015 to equalise the number of lay and MP members on the Committee, as a further attempt to enhance public trust.[53]

The Standards Committee is the only current committee in a Westminster model Parliament to contain lay members.[54] The first three lay members whose term of office ended in 2017 published a report reflecting on their experience,

---

[49] The position of PPSs on the Committee is dealt with more fully later in this chapter. There were other changes to Standing Order No 149 relating to the investigation process, covered in ch 5 of Horne, Drewry and Oliver (eds), *Parliament and the Law* (n 4).

[50] See the section on lay members of the Committee on Standards in ch 7 of Horne, Drewry and Oliver, *Parliament and the Law* (n 4).

[51] See House of Commons Library Standard Note, 'The Code of Conduct for Members—Recent Changes', SN/PC/5127, 22 January 2013.

[52] Committee on Standards, 'Reflections of Lay Members on their first year in post January 2013 to 2014'.

[53] Committee on Standards, 'The Standards System in the House of Commons' HC 2014-14, HC 383, 10 February 2015.

[54] Committee on Standards news, 'Committee welcomes moves to recruit three new lay members', 10 October 2016.

which illustrated diverging views between MPs and lay members on the future direction of the Commons' standards regime.[55] The significance of the lay members is discussed below under Reflections.

V. PARTY FUNDING AND DONATIONS AND LOANS TO MEMBERS

The terms of reference of the CSPL did not originally include party funding. In 1997, however, in the wake of the Labour Government's decision to exempt Formula One from the tobacco sponsorship ban and the receipt of a donation from Formula One by the Labour Party, the new Prime Minister, Tony Blair, came under pressure to reform the rules on donating funds to political parties and to holders of elected office.[56] The CSPL was invited 'To review issues in relation to the funding of political parties, and to make recommendations as to changes in present arrangements'.[57]

The CSPL report of October 1998, recommended clear rules on public disclosure of donations; a ban on foreign donations; a ban on anonymous donations; limits on campaign expenditure; and the creation of an Election Commission to police political donations.[58] The Government issued a White Paper including a draft bill in July 1999,[59] incorporating most of the CSPL's recommendations on donations and the creation of the Electoral Commission.

The Political Parties, Elections and Referendums Bill, introduced on 21 December 1999 included provision to require both political parties and individual candidates to register donations with the Electoral Commission. The Explanatory Notes to the Bill noted the overlap with the House requirements to register in the Register of Members' Interests.

Members were initially alarmed at the extent to which benefits had now to be registered with the Electoral Commission, which used different criteria from the Registrar of Members' Interests. Negotiations began to remedy the discrepancies and to ease the consequent administrative burden. In 2006, the Committee on Standards and Privileges set out the problems that dual reporting caused Members.[60] It called for a single system of notification, operating under

---

[55] Committee on Standards, 'Final Reflections of the first lay members at the end of their appointment period December 2012–March 2017', 28 March 2017.

[56] K Ewing, 'The Disclosure of Political Donations in Britain' in K Ewing and S Issacharoff (eds), *Party Funding and Campaign Financing in International Perspective* (Oxford, Hart, 2006) 58–59.

[57] Letter from Prime Minister, 12 November 1997, and confirmed in HC Deb 12 November 1997, col 899.

[58] Committee on Standards in Public Life, 'The Funding of Political Parties in the United Kingdom' Cm 4057, 1998.

[59] Home Office, The Funding of Political Parties in the United Kingdom: the Government's Proposals for Legislation in Response to the Fifth Report of the Committee on Standards in Public Life, Cm 4413, 1999.

[60] Committee on Standards and Privileges, 'Electoral Administration Bill: Simplification of Donation Reporting Requirements', HC 2005–06, 807, para 1.

the authority of the PCS, to enable Members to discharge both the House's and PPERA's requirements through a single declaration.[61]

Section 59 of the Electoral Administration Act 2006 removed the requirement for Members personally to report recordable donations to the Electoral Commission. It provided for the Electoral Commission to obtain the information it needs for its registers from information supplied by them to the Registrar of Members' Interests. Following alignments of Commons registration requirements,[62] the relevant statutory provisions were brought into force from 1 July 2009.[63]

VI. CONSULTANT LOBBYING AND MEMBERS

Part 1 of the Transparency of Lobbying, Non-Party Campaigning and Trade Union Act 2014 established a Registrar of Consultant Lobbyists. Schedule 1, para 5 of the Act made clear that payment for consultant lobbying does not include salaries or allowances paid to MPs or peers. The paragraph allayed concerns that lobbying by MPs on behalf of constituents might inadvertently be caught. This did not mean that MPs and peers were exempt from registration, simply the mere fact of receiving these payments was not enough to qualify them. The Registrar said in 2015 that:

> [A]lthough the Lobbying Act is not specific on this point, my view is that serving MPs and members of the House of Lords in the context of their normal duties would not be required to register. But if they undertook activities outside their normal duties which might be defined by the Act as consultant lobbying, and where other exemptions, such as VAT registration did not apply, they would be required to register.[64]

The Registrar would expect MPs to register meetings with Ministers under the Act when lobbying on behalf of a paid client and not otherwise exempt. Barry Sheerman is the first MP to be advised to register his not-for-profit company, although it was generally expected that individual MPs would not have to register.[65] The broader question of external employment of Members is explored in Reflections below.

VII. MEMBERS' EXPENSES AND IPSA

On 8 May 2009, *The Daily Telegraph* began publishing a series of articles on Members' expenses claims that continued for several weeks,[66] and eventually led to

---

[61] ibid, para 2.

[62] Committee on Standards and Privileges, 'Ending Dual Reporting of Donations: Interim Report' HC 2007–08, 989; Committee on Standards and Privileges, 'Dual Reporting and Revised Guide to the Rules' HC 2008–09, 208.

[63] Electoral Administration Act 2006 (Commencement No 8 and Transitional Provision) Order 2009, SI 2009/1509.

[64] 'New Whitehall lobbyist register to be launched within weeks', *Guardian*, 25 February 2015, cited in House of Commons Library Briefing Paper 07175, 'The register of consultant lobbyists', 22 January 2016.

[65] 'Labour MP becomes first serving politician to be registered as lobbyist' *Guardian*, 31 July 2017.

[66] The story of the *Daily Telegraph's* obtaining the information and its publication is told in R Winnett and G Rayner, *No Expenses Spared* (London, Bantam Press, 2009).

the creation of an independent statutory body for the administration of Members' expenses and the election of a new Speaker.[67] This was the culmination of a series of events relating to Members' expenses dating back several years, starting with a request under the Freedom of Information (FOI) Act 2000 for information relating to certain Members' expenses claims and including a number of attempts to reform Members' expenses which were only partially implemented. Following recommendations from the Public Administration Select Committee, the Freedom of Information Bill was amended during its passage to include the Commons and Lords on the list of public bodies subject to FOI in 2000. There were absolute exemptions for parliamentary privilege and for confidential advice. A certificate from the Speaker would ensure that the exemptions could not be challenged by the Information Commissioner or the courts. However, the Commons authorities did not expect that the administration of expenses for MPs would fall within these exemptions and Members were advised from the early 2000s that further transparency on allowances would be required.

The Freedom of Information (Amendment) Bill 2006–07 was introduced by David Maclean, a member of the House of Commons Commission. It sought to create a new exemption from FOI for communications between MPs and public authorities; and to exempt both Houses of Parliament from the FOI Act. It was controversial as the House of Commons authorities would no longer be required to disclose information about Members' allowances. The Bill passed the Commons but made no progress in the House of Lords.

A. Arrangements in the House of Commons in Relation to Members' Allowances

Whilst the House of Commons was responsible for Members' allowances, it appointed the Members Estimate Committee (MEC) to codify and keep under review the provisions of the resolutions of the House relating to expenditure charged to the Members Estimate.[68] The MEC appointed the Members Estimate Audit Committee (MEAC) to support the House's Accounting Officer in discharging his responsibilities under the Members Estimate, particularly in maintaining an effective system of internal control.

The MEAC annual report of 2008–09 highlighted a paper prepared by its external members in December 2004, which had called for a review of the rules and had argued that 'a proper system of audit, going behind Members' signatures, should be introduced (taking the form of random checks) to verify the propriety of their

---

[67] The establishment of IPSA is discussed further below and in ch 6, section IV of Horne, Drewry and Oliver, *Parliament and the Law* (n 4).

[68] The MEC, whose members are those Members who serve on the House of Commons Commission, was established in 2004 under Standing Order No 152D to provide oversight of the House of Commons Members Estimate. The scope of the Members Estimate was significantly reduced following the 2010 general election when responsibility for the administration of Members' salaries, expenses claims, travel and certain other costs were transferred to the Independent Parliamentary Standards Authority (IPSA).

use of the money so expended'.[69] In February 2005, the Speaker told the MEAC that the MEC was 'not minded' to pursue such external verification.[70]

Recommendations on Members' allowances from the Senior Salaries Review Body (SSRB) were published in January 2008.[71] The House of Commons referred the SSRB's recommendations to the MEC.[72] But even before that committee could begin its work, the Committee on Standards and Privileges found that Derek Conway, MP had 'misused the Staffing Allowance' in 'paying his son over-generously'.[73]

In a debate in January 2008 Members had expressed 'deep concerns about Members' allowances'.[74] The MEC's review of allowances, published in June 2008, set out detailed recommendations for change: on audit and assurance, including external audit of Members' claims and a receipt threshold set at zero; claims for furniture and household goods were no longer to be accepted; a reduction in the maximum that could be claimed for overnight allowances; and reductions in the amount outer London MPs could claim for overnight expenses.[75] However, its main recommendations were rejected by the House on division on 3 July 2008.[76] On 16 July 2008, the House agreed to ask the Advisory Panel on Members' Allowances (APMA) to rewrite the Green Book (the guide to and rules on Members' allowances).[77] At its meeting on 21 July 2008, the MEC confirmed that 'any changes to the Green Book brought forward by the Advisory Panel on Members Allowances would have to be considered by the MEC before implementation'.[78]

Whilst the APMA was considering revisions to the Green Book, the MEC asked the Members Estimate Audit Committee to 'make proposals on the future role of the National Audit Office as the external auditor of the House of Commons and the House of Commons' own Internal Audit service in providing audit and assurance of spending on the Members' allowances'.[79] The APMA completed its work and a revised Green Book and the MEC's proposals for the auditing of Members' expenses claims were published together in January 2009 by the MEC.[80]

---

[69] House of Commons, 'Members Annual Report, Resource Accounts & Audit Committee Annual Report 2008–09' HC 2008–09, 955, 45–50, para 15.

[70] ibid, paras 16–17.

[71] Review Body on Senior Salaries, 'Review of Parliamentary Pay, Pensions and Allowances 2007', Report No 64, Cm 7270–1, 2008.

[72] HC Deb 24 January 2008, col 1720.

[73] Committee on Standards and Privileges, 'Conduct of Mr Derek Conway' HC 2007–08, 280, para 31.

[74] HC Deb 4 February 2008, col 659.

[75] Members Estimate Committee, 'Review of Members' Allowances' HC 2007–08, 578. Conclusions and recommendations.

[76] Votes and Proceedings, 3 July 2008, item 18; for a discussion of the MEC Review and the background to it, see House of Commons Library Research Paper, 'Members' Allowances', RP 09/60, 25 June 2009.

[77] HC Deb 16 July 2008, cols 314–15.

[78] House of Commons Commission, 'Formal Minutes', 21 July 2008.

[79] Members Estimate Committee, 'Revised Green Book and Audit of Members' Allowances' HC 2008–09, 142, Annex 3, para 1.

[80] Members Estimate Committee, 'Revised Green Book and Audit of Members' Allowances' (n 79).

The House approved the MEC's report and the new rules came into force on 1 April 2009.[81]

B. The MPs' Expenses Scandal 2009

In the intervening period a number of stories about Members' expenses claims were published in the press (prior to *The Daily Telegraph's* more extensive publication of details of Members' expenses). Two of these stories triggered investigations by the PCS, which were considered by the Committee on Standards and Privileges.[82]

The CSPL announced on 23 March 2009 that it would 'be undertaking a wide-ranging review of MPs' allowances' later that year.[83] The Committee agreed to bring forward the review at the request of the Prime Minister, Gordon Brown, and published its report in November 2009,[84] by which time further changes had been made to way in which Members' expenses were reimbursed.

First, in April 2009, the Government announced changes to the allowances system that could 'be enacted sooner' than any recommendations made by the CSPL, tabling a series of motions in the Commons. In addition to a formal written ministerial statement, Gordon Brown, the Prime Minister, outlined the proposals in a video posted on the Downing Street website. The Government proposed a flat-rate daily allowance to replace the Personal Additional Accommodation Expenditure (the 'second home' allowance); that MPs' staff should become direct employees of the House of Commons; and that receipts would be required to support all expense claims. It also made proposals on Members' financial interests—suggesting that Members report what they earned, who paid them, for what and how many hours were worked.[85] When the motions were tabled on 27 April 2009, they did not include proposals for a flat-rate allowance, following the hostile reaction to the initial proposals.

During and before the debate, on 30 April, the Government was also criticised for pre-empting the CSPL's inquiry. Although some of the Government motions were amended, the House agreed to increase the number of constituencies defined as London constituencies (and hence reduce the number of Members qualifying for second home allowances). The House also agreed to the proposed changes on the requirement to register financial interests.[86]

---

[81] HC Deb 22 January 2009, cols 969–70; House of Commons, *The Green Book: A Guide to Members' Allowances* (March 2009).

[82] Committee on Standards and Privileges, 'Jacqui Smith' HC 2008–09, 974; 'Mr Tony McNulty' HC 2008–09, 1070.

[83] Committee on Standards in Public Life, 'Committee on Standards in Public Life to Look at MPs' Allowances' (press notice, 23 March 2009).

[84] Committee on Standards in Public Life, 'MPs' Expenses and Allowances: Supporting Parliament, Safeguarding the Taxpayer (Twelfth Report)' Cm 7724, 2009.

[85] HC Deb 21 April 2009, cols 10WS–11WS.

[86] HC Deb 30 April 2009, cols 1063–142. A fuller description of the Government's proposals and the House's decision can be found in House of Commons Library Standard Note, 'Members' Allowances—the Government's Proposals for Reform' SN/PC/5046, 5 May 2009.

Then, following *The Daily Telegraph's* reporting of expenses claims, immediate changes to the rules were announced on 19 May 2009, following a meeting of political party leaders convened by the Speaker:

> We have today agreed a robust set of interim measures which will take effect at once and do not pre-empt any more substantial changes to be put forward by the Kelly [CSPL] committee.

> Second homes: there will be no more claims for such items as furniture, household goods, capital improvements, gardening, cleaning and stamp duty.

> …

> Designation of second homes: no changes to be made to designation of second homes in the years 2009–10, with a transparent appeal procedure for exceptional cases.

> Capital gains tax: Members selling any property must be completely open with the tax authorities about whether they have claimed additional costs allowance on that property as a second home and are liable for capital gains tax.

> …

> Couples: Members who are married or living together as partners must nominate the same main home, and will be limited to claiming a maximum of one person's accommodation allowance between them.

> Mortgages: all those Members claiming reimbursement must confirm that the mortgage continues, that the payments are for interest only, and the amount claimed is accurate. Mortgage interest claims will be capped at £1,250 per month. In the view of the meeting—and subject to the recommendations of the Kelly committee—this maximum figure should be reduced in the longer term. The same cap will apply to rent and hotel accommodation. Some of these measures I am announcing will require a resolution by the House in the near future; others will be put into effect by administrative action.[87]

A revised edition of the Green Book was issued in July 2009.[88]

On 19 May 2009, the Speaker also informed the House that:

> The meeting [of party leaders] also received a paper from the Prime Minister, which was endorsed by the other party leaders, calling for a fundamental reform of allowances—moving from self-regulation to regulation by an independent body.[89]

The then Speaker, Michael Martin, announced his decision to step down on the same day.[90]

---

[87] HC Deb 19 May 2009, cols 1421–22.
[88] House of Commons, *The Green Book: A Guide to Members' Allowances*, revised edn (July 2009).
[89] HC Deb 19 May 2009, col 1422.
[90] HC Deb 19 May 2009, col 1324.

C. The Passage of the Parliamentary Standards Act 2009

The Government introduced the Parliamentary Standards Bill on 23 June 2009.[91] It passed quickly through both Houses—although it was considerably amended—and received Royal Assent before the Summer Recess on 21 July 2009.[92]

The Parliamentary Standards Bill, as introduced, provided for the establishment of IPSA and gave it responsibility for paying Members' salaries, determining an allowances scheme and paying allowances. The Bill required IPSA to draw up 'MPs' financial interest rules'; and specified how the rules should be enforced. It provided for a Commissioner for Parliamentary Investigations to conduct investigations and stated that 'No enactment or rule of law which prevents proceedings in Parliament being impeached or questioned in any court or place out of Parliament is to prevent' IPSA or the Commissioner carrying out their functions or their use as evidence in proceedings against a Member under the legislation. It also required the House of Commons to have a Code of Conduct.[93]

At second reading on 29 June 2009, Members expressed a number of misgivings about the Bill. They drew attention to concerns the Clerk of the House had raised about the Code of Conduct becoming a statutory requirement and about IPSA's power to question parliamentary proceedings.[94] Clause 6 (MPs' Code of Conduct) and clause 10 (Proceedings in Parliament) were removed from the Bill during its Commons stages. The requirement on IPSA to prepare rules on financial interests was changed to require it to prepare a Code of Conduct relating to financial interests.[95]

Further changes were made in the House of Lords, including the addition of provisions stating that the Bill did not apply to the House of Lords, and that nothing in the legislation would affect Article 9 of the Bill of Rights 1689. Changes were made to investigation procedures: a Commissioner for Parliamentary Investigations was to investigate payments that were not allowed under the scheme and breaches of the statutory code relating to financial interests. An offence of 'providing false or misleading information for allowance claims' was retained but other offences were removed. A sunset clause was added: unless extended by order, provisions relating to the functions of the Commissioner for Parliamentary Investigations were to expire two years after IPSA assumed responsibility for the statutory code.[96] Thus parliamentary self-regulation over the conduct of Members

---

[91] HC Deb 23 June 2009, col 691.

[92] HC Deb 21 July 2009, col 801.

[93] Parliamentary Standards Bill 2008–09 (Bill 121 of 2008–09).

[94] See, eg, HC Deb 29 June 2009, col 47. The Clerk had given evidence on the Bill to the Justice Committee: Justice Committee, 'Constitutional Reform and Renewal: Parliamentary Standards Bill', HC 2008–09, 791.

[95] Parliamentary Standards Bill 2008–09 (Bill 121 of 2008–09), Parliamentary Standards Bill 2008–09 (HL Bill 60 of 2008–09).

[96] Parliamentary Standards Act 2009 as passed; see also House of Commons Library Standard Note, 'The Parliamentary Stages of the Parliamentary Standards Bill', SN/PC5121, 22 July 2009.

was preserved, but investigations of misuse of expenses were passed to an external compliance body. This made sense, as the expenses which might be misused were now to be administered—for the first time—by an external statutory body.

After the CSPL's review of Members' allowances, further changes to the role of IPSA were made in the Constitutional Reform and Governance Act 2010. These amendments to the Parliamentary Standards Act 2009 additionally gave IPSA responsibility for determining Members' pay. Changes were made to the compliance regime. IPSA was removed from any involvement in the Commons Code of Conduct for Members, and the Commissioner for Parliamentary Investigations was replaced by a Compliance Officer who:

— reviews decisions on the payment of expenses if requested to by Members; and
— conducts investigations if he believes payments have been made that should not have been.

The Constitutional Reform and Governance Act 2010 added the following provision on the general duties of IPSA:

3A General duties of the IPSA

(1) In carrying out its functions the IPSA must have regard to the principle that it should act in a way which is efficient, cost-effective and transparent.
(2) In carrying out its functions the IPSA must have regard to the principle that members of the House of Commons should be supported in efficiently, cost-effectively and transparently carrying out their Parliamentary functions.[97]

Additionally, the 2010 Act transferred the administration of the Parliamentary Contributory Pension Fund to IPSA.[98]

As with the Electoral Commission, Members were initially suspicious of a new external regulatory body. Relationships improved as the 2010 Parliament went on, but for many Members, IPSA remains an unwelcome innovation. The new body was considered to be out of touch with the realities of parliamentary life. New Board members were appointed to IPSA in January 2013, following the expiry of the term of office of the original board although the first chair, Sir Ian Kennedy remained in post until 31 May 2016. In the debate on the appointments, some Members expressed the hope that the new board would bring a different approach to its work.[99] Members have continued to express concerns that IPSA makes it difficult for people with families to become Members.[100] New rules came into force in June 2017 banning MPs from employing new family members, technically known as connected parties, indicating that IPSA continues to respond to public concerns.

---

[97] Parliamentary Standards Act 2009, s 3A, as amended.
[98] Constitutional Reform and Governance Act 2010, s 40 and Sch 6.
[99] HC Deb 4 December 2012, cols 831–39.
[100] HC Deb 2 November 2016, cols 407WH–08WH; 23 February 2017, col 1172.

D. Compliance

IPSA appointed an interim Compliance Officer, Alan Lockwood, a former senior military officer, on 4 June 2010.[101] A permanent Compliance Officer, Luke March, was appointed on 31 March 2011 but stayed only a few weeks before resigning on 27 July 2011. Peter Davis, a retired police chief superintendent, was appointed as Compliance Officer on 19 December 2011. Andy McDonald succeeded Davis, who served the full five-year term of his appointment.[102] McDonald took up his post on 8 January 2017. He served in the Metropolitan Police for 30 years, retiring as a Detective Superintendent. The role is a part-time one—the complement of permanent staff of the Office of the Compliance Officer is 'the equivalent of one full-time post'.[103]

The Compliance Officer's remit is defined in statute.[104] It is summarised on the Compliance Officer for IPSA's website:

— conduct an investigation if he has reason to believe that an MP may have been paid an amount under the MPs' Scheme of Business Costs and Expenses (the Scheme) that should not have been allowed; and
— at the request of an MP, review a determination by IPSA to refuse reimbursement for an expense claim, in whole or in part.[105]

The Compliance Officer's role is confined to matters pertaining to the Scheme. He has no power to investigate complaints about expenses that pre-date the creation of IPSA in May 2010. Complaints regarding expense claims prior to May 2010 are usually handled by the PCS.

Once it is confirmed that a complaint falls with the Compliance Officer's statutory remit, the investigation process begins. The investigation process comprises four stages: (i) Assessment; (ii) Investigation; (iii) Statement of provisional findings; and (iv) Statement of findings.

If the complaint is within the Compliance Officer's remit, an assessment is carried out to consider whether there are sufficient grounds to open an investigation. At the conclusion of the assessment, the Compliance Officer may decide that there is sufficient reason to believe that a claim may have been wrongfully paid to an MP and may open an investigation. If there are insufficient grounds to do so, the complaint is closed down. The Compliance Officer may decide not to open an

---

[101] IPSA, 'IPSA has appointed Alan Lockwood to the Post of Interim Compliance Officer' (press release, 4 June 2010).

[102] There is a statutory limit: 'The Compliance Officer is to be appointed for a fixed term not exceeding five years' and a person 'who has been appointed as the Compliance Officer may not be appointed again' (Parliamentary Standards Act 2009, Sch 2 as inserted by the Constitutional Reform and Governance Act 2010, s 26 and Sch 3).

[103] Independent Parliamentary Standards Authority, 'Annual Report and Accounts 2015–2016' HC 2016–17 523, 19 July 2016, Part V: 'Annual Report by the Compliance Officer', para 48.

[104] Parliamentary Standards Act 2009, Sch 2 as inserted by the Constitutional Reform and Governance Act 2010, s 26 and Sch 3.

[105] Website of the Compliance Officer for IPSA, www.parliamentarycompliance.org.uk.

investigation—even if there are grounds to do so—if it is judged that conducting an investigation would be a disproportionate course of action. At the conclusion of an assessment, the MP, IPSA and the complainant, if applicable, are informed of the Compliance Officer's decision.[106]

IPSA's annual report and accounts includes an annual report from the Compliance Officer. His annual report for 2015–16 reports details of complaints handled in the past four years and a commentary on the reviews that were requested by MPs in the previous financial year. During 2015–16, 11 reviews were requested by nine MPs, 'far exceeding any previous financial year'.[107] The vast majority of investigations opened have been "closed prior to an investigation" (see Table 3.2).

Table 3.2: Outcome of all complaints handled by the Compliance Officer since 2012–13

	2012–13	2013–14	2014–15	2015–16
No of complaints received	24	23	40	26
No of investigations opened	1	0	1	3

Source: Independent Parliamentary Standards Authority, 'Annual Report and Accounts 2015–2016 '(HC 2016–17 523), 19 July 2016, Part V: Annual Report by the Compliance Officer, Table 4.

The Compliance Officer's workload has not been onerous, although some of the individual investigations have been time-consuming.

VIII. INVESTIGATION OF MEMBERS' EXPENSES—QUESTIONS OF JURISDICTION—THE LEGG REVIEW

At their meeting on 19 May 2009, following *The Daily Telegraph's* publication of details of the expense claims of numerous Members, the party leaders agreed that:

> All past claims under the former additional costs allowance over the past four years will be examined. This will be carried out by a team with external management; the external manager will be appointed after consultation with the Comptroller and Auditor General. All necessary resources will be made available. The team will look at claims in relation to the rules which existed at that time, and will take account of any issues which arise from that examination which cause them to question the original judgment.[108]

The PCS was already investigating some cases as a result of the press coverage on expenses before *The Daily Telegraph* began its campaign. Police and public prosecutors were also considering prosecutions. On 5 June 2009 Sir Paul Stephenson, the Metropolitan Police Commissioner, and Keir Starmer, then Director of Public

---

[106] Website of the Compliance Officer for IPSA, www.parliamentarycompliance.org.uk.
[107] Independent Parliamentary Standards Authority, 'Annual Report and Accounts 2015–2016', HC 2016–17, 523, 19 July 2016, Part V: 'Annual Report by the Compliance Officer', para 36.
[108] HC Deb 19 May 2009, col 1422.

Prosecutions, issued a joint statement following meetings of the CPS assessment panel:

> The panel's view is that, unless evidence is available which shows individuals deliberately misled the Fees Office, it is highly unlikely that there could be a successful prosecution. Many of those complained about appear to have provided accurate information and therefore the MPS will not pursue a criminal investigation into allegations against them.

> It is for the Commons and the Lords authorities to decide whether they wish to consider these cases under their internal processes and should information come to light that indicates that either Fees Office has been deliberately misled, then they will be able to make a referral back to the MPS for further consideration.

> However, there are a small number of allegations where questions remain about the probity of the claims which will require further information before any decisions regarding investigations could be made. We are therefore continuing to liaise with Parliamentary Authorities in the two Houses over the provision of this additional information so the assessment panel can make informed decisions on these remaining allegations.[109]

The review commissioned by the party leaders was undertaken by Sir Thomas Legg, a former Permanent Secretary, who had served as an independent member on the House of Commons Members Estimate Audit Committee (see above). His review reported to the Members Estimate Committee. His terms of reference were agreed on 1 July, and on 23 November 2009 the MEC agreed that

> any sums recommended for repayment by Sir Thomas should be recovered from Members, preferably voluntarily, but if necessary by deduction from pay and allowances on the authority of a resolution of the House. This was, however, subject to Members having the opportunity to show in an independent appeal process any special reasons why it would not be fair or equitable to require them to make the repayments. The Rt Hon Sir Paul Kennedy agreed to conduct the appeal process.[110]

In his review, Sir Thomas Legg set out his terms of reference:

> To conduct an independent review of all claims made by Members of Parliament (except those who have since died) for the Additional Costs Allowance during the financial years 2004–05 to 2007–08;

> To examine all payments made on such claims, against the rules and standards in force at the time, and identify any which should not have been made, and any claims which otherwise call for comment;

> To allow Members who received such payments or made such claims a fair opportunity to make representations about them;

> Subject to any such representations, to recommend where necessary any repayments which Members should make and otherwise to comment as seems appropriate; and

> To report as soon as possible to the Members Estimate Committee.

---

[109] 'MPs' Expenses: Elliot Morley and David Chaytor Face Police Investigation' *Daily Telegraph*, 5 June 2009.

[110] Members Estimate Committee, 'Review of Past ACA Payments', HC 2009–10, 348, para 2.

Later, in July 2009, the MEC extended the terms of reference to cover 2008–09 but also told him to exclude 'any payments under investigation by the PCS before 20 July 2009, or at any stage by the Police'.[111]

Following an inquiry in 2008, the Committee on Standards and Privileges asked its chairman and the PCS to meet the Commissioner of the Metropolitan Police to 'discuss matters relating to the handling of complaints against Members which might also raise questions of criminal liability'.[112] A statement agreed at 3 April meeting was published on 30 April 2008. It confirmed that:

> [O]ther than in the limited context of participation in proceedings in Parliament, Members of Parliament are in no different position in respect of alleged criminal behaviour than any other person. The Chairman reiterated the Committee's belief in the general principle that criminal proceedings against Members, where these are considered appropriate, should take precedence over the House's own disciplinary proceedings. The meeting discussed how the respective parties might coordinate their activities to ensure the effective delivery of this principle.

The agreement also set out how the PCS and the Committee would liaise with the police.[113]

A. Convictions for Expenses Fraud: The Aftermath

A number of former MPs, one then sitting MP and two members of the House of Lords were convicted on charges of false accounting in respect of the expenses scandal.[114] Full details of the case of *R v Chaytor* and others and subsequent criminal proceedings can be found in chapter two. It is of interest to note that the convictions all related to events before the Parliamentary Standards Act 2009; the Supreme Court confirmed that 'the extent of parliamentary privilege is ultimately a matter for the courts to determine';[115] and those responsible for the disciplinary procedures of the Commons had already agreed with the police an approach for dealing with matters that involved alleged criminal behaviour.

IX. RECALL OF MPs

The May 2010 Coalition Agreement between the Conservatives and Liberal Democrats included a commitment to legislate to introduce a power of recall—

---

[111] ibid, App 1: Sir Thomas Legg, *ACA Review* paras 2 and 4.

[112] Committee on Standards and Privileges, 'The Complaints System and the Criminal Law' HC 2007–08, 523, para 1.

[113] ibid, App.

[114] David Chaytor, Jim Devine, Elliot Morley Eric Illsley, Lord Hanningfield and Lord Taylor of Warwick.

[115] [2010] UKSC 52 [16]; N Parpworth, *Constitutional and Administrative Law*, 7th edn (Oxford, Oxford University Press, 2012) 135.

the power of constituents to unseat an MP. This followed commitments made by all three main political parties in their 2010 manifestos, after the expenses scandal.

The Recall of MPs Act 2015 introduces a recall process.[116] If any of three trigger events occur, the Speaker initiates a petition process. A petition is made available for signing in the MP's constituency for six weeks. If at the end of that period at least 10 per cent of eligible electors have signed the petition, the seat would be declared vacant and a by-election would follow. The Member who was recalled could stand in the by-election.

The three triggers that initiate the petitioning process are:

— the MP has, after becoming an MP, been convicted in the United Kingdom of an offence and sentenced or ordered to be imprisoned or detained, and the appeal period expires without the conviction, sentence or order having being overturned on appeal;
— following on from a report from the Committee on Standards in relation to the MP, the House of Commons orders the suspension of the MP from the service of the House for a period of at least 10 sitting days or a period of at least 14 days;
— the MP has, after becoming an MP, been convicted of an offence under section 10 of the Parliamentary Standards Act 2009 (offence of providing false or misleading information for allowances claims), and the appeal period expires without the conviction having been overturned on appeal.

The recall process is only triggered by misconduct. At second reading, Greg Clark, Minister of State, Cabinet Office, said that:

> We have stopped short of enabling recall on any grounds so that we preserve the freedom of Members of Parliament to vote with their conscience and to take difficult decisions without facing constant challenges ...[117]

During the second reading debate in the Commons, concerns were expressed that the trigger meant that MPs and the courts, rather than voters, took the initial decisions to begin the recall process. However, attempts to introduce a voter-initiated process were rejected at Committee stage and at Report stage in the House of Commons.[118]

X. THE HOUSE OF LORDS

The House of Lords was also affected by a number of scandals relating to expenses and allegations that its members were prepared to accept fees to amend legislation on behalf of clients.

---

[116] Recall of MPs Act 2015.
[117] HC Deb 21 October 2014, col 773.
[118] HC Deb 27 October 2015, cols 51–139; 24 November 2015, cols 649–692.

Its response was quite different from that of the Commons. It continued to emphasise its self-regulating nature, ensuring that, against the Labour Government's original intentions,[119] it was explicitly excluded from the ambit of IPSA. However, its approach to self-regulation of Members' conduct has adapted, with the appointment of a House of Lords Commissioner for Standards. Due to continuing concerns about the ability of the House to impose appropriate penalties against misconduct, Private Members' Bills were successfully introduced which now allow the Lords to expel Members and subject them to unlimited periods of suspension where breaches of the Code of Conduct have been found.

Members of the House of Lords were able to claim a daily subsistence rate and, for those whose main home was outside London, overnight subsistence was available to cover the costs of overnight accommodation in London (or elsewhere, if on official parliamentary business). In 2009 allegations were made that a small number of peers had designated as their main homes, homes outside London that they seldom used, in order to claim overnight subsistence.

Reviews by the Senior Salaries Review Body and by a House of Lords Leader's Group were followed by a report from the House Committee of the House of Lords.[120] On 20 July 2010 the House of Lords debated resolutions to introduce the new single daily allowance from 1 October 2010, and to agree the report of the House Committee.[121] The flat-rate attendance allowance is set at £150 or £300 for each sitting day they attend the House.

A. Appointment of the House of Lords Commissioner for Standards

The background to appointment of the House of Lords Commissioner for Standards is described in his first annual report:

> In May 2009, the then Leader of the House, Baroness Royall of Blaisdon, announced the appointment of a Leader's Group on the Code of Conduct. The Group was appointed 'to consider the Code of Conduct and the rules relating to Members' interests, and to make recommendations'. The Group's creation was directly linked to allegations in the media about the conduct of four peers. The allegations were referred to the Sub-Committee on Lords' Interests for investigation, and resulted in the suspension from the service of the House of two of the four members for having breached the Code of Conduct. That episode, allied to other allegations against peers, and a series of allegations affecting members of the House of Commons, combined to significantly impact on public confidence in Parliament and Parliamentarians.

---

[119] In a statement on constitutional renewal, on 10 June 2009, Gordon Brown, the Prime Minister, told the House of Commons that 'we propose that the House of Commons—and subsequently the House of Lords—move from the old system of self-regulation to independent, statutory regulation' (HC Deb 10 June 2009, col 796).

[120] House of Lords House Committee, 'Financial Support for Members of the House of Lords' HL 2010–11, 18.

[121] House of Commons Library Standard Note, 'Financial Support for Members of the House of Lords', SN/PC/5246, 23 August 2010.

The Leader's Group on the Code of Conduct recommended that the post of Commissioner for Standards be created. The Commissioner would be appointed by the House but be functionally independent. That recommendation was accepted.[122]

A new Code of Conduct was agreed by the House on 30 November 2009,[123] and a Guide to the Code of Conduct contained in the second report of the Committee for Privileges of 2009–10, was agreed by the House on 30 March 2010.[124] Both came into force on 18 May 2010, at the start of the 2010–12 Session of Parliament. The first Commissioner for Standards, Paul Kernaghan, was appointed for 'an initial period of three years' by the House of Lords on 2 June 2010.[125] His term was subsequently extended for a further three years. The second Commissioner is Lucy Scott-Moncrieff, former President of the Law Society, who took up her post in June 2016.

B. Disciplinary Powers of the House of Lords

In 2009, the House of Lords Committee for Privileges reviewed the House's disciplinary powers and the Sub-Committee on Lords' Interests investigated after allegations were made that four members of the House of Lords had been prepared to accept fees to amend legislation.[126] The Committee for Privileges set out its conclusions on the disciplinary powers of the Lords in a short report:

8. We have carefully considered the advice of the Attorney General and Lord Mackay of Clashfern. **We are unanimously in agreement with the advice of Lord Mackay, and accordingly invite the House to agree the following conclusions:**

The House possesses, and has possessed since before the 1705 resolution, an inherent power to discipline its Members; the means by which it chooses to exercise this power falls within the regulation by the House of its own procedures.

The duty imposed upon Members, by virtue of the writs of summons, to attend Parliament, is subject to various implied conditions, which are reflected in the many rules governing the conduct of Members which have been adopted over time by the House.

The House has no power, by resolution, to require that the writ of summons be withheld from a Member otherwise entitled to receive it; as a result, it is not within the power of the House by resolution to expel a Member permanently.

The House does possess the power to suspend its Members for a defined period not longer than the remainder of the current Parliament [emphasis in original].[127]

---

[122] House of Lords, 'Annual Report 2010–2011, Commissioner for Standards', Foreword.

[123] HL Deb 30 November 2009, cols 590–48.

[124] HL Deb 30 March 2010, col 1290.

[125] HL Deb 2 June 2010, col 256.

[126] Committee for Privileges, The Conduct of Lord Moonie, Lord Snape, Lord Truscott and Lord Taylor of Blackburn HL 2009–09, 88-I, App 2, para 1.

[127] Committee for Privileges, 'The Powers of the House of Lords in Respect of its Members', HL 2008–09, 87, para 8.

The House of Lords adopted these conclusions on 20 May 2009. It also considered the Committee for Privileges report on *The Conduct of Lord Moonie, Lord Snape, Lord Truscott and Lord Taylor of Blackburn*. The House agreed with the Committee that Lord Truscott and Lord Taylor of Blackburn had breached the code of Conduct,[128] and suspended the two Lords for the remainder of the 2008–09 Session.[129]

The powers to suspend were subsequently used again in 2010. On 21 October 2010, the House of Lords considered reports from the Committee on Privileges that concluded that three members of the House of Lords—Lord Paul, Lord Bhatia and Baroness Uddin—had incorrectly designated their main home when making claims for expenses made under the Members' reimbursement scheme. The three members of the House of Lords were suspended.[130]

The Lords Commissioner for Standards also recommended suspensions in the cases of Lord Taylor of Warwick and Lord Hanningfield, who were subject to investigation by the House once the criminal proceedings against the peers were concluded. The recommended suspensions were for 12 and nine months respectively, agreed to by the House. Three more suspensions were agreed by the House for peers found to have breached rules on lobbying and use of House facilities in the 2010 Parliament.

Addressing concerns that peers subject to criminal convictions could return to the Lords (since the House had no power to expel its Members) the House agreed in December 2011 that, where a Member has been ordered to repay money and has not repaid it, one month before their suspension ends a motion should be moved inviting the House to agree that the suspension should be extended until the money is repaid, or until the end of the Parliament, whichever is sooner.

C. Suspension and Expulsion of Members of the Lords

Two Private Members' Bills, which gained Government support, subsequently clarified suspension and expulsion powers. The House of Lords Reform Act 2014 allowed for expulsion on two grounds—non-attendance or being subject to a prison sentence of more than a year. This was in the context of more general provisions allowing peers to retire from the Lords for the first time.[131] Subsequently the House of Lords (Expulsion and Suspension) Act 2015 gave the House an extended power of expulsion and a statutory right of suspension for any period of time, so allowing suspensions to continue into a new Parliament. (Previously a new writ of summons could bring to an end a term of suspension.) The House passed standing orders on 15 July 2015 to implement these new powers, which are

---

[128] ibid, para 72, para 89.
[129] HL Deb 20 May 2009, cols 1394–418.
[130] HL Deb 21 October 2010, cols 893–903; *Erskine May* (n 8) 201.
[131] House of Lords Reform Act 2014, s 3.

exercisable when a member has been found to have breached the Code of Conduct. During the Commons Public Bill Committee debates, concerns were expressed by Christopher Chope about the potentially open-ended powers relating to the type of conduct which could give rise to expulsion or suspension. He said:

> It is wrong in principle that hon. Members should allow the other place to have an unlimited power to expel that is dependent only on its Standing Orders, because we should be nervous about their potential misuse.[132]

In response, Sir George Young, who piloted the Bill through the House of Commons, noted that 'It has to be a matter of conduct, and "conduct" appears in the Bill. It cannot be used for matters not relating to conduct'.[133]

XI. REFLECTIONS

Changes in the way in which the conduct of Members of Parliament is regulated have occurred intermittently, usually in response to particular scandals or perceived scandals—such as 'cash for questions' in the 1990s and the 2009 expenses scandal—rather than as part of a grand plan. So the history of regulating Members' conduct is not that different from the history of constitutional changes in the UK, which have as often as not come about in a piecemeal fashion depending on the contingent political pressures of the day. Changes in the regulation of Members' conduct mirror a wider shift in society away from self-regulation to external (in the City, the end of 'my word is my bond' and the establishment of bodies such as the Financial Services Authority, in the medical world the growth of lay members on the General Medical Council, etc). Parliament has not been slow in the past to react to scandals or malpractice in other professions by legislating for a greater degree of external regulation, so perhaps it was inevitable that similar issues would confront Parliament as well.

Changes in regulation have been challenged as an attack on the sovereignty of Parliament—but they tend not to have been prevented. In the 1860s concerns were expressed that Parliament was abdicating its rights in allowing the courts to determine the outcome of contested parliamentary elections. In the 1990s, during the debate on the motion to appoint the first PCS, Sir Nicholas Winterton MP argued that the House was giving up some of its independence in making such an appointment:

> I believe that it is the first time in history that this High Court of Parliament will, to all intents and purposes, have an outsider deciding its behaviour—in short, the behaviour of Members of this House. I do not believe that we should agree to that.[134]

---

[132] Public Bill Committee, 4 February 2015, col 6.
[133] ibid, col 12.
[134] HC Deb 6 November 1995, col 683.

And in the twenty-first century, during the second reading debate on the Parliamentary Standards Bill, Sir Patrick Cormack asked, 'Is it not one thing to have a body that regulates the conduct of elections and another thing entirely to have a body that regulates the conduct of the elected?'[135] But on each occasion, the immediate political and public pressure ('something must be done') ended up taking precedence over the constitutional theory.

The argument against external regulation has not always been on constitutional grounds. On 22 May 1974, when the House of Commons agreed to establish the Register of Members' Interests, some Members argued this was unnecessary. One commented that 'The fact that we are all known to each other is the best safeguard of all against improper conduct. If anyone should unhappily fall by the wayside, the police, the Revenue or this House itself can take the necessary measures'. Another said: 'Parliament is too serious a place to be subjected to such treatment. Disclosure also lowers our dignity. Why should the Press try to look through a keyhole at our private interests?'[136] These comments raise two issues which have affected developments in this field: the decline of deference and the increased expectation of transparency in public life, associated with a more intrusive media.

In the context of the wider shift in society away from self-regulation to external regulation, it is difficult to see how MPs could uniquely be left unaffected. In the same way, MPs can hardly be expected to be exempt from the long-term shift towards greater transparency in public life. This has been aided by the introduction of statutory access to information through the Data Protection Act and especially the Freedom of Information Act. Indeed, in this context it is worth recalling that the initial trigger for the expenses scandal was an FOI request; the large amount of material that was eventually obtained by the *Daily Telegraph* would not have been available to the newspaper had it not been for the fact that the courts had ordered a redacted version of it to be prepared for release, following a series of attempts by the House authorities to resist its disclosure. The 'cash for questions' case in the 1990s was triggered not by an actual case, but by a 'sting' operation by a newspaper against two MPs. So much for preventing the press looking 'through the keyhole'.

The long-term future of standards regulation remains uncertain. The Committee on Standards, with equal numbers of Member and lay members, has had its review of the Code and the Rules, interrupted by an unexpected general election, and so changes are unlikely to be adopted early in the 2017 Parliament. This latest review looks likely to be subject to the same extensive delays in bringing forward recommendations for change as during the 2010 Parliament, due to concerns from party whips.

---

[135] HC Deb 29 June 2009, col 62.
[136] HC Deb 22 May 1974, cols 441 and 484.

The presence of lay members has not stemmed continuing calls in the media and the public for greater transparency and more rigorous rules restricting Members from receiving remuneration other than their salaries.[137] Indeed, the lay members themselves have argued for greater regulation. The appointment of the former Chancellor George Osborne as editor of the London *Evening Standard* in March 2017 crystallised anxieties about outside employment and prompted the CSPL to begin a new review into the current position.[138]

The self-regulating nature of investigations into Members' conduct in both Houses may not survive one more major scandal. The Standards Committee published *The Standards System in the House of Commons* in 2015, which identified the issue of the lack of public trust and its continued impact upon how Members' activities are seen and reported.[139] Pressure appears to be building for external regulation. In 2015 two former Foreign Secretaries, Jack Straw and Sir Malcolm Rifkind, were caught in a media sting offering services which appeared to draw on their experiences in government. Both were eventually exonerated by the Standards Commissioner, since outside employment is permitted under the rules, but she commented that:

[I]f the current arrangements remain, I and my successors will continue to receive allegations concerning external employment and lobbying, which may or may not be justified. On each occasion the reputation of the House and Members risks further damage from the inference that Members are serving their personal interests rather than those of the public.[140]

The 2017 final report from the initial three lay members expressed dissatisfaction with the complex nature of standards regulation in the Commons, which had 'the effect of diluting responsibility, making it difficult to identify leadership in what is already a complex area'. It called for a full review of the system which had evolved since 1995 and noted that the busy lives of MPs made it hard for them to focus on standards issues, making membership of the Standards Committee an onerous responsibility rather than an opportunity to lead. The lay members proposed making failure to register a criminal offence, as in the National Assembly for Wales.[141] This would raise important issues of parliamentary privilege, but the continuing pressure for increased transparency and regulation may lead to completely independent standards machinery.

---

[137] Committee on Standards, 'Martin Williams' (n 38).

[138] Committee on Standards in Public Life, 'MPs' Outside Interests Review—Consultation', March 2017.

[139] Committee on Standards, 'The Standards System in the House of Commons' (n 53).

[140] Committee on Standards, 'Sir Malcolm Rifkind and Mr Jack Straw', HC 2015–16 472, 17 September 2015, Memorandum from the Commissioner, para 12.

[141] Committee on Standards, 'Final Reflections' (n 55), para 50.

IPSA had a somewhat stormy start in 2010. A largely new board took up office early in 2013 and relations with Members gradually improved somewhat. However, there are continuing concerns that IPSA's business costs and expenses scheme does not recognise the complex responsibilities of MPs both to their constituents and to their families.[142] Given the continuing resonance of the expenses scandal, it seems unlikely that the regulation of Members' expenses and salaries would be taken back in-house. But Parliament did eventually change the statute governing the Electoral Commission to redress perceived problems in its operation in 2009 and other regulators or quasi-regulators have been reformed or abolished such as the Audit Commission and the Standards Board for England. The story is not over yet.

---

[142] S Childs, *The Good Parliament* (University of Bristol) July 2016, 20. In its review of its Business Costs and Expenses Scheme, IPSA accepted that 'Our Scheme should not ... discourage individuals from any part of society from seeking to become an MP'. IPSA, 'Review of the Scheme of MPs' Business Costs and Expenses and IPSA's publication policy: Consultation Report and Equality Impact Assessment', March 2017, 6.

Part 2

Parliament: Select Committees and Internal Arrangements

4

The Governance of Parliament

BEN YONG[*]

I. INTRODUCTION

GOVERNING PARLIAMENT HAS always brought challenges, but this has not always been recognised because of the focus on Parliament's relationships with the other branches of government. In *Mid-Victorian Masterpiece*,[1] Sir Barnett Cocks, a former Clerk of the House, described the dawning realisation of a 1950s Commons select committee charged with examining accommodation:

> They were beginning to learn that in a true parliamentary democracy such as that at Westminster, there was no official with absolute authority, nobody wholly in charge and nothing to single out for condemnation except perhaps the inability of Members themselves to achieve what they wanted simply by acting collectively. They were not required themselves to do the work. All that was needed from them was an authorization of perhaps four lines on a piece of paper to be tabled and voted on. It was something which, year after year, remained beyond the capacity of Members of all parties.[2]

Cocks' book is ostensibly about the long process of designing and building the Palace of Westminster, and its management following construction. But the subtitle of the book—'the story of an institution unable to put its own House in order'—is both literal and metaphoric. What Cocks was pointing to was the absence of leadership within Parliament; and the difficulty parliamentarians had—and continue to have—in acting collectively to protect 'Parliament' (a term we must treat with some caution) and its long-term corporate interests.

This chapter is about the governance of the Westminster Parliament. Governance is about the structures through which the Houses of Parliament are each directed, controlled and led.[3] It is about leadership and administration: the internal control

[*] This chapter draws on a much shorter piece co-written with Sarah Petit (in C Leston-Bandeira and L Thompson (eds) *Exploring Parliament*, Oxford, OUP, forthcoming). She is, of course, not responsible for my very different interpretations and conclusions. Of those I can name, I am grateful to Priscilla Baines, Robert Greally, Patrick O'Brien, Louise Thompson and the editors for their comments.

[1] B Cocks, *Mid-Victorian Masterpiece: The Story of an Institution unable to put its own House in order* (London, Hutchinson, 1977).

[2] ibid, 140.

[3] House of Commons Governance Committee, 'House of Commons Governance', HC 297, 2014, 5 ('the Straw Review').

of each House, and (indirectly) how this affects the provision of resources and services to parliamentarians. Issues of parliamentary procedure are thus excluded. For similar reasons, we do not discuss select committees and the Backbench Business Committee.[4] Finally, the chapter does not deal specifically with members' pay, allowances and staffing: this has been dealt with, to some extent, in an earlier edition of this book and in chapter three of this one.[5]

House governance is a subject rarely covered in detail, because it appears to lack the raw excitement of law-making[6] and scrutiny of executive action.[7] Examining how the Houses of Parliament govern themselves is important, because it can tell us about the weakness of the legislature as an institution, relative to the other branches of government. Managing a unique, structurally complex institution like Parliament is a form of public law. Moreover, looking at how Parliament organises and governs itself is a constitutional matter because the support and services to Parliament and its organisation is a necessary, but not sufficient, condition to ensure it carries out its more obvious constitutional functions—legislating, scrutinising, authorising, representing, deliberating—in an effective manner.

The argument of this chapter is that governing Parliament is not easily achievable—and that it is not necessarily or only the executive which hampers the effective working of a legislature. In the language of public choice, Parliament is a deeply complex organisation which has severe problems engaging in collective action.[8] The governance structures of both Houses reflect this. They might be best understood as arrangements of key veto players, where each has the power of initiative but also the power to veto the decisions of the others. The result is, as one might expect, a situation in which the status quo is favoured and change, when it comes, is sporadic, driven by 'exogenous' causes. The long-term corporate interests of Parliament—such as the capacity to organise itself to ensure a well-supported legislature—are haphazardly addressed.

This chapter will proceed in the following fashion. Section II briefly examines the framework through which the Westminster legislature has been viewed: the separation of powers. For the most part, Parliament has been viewed in terms of its relationships with the other branches—in particular, the Executive. In this

---

[4] The Backbench Business Committee is discussed in R Kelly and L Maer, 'Parliamentary Reform and the accountability of Government in the House of Commons' in A Horne and A Le Sueur (eds), *Parliament: Legislation and Accountability* (Oxford, Hart Publishing, 2016) 139, 144–148.

[5] See R Kelly and M Hamlyn, 'The Law and Conduct of Members of Parliament' in A Horne, G Drewry and D Oliver (eds), *Parliament and the Law* (Oxford, Hart Publishing, 2013) 89 and B Worthy 'Freedom of Information and Parliament' in Horne, Drewry and Oliver (ibid) 139.

[6] Contrast with L Thompson, *Making British Law: Committees in Action* (Basingstoke, Palgrave Macmillan, 2015).

[7] For exceptions, see B Winetrobe, 'The Autonomy of Parliament' in D Oliver and G Drewry (eds), *The Law and Parliament* (London, Butterworths, 1998) 14; and M Russell and A Paun, *House Rules? International Lessons for Enhancing the Autonomy of the House of Commons* (London, Constitution Unit, 2007).

[8] T Moe and S Wilson, 'Presidents and Political Structure' (1994) 57 *Law and Contemporary Problems* 1; G Loewenberg, *On Legislatures: the Puzzle of Representation* (Boulder, Paradigm Publishers, 2011).

context, Parliament is regarded as a unitary entity; questions about its internal dynamics are marginalised or obscured.

Section III broadly sets out the peculiarity of Parliament as a public institution: it is expected to represent the polity, and as such members are nominal equals. This makes disagreement almost inevitable, and therefore collective action is particularly difficult. Sections IV and V—the bulk of this chapter—elaborate on this. These set out the governance arrangements in each House of Parliament, and then examine their history. This is followed by details of the dynamics of the key officers and governance units of the two Houses, and the ways in which their organisation creates serious problems of collective action. Section VI returns to the present and looks at the Restoration and Renewal of the Palace of Westminster: a matter currently being debated in Parliament.

As Winetrobe has noted, the 'closer one approaches the apex of the British political system, the more strict law gives way to "non-legal" forms'.[9] The chapter's primary sources are therefore the reports of the two Houses' governance bodies and various domestic committees. As the matters discussed in the various reports are sometimes opaque, and do not explain the political context and institutional dynamics of the issues raised, the chapter also draws on a small number of confidential interviews and discussions carried out in 2016–17 with 15 individuals: five who sat on the House of Commons Commission or on a domestic committee; five who sat on the equivalent bodies in the House of Lords and five senior clerks (three from the Commons; two from the Lords) on House governance. Interviewees were chosen on the basis of their previous or current role in House governance.

II. THE SEPARATION OF POWERS AND THE INTERNAL COMPLEXITY
OF THE BRANCHES OF GOVERNMENT

The doctrine of the separation of powers sits explicitly or implicitly behind most discussions of the legislature. But in various ways it obscures some vital truths about how the legislature works. There are at least three conceptions of the doctrine: there is the 'pure' separation of powers; the checks and balances conception; and the efficiency conception. Most versions of the pure conception insist upon a strict connection between function, personnel and branch, and that functions and personnel in one branch should not overlap with another. Organising institutional power in this way avoids the concentration (and potential for abuse) of power. The checks and balances conception, on the other hand, does not require a rigid connection of functions and personnel to each branch—indeed, to some extent functions can be shared between branches. Its focus is on how each branch can check and balance the others.[10] The 'efficiency' conception allocates function

---

[9] Winetrobe, 'The Autonomy of Parliament' (n 7) 14.
[10] E Barendt, 'Separation of Powers and Constitutional Government' [1995] *Public Law* 599; and R Masterman, *The Separation of Powers in the Contemporary Constitution* (Cambridge, Cambridge University Press, 2011).

on the basis of institutional competence.[11] On this view, the importance of the doctrine lies more in ensuring effective government.

Yet, despite the dominance of the separation of powers as a framework to understand the branches of government, the general view of legal scholarship is that it has serious flaws.[12] There are various objections. First, some conceptions are too stringent in insisting on a link between institution and function—that is, it is impossible to separate functions or even assign a core function to a particular branch of government. Second, it is difficult to reconcile a separation of powers with checks and balances, because the checking function would involve interference with the other branches. Third, the doctrine ignores the modern administrative state, in which some institutions exercise all three 'core' functions of government. Finally, there are conceptual issues in defining the executive, judicial and legislative functions, and what values inform the doctrine.[13]

Yet the doctrine remains, and its persistence means that discussions of Parliament tend to be prefaced by the fusion of executive and legislature—and (what usually follows) various ways in which the executive dominates the legislature (or, at least, the House of Commons).[14] That is, the fusion of executive and legislature is said to hinder the latter in carrying out its proper constitutional functions. There is much truth in this, but it is not the entire story.[15] The doctrine, in most forms, is highly normative. In a recent survey of the separation of powers, for instance, Kavanagh argues that a philosophically justifiable conception of the doctrine must satisfy three criteria. The first criterion is the desideratum of distinctness: it must show the distinctness of the branches without relying on essentialism of function. The second criterion is the desideratum of interaction: it must be able to account for the interaction and interdependence of branches. Finally, these desiderata must be underpinned by the joint enterprise of good government—'coordinated institutional effort between branches of government in the service of good government.'[16]

Thus we can see that the doctrine asks what would be desirable, and not what 'is'—it marginalises the socio-political factors which may animate the action of a particular branch. It also looks outward to explain weakness. The emphasis on the

---

[11] NW Barber, 'Prelude to the Separation of Powers' (2001) 60 *Cambridge Law Journal* 59. In more recent work, Barber has shifted from the term 'efficiency' to 'suitability': NW Barber, 'Self-Defence for Institutions' (2013) 72 *Cambridge Law Journal* 558.

[12] eg E Carolan, *The New Separation of Powers: A Theory for the Modern State* (Oxford, Oxford University Press, 2009) and A Kavanagh, 'The Constitutional Separation of Powers' in D Dyzenhaus and M Thorburn (eds), *Philosophical Foundations of Constitutional Law* (Oxford, Oxford University Press, 2016) 221.

[13] Kavanagh, 'The Constitutional Separation of Powers' (n 12) 222–223.

[14] eg Winetrobe (n 7).

[15] This view of Parliament is now being challenged: M Benton and M Russell, 'Assessing the Impact of Parliamentary Oversight Committees: The Select Committees in the British House of Commons' (2013) 66 *Parliamentary Affairs* 772; M Russell and P Cowley, 'The Policy Power of the Westminster Parliament: The "Parliamentary State" and the Empirical Evidence' (2016) 29 *Governance* 121; and M Russell, D Gover and K Wollter, 'Does the Executive Dominate the Westminster Legislative Process? Six Reasons for Doubt' (2016) 69 *Parliamentary Affairs* 286.

[16] Kavanagh (n 12) 235.

appropriate relationship between branches tends to treat them as if they were unified and coherent actors.[17] *Inter*-branch relationships are the focus: *intra*-branch relationships are ignored. Moreover, the emphasis on interaction emphasises the operation of immunities (such as parliamentary privilege or judicial independence) or the exercise of power (legislative control over the budget, for instance, or judicial review).[18] But the internal coherence of the branch and its capacity to exercise these mechanisms or powers remains largely unexplored.

The importance of recognising internal complexity is better recognised in relation to the executive. Daintith and Page, for instance, noted long ago that at least one reason that the executive acts as it does, and is only weakly accountable to Parliament, is because of its institutional fragmentation.[19] In 'core executive studies' the executive is often characterised as a set of actors operating in a context of resource scarcity. So, for instance, the Prime Minister is in some respects very weak, lacking a large staff or a department of their own, and must cooperate with Cabinet colleagues with far more impressive resources.[20] There is also the long-standing issue about the appropriate relationship between political and administrative staff, and the extent of the latter's duty to the former.[21] In such a context, clear, consistent and coherent development and implementation of policy become far more problematic. In short, we cannot take institutional unity for granted; and this potential lack of unity has implications for institutional action.

This chapter, then, is an attempt to apply this insight to the workings to the legislature. It is a study, not of privileges, immunities and powers, and their exercise against external actors, but of administrative processes, and the interaction between political and administrative actors within the legislative branch. Looked at this way, a different picture of the legislature emerges: one in which the legislature is also hindered by its own internal organisation and dynamics.

III. THE PECULIAR NATURE OF PARLIAMENT

The 2014 Straw Review of the governance arrangements in the House of Commons stated:

> Governance arrangements ... must enable an organisation to meet its primary purposes ... They must deliver clear decision-making, with a high degree of transparency

---

[17]   eg, R Masterman and S Wheatle, 'Unpacking Separation of Powers: Judicial Independence, Sovereignty and Conceptual Flexibility in the UK Constitution' [2017] *Public Law* 469.

[18]   Barber, 'Self-Defence for Institutions' (n 11).

[19]   T Daintith and A Page, *The Executive in the Constitution* (Oxford, Oxford University Press, 1999); and more recently see T Prosser, *The Economic Constitution* (Oxford, Oxford University Press, 2014).

[20]   R Elgie, 'Core Executive Studies Two Decades on' (2011) 89 *Public Administration* 64.

[21]   For two excellent discussions in an executive context, see W West, 'Neutral Competence and Political Responsiveness: An Uneasy Relationship' (2005) 33 *Policy Studies Journal* 131; and H Kaufman, 'Ruminations on the Study of American Public Bureaucracies' (2008) 38 *American Review of Public Administration* 256.

and clarity, whilst incorporating appropriate levels of oversight, challenge and effective personal accountability ... a clear governance structure would have at its apex a single governing body, containing both executive and non-executive roles, with a remit which defines what it is responsible for, and what it has delegated and to whom.[22]

As we shall see, little of this has been present in Parliament. There are very good reasons for this. Jennings' observation that Parliament is a fiction is a useful starting point.[23] The term 'Parliament' presumes that a legal entity with an autonomous and coherent personality, but this is constitutional shorthand, disguising considerable institutional complexity.[24] This stems from particular features of Parliament as a legislature, each of which require some explanation.

First, each House consists of members who are nominally equal: this makes it difficult to impose any kind of hierarchy.[25] This problem of 'the legislative state of nature'[26] has been answered, for the most part, by the evolution of political parties (and to a lesser extent, by committees), but the focus of their collective action remains primarily on short-term, partisan goals. As Tony Wright noted of the House of Commons,

'there is no Parliament, in that collective sense, to insist on anything. There are simply members of Parliament who have preoccupations and inhabit a career structure in which sustained strengthening of the institution is not a central priority.'[27]

Second, there is the obvious institutional fact that in a Westminster parliamentary system, the executive comes from, and exercises significant influence over, the legislature. This is particularly clear in the House of Commons, where usually the Executive commands a majority. Executive influence penetrates almost every facet of parliamentary life: through formal means such as control over the agenda in the Commons;[28] and less formal but equally important means such as whipping and the promise of ministerial office.

Third, 'Parliament' is bicameral: it consists of the House of Commons and the House of Lords.[29] These are quite dissimilar institutions. The House of Commons has 650 elected MPs, who are more driven by immediate political concerns such as re-election, constituency interests, the party and the possibility of ministerial promotion than scrutinising legislation and executive action. By contrast, the Lords currently consists of over 800 peers, mostly appointed, with a rump of

---

[22] Straw Review (n 3) 8–10.
[23] I Jennings, *Parliament*, 2nd ed (Cambridge, Cambridge University Press, 1957) 2.
[24] Winetrobe (n 7) 19.
[25] Loewenberg, *On Legislatures* (n 8) 49.
[26] G Cox, 'The Organization of Democratic Legislatures' in B Weingast and D Wittman (eds), *The Oxford Handbook of Political Economy* (Oxford, Oxford University Press, 2009) 141.
[27] T Wright, 'Prospects for Parliamentary Reform' (2004) 57 *Parliamentary Affairs* 867, 874, quoted in M Russell and A Paun, *House Rules?* (n 7) 13.
[28] eg, House of Commons Standing Order 14(1): 'Government business shall have precedence at every sitting'.
[29] In respect of legislation, there are usually three institutions constituting 'Parliament': the monarch, the House of Commons and the House of Lords. Here we leave the monarch aside.

hereditary peers and bishops. Appointment, coupled with a much higher average age for peers (69, compared with 51 for MPs) means that not only are peers often individuals of expertise, but are also relatively immune to ambition.[30] Moreover, in the Lords, no one party or group has an overall majority. These two features diminish the influence of the Executive. In short, the two Houses do not speak with one voice; their respective members prioritise goals differently.

Fourth, and linked to the previous feature, each House is fiercely protective of its own interests and privileges; and wary of changes which might affect its own autonomy and status. This stance was bolstered by the legal doctrine of exclusive cognisance, which gave each House the exclusive jurisdiction to regulate its own internal affairs without external interference.[31] In practice, however, the possibility that a House might act collectively means that successive administrations and governments in both Houses have been wary of acting on their behalf without first seeking House consent.

Finally, and most importantly, the essence of legislatures is that they represent and contain disagreement.[32] They are riven by partisanship; disagreement is inevitable. Unlike almost any other organisation, there is no 'common purpose' shared by those who work in Parliament. And in Parliament's intensely political environment, and (in Westminster systems) because of its entanglement with the Executive, it is particularly difficult to divorce the corporate concerns of Parliament from partisan concerns. Parliament is the most political of all institutions, but the result is that its administration must act in a non-political way in order to respect all political allegiances.[33]

These features reflect the nature of Parliament as a legislature. The result of them is an institution that has found it very difficult to act in a coordinated, coherent manner where the issue is corporate—such as governance matters. These features also suggest that it is not a simple matter to import private and public sector arrangements into the two Houses.

At Westminster, the governance arrangements in each House reflect the institutional features just discussed. Broadly speaking, in each House, there is a political governance body, a Commission, consisting of key actors in the House (the presiding officer, who usually chairs; the House Leaders of the parties; representation from the backbenches; and more recently, non-executive and staff members) which in principle provides strategic direction for services and administration in the House. It is in turn supported by the House Administration—permanent

---

[30] House of Commons Library, 'Social background of MPs 1979–2015' (CBP 7483, 2016), 5; and 'Membership and principal office holders' at www.parliament.uk/about/faqs/house-of-lords-faqs/lords-members.

[31] L Lawrence Smyth, 'Privilege, Exclusive Cognisance and the Law' in Horne, Drewry and Oliver, *Parliament and the Law* (n 5) 3.

[32] See generally J Waldron, *The Dignity of Legislation* (Oxford, Oxford University Press, 1999).

[33] C Leston-Bandeira, 'The Pursuit of Legitimacy as a Key Driver for Public Engagement: the European Parliament Case' (2014) 67 *Parliamentary Affairs* 415, 421.

House staff. The apex of House Administration is a board, which consists of House staff, and is often chaired by the Clerk, the Accounting Officer of the House.[34] The board implements the policies set by the governance body. The governance body is also supported by a set of domestic committees (so called because they deal with internal matters of house governance rather than matters external to the House), who advise on finances, services and administration.[35] These are composed mostly of parliamentarians, and are a means through which the 'customers' or 'clients' (parliamentarians) of services are connected to the administrative (ie the management board) and political leadership (the Commission). And behind all of these arrangements lies the House itself.

But this formal (and oversimplified) governance structure is inadequate if we wish to know how the Houses are governed, for underneath the formalities lies great ambiguity. Even the titles of key actors suggest conflicting jurisdictional claims: in the Commons, for instance, there is both a Speaker and a Leader of the Commons—who is leading or speaking for the House? In practice, what matters are the relationships between actors: in particular, those between the House, government and the presiding officer (or the absence of a presiding officer, in the case of the Lords); the relationships within the Commission; and that between the Commission and Management Board. These relationships have been rarely expressed in the form of 'law'—at best they may be found in instruments of delegation or memorandums of understanding,[36] but more often than not they take the form of sometimes stable, sometimes shifting practices or understandings, governed by personality.

IV. THE HOUSE OF COMMONS

To some extent, Parliament's governance structures and the way in which responsibilities are allocated is the result of its relatively recent detachment from the executive. The 'modern' history of House governance may be said to begin with the decision in 1965 to pass control over the Palace of Westminster to the two Houses.[37] In fact, the executive continued to play a significant role in the management of the Houses. While day-to-day management of the Palace was

---

[34] Note that as a result of the Straw Review, the administrative structure in the Commons is now different, with a Board which operates under a small Executive Committee, and it is a Director General who now chairs the Board: See Part IV below.

[35] There are also domestic committees for procedure, privilege and conduct, but we are here only concerned with governance matters, not proceedings.

[36] See, for instance, the current 'Instrument of Delegation made by the House of Commons Commission on 15 June 2015', available at: www.parliament.uk/documents/commons-commission/delegation.pdf. This was then amended in 2016: see www.parliament.uk/mps-lords-and-offices/offices/commons/executive-committee/instrument-of-delegation.

[37] There are useful discussions of early Commons governance in M Rush and M Shaw (ed), *The House of Commons: Services and Facilities* (London, George Allen & Unwin, 1983) and more recently, the excellent but as yet unpublished paper of P Baines, 'House of Commons Governance: A Suitable Case for Treatment?' (2017).

transferred to the two Houses' authorities, control over the upkeep of the Palace remained with the Department of the Environment. Control over staffing in the Commons remained formally lodged with the Commission for Regulating the Offices of the House of Commons, which consisted of the Speaker, the Secretary or Secretaries of State, the Chancellor of the Exchequer, the Master of the Rolls, the Attorney and Solicitor General.[38]

Thus, the governance of the Commons remained under the Executive's control, although in practice much was delegated to the Speaker and the Clerk of the House. The Speaker was advised on services in the Commons by the Services Select Committee, a domestic committee set up in 1965 and consisting of 20 members. It had no executive responsibility, but in practice, it assumed a number of executive functions.[39]

Increasing dissatisfaction with the arrangements for House governance in the Commons led to a review by Sir Edward Compton ('the Compton Review'),[40] followed by the Bottomley Committee,[41] which reviewed and modified the recommendations made by Compton. Both reviews noted that the governance arrangements for the House of Commons was unsatisfactory in various ways. The Compton Review had two primary recommendations: the abolition of the Commission appointed under the House of Commons (Offices) Act 1812 (with no replacement body); and the unification of House administration—that is, permanent staff—under the Clerk of the House, following a civil service departmental model (primarily under the supervision of the Chancellor of the Exchequer). The Bottomley Committee agreed to the first in a qualified manner, but not to the second: it was felt that the Compton Review's key recommendations would 'detract from the "self-governing" role of the House'.[42] In relation to the first recommendation, the Bottomley Committee recommended the replacement of the earlier Commission with a new House of Commons Commission ('the Commons Commission'). The Committee stated that:

> [W]e are convinced of the need, in the House of Commons, for an ultimate authority which can express the will of the House in respect of its own services, organisation and staff; which can provide a central thrust for the development of those services; and which can oversee and care for the interests of Members of all parties and where necessary represent those interests to the Executive.[43]

This remains the objective of House governance today. The key (although not immediate) outcome of the Bottomley Committee was the establishment of the

---

[38] House of Commons (Offices) Act 1812, s 2.

[39] Baines, 'House of Commons Governance' (n 37).

[40] 'Review of the Administrative Services of the House of Commons: report to Mr Speaker by Sir Edmund Compton' HC 254, 1974.

[41] House of Commons (Administration), 'Report to Mr Speaker by Committee under Chairmanship of Mr Arthur Bottomley MP', HC 624, 1974–75 ('the Bottomley Report').

[42] ibid, 9.

[43] ibid, 15.

Commons Commission by statute.[44] The Commission consisted of a broader mixture of parliamentary interests: the Speaker; the Leader; and Shadow Leader of the House, and backbenchers. The lack of an inbuilt majority would, in principle anyway, serve to insulate the Commission from the executive. It was primarily responsible for the recruitment, appointment and pay conditions of House staff, and for the preparation of financial estimates for the House.[45] In terms of House administration, a Board of Management was established, but on the whole its organisation remained very much as before, on the basis that it was not delivering a singular policy but rather services to a set of actors.

These changes did not result in a more coherent, strategic approach to governance.[46] Following the Bottomley Committee there were a series of reviews of House governance carried out at relatively regular intervals, all done by external consultants: Sir Robin Ibbs (1990); Michael Braithwaite (1999); and Sir Kevin Tebbit (2007).[47] The first of these, the Ibbs Review, is perhaps the most significant, because later reviews built on its objectives. The Ibbs Review described an organisation in which the governing political body (the Commons Commission) rarely made decisions, and when it did, did so in a non-transparent manner. Moreover, it remained unclear who determined policy for services, or for implementation of policy. This was partly because the Services Select Committee presumed it had an executive role in producing policy, and yet its formal remit was advisory—and that it advised the Speaker, not the Commission.

The Ibbs Review also described an administration which was highly unsatisfactory: it had very limited capacity to monitor—let alone control—financial matters. So, for instance, spending was covered by seven different votes, of which only two were within the remit of Commons authorities. There was simply no readily usable financial information or comprehensive budgets; and no professional financial advice available. The Review concluded: 'A complete overhaul of financial systems is an inescapable necessity'.[48] It was only through establishing financial control over the administration of the Commons (including estates and works) that it could function as a modern public sector organisation.

The Ibbs Review led to a number of changes.[49] On the political side, the key domestic committee, the Services Committee was abolished and replaced with

---

[44]   House of Commons (Administration) Act 1978, s 1.

[45]   House of Commons (Administration) Act 1978, ss 2–3.

[46]   Baines, 'House of Commons Governance' (n 37).

[47]   The House of Commons Commission, 'House of Commons Services', HC 38, 1990/91 ('the Ibbs Review'); the House of Commons Commission, 'Review of Management and Services', HC 745, 1998/99 ('the Braithwaite Review'), and the House of Commons Commission, 'Review of Management and Services of the House of Commons', HC 685, 2007 ('the Tebbit Review'). There was a fourth review, which evaluated the implementation of the Tebbit Review recommendations in 2010: A Jablonowski, *Report on the Implementation of the Tebbit Review Recommendations* (2010). This was also carried by an external consultant, Alex Jablonowski. Unlike the first three, however, this was commissioned by the Commons' Management Board.

[48]   Ibbs Review (n 47) 6.

[49]   Many of these are set out in the Braithwaite Review (n 47).

a smaller Finance and Services Committee to reduce ambiguity of roles. On the administrative side, various reforms were put in place: a clearer remit was set for the Management Board; greater financial management mechanisms and resources were provided. The Review also led to the enactment of the Parliamentary Corporate Bodies Act 1992, which established the Clerks as the corporate officers of the two Houses. This allowed the Clerk of each House to enter into private sector arrangements; and was a necessary condition for full control over the Palace and the surrounding parliamentary estate to be transferred to the two Houses' authorities. That this only happened at the end of the twentieth century is testament to the lack of interest in House governance issues on the part of parliamentarians.

Both the Braithwaite (1999) and Tebbit (2007) Reviews were primarily taken up with modernising and streamlining the management of House administration. The Braithwaite Review recommended the establishment of an Audit Committee and the creation of an Office of the Clerk to support the Clerk's increasing managerial role. The Tebbit Review recommended a streamlined Board of Management (later Management Board), a strengthened Office of the Clerk, and the sharing of Estates and Works.

All three reviews identified perennial problems in both the political and administrative wings of Commons governance. Each review repeated the same criticisms: the Commons Commission lacked transparency, and generally failed to provide strategic direction on House services and administration; its relationships with both the Management Board and the domestic committees were ambiguous; and there was a lack of clarity about who was responsible for determining policy and implementation. In spite of this, the Commons Commission remained unchanged in shape, function and approach.

By contrast, House administration underwent several reforms, in order to meet the manifold and multiplying service demands of members. In time, the reviews resulted in the modernisation and centralisation of House administration; and in doing so consolidated administrative and managerial power in the Commons in the office of the Clerk of the House, effectively making the officeholder the chief executive of all House staff. This was perhaps an inevitable development, given the rise in number of staff working for the House of Commons. In 1979, House staff numbered 550 full time staff; by 2014 well over 1700.[50]

The 2014 Straw Review was significant in being the first review of Commons governance arrangements by members themselves in 40 years (since the 1975 Bottomley Review), which just illustrates the difficulty in getting parliamentarians to think about governance issues. As one MP stated to the Straw Committee, 'People do not become Members of Parliament because they want to run the House of Commons.'[51] Indeed, the establishment of the Review came about, not because of a desire to reform House governance, but from an elixir of particular, contingent events.

---

[50] Straw Review (n 3) 15. Neither figure includes staff employed by MPs, a number which has also increased.

[51] ibid, 15.

In early 2014, Sir Robert Rogers, then Clerk of the House, announced his retirement. The post of Clerk is a Crown appointment—a measure of protection for the independence of the office, since the Clerk is the chief procedural adviser to the Speaker and the House. In theory, then, the Clerk is appointed by the monarch on the advice of the Prime Minister. In practice, however, this has been done following a selection process determined mostly by the Speaker, with the Commission having a much less defined role. This informal division of labour has taken place because the Speaker operationally relies very heavily upon the Clerk, and therefore has a necessary and more immediate interest in the appointment.

Carol Mills, then an Australian parliamentary official, was announced as Sir Robert's successor. It was, however, later revealed that Mills lacked procedural experience, and was under investigation for misleading an Australian parliamentary committee over a possible breach of parliamentary privilege. The selection process was also criticised as procedurally flawed.[52] This allowed some members to launch an attack on the incumbent Speaker, John Bercow MP, who was seen as having increased the power of the Commons relative to the Government. The appointment process was 'paused' (and ultimately an internal candidate was appointed), and an ad hoc committee chaired by Jack Straw MP was established to consider 'the governance of the House of Commons, including the future allocation of the responsibilities for House services currently exercised by the Clerk of the House and Chief Executive'.[53]

It is unclear why the terms of reference were drafted so broadly, given the particular political context from which it emerged. It meant, however, that the Committee was able to examine and address various long-standing issues of House governance—in particular, the lack of strategic direction; and poor relationships between the political and administrative wings of the House.[54] The Review noted, in a passage redolent of any description of most aspects of the UK's constitution:

> The governance arrangements for the House have developed over time often in response to particular issues or events. This has resulted in a situation where the complexities which are inherent in the character of the House as a legislature have been compounded by layers of interventions which have built on and adapted what went before rather than rationalising or restructuring it.[55]

Two external members, an additional backbench representative and two official members (the Clerk and a Director General) were added to the Commission; and the Commission now had a specific statutory duty to set strategic priorities for House services.[56] The rationalisation of House administration continued apace.

---

[52] Some of the public details of this are set out in the Straw Review (n 3) 25–26.

[53] HC Deb 10 September 2014, col 1014.

[54] Details of the implementation of many of the Straw Review's recommendations can be found here: House of Commons Director General's Review, 'Report' (London, 2016).

[55] Straw Review (n 3) 13.

[56] These changes required new legislation: see House of Commons Commission Act 2015, which amended the 1978 Act.

A Director General ('DG') responsible for delivery of services, working under the Clerk, was appointed.[57] An Executive Committee ('ExCo'), consisting of the Clerk, DG and Head of Corporate Services was established. ExCo provides support to the Commission and is an intermediary level body between the Commission and a Board far more operational than the previous management board. Finally, the appointment process for the Clerk was clarified, to some extent: the Straw Review recommended it follow modern recruitment practices for public appointments—that is, it should be open and competitive; and the full selection process should be agreed to and overseen by the Commission.[58]

The key changes brought about by the Straw Review are too recent to evaluate. On the 'political' side, the non-executive and official members have no vote, but the external perspective which they provide may prompt action. The additional backbench member will increase representativeness, and reduce the likelihood of the government enjoying a majority on the Commission (as it had under the coalition Government).[59] But this additional member only reinforces the Commission's fundamental decision-making rule: consensus.

In terms of clarifying the selection process for the Clerk, it seems unlikely to remove the tension between the Clerk's responsibility to the incumbent Speaker and to the House as a whole. On the administrative side, the division of labour between the Clerk of the House and the new DG may alleviate pressures on the Clerk, but this will depend greatly on the relationship between the two office-holders. This relationship will also determine whether ExCo will be effective or not.

More generally, however, the Straw Review and its provenance illustrate the classic problems of House governance: grey and undocumented arrangements; ambiguous relationships between political and administrative staff; struggles for institutional power entangled with partisan politics; and ultimately, change to governance arrangements sparked not by the need for rationalisation or efficiency, but by sometimes quite personal conflict.

A. Key Actors in House of Commons Governance

It is useful at this point to step back and examine more closely the key actors involved in House governance, and their dynamics. This will allow us to see the ways in which governance is 'in fact' exercised, and under what conditions.

The House of Commons Commission is the most important governance body within the Commons, responsible for both the management of House finances

---

[57] The division of labour between the Clerk and the DG are set out in House of Commons Director General's Review, Report (n 54) 34–36.

[58] Straw Review (n 3) 67–68.

[59] ibid, 53.

and personnel.[60] For most of its existence the Commons Commission consisted primarily of politicians: the Speaker; the Leader of the House; a member nominated by the Opposition Leader (usually the Shadow Leader of the House); and three senior backbench members—one from each of the main parties (and since 2015 another to represent the remaining membership). It has, then, been broadly representative of the House, with the government enjoying no inbuilt majority. This has provided the Commission with insulation from the executive, but it also draws the Commission closer to the 'legislative state of nature'. It operates by consensus,[61] which in practice has been difficult to achieve. Inertia is the default position.

The Speaker is the most important actor within the Commission. Within the House, he has a dual role: he is the presiding officer in the Commons, and so resolves issues of procedure; but he is also responsible for the day-to-day administration of the House.[62] The authority that the Speaker derives from being presiding officer bleeds into his administrative role. As Chair of the Commons Commission, the Speaker sets the agenda; he is the actor who spends the longest time in post on the Commission (between 1979 and 2015, Speakers spent an average of eight years in post)[63] and who deals with senior House staff on a day-to-day basis. Many of the Commission's functions have devolved or been delegated to him—in particular, the power of appointment.[64]

Speakers, however, tend to lack the temperament, expertise and time for management and strategic direction of how the House is run. Like most MPs, Speakers have rarely had managerial experience, so they face similar difficulties to parliamentarians thrust into a ministerial role;[65] they also have their procedural responsibilities, and constituency duties as all MPs do. Thus, Speakers can be enormously influential in House governance, but like many ministers, have a tendency to focus on the short term. They are also constrained by other key actors within the governance structure of the House; and tempered by the need to maintain their own neutrality. Thus, the Straw Review noted that the Speaker has 'a position of leadership within the House, without being fully in charge'.[66]

The Leader of the House can be a powerful actor in terms of House administration: the Ibbs Review, for instance, was established in the wake of Sir Geoffrey

---

[60] A useful statement of the Commission's membership, functions and practice can be found at www.parliament.uk/documents/commons-commission/membership-functions-practice.pdf. We do not here deal with the Commission's other corporate role as the Members' Estimate Committee, responsible for oversight over certain aspects of Members' expenditure.

[61] Straw Review (n 3) 52.

[62] There is, in fact, no formal list of the Speaker's administrative powers: see Straw Review (n 3) 16.

[63] Analysis derived using data from D Butler and G Butler, *British Political Facts*, 10th edn (Basingstoke, Palgrave Macmillan, 2010); www.parliament.uk; and House Commission reports 1979–2017.

[64] Instrument of Delegation made by the House of Commons Commission on 15 June 2015, available at www.parliament.uk/documents/commons-commission/delegation.pdf. The Speaker has also always had the power to appoint certain senior staff, including a small retinue of personal staff.

[65] On this, see P Riddell, Z Gruhn and L Carolan, *The Challenge of being a Minister* (London, Institute for Government, 2011).

[66] Straw Review (n 3) 16.

Howe's brief tenure as Leader on the Commission;[67] and modernisation of the Commons (mostly in terms of procedure) took place under Robin Cook. However, Leaders have a dual role: they are expected to ensure that the legislative agenda of the Government is met in the Commons, as well as representing the House where appropriate. Almost inevitably, the former role dominates over the latter. The rare Leader committed to reform faces formidable challenges, not least from their own whips and an indifferent to hostile Prime Minister.[68] Leaders tend to be members on their way down, rather than up, which can restrict their influence. The Leader's Office has very small resources (with a staff in the twenties, compared to the thousands who staff the large Whitehall departments).[69] Tenure for Leaders of the House is low: between 1979 and 2017, the average time in office was two years.[70]

A similar analysis applies to the Shadow Leader of the House, whose average time in post is even shorter: 1.5 years in the same period.[71] To a large extent, then, the Leader (and the opposition's counterpart) acts as a veto player, and only rarely exercises any power of initiative. Backbench members of the Commission—chosen by the Whips—have tended to support the status quo. Although one member is Chair of the Finance Committee, backbench members as a group have lacked the institutional authority of the Speaker or the Leaders.[72] Finally, we need note that the Leader and Shadow Leader are part of another set of key actors—the 'usual channels', who prefer—all things considered—the status quo. The usual channels are also responsible for the appointment of the backbench members of the Commission, and those who sit on the domestic committees.[73]

Broadly, then, the Commons Commission, composed primarily of politicians with multiple, conflicting priorities, and having a high turnover, is predisposed towards inaction on issues with long-term implications. This is compounded by members' fear of negative publicity, which prompts them against action. At the same time, however, being composed of politicians, the Commission has the tendency to be reactive, focusing on routine matters and the short term. In this respect, it is often the Speaker who dominates, because of a lack of focused engagement from the other actors.

The domestic committees were established as a means by which concerns about administration and governance could be 'fed up' to permanent House staff and to the Commission. Chairs and members of the domestic committees remain chosen via party whips and the usual channels.[74] There has long been confusion over

---

[67] Baines, 'House of Commons governance' (n 37).

[68] On the Leader of the House, see G Power, 'The Politics of Parliamentary Reform: Lessons from the House of Commons (2001–2005)' (2007) 60 *Parliamentary Affairs* 492.

[69] J Straw, *Last Man Standing: Memoirs of a Political Survivor* (London, Macmillan, 2012), 469.

[70] Analysis derived using data from Butler and Butler *British Political Facts* (n 63); www.parliament. uk; and House Commission reports 1979–2017.

[71] ibid.

[72] John Thurso MP was perhaps an exception.

[73] M Rush, C Ettinghausen, I Campbell and A George, *Opening up the Usual Channels* (London, Hansard Society, 2002).

[74] Membership of these committees is not subject to the Wright reforms. eg, House of Commons Standing Order 122B.

the jurisdictional boundaries between the domestic committees, the Commons Commission and the Management Board. Committees have often thought of their role as executive in nature, whereas committee terms of reference have long stated that their function is advisory. Moreover, absenteeism and turnover in these committees has traditionally been high.

Thus, House governance have often fallen by default on the shoulders of the administrative wing—that is to say, on House staff and the Management Board. The board has traditionally supported the Commons Commission and implemented its decisions. However, the relationship between the Commission and the Board (and House staff) is complicated, for two key reasons. These complications are inherent in all public bureaucracies, although the legislative context adds a unique twist.

The first is the tendency towards compartmentalisation (like 'siloism' in the executive), which plagues all organisations.[75] House administrative organisation has, for much of its existence, lacked unity because of the functional specialisation of House staff: for decades House services had a federal structure with the Clerk of the House operating as *primus inter pares*, but who shared administrative control with powerful department heads such as the Serjeant-at-Arms. Thus, until the late 1990s we have seen that the Board acted as 'a forum for discussion and compromise, rather than for strategy and decision.'[76] It was not a 'supra-departmental' body that acted collectively. The various consolidations brought about by successive reviews, however, have now made the Board and House administration far more cohesive, but concerns about coordination persist.[77]

But there is a more fundamental tension lying at the heart of the relationship between the political wing and the permanent House administration: the constitutional (and prudent) necessities for permanent staff to be *both* responsive *and* politically impartial. House staff must be responsive to each and every member, but balance this with their responsibility to the House as a corporate entity which exists across time. So, for instance, the Clerk of the House is responsible to the Speaker and the Commission, but he is also Accounting Officer for the House, responsible for the proper use of public money.[78] Navigating between the twin necessities of responsiveness and impartiality can be difficult: in the intensely political environment of the Commons, 'acts undertaken as impartial management initiatives can quickly assume unintended political significance'.[79]

Indeed, this duty of political impartiality, or perhaps constrained responsiveness, takes on a special importance in a legislative context: it is not always clear who the legitimate representative of 'the House' is. Ultimately, civil servants in a

---

[75] See generally B Guy Peters, *Pursuing Horizontal Management* (Kansas, University Press of Kansas, 2015).

[76] Braithwaite Review (n 47) 41.

[77] Straw Review (n 3) 22–24.

[78] The Clerk is appointed as accounting officer by the Commons Commission under the House of Commons (Administration) Act 1978, s 3(2).

[79] Braithwaite Review (n 47) 9.

department can turn to their Secretary of State as representative of the department to resolve a thorny issue. Not so for House staff. As we have seen, they generally have no identifiable 'leader' in the way that civil servants have. The Commission is legally their employer (although management is delegated to the Board), but in practice, political authority is not often forthcoming, or comes from a some-what imperfect representative, the Speaker. House staff are expected to be politi-cal impartial and loyal to the vague entity that is 'the House' (and noticeably, not Parliament).[80] For all these reasons, permanent staff are less wont to act, or act in a manner which can frustrate those on the Commission, the domestic committees and members generally. What Kaufman said of politico-administrative relations in an executive context is equally true in a legislative context:

> [T]he system is so loaded with ambiguity that what looks like wilful insubordination and evasion from one standpoint may seem like defensible and even dutiful behavior from another. It is difficult to be sure which is which because of the plethora of commands.[81]

Political impartiality acts as a necessary shield for staff in the face of competing and conflicting partisan demands, but it can result in apparent inaction or a stud-ied passivity. It may be no surprise, therefore, that relations between the political and administrative wings of House government are not always sweetness and light.

This brings us on to the House itself, which all key actors recognise as 'sovereign'. It rarely intervenes in governance matters in a decisive way. This is partly because its composition is constantly changing, but at every election: between 1979 and 2015 the average turnover following each general election was roughly a quarter of the House.[82] With such a turnover, 'its' institutional memory and willingness to address long-term governance issues is very limited.[83] That said, the history of Commons governance illustrates that successive Commissions and governments have been wary of acting without first seeking the House's views and consent.

The result of this tangled state of affairs is that changes in governance have come about slowly; or abruptly changed following an exogenous 'shock' to the system.

V. THE HOUSE OF LORDS

Limited space allows for only a brief examination of the governance structure in the Lords, but it provides a useful comparator for the Commons.[84] For the most

---

[80] House of Commons, *Staff Handbook*, 6th edn (2013), paras 5.1–5.2.

[81] Kaufman 'Ruminations' (n 21) 261.

[82] Statistics drawn from House of Commons Library, 'Research Paper: UK Election Statistics: 1918–2012', 12/43, 2012 and House of Commons Library, 'Social background of MPs 1979–2015', CBP 7483, 2016.

[83] This turnover obviously also affects the composition of the House Commission and domestic committees.

[84] There is an excellent standard note from the House of Lords Library which covers many of these matters: House of Lords Library, 'The Governance and Administration of the House of Lords', LLN 2015/004, 2015.

part, the dynamics in the Lords replicate those in the House of Commons, but the Lords' arrangements have been much less formal in nature, and far slower to change. This has been primarily due to the Lords' unelected, subordinate status within Parliament—for most of the twentieth century there was little internal or external pressure to reform governance arrangements.[85] The focus of political and public attention has been primarily on reforming the composition of the Lords, not its inner workings. The result was that for decades House services in the Lords were run in a semi-autonomous fashion by permanent staff, with limited oversight by members.

The primary catalysts for change in House governance in the Lords have been exogenous—that is to say, sparked by factors external to the House: changes to governance arrangements in the 'other place'; and the removal of most hereditary peers in 1999, shifting the composition of the House towards appointed peers; and increasing numbers of life and working peers appointed by successive Prime Ministers. The last catalyst in particular has put pressure on scarce resources in the House, encouraging greater rationalization of governance structures.[86]

The 'modern' governing arrangements for the Lords begins with the 2002 Tordoff Review.[87] The Review had been established in the wake of the Commons' 1999 Braithwaite Review. A major reason for the Tordoff Review was to evaluate the administrative financial mechanisms put in place in the Lords following Ibbs, but equally as important was the dissatisfaction of peers with the then current governance arrangements—'there was a prevailing sense that the system [had] failed ... [and] a widespread distrust of the existing system'.[88]

The Tordoff Review was scathing. It bluntly stated the Select Committee on the House of Lords Offices (then the functional equivalent of the Commons Commission) was dysfunctional. It consisted of an extraordinary 28 members, including the Chairman of Committees; the Leaders, Deputy Leaders, Chief Whips of the three main parties, the Convenor of the Crossbenchers; and the chairs of all the 'domestic' subcommittees.[89] The lack of clearly defined responsibilities, and the size and organisation of the Offices Committee meant that it acted as a 'post box' for decisions made by its various subcommittees (the equivalent of

---

[85] The Lords have had far less pressure in terms of resource and staff: resource and capital costs of the Lords at present, for instance, are just over half that of the Commons; and if MPs' salaries and expenses are included, the cost of the Lords is less than a third of that of the Commons: R Walters and R Rogers, *How Parliament Works*, 7th edn (Abingdon, Routledge, 2015) 73.

[86] eg, M Russell, *House Full: Time to get a Grip on Lords Appointments* (London, UCL, 2011).

[87] Named after the chair of the committee carrying out the review, the then Chairman of Committees, Lord Tordoff: see Select Committee on the House of Lords' Offices, Fifth Report, HL 105, 2002 ('the Tordoff Review'). The Lords' governing arrangements had already been reformed once in order to conform with changes to financial management in the Commons following the 1991 Commons Ibbs Review, but there is limited documentation on this change, and indeed governance of the Lords prior to 2000.

[88] ibid, App 2, para 10.

[89] In fact, the Offices Committee numbered *twice* this size prior to the Ibbs Review. See ibid, App 2, para 13.

domestic committees). The Review's evaluation of the political wing of the Lords' governance arrangements strikes a familiar note:

> The size of the Offices Committee, the infrequency of its meetings, and the way issues reach it, all mean that it is incapable of providing leadership for the domestic administration of the House. It does not develop a coherent strategy or set an agenda for the more specialised Sub-Committees and for the administration as a whole. In the absence of such leadership the Sub-Committees are reactive—they respond to proposals put before them and rarely take a strategic view of the requirements of the House and how to meet them. This has a knock-on effect on staff: without political guidance from the Committee structure, the staff prepare papers for Sub-Committee meetings which concentrate on specific proposals or particular complaints, rather than medium or long-term policies for improving the administration of the House as a whole.[90]

In short, the need to ensure representation (and therefore the requirement of consensus) replicated the legislative state of nature and paralysed effective governance. Moreover, the lack of leadership and clearly defined responsibilities within the Lords meant that the Lords could neither assert itself in relation to the Commons, nor engage in meaningful discussion about shared services. Thus we can see that organisation and institutional arrangements matter: the absence of a clear, hierarchical governance structure meant that the Lords was hampered in its capacity to carry out its basic constitutional functions—or even seek clarity on what these functions might be.

On the administrative side, there was again a familiar refrain. The Tordoff Review pointed out that there was no centralised management board to provide support to the Offices Committee on strategy or a business plan—there were 15 administrative offices (compared with the five departments in the Commons). Given this fragmentation it was difficult for the administration to provide focused support to the Offices Committee.

The Tordoff Review made a number of recommendations which were mostly implemented. The Offices Committee was replaced with a relatively smaller House Committee of 12 peers, which was expected to provide leadership and policy direction for House administration. The subcommittees were reconstituted as domestic committees. Their primary role was to advise the House Committee; and to act as 'user groups' to allow peers to discuss House services. An Audit Committee with external members and a management board were established. Thus, governance arrangements were rationalised, with power explicitly centralised within the House Committee.

Between the 2002 Tordoff Review and the 2016 Shephard Review (see below), there were a series of reviews. The 2007 Parker Review[91] mostly focused on House administration: the Management Board was regarded as reactive and responding to the short-term and the routine. It recommended the appointment of non-executive

---

[90] ibid, App 2, para 15.
[91] Sir J Parker and H Mahy, 'Review of the Management Board of the House of Lords' (2007).

members to the Board.[92] The 2007 Tordoff-Hunt Review,[93] on the other hand, focused primarily on the political side of governance. It concluded that the governance structures needed only incremental tweaking—in particular, tighter terms of reference and better relationships between the House Committee, management board and the domestic committees. The 2011 Thomas and Makower Review[94] returned to issues of administration, recommending a smaller Management Board, a non-executive element, rationalisation and reduction in the number of free-standing administrative offices, and greater support to the Office of the Clerk of the Parliaments.

Reading all reviews more closely, however, it is clear that while the 'excesses' of the pre-Tordoff years had ended, fundamental problems remained. The political wing failed to provide leadership, remained unable to decide, or focused on routine matters at the expense of thinking more long term; while the House administration remained mostly reactive, limited by the passivity of the political wing and the continued fragmentation of its services, which were organised along both functional and task lines.

By far the most public change to House governance in this period was the establishment of the Lord Speaker in 2005, which resulted from Prime Minister Blair's decision to 'reform' the post of Lord Chancellor. Here was an opportunity to address the absence of a Commons-style Speaker, a figure to whom administrative concerns could also be directed. The House, however, was concerned that a Commons-style Speaker would upset the principle of self-regulation. Thus, what was created only served to blur the lines of accountability within the Lords, with the Lord Speaker's functions and duties carved out from the existing duties of the Lord Chancellor and the Chairman of Committees.[95] The Lord Speaker was an elected post, the public face of the Lords, and Chair of the House Committee; but at the same time the Lord Speaker had little connection with the administrative staff of the House, except in matters of security. The Chairman of Committees (on whom, see more below) remained the key link between peers and the administration. Thus, there is now a triumvirate of officers with vested roles in administration and governance: the Lord Speaker, the Chairman of Committees and (to a lesser extent) the Leader of the Lords. This diffusion of functions has meant a lack of clarity over responsibility for governance.[96]

In 2016 the Leader's Group on Governance published a report (the 'Shephard Review', named after the Group's chair) recommending various changes to

---

[92] This was rejected by the Tordoff-Hunt Review: House of Lords House Committee, 'Internal Governance' H/07-08/1, 2007. This was chaired by Lord Tordoff and Lord Hunt of Wirral.

[93] ibid.

[94] M Thomas and A Makower, 'Report of a Review of the Structure of the House of Lords Administration and the Operation of the Management Board' (2011).

[95] Select Committee on the Speakership of the House, 'The Speakership of the House of Lords', HL 92, 2005.

[96] Thus, when Lord Sewel (then Chairman of Committees, 2012–15) abruptly left the House of Lords following a scandal, it was initially unclear who was responsible for managing the aftermath.

governance.[97] The Review stems from various incidents demonstrating that the current arrangements had become unsustainable; the 2014 Straw Review; and more broadly, because of anxiety about increasing public and media scrutiny, the pressures on resources brought about by increasing numbers of appointed peers; and the impending Restoration and Renewal programme of the Palace of Westminster (see below).

The Shephard Review's recommendations were mostly accepted by the House.[98] The House Committee—renamed the House of Lords Commission ('the Lords Commission')—was now explicitly responsible for the strategic direction of House services. The Lords Commission remained 12 in number, but two backbench members were replaced by two non-executive members to provide an external challenge. The key domestic committees were reduced in number, with new Finance and Services Committees advising the Commission. Clearer terms of reference for all committees and the Commission were set down. The Chairman of Committees would no longer sit as *ex officio* chair of either the new Finances or Services Committees. As a result, the Lords' governance structure—particularly the House Commission and domestic committees—now neatly mirrors the arrangements in the Commons. This was deliberate, and may allow the two Houses to work together in a more coherent fashion, particularly given Restoration and Renewal.

A. Key Actors in House of Lords Governance

If we once again step back to examine the dynamics between the key actors, we see a similar picture to the Commons. The primary difference is that underlying House governance is the absence of a government majority: this makes the criterion of consensus even more critical.

The Lords Commission is the key political body in relation to governance matters. It suffers from the same defects as its Commons counterpart: it is a body of limited capacity and effectiveness because of its composition and decision-making process. It is almost twice as large as the Commons Commission, consisting of 12 members: the Lords Speaker (and prior to 2005, the Lord Chancellor); the Chairman of Committees; the leaders of the Conservatives, Labour and the Liberal Democrats; the Convenor of the Crossbench Peers; four backbench peers; and, as of 2016, two non-executive members. Unlike its Commons counterpart, however, the Lords Commission and its predecessors have had no statutory basis; its existence has depended on the will of the House.

---

[97] Leader's Group on Governance, 'Governance of Domestic Committees in the House of Lords', HL 81, 2016 ('the Shephard Report').

[98] Details can be found here: House Committee, 'Implementing the Recommendations of the Leader's Group on Governance' HL 19, 2016; and see HL Deb 21 July 2016, col 743.

Within the Commission itself, the key actors are the Lord Speaker, the Leaders and the Chairman of Committees, and more broadly, the usual channels. Prior to the establishment of the Lord Speaker, it was the Lord Chancellor who had a quasi-presiding officer function, who sat by dint of that role in the Offices Committee (later the House Committee). However, the Lord Chancellor was notorious for the number of hats held—as titular head of the judiciary, Cabinet minister and quasi-presiding officer of the Lords. Although the average time in post between 1979 and 2007 was five and a half years,[99] the burdens of this office (primarily judicial work prior to the Constitution Reform Act 2005) meant that the administration of the House was a low priority for successive Lord Chancellors.

We have already discussed the Lord Speaker. Although office-holders are elected, and would seem to have an independent source of authority, it is a new office, and its functions are primarily directed outwards rather than internally. Office-holders have had limited connection with the administrative staff of the House, except in matters of security.

Instead, it has been the Chairman of Committees[100] who has been the key link between peers and the administration. Chosen via the Committee of Selection (that is, by the usual channels), and expected to maintain a non-partisan stance, the Chairman exercises the effective equivalent of the Speaker's administrative role by dint of his role as *ex officio* chair of key domestic committees,[101] his office's physical proximity to key House staff and long periods of tenure.[102] It was for these reasons that the 2002 Tordoff Review recommended the Chairman should provide leadership as the chair of the Lords Commission's predecessor, the House Committee.[103]

Leaders of the Lords suffer from similar problems to their Commons counterparts. They have divided responsibilities, and historically they have not stayed for long in office: they have had a tenure similar to their Commons counterparts (2.3 years in the period 1979–2017).[104] Moreover, in the past they shared the authority of government with another government minister, the Lord Chancellor. To the extent, then, that there is leadership in the Lords, it is exercised unevenly, mediated through several veto players. The Leaders (and formerly the

---

[99] Figures calculated using Butler and Butler, *British Political Facts* (n 63); and www.parliament.uk. The period ends with the establishment of the office of Lord Speaker in 2005.

[100] Following the implementation of the Shephard Report, the Chairman of Committees is now known as the Senior Deputy Speaker, but he remains formally appointed as the Chairman of Committees to avoid the need to amend relevant legislation.

[101] However, as already noted, since 2016 the Chairman's institutional power has now been weakened because he no longer sits as chair of the two key domestic committees dealing with finance and services.

[102] If we exclude those who died in office (Lord Mackay of Ardbrecknish), left because of scandal (Sewell) or served as temporary replacements (Tordoff, Laming), Lord Aberdare served for 16 years (1976–92) and Lord Brabazon for 10 (2002–12).

[103] Tordoff Review (n 87) App 2, para 27. The Chairman did so until the establishment of the Lords Speaker in 2005.

[104] Figures calculated using Butler and Butler, *British Political Facts* (n 63); and www.parliament.uk.

Lord Chancellor) are all members of the usual channels, and along with the party Whips are mostly likely to exercise their influence in favour of the status quo. The Lord Speaker, Chairman of Committees and the Convenor of the Crossbenchers are expected to be non-partisan and must therefore tread carefully. And, as in the Commons, all key political actors are constrained by the fear of negative publicity.

From our brief historical overview, we have seen that House administration in the Lords have gone through similar changes to those in the Commons (indeed, much of it driven by those changes): a slow process of rationalisation, with a particular emphasis on financial management. House staff in the Lords are also in a similar invidious position to staff in the Commons: they are expected to be politically neutral, and yet they may be understood as the 'stewards' of the House (and again, not to the notional entity, 'Parliament').[105] The result has been a mixture of deferential behaviour and frustrated attempts to press peers towards greater modernisation.[106] Noting the absence of direction from the political wing—a 'strategic vacuum'—one review of House administration commented that

> officers will usually attempt to plug critical gaps of thinking. But the relationship is fragile, and extends only to certain topics. This is one of the reasons why parliaments have tended to lag behind even the broader public sector in their adoption of new working methods.[107]

Finally, there is the House itself. In the Lords the influence of the House is subtly stronger—this is particularly so in the twenty-first century, as the government enjoys no majority in the Lords. The corollary of this, however, is that a cross-party consensus is necessary to achieve change. The quasi-constitutional status of the principle of 'self-regulation', which underlies the everyday operations of the Lords, is testament to this.[108] Self-regulation, however, tends to translate into a fear that new structures or reforms will interfere with or undermine that much-vaunted principle—as was the case with the establishment of the Lord Speaker.

The governance landscape in the Lords is therefore what the Commons governance arrangements would have been, but for the far more intense public and political pressures put on the Commons, and the presence of a government majority. In the Lords, there is an even greater dispersal of accountability—for instance, the equivalent functions of the Commons Speaker are shared between three different actors in the Lords. The reforms adopted have usually mirrored those in the Commons, but have taken longer to be accepted by the House.

---

[105] House of Lords, *Staff Handbook* (2012), para 12.1.

[106] Emma Crewe argues that many of the recommendations of the Tordoff Committee were the work of clerks: E Crewe, *Lords of Parliament* (Manchester, Manchester University Press, 2005), 175.

[107] Thomas and Makower, *House of Lords* (n 94) 22.

[108] eg, House of Lords, *Companion to the Standing Orders and Guide to the Proceedings of the House of Lords*, 25th edn (2017), 47.

The House itself has been somewhat more interventionist in governance matters, but not necessarily in a positive fashion.[109]

VI. RESTORATION AND RENEWAL

In this final section we return, full circle, to the subject matter and themes of *Mid-Victorian Masterpiece*, with the recent debate over the restoration and renewal ('R&R') of the Palace of Westminster.[110] We shall not delve into all the details of R&R here, given its complexity, but also because at the time of writing, the issue remains live. It does, however, illustrate the difficulties Parliament has in engaging in collective action on corporate issues.

The Palace of Westminster was designed in the 1830s but construction was only completed in the 1860s.[111] It was damaged during World War Two and rebuilt in the period 1945–50. Since then there has been no general renovation of the Palace, although there have been many incremental upgrades. Over time, the parliamentary estate expanded to include a number of properties in and around Westminster. As noted earlier, control over the Palace shifted to Parliament over a period of 30 years. The Palace is now an iconic building, classed as a World Heritage site, under the control of the two Houses' authorities. It continues to accommodate many MPs and peers.

From the beginning of the twenty-first century, there were increasing concerns about the deteriorating physical state of the Palace.[112] In 2012, a study group established by the two Houses' management boards published a pre-feasibility study and business case for the long-term maintenance of the Palace of Westminster.[113] It stated bluntly that 'If the Palace were not a listed building of the highest heritage value, its owners would probably be advised to demolish and rebuild [it],'[114] and 'it is remarkable that it continues to function.'[115]

In spite of this, two initial assumptions were made, which remain fundamental to this day. The first was that the Palace had to remain as a central site for the work of Parliament. The second was that in carrying out R&R, the legislative and

---

[109] The Lords has been less amenable to the work of external consultants, for instance. The House rejected with the Office Committees' recommendation to allow Michael Braithwaite to review their governance arrangements in 2002: see Tordoff Review (n 87) App 2, para 2. The recommendations of Sir John Parker and Helen Mahy were rejected by members in the Tordoff-Hunt Review: contrast this with Parker and Mahy, *Review of the Management Board* (n 91).

[110] Key reports on the R&R project can be found on the Houses of Parliament Restoration and Renewal website: www.restorationandrenewal.parliament.uk.

[111] This is discussed in Cocks, *Mid-Victorian Masterpiece* (n 1).

[112] Much of the history is laid out in the Pre-Feasibility Study: House of Commons, House of Lords Study Group, *Restoration and Renewal of the Palace of Westminster: Pre-Feasibility Study and Preliminary Strategic Business Case* (2012), Annex 1.

[113] ibid.

[114] ibid, 5. This was because the cost of refurbishment alone (not renewal) was far in excess of the insurance reinstatement value of £1.8 billion.

[115] ibid, 27.

political work of the two Houses should not be impeded, or as little as possible. With these in mind, the study set out a number of initial options, including continuing repairs and replacement over an indefinite period of time; a rolling programme over a defined period of time; repairs and replacement in a shorter period of time, and with parliamentary activity shifted elsewhere.

Successive reports confirmed the initial study's findings of a looming crisis. Following the pre-feasibility study, the Commons Commission and Lords' House Committee agreed to have an external review of the various options for the restoration and renewal of the Palace. An Independent Options Appraisal (IOA) Report was published in mid-2015.[116] The IOA Report set out the costs of a rolling programme (minimal work, with Parliament occupied); a partial decant (the Commons then the Lords moving to temporary accommodation); and full decant (with both Houses vacating). Broad details of each are set out in Table 4.1 below.

Table 4.1: The options for Restoration and Renewal of the Palace of Westminster

	Projected time (years)	Projected cost (£ billion)
Rolling programme	32	5.7
Partial decant	11	3.9–4.4
Full decant	6	3.5–3.9

Source: Deloitte, AECON and H&K, 'Palace of Westminster Restoration and Renewal Programme Independent Options Appraisal'—Final Report (2014) 10.

A Joint Committee was then appointed in late 2015 to consider the IOA and R&R project. It reported back in late 2016.[117] The Committee recommended that there was a 'clear and pressing need' to carry out R&R, and that of the three options, a full decant was seen as the least disruptive and most cost-effective option overall.[118] It also recommended the establishment of an arm's length delivery authority, overseen by a sponsor board, to test the options and produce the final detailed designs and business case. The Committee exhorted both Houses to make a decision on this as soon as possible. The Public Accounts Committee published a report supporting the recommendations of the Joint Committee,[119] but the Treasury Committee announced in early 2017 it would carry out an inquiry into the options examined by the Joint Committee.[120] And at the time of the announcement and

---

[116] Deloitte, AECON and H&K, 'Palace of Westminster Restoration and Renewal Programme Independent Options Appraisal—Final Report' (2014).

[117] Joint Committee on the Palace of Westminster, *Restoration and Renewal of the Palace of Westminster*, HC 659, 2016–17.

[118] ibid, 10.

[119] House of Commons Committee of Public Accounts, *Delivering Restoration and Renewal*, HC 1005, 2017.

[120] www.parliament.uk/business/committees/committees-a-z/commons-select/treasury-committee/inquiries1/parliament-2015/restoration-and-renewal-palace-of-westminster-16-17.

confirmation of the general election in late April 2017, there had been no debate on the Joint Committee's report. Thus, there will be no consideration of R&R in the immediate future.[121]

Two points emerge. First, the role of the Executive in this (and indeed in the history of House governance) is fundamental, but lacks transparency. So, for instance, the Treasury Committee's queries on the costs of R&R were addressed to David Lidlington, the incumbent Leader of the Commons—not to the respective House Commissions.[122] It is unthinkable that the Government's backing would not be required for such a major capital investment; and yet there is very little explicit public acknowledgement of this role.

The second point is that there is a history of parliamentary indecision over estates and accommodation: the construction of the Palace of Westminster; the acquisition of surrounding property for parliamentary use. It is no different here. Concerns over the Palace's deteriorating state and its effect on the operations of Parliament have been voiced since at least 2000. The Commissions of the Houses have been slow in responding to this impending crisis over parliamentary infrastructure; and, in spite of two independent reports and two separate select committee reports urging immediate action, the Houses and their governance bodies have so far failed to make any collective decision. At the very least, this failure to make a decision will increase the overall cost of implementation; but at its worst may result in a serious accident.

There is a common denominator linking both points together: the fear of negative publicity. No one wants to be seen to be taking the decision to spend so much money on essentially themselves. Although this chapter has eschewed the matter of members' pay, allowances and staffing, the parallels between the 2008 expenses crisis and R&R are too marked to be ignored. The expenses crisis came about because of a long-term failure on the part of successive House of Commons administrations and the executive to address the cost of democratic governance in a transparent way for fear of how this would be interpreted by the media and the public.[123] Even when it became clear that the Freedom of Information Act applied to the Commons, there was great difficulty securing collective agreement from key actors—the Commission (and particularly the Speaker), the Management Board, the Executive, and MPs themselves. It was only following the *Telegraph's* reportage on the non-redacted data on MPs' expenses that their hands were forced; and in fact the proposed 'solution' (the establishment of the Independent Parliamentary Standards Authority) came not from the Commons, but the Executive. The reactive nature of parliamentary governance—and in particular the unwillingness

---

[121] Indeed, *the Times* suggests R&R will not be dealt with in the new Parliament: 'MPs delay Westminster repairs to shore up May', *The Times* (15 June 2017).

[122] ibid.

[123] See A Kelso, 'Parliament on its Knees: MPs' Expenses and the Crisis of Transparency at Westminster' (2009) 80 *Political Quarterly* 329 and Worthy 'Freedom of Information and Parliament' (n 5) 155–56.

or inability of parliamentarians and key governance bodies to press the issue to resolution—threatens to cause yet another crisis in democratic governance.

VII. CONCLUSION

Our claim in this chapter has been that to understand how 'Parliament' works, we should examine not just its external relationships with the other branches, but also its internal administrative structures and processes. We do not deny that the executive plays an important, even dominating, role in determining the scope and limits of legislative action. The argument is rather that even if there was no fusion between the executive and the legislature, the latter would still have serious issues in ensuring collective action. The need for consensus, the requirement of impartiality, the intensely political environment of both Houses and concern about media scrutiny and public disapproval have been a recipe for inertia and inaction.

Of course, it is clear that in some respects 'Parliament' *has* been able to act 'collectively'. But we have to treat some examples of these with caution. In the passing of legislation, for instance, Parliament acts collectively, but this occurs primarily because of political parties, which aggregate political preferences.[124] Select committees and procedural matters have not been addressed in this chapter, but there has clearly been an increase in what the late Anthony King called the 'cross-party mode' in the growth and increasing sophistication of select committees; and in the establishment of the Backbench Business Committee.[125] It is at least arguable, however, that much of this has occurred because of highly specific, exogenous circumstances. There are at least three conditions for successful 'efficiency' reforms (ie, reforms which benefit the legislature rather than the executive):[126] a window of opportunity, usually at the beginning of a Parliament; a reform agenda; and leadership.[127] These may be necessary, but not sufficient conditions.[128] This was certainly the case with the Wright reforms, which were a response to the 2008 expenses scandal.

Our examination of intra-branch relationships suggests that a significant reason for Parliament's sluggish nature is the lack of an accepted hierarchy or an identifiable, active leadership. The executive, in spite of its own endemic coordination problems, can rely on party cohesion and collective cabinet responsibility in the political context, and individual ministerial responsibility (which requires civil service loyalty) in the administrative context, to ensure a

---

[124] Cox, 'The Organization of Democratic Legislatures' (n 26).

[125] A King, 'Modes of Executive-Legislative Relations: Great Britain, France and Germany' (1976) 1 *Legislative Studies Quarterly* 11.

[126] A Kelso, *Parliamentary Reform at Westminster* (Manchester, Manchester University Press, 2009).

[127] P Norton, 'Reforming Parliament in the United Kingdom: The Report of the Commission to Strengthen Parliament' (2000) 6 *Journal of Legislative Studies* 1.

[128] M Russell, '"Never Allow a Crisis Go To Waste": The Wright Committee Reforms to Strengthen the House of Commons' (2011) 64 *Parliamentary Affairs* 612, 631–32.

unified stance. The judiciary, too, has its own sources of cohesion and coordination resolution mechanisms: long immersion in the law; a very clear judicial hierarchy; and most recently, a strong judicial administrative organisation.[129] To put it another way: the executive and judiciary are strong relative to the legislature because they are unified institutionally in a way that the legislature can only rarely be.[130]

Rather than focusing on conflict between branches, examining the 'mundanity' of administration and internal issues of capacity may be an equally important way for us to evaluate the strengths and/or autonomy of each branch. What is striking, in examining the various governance reports of the Houses of Parliament, is the extent to which a driver of Parliament's growing autonomy has been the need to work through everyday matters such as accommodation, estates and services. It is in responding these issues that the Houses have been forced to bolster their financial and management capacity, and to some extent work together in a more unified manner.[131] These changes, as Winetrobe perceptively noted, 'have not generally been motivated by questions of constitutional principle and propriety'.[132] The ground-breaking Ibbs Review, for instance, did not justify its recommendations in terms of the Commons' constitutional functions or roles; this was simply a matter of ensuring a public sector organisation followed standard business practice. It was only later that those tasked with governance reforms began to recognise the constitutional significance of administrative issues.[133] Future students may wish to turn to issues such as estates security and the R&R programme to understand the weaknesses and strengths of the legislature rather than look to legislative clashes with the judiciary or the executive.

None of this suggests what the 'proper' role or capacity of Parliament should be, or what is desirable. That question is far too complex to be dealt with in one chapter, for there are various competing values which underlie the governance of the legislature that require careful evaluation. The most obvious set of values is that between supporting the government (governing), and scrutinising its action and legislative proposals (accountability). But there is also a tension between the democratic value of representation—the need to accommodate and support the representatives of the constituencies and interests of the UK, and the value of organisational efficiency—the administrative drive towards the provision of coordinated, coherent institutional action. These values are not easily reconciled.[134] But we should expect no less: conflict is the central characteristic of all legislatures.

---

[129] G Gee, R Hazell, K Malleson and P O'Brien, *The Politics of Judicial Independence in the UK's Changing Constitution* (Cambridge, Cambridge University Press, 2015).

[130] Moe and Wilson 'Presidents and Political Structure' (n 8).

[131] Winetrobe (n 7) 31.

[132] ibid, 18.

[133] See Braithwaite Review (n 47) 9; Tebbit Review (n 47) 10; Straw Review (n 3) 13.

[134] That said, redundancy caused by representation is not necessarily a negative characteristic. Having particular problems examined by different and overlapping 'constituencies' or organisational units may be wise—not least because it is entirely possible one of these may miss the problem entirely. See generally B Guy Peters, *Pursuing Horizontal Management* (n 75).

5

Select Committees: Powers and Functions

CHRISTOPHER JOHNSON

I. INTRODUCTION: COMMITTEES AND THE CHAMBER

A. Origins

IN THE WORDS of a former edition of *Erskine May*, 'in both Houses of Parliament the practice of delegating to small bodies of Members, regarded as representing the House itself, the consideration of detailed or technical questions, is as old as any part of their settled procedure'.[1]

This passage, while accurately reflecting the antiquity of committees, perhaps gave a misleading impression of the scope of their work, even when it was written, in 1989. As long ago as 1571 the House of Commons was recorded as appointing committees to investigate elections and religion,[2] neither of which would normally be regarded as 'detailed or technical questions'.

A clue as to the reason for the emergence of committees can be found in one of the earliest Standing Orders of the House of Lords, codified in 1621 and still in force today as SO No 62: 'To have more freedom of debate, and that arguments may be used (pro and contra), Committees of the Whole House are appointed, sometimes for Bills, sometimes to discuss matters of great moment.' The committee format provided greater 'freedom of debate', the possibility to innovate in ways that would be inconceivable in plenary session.

While SO No 62 refers to Committees of the whole House, rather than select committees, in the early days there was no hard distinction between the two formats. Many bills, for instance, were committed to committees of named (or 'select') membership. But those members may just have been those who happened to be present on the day, or who volunteered to participate. There were also committees

---

[1] *Erskine May: Parliamentary Practice*, 21st edition (London, Butterworths, 1989) 604.
[2] See 'The History of Parliament Online' for 1571, at www.historyofparliamentonline.org/volume/1558-1603/parliament/1571#footnote4_g9rh143.

of open membership, lasting in the Lords until the mid-twentieth century, and functioning in effect as Committees of the whole House.

Notwithstanding this uncertainty over their procedural status—perhaps partly because of it—the practical value of committees was obvious, and in their diverse formats they quickly became a vital component in the work of both Houses. There were committees of inquiry, addressing key issues of the day, such as the conditions in London gaols, or the slave trade. Where there were disagreements between the Commons and Lords, the two Houses appointed committees to engage in conferences (the ancestors of today's Reasons Committees). Secret committees were even appointed to deal with disagreeable subject matter, such as the allegations of adultery against George IV's consort, Caroline of Brunswick.

The mid-nineteenth century saw select committees taking root in something closer to their modern form. In 1854 the Committee on the Army before Sebastopol, described by the then Clerk of the House, Sir Robert Rogers (now Lord Lisvane), as the first modern investigative committee,[3] was appointed to review the conditions endured by soldiers in the Crimean War: its mere appointment, after a vote in the House of Commons, was sufficient to cause the resignation of the Prime Minister, Lord Aberdeen. In 1857, as the scope and complexity of government operations grew, the House of Commons established a Select Committee on Public Monies, to inquire into 'the Receipt, Issue and Audit of Public Monies in the Exchequer, the Pay Office, and the Audit Department'. In 1861 this Committee became the first permanent select committee, the Public Accounts Committee, and its role was confirmed by the adoption of a Standing Order in 1862:

> That there shall be a Standing Committee of Public Accounts; for the examination of the Accounts showing the appropriation of sums granted by Parliament to meet the Public Expenditure, to consist of nine members, who shall be nominated at the commencement of every Session, and of whom five shall be a quorum.

While the Commons was developing committee procedures to strengthen its oversight of public finances, the Lords struggled, from the 1820s onwards, to establish an Appellate Committee that would allow it to exercise its distinct judicial functions more efficiently.[4] In a pattern that will be familiar to students of House of Lords reform, attempts to improve internal procedures were lost in a wider debate on whether or not the House should exercise any judicial role at all. This reached its peak in the 1870s, leading to the passage of the Appellate Jurisdiction Act 1876,[5] which established the 'Lords of Appeal in Ordinary'—but it

---

[3] Written evidence submitted by the Clerk of the House to the Liaison Committee, 9 July 2012: www.publications.parliament.uk/pa/cm201213/cmselect/cmliaisn/697/697we36.htm. An isolated instance in the seventeenth century was the appointment in 1667 of a committee to inquire into the disastrous Anglo–Dutch war earlier the same year.

[4] See G Dymond, 'The Appellate Jurisdiction of the House of Lords', House of Lords Library Note (2009), www.parliament.uk/documents/lords-library/lln2009-010appellate.pdf.

[5] See D Steele, 'The Judicial House of Lords: Abolition and Restoration 1873–6' in L Blom-Cooper, B Dickson and G Drewry (eds), *The Judicial House of Lords, 1876–2009* (Oxford, Oxford University Press, 2009) 13–29.

was only in 1948 that the disruptive effect of post-war building works persuaded the House to appoint an Appellate Committee, so that these professional judges could meet outside the House of Lords Chamber to hear legal arguments.[6] Even as recently as 2009 (when a Supreme Court was finally established, under the terms of the Constitutional Reform Act 2005), the Appellate Committee would return to the Chamber to hand down judgments and, at set times of year, to hear Counsel—occasions that any Member of the House, legally qualified or not, was entitled to attend, though not to participate in.

A key attribute of committees, and one of the reasons they were so suited to dealing with technical matters, was the involvement of non-members—indeed, the Commons committee on religion in 1571 was appointed specifically 'to confer with the bishops'. This begged a fundamental question: were non-members called upon to assist either the House or its committees in their work protected by the privileges of the House?

The Commons partially answered the question in a resolution agreed on 8 March 1688: 'That it is the undoubted right of this House that all witnesses summoned to attend this House, or any committee appointed by it, have the privilege of this House in coming, staying and returning'.[7] This addressed the grosser and more immediate forms of interference with witnesses,[8] but did not necessarily protect them from the adverse consequences of giving honest evidence. Only in 1818 did the Commons address the status of witnesses' evidence in terms, resolving on 26 May: 'That all witnesses examined before this House, or any committee thereof, are entitled to the protection of this House in respect of anything that may be said by them in their evidence'.[9]

With this protection in place, the way was open for the development of investigative committees in the 1850s—though the privilege claimed by the Commons was in fact not formally confirmed by the courts until 1881.[10]

It is notable, nevertheless, that as recently as the 1980s, in the notorious case of *R v Murphy*, two judgments of the Supreme Court of New South Wales[11] reversed the conventional view of the status of committee proceedings, allowing witnesses who had given evidence given to a Senate committee investigating alleged malpractice by a Justice of the High Court to be cross-examined in court on that evidence. This led the Australian Parliament to place the privileged status of committee proceedings beyond doubt, by means of the *Parliamentary Privileges Act 1987*.[12]

---

[6] See L Blom-Cooper and G Drewry, *Final Appeal: A Study of the House of Lords in its Judicial Capacity* (Oxford, Oxford University Press, 1972) 111–13.

[7] See *Erskine May*, 19th edition (London, Butterworths, 1976) 156; *House of Commons Journal* (1688–93) 45.

[8] For instance, in Goodall's case, the arrest of a person who had been summoned to appear as a witness before the 'Committee of Poll-money' (see *House of Commons Journal* (1640–42) 454.

[9] *House of Commons Journal* (1818) 389.

[10] *Goffin v Donnelly* (1881) 6 QBD 307.

[11] The first judgment was not reported; the second is in (1986) 5 *NSWLR* 18.

[12] See *Odgers' Australian Senate Practice*, 14th edn (Canberra, Department of the Senate, 2016) ch 2 (online at www.aph.gov.au/About_Parliament/Senate/Powers_practice_n_procedures/Odgers_Australian_Senate_Practice).

But the fact that such a collision between legislature and judiciary occurred in the first place, following a committee inquiry into allegations of criminal conduct (in other words, a matter normally reserved to the courts), underlines that some of the tensions inherent in the committee model are still to be fully resolved. On the one hand, there is Parliament's desire for procedures that allow flexibility and informality, the ability to address new issues in unconventional ways; on the other, there is the risk that Parliament may over-reach itself, and that the very informality of such proceedings may ultimately compromise their legal status as 'proceedings in Parliament'.

B. Developments in the Late Twentieth Century

Two developments led to the establishment of the present system of House of Commons departmental select committees in 1979. The first was the progressive (and, from 1945 onwards, rapid) increase in the range of governmental activity. The second was the growing strength of party discipline. The two factors combined led to a general recognition, by the 1970s, that the traditional forms of parliamentary scrutiny, such as plenary debate, were no longer adequate. New tools were needed to enable parliamentarians to conduct detailed, expert and responsive scrutiny of government.

There were various experiments. The House of Commons Estimates Committee, originally appointed in 1912 and re-established in 1945, broadened out from its original remit, appointing sub-committees to investigate the efficiency of the departments and organisations responsible for spending the nation's money. It was followed in the 1950s by the Nationalised Industries Committee. Then the 1966 Labour Government encouraged the appointment of a range of select committees with broad responsibilities such as agriculture, science and technology, or race relations and immigration. They enjoyed mixed success, and further Procedure Committee reviews led ultimately to the establishment in 1979 of the departmental select committee system.

Proposing the appointment of the committees, the Leader of the House, Norman St John-Stevas, articulated what had become a widely accepted view. He presented his proposals as helping 'to redress the balance of power' between the House and the Executive. The committees would provide 'more effective scrutiny of government', involving Members on 'both sides of the House', and contributing to 'greater openness in government'.[13]

But while St John-Stevas' arguments reflected a widely held view, there were dissenting voices. Michael Foot, Leader of the House in the run-up to the 1979

---

[13] See P Baines, 'History and Rationale of the 1979 Reforms' in G Drewry (ed), *The New Select Committees*, 2nd edn (Oxford, Oxford University Press, 1989) 15.

election, had expressed concerns when the Procedure Committee's report was first debated:

> I believe that access to the Chamber by an individual Member, throughout his whole parliamentary career, is the supreme attribute of the House of Commons which distinguishes it and makes it the place that it ought to be ... if that attribute is broken, injured or impaired, great injury will be done to the House.[14]

Enoch Powell, though by 1979 he supported the reforms, had previously highlighted similar dangers:

> Everything which diminishes true debate on the Floor of the House of Commons strengthens the Executive and weakens Parliament ... our experience is as politicians and would-be Ministers facing other politicians and actual Ministers, to ... fight it out. We can only do that through debate, we can only do that on the Floor of the Chamber.[15]

Powell and Foot were harking back to a romantic vision of the House of Commons chamber, as the field on which the battle of ideas and parties was fought out, and on which governments stood or fell, as the debate determined. But their nostalgia illustrates a genuine tension between committees and the House.

The rationale for the establishment of departmental select committees was based on a combination of flexibility and specialisation. Put the two together, and committees would be a powerful tool for finding new and innovative ways to scrutinise and hold the executive to account.

The risk of specialisation, though, was that members would be distracted from debating the great issues of the day on the floor of the House; and allied to this was the possibility that committee work would become academic, lacking any real impact—essentially a displacement activity. Some of these concerns were articulated by the present author's father, writing in 1977:

> Many of the protagonists of more select committees ... have just failed to see that as such committees have no real power and are detached from party interests, they are thus committed to fundamentally academic exercises ... Scrutiny therefore becomes an activity which keeps a growing number of back-benchers out of mischief: its end product is a growing quantity of paper.[16]

If, on the other hand, such concerns were misplaced, and committees did come to possess 'real power', what would be the basis of that power? How would it relate to the power of the two Houses, and how, given the flexibility inherent in committee working practices, would it be controlled?

The following sections outline the main types of committee, their functions, and their powers. At the end of the chapter I revert to the questions of principle just posed.

[14] House of Commons Debates, 20 February 1979.
[15] Quoted by Baines, '1979 Reforms' (n 13) 17, and taken from a Granada Television series, the transcript of which was published as *The State of the Nation: Parliament*, ed. D Crow (London, Granada Television Ltd, 1973).
[16] N Johnson, *In Search of the Constitution* (Oxford, Pergamon Press, 1977) 58–59.

II. THE MAIN TYPES OF COMMITTEE

A. Ad hoc Committees

As indicated earlier, the first committees were appointed by one or other House on an ad hoc basis, to consider specific issues, and ever since the Committee on the Army before Sebastopol in 1854 the investigation of instances of scandalous maladministration has been a major driver of committee work.

The key risk facing such committees is that they become victims of party political bias. This risk was realised in 1913, following allegations that members of the Liberal Government had been guilty of what would now be called 'insider trading', buying shares in the Marconi Company shortly before the Government awarded the company a lucrative contract. The committee appointed to investigate the Marconi scandal split along party lines, with Liberal members clearing ministers of blame, and others accusing them of grave impropriety.

The Marconi scandal was one of the factors leading to the enactment of the Tribunals of Inquiry (Evidence) Act 1921. This made statutory provision for independent, judge-led inquiries into matters of 'urgent public importance',[17] and gave such inquiries the power to enforce the attendance of witnesses or the production of documents, and to examine witnesses on oath. Since that time Parliament has faced increasing competition from public inquiries, which can now be set up under a consolidated statutory basis, the Inquiries Act 2005. Nevertheless, judge-led statutory public inquiries remain rare—perhaps because Ministers are put off by the example of the Bloody Sunday inquiry, chaired by Lord Saville of Newdigate, which lasted more than 12 years and cost a total of £191.5 million.[18]

The great benefits of parliamentary ad hoc committees, in contrast, are their low cost, speed and flexibility. The structures, the staff, the processes and facilities—all are ready to go at a moment's notice, and can be adapted to fit the exact circumstances. There is also, notwithstanding the Marconi scandal, what might be called Parliament's 'brand'—its independence of Government, and its media profile, both of which, in different ways, help to protect Ministers from accusations of whitewash.

The pros and cons of ad hoc committee inquiries were aired most fully in a heated debate on 5 July 2012, in the wake of the LIBOR scandal. The Opposition proposed the establishment of a 'forensic, judge-led public inquiry' under the terms of the Inquiries Act 2005, but the Chancellor of the Exchequer, George Osborne, resisted this approach, arguing that 'judge-led public inquiries take an incredibly long time to conclude'.[19] He continued: 'We have in Parliament the skills, the expertise and the mandate to do the job … let us get on with it'.[20]

---

[17] Tribunals of Inquiry (Evidence) Act 1921, s 1(1).
[18] For a list of public inquiries since 1990, with timings and costs, see the report of the House of Lords Select Committee on the Inquiries Act 2005, Session 2013–14, HL Paper 143, App 4.
[19] HC Deb 5 July 2012, col 1134.
[20] ibid, col 1136.

His arguments persuaded the House to support the establishment of the Parliamentary Commission on Banking Standards.[21]

Ad hoc committees may be set up by either House, or by both acting in concert. In some cases (such as the Banking Commission) they focus on specific issues or events, while in less time-critical circumstances they may be called upon to consider Government proposals (such as the 2013 Joint Committee on the Draft Voting Eligibility (Prisoners) Bill, which considered various options for addressing the entitlement of prisoners to vote).

The House of Lords also establishes a number of ad hoc committees (currently four) each session, to consider broad cross-cutting themes, or to conduct post-legislative scrutiny of selected Acts of Parliament. Topics are recommended by the Liaison Committee, drawing on suggestions by Members of the House. The process is not controlled by the Government (though the Leader of the House and the Government Chief Whip, with their opposite numbers from other major parties, sit on the Liaison Committee). The reports of House of Lords ad hoc committees are typically detailed, evidence-based and analytical, and the conclusions are reached on a cross-party basis.

B. Investigative Committees

The term 'investigative committee' has no formal procedural definition, but is used here to describe permanent committees, which conduct thematic inquiries on topics falling within their remit. They may also have a range of other functions, including scrutinising bills, and conducting post- and pre-legislative scrutiny. They may also, in the case of Commons departmental select committees, conduct pre-appointment hearings, as well as regularly interrogating Ministers and senior officials.

Inquiries generally begin with a 'call for evidence': a public document setting out the scope of a new inquiry, identifying key questions, and inviting anyone with an interest to submit evidence. On the basis of that written evidence, and of oral evidence collected during public meetings, the committee prepares a report, which normally includes recommendations to Government and others.

C. Legislative Committees

The core scrutiny of public bills is largely still conducted by the two Houses, rather than by select committees. But such scrutiny is increasingly supported and informed by select committee analysis. Thus the Joint Committee on Human

---

[21] For a discussion of the innovative working practices of the Banking Commission (which have yet to be adopted by other committees), see R Kelly, 'Select Committees: Powers and Functions' in A Horne, G Drewry and D Oliver (eds) *Parliament and the Law* (Oxford, Hart, 2013) 178–79.

Rights scrutinises all bills to assess their compatibility with the rights protected by virtue of the European Convention on Human Rights, the Human Rights Act 1998, the common law and any UK international obligations,[22] while in the House of Lords the Constitution Committee examines all bills for their constitutional implications.

While both these committees divide their time between legislative scrutiny and thematic inquiries, other committees focus solely on legislative scrutiny. For instance, the House of Lords Delegated Powers and Regulatory Reform Committee is appointed 'to report whether the provisions of any bill inappropriately delegate legislative power, or whether they subject the exercise of legislative power to an inappropriate degree of parliamentary scrutiny'.[23]

Domestic secondary legislation also receives committee scrutiny. The Joint Committee on Statutory Instruments conducts technical scrutiny of all statutory instruments (SIs) laid before Parliament, though it does not address the merits of such instruments, or the underlying policy objectives. In contrast, the Lords Secondary Legislation Scrutiny Committee reviews all SIs subject to either affirmative or negative procedure, and draws the attention of the House to any issues of public policy that are likely to be of interest to the House.

Secondary legislation that is subject to enhanced parliamentary scrutiny (such as Legislative Reform Orders) is also reviewed by select committees in both Houses.[24] Specific arrangements have been introduced for other secondary legislation or quasi-legislation, such as Public Bodies Orders and National Policy Statements.

Other types of legislation receive other types of scrutiny. Since the UK joined the European Economic Community in 1973 (and pending its withdrawal from what is now the European Union), scrutiny committees in both Houses[25] have been tasked with considering all draft European laws, and with reviewing the position taken by Government Ministers in the Council of Ministers, which shares responsibility for legislating at European level with the European Parliament.

D. Domestic and Statutory Committees

The work of domestic committees (those responsible for the internal administration of the two Houses, and for aspects of parliamentary business or procedure), and of statutory committees (bodies analogous to select committees that are

---

[22] For more on this, see ch 10.

[23] See House of Lords Minutes of Proceedings, 25 May 2016.

[24] The Commons Regulatory Reform Committee and the Lords Delegated Powers and Regulatory Reform Committee.

[25] The European Scrutiny Committee in the House of Commons, and the European Union Committee in the Lords.

appointed under statute, such as the Ecclesiastical Committee and the Intelligence and Security Committee)[26] falls outside the scope of this chapter.

III. THE FUNCTIONS OF COMMITTEES

A. Legislative Scrutiny

The description already given of the key committees tasked with supporting the work of the two Houses in scrutinising legislation illustrates the substantial overlap between different types of committee work. Many committees, like the Joint Committee on Human Rights, undertake both thematic inquiries and legislative scrutiny.

This overlap is most apparent in those elements of scrutiny that fall outside the formal legislative process that follows the introduction of a Bill. For instance, bills that are published in draft are subject to committee scrutiny, in most cases by Commons departmental select committees. Only in the case of particularly complex or high-profile draft bills is such pre-legislative scrutiny undertaken by an ad hoc Joint Committee.[27] Such pre-legislative scrutiny is typically conducted to a tight time-table, but still gives committees the opportunity to gather evidence from key stakeholders and to reflect that evidence in recommendations to Government.

Acts of Parliament may also be subjected to post-legislative review. In response to a Law Commission report in 2006[28] the Government agreed that departments should, in most cases, publish a memorandum three to five years after an Act receives Royal Assent, reviewing its impact. The Government resisted the Commission's proposal that such Acts should then be reviewed by a permanent Joint Committee, and instead memoranda are submitted to Commons departmental committees in the first instance. Take-up by those committees has been patchy (in 2013 the Government noted that while 58 memoranda had been published, only three had been the subject of dedicated inquiries[29]), but has been supplemented in recent years by the House of Lords, which normally appoints one ad hoc post-legislative scrutiny committee each session.

---

[26] The role of the Intelligence and Security Committee is considered elsewhere (see, eg, A Horne and C Walker, 'Parliament and National Security' in A Horne and A Le Sueur (eds) *Parliament: Legislation and Accountability* (Oxford, Hart, 2016) 221–26 and H Bochel, A Defty and J Kirkpatrick, 'New Mechanisms of Independent Accountability: Select Committees and Parliamentary Scrutiny of the Intelligence Services' (2015) 68 *Parliamentary Affairs* 314.

[27] See for instance the Joint Committee on the draft Modern Slavery Bill, which reported in April 2014.

[28] The Law Commission, 'Post-legislative scrutiny' (2006), Cm 6945: www.lawcom.gov.uk/wp-content/uploads/2015/03/lc302_Post-legislative_Scrutiny.pdf.

[29] See 'Post-legislative scrutiny', House of Commons Standard Note, 23 May 2013, 9: http://research-briefings.parliament.uk/ResearchBriefing/Summary/SN05232#fullreport.

B. Holding the Government to Account

One of the key drivers behind the establishment of departmental select committees of 1979 was a desire to scrutinise Government more effectively and expertly than was possible in plenary sittings. Such scrutiny has become increasingly central to the work of committees in the House of Commons. Indeed, the most recent edition of *Erskine May*, in marked contrast to the 1989 edition's emphasis (quoted at the start of this chapter) upon the 'detailed and technical' character of committee work, begins its account of committees by stating that 'they have become over recent years the principal mechanism by with the House discharges its responsibilities for the scrutiny of government policy and actions'.[30]

Some committees undertake cross-cutting scrutiny: the Public Accounts Committee, for instance, is responsible for 'the examination of the accounts showing the appropriate of the sums granted by Parliament to meet the public expenditure, and of other such accounts laid before Parliament as the committee may think fit'. In contrast, departmental select committees are appointed under SO No 152 'to examine the expenditure, administration and policy of the principal government departments ... and associated public bodies.'

To take a typical example: the Education Committee in 2016–17 held two public meetings with the Secretary of State for Education, in April and September, questioning her on her priorities and policies; it monitored the performance of key agencies that report to the Department, holding a public meeting with the head of Ofsted (the Chief Inspector of Education, Children's Services and Skills) in July; it considered and published the Department's Estimate for the 2016/17 financial year, and the subsequent Supplementary Estimate. Taken as a whole, the Committee's work amounts to a steady, if not intense, programme of scrutiny and questioning, at both strategic and administrative levels.

Pre-appointment hearings for certain high-profile public appointments are a relatively recent addition to the armoury of Commons select committees. Such hearings can be traced back to 1998, when the Treasury Committee, following the Government's announcement the previous year of the independence of the Bank of England, first scrutinised appointments to the Bank's Monetary Policy Committee. Only in 2007, however, after Gordon Brown's Labour Government published the *Governance of Britain* Green Paper,[31] did the practice become general, and the Liaison Committee subsequently adopted guidelines for the conduct of hearings.[32] But while they have become a regular feature of select committee

---

[30] *Erskine May*, 24th edn (London, LexisNexis, 2011) 799.
[31] *The Governance of Britain*, CM 7170, July 2007, 28–30: www.gov.uk/government/uploads/system/uploads/attachment_data/file/228834/7170.pdf.
[32] See www.parliament.uk/business/committees/committees-a-z/commons-select/liaison-committee/role/pre-appointment-guidelines. For a fuller discussion of pre-appointment hearings, see R Kelly, 'Select Committees: Powers and Functions' in Horne, Drewry and Oliver *Parliament and the Law* (n 22), 174–78, and R Hazell, M Chalmers and M Russell, 'Pre-Appointment Scrutiny Hearings in the British House of Commons: All Bark, or Some Bite?' (2012) 18 *Journal of Legislative Studies* 222.

scrutiny, they also illustrate the limits of Parliament's authority over the executive: committee findings are politically persuasive, but are in most cases formally non-binding.[33] When the Education Committee in 2016 found the Government's nominee for the position of Chief Inspector of Education, Children's Services and Skills to be unsuitable, the Secretary of State dismissed its concerns and made the appointment regardless.[34]

In contrast with the House of Commons, committees in the House of Lords were not established primarily to conduct scrutiny of Government departments. The different constitutional relationship between the House of Lords and the Government is reflected in the broad terms of reference given to Lords committees (for instance 'to consider science and technology'[35]), and the long-standing presumption, repeatedly endorsed by the House, that Lords committees should be cross-cutting in remit, rather than shadowing particular departments of state.[36]

C. Promoting Public and Parliamentary Debate

Committees spend most of their time conducting inquiries, sometimes narrowly focused, but sometimes wide-ranging, into relevant policy areas. In the Commons such inquiries are typically an extension of committees' scrutiny function, a means of considering an important matter of public policy in more detail than is possible in a one-off meeting with a Minister or official. For instance, in 2016 the House of Commons Health Committee conducted a short inquiry into winter pressure in hospital A&E departments, publishing its report in October of that year.[37]

In the Lords, in contrast, committees generally adopt wider horizons, focusing on what the 2011 Leader's Group on Working Practices described as the House's third core function, namely providing 'a forum for public debate and inquiry'.[38] That public debate is in part stimulated by inquiries themselves, which may raise the profile of a particular issue—Lords committee inquiries often last several months, and committees receive and publish large quantities of written evidence, as well as holding a dozen or more public meetings. Reports, which are wide-ranging, evidence-based and detailed, are later debated on the floor of the House.

---

[33] One exception is the role of Information Commissioner, where the Government made a commitment in 2011 to accept the recommendation of the Justice Committee (see https://hansard.parliament.uk/Commons/2011-02-16/debates/11021645000022/InformationCommissioner).

[34] See Education Committee, 1st Special Report of Session 2016–17, HC 674. Most pre-appointment hearings have led to positive findings, but in two instances a negative finding has been followed either by the candidate's withdrawal or by non-appointment. See www.parliament.uk/documents/commons-committees/liaison/Pre-appointment-table-by-department-to-March-2017.pdf.

[35] The House of Lords Science and Technology Committee was first established in 1979, in response to the decision of the House of Commons to abolish its own cross-cutting Science and Technology Committee as part of the wider reform leading to the establishment of departmental select committees.

[36] This presumption dates back to the 1992 Jellicoe Committee on the committee work of the House.

[37] House of Commons Health Committee, 3rd Report of Session 2016–17, HC 277.

[38] Report of the Leader's Group on Working Practices, 2010–12, HL Paper 136, 8.

D. Limitations to Committee Work: The *sub judice* Rule

The relationship between Parliament and the Courts is governed by what has been described as 'a mutuality of respect between two constitutional sovereignties'.[39] This principle of respect and comity is partially codified in statute (notably in Article 9 of the Bill of Rights 1689, which codifies the immunity of things said or done in the course of parliamentary proceedings), but is also reflected in long-standing conventions and in resolutions agreed by the two Houses. In particular, both Houses have adopted a *sub judice* rule, under which, in the words of the House of Lords *Companion to the Standing Orders*, they 'abstain from discussing the merits of disputes about to be tried and decided in the courts of law'.[40]

The rule applies by extension to committees of both Houses. It applies to all cases that are active[41] before United Kingdom courts, and is mandatory—such cases are not to be referred to in any motion, debate or question. *Erskine May* notes that committees have suspended inquiries 'because a witness had been charged with criminal offences related to the subject-matter of the inquiry'.[42]

Even when cases are not technically active (for instance, during a police investigation that may lead to charges being brought) committees are expected to exercise caution—the Joint Committee on Parliamentary Privilege noted in 2013 that 'Committees are careful to avoid actions which could prejudice legal processes, even when investigations are at too early a stage for *sub judice* considerations to apply'.[43]

IV. COMMITTEE POWERS

To exercise the functions just described, committees require certain powers. Procedural principle requires that committees possess only those powers conferred upon them by the House, so all powers exercised by committees are set out either in Standing Orders (particularly in the Commons) or in the specific orders of reference establishing the committee (the practice in the Lords). The main powers conferred upon committees are summarised in this section.

---

[39] Lord Woolf MR, quoting Sedley J, in *R v Parliamentary Commissioner for Standards ex parte Mohamed Al Fayed* [1998] 1 All ER 93.

[40] House of Lords, *The Companion to the Standing Orders* (2017) 59. The rule is subject to a number of qualifications: it does not restrict the right of either House to legislate on any matter or to discuss delegated legislation, and it does not apply to judicial review cases, in which ministerial decisions are in question. The Speaker of the House of Commons and the Lord Speaker have power to waive the *sub judice* rule in specific cases.

[41] Cases are 'active' from the point when, in criminal cases, 'a charge has been or a summons to appear has been issued', and, in civil cases, when 'arrangements for a hearing' have been made.

[42] *Erskine May* (n 30) 813.

[43] Joint Committee on Parliamentary Privilege, Report of Session 2013–14, HL Paper 30, HC 100, para 68.

A. Power to Report

Under Commons SO No 133, each select committee 'shall have leave to report to the House its opinion and observations upon any matters referred to it for its consideration, together with the evidence taken before it'. This power may be exercised by a committee even though it is not expressly directed to do so by its order or reference.[44] In the Lords, a committee may be appointed either to report on a particular matter (in other words, as an ad hoc committee, which ceases to exist once its report has been agreed), or to report 'from time to time', in which case it can make multiple reports.

B. Power to Appoint Sub-committees

Committees need the express permission of the House to appoint sub-committees or to entrust to those sub-committees tasks falling within their orders of reference. Most Commons committee have been given such permission under Standing Orders—for instance, under SO No 152(3) each departmental select committee may appoint one sub-committee.

In the Lords the power to appoint one or more sub-committees is set out in the appointment motion, and is kept under regular review. The Economic Affairs Committee is empowered to appoint one sub-committee (which each year scrutinises the Finance Bill), whereas the European Union and Science and Technology Committees have the power to appoint more than one (though the Science and Technology Committee has not used this power since 2012).

Lords committees that possess the power to appoint sub-committees are also given the power to co-opt members of the House to serve on those sub-committees. Thus the European Union Committee, which has 19 members, appoints six sub-committees, each 12-strong, a large majority of whose members are co-opted. In the Commons, in contrast, only members of the parent committee serve on sub-committees: thus in 2016 the Environment, Food and Rural Affairs Committee appointed six of its number to conduct an inquiry into forestry in England.[45]

C. Power to Send for Persons, Papers and Records

Committees rely heavily upon written and oral evidence, and thus a key backstop for committees is the power to 'send for persons, papers and records'. Committees begin by inviting witnesses to give evidence or to supply documents, and witnesses usually cooperate willingly. But this power means that in the rare event that a witness refuses to provide evidence, a committee may issue a formal order to

---

[44] *Erskine May* (n 30) 830.
[45] See Environment, Food and Rural Affairs Committee, 5th Report of Session 2016–17, HC 619.

attend or supply documents, signed by the chair. Failure to comply with such an order may be reported to the House as a prima facie contempt. It would then be for the House to decide how to exercise its inherent penal powers in investigating and punishing the contempt.

In the Commons the power to send for persons, papers and records is embodied in the Standing Order under which a committee is established—SO 152(4) in the case of departmental select committees. In the Lords, the power, previously reserved to the House, has been included in the appointment motions for all select committees since 2009.

It is important to note that the power to summon persons is subject to certain conventional limitations. The Cabinet Office's *Giving evidence to Select Committees: Guidance for Civil Servants* (the 'Osmotherley Rules') asserts a general principle that 'civil servants are accountable to Ministers who in turn are accountable to Parliament', and, while acknowledging the 'formal position' that a committee could insist on the attendance of a named official, makes it clear that in normal circumstances 'the decision on who is best able to represent the Minister rests with the Minister concerned'.[46]

Restrictions also apply to judges: the Judicial Executive Board has issued guidance indicating that their appearance before committees 'should be regarded as exceptional', and outlining a number of issues (including the merits of individual cases, or the effect of bills currently before Parliament) on which they should not comment. When a committee does request the attendance of a member of the judiciary, it is dealt with by the Private Office of the Lord Chief Justice.[47]

Neither the Osmotherley Rules nor the guidance published by the Judicial Executive Board has been endorsed by Parliament, and the Joint Committee on Parliamentary Privilege in 2013 saw no reason formally to acknowledge an exemption from the power to summon in either case.[48]

Some of the procedural and reputational complications attaching to committees' power to send for persons, papers and records are considered in the final section of this chapter.

D. Power to Take and Publish Evidence

Committees are given the power to publish evidence 'from time to time'. This allows committees to publish written evidence and transcripts of oral evidence as an inquiry progresses, without having to wait for the publication of a report.

---

[46] 'Giving Evidence to Select Committees: Guidance for Civil Servants' (October 2014), paras 4, 12–13: see www.gov.uk/government/uploads/system/uploads/attachment_data/file/364600/Osmotherly_Rules_October_2014.pdf.

[47] 'Guidance to Judges on Appearances before Select Committees' (October 2012), paras 1–2: see www.judiciary.gov.uk/wp-content/uploads/JCO/Documents/Guidance/select_committee_guidance.pdf.

[48] Joint Committee on Parliamentary Privilege, Report of Session 2013–14, HL Paper 30, HC 100, paras 86–88.

The Parliamentary Witnesses Oaths Act 1871 empowers the House of Commons and its committees to administer oaths to witnesses, and under SO No 132 such oaths are administered by the chair or the clerk. False evidence given under oath would be punishable under the Perjury Act 1911—raising the risk that committee processes could, notwithstanding the general principle of parliamentary privilege, come before the courts.[49]

The power to administer oaths is controversial and rarely used. The most recent example was on 7 November 2011, when the Chair of the Public Accounts Committee, Margaret Hodge, decided in the middle of a meeting with Anthony Inglese, a senior lawyer at HMRC, to require him to give evidence on oath. This led to a widely reported dispute between Ms Hodge and the outgoing Head of the Civil Service, Sir Gus O'Donnell (now Lord O'Donnell), in which he expressed concern that appearances of civil servants before the Public Accounts Committee had been turned into a 'theatrical exercise in public humiliation'.[50]

While the House of Lords has always had the power to take evidence on oath, and to treat false evidence as perjury, a resolution of 1857, which stated that committees should 'examine witnesses without their having been previously sworn, except in cases in which it may be otherwise ordered by the House', still applies.[51]

E. Power to Travel

Most committees are given the power 'to adjourn from place to place', without which they would be required to meet exclusively within the precincts of the House. In practice this power is used not only to conduct formal meetings and to take evidence outside Westminster, but to conduct informal visits relating to current inquiries.

In the House of Commons, the power to 'adjourn from place to place' is provided for in Standing Orders, and is typically unlimited (though in the case of the Joint Committee on the National Security Strategy it is limited to travel 'within the United Kingdom'). Applications for travel overseas are then considered by the Liaison Committee, under delegated authority from the House of Commons Commission.

In the Lords, most committees are given the power to 'adjourn from place to place' in their motions of appointment. In some cases, particularly in the case

---

[49] See A Horne, 'Evidence under oath, perjury and parliamentary privilege', *UK Const L* blog (29 January 2015) available at: http://ukconstitutionallaw.org.

[50] For the transcript of the meeting, see www.publications.parliament.uk/pa/cm201012/cmselect/cmpubacc/1531/11110701.htm. See also R Syal, 'Ex-civil service chief accused of acting as "shop steward"' *The Guardian* (15 March 2012), www.theguardian.com/politics/2012/mar/15/ex-civil-service-chief-accused.

[51] House of Lords Journal (1857) 60.

of ad hoc committees with clearly domestic remits, the power is limited to travel within the United Kingdom.[52]

F. Power to Appoint Specialist Advisers

Specialist Advisers are appointed, in the words of House of Commons Standing Orders, 'either to supply information which is not readily available or to elucidate matters of complexity within the committee's order of reference'. They are often academics, lawyers, or sometimes retired public servants, with a particular expertise in the subject matter of an inquiry. They are not employees of the House, but are contractors, appointed on a daily rate, and support committee staff in briefing the committee, identifying witnesses, suggesting lines of questioning, and drafting reports.

V. REFLECTIONS

The rationale of the reforms of the 1970s was that committees were needed to improve Parliament's capacity to scrutinise an increasingly complex executive. There were, admittedly, concerns that such scrutiny would lack teeth, that it would be academic and bureaucratic, and that it would distract members from their core task of debating and deciding on the vital issues of the day in the House of Commons chamber. But the consensus was that more specialised, granular analysis in select committees would enhance the work of Parliament as a whole.

Though brief, the previous sections have shown that committee work today is far more diverse than the reformers of the 1970s could have imagined. Committees supplement the work of both Houses in legislative scrutiny, including scrutiny of the huge quantities of secondary legislation that would otherwise receive next to no parliamentary attention. They have moved into the territory of public inquiries, investigating wrong-doing and scandal in both public and private sectors. They hold departments and public bodies very visibly to account, including through pre-appointment hearings and regular meetings with ministers.

Perhaps the most striking demonstration of the expansion of committee responsibilities is the fact that since 2002 the Prime Minister has given oral evidence to the House of Commons Liaison Committee—a degree of personal accountability to a committee that Norman St. John-Stevas could hardly have contemplated in 1979.[53]

The reason this change has been possible is because of the flexibility and informality inherent in committees, their ability and readiness to innovate. They rely

---

[52] For instance, the Charities Committee, appointed on 25 May 2016.
[53] The Liaison Committee does not, however, produce reports following its meetings with the Prime Minister: the meetings are an end in themselves.

ultimately upon the ancient rights, powers and privileges of Parliament itself. Yet the committee, in its simplest form, is just a small group of parliamentarians, tasked with investigating an issue, meeting largely in private, and able to a large extent to make up their own rules as they go along.

Thus, without any formal change in committee powers, successive reforms have enhanced and expanded the role and importance of committees. In 2000 the House of Commons Liaison Committee noted the willingness of some committees to 'experiment and innovate', in areas such as scrutiny of draft bills or the holding of confirmation hearings, holding this up as 'best practice'.[54] It raised new possibilities, including the remuneration of committee chairs, to further bolster the authority of committees.

Although the Liaison Committee's recommendations were resisted by the Government, it found an ally after the 2001 election in the new Leader of the House of Commons, Robin Cook. He used the Modernisation Committee to push through reforms, which included the remuneration of chairs, thereby creating an 'alternative career structure' for backbench MPs. The Modernisation Committee also focused on outreach, including such issues as the accessibility and design of reports, recommended an increase in committee resources, and for the first time proposed the adoption of 'an agreed statement of the core tasks' of all departmental select committees.[55]

The Liaison Committee on 20 June 2001 duly adopted a list of 10 core tasks for departmental select committees, and these, supplemented by the practice of annual reporting by committees, have been a powerful driver for improving the effectiveness of committee work. More recent reforms have strengthened committees more overtly—in particular, the direct election since 2010 of most committee chairs, which, along with the salary granted them, has hugely increased their authority and independence.

The House of Lords has been slow to follow down the path of reform. Nevertheless, since the publication of the report of the Royal Commission on the House of Lords in 2000 there has been a marked expansion of committee work. The Royal Commission itself recommended three new committees, on the Constitution, Economic Affairs, and the Merits of Statutory Instruments. All three have become well established, and the third (now the Secondary Legislation Scrutiny Committee) identified an area of scrutiny that remains largely untouched by Commons committees. More recent expansions have seen the appointment of a Communications Committee, and the appointment each session of four ad hoc committees. But while the quantum of committee work has increased, the Lords Liaison Committee has not shown the reforming zeal of its Commons counterpart, and the working practices of Lords committees have changed little.

---

[54] Liaison Committee, 'Shifting the Balance: Select Committees and the Executive', First Report, 2000–01, HC 300, para 24.

[55] Committee on Modernisation of the House of Commons, Select Committee's First Report, 2001–02, HC 224.

Thus the working practices of Commons committees have evolved, and their important role in scrutinising the executive is generally acknowledged. But the fundamental questions posited earlier in this chapter remain: do they have any real power, and if so, is that power legitimate? What do committees actually achieve?

In parallel with the reforms of the last 20 years has come an increasing consciousness of the need to demonstrate, and measure, 'impact'. The difficulty of devising accurate measures, in a shifting, multi-dimensional political environment, is immense. Some committees have experimented with simple quantitative measures: the Home Affairs Committee, for instance, in 2012 introduced a 'traffic light' system for measuring the effectiveness of its reports: 'Recommendations are coded green if, in our view, the Government has accepted them; red if they have been rejected; and yellow if they have been partially accepted, or if the Government has undertaken to give them further consideration.'[56] This approach was later rejected by the Liaison Committee, which argued that 'a bald count of recommendations accepted and rejected does not allow for the recommendations which are easy to accept or the harder ones which are rejected initially but implemented eventually'.[57]

Other measurements of effectiveness may be more intellectually defensible, but are also more elusive. The Liaison Committee cited 'the assessment of stakeholders and academics'. In so doing it drew on what remains the most comprehensive study of committee effectiveness, by the Constitution Unit in 2011, which described committee influence as a 'very slippery subject'.[58] The authors concluded that the acceptance of recommendations by government probably captured only half of committee influence. Among the other forms of influence, the most potent was probably the 'fear factor', which was largely prospective and dissuasive: 'Comments such as those from ministers and officials in this study that "you've always got to think, how would I explain that to the committee?" are probably the clearest indicators of this crucial form of influence that scholars will ever be able to find.'[59]

What the reformers of the 1970s could not have anticipated, and what underlies the ability of committees to generate fear, is the impact of technology, particularly the explosion of news media over recent decades. While proceedings in the two chambers are often poorly attended and procedurally obscure, committee proceedings, now all streamed live on the Internet, can have an intimacy and drama all their own, one that appeals to online consumers of information—which we all now are. The election of committee chairs in the Commons was also a critical development, not just because it loosened the grip of party managers, but because

---

[56] Home Affairs Committee, 'Effectiveness of the Committee in 2010–12', First Report of Session 2012–13, HC 144.

[57] Liaison Committee, 'Legacy Report', First Report of Session 2014–15, HC 954.

[58] M Russell and M Benton, *Selective influence: the policy impact of House of Commons select committees* (London, Constitution Unit, 2011) 96.

[59] ibid, 97. See also ch 10.

it created an alternative to ministerial office as a source of parliamentary status and celebrity.

The 2010 Parliament saw a huge increase in coverage of committees, led by two of the new breed of 'celebrity chair', Margaret Hodge, of the Public Accounts Committee, and Keith Vaz, of the Home Affairs Committee. Alongside the increase in coverage came a multiplication of the number of concurrent inquiries, many launched in response to breaking news stories, and an extraordinary increase in their reach, straying into areas of public and private life far removed from committees' core task of scrutinising the executive.

But by 2015 it was becoming increasingly clear that the 'fear factor' was open to abuse. One commentator described committee proceedings as 'a mix of slapstick and ritual humiliation … the national stocks, in which the villain of the day can be arraigned and pelted with impudent questions to see whether they crack'.[60] The appearance of Rona Fairhead before the Public Accounts Committee in March 2015 was arguably a tipping point: appearing as a non-executive director of HSBC, she had recently taken on the unrelated role of Chair of the BBC Trust. During the meeting the chair, Margaret Hodge, described her as 'totally incompetent', telling her she should resign from her BBC role. This led to accusations that Ms Hodge had launched an 'abusive and bullying attack', bringing Parliament itself into disrepute.[61]

Since 2015 the personnel may have changed, but the pattern of committee behaviour has not. If anything, committees have become more assertive in using the powers conferred upon them by the House, in pursuit of ever greater 'impact'. The issuing of formal summonses to reluctant witnesses, once exceptional, has become relatively commonplace. This has in turn focused attention upon the ultimate source of committee powers, namely the centuries-old power of both Houses to punish those guilty of contempt, including by fines or imprisonment.

The most high-profile case involved the Culture, Media and Sport Committee's inquiry into allegations of phone-hacking by employees of News International, which was revived in 2011 following the closure of the *News of the World*. The committee issued a formal summons requiring the attendance of the proprietors of News International, Rupert and James Murdoch, and the fiasco of Rupert Murdoch's appearance, when he was assaulted by a member of the public, was captured live on television and received enormous media coverage. Perhaps more significant in the longer term, though, was the committee's subsequent finding that three employees of News International, and the company itself, had knowingly misled the committee.[62] After a long investigation, the Committee of Privileges in 2016 found that two of the employees had indeed knowingly misled

[60] 'Have Select Committees become an abuse of power? Discuss …' *The Independent*, 29 May 2015.
[61] 'Margaret Hodge accused of 'abusive and bullying' attack on BBC Trust chair', *The Guardian*, 11 March 2015.
[62] Culture, Media and Sport Committee, 'News International and Phone-hacking', Eleventh Report, 2010–12, HC 903, 84.

the committee, and were thus guilty of contempt of the House.[63] Acknowledging that the only feasible sanction was formal admonishment, it recommended such admonishment be made by means of a resolution of the House, rather than (as used to be in the case) to the culprit in person and at the bar of the House. The resolution was duly agreed by the House on 27 October 2016.

Another extreme case was that of the Business, Innovation and Skills Committee, which in January 2016, following media reports on working conditions at Sports Direct, decided to invite the company's founder, Mike Ashley, to give evidence. In reply, Mr Ashley invited the Committee to visit the company's premises at Shirebrook, and when this was refused, Mr Ashley's response was to accuse the Committee of 'abusing parliamentary procedure in an attempt to create a media circus at Westminster'. The Committee then issued a formal summons, dated 15 March 2016, to appear before the Committee on 7 June. There followed a protracted correspondence, largely conducted in the glare of publicity, during which Mr Ashley sought clarification of the legal status of the proposed meeting, and of the measures in place to protect his fundamental rights. Only on 5 June did he confirm that, to avoid a 'lengthy legal battle', he would attend the committee.[64]

These events beg a number of questions. In an earlier case, in 2011, the Business, Innovation and Skills Committee attacked the 'dismissive' refusal of the CEO of Kraft Foods to give evidence personally—but in that instance it was unable to issue a summons, as the individual concerned was not a UK resident, and was therefore outside the House's jurisdiction.[65] What would have happened if Mike Ashley, who was a UK resident and was therefore in theory subject to the committee's jurisdiction, had similarly called its bluff? And is the threat of admonishment (the maximum penalty contemplated in the News International case) sufficient to ensure cooperation with committees in future?

Such questions have been repeatedly asked in recent years. In written evidence to the Liaison Committee in 2012, Sir Robert Rogers raised the possibility that the House's powers, upon which committees rely, were a 'paper tiger'. He offered three options: to do nothing; to reassert existing powers and establish more robust procedures for using them in Standing Orders (which could be seen as 'merely exhortatory'); or to provide coercive and penal powers in statute (which could expose committees to the 'intrusive and unwelcome' oversight of the courts).[66] One year later, the Joint Committee on Parliamentary Privilege essentially endorsed Sir Robert's second approach, noting that the House's powers, though in many

---

[63] Committee of Privileges, 'Conduct of witnesses before a select committee: Mr Colin Myler, Mr Tom Crone, Mr Les Hinton, and News International', First Report of Session 2016–17, HC 662.

[64] The correspondence is published on the committee's website at www.parliament.uk/business/committees/committees-a-z/commons-select/business-innovation-and-skills/inquiries/parliament-2015/working-practices-at-sports-direct-inquiry-16-17/publications.

[65] See Business, Innovation and Skills Committee, 'Is Kraft working for Cadbury?', Sixth Report of Session 2010–12, HC 871.

[66] Written evidence submitted by the Clerk of the House to the Liaison Committee, 9 July 2012: www.publications.parliament.uk/pa/cm201213/cmselect/cmliaisn/697/697we36.htm.

cases not exercised since the nineteenth century, remained in existence; it also proposed draft Standing Orders for consideration by the House of Commons.

Most recently, in response to the News International case, the Committee of Privileges has launched yet another inquiry into select committee powers. The committee has published a comprehensive paper by Sir Robert's successor as Clerk of the House, David Natzler, outlining the same issues that have preoccupied so many committees. His paper elegantly encapsulates the current dilemma:

> The fear is always that a particular crisis will reveal that the Emperor has no clothes and that the consequent damage to committees' ability to scrutinise public policy and hold the Government and other public bodies to account will suffer far-reaching damage. That this has not so far happened does not mean that it will not or cannot in future. On the other hand, when it has come down to it, the Emperor has in fact proved to be quite effectively attired, not perhaps with the historic powers to take into custody or to commit individuals, but with other softer, but sometimes equally persuasive, means: the pressure of public opinion; the requirements on individuals to demonstrate that they are 'fit and proper persons'; the risk that failure to co-operate will be interpreted against them.[67]

The reality is that Mike Ashley came within 48 hours of challenging the Emperor's nakedness—the next high-profile witness with good legal advisers may decide to try his or her luck. And publicity, though it has become the most potent weapon in committees' armoury, may turn out to be double-edged, particularly if committees are seen to be abusing their powers by bullying helpless witnesses in the 'national stocks'.

At heart, privilege is a special right or power, an exception to the general run of the law, and as such, it needs to be exercised with restraint. Indeed, the survival of such privileges across society is open to question, thanks to international law obligations, such as the European Convention on Human Rights[68] and its domestic corollary, the Human Rights Act 1998, and to domestic laws, such as the Data Protection Act 1998 and the Freedom of Information Act 2000, which give citizens legally enforceable mechanisms to defend their personal rights and to hold public bodies, including Parliament, to account. Against this backdrop, Parliament's continuing possession of ancient, uncodified and largely dormant penal powers seems anomalous.

Committees are at the sharp end of these developments, precisely because of the flexibility that has enabled their expansion and undeniable success over the last 40 years. That flexibility has allowed them to devise new working practices, allowing them to hold the Government to account and to scrutinise legislation

---

[67] Written evidence submitted by the Clerk of the House to the Committee of Privileges, February 2017: http://data.parliament.uk/writtenevidence/committeeevidence.svc/evidencedocument/committee-of-privileges/select-committee-powers/written/48435.pdf.

[68] The European Court of Human Rights has in fact twice ruled that national parliaments have over-reached themselves in exercising penal powers, both in respect of non-members (*Demicoli v Malta (Application no) 13057/87*) [1991] 14 ECHR 47) and opposition members (*Karácsony and Others v Hungary (Application nos) 42461/13 and 44357/13* [2016] ECHR).

more effectively. It has allowed them to extend their remit, beyond what was once a narrow and largely technical focus on Government policy and administration, and committees today regularly conduct quasi-judicial inquiries into the scandals of the day. The sceptics of the 1970s have been proved wrong.

Finally, committees and their increasingly powerful chairs have used the flexibility of their working practices to help them harness an alternative source of power in the news media, raising their profile and inspiring fear in alleged wrong-doers. But in so doing they tread a tight-rope. The question is whether, in the absence of statutory codification of their powers and responsibilities, they will keep their balance.

6

Relationship between the Two Houses

LORD NORTON AND LUCINDA MAER

THE UK PARLIAMENT comprises two Houses, but each is a largely discrete entity and the relationship that does exist between them is largely governed by an acceptance of the unelected House of Lords that the elected House, the House of Commons, enjoys primacy.

The principal means of formal interaction between the two Houses has been by message. 'A message is the most simple mode of communication … Messages are carried from one House to the other by one of the Clerks of the House which sends the message. The reception of a message does not interrupt the business then proceeding'.[1] There is also now communication by joint committees as well as by select committees of both Houses communicating with one another. As we shall, there is also informal interaction between members of both Houses. However, each House remains master of its own proceedings and most communication, such as a Bill passing from one House to another or amendments to a Bill, is by message. In practice, the conveying of a message by hand is complemented now by it being sent also in electronic form.

Each House is vested with power by virtue of being a House of Parliament. The two Houses were essentially co-equal in powers (although the Commons enjoyed pre-eminence in the granting of supply) until the twentieth century. The early part of the twentieth century saw a struggle between the two resolved in favour of the Commons. The latter half of the century was marked by the Lords reinventing itself as a chamber of legislative scrutiny, seeing itself as a chamber complementary to, rather than duplicating or competing with, the House of Commons.

The relationship between the two Houses is governed by statute, by conventions and by practice. The House of Lords is formally constrained, but it also exercises a degree of self-restraint. We focus on the constraints on the House of Lords before addressing the means of cooperation between the two Houses. Cooperation, similar to the constraints, takes the form of formal procedures and informal interactions.

---

[1] *Erskine May: Parliamentary Practice* (hereafter *Erskine May*), 24th edn (London, LexisNexis, 2011) 171–72.

I. CONSTRAINTS

The constraints, underpinning the system of asymmetrical bi-cameralism, may be grouped under the headings of statutes, conventions and practices.

A. Statutes

The principal limit on the powers of the House of Lords derives from the Parliament Acts 1911 and 1949. They enshrine the supremacy of the House of Commons.

The Commons for most of its history enjoyed primacy in granting supply. Henry IV in 1407 affirmed its right to originate proposals for taxation. After the Restoration in 1660, the Commons also began to deny the right of the Lords to amend money Bills. In 1678 the Commons passed a motion

> That all aids and supplies, and aids to his Majesty in Parliament, are the sole gifts of the Commons; and all bills for the granting of any such aids and supplies ought to begin with the Commons; and that it is the undoubted and sole right of the Commons to direct, limit, and appoint in such bills the ends, purposes, considerations, conditions, limitations, and qualifications of such grants, which ought not to be changed or altered by the House of Lords.[2]

However, the Lords remained coequal with the Commons in matters other than finance and even with money Bills the restraint was on amendment and not rejection. In 1909, the Lords rejected the budget. The result was the enactment of statutory constraints on the House, accepted by the Lords under threat of a sufficient number of new peers being created in order to ensure the Bill's passage.[3] The Parliament Act 1911 is the principal statute governing the relationship between Lords and Commons.

A Money Bill is one that deals exclusively with national taxation, public money or loans or their management, and certified as such by the Speaker. Under the provisions of the Act, a Money Bill can be sent up for Royal Assent without the agreement of the Lords if sent up to the Lords at least one month before the end of the session and if not agreed within the course of one month. The Lords can amend such Bills,[4] but the Commons is not obliged to consider such amendments. In practice, the Lords may debate such Bills, but after the Second Reading has been agreed, the remaining stages are taken formally.

The Lords retained greater latitude in respect of Bills not certified as money Bills. (Given that Bills with financial provisions often include other matters,

---

[2] *Erskine May* (n 1) 786. As it records, the principles have been amplified in subsequent motions.
[3] See C Ballinger, 'Hedging and Ditching: The Parliament Act 1911' (2011) 30 *Parliamentary History* 19; P Norton, 'Parliament 1911 in its Historical Context' in D Feldman (ed), *Law in Politics, Politics in Law* (Oxford, Hart Publishing, 2013) 155–69.
[4] The same is not the case with Supply Bills, which are not the same as Money Bills. As they may not be amended, committee stage is negatived.

they do not qualify as money Bills and so relatively few Bills are certified by the Speaker.) Bills, other than money Bills, rejected by the Lords would, if passed by the Commons in three successive sessions, be presented for Royal Assent, unless the Commons directed otherwise. At least two years had to elapse between the Second Reading of the Bill on the first occasion and Third Reading in the third session. The Parliament Act 1949 reduced the period from three sessions to two. As a Bill has to be sent up to the Lords at least one month before the end of the second session, the Lords can thus delay a Bill for a maximum of one year and one month.[5] For the purposes of the Act, a rejection by the Lords encompasses a failure to pass the Bill.[6]

The provisions of the Parliament Act do not apply to Bills that are introduced in the Lords, to secondary legislation, or to Bills that seek to extend the life of a Parliament.[7] A government introducing a contentious measure that may run into trouble in the Lords will thus normally ensure it begins life in the Commons.

In practice, the Government rarely has recourse to the provisions of the Parliament Act. Only three Bills were enacted under the provisions of the Parliament Act 1911: the Government of Ireland Act 1914; the Welsh Church Act 1914; and the Parliament Act 1949. Four measures have been given Royal Assent under the provisions of the 1949 Act: the War Crimes Act 1991; the European Parliamentary Elections Act 1999; the Sexual Offences (Amendment) Act 2000; and the Hunting Act 2004. What is noteworthy is that most of the Bills passed under the provisions of the 1949 Act have represented disagreement between members of the two Houses rather than a conflict between the Government and the House of Lords. Other than the European Parliamentary Elections Bill, the Bills were seen as falling within the (largely undefined but generally understood) category of 'conscience issues' and left for members to vote as they deemed appropriate.

The Parliament Acts thus constitute the formal constraint on the legislative capacity of the House of Lords. The House has the power of delay (other than in exceptional cases), but its behaviour is characterised by a large measure of self-restraint, to the extent that the exercise of a formal over-ride by the Commons is a rarity.

B. Conventions

The self-restraint of the House of Lords is given shape by convention and practice. Whereas the Parliament Acts constitute constraints imposed on the House, these

---

[5] On the timescale, see the House of Commons Library Briefing Paper, 'The Parliament Acts', SN00675, February 2016.

[6] The Sexual Offences (Amendment) Bill in 2000, rejected by the Lords in the previous session, was given a Second Reading by peers in the second, but the House then made amendments to it and the Government decided not to make further progress with it. It waited until the end of the session, when the Bill qualified for presentation for Royal Assent.

[7] The Fixed-term Parliaments Bill in 2011 included a provision that would allow the life of a Parliament to be extended by one month. Given that provision, the Bill did not qualify for enactment under the terms of the Parliament Act.

are generated by the House itself and it remains within its gift to enhance, modify or abandon.

The principal convention governing the relationship between the two Houses is the Salisbury convention. A number of practices adopted by the House are also variously designated as conventions (including by the Joint Committee on Conventions, which reported in 2006),[8] but they fail to meet the criteria of conventions, namely, binding rules of behaviour accepted by those at whom they are directed. A practice that is not invariable does not qualify.

The Salisbury convention derives from a statement made by Viscount Cranborne (later the Marquess of Salisbury), Conservative leader in the House of Lords, in August 1945. It had its origins in the referendal doctrine developed by his grandfather, the 3rd Marquess. That contended that the House of Lords was entitled to reject a measure of major import where it was not clear that the measure had the consent of the people. When, through an election at which the measure had been part of the Government's programme, the Government had received a majority, and hence the mandate of the people, the logic of the doctrine was that the Lords therefore could no longer resist the measure.[9] The doctrine was used as a basis for rejecting the Irish Home Rule Bill in 1893. It also was applied in respect of the Irish Church Bill, debate on which had dominated the general election of November 1868. Given that the Liberals won the election, and could claim a mandate for the Bill, Salisbury accepted that the Lords could not block its passage. He voted with 36 other Tory peers to ensure the Bill received a Second Reading.

In 1945, faced with a Labour government that had been elected with a large majority on a programme embodied in its manifesto, *Let Us Face the Future,* his grandson declared in the House that:

> [W]e should frankly recognise that their proposals were put before the country at the recent General Election and that the people of this country, with full knowledge of these proposals, returned the Labour Party to power ... I believe that it would be constitutionally wrong, when the country has so recently expressed its view, for this House to oppose proposals which have been definitely put before the electorate.[10]

A doctrine that had been used to reject measures of earlier Liberal governments was now used to uphold measures introduced by a Labour government. The explanation was to be found in the development of detailed election manifestos and the recognition by Cranborne that it was politically as well as constitutionally unwise of the Lords to challenge a government enjoying such a large majority in the elected House.

---

[8] Joint Committee on Conventions, 'Conventions of the UK Parliament', Vol 1, Session 2005–06, HL Paper 265-I, HC 1212-I.

[9] See C Comstock Weston, 'Salisbury and the Lords, 1868–1895' (1982) 25 *Historical Journal* 103, reproduced in C Jones and DL Jones (eds), *The House of Lords, 1603–1911* (London, The Hambledon Press, 1986) 461–88.

[10] HL Deb 16 August 1945, col 47.

The doctrine enunciated by Cranborne was followed by Tory peers, refraining in that Parliament from blocking measures, even those that they heartily disliked, and maintained the practice in subsequent Parliaments. It thus took on the form of a convention.

The convention is that the House of Lords does not reject at second or third reading, or pass an amendment that would amount to wrecking, any Government Bill brought from the Commons which was promised in the Government's election manifesto. As with other conventions, there is some debate as to its contours—the precise definition of a wrecking amendment has never been established—but the essential point is that it has become an invariable practice.

The convention has occasionally been queried, the Liberal Democrats having argued that it was no more than an agreement between the Government and the Opposition. Rodney Brazier has argued that there is a widespread view that the convention ceased after the House of Lords Act 1999 took effect, removing most hereditary peers from the House.[11]

Despite the disputes as to the contours or indeed the existence of the convention, the House has not rejected a manifesto Bill, either through denying it a Second or Third Reading or passing a wrecking amendment, since Cranborne made his statement at the Opposition despatch box in 1945. The Joint Committee on Conventions also recorded that the convention had evolved and now extended to manifesto Bills introduced in the House of Lords. It also recorded that, despite being contested by the Liberal Democrats, it was recognised by the whole House, unlike the original doctrine.[12] In effect, this was a statement not that the convention had evolved, but that the practice enunciated by Cranborne had evolved into a convention.

Indeed, the convention has not only been followed, but also the practice has developed of the House not rejecting Bills that are in the Government's programme for the session.[13] The practice has not evolved into a convention, in that on occasion Government Bills have been the subject of divisions. The Joint Committee on Conventions in 2006 recorded that in the previous 25 years, there had been 13 attempts to defeat Government Bills at Second Reading, five of them successful. As it went on to note:

> But the list must be compared with the much longer list of government Bills, many of them controversial, to which the Lords have given an unopposed Second Reading over this period. It is evidently uncommon for a government Bill to be assailed at Second Reading in the Lords, and very uncommon for such an attack to succeed.[14]

The Clerk of the Parliaments, in evidence to the committee, said that there was not a convention that the House did not vote against Second Readings, but that the House did not vote against without giving notice.

[11] Joint Committee on Conventions (n 8) paras 93, 30.
[12] ibid, paras 31–32.
[13] ibid, paras 94–95, p 31.
[14] ibid, para 95, p 31.

The House thus adheres to the convention that a Bill deriving from a manifesto commitment of the Government is not rejected, whether introduced in the Commons or Lords. It has also developed the practice of not rejecting on Second Reading Bills that are in the Government's programme for the session, even if not in the manifesto.

C. Practices

The foremost practices governing the relationship are to be found in the legislative process. These are notably in respect of resolving disputes between the two chambers ('ping-pong'), the financial privilege of the Commons, the Lords not rejecting statutory instruments, and the Government getting its business in reasonable time. Though some politicians have elevated these practices to the status of conventions or rules, they fail to meet the criteria for either. Even in respect of what may seem a well-established rule in respect of 'double insistence' in the process of ping-pong, there is nothing that binds the two Houses to the practice. There is, as *Erskine May* records, 'no binding rule of order which governs these proceedings in either House'.[15] It would be possible, as it records, for the two Houses to find some means of varying the practice if both were keen to save a Bill. There may also be a more practical reason for variation. The rules governing the exchanges between the two Houses are, as the Clerk of the House of Commons told the Joint Committee on Conventions, 'exceedingly complex'.[16] At times, when amendments have been the subject of several exchanges between the Houses, it has proved difficult to keep abreast of the status of amendments moved as alternatives (amendments in lieu). As one Clerk admitted to the author, with one Bill in recent years, the Clerks came close to losing control of the process.

i. 'Ping-pong'

Bills have to be agreed in identical form by the two Houses in order to be presented for Royal Assent. Once a Bill has cleared all its stages in one House, it then goes to the other. The other House may make amendments and these then have to be agreed by the House in which the Bill originated. As most Bills are introduced in the Commons, this mostly means amendments made by the House of Lords. Most Lords' amendments that are agreed are Government amendments—though their genesis may be, and frequently is, amendments moved by the Opposition or backbench peers at earlier stages[17]—and as such prove acceptable to the Commons.

---

[15] *Erskine May* (n 1) 636.
[16] Joint Committee on Conventions (n 8), para 169, p 48.
[17] Research by Meg Russell found that a majority of substantive Government amendments (55%) made to 12 Government Bills in the years from 2005 to 2012 could be traced to amendments moved earlier by peers, with others attributable to reports from committees or pressure from MPs. M Russell, *The Contemporary House of Lords* (Oxford, Oxford University Press, 2013) 173.

However, if the Commons rejects an amendment moved by the Lords, or proposes an alternative, it is then up to the Lords to agree or disagree with the Commons' action. If it does not insist on its original amendment, the Bill is passed.

Where disagreement persists between two chambers, some legislatures employ the practice of a conciliation or conference committee, comprising some members of both Houses meeting to try to reach agreement. This was an option considered in 1910 in the discussions that led to the Parliament Act 1911,[18] but was rejected in favour of an amendment going back and forth between the two Houses until agreement is reached or the Bill falls. This process is known in France as 'navette' (shuffle), but in the UK is colloquially known as 'ping-pong'. An amendment rejected by one House returns to the other and exchanges continue until agreement is reached, either on the rejection or acceptance of the amendment or an alternative.

The principal rule governing 'ping-pong' is that known as 'double insistence'. If a House insists on an amendment to which the other has disagreed, and the other insists on its disagreement, with neither having offered an alternative ('an amendment in lieu'), the Bill is lost.[19] In practice, it is rare for the Lords to insist and usually accepts the Commons rejection of an amendment on the first occasion it happens. This is especially the case where the Commons has rejected the amendment, by a clear majority and the Government benches are united in resisting it. In 2017, for instance, the Lords passed two amendments, by substantial majorities, to the European Union (Notification of Withdrawal) Bill, a Bill that had cleared the Commons without amendment. When the Commons rejected both amendments, with the Government standing firm in its resistance, the Lords did not insist on their amendments.

The situation is different where peers detect that the Government party is not united in the Commons, and/or where it feels there is an important principle at stake (and one that may resonate with the public). The European Parliamentary Elections Bill, introduced in 1997, provided for a regional list system of elections for the European Parliament, with a closed rather than an open list. The Lords passed an amendment providing for an open list and insisted on its amendment, arguing that the principle of voter choice was important, and resisting Commons amendments in lieu. On the fourth occasion that the Lords discussed Commons reasons for disagreeing with the Lords amendment, the Government announced it would be reintroduced in the following session, to be enacted under the provisions of the Parliament Act.

As the Joint Committee on Conventions noted, the process of resolving differences has been complicated at times by the practice of packaging amendments for the purpose of agreeing or disagreeing.[20] This is seen as acceptable where amendments are closely connected. It is more problematic where amendments

---

[18] C Ballinger, *The House of Lords 1911–2011* (Oxford, Hart Publishing, 2012) 17–19, 27; Norton, 'Parliament Act 1911' (n 3) 163–64, 166.

[19] *Erskine May* (n 1) 636.

[20] Joint Committee on Conventions (n 8), paras 171–78, pp 49–50.

appear to be grouped purely for reason of convenience or to avoid compromise on a particular amendment in the package, avoiding the problem of double insistence by proposing an amendment in lieu to one of the other amendments.

ii. Financial Privilege

The House of Commons, as we have seen, has long asserted primacy in the raising and spending of money. When the House of Lords makes amendments that have financial implications, this is deemed to engage the financial privilege of the Commons. The Clerk of Legislation advises when such privilege is engaged.

If the amendment is such as to require a Money or Ways and Means Resolution, then the amendment is summarily rejected by the Commons, on the instructions of the Speaker.[21] This is an assertion of what has been termed 'unwaivable financial privilege'.[22] Where amendments are within the scope of a Money or Ways and Means resolution, then it is open to the Commons to agree to the amendment (in which case the House is deemed to have waived its privilege) or propose an amendment in lieu (in which case the issue of privilege does not arise). However, if the Commons rejects an amendment that has financial implications, the practice is for the House to disagree on grounds of privilege alone (even if it has debated the substance of the issue) and to inform the Lords that the amendment involves a charge upon public funds and do not offer any further reason, 'trusting that the reason given may be deemed sufficient'.[23]

The practice of the Lords is, as recorded in the *Companion to the Standing Orders*, not to insist on its amendment, though it may offer an amendment in lieu. The last time the Lords insisted on its amendments, where financial privilege was engaged, was in 1930. However, the use of financial privilege, and the passing of amendments in lieu which may engage financial privilege, has proved controversial in recent years.

The Lords variously offers amendments in lieu where financial privilege has been engaged. Russell and Gover record that of 160 amendments to which financial privilege was invoked in the period from 1974 to 2013, the Lords responded in 19 cases by agreeing one or more amendments in lieu (representing 22 amendments in total).[24] Conflict has arisen where the amendments in lieu continue to engage financial privilege. The Joint Committee on Conventions concluded that 'If the Commons have disagreed to Lords Amendments on grounds of financial privilege, it is contrary to convention for the Lords to send back Amendments in lieu which clearly invite the same response'.[25] Given that almost all of those amendments in lieu proposed in 1974–2013—19 of the 22 identified by Russel and Gover—engaged

---

[21] *Erskine May* (n 1) 793.
[22] Constitution Committee, House of Lords, *Money Bills and Commons Financial Privilege*, Tenth Report of Session 2010–11, HL Paper 97, App 2, para 12, p 9.
[23] *Erskine May* (n 1) 792.
[24] M Russell and D Gover, *Demystifying Financial Privilege* (London: The Constitution Unit, 2014) 13.
[25] Joint Committee on Conventions (n 8) para 252, p 67.

financial privilege (including two proposed by the Government),[26] the assertion of a convention appears unfounded and, indeed, may not bear the weight of being included under the heading of practice. The practice has been to offer amendments in lieu that do engage financial privilege.

What has developed as a practice has been not to insist on amendments when an amendment in lieu has been offered by the Lords and rejected by the Commons on the grounds of financial privilege. In considering the Welfare Reform Bill in 2012, the Lords offered seven amendments in lieu that engaged financial privilege. Five of these had Government support, so not surprisingly were accepted by the Commons. The remaining two had been passed against the wishes of the Government and were rejected by the Commons on grounds of financial privilege. The Lords did not then persist in their disagreement.[27] In the same year, there was a similar disagreement over an amendment to the Legal Aid, Sentencing and Punishment of Offenders Bill. When the amendment in lieu was rejected by the Commons on grounds of financial privilege, again the Lords did not persist in their disagreement.[28]

Whereas the willingness of the Lords on occasion to offer amendments in lieu where financial privilege has been engaged has proved contentious, so on occasion has been the Commons' claim to privilege in rejecting Lords amendments. As Russell and Gover show, this was especially the case with the Counter-Terrorism Bill in 2008, the Identity Documents Bill in 2010 and the Welfare Reform Bill in 2012.[29] On the last of these, one peer claimed that financial privilege had been invoked in a way that was 'completely contrary to the conventions of the constitution'.[30] There was no convention to be broken. As Russell and Gover demonstrate, financial privilege is a concept little understood—the process is opaque and involves no explanation of the reason for why privilege is invoked—but the problem in recent years has not been process, but the increase in defeats in the Lords on contentious social legislation, where more than in previous years have been on amendments that engage financial privilege.[31]

iii. Statutory Instruments

The House of Lords usually approves statutory instruments (SIs), but it is not an invariable practice. The House has asserted its right to reject such instruments and has on occasion exercised it. The House therefore does not regard itself as bound, and has not been bound, by a moral imperative that it should not reject statutory instruments. So long as that is the case, there is no convention. The Joint Committee on Conventions recognise that no convention was breached if the

---

[26] Russell and Gover, *Demystifying* (n 24) 14.
[27] ibid, 11.
[28] ibid, 11.
[29] ibid, 9–10.
[30] ibid, 10.
[31] ibid, 31–32.

House defeated a statutory instrument. As it reported, 'The Government appear to consider that any defeat of an SI by the Lords is a breach of convention. We disagree'. It continued:

> It is not incompatible with the role of a revising chamber to reject an SI, since (a) the Lords (rightly or wrongly) cannot exercise its revising role by amending the SI or in any other way, (b) the Government can bring the SI forward again immediately, with or without substantive amendment, as described by the Clerk of the Parliaments, and (c) the power to reject SIs gives purpose and leverage to scrutiny by the Joint Committee on SIs, and by the new Lords Committee on the Merits of SIs. The Government's argument that 'it is for the Commons as the source of Ministers' authority, to withhold or grant their endorsement of Ministers' actions' is an argument against having a second chamber at all, and we reject it.[32]

In October 2015, the Lords withheld agreement to the Tax Credits (Income Threshold and Determination of Rates)(Amendment) Regulations 2015 until certain conditions were met.[33] The failure to approve the regulations proved politically controversial and the Prime Minister, David Cameron, asked a former Leader of the House of Lords, Lord Strathclyde, to undertake a review of SIs and to consider how more certainty and clarity could be brought to their passage through Parliament. Lord Strathclyde published his report in December 2015.[34] In response to what he perceived as a 'fraying' of 'the Lords convention on statutory instruments', he advanced three options: to remove the Lords from the SIs procedure altogether; to retain a role, but with the House adopting a resolution detailing restrictions on its power to withhold approval or to annul an SI; or to provide for a new procedure, set out in statute, allowing the Lords to invite the Commons to think again when a disagreement exists, but enabling the Commons to insist on its primacy.

The review was subject to considerable criticism in the Lords[35] and was accused of being internally contradictory. The fact that there is no convention was borne out by the words of Lord Strathclyde in the course of asserting that there is:

> The convention that the House of Lords should not, *or should not regularly*, reject SIs is longstanding but has been interpreted in different ways, has not been understood by all, and has never been accepted by some members of the House.[36]

The very wording draws attention to the absence of any agreement and thus negated the claim that there is a convention governing how the House deals with secondary legislation. Even if there was an invariable practice of not rejecting SIs, the action of the Lords in dealing with the Tax Credits Regulations would not have been caught by it. A motion to reject the Regulations was rejected by the House.[37]

---

[32] Joint Committee on Conventions (n 8) para 228.
[33] HL Deb 26 October 2015, cols 1035–42.
[34] 'Strathclyde Review: Secondary Legislation and the primacy of the House of Commons', Cm 9177, December 2015.
[35] See HL Deb 13 January 2016, cols 272–380.
[36] 'Strathclyde Review' (n 34), 15. Emphasis added.
[37] HL Deb 26 October 2015, cols 1031–33.

The motions that were passed provided that they be delayed until certain conditions were met.

The Joint Committee on Conventions quoted the Clerk of the Parliaments as saying 'There is no generally accepted convention restricting the powers of the Lords on secondary legislation'.[38] It then goes on to state, 'There was once a loose convention against voting down SIs, but no longer'. However, the problem here is the very concept of a 'loose convention' because it is either a convention or it is not. Because it entails an invariable practice, there cannot be any variation.

It has therefore been the practice of the House not to withhold consent to SIs, but there is no convention. Following debate on the Strathclyde Report, the Government took no action on its recommendations.

In terms of scrutiny of secondary legislation, there is a notable difference between the two Houses, not in respect of powers, but in terms of scrutiny of SIs.[39] SIs are subject to consideration by the Joint Committee on Statutory Instruments (see below)—for SIs subject only to Commons approval, MPs sit as a Commons' committees—and SIs to give effect to EU directives are considered by the European Committees in each House. Otherwise the Commons employs no permanent committees for the consideration of secondary legislation. The Lords utilises the Delegated Powers and Regulatory Reform Committee for examining the input side of secondary legislation, that is, the order making powers included in Bills. It employs the Secondary Legislation Scrutiny Committee (formerly the Merits of Statutory Instruments Committee) for examining the output side, that is, the SIs laid before the House. Both committees are empowered to report to the House.

iv. Getting the Government's Business in Reasonable Time

There is a Lords' practice of considering Government business 'in reasonable time'. This affects the relationship between two Houses in that it determines when the Commons will receive and have time to consider a Government Bill introduced in the Lords and how the Lords considers a Government Bill brought up from the Commons. The Commons recognise the role of the Lords as a chamber of detailed scrutiny, but would likely regard undue delay in considering a Bill, especially if it had the potential to prevent the Bill being enacted, as impinging on its primacy.

Both the Royal Commission on the Reform of the House of Lords[40] and the Joint Committee on House of Lords Reform[41] asserted as a convention that the Government was able to gets its business in reasonable time. The form of words has varied: 'considered within a reasonable time' (Royal Commission), 'considered

---

[38] Joint Committee on Conventions (n 8), para 217, 60.

[39] See ch 14, by Adam Tucker, for consideration of draft legislation.

[40] Royal Commission on the Reform of the House of Lords, 'A House for the Future', Cm 4534, January 2000, para 4.20.

[41] Joint Committee on House of Lords Reform, First Report of Session 2002–03, HL Paper 17, HC 171, para 12.

without undue delay' (Joint Committee), 'consider the Government's business without unreasonable delay' (Hunt Report; see below). However, it is a practice rather than a convention, since there has never been a definition of what constitutes 'reasonable time'. It is a concept not addressed in the Lords' *Companion to the Standing Orders* or in *Erskine May*.

The practice of the House has been to follow the Government's scheduling of its business, usually agreed by negotiation through the usual channels. It has not therefore usually been an issue. However, it did become a matter of contention in the 2001–05 Parliament. In March 2002, the Lords voted to delay committee stage of the Animal Health Bill until a consultation and two inquiries had been completed. The result was that the Bill did no go into committee until just before the summer recess. The last occasion on which such a dilatory amendment had been passed was in 1887. In March 2004, the House also voted to refer the Constitutional Reform Bill, a measure to abolish the office of Lord Chancellor and establish a Supreme Court, to a select committee and to carry it over from one session to the next. The same month the Government dropped a House of Lords Reform Bill to remove the remaining hereditary peers from the House after the Opposition Leader, Lord Strathclyde, had threatened a 'major fight' on the issue.

The issue was addressed by a working group of Labour peers, chaired by Lord Hunt of King's Heath, which reported in July 2004. It argued that a balance had to be struck between the need for the Lords to have enough time to consider a Bill properly and for the Government to get its business in reasonable time. It followed the 1968 White Paper on House of Lords Reform in recommending that the House should have sixty sitting days to consider a Bill or rather 'most bills'. The recommendation was subsequently embodied in the Labour Party's 2005 election manifesto.

In practice, no action was taken on the recommendation. As the Joint Committee on Conventions observed, the Government softened its stance in its evidence to the Committee.[42] The debate on the subject highlighted the absence of agreement on the meaning of 'reasonable time'. For the Clerk of the Parliaments and Opposition Leader, Lord Strathclyde, it meant getting the business by the end of the session. For Government, it was a shorter period, though it moved to suggesting an outside limit of 80 sitting days. There was also the problem that a delay in the passage of a Bill may not be the result of the actions of the House, but the actions of Government. This was illustrated in the subsequent Parliament, when in 2013 the Government chose to 'pause' consideration of the Transparency of Lobbying, Non-Party Campaigning and Trade Union Administration Bill for a period of six weeks so that more consultation could take place. Other practical problems variously identified, where a time limit could prove problematic, were in cases of long and complex Bills, where there were numerous Government amendments, where a Bill may be re-committed, and even in cases where Opposition front-benchers

---

[42] Joint Committee on Conventions (n 8) para 132, p 39.

leading on a Bill may be unavailable. There was also the objection that imposing a limitation by statute would render the procedure amenable to judicial review.

In evidence to the Joint Committee on Conventions, the Clerk of the Parliaments observed that it was not self-evident that 60 days and 'reasonable time' were synonymous: in the 2005–06 session, up to 26 May, he reported, 13 Bills had taken longer than 60 days 'without any suggestion that this was unreasonable'.[43]

The result is that there has been no change to the existing arrangements. It remains the practice that a Government Bill is considered in reasonable time, but without there being any agreed definition of what constitutes reasonable time. Rather, so long as there is agreement between the usual channels, there is no challenge of unreasonableness.

II. COOPERATION

Conflict between the two chambers is a relatively infrequent feature of parliamentary life. Cooperation is a more consistent feature. As we have seen, agreement is normally reached on amendments to Bills. There is formal cooperation in the formation of joint committees. There are three permanent committees, established by standing orders of each House: the Joint Committee on Consolidation Etc Bills; the Joint Committee on Statutory Instruments; and the Joint Committee on Human Rights.

The Joint Committee on Consolidation Etc Bills considers Consolidation Bills as well as Statute Law Revision Bills and certain other categories of Bills, including those recommended by the Law Commission to repeal obsolete legislation. The Bills are introduced in the House of Lords and are referred without motion to the Joint Committee. After the committee report on a Bill, it is then re-committed to a Committee of the Whole House. In practice, Consolidation Bills are relatively few in number and by their nature rarely controversial.

The task of the Joint Committee on Statutory Instruments is to ensure that SIs that are subject to approval by both Houses are *intra vires* (within the powers granted) and are not deficient in terms of drafting. (Instruments that are subject only to approval by the Commons are considered by the MPs on the committee sitting separately as the Select Committee on Statutory Instruments.) The committee reports on the SIs, but it has no formal powers and it is not unknown for an SI to be approved before the Committee has reported. As with the Joint Committee on Consolidation Etc Bills, service on the committee is not seen as high profile or sought after.

The Joint Committee on Human Rights was established in 2000[44] and constitutes a notable attempt by Parliament to adapt to the changes wrought by the Human

---

[43] Joint Committee on Conventions (n 8) para 142, p 41. See also ch 10 on Parliament and Human Rights.

[44] See P Evans, 'The Human Rights Act and Westminster's Legislative Process in A Brazier (ed), *Parliament, Politics and Law Making* (London, The Hansard Society, 2004) 84–93.

Rights Act 1998. The terms of reference of the committee were widely drawn. It can consider and report on matters relating to human rights in the United Kingdom (though not individual cases).[45] It has served to scrutinise the compliance of government departments with the Act and to raise the profile of human rights, not least with Parliament as well as Government. It has helped create within Government what its first chair described as a 'culture of justification',[46] with departments knowing that in the generation of measures they have the Joint Committee ready to check thoroughly that it has complied with the provisions of the Act. It has proved a prolific committee. In the 2005–10 Parliament, it published 129 reports and also saw a remarkable increase in references to human rights in both chambers, though more so the House of Lords than the House of Commons.[47]

The committee comprises six members drawn from each House and its work has been facilitated by a willingness to appoint senior figures. On the Lords side, these have included senior QCs, such as Lord Lester of Herne Hill (widely credited as the father of the Human Rights Act), Lord Faulks and Baroness Kennedy of the Shaws. It has also included others with experience in the field, such as Baroness O'Loan, a former law lecturer and Police Ombudsman for Northern Ireland. The committee is chaired by an MP, the first chair being Jean Corston, a former chair of the Parliamentary Labour Party, and in the 2015–17 Parliament former Cabinet minister and Solicitor-General Harriet Harman. The members have served to raise the profile of human rights issues in each chamber. In their research, Hunt, Hooper and Yowell found that seven parliamentarians were especially prolific in their references to human rights, each making 30 or more references to committee reports. These comprised two MPs and five peers; all bar one of these were members of the JCHR.[48] The JCHR has thus served to draw on the strengths of the membership of the two Houses in order to carry out the tasks ascribed to it.[49] Utilising especially those with a legal background has facilitated it as an intermediary between courts and the executive, enabling it to contribute to what Alison Young has characterised as a 'democratic dialogue' between institutions,[50] the courts and Parliament complementing one another in the protection of rights.[51] By creating a joint committee, the two Houses may be seen to be playing to their strengths.

---

[45] It is also required to examine and report on remedial orders (a fast-track system for correcting incompatibilities in existing legislation that are identified by the courts), but in practice few such orders are ever made. Evans (n 44) 87.

[46] Constitution Committee, House of Lords, 'Parliament and the Legislative Process', 14th Report of Session 2003–04, HL Paper 173-II, 164.

[47] M Hunt, H Cooper and P Yowell, *Parliament and Human Rights: redressing the democratic deficit* (Swindon, Arts and Humanities Research Council, 2012) 19–22.

[48] Hunt, Hooper and Yowell, *Human Rights* (n 47) 24–26.

[49] P Norton, 'A Democratic Dialogue? Parliament and Human Rights in the United Kingdom' (2013) 21 *Asia-Pacific Law Review* 157.

[50] A Young, *Parliamentary Sovereignty and the Human Rights Act* (Oxford, Hart Publishing, 2009), esp 128.

[51] Norton, 'A Democratic Dialogue?' (n 49) 143.

Joint committees have also become a more regular feature as a result of the greater use of the pre-legislative scrutiny of Bills. Since 1997, successive governments have published some Bills in draft—a total of 76 in the period from 1997 to 2010—and submitted most to Parliament for scrutiny. Not all are subject to parliamentary scrutiny, either because they are published too late or the relevant departmental select committee in the Commons has been too busy to undertake the task. However, most are subject to pre-legislative scrutiny and most by Commons' departmental select committees. Some, though, are referred to a joint committee for consideration. Since 1997, 24 Bills have been considered by joint committees.

Formally, joint committees constitute two separate select committees, appointed by each House to work together, but, as *Erskine May* records, they operate as a single committee, with one chair and with all decisions made jointly.[52]

Referral of a draft Bill to a joint committee normally takes place where the Bill is of constitutional significance or where its subject matter may benefit from drawing on the experience and knowledge of peers as well as MPs. Constitutional measures subject to pre-legislative scrutiny by joint committees have included the draft Civil Contingencies Bill in 2003, the draft Constitutional Renewal Bill in 2008 (enacted as the Constitutional Reform and Governance Act 2010), the draft House of Lords Reform Bill in 2012, and the draft Voting Eligibility (Prisoners) Bill in 2013. Other draft Bills have been within fields such as terrorism, deregulation, corruption, defamation, care, charities, and disability.

Utilising joint committees is efficient in that it may facilitate passage of the measure in both Houses, the nature of the scrutiny potentially reducing the need for extensive scrutiny in each, and with each having members who can comment authoritatively on the measure. The use of joint committees also widens the pool from which the membership may be drawn. The Joint Committee on the draft Voting Eligibility (Prisoners) Bill included an MP who had been prisons minister, another who had served as an assistant prison governor, and a peer who had been President of the Supreme Court.

Joint committees may also be employed to report on particular issues, not least those directly affecting Parliament. These have included proposals for the reform of the House of Lords. Such proposals obviously affect directly the Lords, but also necessarily affect the relationship between the two Houses and the place of Parliament in the political system.[53] In May 2006, the two Houses agreed to a joint committee to consider 'the practicality of codifying the key conventions on the relationship between the two Houses of Parliament which affect the consideration of legislation'. It reported in November 2006.[54] There have also been two joint committees on the issue of parliamentary privilege.[55]

---

[52] *Erskine May* (n 1) 911.

[53] See P Norton, *Reform of the House of Lords* (Manchester, Manchester University Press, 2017).

[54] Joint Committee on Conventions (n 8).

[55] Joint Committee on Parliamentary Privilege, First Report of Session 1998–99, HL Paper 43-I, HC 214-I; Joint Committee on Parliamentary Privilege, Report of Session 2013–14, HL Paper 30, HC 100.

However, one of the most innovative uses of such committees was the appointment in 2012, as a joint committee, of the Commission on Banking Standards. This comprised 10 members, chaired by the chair of the Treasury Committee, Andrew Tyrie, and including the Bishop of Durham—who had previously worked in industry and who, in the course of proceedings, became the Archbishop of Canterbury—former Chancellor of the Exchequer, Lord Lawson, former Treasury economist and Cabinet Secretary, Lord Turnbull, and Lord McFall, who, as an MP, had been the long-serving chair of the Treasury Committee. It had a substantial support staff and worked through 11 panels (some of which comprised one or two members), covering subjects such as corporate governance, mis-selling and cross-selling, financial exclusion and basic bank accounts. It was asked to report by December 2012 before publication of a Banking Reform Bill. Its reports underpinned regulatory reform and banking regulation.

The creation of a joint committee requires each House to pass a motion agreeing to such a committee. One House will normally propose such a committee (in the case of a Bill, it will originate in the House in which the Bill is pending) and the other House then responds. In most cases, the response is positive, though there have been occasions when one House has rejected or not acted on a proposal of the other. In July 2015, for example, the Lords (against Government advice) passed a motion proposing a joint committee to consider and report on the constitutional implications of the Government's proposals to change the Standing Orders of the House of Commons in order to give effect to English Votes for English Laws, but the Commons took no action.

The appointment of a joint committee entails discussion between the authorities of both Houses, not only to reach agreement to appoint a committee, but also its terms of reference and its size. Joint committees have varied in size between 10 members, as on the Joint Committee on Banking Standards, to 26, as on the draft House of Lords Reform Bill. MPs are appointed, as with select committees, on the basis of party strength in the chamber. The party proportions may thus vary from Parliament to Parliament. Peers are appointed on a less variable formulaic basis. If 12 peers are to be appointed, it is on the basis of four Conservative, four Labour, two Liberal Democrat, and two cross-bench peers. Appointing 13 peers, as with the draft House of Lords Reform Bill, enables a Bishop to be appointed (in this case, the Bishop of Leicester). The quorum for Lords' members is three. The quorum for Commons' members is three or a quarter of the Commons' membership, whichever is the greater, unless another number is set by the order of the House. On occasion this matters, not least given the demands made especially on MPs' time.

All the members of joint committees are nominated by the Committee of Selection in each House, the names put forward through the usual channels. Joint Committees elect their own chair and, other than in one case, adopt House of Lords procedure. (The exception was the Joint Committee on Tax Law Rewrite Bills, where both Houses agreed to the use of Commons' procedures.) In practice, agreement is reached in advance between the parties as to who should be nominated to chair. The use of Lords' procedure makes little significant manifest difference, compared to Commons' procedure, other than in respect of deciding the issue if there is a tied vote.

Other than cooperation through the formation of joint committees, there is also cooperation through delegations to international organisations, such as the North Atlantic Treaty Organisation (NATO) Parliamentary Assembly, comprising 13 MPs and five peers, and the Organisation for Security and Cooperation in Europe (OSCE) Parliamentary, with 10 MPs and three peers. Members of both Houses also serve on delegations to visit other parliaments. There is also cooperation at a political level between the usual channels in the two Houses as well as cooperation at official level. Clerks of committees of the two Houses communicate in order to ensure that a committee in one House does not clash with another in terms of subject coverage. There is also liaison in order to keep abreast of what committees in the same field are doing. This has been especially important in the field of European legislation, given the complementary roles of the European Scrutiny Committee in the Commons and the European Union Committee in the Lords.

Formal cooperation between the two Houses is complemented by informal cooperation between MPs and peers. This takes the form of contact through all-party parliamentary groups, party groups and by members occupying shared social space.

A. All-Party Parliamentary Groups (APPGs)

APPGs are cross-party bodies that have to be registered, and abide by rules established by the House of Commons,[56] but which have no formal status. Each Group is an informal group of MPs and peers who come together to consider a shared interest in a particular subject. Although designed for members of both Houses, an APPG may invite others to attend and be involved in meetings.

APPGs have grown over the decades, since the first such group was formed in 1933.[57] In 1988 there were 103 subject groups and 113 country groups.[58] By the end of the 2015–17 Parliament, there were 496 subject groups, 132 country groups and three clubs (football, hockey and rugby union football). To qualify as an APPG, it must be open to members of both Houses, regardless of party affiliation. Given that the formal responsibility of the groups rests with the House of Commons, the Chair and Registered Contact must be an MP. Each group must

---

[56] *Guide to the Rules on All-Party Parliamentary Groups* (London, Office of the Parliamentary Commissioner for Standards, 2015).

[57] C Powell, *The Parliamentary and Scientific Committee. The First Forty Years 1939–1979* (London, Croom Helm, 1980).

[58] JB Jones, 'Party Committees and All-Party Groups' in M Rush (ed), *Parliament and Pressure Politics* (Oxford, Clarendon Press, 1990) 125.

have at least four officers, of which at least two must be MPs. Peers may serve as officers, other than as the Chair and Registered Contact. Some peers serve as co-chairs. Groups must hold annual general meetings, as well as at least one other meeting during the year. The quorum for a meeting is five members drawn from either House, one of which must, for the purposes of the annual general meeting, be an MP.

The introduction at the end of the 2010–15 Parliament of the position of Chair and Registered Contact meant that peers could no longer serve as the sole chair, but in practice some have continued to run APPGs as co-chairs or vice-chairs. Thus, for example, the APPG on drugs policy reform, led for many years by Baroness Meacher, elected Green MP Caroline Lucas to be Chair and Registered Contact, while Baroness Meacher continued in effect to take the lead, having established international as well as national contacts to press for an evidence-based review of drugs policy.

APPGs constitute a valuable means of bringing members together from the two Houses on issues of mutual interest. Some exist in little more than paper form, others are active and sustained by members of both Houses. Whereas some draw MPs and peers to discuss issues of shared concern, some are more social in nature, such as the bridge and golf groups, given an opportunity for members from both Houses to mix socially.

B. Party Groups

Each parliamentary party has its own organisation, electing officers and hold-ing regular meetings.[59] The Conservative and Labour parliamentary parties also appoint committees or subject groups. The main organisation is to be found in the Commons, but each party in the Lords also hold weekly meetings.

The Parliamentary Labour Party (PLP) comprises all Labour representatives in Parliament and Labour peers are thus deemed members of the PLP and are eligi-ble to attend weekly PLP meetings.[60] Some do attend, though MPs dominate and most PLP activity is discussed in terms of MPs. There is also representation of MPs and peers on the party's Parliamentary Committee, which serves when Labour is in office to maintain, according to the PLP's Standing Orders, 'an effective two-way channel of communication between Government and Back-benchers in both Houses'. Of the 15 members, six are elected back-bench MPs and one is a Labour peer elected by the Labour Peers Group.[61] Labour peers are also entitled to attend the departmental committees of the PLP.

---

[59] P Norton, 'The Organization of Parliamentary Parties' in SA Walkland (ed), *The House of Commons in the Twentieth Century* (Oxford, Clarendon Press, 1979) 7–68.

[60] L Minkin, *The Blair Supremacy: A study in the politics of Labour's party management* (Manchester, Manchester University Press, 2014) 416.

[61] Minkin, *Blair Supremacy* (n 60), 406.

A similar though not identical position exists in the Conservative Party. The 1922 Committee comprises all Conservative private members in the House of Commons, that is, all MPs bar the Leader in Opposition and all back-bench MPs when in Government, though ministers may now attend as observers.[62] In 1969, it was agreed that, as a means of strengthening links with Conservative peers, two peers should be invited to attend meetings. The practice has since developed of any Conservative peer who wishes to attend may do so. There are few who attend on a regular basis, though an important meeting, such as an address by the party leader, may draw a good number. The practice has also developed of the chairman of the Association of Conservative Peers (ACP) giving a short report at each 1922 Committee meeting on what is happening in the Lords and a member of the executive of the 1922 Committee giving a brief report at the start of each weekly meeting of the ACP.

When the 1922 Committee decided in the 2015–17 Parliament to resuscitate party committees, which had been active in the period from the 1920s to the 1990s, one notable innovation was to appoint peers as vice-chairs of the committees. The executive of the ACP nominated the peers who were to serve. The process of appointing the committees was a slow one, delayed by the creation of new Government Departments (which the party committees shadowed) and it was not until the Parliament returned in 2017 that the creation of the committees got under way.

Liberal Democrat peers may also attend meetings of the Parliamentary Liberal Party. The difference between the Liberal Democrats and the other parties is that the party's peers outnumber the MPs, notably so in the Parliament returned in 2015. Under the coalition Government of 2010–15, the parliamentary party created back-bench party committees, each co-chaired by an MP and a peer, in order to ensure the party retained a distinctive voice, with the chairs able to express a party view.

Party organisation is a means of facilitating contact between members in the two Houses, enabling them to share concerns from a party perspective, though also keeping them abreast of developments in the other House. There is, though, an obvious bias in that many peers have previously sat in the House of Commons. They are thus are more aware of the practices and activities of the Commons than is the case with MPs, who—with one exception in the period from 2001 to 2015— have no experience of sitting in the Lords.[63]

Other than through party meetings, MPs and peers of the same party mix also informally, not least through dining and other social outlets. Former MPs

---

[62] P Norton, *The Voice of the Backbenchers. The 1922 Committee: the first 90 years, 1923–2013* (London, Conservative History Group, 2013) 37–40.

[63] The exception was John Thurso, Liberal Democrat MP for Caithness, Sutherland and Easter Ross (2001–15) who had sat in the Lords as Viscount Thurso until excluded under the House of Lords Act 1999. Following his defeat in the 2015 general election, he returned to the Lords as an elected hereditary peer.

enjoy certain dining rights and access to certain Member-only facilities in the Commons.

C. Social Space[64]

Formal space essentially constitutes space occupied by the chamber and committees, governed by formal rules and constituting a recognised and usually recorded part of parliamentary proceedings. It may also be taken to extend to all-party groups and parliamentary party organisation in that these encompass activities that are formally scheduled, have officers and with these officers having some recognition for parliamentary and party purposes. None of these characteristics apply in the context of social space.

Social space is not governed by formal rules and minutes and is where contact between members and between members and others (members of the other House, staff, and the public) is informal, but contact nonetheless that can affect parliamentary behaviour. The methodological problem is that it is not measurable, but it is important for socialisation into the institution, for information exchange, and for lobbying. That information exchange and lobbying can take place between members of both Houses.

Social space has always been important. There has always been space that has been exclusive to Members—in the Commons, for example, the Members' tea room, the smoking room, and the Members' dining room. In the Lords, there is the Bishop's Bar and the Long Table in the dining room. These spaces have been important for political discourse and have featured in memoirs as the sites employed by political leaders to curry favour. Margaret Thatcher, for example, as Conservative party leader would occasionally descend on unsuspecting Conservative Members in the tea-room in order to find out their concerns. It could be argued that Edward Heath's neglect of the tea-room contributed to his loss of the Conservative party leadership in 1975.

The nature of the space has differed between the two Houses. MPs, unlike peers, normally dine on a party basis, so there is little interaction between parties. However, there is some interaction between members of the two Houses, in that peers who are former MPs enjoy dining rights and variously join with colleagues still sitting in the Commons.

Social interaction between members of both Houses has been facilitated by what is, in terms of social space, arguably the most significant change since the Palace was constructed in the 1850s. That is the opening in 2001 of a new parliamentary building, Portcullis House. This was important for three reasons. First, it meant

---

[64] This section derives largely from Philip Norton, presentation at the panel '"Designing for Democracy"—The Role of Architecture and Design in Parliamentary Buildings', 67th Political Studies Association Annual International Conference, University of Strathclyde, Glasgow, 11 April 2017.

that each MP had an individual office: it has offices for 213 members. Having individual offices limits interaction with other members, never mind members of the other House. Second, and offsetting this, it created a major social space in the form of the Atrium, a large space in the centre of the building, with attendant meeting and eating facilities. Furthermore, this space exists at the intersection of various parliamentary buildings, linking these building (1 Parliament Street, Norman Shaw North and South), with the rest of the Palace. MPs from these buildings pass through the Atrium on the way to the chamber. Third, and of primary relevance for our purposes, the social space is not confined to MPs. Peers and staff can use it; members and staff can use it to meet people from outside Parliament.

It is, in short, a major social space—crowded on most days of the parliamentary week—and one for which there was no previous parallel in the Palace of Westminster. There are meeting rooms and dining rooms, but nothing comparable to the Atrium in Portcullis House. It is a unique social space, facilitating interaction between members of both Houses as well as between members and others—staff, journalists, representatives of outside organisations, and members of the public. It has arguably transformed the dynamics of Parliament. It has shifted the emphasis from the Palace to Portcullis House. It is the place to be to find out what is going on and for social and unscheduled meetings, including between MPs and peers.

Such social interaction may have consequences for legislation and public policy. Chance or not so chance encounters may alert members of one House to particular developments in the other or lead to cooperation in pursuing or not pursuing a particular approach to a measure going through Parliament.

Informal interaction between officials in the two Houses may also prove helpful in keeping abreast of developments within Westminster. This may encompass chance encounters, but can take the form of attending seminars organised by organisations such as the Hansard Society. There is more structured interaction through the annual conference of the Study of Parliament Group, an organisation that draws together academics with an interest in Parliament (or parliaments) and clerks and other officials of the two Houses (and devolved legislatures). There is a sharing of information, not only between those working in the two Houses, but also with those outside who study the institution.

III. CONCLUSION

The formal relationship between the two Houses works largely on trust. The House of Lords is constrained by the Parliament Acts, but could cause major disruption to the legislative process if it were not prepared to work within non-statutory rules and practices. The conventions and practices derive from the Lords fulfilling the role, in many respects a self-ascribed role, of a complementary, rather than a competitor, chamber to the Commons.

The relationship is marked not only by restraint, but also by cooperation. Other than formal contact through sending messages, contact and cooperation have been enhanced over the years by the greater use of joint committees and through more informal contact through party structures and the enlargement of social space. The two chambers remain somewhat distant from one another, not only physically but also politically (no party enjoying an overall majority in the Lords) and in their procedures, but the interaction of MPs and peers has been enhanced in recent years. Each is still somewhat unfamiliar to the other, but arguably not to the extent that was the case in the mid-twentieth century.

7

Public Legal Information and Law-making in Parliament

JACK SIMSON CAIRD[1]

PUBLIC LEGAL INFORMATION (PLI) on Bills and statutory instruments (SIs) plays an increasingly significant role in the legislative process in Parliament. In the first edition of *Parliament and the Law*, published in 2013, Andrew Kennon's chapter on legal advice noted that Parliament's need for legal expertise was 'varied' and 'growing'.[2] This chapter examines the connected but distinct role of PLI within the specific context of the legislative process in Parliament.[3] When primary or delegated legislation is scrutinised in Parliament, it will be accompanied by a number of forms of PLI, produced by both lawyers and officials working for either Government or Parliament, to inform parliamentary debate. PLI refers to the disparate category of published material produced by Government and Parliament, which informs debate on the content of a legislative proposal. The primary examples of PLI covered are the Government's explanatory notes and memoranda, and Parliament's committee reports and library briefings.[4] Each has distinct origins and purposes, but conceived of as a collective they represent a form of inter-institutional communication that complements and underpins parliamentary debate on legislative proposals.

Legislative proposals are often complex, and their implications are not always clear from the face of the text itself. As Matthew Williams' research on the language of legislation has shown, legislation in the UK is 'increasingly indeterminate'.[5]

---

[1] All views expressed here are entirely my own. Thanks to Ben Yong, Matthew Purvis, Justin Leslie, Edward Wood, Gabrielle Appleby, Anna Olijnyk, Mary Liston and Grant Hoole for their comments—the usual disclaimers apply.

[2] A Kennon 'Legal Advice' in A Horne, D Oliver and G Drewry (eds), *Parliament and the Law* (Oxford, Hart Publishing, 2013) 137.

[3] There are other important examples of public legal information that inform Parliamentary debate, see for example in the context of the exercise of the war prerogative, where the Attorney-General released a version of his legal advice on the legality of military intervention ahead of the debate on intervention in Libya.

[4] Other materials published to accompany Bills and SIs that could qualify as PLI include Equality Assessments and Impact Assessments, and these are not addressed in detail here.

[5] M Williams, 'The Grammar of Politics: A Brief History of Legislative Language in Britain' (2017) 88 *Political Quarterly* 2, 255.

Further, Parliament only has limited time to debate and consider a proposal before it is enacted. These two factors make PLI a vital resource for those engaged in scrutiny in Parliament, as well as for any of the public that are interested in understanding the effect of what is proposed. PLI can provide a platform for the detail of the legal implications of a proposed legislative change, which might otherwise only be known within government, to be exposed at an early stage in the parliamentary process, which in turn can facilitate effective scrutiny and public engagement.

The first aim of this chapter is to outline the value and purpose of PLI to the legislative process in Parliament. The second is to consider how the nature and character of PLI is conditioned by the UK's shifting constitutional framework, and even more fundamentally by the relationship between politics and law in our political system. The first value of PLI is that it provides a platform for the legal implications of the proposal to be disseminated and examined in Parliament. PLI is in effect a means for a collaborative dialogue to take place between government and parliamentary officials that uses interpretive analysis to bring legal detail, particularly the Government's own legal analysis, out into the open so that it can be used by parliamentarians, and others, engaged in the scrutiny process. The second value of PLI is that it creates a publicly accessible resource that explains the content of a legislative proposal that can be used by any interested party, including the courts, civil society, the private sector and any member of the public, who might want to understand what the provisions are intended to achieve. Both of these benefits serve to highlight that the parliamentary legislative process is more than just a political forum whereby parliamentarians can seek to change the content of the law. While PLI can feature competitive disputes between Government and Parliament over the meaning of a proposal, it can also act as a collaborative exercise between Government and Parliament to publicly communicate important information about the legal effect of a change to the statute book.

A close examination of PLI provides a novel angle through which to consider the function of the law-making process in Parliament. The legislative process in Parliament is typically analysed through a primarily political lens. For example, Russell and Gover's major work on the legislative process, published in 2017, identifies the different forms of political influence on Bills within Parliament.[6] But it is also worthwhile to look at the legislative process through a legal lens, to see the parliamentary process as a mechanism for exploring and elucidating the legal effect of a legislative proposal. One of the functions of the parliamentary law-making process is to provide a public forum to inform all participants in the democratic process, including the public, of the legal implications of a proposal to change the law. Seen through this lens, the importance of PLI, which offers interpretive analysis on the content of a legislative proposal is more readily apparent.

---

[6] M Russell and D Gover, *Legislation at Westminster* (Oxford, Oxford University Press, 2017).

The primary purpose of PLI is clearly political, to enable debate and scrutiny, but its growing importance highlights the constitutional shifts that have made legal issues and 'legal politics', as Rick Rawlings has referred to it, increasingly prominent in Parliament.[7] For example, both devolution and human rights legislation have led to the inclusion of subject specific explanatory material for legislative proposals.

Scrutiny of Brexit legislation is likely to depend upon dialogue through PLI. For example, in March 2017, the House of Lords Committee on the Constitution called for the Government to produce an explanatory memorandum with a wealth of information to accompany SIs enacted in order to prepare for Brexit.[8] Each memorandum should include, for example, an explanation of how the instrument would alter the EU law to which it relates.[9] At the time of writing the arrangements for scrutinising Brexit SIs have not yet been finalised, but it is clear that the complexity of many of the SIs, and the limited time to examine them, will mean that the nature of the PLI supplied will be significant.

A final introductory point is that the role of PLI in the legislative process in Parliament is connected to how it is treated by the courts. Parliamentary privilege, a fundamental principle of the UK's constitution, limits the courts' ability to use PLI, and the broader parliamentary record, as a means of determining questions of statutory interpretation. In many other democracies, notably the United States and Belgium, for example, the judiciary regularly use legislative history, including explanatory materials produced and parliamentary debate, to inform questions of statutory and constitutional interpretation.[10] In constitutional contexts where parliamentary sovereignty does not apply, and courts review the constitutionality of legislation, there is greater incentive for the courts to use this material to inform their interpretive judgements.

The first section of this chapter examines the Government's explanatory notes and memoranda for both primary and secondary legislation. This material is the main form of PLI in the legislative process, and is widely used by those engaged in scrutiny. The second section consider Parliament's primary forms of public legal information: committee reports on bills and library briefings. This parliamentary material serves a number of functions, of which providing information on the content of a Bill is just one. Seen as a form of PLI, it represents an alternative to the Government's interpretive analysis of a bill, which highlights its constitutional

---

[7] R Rawlings, 'Review, revenge and retreat' (2005) 68 *Modern Law Review* 378, 409.

[8] The House of Lords Select Committee on the Constitution, 'The "Great Repeal Bill" and delegated powers', 2016–17, HL 123, para 102.

[9] ibid.

[10] For the United States see L Eig, 'Statutory Interpretation: General Principles and Recent Trends', Congressional Research Paper (2011) 43–46; WN Eskridge, *Dynamic Statutory Interpretation* (Cambridge, Harvard University Press, 1994) 205; JR Siegel, 'The Use of Legislative History in a System of Separate Powers' (2000) 53 *Vand. L Rev* 1457; for Belgium see P Popelier and J De Jaegere, 'Evidence-based judicial review of legislation in divided states: the Belgian case' (2016) 4 *The Theory and Practice of Legislation* 2, 187.

significance. The third section is a case study on the discussion of PLI in the judicial review proceedings in *Miller*.[11] The fourth and final section draws out the main constitutional values of PLI to the legislative process. The legislative process is more than just an opportunity to amend legislation. The exposure to parliamentary scrutiny is also an opportunity for an interpretive dialogue that enables the implications of a legislative proposal to be explored and subject to public debate.

I. THE GOVERNMENT'S PLI

The explanatory notes and memoranda supplied by Government that accompany Bills and SIs are the main sources of information, beside the text of the proposal itself, available to participants in the legislative process and the public on the legal effect of the proposed change to the law. For primary and secondary legislation these are written by the government department responsible for the bill. The notes to a bill are printed by the House in which the bill is introduced, and published alongside the bill and revised when the bill reaches the other House. The timing and provenance of these notes and memorandum means those engaged in scrutiny, and those responsible for authoring Parliament's PLI, read the notes with the bill to assist in their understanding of its legal effect. This means that this material has the potential to exert significant influence over how the content of a Bill is understood. In the case of most provisions, if not the vast majority, the explanatory material produced by the Government will not change how the text of the proposal is understood. However, when there is some interpretive uncertainty over the legal implications of a provision, any additional information produced by the Government on the thinking behind the detail can prove influential.

Constitutional legislation often contains important provisions with interpretive ambiguity. In such situations the explanatory material represents an opportunity for the Government to offer some clarity and direction over how it intends the provision to work in practice. A prominent example of such a provision is section 2(4) of the European Communities Act 1972 (ECA). The provision was central to the 1972 Act's scheme of enabling the supremacy of EU law over UK law in domestic courts. However, Danny Nicol argues that when then the provision was being considered by Parliament, very few parliamentarians appeared to be aware of the constitutional significance of the provision. According to Nicol, this was in part attributable to the fact that 'Parliament was ill served by Government and by Whitehall's army of lawyers'.[12] Nicol argues that the Government could have informed parliamentarians on the constitutional implications of the ECA, but instead the Government were 'more concerned to "get their way" on EEC

---

[11] *R (Miller) v Secretary of State for Exiting the European Union* [2016] EWHC 2768 (Admin); *R (on the application of Miller and another) v Secretary of State for Exiting the European Union* [2017] UKSC 5.
[12] D Nicol, *EC Membership and the Judicialisation of British Politics* (Oxford, Oxford University Press, 2001) 256.

membership than furnish MPs with a realistic assessment of the constitutional shape of things to come'.[13] At the time when the ECA was enacted, the Government did not make explanatory notes available to MPs or the public. Even if it had, this would not necessarily have made the constitutional implications clear. The broader point is that the Government is not under a formal duty to present impartial analysis of its own legislation, and its account of a Bill does not always provide parliamentarians with a balanced perspective on its legal implications.

Nicol's criticisms of the passage of the ECA do not map on to how Parliament examines major constitutional bills today. The introduction of explanatory notes is one reason, but arguably the most important change has been the creation of subject specialist parliamentary committee charged with legislative scrutiny. These committees enable a dialogue to occur between the executive and legislative branches on the detail of a Bill, and this has prompted developments in how the Government presents explanatory notes and memorandums. Whereas in 1972 the Government's justification for the detail of a bill, and the legal advice that lay behind it, could only be extracted through parliamentary debate, today the presence of explanatory notes and the demands of parliamentary committees means that before a debate is held a considerable amount of detail on a legislative proposal is available for those engaged in scrutiny.

The significance of this material, and the insight it can provide into the Government's approach to particular provision, must be seen in the context of opacity of the internal legal procedures within Government that lead to legislative proposals being put before Parliament. So while government's approach to explanatory material on legislation has changed since 1972, it remains fiercely committed to the constitutional convention that the legal advice obtained from the Law Officers on legislation is confidential. The Ministerial Code states:

> The fact that the Law Officers have advised or have not advised and the content of their advice must not be disclosed outside Government without their authority.

If a Bill raises issues of constitutional or legal complexity, a legal opinion from the Law Officers is almost certain to have been sought. This advice will complement and inform the memorandum on legal and constitutional issues that is prepared for ministers for every Bill.[14] The Cabinet Office's *Guide to Making Legislation* states that for each Bill a legal issues memorandum is produced for the Cabinet's Public Bill Committee. This memorandum is likely to contain content based on internal legal advice on any complex constitutional issues, for example ECHR compatibility. This memorandum is not published.

As the constitution has changed and become more legally complex and multi-layered, through, for example, devolution and the Human Rights Act 1998, the importance of the Law Officers' advice and the legal memorandum has, in terms of external justification of the Bill, arguably grown. However, the UK Government's

---

[13] ibid.
[14] Cabinet Office, 'Guide to Making Legislation' (2017) 3.23.

default position is that its own legal advice on legislation should remain private. The result is that much of the debate on the constitutionality of legislation is, by contrast to other constitutional systems, largely internalised within Government, in what Hazell has referred to as 'private public law'.[15] This contrasts with systems elsewhere, for example in New Zealand, where the Attorney-General provides a detailed statement on the Human Rights compatibility of a Bill to Parliament.[16] The UK Government argues that confidentiality is necessary 'because of the importance of the government being able to consult its most senior legal advisers without fear that either the advice itself, or the fact that the advice was requested will be disclosed'.[17] This convention means that it is not possible to know when the Government's internal legal advice is being disseminated through PIL or elsewhere. Nevertheless it is at least arguable that the current arrangements, whereby various committees request particular information on a Bill, and the standardised use of PLI, provide greater opportunity for that the substance of that advice to be made available for public debate.

This section discusses the explanatory notes and memoranda produced by Government and looks at some examples to illustrate their value to the legislative process. The value of this material to a particular debate will depend on the nature of the Bill and the approach taken to the notes themselves. The variety of approaches taken to the notes has been criticised, and recently the Government has sought to improve the quality of explanatory notes through the Cabinet Office's Good Law initiative.[18] In the context of the notes and memoranda for secondary legislation, the discussion focuses on the role of parliamentary committees in the development of memoranda.

A. Explanatory Notes

In 1997 the Select Committee on Modernisation agreed a proposal for 'Explanatory Notes'.[19] They recommended that they should be 'neutral in tone' and 'not try to promote the Bill and the policy underlying it'.[20] The notes themselves have no formal legal status. On the first page, they come with a warning that the notes 'do not form part of the Bill and have not been endorsed by Parliament'. Instead their

---

[15] R Hazell, 'Out of Court: Why have the courts played no role in resolving devolution disputes in the United Kingdom' (2007) 37 *The Journal of Federalism* 4, 589; C McCorkindale and J Hiebert, 'Vetting Acts of Scottish Parliament for Legislative Competence' (2017) *Edinburgh Law Review Hazell* (forthcoming).

[16] See A Geddis, '"Declarations of Inconsistency" under the New Zealand Bill of Rights Act 1990' *UK Const L* blog (19 June 2017) (available at https://ukconstitutionallaw.org)); Section 7 of the New Zealand Bill of Rights Act 1990 and Standing Order 261 of the Standing Orders of the House of Representatives.

[17] *HM Treasury v The Information Commissioner & Anor* [2009] EWHC 1811.

[18] www.gov.uk/guidance/good-law.

[19] Select Committee on Modernisation of the House of Commons, Second Report 1997–98; D Greenberg (ed) *Craies on Legislation* (London, Sweet & Maxwell, 2017) 466–67.

[20] Greenberg, *Craies on Legislation* (n 19) 466–67.

purpose is limited to outlining what the Bill will mean in practice, setting out the policy background and identifying how the Bill will change other statutes.

In basic terms the value of the notes is that they can use forms of communication that the Bill cannot.[21] As Sir Christopher Jenkins QC noted in his evidence to the House of Commons Select Committee on Modernisation of the House, 'a Bill is not there to inform … its sole reason to exist is to change the law'.[22] The nature of legislation constrains its ability to prioritise clarity.[23] A more cynical view for this approach was put forward by Lord Hewart, who suggested in 1939 that Bills were drafted to be deliberately complex so as not to 'expose too large a surface areas for possible attack' in the Commons.[24] He added 'to be intelligible is to be found out, and to be found out is to be defeated'.[25] Even if such a cynical view is rejected, it is the case that legislation is often difficult to understand, even for expert readers. This makes the explanatory notes a potentially vital mechanism for the transparency of Government policy; accountability in terms of enabling parliamentary and public scrutiny; but also for promoting the rule of law by enhancing the clarity and accessibility of the law.[26]

Explanatory notes protest that they are not authoritative but, as Greenberg points out, that somewhat masks their significance.[27] Their importance is reflected in the fact that both the courts and those that have to interpret the Bill during its passage through Parliament, rely on them as a 'promising source of background material in the context of which the legislative intention may be deduced'.[28] The courts have clearly stated that the explanatory notes can be used to inform questions of statutory interpretation. The leading case is on this matter is *Westminster City Council v National Asylum Support*, where Lord Steyn provided a detailed analysis on the role of explanatory notes.[29] Lord Steyn outlines that the notes are 'always admissible aids to construction'.[30] Lord Steyn adds that Explanatory Notes 'will sometimes be more informative and valuable than reports of the Law Commission or advisory committees, Government green or white papers, and the like'.[31] This is because the 'connection of Explanatory Notes with the shape of the proposed legislation is closer' than other admissible aids to construction.[32] Lord Steyn then turned to what the notes could not be used for:

> What is impermissible is to treat the wishes and desires of the Government about the scope of the statutory language as reflecting the will of Parliament. The aims of the

---

[21] Greenberg (n 19) 468.

[22] Select Committee on Modernisation of the House of Commons, Second Report 1997–98, Memorandum by First Parliamentary Counsel, para 9.

[23] D Greenberg, *Laying Down the Law* (London, Sweet & Maxwell, 2011) 228.

[24] Lord Hewart, *The New Despotism* (London, Benn, 1929) 77–78.

[25] ibid.

[26] Greenberg, *Laying Down the Law* (n 23) 227.

[27] Greenberg (n 23) 227.

[28] Greenberg (n 23) 227.

[29] *Westminster City Council v National Asylum Support Service* [2002] UKHL 38, 5–6.

[30] ibid.

[31] ibid.

[32] ibid.

Government in respect of the meaning of clauses as revealed in Explanatory Notes cannot be attributed to Parliament. The object is to see what is the intention expressed by the words enacted.[33]

This approach reflects the constitutional status of the notes, and in particular the fact that even if they are published by one of the Houses of Parliament, they are not subject to parliamentary approval, nor part of the legislative text, and so they should not be treated as indicative of Parliament's intention. From a separation of powers perspective, the courts' recognition of the notes' constitutional status is critical. Explanatory Notes are indicative of what the Governments thinks the law means, and only the courts have the constitutional authority to determine the meaning of the law. The executive branch should not be able to dictate the meaning of the law, and the way it is interpreted in the courts, through a document that is not scrutinised or voted on by Parliament.[34] However, reliable evidence of what Government sought to achieve through its legislation is valuable for the tasks facing the courts. As Steyn implies, Explanatory Notes are the most reliable element of an Act's parliamentary history. This can partly be explained by the fact that they are authored by the civil servants that are directly responsible for devising the content. The critical point is that their relevance is understood in the context of their constitutional status. If the courts were to rely on them extensively this could make the authors of the notes reluctant to include detail that could influence the courts in the way in which Steyn describes.[35] This in turn could make them less useful for their primary audience: those engaged in parliamentary scrutiny of legislative proposals. Alternatively, government lawyers might take the opportunity to provide examples of how a provision would work. One can see that for delegated powers, this might be helpful for both parliamentary scrutiny and the courts.

Even without the risk of intervention from the courts, writing good Explanatory Notes is challenging. The notes exist within, and reflect, a delicate relationship between Government and Parliament at the heart of the legislative process. Rules in the House of Commons prevent overtly political or justificatory language from being used.[36] If the notes simply paraphrase or describe the text they risk falling victim to Greenberg's criticism that they are 'bland' and 'pointlessly repetitive'.[37] If they add too much context and background they might risk proving a distraction

---

[33] ibid; *R (S) v Chief Constable of South Yorkshire Police* [2004] 1 WLR 2196, 2199, HL; Lord Steyn stated that the notes are more 'immediate and valuable material' than other material regularly used by courts, such as Green Papers, and are therefore to be considerable admissible aids of construction for a statute.

[34] A Kavanagh, 'Pepper v Hart and Matters of Constitutional Principle' (2005) 120 *Law Quarterly Review* 98.

[35] *Solar Century Holdings Ltd & Ors v Secretary of State for Energy & Climate Change* [2014] EWHC 3677.

[36] *Erskine May: Parliamentary Practice*, 24th edn (London, LexisNexis, 2011); Greenberg, *Laying Down the Law* (n 23) 227–34.

[37] Greenberg (n 23) 229.

from the text of the Bill. The notes cannot directly engage in political debate, but nor are they independent or impartial. Adding useful context within this analytical frame is a difficult balance. Greenberg cites the notes to the Gambling Act 2005 as an example of how they should be drafted.[38] They examine the underlying intention of the social and legal background to the changes made by the legislation.[39] These notes, he argues, are the 'exception rather than the norm'.[40] Greenberg explains that such an approach requires significant investment of time and resources. Once the Bill is enacted, the Government has more time to develop the notes, and is not constrained by the same requirements that apply to the Commons' Public Bill Office.

The Office of Parliamentary Counsel, as part of the Good Law project, undertook a review of Explanatory Notes in 2013. A survey of users of the notes highlighted some suggestions for improvement. Those surveyed asked for the notes to include more practical examples of how the law will work once enacted, information on 'why' the law was passed, rather than just what it will do, and stated that the notes are not useful when they simply paraphrase the legislation.[41] Demands for both more contextual information and explanation of purpose of the provisions highlights the effect of the constraints that apply to Explanatory Notes. It is understandable that users of the notes, parliamentarians and parliamentary officials might all wish for notes that reveal more of the Government's thinking that lies behind the provisions, as this might make it easier to understand and scrutinise the legislation. However, this is not necessarily sufficient to persuade the Government. The courts' willingness to use the notes as interpretive aids, the additional resources required to provide useful explanatory material, and the potential to increase the strength of scrutiny all point to why the Government might not want to provide more informative notes.

An additional difficulty is how such information can be provided, while at the time maintaining a neutral tone that does not 'sell' the Bill. Providing more detail and addressing more 'why' questions could make it harder to maintain a technical and neutral tone. The reasons for certain provisions may be intrinsically political, for example based on a manifesto commitment, and referring to, or elaborating on, the political context may not deemed be appropriate for Explanatory Notes.

---

[38] Gambling Act 2005, Explanatory Notes.

[39] Greenberg (n 23) 229.

[40] ibid.

[41] The Office of Parliamentary Counsel piloted a new format for Explanatory Notes in 2014–15. This new format includes headings on policy background and legal background. They also experimented with different ways of presenting the territorial extent and application of a Bill. In the response to the consultation, the Office of Parliamentary Counsel noted the positive feedback on the headings on policy and legal background, and decided to adopt it for 2015. The consultation response also decided that extent and application should be presented in tabular form, and that the commentary on each provision should include a sentence on territoriality, Office of Parliamentary Counsel, 'Explanatory Notes Pilot: Office Of The Parliamentary Counsel Response To Consultation' (2014) 3.

It is possible to address 'why' a provision is needed without being overtly political, but it is not straightforward. In a broader sense, the need to keep internal legal advice confidential is another potential barrier to a more open approach. Revealing the detailed legal analysis that lies behind a provision might create a risk that internal legal advice becomes politicised. This could then have a negative effect on the way that such advice is provided. Explanatory Notes operate within a complex web of constitutional and practical limits, and this makes a more expansive approach difficult to achieve.

One example of a set of notes that engages, albeit briefly, with its constitutional context, was the notes prepared for the Fixed-term Parliaments Bill.[42] The notes outlined some of the constitutional effect of the provisions, which is not necessarily apparent from the text of the Bill itself. The Fixed-term Parliaments Bill was designed to introduce fixed days for parliamentary general elections, and to convert what were at the time prerogative powers, to call an election and to dissolve Parliament, into statutory form. The text of the Bill did not explicitly engage with the impact on the residual status of the prerogative powers, the question of whether they are abolished or whether are in abeyance and can be revived. The notes that accompanied the Bill when it was introduced stated that 'The Queen does not retain any residual power to dissolve Parliament'.[43] This indicated that the power is abolished and is not in abeyance. It could be argued that this follows logically from the statement in the text of the Bill that 'Parliament cannot otherwise be dissolved'. The notes published to accompany the Act, are notably more explicit on the impact on the prerogative than the notes that accompanied the Bill:

> The prerogative power to dissolve Parliament before the maximum five-year period was exercised by Her Majesty, conventionally on the advice of the Prime Minister. This prerogative power was abolished by this Act.[44]

During the debate on the Bill in Parliament, the question of whether the prerogative could be reinstated was used by the Government to argue against an amendment tabled in the Lords. In the Commons, the Minister responsible for the Bill said:

> They clearly assume that it would be possible for the Prime Minister to regain the option of asking Her Majesty the Queen to dissolve Parliament, but it is entirely possible that, by failing to provide for the prerogative power to dissolve to be reinstated, they have left matters in the position where neither the rules in the Bill nor the previous prerogative powers can have effect. Indeed, it is worth asking whether it is possible to reinstate a prerogative power that has been removed.[45]

---

[42] Fixed-Term Parliaments Bill Explanatory Notes 64—EN 55/1.
[43] ibid.
[44] Fixed-Term Parliaments Act 2011 Explanatory Notes.
[45] HC Deb, 8 September 2011, col 582.

There is a live debate on whether repealing the Act would revive the prerogative.[46] The Conservative manifesto for the 2017 general election included a commitment to repeal the Act.[47] The notes' statement that the prerogative has been abolished could influence political debates over the options for repeal. They could also prove relevant should the impact of the Act come before the courts. Moreover, the statement demonstrates the potential of notes to an Act to be used as mechanism for suggesting how the legislation should be interpreted.

The notes to the Bill also made direct reference to the proposal's political origins. In the section on the background, the notes refer to 'The Coalition: our programme for government' and provides an extract that refers to the original plans to 'provide for dissolution if 55% or more of the House votes in favour'.[48] That is as far as the notes go to refer to the political context. During parliamentary debate, much of the focus was on whether it was appropriate to enact constitutional change in order to provide stability for the particular circumstances facing the coalition Government formed after the 2010 general election. This minimalist approach to political context ensures that the notes are not the subject of debate. Going any further might prove incompatible with the need to maintain a 'neutral' tone.

The Explanatory Notes for the European Union Referendum Bill interpreted the Bill's constitutional effect in a narrow literal sense.[49] The political restrictions on the notes appear to frame the way in which the legal implications are presented. The notes state that the origin of the proposal was the Queen's Speech in 2015, and that is as far as they go in terms of outlining the policy background. In terms of legal background, the notes do not refer to the wider constitutional context, and simply reflect the fact that the content of the Bill was exclusively concerned with providing the legal machinery for the referendum to take place. The potential legal impact of the outcome of the referendum was not referred to by the notes. In the context of the highly charged political debate on the UK's membership of the EU, engagement with matters beyond those strictly engaged with by the Bill would risk creating a distorting impression of the aims of the Bill. The minimalist approach in this context serves to leave the maximum space for Members to determine the political implications of the text of the Bill. The risk of such an approach is that some of the constitutional and legal implications of the Bill, which may politically controversial, are not addressed by Members as their attention is not drawn them by the Government. This risk is one that is in keeping with the political character of the UK constitution. The absence of a codified constitution and the presence

---

[46] See A Horne and R Kelly, 'Prerogative Powers and the Fixed-term Parliaments Act' *UK Const L* blog (19 November 2014); R Craig, 'Zombie Prerogatives Should Remain Decently Buried: Replacing the Fixed-term Parliaments Act 2011 (Part 1)' *UK Const L* blog (24 May 2017); R Craig, 'Zombie Prerogatives Should Remain Decently Buried: Replacing the Fixed-term Parliaments Act 2011 (Part 2)' *UK Const L* blog (25 May 2017).

[47] The Conservative Party Manifesto 2017.

[48] Fixed-Term Parliaments Bill Explanatory Notes 64—EN 55/1, para 6.

[49] European Union Referendum Bill Explanatory Notes Bill 2—EN 56/1.

of parliamentary sovereignty can be defended on the basis that they ensure that it is elected representatives that set the agenda of political debate, and this fits with a minimalist approach to Explanatory Notes. Changes to the constitution, particularly devolution, human rights and Brexit combined with an increasing focus on constitutional issues through parliamentary committees, has led to a countervailing pressure to include more legal analysis in the Explanatory Notes. Balancing these pressures has led to innovation.

B. Explanatory Memoranda for Bills

In order to supplement the explanatory material provided by the note, and particularly in order to meet demands of parliamentary committees, the Government prepares memorandums for particular committees on particular aspects of Bills. As chapter 10 notes, memoranda enable the Government to provide legal analysis for the Joint Committee on Human Rights (JCHR) that might be considered too argumentative in tone for the Explanatory Notes.[50] As these are published by the Government rather than by either House, there are able to contain more justificatory material, which committees find particularly useful for evaluating the substance of the change to the law that is proposed. As Horne and Conway note, these memoranda are a sign that human rights scrutiny has become more ingrained in the legislative process, and offers Government an opportunity to demonstrate that it has engaged with the human rights implications of changes proposed, which can make for a smoother passage in both Parliament and the courts.[51]

As well as for the JCHR, the Government provides a memorandum on the delegated powers in a Bill for the House of Lords Delegated Powers and Regulatory Reform Committee (DPRRC). The Cabinet Office Guide to Making Legislation explains that it should justify the inclusion of any delegated powers and address any concerns that might be raised.[52] The case for powers to enact secondary legislation, even if it does not engage in substantive political questions in the same way as human rights, requires justificatory language not suitable for Explanatory Notes. The Guide also suggests that special focus should be given to Henry VIII powers, which reflects the level of attention given to these powers by the DPRRC and the Lords.[53]

The Guide advises those responsible for the Memorandum to consult the DPRRC's guidance. This is evidence of the value of a pro-active approach to parliamentary scrutiny, as it enables the Committee to influence the legislative process 'upstream' in Government.[54] The DPRRC's guidance covers procedure

---

[50] See ch 10.
[51] ibid.
[52] Cabinet Office, Guide to Making Legislation (2017) 3.15.
[53] ibid.
[54] D Oliver, 'Improving the Scrutiny of Bills: the Case for Standards and Checklists' [2006] *Public Law* 219, 243.

and practical matters, such as how the memorandum should be formatted. In terms of substance the Guidance outlines that the Memorandum should:

— fully explain the purpose of the power
— describe why the matter that is the subject of the power has been left to delegated legislation rather than included in the bill
— fully explain the choice of parliamentary scrutiny procedure provided for each power; and, if there is no scrutiny, the justification for its absence.[55]

In terms of explanation, the memorandum should justify why the power is needed, and why primary legislation cannot be used, why the breadth of the power is required and why it has been conferred on a particular person.[56] The Guidance also outlines principles that it applies to powers, including: that each Henry VIII power must be identified; and if any procedure other than affirmative is used for a Henry VIII power then special justification is needed; justification for the adoption of a 'skeleton bill structure'; and if a power enables the setting of a criminal penalty by secondary legislation.[57] These principles demand a level of justification that goes further than the nature of Explanatory Notes would allow. This material accelerates the scrutiny process, as it enables the Committee to scrutinise the Government's reasoning for a power. Without the Memorandum, the Committee would not be able to probe the reasons for including the powers *before* the second reading of the Bill in the Lords. Getting the timing right is an important element of effective legislative scrutiny, and in this context it means getting as much relevant information as possible at the disposal of parliamentarians as early as possible.

Scrutiny of the memoranda is a regular feature of the DPRRC's scrutiny reports. The Committee's report of the Investigatory Powers Bill, published in 2016, stated that a particular power was 'inappropriate' as it enabled ministers to make changes to future enactments.[58] The Committee's conclusion was underpinned by their dissatisfaction with the Government's justification for the breadth of the power in the memorandum. The DPRRC argued that a power that applies to future legislation needs 'a convincing case to be made'.[59] The memorandum stated that the power was necessary 'because other Bills before Parliament at the same time as this Bill touch upon the powers and public authorities covered by this Bill' and as such this power was needed to enable consequential amendments that might be needed when those Bills are enacted.[60] The Memorandum also claimed that the

---

[55] House of Lords Delegated Powers and Regulatory Reform Committee Guidance for Departments on the role and requirements of the Committee, July 2014, 28.

[56] ibid.

[57] ibid, 36.

[58] Delegated Powers and Regulatory Reform Committee, Second Report of Session 2016–17, 8 July 2016, HL Paper 21, para 16.

[59] ibid, 14.

[60] Delegated Powers and Regulatory Reform Committee Investigatory Powers Bill Memorandum By The Home Office (2014) 124, 125.

power was limited and could not be used to amend legislation 'at any point in the future'.[61] The DPRRC found that this was not satisfactory:

> We found this paragraph difficult to understand. It seems to be saying that, because the scope of the power is limited to making consequential provisions, in practice the power will be exercised shortly after enactment and not at any more distant point of time in the future. We are not convinced that this is necessarily right. But even if it were right, it suggests that the Department itself considers that the power to amend future enactments is not needed.[62]

This illustrates the form of engagement facilitated by the memoranda, and in particular the use of justificatory language in relation to matters of legal and constitutional significance. This dialogue and difference of opinion between the branches on the detail within the Bill provides resources that can be taken up during committee and report stage in the Lords through amendments.[63] In this case the Government accepted the case to restrict the scope of the power and agreed, in their response to the report, to bring forward amendments to reflect the Committee's position.[64]

The Committee's report on the Transparency of Lobbying, Non-party Campaigning and Trade Union Administration Bill 2014 was extremely critical, stating that the 'very poor quality of the memorandum' had impeded their scrutiny of the powers.[65] The Hansard Society has identified the poor quality of memoranda as a barrier to MPs and peers engaging with scrutiny of delegated powers.[66]

Explanatory memoranda enable the Government to include argumentative content on the detail of a Bill, which might otherwise not be covered until the committee stage, at an earlier stage in the parliamentary process. In practice, however, the memoranda do not always meet their potential in terms of facilitating scrutiny and engagement.

C. Explanatory Notes and Memoranda for SIs

Explanatory Notes and Memoranda are also supplied for SIs. The notes are, like Explanatory Notes for Bills, authored by the relevant government department responsible for the instruments. Again, like primary legislation, they highlight that they are not themselves part of the law: each note is preceded by the words 'This note is not part of the Order'. However, unlike with primary legislation, they are appended to the instrument itself. In the context of delegated legislation, where there is limited opportunity for debate and the substance is often particularly

---

[61] ibid, 125.

[62] Delegated Powers and Regulatory Reform Committee (n 60) para 15.

[63] For highlights of recent amendments see Delegated Powers and Regulatory Reform Committee, Twenty Third Report of Session 2016–17, 16 March 2017, HL Paper 143.

[64] Delegated Powers and Regulatory Reform Committee, Fourth Report of Session 2016–17, 9 September 2016, HL Paper 43, App 1: Investigatory Powers Bill: Government Response.

[65] House of Lords, Delegated Powers and Regulatory Reform Committee, Seventh Report of the Session 2014–2015, Special Report: Quality of Delegated Powers Memoranda, HL Paper 39, 36–37.

[66] J Blackwell and R Fox, 'Devil in detail: Parliament and delegated legislation' (2015) 214.

technical, the explanatory material produced by Government plays a major role in facilitating parliamentary scrutiny.

In the context of Brexit there is an increasing interest in Parliament's scrutiny of SIs. As soon as the Government confirmed that Brexit would require a large number of SIs to be enacted in a short timeframe, this prompted debate over whether Parliament would have the capacity to rise to the challenge of scrutinising these changes. As noted above, the Lords' Constitution Committee highlighted that the content of the Explanatory Memoranda would have to be tailored to the specific demands of Brexit.

The Government's use of delegated legislation, and Parliament's perceived inability to scrutinise it effectively, has long prompted criticism of a shift in power away from Parliament towards the Government, from Lord Hewart's claim in 1929 that reliance on delegated legislation was evidence of a 'new despotism',[67] to Lord Hailsham's 'elective dictatorship' in 1976,[68] to Lord Judge's claim in 2016 that every Henry VIII power is a 'self-inflicted blow' that boosts the power of the executive.[69] Part of this argument is that Parliament is not equipped to scrutinise the scale of delegated legislation that is produced by Government.

In 2017, Parliament has in place a complex set of procedures to scrutinise delegated legislation, and PLI forms an integral part of those arrangements. PLI arguably plays a bigger role in Parliament's scrutiny of delegated legislation than it does in relation to primary legislation. Delegated legislation is often characterised as being technical in nature. This is in part because delegated legislation can only be made when a provision of primary legislation gives the Government an explicit power to do so. They are defined by the fact that they are restricted in scope, and this means that they are often concerned with the detailed regulations that implement a particular policy in a specific area. However, it is important to note that this narrow scope is not a barrier to political controversy, and delegated legislation can concern highly controversial policy changes in high-profile areas.[70] In part it is the number of instruments enacted, and the technical nature of language and procedures used that secures its position outside of the mainstream of politics. Page's major work on delegated legislation memorably characterised the process of enacting delegated legislation as 'politics in seclusion'.[71] Parliamentary scrutiny of delegated legislation is an opportunity, through both the notes and memoranda produced by Government, and the parliamentary reports produced by the JCSI and the Secondary Legislation Scrutiny Committee (SLSC) in response, to move issues out of obscurity and into the 'world of inter- and intraparty political conflict'.[72]

---

[67] Lord Hewart, *The New Despotism* (London, Benn, 1929).

[68] Lord Hailsham, *The Dilemma of Democracy* (London, Collins, 1978).

[69] Rt Hon Lord Judge, 'Ceding power to the Executive: the Resurrection of Henry VIII', King's College London lecture, 12 April 2016.

[70] Tax credits reference to article.

[71] E Page, *Governing by numbers: delegated legislation and everyday policy making* (Oxford, Hart Publishing, 2001).

[72] ibid, 175.

The technicality of the language of most SIs, and routine way in which they are produced, with little in the way of political attention, means that explanatory material can be a major factor in enhancing the transparency and accessibility of both the process and substance of delegated legislation. Explanatory material is central to the dialogue with committees, which in the absence of parliamentary debate, represent the principal sources of parliamentary scrutiny of delegated legislation.

The Explanatory Note appended to an instrument is normally a plain language description of the effect of an instrument. The note is neutral in tone. For similar reasons to those explored above in relation to primary legislation, both the JCSI and the SLSC rely on an Explanatory Memorandum, which supplements the note, as an integral part of their scrutiny.

There are two main forms of scrutiny of SIs in Parliament. The JCSI engages in technical scrutiny.[73] The Standing Orders set out the grounds under which it scrutinises SIs. These include 'defective drafting' and whether it is within the power in the parent act, as well a number of other technical grounds.[74] The House of Lords SLSC, by contrast, examines the merits of SIs. The relevant Standing Orders set out a number of grounds for its scrutiny including whether an instrument 'is politically or legally important or contains policy likely to be of interest to the House', and interestingly for the focus of this chapter whether the 'supporting material is inadequate in explaining the policy intention'.[75]

To inform scrutiny by both the JCSI and the SLSC, the Government publishes an explanatory memorandum for instruments laid before Parliament. The memorandum is published by the Government alongside the instrument and sets out information for both committees, including the purpose of the instrument, the policy background, and information on the vires of the instrument and whether it complies with the ECHR.

The JCSI uses the content of these memoranda in the analysis within their reports on instruments. In their report on the Non-Contentious Probate Fees Order 2017, a draft instrument, the Committee reported that 'if it is approved and made, there will be a doubt whether it is intra vires'.[76] The report notes that the memorandum stated that the change to fees to be made by the instrument was based on 'the need to make sure that Her Majesty's Court and Tribunal Service is properly funded'.[77] As a result, the JCSI asked, in correspondence, prior to the publication of the report, for further clarification as to whether the change was actually imposing a tax, which would be of doubtful vires. The Ministry of Justice

---

[73] It is composed of seven peers and five Members. Its staff includes seven advisory counsel (lawyers), four from the Commons and three from the Lords.

[74] House of Commons Standing Order No 151 and House of Lords Standing Order No 73.

[75] Greenberg (n 24) 351.

[76] Joint Committee on Statutory Instruments, Twenty-sixth Report of Session 2016–17, HL 152, HC 93-xxvi, para 1.4.

[77] Explanatory Memorandum to The Non-Contentious Probate Fees Order 2017, SI 2017, para 7.1.

supplied a further memorandum, appended to the JCSI's report, which set out in some detail their position that the order was within the powers allocated by the parent Acts. In the supplementary memorandum the Government advanced the view that there was a precedent of these powers being used to impose an analogous fee for issuing a money claim. The JCSI rejected this comparison:

> Applying for probate is not to be compared with the commencement of proceedings. A person can choose whether to litigate, and therefore whether to incur the fees payable on issuing a claim—which may be recoverable from the defendant if the case succeeds. In contrast, executors have to obtain probate to allow them to administer an estate, and the fee for doing so is not refundable. This is an administrative process, akin to the registration of a life event. Nobody applying for an uncontested probate would think for a moment that they were engaging in litigation.[78]

This form of interpretive analysis is central to the scrutiny undertaken by the JCSI, but is only possible as a result of the explanatory material supplied by Government. The publication of supplementary memoranda, as in this case, answering queries from the JCSI, enables the report to contain a thorough examination of the Government's position, which can then inform parliamentarians' view of the instrument. Further, this particular example highlights that the sort of technical scrutiny facilitated by PLI can engage matters of political controversy. As Page observed, the dividing line between scrutiny of legality and policy 'is not always a technical matter'.[79] It involves 'an interpretation of what Parliament intended when it passed the parent legislation'.[80] Questions of statutory interpretation are certainly questions of law, but as the practice of judicial review around the world shows, they also involves value judgments that engage with policy questions.

The SLSC has played a major role in demanding improvements in the quality of the explanatory memoranda on SIs. They describe their work as a 'news service to the House'. The scale of their work is enormous: they examine every instrument subject to a parliamentary procedure—around 1000 a year. The vast majority do not produce a comment, but to be able to identify those that do relies on explanatory material. Their guidance to departments is clear about why they need this material:

> The purpose of the EM is to provide members of Parliament and the public with a plain English, free-standing, explanation of the effect of the instrument and why it is necessary. It is not meant for lawyers, but to help people who may know nothing about the subject quickly to gain an understanding of the SI's intent and purpose. Legal explanations of the changes are already given in the Explanatory Note which form part of the actual instrument.[81]

---

[78] Joint Committee on Statutory Instruments (n 76) para 1.9.
[79] Page, *Governing by numbers* (n 71) 157.
[80] Page (n 71) 157.
[81] Guidance For Departments Submitting Statutory Instruments To The Secondary Legislation Scrutiny Committee (July 2016) 5.

This focus on material that is not legal highlights the value of the complementary division between the JCSI and the SLSC. The focus on the non-legal is particularly important for highlighting the political context which is so central to engaging parliamentarians and the public. The Guidance sets out a number of common faults with Explanatory Memoranda including 'Writing it like a press notice' and 'gaps in logic'.[82] The Committee has registered concerns over the consistency and quality of Explanatory Memoranda. The SLSC's complaints were such that the Procedure Committee added criticism of the Explanatory Materials to the SLSC's terms of reference.[83] During an evidence session on this matter in 2016, Chris Wormald, Head of Government Policy Profession and Permanent Secretary at the Department of Health, concluded after examining the approach to Explanatory Memoranda that the Government does not do enough to ensure a consistent level of quality.[84] Driving up the quality of the Explanatory Memoranda is one of the Committee's main contributions to the work of the House.

The Hansard Society has argued that the SLCS' lack of teeth, and the absence of political pressure, leaves the Committee in an 'attritional relationship with Whitehall', whereby the committee is engaged in constant to-and-fro with Government over the quality of memoranda.[85]

II. PARLIAMENT'S PLI

Parliament produces two main forms of PLI: committee reports on Bills; and briefing papers from the libraries of both Houses. While these are very different forms of PLI, they are united by the fact that they are parliamentary in origin. In a parliamentary system, whereby the legislative process is driven by the Government, and reliant upon close working between the executive and the legislative branches, distinctive parliamentary sources of material on legislative proposals can serve to bolster Parliament's contribution. The presence of such institutional support can enhance the ability of parliamentarians to delve into the detail of a proposal and ask the difficult questions that hold the Government to account.

A. Committee Reports

Committee reports on Bills are more than just information, as they represent a political output by a group of parliamentarians, but in practice they also serve to inform parliamentarians and the public about the substance of the

---

[82] ibid, 6–7.
[83] Blackwell and Fox, *Devil in detail* (n 66) 213.
[84] The Select Committee on Secondary Legislation Scrutiny Inquiry On The Quality Of Information Provided In Support Of Secondary Legislation Evidence, Session No 1, Tuesday 12 July 2016.
[85] Blackwell and Fox (n 66) 215.

proposed legislation. Their reports are not impartial or neutral but instead represent the view of the parliamentarians that sit on the committee in question. Their role is vital as it serves to create a political dialogue, between government and Parliament, outside of a strictly partisan context, on the detail in a Bill. The role of these committees is documented elsewhere,[86] and so I do not propose to describe their work in detail. Instead the aim in this short section is to highlight how their reports can serve as forms of PLI, and in particular how they do more than just support scrutiny within Parliament, but serve a broader purpose of producing a public record on the meaning of a legislative proposal.

Parliamentary committees have been the main drivers of the development of the PLI produced by government. Even if PLI is not a formalised part of the parliamentary process, in certain areas, for example scrutiny of secondary legislation, it has become central to how parliamentary scrutiny operates. On delegated legislation there is limited scope for parliamentary debate, and committees rely on a collaborative approach from Government to supply them with the material so that they can engage in a dialogue on the detail of what is proposed.

The role of these committees, in particular the JCHR, the DPPRC and the House of Lords Constitution Committee, make a major contribution to information available on a Bill to both parliamentarians and the public. The ability to issue reports on a Bill puts committees in a privileged position within the Parliament–Government dialogue. A conflict on the substance of a Bill can serve to publicise the content of a proposed change to the law. Reports on Bills enable a form of analysis that would not otherwise have the opportunity to be heard, as a speech in a debate does not provide the same type of opportunity to set out an analytical position on a Bill. Within a report, a committee is able to address the detail of a Bill using sources and evidence. Further, a report from a parliamentary committee can become a point of reference within parliamentary debate. This fills an important gap in legislative reasoning within Parliament.[87] The ability of a committee (through its clerks and advisers) to write what is effectively an 'essay' or 'judgment' on the constitutional effect of a Bill, means that Parliament has its own internal source of constitutional analysis and is not reliant on the Government or the views of individual parliamentarians. The availability of well-reasoned analysis from a respected parliamentary source creates an opportunity for those on the floor of either House respond by proposing amendments. Another feature is the prompting of Government responses.[88] It is normal practice for a committee report to

---

[86] A Horne and M Conway (Chapter 10); A Le Sueur and J Simson Caird, 'The House of Lords Select Committee on the Constitution' in A Horne, D Oliver and G Drewry (eds), *Parliament and the Law* (Oxford, Hart, 2013).

[87] M Tushnet, 'Interpretation in Legislatures and Courts; Incentives and Institutional Design' in R Bauman and T Kahana (eds), *The Least Examined Branch* (Cambridge, Cambridge University Press, 2006) 371–72.

[88] D Feldman, 'Parliamentary Scrutiny of Legislation and Human Rights' [2002] Public Law 323–348, 333.

prompt a direct Government response after the report is published.[89] The Government response often shows that those responsible for the Bill, within the Bill team, have contributed to the analysis. Prompting such a response serves to create an additional source of PLI, which is likely to raise the overall level of detail available to parliamentarians and other interested parties.

We have already seen that the DPRRC drives forward the format of Government's memoranda and Chapter 10 outlines that the JCHR has done the same. The Constitution Committee is yet to prompt the use of memoranda. The Committee has though made a change to the way that explanatory notes are formatted. The Government has followed a recommendation in the Constitution Committee's report on *Fast-Track Legislation*,[90] that the Explanatory Notes should respond to eight specific questions designed to extract the Government's reasoning for using the special procedure, which limits the opportunity for scrutiny. This information serves as basis for the Committee's scrutiny of Bills that are fast-tracked.[91]

The European Scrutiny Committee is another parliamentary committee that relies upon Explanatory Memoranda in its scrutiny of deposited EU documents.[92] The Cabinet Office provides guidance on what the Explanatory Memoranda should contain, including the impact on EU law. These Explanatory Memoranda and the legal resources of the Committee, two legal advisers and six 'clerk advisers', reflect the size and complexity of the Committee's workload, typically examining over 1000 documents per annum, covering the full breadth of the EU's competence.[93] Whatever arrangements are adopted for scrutinising SIs designed to deal with the UK's new relationship with the EU, specifically designed explanatory material, as the Constitution Committee has recommended, would facilitate more effective scrutiny. Greenberg notes that in the context of Brexit legislation a 'clear audit trail' will be needed so that Parliament can identify the precise effect of particular SIs.[94] This is particularly important, where Parliament will need to be able to distinguish between SIs that disentangle UK law from EU law and those introduce new domestic policy.[95] The possibility of 'mixed motive' instruments that do both will make high-quality explanatory material vital for those attempting to identify those elements that might require close scrutiny.[96]

Pre-legislative scrutiny can provide an additional form of PLI. Pre-legislative scrutiny of a draft Bill is undertaken by a parliamentary committee, either an ad

---

[89] *Erskine May* (n 36) 836.

[90] House of Lords Select Committee on the Constitution, 'Fast-Track Legislation: Constitutional Implications and Safeguards', HL 2008–09, 116, para 186.

[91] J Simson Caird and D Oliver, 'Parliament's Constitutional Standards' in A Horne and A Le Sueur (eds), *Parliament: Legislation and Accountability* (Oxford, Hart, 2016).

[92] P Hardy, 'European Scrutiny' in Horne and Le Sueur (ibid) 98.

[93] ibid, 97.

[94] D Greenberg, 'Brexit and legislating for withdrawal: two steps forward …' *Practical Law UK*, 4 April 2017.

[95] ibid.

[96] ibid.

hoc committee or an existing departmental select committee, which will then produce a report setting out its views on the Bill. When the resulting Bill is formally introduced to Parliament, the report of the pre-legislative committee can serve as a scrutiny resource for parliamentarians.[97]

Committee reports on Bills and SIs are normally agreed with cross-party support, and in this sense normally operate outside of the political conflict between parties. The work of the DPRRC and the JCSI in particular is sometimes characterised as being 'technical' in nature. Such a description is designed to capture the fact that the scrutiny is motivated by the efficacy of the drafting, or the constitutional and legal propriety of the approach taken, rather than a judgment of the substantive merits of the policy content of the proposal. From a public law perspective, the 'technical' label seems over-simplistic. Even the scrutiny for vires that the JCSI engages in requires a level of interpretive reasoning that will sometimes entail value judgments. In judicial review proceedings a judge's approach to a question of vires is not considered to a purely 'technical' exercise.[98] In the parliamentary context, this characterisation is intended to categorise different forms of political activity, which is an understandable approach, but one should be cautious in regarding any form of legislative scrutiny as 'technical' or 'neutral' as it risks understating its own political importance.

B. House of Commons Library Briefing Papers

The House of Commons Library provides an impartial research service for MPs. A core element of this service is producing briefings on Government Bills before the House of Commons. The Library produces a detailed briefing on every public Bill at least two working days before the second reading debate is held.[99]

The timing of the publication of the Bill briefings is designed to inform the debate on second reading. If a Bill starts in the Commons, the main opportunity for Members to engage in scrutiny is the second reading debate, when the overall policy of a Bill is debated and subject to a vote. The Government ministers responsible for the Bill in the Commons have the benefit of briefings, including the legal memorandum, from the Bill team and parliamentary counsel responsible for the Bill. Members of Parliament that are scrutinising the Bill will not have access to this internal government material. MPs have their own staff, who may be able to support them in their preparation. The scale and speed of the task makes

---

[97] The passage of the Modern Slavery Bill contained a number of examples of this practice and these are detailed in J Mulley and H Kinghorn 'Pre-legislative Scrutiny in Parliament' in Horne and Le Sueur (n 91) 47–51.

[98] JAG Griffith, *The Politics of the Judiciary* (Manchester, Manchester University Press, 1977).

[99] The Commons Library also provides an enquiry service for Members and their staff. Members and their staff can use this service to request bespoke briefings to support their legislative scrutiny work. These briefings are confidential and are not published and so do not fit my definition of PLI.

overcoming the imbalance of legal resources difficult. This makes library briefings on bills particularly important, as they provide impartial information on the proposed change to law, and as such represent an institutional counter-balance to the Government's access to officials. For MPs from the front-bench teams in the official opposition and other parties this is especially useful as the briefing can support them in developing their analysis on the detail of the Bill for responding to the Government minister's speech at second reading.[100]

The distinguishing feature of Commons' briefings on Bill, as examples of PLI, is that their content is strictly impartial. Library clerks, who author these briefings, are required as a condition of their employment to be politically impartial.[101] As such, the role of the briefings is not to provide a critical commentary on the Government's legislative proposal, which pressure groups often supply, nor to provide a supportive justificatory analysis. Instead the briefings provide a balanced analysis of the content of a Bill. In practice, this will mean including a range of political and expert views on the matters covered in a Bill. In this sense the briefings serve as a mechanism for transmitting analysis and research relevant to a Bill to Members in order to inform their scrutiny of a Bill. The papers can also contain some independent analysis of the detail in the Bill. In producing this analysis, the Library clerks will themselves rely on the Government's Explanatory Notes, and seek to add value by building on the material they contain.

C. House of Lords Briefing Papers

Like the Commons Library, the House of Lords Library produces impartial, authoritative, politically balanced briefings for its Members for all government and private member's bills that receive a second reading in the House of Lords. Typically, these briefings will provide a digest of the content of the bill, the proposer's rationale for particular clauses and stakeholder reaction to them. In addition, where a Bill has arrived following scrutiny in the Commons, Lords Library briefings identify passages of the bill that are manifesto commitments, where the bill has been amended and how and where the Government has undertaken to return with amendments in the Lords. The briefing will also typically flag up issues that MPs indicated at report or third reading would benefit from specific careful consideration in the Lords.

The briefings are prepared in order to be made available to all members at least three days before the debate in question. The availability and timeliness is an important element. Few members of the Lords have full-time staff and even those who do are often unable to call upon expert research support to assist their preparation for a bill's scrutiny. Moreover, members of the Lords

---

[100] Members and their staff can also request bespoke confidential briefings on Bills.
[101] House of Commons Staff Handbook, 5.2–5.3.

receive numerous representations from pressure and lobby groups ahead of a Bill's passage through the Lords, much of which may be difficult to judge as authoritative or to navigate efficiently. Consequently, members value the timely availability of a briefing which concisely sets out the legal, political and stakeholder considerations at play.

III. A CASE STUDY OF PLI AS CONSTITUTIONAL DIALOGUE—THE EUROPEAN UNION REFERENDUM ACT 2015

A number of the forms of PLI examined in this chapter came under scrutiny following Brexit. This short case study highlights the role of the PLI that accompanied the European Union Referendum Bill 2015 as examined in the *Miller* judicial review proceedings. The case study demonstrates the way in which PLI can facilitate a constitutional dialogue between all the branches of state.

The Government introduced the European Union Referendum Bill on 28 May 2015. On the same day the Explanatory Notes, considered above, on the Bill were published. The notes did not engage with the possible constitutional implications of the Bill.

On 3 June 2015, the House of Commons Library published its briefing on the Bill, six days before the second reading debate in the Commons on 9 June 2015.[102] The briefing provided context of the UK's relationship with the EU and detailed commentary on each of the clauses. The commentary contextualised the provisions by reference to other referendums held in the UK. Section 5 of the briefing analysed the typology of referendums held in the UK, and explained how the referendum proposed in the Bill compared with previous ones:

> It does not contain any requirement for the UK Government to implement the results of the referendum, nor set a time limit by which a vote to leave the EU should be implemented. Instead, this is a type of referendum known as pre-legislative or consultative, which enables the electorate to voice an opinion which then influences the Government in its policy decisions. The referendums held in Scotland, Wales and Northern Ireland in 1997 and 1998 are examples of this type, where opinion was tested before legislation was introduced ... In contrast, the legislation which provided for the referendum held on AV in May 2011 would have implemented the new system of voting without further legislation, provided that the boundary changes also provided for in the Parliamentary Voting System and Constituency Act 2011 were also implemented.[103]

The commentary was not cited during the debate on the Bill. The provisions of the Bill did not engage with the legal implications in the event of a leave vote, and as such they were not the focus of debate during the Bill's passage through the Commons.

---

[102] European Union Referendum Bill 2015–16, Number 07212, 3 June 2015.
[103] ibid, 25.

A. The *Miller* Case

The result of the referendum on 23 June 2016 turned the focus to the question of whether or not the Government had the necessary legal authority to give effect to the result of the referendum. The *Miller* judicial review challenge led to the examination of a wide range of features of the UK constitution. Before both the High Court and the Supreme Court, the Government argued that the European Union Referendum Act 2015 and the referendum itself should be read as legally relevant to the main question of the case, whether the Government had legal authority to use the prerogative to trigger Article 50 of the TFEU.

Unusually this led to the substance and status of the Commons' Briefing Paper to be raised repeatedly in the Miller challenge before both the High Court and the Supreme Court. The UK courts' general position is that when interpreting a statute Parliament's intention is established by giving effect to the words of the statute.[104] Parliament votes on and enacts only those words, and is not asked to endorse any of the other material. However, in certain contexts the UK courts have begun to make increasing use of a number of elements of legislative history, including Hansard, explanatory notes and committee reports.[105] The courts' engagement with examples of PLI is an important subtext to understanding its constitutional significance, as this could in turn influence how, for example, the Government approaches its explanatory material.[106] All material that might be indicative of legislative intent is likely to be particularly important when the legislation is constitutionally significant, and where questions of parliamentary intent could become a matter of intense legal and political debate.

On 17 October 2016, David Chambers QC, who represented Mr Santos, one of the lead claimants in the judicial review proceedings, argued before the High Court that the Commons briefing paper was relevant to understanding the legal implications of the European Union Referendum Act 2015. Mr Chambers argued that the paper 'expressly set out the legal position as it then was' and then referred to the passage of the briefing which explained that the referendum that the Bill would provide for was not legally binding and was instead consultative.[107] This, Mr Chambers argued, demonstrated 'that when the 2015 Act was passed, Parliament made the informed decision that the result of the referendum would not be legally binding'.[108]

This reference to the Commons Library briefing was picked up in the High Court's judgment, which found that the Government could not use the Crown's

---

[104] *Warburton v Loveland* (1832) 2 D &Cl (HL) 480, 489; Greenberg (n 24) 741.

[105] Greenberg (n 24) 953; *Pepper (Inspector of Taxes) v Hart* [1993] AC 593 (HL); for analysis see: A Kavanagh, 'Pepper v Hart and Matters of Constitutional Principle' (2005) 120 *Law Quarterly Review* 98.

[106] See Popelier and De Jaegere, 'Evidence-based judicial review of legislation in divided states' (n 10) 187.

[107] *The Queen On The Application Of: Santos & Miller Applicants V Secretary Of State For Exiting The European Union Respondent*, 13 October 2016, Transcript 181.

[108] ibid, Transcript 183.

prerogative powers to give notice under Article 50. The judgment, delivered by the Lord Chief Justice of England and Wales, the Master of the Rolls and Lord Justice Sales, stated that the European Union Referendum Act 2015 did not provide a statutory power for the Government to implement the referendum result. The 2015 Act did not contain provisions on how the result should be implemented, and as a result the referendum was in legal terms only advisory and therefore did not bind Parliament.[109] This fact was reinforced by the Briefing according to the Court:

> Further, the 2015 Referendum Act was passed against a background including a clear briefing paper to parliamentarians explaining that the referendum would have advisory effect only.[110]

In the Supreme Court, the Briefing Paper was again raised in oral argument, in response to the Government's argument that the Court should take into account Parliament's intention in enacting the 2015 Act. The Government argued that the legislative scheme on the UK's relationship with the EU, including the 2015 Act, demonstrated that specific legislative authority for giving the Article 50 Notice was not required. The 2015 Act's silence on the need for specific legal authority was evidence that 'the Government's power to give the Article 50 notice' had not been removed by Parliament:[111]

> The premise of the 2015 Act was the continued existence of the Government's prerogative powers to act on the international plane—including, specifically, to give Article 50 notice as the first step in implementing a 'leave' vote.[112]

This, the Government claimed, was the 'clear understanding of all concerned'. The speech of the Minister responsible for Bill, David Liddington MP, was cited as evidence for this. Mr Liddington said that the Bill had one purpose: 'to deliver on our promise to give the British people the final say on our EU membership in an in/out referendum'.[113] In oral argument James Eadie QC, representing the Government, pointed out in response to a question from Lord Clarke on the Briefing:

> It is a House of Commons Library briefing paper, not written by Government but by a member of House of Commons staff. It tells one nothing, therefore, about the intention of Government. It is not an assurance to Parliament by Government, it is not anything that would bear on parliamentary intention. It is not a legitimate aid to interpretation.

The Government's argument in relation to the 2015 Act was that its silence was 'compelling' in that it demonstrated that Parliament intended to leave the Government's legal authority to trigger Article 50 in place. David Chambers QC,

---

[109] *R (Miller) v Secretary of State for Exiting the European Union* [2016] EWHC 2768 (Admin), paras 105–08.

[110] ibid, para 107.

[111] Supreme Court Printed Case of the Secretary of State for Exiting the European Union (18 November 2016) 6.

[112] ibid, 14.

[113] HC Deb, Hansard, 9 June 2015, col 1047.

representing Mr Santos before the Supreme Court, again made reference in oral submission to the Briefing Paper to make the argument that the 2015 Act did not support the view that the Government held legislative or prerogative power to trigger Article 50. He explained why in the following terms:

> we relied on this briefing paper in the divisional court to evidence the historical fact that during the passage of the bill which became the 2015 Act, parliamentarians were informed that under the form of the bill, the result of the referendum would be advisory only. Which was consistent in our submission, which was the law as it then stood or the law as it was then understood by those who were going to consider this legislation. When the referendum is referred to as advisory only, what that means is that it was not legally binding.[114]

In response, the President and Lord Mance questioned the relevance and admissibility of the Briefing Paper. The Supreme Court judgments in *Miller* did not make any reference to the Briefing in their analysis of the 2015 Act.

The majority judgment of the Supreme Court, which supported the High Court's conclusion, rejected the Government's analysis of the 2015 Act. The Court did not accept the Government's view that the 2015 Act was understood at the time, as evidenced by the statement of Mr Liddington in the Commons, to be legislating in a context where the Government had the necessary constitutional authority to trigger Article 50 and that therefore no further Parliamentary authorisation for triggering Article 50 was required:

> There are two problems with this argument. The first is that it assumes what it seeks to prove, namely that the referendum was intended by Parliament to have a legal effect as well as a political effect. The second problem is that the notion that Parliament would not envisage both a referendum and legislation being required to approve the same step is falsified by sections 2, 3 and 6 of the 2011 Act, which, as the Explanatory Notes (quoted in para 111 above) acknowledge, required just that—albeit in the more elegant way of stipulating for legislation whose effectiveness was conditional upon a concurring vote in a referendum.[115]

The majority position highlights that the Explanatory Notes of a Bill can represent an opportunity to engage with the wider constitutional context. Such engagements can have beneficial political consequences, in the sense of affecting the way in which the provisions in a Bill are understood. The majority referred to the Explanatory Notes to the European Union Act 2011 which *did* engage directly with the constitutional context, and served to clarify how the provisions should be understood to engage with Parliament and the legislative steps that would be required. For the majority, therefore, the notes for the 2015 Act's silence counted against the Government's position. This silence clearly left space for contrasting

---

[114] Supreme Court Transcript of proceedings in *R (on the application of Miller and Dos Santos) v Secretary of State for Exiting the European Union* 16 December 2017, 105–08.

[115] *R (on the application of Miller and another) v Secretary of State for Exiting the European Union* [2017] UKSC 5, 20.

interpretation. Lord Reed's dissent argued that the 2011 Act's explicit provisions on further parliamentary engagement made it unlikely that further engagement could be implicitly read into the silence of the 2015 Act.[116]

The provisions of the 2015 Act did not engage the broader constitutional context, and this provided an opportunity for the explanatory notes to outline how the Bill's silence should be interpreted. The absence was analysed by the Library briefing, which informed Members of a potential legal vacuum. The Briefing Paper did not though supply any evidence of Parliament's intention when it enacted the 2015 Act, and the way it was used by counsel showed a misunderstanding of the role of Library briefings in the legislative process. The use of PLI in *Miller* does highlight its potential constitutional significance. However, it should be noted that the circumstances of *Miller*, where the silence of a constitutional Bill is put under such an intense spotlight, were unusual.

This experience might serve as a lesson that if the Government thinks that provisions have a particular constitutional effect, it is better off saying so in the notes. *Miller* might incentivise the Government to provide more detail, and this could serve to the benefit of the PLI produced by Parliament. The examination of the Library's briefing shows that when there is interpretive doubt, or constitutional implications that are not fully explained then it falls upon parliamentary actors to identify those issues to draw them to the attention of Members. Independent parliamentary and impartial interpretive analysis of a Bill can mitigate the Government's reticence to explore the constitutional implications of its own legislation.

IV. THE CONSTITUTIONAL VALUE OF PLI

The purpose of PLI is to enhance parliamentarians' understanding of the legislative provisions before them. Major policy bills will often be preceded by White Papers and consultations that can inform debate in Parliament. These papers provide helpful policy background but do not provide detailed material on the legal effect of provisions in a major Bill. Parliament enacts law not policy, and as such PLI, produced by officials in Government and Parliament, on the implications of all the provisions in a Bill or SI has become an established feature of the legislative process. PLI is designed to support legislative scrutiny, and the examples discussed in this chapter have shown how it enables communication between Government and Parliament on the content of the Bill.

Parliamentary committees' increasing engagement in legislative scrutiny has driven the development of the Government's PLI. Committees use the Government's PLI to inform their scrutiny of Bills and SIs, but they also use them as a mechanism for communicating with the Government, requesting

---

[116] ibid, 214.

further memoranda on particular points, and issuing guidance to demand that memoranda cover specific points. Improving the quality of PLI is a tangible benefit of the work of these permanent parliamentary legislative scrutiny committees. Their ability to challenge the Government's analysis of the legal implications of their proposals, as set out in their Explanatory Notes and Memoranda, serves as a valuable check on the Government's legislative power. The ability to produce a report, with cross-party support, that includes critical analysis of the reasons put forward by Government to justify, for example the inclusion of delegated powers, illustrates how PLI can serve to enhance Parliament's ability to hold the Government to account. Further, it can make the legislative process more transparent, by prompting the Government to provide more detail on the thinking behind its legislative choices.

Improving the quality of PLI on legislative proposals may seem like a relatively minor achievement for scrutiny, when most associate effective impact with securing amendments, but it must be seen in the light of the inaccessibility of the Government's internal procedures for producing legislation. In this context, raising the quality and level of detail of PLI on legislative proposals should be seen as a significant achievement.

Raising the level of justification within the Government's explanatory memorandum is particularly important achievement in the UK constitutional context. The nature of the UK constitution and in particular parliamentary sovereignty gives the Government considerable freedom in how it drafts legislation, and in particular, how it drafts constitutional legislation. In the absence of a specific procedure for constitutional amendments, or formalised constitutional review, the Government does not have to justify the constitutionality of its legislation, in particular, how it fits within and relates to the existing constitutional framework. This freedom extends to the Government's explanatory material, and given the choice, it is not surprising that the Government tends to adopt a rather minimalist approach in the way that explains most legislation and even constitutional legislation. Nevertheless, it should also be noted that explanatory material can be used tactically to advance a particular interpretation of provisions.

Library briefings on Bills are an additional counterbalance to the reliance on the Government for detailed information on legislative proposals and their occasional tendency to supply PLI that is thin on political context. The impartial content of Library briefings and their ability to harness external expertise strengthens the depth and breadth of the PLI. While authors of Library Briefings may have more freedom in terms of the content they include than Government lawyers do when authoring explanatory notes, they also operate in a constrained environment. Producing politically impartial content on bills, which can often contain contentious content, for a deeply political environment requires a degree of sensitivity and awareness that is only achieved by cautious and considered drafting.

The value of PLI is more apparent when the parliamentary law-making process is seen as a mechanism for enhancing the transparency and accountability of the

Government's legislative output. In this context, high-quality explanatory material is more than just a by-product of effective scrutiny, and is essential to the legitimacy of the legislative process. The Commission on Parliamentary Reform's Report on the Scottish Parliament, published in 2017, called for more accompanying documentation with Bills to be published by the Scottish Government in order to 'facilitate effective scrutiny' and to improve 'the clarity of intent' of legislation. The Report also notes that such material serves to 'support people to engage with the legislative process on a more informed basis'.[117] While PLI has clear instrumental value in enabling effective scrutiny, it also plays a broader role in making the legislative process more accessible.

The parliamentary law-making process is a public service. Material on legislative proposals written in plain accessible language enables public engagement with Parliament, so that the public can engage with what is being debated, and to make content of the law more readily understandable. Publicising changes to the law, through PLI, is a procedural manifestation of a core element of the rule of law: the accessibility of the law. In Lord Bingham's view this meant that the law must be intelligible, clear and predictable.[118] The quantity and complexity of legislation mean that in reality understanding the law by reading the plain text of a bill is difficult even for legal experts. Legislation has, according to Williams, moved away from 'the logic of communication' and now builds meaning through analogy.[119] The extent of the inaccessibility of legislative drafting is the subject of debate, and as Greenberg notes, 'there are limitations on the extent to which good legislative drafting can utilise natural English expressions in a natural English way'.[120] The body of PLI created by Government and Parliament creates a public record that provides an invaluable resource for understanding the content and purpose of the law.

The presence of subject specific legislative committees that operate outside of the central Government and opposition dynamic has prompted the Government to reveal more legal information through explanatory memoranda. These exchanges represent a form of dialogue that can go further than parliamentary debate in addressing the content of a bill. This is not a problem: ideally the two should complement each other, as they often do when reports are taken up through amendments in either House. At the same the distinct nature of PLI is reflected in the fact that the courts seem more willing to rely upon it than Hansard, particularly the Government's Explanatory Notes and committee reports, when engaged in detailed analysis of legislative provisions. Using this material comes with risks, not least in potentially informing the way in that such material is prepared.

---

[117] Commission on Parliamentary Reform, Report on the Scottish Parliament (2017) 21.
[118] T Bingham, *The Rule of Law* (London, Allen Lane, 2009) 37.
[119] M Williams, 'The Grammar of Politics: A Brief History of Legislative Language in Britain' 88 (2017) *Political Quarterly* 2, 256.
[120] ibid, 224.

There is a case for further explanatory material to be produced by both Government and Parliament. Creating a publicly available record on the detail of a proposal can also serve a number of other practical constitutional functions. The first is that it means that those responsible for enforcing and interpreting a statute, most obviously the courts, but also other public bodies, have a resource that can they can draw upon in order to enhance their understanding of the statutes. Certain statutes, particularly those that are not designed to be judicially enforced, depend on being accessible in order to be effective, and in such situations, if they are ambiguous, the PLI assumes an important role. A connected benefit is that parliamentary scrutiny benefits from an accessible record of past scrutiny of legislation that can be used to inform subsequent scrutiny. For example, the Government's past justification for delegated powers is a vital resource for the DPRRC's scrutiny, as it enables them to assess whether the Government is seeking to extend the use of such powers.

The legislative process in Parliament is the interface between law and politics in our constitutional system. The process of enacting legislation can often appear to be a largely technical exercise, and the nature of the Government's PLI does not always encourage political debate on the detail within a Bill. The primary role of Committee reports and Library Briefings in that context is to bring the detail within the reach of political and public debate by contextualising and explaining the legal implications of what it is proposed. PLI on legislative proposals enlarges the scope for political debate and public engagement with the legislative process and the content of the law. These are both major constitutional goods, which should drive any future improvements to the way Government and Parliament produce material on legislative proposals. The legislative process and the content of the law benefit from deep disagreement and the largest possible audience. PLI is an essential tool for achieving both.

In practice, the actual contribution of this material to the rule of law depends on the approach taken by those responsible for drafting the material. PLI relies upon a collaborative relationship between Parliament and Government, particularly between parliamentary committees and government bill teams. If the Governments takes a proactive and candid approach this can help those responsible for Parliament's PIL. There is a cyclical quality to PLI. When this communication channel works well it can facilitate the quality and quantity of committee scrutiny and external expert commentary on a Bill, which in turn inform Library Briefings, as well making the task of analysing the content easier for the public. These constitutional goods are important, but this should not obscure the fact that achieving them is not a primary purpose of the parliamentary legislative process.

The PLI produced by Government, and scrutiny of them within Parliament, can have the effect of drawing attention to and politicising elements of legislative proposals. Advocates of the rule of law, and those who favour enhanced legislative scrutiny, should not assume that the case for revealing more legal background of legislative proposals is axiomatic.

The UK constitution and Parliament do not seek to prioritise legal issues in parliamentary scrutiny and political debate, and it could be argued that such matters are best reserved for internal discussions within Government. Parliament, by contrast, should concentrate on the broader policy debates, rather than focus on legal issues that are best left to those responsible for designing and implementing the law. For Greenberg, Parliament's role is not to engage with technical legal matters: instead, they are 'elected to participate in debates about, and to participate in decisions about, general social policy, and not as an expression of confidence in their technical ability in the matter of the drafting and application of legislation'.[121] Greenberg warns that MPs should not mistake their participation in the law-making process as giving them expertise in legislation, as doing so would risk them 'becoming back-seat drivers of the worst and most dangerous kind'.[122]

It might be assumed by some that more legislative scrutiny, even of a technical character would be a good thing. However, preserving the political character of parliamentary debate, rather than seeing it dominated by legal and constitutional technicalities, has been defended as a strength of the political constitution. Thought of in this way, prioritising the political should restrict the way in which legal issues are considered, and there is some evidence of this dynamic in the way that political norms within Government and Parliament influence the arrangements for PLI.

Parliament's role in the law-making process is not to obstruct the elected Government's legislative business. The arrangements that support scrutiny, including PLI, reflect a careful balancing act between enabling Government to govern through legislative enactments, and ensuing that the Government's legislative agenda is scrutinised. Any changes to PLI that might shift that balance will need careful consideration.

Professor John Griffith, author of 'The Political Constitution',[123] the seminal article on the nature of the UK constitution, argued that Parliament and the legislative process are not solely designed around the scrutiny and accountability of Government.[124] Griffith argued that Parliament 'is also the forum for defence, approval and congratulation of the Government'.[125] Instead of framing the central relationship as between the Government and Parliament, Griffith argued that the central conflict was between Government and opposition, and as a consequence much of the legislative scrutiny that takes places is designed not to improve a Bill, but 'to make the Government less acceptable'.[126] Griffith's perspective is a reminder

---

[121] Greenberg (n 23) 107.
[122] Greenberg (n 23) 108.
[123] JAG Griffith, 'The Political Constitution' (1979) 42 *Modern Law Review* 1, 19.
[124] See JAG Griffith, 'The Place of Parliament in the legislative process, Part I' (1951) 14 *The Modern Law Review* 279; 'The Place of Parliament in the legislative process, Part II' (1951) 14 *The Modern Law Review* 425.
[125] ibid.
[126] Griffith, 'Part I' (n 124) 279; 'Part II' (n 124) 425.

that the law-making process in Parliament is not designed to be consensual, and this is reflected in the Government's approach to explanatory material.

In practice, the increasing scope of PLI shows that justificatory standards in the legislative process can be raised without altering the existing constitutional framework. Even if core principles and attitudes are left untouched, requiring more information on legislative proposals raises fundamental questions about the purpose of the parliamentary law-making process and the proper relationship between law and politics. Any form of constitutionalism requires such questions to be posed frequently and to be deliberated frankly.

Part 3

Devolution and the English Question

8

Devolution and the UK Parliament

SIR PAUL SILK

I. INTRODUCTION

JOHN McELDOWNEY'S LAST sentence in the previous edition of this book—'the devolution settlement will inevitably continue to evolve'—has proved something of an understatement. Reviews, Brexit and crises of one sort or another have meant continuing devolutionary development over the last five years. Despite the often-expressed wish that the constitutional debate would stop so that political leaders could concentrate on the delivery of services, the inevitability of future further change has hardly diminished. This chapter will first describe what has happened in Scotland, Wales, Northern Ireland and England since the last edition. It will then discuss a number of themes that cut across the jurisdictions. More questions are asked than are answered, but that is unavoidable when devolution is both so fluid and so dynamic.

II. WHAT HAS HAPPENED IN SCOTLAND?

The previous edition of this book was produced after the Edinburgh agreement of November 2012 that there should be a referendum on Scottish independence, but before the campaign had begun in earnest. That campaign dominated Scottish politics through 2013 and 2014 and the unexpected closeness of the result has dominated the politics of the Union ever since.

The Edinburgh agreement led to considerable legislative activity. The UK Parliament passed the Scotland Act 1998 (Modification of Schedule 5) Order 2013[1] in early 2013. This provided that a referendum on the independence of Scotland from the rest of the UK was not to be a reserved matter subject to three main conditions: that the referendum could not be held on the same day as the anticipated EU referendum; that it should be held no later than 31 December 2014, and that the ballot paper should give the voter a choice between only two responses.

---

[1] SI 2013/242.

The Scottish Parliament subsequently passed the Scottish Independence Referendum Act 2013[2] setting the question ('Should Scotland be an independent country?'), providing for the Scottish Ministers to fix the date of the poll and otherwise to regulate the conduct of the referendum. A separate Scottish Independence Referendum (Franchise) Act 2013 dealt mainly with the enfranchisement of 16- and 17-year-olds for the purposes of the referendum.[3] The date of the referendum was set as 18 September 2014.

Opinion polls had shown a consistent lead for opponents of independence through 2013 and 2014, though two Sunday newspaper polls in the fortnight before voting showed a majority for independence and duly caused political alarm among unionists. In the event, 44.7 per cent of those voting believed that Scotland should become an independent country. Turnout was an extraordinary 84.6 per cent—the highest figure in any referendum or general elections since the introduction of universal suffrage. The holding of a referendum on the territorial boundaries of the state is an appropriate matter for decision by referendum according to the House of Lords Constitution Committee.[4] However, the contrast between the enthusiasm for participatory democracy demonstrated in the engagement in the Scottish referendum process—not just at the final voting stage—and the disenchantment with conventional parliamentary politics was stark, and it is certainly arguable that it was a warning sign for the EU referendum to be held in 2016.

In the week before the referendum, a striking story appeared on the front page of the *Daily Record*.[5] The Prime Minister, Deputy Prime Minister and Leader of the Opposition used the newspaper to make a vow to the people of Scotland—about the Constitution, about fairness and about the NHS. The vow on the Constitution was that Holyrood would be strengthened with extensive new powers, on a timetable beginning on 19 September, with legislation in 2015, and that the Scottish Parliament would be 'a permanent and irreversible part of the British constitution'. Characterised by some as a panic reaction, and credited by others as a decisive intervention, the vow was followed by an early morning statement from the steps of 10 Downing Street as soon as the result of the referendum was clear on 19 September. David Cameron's statement[6] confirmed the vow and announced that Lord Smith of Kelvin would oversee the process to take forward the commitments, reporting by November 2014 and with draft legislation by January. As far as independence was concerned, the Prime Minister's view was that the question

---

[2] Royal Assent on 17 December 2013.

[3] The disenfranchisement of convicted prisoners from voting in the referendum was found to be lawful by the Supreme Court in *Moohan and another (Appellants) v The Lord Advocate (Respondent)* [2014] UKSC 67.

[4] Select Committee on the Constitution, 'Referendums in the United Kingdom' 12th Report of Session 2009–10, HL Paper 99.

[5] www.dailyrecord.co.uk/news/politics/david-cameron-ed-miliband-nick-4265992.

[6] www.gov.uk/government/news/scottish-independence-referendum-statement-by-the-prime-minister.

had been settled for a generation. Pledges were also made for Wales and Northern Ireland, and—most controversially—for the settlement of the West Lothian question with English laws to be decided by English votes.[7]

The Smith Commission was set up within a week. Each political party in Scotland nominated members. Its unanimous report[8] was produced on 27 November—an extraordinary achievement, though inevitably the complexity of the issues considered could not be fully addressed in the time and in 28 pages of text. Under the Smith proposals, the Scottish Parliament and Scottish Government were to be made permanent in UK legislation, with the Parliament given powers over how it was elected and run. The Parliament would also assume a range of new and important powers in policy areas such as taxation, welfare, employability, transport and energy. Several other interesting recommendations on intergovernmental cooperation, intra-Scotland devolution, strengthened oversight by the Scottish Parliament and greater awareness of its work were also made. Essentially, the work of the Calman Commission was to be superseded and the modest fiscal changes made by the Scotland Act 2012 were to be substantially expanded.

A White Paper containing draft clauses for a Scotland Bill (and making clear the need to agree a fiscal framework) was published in January 2015.[9] This was followed by Reports from the Commons Scottish Affairs and Political and Constitutional Reform Committees and the Lords Constitution Committee.[10] The Bill was introduced in the Commons on 28 May 2015. The arguments for and against the de-reserving of particular areas of public policy are beyond the scope of this book, as are the arguments in respect of the striking extent of the devolution of fiscal and welfare powers proposed in the Bill (and eventually enacted). Under them, Scotland has a level of fiscal control not paralleled in many federal systems.

Three proposals contained in the Bill—and subsequently enacted in the Scotland Act 2015—are, however, very much within this book's scope. The first is one that has received less attention than the other two. This is the requirement for a two-thirds majority in the Scottish Parliament for any legislation that deals with elections to the Scottish Parliament, the franchise for elections, the electoral system, the number of constituencies and regions and the numbers of MSPs for each constituency or region. The section also provides for disputes to be determined in

---

[7] See ch 9.

[8] Smith Commission, Report of the Smith Commission on further devolution of powers to the Scottish Parliament, November 2014, www.smith-commission.scot.

[9] 'Scotland in the United Kingdom: An enduring settlement' Cm 8990, www.gov.uk/government/uploads/system/uploads/attachment_data/file/397079/Scotland_EnduringSettlement_acc.pdf.

[10] Scottish Affairs Committee, 'The Implementation of the Smith Agreement', HC-835 2014–15, 10 March 2015; Political and Constitutional Reform Committee, 'Constitutional implications of the Government's draft Scotland clauses', 22 March 2015, HC 1022, 2014–15; House of Lords Constitution Committee, 'Proposals for the devolution of further powers to Scotland', HL-145 2014–15, 24 March 2015.

the Supreme Court.[11] As the Lords Constitution Committee noted,[12] the existence of such a provision in respect of Scotland (and, later, Wales) may well encourage others to argue that Parliament itself should similarly be bound by super-majorities in certain defined areas of constitutional enactment.

The other provisions noteworthy from a constitutional law viewpoint are the declaratory clauses 1 and 2. Both were, and remain, the subject of much debate. Clause 1 was intended to insert statutory statements into the Scotland Act 1998 that the Scottish Parliament and the Scottish Government were each a 'permanent part of the United Kingdom's constitutional arrangements'. The constitutional difficulty of entrenchment and the wish to buttress statements of intent with extra-legal brickwork meant that this Clause was substantially amended. Thus section 1 still provides that the Scottish Parliament and the Scottish Government are a permanent part of the United Kingdom's constitutional arrangements, but also states that they are not to be abolished except on the basis of a decision of the people of Scotland voting in a referendum. Subsection (2) of section 1 makes the further declaratory announcement that the purpose of the section is 'to signify the commitment of the Parliament and Government of the United Kingdom to the Scottish Parliament and the Scottish Government'.

Clause 2 was enacted without alteration as section 2 of the Scotland Act 2016. It enshrines in law part of the 'Sewel Convention' (the convention that has developed that the Scottish Parliament is asked to pass a consent motion in respect of any proposed legislation on devolved Scottish matters at Westminster).[13] It does this by stating that 'the Parliament of the United Kingdom will not normally legislate with regard to devolved matters without the consent of the Scottish Parliament'. The section does not, however, deal with the part of the Sewel Convention that is taken to require Scottish Parliament consent for legislation affecting the competences of the Scottish Parliament or Government. It also contains the rather legally slippery word 'normally'.[14]

The Scotland Bill was intensively debated in both Commons and Lords. Between the conception of the Bill and its progress through Parliament, the 2015 general election had delivered a set of 56 Scottish National Party (SNP) members out of 59 MPs representing Scottish seats. This had many interesting consequences for the House of Commons where, for example, the Scottish Affairs Committee now contained a majority of MPs representing seats in England, while almost all other select committees, as well as the House of Commons Commission, contained an SNP MP. The numbers of SNP MPs certainly ensured that the Bill's progress

---

[11] Section 11 of Scotland Act 2016.

[12] House of Lords Constitution Committee, 'Proposals for the devolution of further powers to Scotland', HL-145 2014–15, 24 March 2015, para 92. The Committee also noted that a super-majority is required by section 2 of the Fixed-term Parliaments Act 2011.

[13] See further discussion of Sewel and Legislative Consent Motions below.

[14] As the former Lord Chief Justice, Lord Judge, said in the House of Lords: 'The word "normally" ... is a weasel word. It does not mean anything very much in legislative terms'. Official Report, 31 October 2016, col 465.

through Committee of the whole House was lively. It is, however, striking that there is no member of the House of Lords who represents the SNP, principally because of the party's opposition to a non-elected House, and that inevitably skewed that House's consideration of the Bill.

The Scotland Bill was also debated in the Scottish Parliament, particularly as part of the work of the Devolution (Further Powers) Committee of the Parliament—a Committee originally set up to consider the Scotland Act 1998 (Modification of Schedule 5) Order 2013, but whose remit had been extended to keep a watch on the legislation to implement the Smith Commission recommendations. At the same time, extensive bilateral discussions were taking place between the London and Edinburgh Governments about the fiscal framework that was necessary to underpin the fiscal measures contained in the Scotland Bill. Those discussions were concluded on 25 February 2016, and this in turn allowed the Scottish Government to recommend to the Scottish Parliament that it consent to the Scotland Bill,[15] though the recommendation made clear the Scottish Government's view that 'the Scotland Bill and the Smith Commission report could have delivered more effective and coherent powers to the Scottish Parliament'. Legislative consent was given in Holyrood on 16 March 2016 and the Scotland Bill received Royal Assent on 23 March. By the end of 2016, the Act had largely been brought into force and the Scottish Government and Parliament (where the SNP had lost its majority in the General Election of May 2016, though it remained the party of government) were actively working on its implementation.

Meanwhile, discussion of Scottish independence[16] revived following Scotland's vote in the Brexit referendum (by 62.0 per cent to 38.0 per cent) to remain within the EU, thus proving right those Remain supporters who had argued that a decision to leave the EU in the Brexit referendum might exacerbate Scottish autonomist demands. The Scottish Government duly published in October 2016 a draft Referendum Bill for consultation,[17] and this was followed in December by a detailed proposal on Scotland's Role in Europe.[18] The Scottish Parliament voted on 28 March 2017 by 69 votes to 59 to request the UK Government to make a second section 30 Order to allow a binding independence referendum between Autumn 2018 and Spring 2019.[19] The request was speedily rebuffed, with the Secretary

---

[15] www.parliament.uk/documents/commons-public-bill-office/2015-16/legislative-consent-resolutions/Scotland-Bill2-LCM-160316.pdf.

[16] See also ch 8, s VI.

[17] www.gov.scot/Publications/2016/10/8279.

[18] www.gov.scot/Resource/0051/00512073.pdf.

[19] The full text of the resolution was: 'That the Parliament acknowledges the sovereign right of the Scottish people to determine the form of government best suited to their needs and therefore mandates the Scottish Government to take forward discussions with the UK Government on the details of an order under section 30 of the Scotland Act 1998 to ensure that the Scottish Parliament can legislate for a referendum to be held that will give the people of Scotland a choice over the future direction and governance of their country at a time, and with a question and franchise, determined by the Scottish Parliament, which would most appropriately be between the autumn of 2018, when there is clarity over the outcome of the Brexit negotiations, and around the point at which the UK leaves the EU in spring

of State for Scotland suggesting that any discussion of a referendum would not begin until after Brexit had taken place, with no vote happening in any case for some time after that so that Scottish voters could properly appreciate what the consequences of Brexit had been.[20] The June 2017 General Election was fought in Scotland partly as a reprise of the independence referendum, with the SNP arguing that if it gained a plurality of seats in Scotland, that would fortify its mandate for a further referendum, albeit at the end of the Brexit process. The Conservative manifesto did not rule out a referendum but confirmed that it should not happen until after Brexit, and only if there was 'public consent'. The SNP did achieve a plurality of seats, but pro-union parties received well over 60 per cent of votes cast. It remains to be seen whether calls for independence will be muted over the next few years: Nicola Sturgeon was seen by some to have backed down when she made a post-election statement to the Scottish Parliament on 27 June 2017 deferring the date the Scottish Government proposed for the referendum.[21]

III. WHAT HAS HAPPENED IN WALES?

The Welsh devolution 'settlement' has hardly qualified as settled at any time since powers were first devolved. The last 20 years have seen a giddy succession of changes of powers and structures. Since the previous edition of this book there have been two Westminster Acts giving major further powers to the National Assembly for Wales (NAW). Both flowed from the recommendations of the Commission on Devolution in Wales (the 'Silk Commission').[22] That Commission, containing nominees of the four political parties at that time represented in the NAW, together with non-political members, had been appointed by the UK Coalition Government in 2011. Its first report on fiscal matters[23] resulted in the Wales Act 2014—though the controversy within the UK Government over how fiscal powers should be devolved to Wales can be surmised from the delay between the Commission's report and the Government's response. The Commission's

---

2019; believes that this gives people in Scotland a choice at a time when there is both the most information and most opportunity to act; further believes that 16 and 17-year-olds and EU citizens, who were excluded from the EU referendum, should be entitled to vote, and considers that this referendum is necessary given the Prime Minister's decision to negotiate a hard exit from the EU, including leaving the single market, which conflicts with assurances given by the UK Government and prominent Leave campaigners, and which takes no account of the overwhelming Remain vote in Scotland.'

[20] www.heraldscotland.com/news/15187649.Mundell_suggests_May_will_not_discuss_another_independence_referendum_until_after_2021.

[21] www.parliament.scot/parliamentarybusiness/report.aspx?r=11035. It is to be hoped that any dispute as to whether a referendum should take place will be resolved politically, not through the Courts—see centreonconstitutionalchange.ac.uk/blog/second-scottish-independence-referendum-without-s30-order-legal-question-demands-political.

[22] The author of this chapter declares his interest as the Chair of the Commission.

[23] The Commission on Devolution in Wales, 'Empowerment and Responsibility: Financial Powers to Strengthen Wales', November 2012.

second report on wider constitutional matters[24] led to the Wales Act 2017—again, there was argument within government and outside, and by no means all the Commission's recommendations were adopted.

The principal provisions of the 2014 Act gave the NAW and Welsh Government new powers in taxation and borrowing. Stamp duty was replaced in Wales by a new Welsh tax on land transactions, and landfill tax was also devolved. New taxes might also be devolved. More significantly, some control over income tax was devolved, though the income tax provisions were not to come into force unless endorsed in a referendum. The original UK Government proposals on income tax were heavily criticised as not offering the Welsh Government the flexibility necessary to use income tax as a policy instrument—there was a so-called 'lock-step' provision that would have required each rate of tax to be changed by the same amount. This restriction was removed by government amendment during the Bill's progress through Parliament—though the Legislative Consent Motion had been passed in the NAW before this happened.[25] The 2014 Act also gave the NAW new powers over its own budgetary procedures.

There were also some important provisions in the Act that did not emanate from the Silk Commission. The Assembly term was increased to five years; dual membership of the NAW and the House of Commons was banned; and the restriction that had been introduced in 2006 (uniquely in Wales) that prevented candidates from standing both for constituency and regional list seats at elections was removed. The Law Commission was also given a statutory relationship with the Welsh Ministers—seen by some as a prelude to a Welsh legal jurisdiction.[26]

The Bill that became the Wales Act 2014 was introduced in the same month as the Silk Commission produced its second report, but decisions on whether to legislate for any of the Commission's recommendations in that report were deferred. The second report was wide-ranging: it set out a set of principles that should, in the Commission's view, determine whether an area of policy should be devolved or not, and, using those principles, the Commission recommended further devolution in a range of areas including broadcasting, transport, energy, water and (most radically) policing and justice. Better intergovernmental cooperation

[24] The Commission on Devolution in Wales, 'Empowerment and Responsibility: Legislative Powers to Strengthen Wales', March 2014.

[25] The LCM was passed on 1 July. The amendments were made in the Lords in October after Stephen Crabb had replaced David Jones as Secretary of State for Wales.

[26] The debate about the possible creation of a separate Welsh jurisdiction has continued for some time. The Welsh Government consulted on the issue in 2012: https://consultations.gov.wales/consultations/consultation-separate-legal-jurisdiction-wales. A Report from the NAW Constitutional and Legislative Affairs Committee on was published in the same year in: www.assembly.wales/Laid%20Documents/CR-LD9135%20-%20Constitutional%20and%20Legislative%20Affairs%20Committee%20-%20Inquiry%20into%20a%20Separate%20Welsh%20Jurisdiction-12122012-241484/cr-ld9135-e-English.pdf. The Silk Commission pointed out that several of the elements of a separate jurisdiction already exist in Wales, but they did not recommend the creation of a separate jurisdiction, or a separate courts system or separate legal professions. A useful recent summary of the issues is at www.geldards.com/the-law-in-wales---is-it-time-for-a-separate-legal-jurisdiction.aspx (accessed 2 June 2017). The Welsh Government announced in September 2017 that the former Lord Chief Justice, Lord Thomas of Cwmgiedd, would chair a Commission on the issue.

was also recommended. The Commission also argued that the Welsh devolution arrangements should be brought into line with those of Scotland and Northern Ireland, with the 'conferred powers' model (where Wales has only the powers conferred upon it by UK legislation) replaced by the 'reserved powers' model (where Wales has powers in all areas not reserved by legislation to London). Such a model had been argued to be incompatible with the single England and Wales legal jurisdiction[27]—an argument with which the Commission disagreed. Finally, the Commission made a number of recommendations about the Assembly itself: its size should be increased (though the Commission did not recommend a specific size, nor did it discuss the new electoral arrangements that would be necessary); inappropriate powers of the Secretary of State to intervene in proceedings should be removed and other obligations and restrictions on the NAW should be reviewed with the aim of bringing the Assembly in line with the Scottish Parliament; the Assembly should be able to call itself a Parliament, if it wished; there should be improved inter-parliamentary cooperation; the House of Lords should ensure adequate consideration of Welsh matters, and future appointments to that House should fairly represent Welsh-domiciled people; and the permanence of the NAW should be recognised.

The Prime Minister's statement on the day after the Scottish referendum had referred to the need for a new settlement in Wales (and Northern Ireland) as well as Scotland. The Silk Commission had produced a template, and the Secretary of State instituted a series of meetings between Westminster representatives of the political parties in November 2014 to consider the Commission's proposals. It was agreed at those meetings that only the recommendations on which there was a consensus should proceed—this meant, in effect, that either Conservative or Labour representatives could veto recommendations since both Plaid Cymru and Liberal Democrat parties were in favour of adopting all the Commission's proposals. A White Paper was produced just before St David's Day 2015, thus giving the process the title of the St David's Day Agreement.[28] Many of the Commission's recommendations were agreed, particularly the proposal to move to the reserved powers model. Notably, however, the policing and justice transfers were not agreed. The White Paper also promised to give Wales a similar package of constitutional powers as were being given to Scotland in response to the Smith Commission. And in anticipation of a referendum on income tax powers, a funding floor for Wales was announced, so dealing with one aspect of Welsh grievance about the Barnett formula.

A draft Wales Bill to implement the White Paper was produced for pre-legislative scrutiny on 20 October 2015. The draft Bill was considered by the Welsh Affairs Committee, which held one of its evidence sessions jointly with the NAW's

---

[27] Most notably in a joint Memorandum from the then First Minister and then Secretary of State to the Welsh Affairs Committee—Welsh Affairs Committee (2005) 'Government White Paper: Better Governance for Wales', Ev62.

[28] 'Powers for a Purpose: Towards a Lasting Devolution Settlement for Wales', Cm 9020. The word 'Agreement' has rankled some, particularly in Plaid Cymru.

Constitutional and Legal Affairs Committee. Both Committees' reports were highly critical of the draft Bill, as was an academic study that described the draft as 'constricting, clunky, inequitable and constitutionally short-sighted'.[29] Essentially, criticism focused on the apparent absence of principle in drawing up the list of reservations and the restrictions imposed on the NAW's freedom to legislate in order to preserve the single England and Wales jurisdiction, particularly a 'necessity test' that the authorities in Wales would need to apply before legislating. The Welsh Government also published its own, very different draft Westminster Bill: the Government and Laws in Wales Bill.[30] Much to his credit, the then Secretary of State recognised the validity of much of this criticism and undertook to revise the Bill extensively. This was a powerful vindication of the value of pre-legislative scrutiny—but also of its dependence on the open-mindedness of the Minister whose legislation is being scrutinised.

Assembly elections took place on 5 May 2016. Labour was the largest party, with 29 out of the NAW's 60 seats. Plaid Cymru had 12 seats and the Conservatives 11. UKIP became the first new party to join the Assembly, winning seven regional seats, thus giving itself its highest representation in any legislature in the UK. The Liberal Democrats retained only one seat. Six Assembly Members (AMs) have served as MPs; seven MPs elected in 2015 had served as AMs.[31] After a vote on the appointment of a First Minister where the result was a tie between the Leaders of Labour and Plaid Cymru, a compromise was reached where the sole Liberal Democrat was appointed to the Cabinet (all Cabinet members were restyled as 'Cabinet Secretaries') and liaison arrangements were agreed between the Government and Plaid Cymru. This has so far meant that the precarious arithmetic of the NAW has not led to unstable government.

The Wales Bill was introduced on 7 June 2016. Although much improved on the draft Bill, it was still heavily criticised both in Parliament and the NAW and outside and its progress was slow. Particularly noteworthy were Reports from the NAW's Constitutional and Legal Affairs Committee and from the Lords Constitution Committee (the two Committees held a meeting together).[32] Interestingly, the NAW's Presiding Officer, the Welsh Government and the Constitutional and Legal Affairs Committee all put forward amendments that were taken up by parliamentarians at Westminster. A number of concessions were made during the Bill's

---

[29] Welsh Affairs Committee, 'Pre-legislative Scrutiny of the draft Wales Bill', First Report of Session 2015–16, HC 449; Constitutional and Legislative Affairs Committee, 'Report on the UK Government's Draft Wales Bill', December 2015; Wales Governance Centre, Cardiff University and Constitution Unit, University College London, 'Challenge and Opportunity: The Draft Wales Bill 2015', February 2016.

[30] This Bill had, of course, no formal status at Westminster.

[31] Since their election, three AMs have left their former groups, including one who is a current MEP (Nathan Gill from UKIP), one who is a former MP and current Peer (Dafydd Elis Thomas from Plaid Cymru) and one who is a former MP (Mark Reckless from UKIP). In such a small Assembly, this has all created difficulties for allocations to committee and so on.

[32] Constitutional and Legal Affairs Committee, Report on the UK Government's Wales Bill, October 2016 www.assembly.wales/laid%20documents/cr-ld10771/cr-ld10771-e.pdf; House of Lords Select Committee on the Constitution, 'Wales Bill', Fifth Report of Session 2016–17, HL Paper 59.

parliamentary passage, especially further to restrict the number of reservations.[33] A Legislative Consent Motion was agreed only on 17 January 2017 after brinksmanship by both Westminster and Cardiff Governments, and the Bill received Royal Assent a fortnight later. The Act replicates the Scotland Act 2016 in providing for the permanence of the NAW and Welsh Government, and by providing that Parliament would not normally legislate 'with regard to' devolved matters without the consent of the NAW. As in Scotland, powers over the size of, the electoral system for, and elections to the NAW were transferred to Wales, and subjected to a supermajority requirement. The reserved powers system was introduced, together with a somewhat curious requirement for a Justice Impact Assessment to accompany NAW draft Bills.[34] Some existing statutory constraints on the NAW (such as on the composition of its committees) were, however, removed. Controversially as far as UKIP and some Conservatives were concerned, the requirement in the 2014 Act for a referendum before income tax powers came into effect was removed. This was acceptable to the Welsh Government once they had secured an agreement on a fiscal framework.

The Assembly Commission promptly established an Expert Panel to advise it on the size of the NAW and the electoral method for it (as well as whether the franchise should be extended to 16- and 17-year-olds); and, following a consultation, legislation to change the NAW's name to 'Senedd' or 'Parliament' is to be brought forward.[35] An active debate also continues as to whether there should be an entirely separate Welsh legal jurisdiction, or a distinct Welsh jurisdiction within an England and Wales jurisdiction, or whether the interests of citizens are best safeguarded by preservation of a single jurisdiction with two legislatures (an international anomaly). Meanwhile, the Assembly's Constitutional and Legal Affairs Committee remains an active monitor of Welsh devolution. At the UK level, the Conservative Party manifesto for the June 2017 General Election laid particular emphasis on cross-border cooperation, while the Labour Party's manifesto endorsed the Welsh Government's Government and Laws in Wales Bill as a way forward.

IV. DEVELOPMENTS IN NORTHERN IRELAND

Northern Ireland is often a rather awkward element of the devolution discussion: it cannot be described as a nation in the way that Wales and Scotland can, but

---

[33] See, for example, HL Deb 14 December 2016, col 1264ff where the Government made concessions on matters including water, sewerage and fixed-odds betting terminals.

[34] The reserved powers model also will have the effect of limiting the NAW's powers in some areas by reserving matters that might have been regarded as 'related to' conferred powers previously. See later discussion of the Supreme Court's decision in *Agricultural Sector (Wales) Bill—Reference by the Attorney General for England and Wales* [2014] UKSC 43, and the Welsh Government's hasty introduction of the Trade Union (Wales) Bill before the Wales Act 2017 could come into effect (discussed further below).

[35] www.bbc.co.uk/news/uk-wales-politics-40263684 (accessed 20 August 2017).

yet arguably has a more distinct identity in the UK than either of those nations. The first edition of this work described succinctly and masterfully, in the way that only a Northern Irishman could, the tensions inside a settlement that is itself built upon inter-community divisions and differing aspirations. Those tensions have continued over the past four years.

What was to become the Northern Ireland (Miscellaneous Provisions) Act 2014 was introduced in the Commons as a Bill on 9 May 2013, a draft having been published for consultation on 11 February.[36] The Bill received Royal Assent on 13 March 2014. As with all Acts with such a title, there are many disparate elements to the legislation, but several were of considerable importance for the Assembly. Paralleling what had already happened in Scotland and Wales, the Assembly's term was extended to 2016 to avoid a clash between Stormont and Westminster elections. The Act also banned 'double jobbing' so that Members of the Assembly (MLAs) could not also be MPs or members of the Dáil Éireann (the lower House of the Irish Parliament).[37] Finally, the Act made a tentative step towards a reduction in size for the Assembly. The Assembly was made up of 108 members elected by proportional representation (single transferable vote) with each Westminster constituency returning six MLAs. Under the Act, the size of the Assembly became a 'reserved matter', meaning that it was a matter on which the Assembly could legislate subject to the consent of the Secretary of State and the approval of both Houses of Parliament. However, as well as that constraint on the Assembly's legislative freedom, any amendment of size was limited to a reduction to five MLAs for each Westminster seat; every Westminster seat must have the same number of MLAs and change could only happen if there is cross-community support.

The legacy of the years of unrest was still manifest on the streets of Belfast, and there was a new source of tension between the Governments in London and Belfast because of the refusal by Sinn Féin to implement the reforms to the benefit system that had been introduced in Great Britain by the Welfare Reform Act 2012. Northern Ireland had theoretically had a separate social security system since the days of the Northern Ireland Parliament, but had always marched in step with London previously. Because of the requirement for cross-community agreement, Sinn Féin's refusal to implement the reforms meant that their partners in the Northern Ireland Executive, the Democratic Unionists (DUP), were also unable to do so. The inherent tension between theoretical legislative power and the reality of where financial power lies has never been more starkly illustrated since devolution began. Another issue was the desire across parties in Northern Ireland that corporation tax should be devolved to Northern Ireland to allow the Northern Ireland

---

[36] Cm 8563.
[37] The recommendation to ban double-jobbing between Stormont and Westminster was made by the Commission on Standards in Public Life in its 2009 'Report on MPs' Expenses and Allowances'. The Commons Northern Ireland Committee in its Report on the draft Bill recommended that the ban should be extended also to the Dáil Éireann (Second Report of Session 2012–13, HC 1003).

tax regime to compete with that in the rest of Ireland. These, and a number of other issues, were discussed between the political parties in Northern Ireland and the UK and Irish Governments. The result was the Stormont House Agreement of 23 December 2014. The Agreement deals with matters from flag-flying to oral history. But it sought to bring the welfare issue to an end. It also elicited a commitment to legislate for the devolution of corporation tax and to consider other tax devolution—Air Passenger Duty in respect of longer flights had already been devolved to Northern Ireland.[38] The Agreement further promised that the reduction in the size of the Assembly would be taken forward for the then-expected 2021 election; that arrangements would be put in place by the Assembly by March 2015 to enable those parties which would be entitled to ministerial positions in the Executive, but choose not to take them up, to be recognised as an official opposition and for their work to be facilitated; that statements to the Assembly should make clear whether they reflected an agreed Executive position; and that there should be a more transparent and robust system for MLAs' salaries and expenses. Several deadlines for implementation were missed, and the Stormont House Agreement needed rebooting in 2015 in the wake of further inter-communal tensions and a sense of crisis in Northern Ireland's political institutions. The Fresh Start Agreement, which aimed to do what its label said, was concluded on 17 November 2015.[39]

Westminster and Stormont legislation has flown from these two Agreements. At Westminster, the Corporation Tax (Northern Ireland) Act 2015 went through its parliamentary stages during the first three months of the year. Under its provisions, the Northern Ireland Assembly can fix the rate of corporation tax for small and medium enterprises based in Northern Ireland. The Northern Ireland (Welfare Reform) Act 2015 was intended to resolve the welfare dispute, and was speeded through Parliament, being introduced in the Commons on 19 November 2015 and enacted five days later. The Northern Ireland (Stormont Agreement and Implementation Plan) Act 2016 contained provisions requiring the Northern Ireland Executive not to set a budget in excess of its funding, and lengthening the period allowed for appointing Ministers after an Assembly election. There are also provisions about paramilitarism, including a requirement placed upon MLAs to make an undertaking:

— 'to support the rule of law unequivocally in word and deed and to support all efforts to uphold it;
— to work collectively with the other members of the Assembly to achieve a society free of paramilitarism;
— to challenge all paramilitary activity and associated criminality;

---

[38] Under the Finance Act 2012, and implemented in Northern Ireland by the Air Passenger Duty (Setting of Rate) Act 2012.

[39] www.gov.uk/government/news/a-fresh-start-for-northern-ireland.

— to call for, and to work together with the other members of the Assembly to achieve, the disbandment of all paramilitary organisations and their structures;

— to challenge paramilitary attempts to control communities;

— to support those who are determined to make the transition away from paramilitarism;

— to accept no authority, direction or control on my political activities other than my democratic mandate alongside my own personal and party judgment.'

Understandable as this requirement may be, it is still an exceptional way for the Westminster Parliament to seek to restrict membership of a devolved legislature— and there is, of course, no parallel provision for MPs or Peers from Northern Ireland.

At Stormont, the Assembly and Executive Reform (Assembly Opposition) Act was passed on 23 March 2016. The Act was one of the few non-Executive Bills that has become law, appropriately being sponsored by the independent MLA, John McCallister. It followed the Stormont House Agreement's provisions relating to the formation of an Opposition. As the Explanatory Memorandum made clear, the legislation was more a clear statement of intent to implement those provisions rather than something that needed strictly to be done by legislation— indeed, the necessary new standing orders were passed before the Act became law. The Departments Act (Northern Ireland) 2016 reduced the number of Executive Departments, and hence of the Assembly's statutory committees, from 12 to nine. The Assembly Members (Reduction of Numbers) Act (Northern Ireland) 2016 became law on 22 July 2016 and meant that five MLAs, rather than six, would be returned by each Westminster constituency at the next Assembly elections.

Those elections came sooner than expected. The previous elections to the Northern Ireland Assembly had taken place on 5 May 2016. Overall there was little change, with the DUP retaining the same number of seats and its leader, Arlene Foster, continuing as First Minister. Sinn Féin lost one seat, but its leader, Martin McGuinness, continued as Deputy First Minister in the power-sharing Executive. However, on 9 January 2017, Martin McGuinness resigned because of a dispute over mismanaged expenditure under a renewable energy scheme. When Sinn Féin nominated no replacement within the seven-day period of grace allowed, an election was called for 2 March 2017. This election saw a substantial increase in turnout, with a 3.9 per cent increase in Sinn Féin support, and a 1.1 per cent fall in support for the DUP, which remained the largest party with 28 seats of the Assembly's 90 seats to Sinn Féin's 27. However, the two parties were unable to agree on power-sharing. The deadline for forming an administration passed, but talks between the parties and involving both the British and Irish Governments were underway in April 2017, with the UK Government hoping that a return to direct rule could be avoided. The calling of the UK general election interrupted that process. The result of the election enormously strengthened the position of the DUP in relation to the UK Government. This was concerning to Sinn Féin, and no obvious progress in re-establishing the Assembly had happened by August 2017. Assembly engagement with the pressing post-Brexit issue of the Irish border is crucial.[40]

V. DEVOLUTION'S DIFFERENT PATH IN ENGLAND

A tidy-minded approach to the British territorial constitution might suggest a federation of four countries as a way forward. But any suggestion that a federal system could be introduced in the UK runs aground on a very jagged rock: England has over 84 per cent of the population and an even higher percentage of the wealth. Though there are even more lop-sided union states (Tanzania or Trinidad and Tobago) there is no federation where one element is so dominant. Moreover, as the Lords Constitution Committee has pointed out, the creation of an English Government would do little to meet the argument that devolution brings government closer to the governed.[41] So, despite the long-standing advocacy of the Campaign for an English Parliament and the growth of a sense of English identity—and grievance,[42] there is little likelihood of a Parliament for England coming into being.[43] If England showed any desire to embrace regional government, a federal structure might be conceivable—but there appears to be no desire for this either.[44] Nevertheless, there has been increasing evidence of a sentiment in England that devolution has resulted in advantages for Scotland, Wales and Northern Ireland but not to England.[45] One result has been the clamour for 'English votes for English laws' (EVEL)—a matter dealt with elsewhere in this book.[46] A second result has been that the word 'devolution' has been used increasingly in political dialogue in relation to England.

However, devolution in relation to England means something very different from devolution to Scotland, Wales and Northern Ireland. Essentially the 'devolution

---

[40] Both the Prime Minister in her letter to the President of the European Council triggering Article 50, and the EU response, acknowledged the particular importance of avoiding adverse cross-border Brexit consequences in Ireland. Following the majority vote in Northern Ireland in favour of remaining in the EU, Sinn Féin had called for a poll on Irish unification. This request was rejected by the UK Government. The Social Democratic and Labour Party (SDLP) also called for a border poll in their manifesto for the UK general election.

[41] Committee on the Constitution, 'The Union and Devolution', Tenth Report of Session 2015–16, HL Paper 149, para 376.

[42] C Jeffery, R Wyn Jones, A Henderson, R Scully and G Lodge, 'Taking England Seriously: The New English Politics—The Future of England Survey 2014', www.centreonconstitutionalchange.ac.uk/sites/default/files/news/Taking%20England%20Seriously_The%20New%20English%20Politics.pdf.

[43] Though it is noteworthy that the Constitution Unit at University College London is undertaking a research project on Options for an English Parliament. This is due to report in winter 2017.

[44] 'The Union and Devolution' (n 41) para 382.

[45] See www.birminghammail.co.uk/news/midlands-news/labour-hopes-english-nationalism-win-12484212#ICID=sharebar_twitter as an example of the 'English backlash'.

[46] EVEL has even been seen by some as the creation by stealth of a devolved legislature for England within Parliament.

deals' in England involve a negotiation between the Government in London and a set of councils (or sometimes a single council) that results in a tailor-made set of powers being decentralised and vested in a new regional authority, normally led by an elected Mayor. London has had its own system of government of this type since 2000 and the perceived success of that model may have been a precedent for the devolution deals. The first and most prominent devolution deal was indeed for a similar metropolitan area—Greater Manchester, where in October 2014, the UK Government and local civic leaders agreed that a 'metro-mayor' with extended powers over transport, housing, planning and policing would be created. Health and social care were later brought within his or her ambit.

In a White Paper of July 2015,[47] the UK Government proposed the extension of the model. This argued that cities were essential drivers of growth and that 'devolution of significant powers will rest on cities agreeing to rationalise govern-ance and put in place a mayor to inspire confidence'. Other 'city deals' with several northern cities were contemplated. Unlike Scotland, Wales and Northern Ireland, there was no proposal for legislative devolution, nor any proposal that the new forms of governance should be endorsed by local referendum. Indeed, the system has been characterised by one academic as concentrating power in 'closed political and business elites' rather than enhancing democracy.[48]

Further devolution deals have since been announced for more diverse areas including Cornwall, East Anglia, Liverpool, Sheffield, Tees Valley, the West Country and the West Midlands. Some deals have been rejected, including those for Greater Lincolnshire and the North East. Each deal is different, though most give powers over the further education system, business support, the Work Programme, the use of EU structural funds and planning and land use with various appropriate local add-ons. The widest-ranging deals have involved health and policing. The asymmetry between deals is seen by some as sensible pragmatism, and by others as creating a potentially chaotic system of government in England. Concern appears to have been recognised in the Conservative manifesto for the June 2017 election, with its promise to 'consolidate our approach, providing clarity across England on what devolution means for different administrations so all authorities operate in a common framework'. Earlier speculation that Theresa May was less enthusiastic about devolution deals had been quashed by the commitment in the Autumn Statement of 23 November 2016 that 'the government remains commit-ted to devolving powers'—albeit that this was 'to support local areas to address productivity barriers'.[49] In May 2017, combined authorities in Cambridgeshire and Peterborough, Greater Manchester, Liverpool City Region, Tees Valley, West of England and West Midlands elected Mayors, as did the single local authorities of Doncaster and North Tyneside.

---

[47] HM Treasury, 'Fixing the Foundations: creating a more prosperous nation', Cm 9098, July 2015.
[48] J Tomaney 'Limits of Devolution: Localism, Economics and Post-democracy' (2016) 87 *The Political Quarterly* 546.
[49] www.gov.uk/government/publications/autumn-statement-2016-documents/autumn-statement-2016.

The current statutory basis for the devolution deals is the Cities and Local Government Devolution Act 2016. This amends the Local Democracy, Economic Development and Construction Act 2009 and the Localism Act 2011. The 2016 Act has been criticised by the Lords Constitution Committee because of the wide-ranging powers it gives to Ministers by secondary legislation to change local government structures, create mayors and transfer public functions. The legislation was also compared unfavourably by the Committee with the devolution legislation for Scotland, Wales and Northern Ireland.[50] This might be a little unfair in view of the absence of any devolution of primary legislative powers under the deals inside England—it is, after all, the legislative process in Scotland, Wales and Northern Ireland that has elevated their actions expressed in primary legislation, at least in the eyes of the Supreme Court,[51] above the actions of other statutory bodies, including the new English devolved bodies. However, the general criticism is valid—that Parliament is too willing to give powers in important areas away to Ministers.

It is conceivable that Mayors will in the future seek legislative powers—for example, the statutory powers over certain taxes exercised in Scotland, Wales and Northern Ireland is envied by London and that envy may spread. The Labour Party in its manifesto for the 2017 general election called for a Minister for England. So devolution in England is likely to be, as it has been elsewhere in the UK, a 'process, not an event'. Variety will show what is successful and what is not—and the Secretary of State's annual report on devolution in England, a requirement inserted into the 2016 Act during its parliamentary progress,[52] will be a useful quarry of information. Parliament will also need to be ready to develop its own processes and structures to deal with increased English devolution—one consequence of the form of devolution in England is that there is no institutional response in Parliament to the devolved structures in England, other than the Communities and Local Government Select Committee and other mechanisms to hold Ministers involved in the devolution deals to account. But it is hard to dissent from the words with which the Lords Constitution Committee concluded its mammoth Report on the Union and Devolution: 'what is clear is that the English Question remains one of the central unresolved issues facing decision-makers grappling with the UK's territorial constitution.'[53]

VI. SOME ISSUES

A. The Problems of Two Legislatures

The legislatures at the central and devolved levels are co-legislators for their territories, and should form, in the words of the McKay Commission,

---

[50] 'The Union and Devolution' (n 41) para 393.
[51] See Lord Hope at para 49 in *AXA General Insurance Limited v The Lord Advocate* [2011] UKSC 46.
[52] Section 1.
[53] *The Union and Devolution* (n 41) para 430.

a 'legislative partnership'.[54] That is not always the case. Instead it has been a common complaint that relations between the devolved legislatures and Westminster are not as good as they ought to be. The Westminster Parliament has set up few structures that respond adequately to devolution, and opportunities for Committees in London and Edinburgh/Cardiff/Belfast to work cooperatively together have, with a few notable exceptions,[55] rarely been taken. There are no formal mechanisms for the scrutiny of inter-governmental relations. Simple matters like Ministers willingly giving evidence to Committees at the other legislature, or access passes to Westminster for parliamentarians from the devolved legislatures, have not happened. One particularly unsatisfactory area of potential tension between legislatures is the way in which the devolved administrations increasingly have powers to raise their own taxation subject to an agreed fiscal framework, while they receive funding under the non-statutory and inherently unsatisfactory Barnett formula—a formula that is often perceived in England as unfairly benefitting Scotland in particular.[56]

This is compounded by ignorance about the rather confusing delineation of responsibilities. Even in areas like health that have now been devolved for almost 20 years, there remains uncertainty among citizens and civil society about the respective responsibilities of central government and the devolved governments. English issues, like health and social care, figured strongly in the UK general election of June 2017. This confusion is particularly acute in Wales with its weak local media and closer cross-border integration. All four Parliaments have done good work through their outreach services to counter these misapprehensions, but individual parliamentarians representing the same geographical area in Westminster, or in one of the devolved nations, have not always been so keen to point out the limits of their responsibilities, especially when the parliamentarian representing the same area in the other legislature is drawn from a different political party.

With capacity at the devolved level an issue, especially in Wales but also in Scotland, innovative means of cooperation and joint scrutiny could produce a solution that would be mutually beneficial. The McKay Commission recommended a Devolution Committee of the House of Commons that could consider the consequences of United Kingdom decisions on cross-border effects, hold United Kingdom/English ministers to account, evaluate Legislative Consent Motions and how they work in practice and raise awareness of the implications of devolution. This could become a wider Committee with representatives of the devolved legislatures for some at least of its work. Indeed, the Scottish Conservatives have in the past proposed a Standing Committee of the Parliaments and Assemblies,[57]

[54] See Part VII of the Report of the Commission on the Consequences of Devolution for the House of Commons, chaired by Sir William McKay.
[55] The Lords Constitution Committee and the Welsh Affairs Committee in the Commons, for example.
[56] For a comprehensive analysis of the strengths and weaknesses of the Barnett formula, see House of Lords Select Committee on the Barnett Formula, Report of Session 2008–09, HL 139.
[57] See Scottish Conservatives 'Commission on the Future Governance of Scotland: Report', May 2014, 18.

while the British/Irish Parliamentary Assembly could be developed into a more effective body, not least in the context of the concerns about the consequences of Brexit for the border between Northern Ireland and the Republic.

B. Legislative Consent

In the Scottish Parliament, a Bill under consideration in the UK Parliament which makes provision applying to Scotland for any purpose within the legislative competence of the Scottish Parliament, or which alters that legislative competence or the executive competence of the Scottish Ministers, must be subject to a legislative consent memorandum (LCM) from the Scottish Government. This Memorandum is considered by the relevant Scottish Parliament committee before the motion itself is considered in plenary.[58] A relatively large number of Westminster Bills are subject to the procedure: 13 in Session 2012–13; 11 in Session 2013–14; seven in Session 2014–15 and four in Session 2015–16. The NAW follows similar procedures to those in Scotland. The Welsh Government tables a legislative consent memorandum in respect of any relevant Bill, with the memorandum normally being considered in the appropriate committee. A relevant Bill is one under consideration in the UK Parliament which makes provision in relation to Wales for any purpose within the legislative competence of the Assembly or which modifies the legislative competence of the Assembly. Since 2012, over 30 Westminster Bills have been subject to legislative consent procedures. In addition, in Wales, the Welsh Government must lay a written statement setting out its view of any Westminster Bill that modifies the functions of the Welsh Ministers, the Counsel General, the Assembly or the Assembly Commission.[59] Under the procedures of the Northern Ireland Assembly, an LCM is a motion that seeks the agreement of the Assembly to the UK Parliament considering provisions of a Bill that deal with a devolution matter. This is defined to mean either a transferred matter or a change to the Assembly's legislative competence, or the executive functions of a Minister or a department.[60] One added complication in Northern Ireland is that the Minister proposing the LCM must have cross-community agreement in the Executive to do so.

Most LCMs are uncontroversial and are passed because it is simply more convenient for legislation covering a matter that is devolved to be passed for the whole of the UK (or for Great Britain) in Parliament. This is not always the case. The NAW rejected an LCM in respect of the Trade Union Bill on 26 January 2016. It was the UK Government's position that an LCM was not necessary because industrial relations were outwith the Assembly's powers. The Welsh Government, relying on the way in which the Supreme Court had interpreted the

---

[58] Chapter 9B of the Standing Orders.
[59] Standing Orders 29 and 30.
[60] Standing Order 42A.

Agricultural Wages case,[61] believed the contrary. Despite the refusal of the LCM, the Trade Union Act 2016 was passed in the UK Parliament. Early in 2017, the Welsh Government introduced the Trade Union (Wales) Bill to repeal certain sections of the UK Act in respect of Wales. This was passed on 18 July 2017 before the relevant sections of the Wales Act 2017 came into force and before therefore industrial relations became a reserved matter. It had been expected that the law-fulness of the Trade Union (Wales) Act would be referred to the Supreme Court by the Attorney-General (the Welsh Government's Finance Secretary has said that any attempt to reverse the Bill would be a 'democratic outrage'). The refer-ence, in fact did not happen—though the Secretary of State for Wales promised that the UK Government would 'at the next available opportunity' take action to ensure that the safeguards in the Trade Union Act 2016 applied throughout Great Britain.[62] This may conceivably involve Westminster reversing the Assembly Act.

As mentioned earlier,[63] some (but not all) of the matters covered by LCMs are now mentioned in statute: section 2 of the Scotland Act 2016 inserts the words 'But it is recognised that the Parliament of the United Kingdom will not nor-mally legislate with regard to devolved matters without the consent of the Scottish Parliament' into the Scotland Act 1998. A parallel provision is made by section 2 of the Wales Act 2017. The effect of these provisions was determined by the Supreme Court in *Miller*. Commenting first that 'Judges … are neither the parents nor the guardians of political conventions; they are merely observers', the Court was of the view that 'the purpose of the legislative recognition of the convention was to entrench it as a convention'. But even entrenched conventions were not matters for the courts to determine: 'the Sewel Convention has an important role in facili-tating harmonious relationships between the UK Parliament and the devolved legislatures. But the policing of its scope and the manner of its operation does not lie within the constitutional remit of the judiciary, which is to protect the rule of law'.[64] The conclusion that these statutory provisions are examples of legislation that is not within the fence of the rule of law and hence of judicial protection is certainly striking, not least because a reasonable assumption might be that Parlia-ment had intended to create a justiciable rule. It also opens the question as to what the purpose is of putting a convention in a statute if it is not to be justiciable, and how an entrenched convention is to be distinguished from a convention that is not entrenched.[65]

---

[61] *Agricultural Sector (Wales) Bill—Reference by the Attorney General for England and Wales* [2014] UKSC 43—see s D below.

[62] www.bbc.co.uk/news/uk-wales-politics-39513747 and letters from the Attorney-General and the Secretary of State for Wales to the Clerk and Chief Executive of the NAW of 10 August 2017 published at http://senedd.assembly.wales/mgIssueHistoryHome.aspx?IId=16591.

[63] See ch 8, ss II and III.

[64] [2017] UKSC 5, paras 136 to 151.

[65] For a discussion of the issues, see E Velasco and C Crummey, 'The Reading of Section 28(8) of the Scotland Act 1998 as a Political Convention in Miller', *UK Const L* blog (3 February 2017) (available at https://ukconstitutionallaw.org) and J Atkinson, 'Parliamentary Intent and the Sewel Convention as a Legislatively Entrenched Political Convention', *UK Const L* blog (10 February 2017) (available at https://ukconstitutionallaw.org).

Without the protection of the Courts, and in the absence of any satisfactory procedural notice being taken in Parliament of the willingness or otherwise of the devolved legislatures to approve LCMs,[66] there is something inherently unsatisfactory in the LCM process. As one commentator[67] appositely wrote after the Supreme Court judgment, 'the court may simply be an observer, watching on as the children fight. But something should be in place to try and avoid, or at least minimise, such fights in the future if we are to maintain anything that resembles a harmonious, coherent, stable and workable devolution settlement'. This concern is only likely to grow as legislation to implement Brexit is brought forward, especially when it is likely that that there will be legislation that will be argued to cover devolved matters and that will be objectionable to one or more of the devolved legislatures. Brexit means an increased likelihood that LCMs will be refused.[68]

C. Brexit

The result of the referendum on the UK's membership of the EU will overshadow all British politics for decades. But there is also a devolution dimension that may result in profound constitutional change within the union of Great Britain and Northern Ireland. The referendum showed Wales and England voting in very similar ways—52.5 per cent and 53.4 per cent respectively voted to leave the EU. However, every electoral region in Scotland voted to remain within the EU, with 62.0 per cent of Scottish voters overall in favour of EU membership. There was also a majority to remain within Northern Ireland where 55.8 per cent voted to remain, with a correlation between nationalist areas voting to remain and unionist areas voting to leave.

Four issues have emerged. The first is the extent to which the devolved nations should be involved in the Brexit process. The second is the extent of any effective power that they might hold to affect that process. The third is the way in which their competences may be changed. The final issue is what Brexit may do to the future constitution of the UK.

At an extraordinary session of the British Irish Council on 22 July 2016, Carwyn Jones suggested that all four Parliaments of the UK should ratify any post-Brexit deal.[69] A letter to the Prime Minister to this effect was endorsed by Nicola

---

[66] The Lords Minute contains a daily list of Bills in progress which refers to LCMs, while the Commons Order Paper mentions LCMs as Notes to Bills. Hard copies of LCMs are available on demand in the Vote Office and their texts are published among Bill documents on the Bills before Parliament web pages.

[67] P Reid, 'Time to Give the Sewel Convention Some (Political) Bite?', *UK Const L* blog (26 January 2017) (available at https://ukconstitutionallaw.org).

[68] For a full discussion of the particular potential problems in Northern Ireland (though with a read-across to Scotland and Wales) see C Harvey and D Holder, 'The Great Repeal Bill and the Good Friday Agreement—Cementing a Stalemate or Constitutional Collision Course?', *UK Const L* blog (6 June 2017) (available at ukconstitutionallaw.org).

[69] See also his speech to the Chicago Council on Global Affairs, 9 September 2016.

Sturgeon and sent in advance of a meeting of the Joint Ministerial Council on 24 October 2016. Meanwhile, an Institute for Government report suggested that while Parliament might be sovereign, to ignore the will of the devolved legislatures would be a 'reckless strategy for a government committed to the union'.[70] The first report from the Commons Exiting the European Union Committee[71] concluded that it was 'essential that all the devolved governments, and the different regions of England, are duly involved in the process and have their views taken into account'. However, an amendment that would have called for the devolved legislatures, as well as Parliament, to endorse the final deal was only supported by SNP, Plaid Cymru, SDLP and Liberal Democrat Committee members and was therefore rejected in the Committee. The issue was subsequently raised in debate on the European Union (Notification of Withdrawal) Bill, when Labour MPs joined other opposition MPs in supporting a new clause (rejected by 333 votes to 276) that would have required strengthened powers for a Joint Ministerial Council in the Brexit negotiations.[72]

There has been an undertaking by the UK Government of serious engagement with the Scottish Government (as well as those in Wales and Northern Ireland) on Brexit, and regular meetings have been held of a new intergovernmental committee.[73] However, following the Supreme Court's dismissal of any argument that the devolved legislatures had a legislative competence in respect of EU withdrawal parallel to that of the UK Parliament,[74] it is unlikely that the wishes of the devolved Governments and Parliaments will prevail where they are at odds with the wishes of London. Consultation but no ceding of control appears the UK Government stance. However, a minority Government that depends on DUP votes may need to make concessions that a majority Government would have hoped to avoid.

The devolution settlements were, of course, predicated on the UK's membership of the EU (and provided that the devolved nations had to comply with EU law) with the constraints that imposed on aspects of domestic policy-making that are now devolved—for example state aids, the VAT regime or agricultural support. There is a potential here for substantial new powers to pass to the devolved administrations. Indeed, the Prime Minister has spoken clearly about the 'significantly increased decision-making powers' that will flow to the devolved administrations as a consequence of Brexit.[75] However, the White Paper 'Legislating for the United Kingdom's Withdrawal from the European Union'[76] emphasised

---

[70] www.instituteforgovernment.org.uk/node/3013.

[71] Exiting the European Union Committee, First Report of Session 2016–17, HC 815, www.publications.parliament.uk/pa/cm201617/cmselect/cmexeu/815/815.pdf.

[72] HC Deb, 6 February 2017, col 130ff.

[73] JMC (EN); see www.gov.uk/government/news/pm-to-meet-ministers-from-devolved-nations-at-first-jmc-meeting-in-wales.

[74] [2017] UKSC 5, para 130.

[75] HC Deb 29. March 2017.

[76] Cm 9466, www.gov.uk/government/uploads/system/uploads/attachment_data/file/604516/Great_repeal_bill_white_paper_accessible.pdf; see pages 27 and 28.

the importance of maintaining a single market within the UK and of common frameworks within the UK. This was confirmed in the Conservatives' June 2017 election manifesto—a document characterised by the Institute for Government as 'assertive unionism'.[77] Hence it is likely that there will be areas where competences are ostensibly fully devolved but where the powers repatriated from Brussels may well eventually be held in London rather than passed to Edinburgh, Cardiff and Belfast.[78] The new political arithmetic in Westminster after 8 June 2017, and the Conservatives' dependence on the DUP, may change this, though Nicola Sturgeon and Carwyn Jones issued a joint statement on publication of the European Union (Withdrawal) Bill in July 2017 claiming that the Bill was a 'naked power grab'.[79]

The decision by the Scottish Government to call for a second independence referendum demonstrated a belief that the result of the Brexit process is likely to bolster support for independence. Despite the vote on 8 June, that is certainly a possible future, and it is also possible that support for a united Ireland will grow (Sinn Féin and the SDLP have called for a border poll). But Brexit could also boost unionism, and even be a threat to devolution, especially in Wales: Andrew RT Davies, the Leader of the Welsh Conservatives, said soon after the referendum that the anti-establishment, post-Brexit mood might mean that a majority in Wales would, if asked, vote to abolish the Assembly.[80] A more nuanced view from Labour AM Jeremy Miles, that anti-establishment disillusionment might affect it over time, might equally apply in Scotland.[81]

One other consequence of Brexit needs to be mentioned: the devolved legislatures and governments will, of course, face similar challenges to their London equivalents as legislation inside the UK is adjusted to take account of British withdrawal from the EU—and the same concerns about Henry VIII powers in London will apply equally in Edinburgh, Cardiff and Belfast.

D. Role of the Supreme Court[82]

Aside from *Miller*, four other important devolution cases over the past three years have shown how the Supreme Court has undertaken the role of determining the

---

[77] www.instituteforgovernment.org.uk/blog/devolution-and-manifestos-four-key-questions (accessed 18 August 2017).

[78] See G Peretz, 'Storm Clouds over the Welsh Mountains: Agriculture and Devolution' *UK Const L* blog (30 March 2017) (available at https://ukconstitutionallaw.org).

[79] https://news.gov.scot/news/eu-withdrawal-bill (accessed 21 August 2017).

[80] Institute of Welsh Affairs, 'Click on Wales', 28 August 2016, www.iwa.wales/click/2016/08/welsh-assembly-swept-away-anti-establishment-tide.

[81] Tweet retrieved 29 August 2016: https://twitter.com/Jeremy_Miles. There has also been some polling evidence that people is Wales are 'indycurious'—see www.iwa.wales/click/2017/06/indycurious-wales/#.WTFQY2YC9g8.twitter.

[82] For a full discussion of the Supreme Court and Devolution, see House of Commons Library Briefing Paper No 07670 of 27 July 2016 (Jack Simson-Caird).

devolution settlement. The first was the case of the Agricultural Sector (Wales) Bill[83]—a reference to the Court by the Attorney-General under section 112(1) of the Government of Wales Act 2006. The UK Government had abolished the regime for regulating agricultural wages under the Enterprise and Regulatory Reform Act 2013. The Agricultural Sector (Wales) Bill sought to reinstate that system in Wales. Agriculture was a conferred matter under the Government of Wales Act, and the Welsh Government argued that agricultural wages were a 'related matter' to agriculture. The Attorney-General disagreed, submitting that the Bill did not relate to agriculture but to employment and industrial relations, which were not devolved. The court found unanimously against the Attorney-General. The second case was the reference to the court by the Counsel General under section 99(1) of the Government of Wales Act 2006 of the Recovery of Medical Costs for Asbestos Diseases (Wales) Bill.[84] In this case, two issues were before the court: whether the Bill interfered with the rights of the insurers under the European Convention on Human Rights (ECHR) to the peaceful enjoyment of their possessions; and whether the Bill was within the competence of the NAW. On the first issue, the court found that the retrospective effect of the Bill required special justification, but that this was absent. On the second issue, the court decided that the subject matter of the Bill was not sufficiently 'related to' the 'organisation and funding of [the] national health service' to be within competence (though the justices were divided on this issue). The third case was one from Scotland.[85] In this case, four registered charities with an interest in family matters, and three individual parents, challenged Part 4 of the Children and Young People (Scotland) Act 2014 on the basis that it was outside the legislative competence of the Scottish Parliament because it related to matters which were reserved to the UK Parliament, and that it was incompatible with rights under the ECHR and/or EU law. The court found that the Act was within competence of the Parliament, but incompatible with the ECHR. The Court invited written submissions as to the terms of its order under section 102 of the Scotland Act in order to give the Scottish Parliament and Scottish Ministers an opportunity to address the matters raised in the judgment. In the meantime, since the defective provisions of Part 4 of the 2014 Act were not within the legislative competence of the Scottish Parliament, they could not be brought into force. In a further Scottish case, the Supreme Court found that a provision in the Sexual Offences (Scotland) Act 2009 was not compatible with the ECHR, and that it was not possible to interpret the statute narrowly so that it would be compatible. Therefore, in accordance with section 29 of the Scotland Act 1998, the provision was outside the competence of the Scottish Parliament and was not law.[86]

---

[83] *Agricultural Sector (Wales) Bill—Reference by the Attorney General for England and Wales* [2014] UKSC 43.

[84] *Recovery of Medical Costs for Asbestos Diseases (Wales) Bill: Reference by the Counsel General for Wales (Applicant) and The Association of British Insurers (Intervener)* [2015] UKSC 3.

[85] *The Christian Institute and others (Appellants) v The Lord Advocate (Respondent) (Scotland)* [2016] UKSC 5.

[86] *AB (Appellant) v Her Majesty's Advocate (Respondent) (Scotland)* [2017] UKSC 25.

In a lecture delivered in October 2016 on the constitutional role of the Supreme Court in the context of devolution in the UK,[87] the President of the Court, Lord Neuberger, argued that 'the Supreme Court has been conceived, born and brought up at a time of constitutional changes which have required the judges in the UK, and particularly its top court, to have an ever-increasing constitutional role'—and that this had been particularly apparent in its role of determining the lawfulness of devolved legislation. Though he argued against the need for a separate Constitutional Court, it is increasingly apparent that the way in which the powers of the legislatures and governments of the UK relate to one another will become matters for the arbitrament of the Supreme Court, and pressure may grow for disputes between central and devolved Governments to be resolved in the Court, as happens in other federal systems. There may even be pressure for the devolved governments to be able to challenge Westminster legislation as the Westminster Government is able to do in the case of devolved legislation—with the inevitable consequence that the protection of Westminster proceedings under Article IX of the Bill of Rights would need to change.[88]

E. Rebalancing the Constitution

Devolution has developed in the UK in a piecemeal and pragmatic way. Many regard that as a problem. In the opinion of the Lords Constitution Committee, 'there is no evidence of strategic thinking in the past about the development of devolution. There has been no guiding strategy or framework of principles to ensure that devolution develops in a coherent or consistent manner'.[89] But the turbulence in the relationship between the nations of the UK has also led some unionists to call for something more fundamental than devolution based on consistent principles. For example, former Prime Minister Gordon Brown has on several occasions expressed support for some form of federalism—an idea endorsed in the Labour Party's manifesto for the 2017 general election,[90] while the cross-party Constitution Reform Group, chaired by Lord Salisbury, but also containing senior politicians from the Conservative, Labour, Liberal Democrat and Ulster Unionist parties, has published a draft Act of Union Bill under which each of England, Scotland, Wales and Northern Ireland would determine its own affairs to the extent that it considers it should, but would also be free to choose to share, through the United Kingdom, functions which are more effectively exercised on a shared basis.[91]

---

[87] www.supremecourt.uk/docs/speech-161014.pdf.

[88] This suggestion was made by one Plaid Cymru AM. See www.walesonline.co.uk/news/politics/demand-powers-challenge-increasingly-dangerous-12388162.

[89] *The Union and Devolution* (n 41).

[90] For example, at the 2016 Edinburgh Book Festival. See also www.theguardian.com/politics/2017/mar/18/gordon-brown-to-push-patriotic-third-option-for-more-powerful-scotland-after-brexit.

[91] www.constitutionreformgroup.co.uk. The author of this chapter declares his interest as a member of the group.

Constitutional change will happen. A federal constitution, new judicial powers, curtailed parliamentary competence, and a potential new role for a House of Lords reconstituted as a Senate are all possible. The dissonance between fiscal independence for the devolved nations and their dependency on fiscal transfers from the wealthier parts of England will need resolution. The absence of any apparent desire for English legislative devolution may change when powerful mayors are in post throughout England. The break-up of the UK also remains a possibility. Any radical constitutional development has profound consequences for Parliament. The sticking-plaster of EVEL will be discussed in another chapter. But whatever its merits may be, EVEL is unlikely to save the Union in its present form and Parliament should be ready for more fundamental, devolution-inspired, change.

9

'English Votes for English Laws'

LIAM LAURENCE SMYTH

I. INTRODUCTION

ENGLAND HAS NO Parliament. The Acts of Union, with Scotland in 1707 and with Ireland in 1801, created a unitary Parliament for a United Kingdom dominated by England, with Members for English constituencies holding by far the greatest number of seats.

The uncodified British Constitution now includes statutory legislatures for Northern Ireland, Scotland and Wales with differing but very substantial competences.[1] The asymmetry in legislative jurisdiction results in MPs for Scottish constituencies being entitled to vote, perhaps decisively, on matters affecting England when such matters in Scotland are decided not at Westminster but by the devolved Scottish Parliament. Enoch Powell, by then an Ulster Unionist, dubbed this asymmetry the West Lothian Question in tribute to the constituency of Tam Dalyell who, along with Neil Kinnock in Wales, was among the foremost Labour opponents of devolution in the late 1970s.

The failure of the Scottish and Welsh referendums in 1979 to reach the required threshold for a Yes vote precipitated the fall of the Callaghan Government in a motion of no confidence moved by Mrs Thatcher, whose subsequent Government from 1979 to 1990 showed no interest in reviving plans for devolution of powers to Scotland or Wales. The troubled Northern Ireland Assembly which existed from 1982 to 1986 failed to make headway in ending direct rule of the Province, despite the 1985 Anglo–Irish Agreement. A halving of the number of seats held in Scotland by Conservatives over the period of the Thatcher and Major Governments exacerbated the gulf between a Labour-dominated Scotland and a comfortable Conservative majority in England.[2]

---

[1] See ch 8 by Sir Paul Silk in the present volume for more on devolution and the UK Parliament.

[2] The number of seats in Scotland won by Conservatives in 1979 was 22, and broadly the same at 21 in 1983, but fell to 10 in 1987 remaining steady at 11 in 1992 followed by a complete wipe-out of Conservative MPs in Scotland in the 1997 New Labour landslide.

Under John Major, Prime Minster from 1990 to 1997, the Conservative Government responded to demands for a greater distinctive voice for Scotland at Westminster by extending the scope of proceedings in the Scottish Grand Committee which began to meet occasionally in Scotland as a debating forum comprising all MPs for Scottish constituencies.

The new Labour Government which swept to power in 1997 under Tony Blair succeeded in establishing a new Scottish Parliament and a weaker and initially less popular National Assembly for Wales.[3] The 1998 Good Friday Agreement led to another Northern Ireland Assembly, an ingenious piece of constitutional machinery intended to generate permanent power-sharing in both the executive and legislative branches of government. An effort to pave the way for regional assemblies in England fell at the first hurdle in November 2004, with the failure of a referendum in the North-East, which had been thought to be the most promising part of England in terms of a desire to express a strong sense of regional identity.

Under Gordon Brown, the Labour Government introduced English regional select and grand committees,[4] but his attempt to revitalise the grand committee system proved no more long-lasting than had that of John Major. The English regional select and grand committees were not continued into the 2010 Coalition Parliament.

How to respond to the West Lothian Question was among the topics on which the coalition parties had differing views. A Commission under Sir William McKay, a former Clerk of the House of Commons, was appointed in February 2012 and reported in March 2013.[5] The McKay Commission recommended that MPs from outside England should continue to vote on all legislation but with prior knowledge of the view from England.[6] The McKay Commission concluded that:

> If perceived concerns and political expectations in England are to be met, any new procedures should be simple, comprehensible and accessible. Proposals must be widely regarded as fair, go with the grain of parliamentary procedure and practice, give politics the chance to work, and respect the prerogatives of all MPs.[7]

The coalition Government could not agree which items to take forward from the menu of proposals from the McKay Commission.

---

[3] In the referendums held in 1997, the Scottish Parliament was supported by 44.7% of the electorate (74.3% of those who voted) while the National Assembly for Wales secured no more than 25.2% (50.3% of those who voted).

[4] Regional grand committees and regional select committees were established for East Midlands, East of England, North East, North West, South East, South West, West Midlands and Yorkshire and the Humber on 12 November 2008, with a regional select committee on London being added on 25 June 2009.

[5] Commission on the Consequences of Devolution for the House of Commons (chair: Sir William McKay), Report on the Consequences of Devolution for the House of Commons, March 2013, at http://webarchive.nationalarchives.gov.uk/20130403030652/http://tmc.independent.gov.uk/wp-content/uploads/2013/03/The-McKay-Commission_Main-Report_25-March-20131.pdf.

[6] ibid, Executive Summary, para 15.

[7] ibid, para 18.

II. ENGLISH VOTES FOR ENGLISH LAWS

A. The Return of EVEL

William Hague had used the slogan 'English Votes for English Laws' (EVEL) during his spell as one of the series of Conservative leaders of the Opposition facing Tony Blair.[8] He revived the term during his last period of ministerial office, as Leader of the House in the final phase of the 2010–15 coalition Government. In December 2014 the coalition Government published a consultation paper which unusually outlined separate party proposals, with three Conservative options and a distinct alternative approach from the Liberal Democrats.[9] The Conservative manifesto in 2015 promised 'we will introduce English votes for English laws, answering the longstanding West Lothian Question in our democracy'.[10] It fell to Chris Grayling as Leader of the House in the incoming Conservative Government to implement EVEL in practice.

B. The Grayling Approach

There were two key decisions taken by Chris Grayling on implementing EVEL: that it should be a Commons-only procedure governed by Standing Orders, rather than a statutory reshaping of the powers of the House of Commons; and that EVEL decisions should be effective and not merely advisory.

The Standing Orders of the House of Commons were brought together in the mid-nineteenth century as a selection of significant resolutions of the House of Commons governing aspects of parliamentary procedure which had been given continuing ('standing') effect lasting indefinitely beyond the Session in which they were adopted. Standing Orders in the British Parliament persist beyond Dissolution from one Parliament to the next.

While House of Commons Standing Orders have grown considerably in length, and have been subject to periodic revision, they are still far from a comprehensive codification of parliamentary procedure. They can be repealed, amended and disapplied or varied in a particular case by a decision of the House requiring no more than a simple majority. Bringing in EVEL by Standing Orders was simpler, quicker and more flexible than doing so by primary legislation which would have taken far longer, possibly displacing other priorities in the legislative programme,

---

[8] For example, in a speech at the Centre for Policy Studies on 15 July 1999. See also the Report of the Commission to Strengthen Parliament (July 2000) chaired by Lord (Philip) Norton of Louth and 'Answering the question: devolution, the West Lothian Question and the future of the Union', the Report of the Conservative Democracy Task Force (2008) headed by Kenneth Clarke.

[9] 'The Implications of Devolution for England', Cm 8969, 2014.

[10] A more detailed review of the historical backdrop to the 2015 Standing Orders may be found in M Kenny and D Gover, 'Finding the Good in EVEL: An Evaluation of "English Votes for English Laws" in the House of Commons', Mile End Institute at Queen Mary University of London, November 2016.

and which would have entailed securing the far from certain acquiescence of the Lords where the Conservatives alone could not command a majority. The corollary of the flexibility of Standing Orders is the readiness with which another Government could get rid of EVEL by repealing the relevant Standing Orders, assuming it had a majority in the Commons.

The McKay Commission's approach had been that any consequences of the House over-riding the majority view of Members for constituencies in England should follow through political and democratic accountability. In other words, a Government would have to face the political consequences of relying on non-English MPs to pass measures affecting England. The Grayling approach of making EVEL decisions effective meant that the EVEL Standing Orders had to be quite lengthy and complicated in order that differences on the text of Bills between the House as whole and English MPs as a group could be resolved in a kind of internal 'ping-pong'.

Despite the apprehensions to which the slogan 'English Votes for English Laws' gave rise, the Standing Order package brought forward by Chris Grayling did not provide for a new legislative process for English legislation. Instead, it allowed a majority of MPs for constituencies in England to block primary or secondary legislation applying to England. The 'V' in EVEL should really stand for 'veto'.[11]

The courts are bound by the principle expressed in Article IX of the Bill of Rights not to 'impeach or question' proceedings in Parliament. The fact that EVEL affords a veto power only makes it even less likely that this aspect of the internal processes of the House of Commons will come before the courts. Any primary legislation made by Parliament must still be passed by the House of Commons; any secondary legislation subject to the affirmative procedure must be approved by the House of Commons; and any secondary legislation subject to annulment may be annulled only by the House of Commons.[12] So at the most EVEL might result in legislation not including provisions which were vetoed at some stage under EVEL procedures in the Commons.

C. Debating EVEL

The Government's approach to EVEL was vigorously contested on the floor in both Houses and also subjected to scrutiny by several select committees. As Leader of the House Chris Grayling gave evidence to the House of Commons Procedure Committee on 8 September 2015 and to the House of Commons Public

---

[11] There has been no case yet of a Bill certified as relating wholly to England, which would under Standing Order No 83K be considered by a public bill committee not only confined to Members for constituencies in England but reflecting party strengths among Members for constituencies in England. The Standing Orders make no comparable provision for Bills such as the Charities (Protection and Social Investment) Bill [Lords] of Session 2015–16, the only Bill to date certified as relating wholly to England and Wales.

[12] The House of Lords, whose powers are unaffected by the House of Commons EVEL Standing Orders, may also annul statutory instruments subject to the negative procedure. Most affirmative statutory instruments require also the approval of the House of Lords. And, barring the exceptional cases where the Parliament Act is brought to bear, primary legislation is passed also by the House of Lords.

Administration and Constitutional Affairs Committee on 10 November 2015. His successor David Lidington gave evidence to the House of Lords Constitution Committee on 14 September 2016. In addition to regular weekly scrutiny at Business Questions every sitting Thursday, and the Ministerial Statement on 2 July, there were debates in the House of Commons on 7 and 15 July 2015, in the House of Lords on 16 July 2015 and in the House of Commons again on 22 October 2015.

On 2 July 2015 the Leader of the House announced at Business Questions that there would be two days of debate on Standing Order changes relating to English votes for English laws, with the first taking place on 15 July 2015. The Leader of the House made a statement the same day after Business Questions on the Government's proposals.[13]

Alistair Carmichael, one of the few Liberal Democrats remaining in the House after the 2015 general election, and one of only three non-SNP MPs elected in Scotland in 2015,[14] successfully applied on 6 July 2015 for an emergency debate on the decision to introduce EVEL through Standing Orders. The debate was held on 7 July 2015 and ended in a Division on which the Government abstained.[15]

The first day of debate in Government time took the form of a general debate on an unamendable motion, 'That this House has considered the matter of English votes for English laws', on 15 July 2015.[16] The House of Lords debated the Government's proposals for the EVEL changes in House of Commons procedure on 16 July 2015 and, on 21 July 2015, voted by 320 to 139 to support a motion to establish a Joint Committee 'to consider and report on the constitutional implications' of the proposed new EVEL procedures.[17] The Message from the Lords was printed in the House of Commons Votes and Proceedings for 21 July 2015 but no further action was taken until Graham Allen (Labour, Nottingham North) unsuccessfully moved, as an Amendment to the package of Standing Order changes agreed by the House on 22 October 2015, that the Commons agree to the Lords proposal to establish a joint committee.[18]

Updated proposals were published by the Government on 15 October 2015, when the Leader of the House announced that the second and decisive day of debate on the Standing Order changes would be held on 22 October 2015. The final

---

[13] The Government's paper, 'English Votes for English Laws: Proposed Changes to the Standing Orders of the House of Commons and Explanatory Memorandum', 2 July 2015, was succeeded on 14 July 2015 by a revised version which was the basis for the debate on 15 July 2015. The revisions concerned the applicability of the new procedures to Supply Bills, money resolutions and ways and means motions.

[14] The others were David Mundell (Dumfriesshire, Clydesdale & Tweeddale, Conservative) and Ian Murray (Labour, Edinburgh South).

[15] Ayes 2; Noes 291.

[16] The motion was not amendable because under Standing Order No 24B, where a motion, 'That this House has considered a matter', is expressed in neutral terms, no amendments to it may be tabled. The motion was agreed to without a Division after hours of debate; the Government had tabled a business motion to extend the debate to 10pm instead of the normal moment of interruption on a Wednesday at 7pm.

[17] HL Deb 21 July 2015, cols 1007–31.

[18] Ayes 215, Noes 312.

text of the proposed Standing Order changes was tabled on 19 October 2015 after the publication of the report of the House of Commons Procedure Committee.[19]

The changes to Standing Orders were adopted on 22 October 2015 by 312 votes to 270.[20] The EVEL Standing Orders as adopted on 22 October 2015 applied to most Government Bills receiving a Second Reading in the Commons after that date. Private Members' Bills, Law Commission Bills and Supply Bills are not covered by the EVEL procedure.

III. EXTENT AND APPLICATION

Although the EVEL slogan, and the present chapter up to this point, referred to 'English' laws, the policy also gives a veto to MPs for constituencies in England or Wales on matters within devolved legislative competence which relate only to England and Wales. There is no comparable veto for MPs with constituencies in Wales on matters within devolved legislative competence relating only to Wales.

There is no legal jurisdiction extending only to England. Laws may extend to the United Kingdom, to Great Britain (England and Wales, and Scotland), to Northern Ireland, to Scotland or to the single legal jurisdiction of England and Wales. Laws which extend to England and Wales may apply in the whole of England and Wales, or only in England, or only in Wales. The test in Standing Order No 83J is whether provisions 'relate exclusively' to England, or to England and Wales, so it is necessary to determine to which territory each clause, schedule, amendment or Lords Amendment applies.

IV. THE EVEL STANDING ORDERS

The new EVEL Standing Orders are numbered Nos 83J to 83X and appear after Standing Orders Nos 83A to 83H, which deal with the programming of Bills. The EVEL Standing Orders are not entirely self-contained: consequential amendment was required to several other Standing Orders.[21]

---

[19] Minor adjustments to the Standing Orders reflected or anticipated the views of the Procedure Committee, removing the ban on the Speaker giving reasons for his decisions, allowing the Speaker to consult two Members appointed by the Committee of Selection and most significantly allowing all Members of the House to speak in any Legislative Grand Committee while reserving the right to move motions and vote to only Members from the relevant ('qualifying') constituencies.

[20] Similar majorities of 312 to 269 were recorded on votes rejecting two of the three Amendments to the Government's package selected by the Speaker. The other Amendment voted on, Graham Allen's proposal to concur with the Lords proposal that a joint committee be appointed, was lost by a larger margin of 312 to 215.

[21] For the EVEL changes made on 22 October 2015, see the Hansard Official Report or the Votes and Proceedings of the House of Commons for that day. The changes were published immediately as a separate Addendum (www.publications.parliament.uk/pa/cm201516/cmstords/soadd2210.pdf) and incorporated in subsequent editions of the Standing Orders.

Standing Order No 83J requires the certification of a Bill's provisions before Second Reading according to two basic criteria for EVEL to apply: relating exclusively to England, or to England and Wales; and on a matter of devolved legislative competence.

Standing Order No 83K deals with Bills certified as wholly relating exclusively to England and being within devolved legislative competence.

Standing Order No 83L provides for recertification of a Bill's provisions before Third Reading.

Standing Order No 83M requires the relevant Legislative Grand Committees for England and Wales and for England to agree motions consenting to the respectively certified provisions before Third Reading may take place.

Standing Order No 83N provides for reconsideration of Bills in the absence of consent from a Legislative Grand Committee.

Standing Order No 83O deals with the certification of motions relating to Lords Amendments.

Standing Order No 83P deals with the certification of entire statutory instruments.

Standing Order No 83Q provides that a statutory motion on a certified statutory instrument is agreed to only if, of those voting in the division, both a majority of Members and a majority of Members representing qualifying constituencies (England or England-and-Wales), vote in support of the motion.

Standing Order No 83R provides that a double majority is required to approve the annual police grant, which does not require a Speaker's certificate because it can apply only to England and Wales, and to approve certain other delegated legislation which does not require a certificate because it can apply only to England, including the annual local government finance reports, annual revenue support grant reports and motions on student fees under the Higher Education Act 2004.

Standing Order No 83S modifies the application of Standing Orders Nos 83J to 83N in their application to Finance Bills, which may be certified as relating exclusively to England and Wales and Northern Ireland.

Standing Order No 83T provides for a statutory instrument to be certified as relating exclusively to England and Wales and Northern Ireland if its parent primary legislation parent is a Finance Act.

Standing Order No 83U requires the Budget's Ways and Means Resolutions to be considered for certification in relation to England and Wales and Northern Ireland, or in relation to England and Wales.

Standing Order No 83V requires a double majority for certified Budget Resolutions.

Standing Order No 83W establishes the three Legislative Grand Committees, for England, for England and Wales and for England and Wales and Northern Ireland.

Standing Order No 83X applies Committee of the whole House procedure to Legislative Grand Committees.

Implementing the Standing Orders required new processes at a practical level, such as double-recording on certain Divisions, which have been well described in an article by Matthew Hamlyn, House of Commons Clerk of Bills.[22]

The EVEL Standing Orders have been amended only once. On 7 March 2017 the implied reference to Scottish rates of income tax was simplified in order to remove a possible ambiguity arising from the non-resident status of certain taxpayers.

V. SELECT COMMITTEE SCRUTINY

The House of Commons Procedure Committee produced its interim report on EVEL in October 2015 just before the EVEL Standing Orders were adopted.[23] The Committee drew the attention of the House to the risk of a successful challenge to a certificate issued by the Speaker, despite the prohibition expressed in Article IX of the Bill of Rights on courts' questioning or impeaching proceedings in Parliament.[24] The Committee's recommendation that the EVEL procedures should not be applied to any Bill in the 2016–17 Session until after the Committee had reported on its evaluation of EVEL in practice during the 2015–16 Session[25] proved to be a forlorn hope.

In its report published in February 2016, the House of Commons Public Administration and Constitutional Affairs Committee (PACAC) expressed its 'significant doubts that the current Standing Orders are the right answer or that they represent a sustainable solution'.[26] In PACAC's view, the EVEL Standing Orders may be unlikely to survive the election of a Government that cannot command a double majority of both English and UK MPs. The Committee recommended that the Government should develop proposals that would be more comprehensible, more likely to command the confidence of all political parties represented in the House of Commons, and therefore more likely to be constitutionally durable.[27]

PACAC concluded that the devolution test for certification is not a 'very simple test' and, alongside the instruction that 'minor or consequential effects' be disregarded, risks putting the Speaker in an unnecessarily controversial position. The Committee thought it highly likely that interested parties from inside and outside the House would want to make representations on where the devolution boundaries lie, and whether the effects of a Bill, or a clause or schedule of a Bill, were more than minor or consequential.[28] PACAC considered that the UK

---

[22] M Hamlyn, *English Votes for English Laws* (2016) 84 *The Table* 9.

[23] Procedure Committee, 'Government proposals for English votes for English laws Standing Orders: interim report', First Report of Session 2015–16, HC 410.The Procedure Committee had already published in September 2015 a letter from its Chair to the Leader of the House indicating the Committee's initial findings.

[24] ibid, para 49.

[25] ibid, para 105.

[26] Administration and Constitutional Affairs Committee, 'The Future of the Union, part one: English Votes for English laws', Fifth Report of Session 2015–16, HC 523, para 72.

[27] ibid, para 72.

[28] ibid, para 63.

Supreme Court decisions on referred Welsh legislation[29] were a worrying portent of the potential controversy that may arise from attempts to adjudicate both where the devolution boundaries lie and working out what minor or consequential effects on devolved competence might be.[30]

PACAC agreed with the Procedure Committee that the Speaker should establish and publish a more thorough set of guidelines regarding how representations should be made to the Clerk of Legislation on certification issues.[31] The Committee sided with two former Clerks of the House of Commons, Sir William McKay and Lord Lisvane (Sir Robert Rogers), in criticising the obscurity of the EVEL Standing Orders which had been drafted like legislation, by Government Parliamentary draftsmen.[32] Both Clerks had emphasised the primary requirement for Standing Orders to be understood by Members affected by them: the Procedure Committee pronounced that 'Never again should Standing Orders be drafted by the Government, rather than Clerks'.[33]

In its report published in November 2016, the House of Lords Select Committee on the Constitution was 'confident that the Speaker's decisions on certification are protected by Article 9 of the Bill of Rights and that no legal challenge to his decisions should be entertained by the courts'.[34] The Committee recognised 'concerns that should the EVEL procedures be set in statute they would be opened up to challenge and interpretation in the courts. In that event, we recommend that the legislation be drafted in a way that protects the operation of Article 9 of the Bill of Rights, which prevents the courts from questioning proceedings in Parliament'.[35] The Committee also found that 'There is no evidence that legislation is being drafted differently, or that the legislative programme has changed, following the introduction of EVEL'.[36]

Having published its interim Report as described above in the autumn of 2015, the House of Commons Procedure Committee published its technical evaluation of the first year of operation of the 'English votes for English laws' procedures in December 2016.[37] The Committee made suggestions to improve the operation of the procedure, including eliminating the frequently otiose legislative grand committee stage unless there was a demand for debate on the consent motions.[38] The Committee reiterated its criticism of the drafting of the EVEL standing orders, and

[29] *Local Government Byelaws (Wales) Bill 2012– Reference by the Attorney General for England and Wales* [2012] UKSC 53 and *Agricultural Sector (Wales) Bill—Reference by the Attorney General for England and Wales* [2014] UKSC 43 were cited by PACAC. See also *Recovery of Medical Costs for Asbestos Diseases (Wales) Bill—Reference by the Counsel General for Wales* [2015] UKSC 3.

[30] 'The Future of the Union, part one' (n 26) para 60.

[31] ibid, para 63.

[32] ibid, para 50.

[33] ibid, para 50.

[34] Select Committee on the Constitution, 'English votes for English laws', Sixth Report of Session 2016–17, HL Paper 61, para 81.

[35] ibid, para 136.

[36] ibid, para 112.

[37] Procedure Committee, 'English votes for English laws Standing Orders: report of the Committee's technical evaluation', Third Report of Session 2016–17, HC 189.

[38] ibid, para 54.

drew attention to the lack of support for the new procedures in the House from every party except the party of government.[39]

The Government addressed the Procedure Committee's conclusions and recommendations in its response to the technical review of the procedures on 30 March 2017. The Procedure Committee found the Government's response disappointing because it 'missed several opportunities to make practical improvements to the operation of the present procedures, and failed to acknowledge the widespread dissatisfaction with them which we have observed in the House'.[40] The Procedure Committee recommended that its successor Committee in the 2017 Parliament continue to keep the operation of 'English votes for English laws' procedures, insofar as they are continued by the present or any future administration, under regular review.[41]

VI. CERTIFICATION OF BILLS

Despite the apprehensions raised in debate and by select committees, there has been little comment on the Speaker's certification decisions in bills, set out in Table 9.1. The Clerk of Legislation prepares procedural advice for the Speaker, drawing principally on information published by the Government in its Explanatory Notes and other departmental memoranda announced in Written Ministerial Statements and published online for each Bill on the Bills before Parliament webpages. The Office of Speaker's Counsel provides separate but coordinated legal advice for the Speaker. Decisions on SO No 83J certificates before Second Reading are generally made at a regular Wednesday morning meeting shortly before the date scheduled for Second Reading.

The Speaker's decisions have on occasion not matched the Government's own conclusions in its Explanatory Notes. For example, the Speaker certified relatively few of the provisions in the Higher Education and Research Bill as relating 'exclusively' to England owing to the relevant definitions in the Bill of English higher education courses being 'in, or mainly in' England.

On competence, England-only provisions relating to sharing information by HMRC, for example in relation to eligibility for childcare or social housing subsidies, have been judged to be beyond devolved legislative competence.

Decisions have to be made swiftly sometimes: because Standing Order No 83L certificates before Third Reading cannot be made till the Report stage has concluded, the House has to suspend for a few minutes in order to allow the Speaker to sign the certificate and for the matching consent motion(s) to be circulated for consideration in the Legislative Grand Committee(s). The Public Bill Office

---

[39] ibid, para 71 and 76.
[40] Procedure Committee, 'Matters for the Procedure Committee in the 2017 Parliament', Seventh Report of Session 2016–17, HC 1091, para 27.
[41] ibid, para 28.

Table 9.1: EVEL certificates for Bills in Sessions 2015–16 and 2016–17 Numbers of certified Clauses, Schedules, Amendments made in Committee or on Report, and Motions relating to Lords Amendments

Session	Bill	2R SO No 83J	3R SO No 83L(2)	3R SO No 83L(4)	LAs SO No 83O (2)	LAs SO No 83O (4)
2015–16	Housing and Planning	107 (E) 40 (E&W)	40 (E&W) 135 (E)	4 (E&W) 5 (E)	18 (E) 3 (E&W) —— 5 (E) 1 (E&W) —— 1 (E&W)	1 (E)
2015–16	Charities (Protection and Social Investment) HL	Whole Bill (E&W)	Whole Bill (E&W)	—	—	—
2015–16	Childcare HL	3 (E)	3 (E)	1 (E)	—	—
2015–16	Energy HL	1 (E&W)	1 (E&W)	—	—	—
2015–16	Enterprise HL	3 (E) 3 (E&W)	4 (E&W) 7 (E)	2 (E&W) 9 (E&W)	—	—
2015–16	Policing and Crime	11 (E) 58 (E&W)	—	—	—	—
2016–17	Policing and Crime (*carried over*)	—	71 (E&W) 11 (E)	1 (E&W)	5 (E) 20 (E&W)	1 (E&W) 1 (E + E&W)
2016–17	Higher Education and Research	8 (E)	1 (E&W) 2 (E)	4 (E)	1 (E)	—
2016–17	Neighbourhood Planning	12 (E) 20 (E&W)	20 (E&W) 18 (E)	7 (E) 2 (E&W)	—	—

(*continued*)

Table 9.1: *(Continued)*

Session	Bill	2R SO No 83J	3R SO No 83L(2)	3R SO No 83L(4)	LAs SO No 83O (2)	LAs SO No 83O (4)
2016–17	Technical and Further Education	2 (E) 40 (E&W)	40 (E&W) 2 (E)	4 (E) 2 (E&W)	—	—
2016–17	Digital Economy	1 (E)	—	—	—	—
2016–17	Children and Social Work HL	3 (E&W) 57 (E)	62 (E) 2 (E&W)	1 (E&W)	—	—
2016–17	National Citizen Service HL	10 (E)	9 (E)	1 (E)	—	—
2016–17	Local Government Finance	39 (E)	*Dropped at 2017 general election*			
2016–17	Bus Services HL	18 (E)	19 (E)	—	—	—
2016–17	Health Service Medical Supplies (Costs) Bill	—	—	—	1 (E)	—
2016–17	Prisons and Courts	23 (E&W)	*Dropped at 2017 general election*			

Source: Votes and Proceedings of the House of Commons.

publishes in advance on the Bills before Parliament web pages, and with the Speaker's provisional selection of amendments, a *provisional* SO No 83L certificate drawn up in anticipation that all and only Government-sponsored changes will be made to the Bill at report stage. But even that provisional certificate cannot be prepared until the Government has tabled all its proposals for report stage for which the deadline is only two working days in advance. At Lords Amendments and subsequent stages, the interaction of EVEL and programming means that it is usually not practical for the Speaker to sign an SO No 83O certificate other than retrospectively, once it is known which motions on Lords Amendments were actually put to the House. As with report stage, it is normally possible to indicate provisionally in advance which Lords Amendments would be the subject of certified motions.

VII. BUDGET PROCEDURE

For devolved financial matters such as stamp duty land tax or landfill tax, Standing Orders Nos 83S and 83U bring into play a different permutation, to afford a veto for Members with constituencies in England or Wales or Northern Ireland. Following the March 2016 and March 2017 Budgets, ways and means motions on those taxes were certified (see Table 9.2), but those motions were not divided upon and nor were the certified Clauses founded on those motions the subject of any discussion in the enlarged (England, Wales and Northern Ireland) Legislative Grand Committee after report stage.

Table 9.2: EVEL certificates for Finance Bills, etc in Sessions 2015–16 and 2016–17 Numbers of Ways and Means Motions, Clauses, Schedules and Amendments made in committee or on Report certified in relation to England and Wales and Northern Ireland

Session	Bill	Ways & Means Motions	2R SO No 83J	3R SO No 83L(2)	3R SO No 83L(4)
2015–16	Finance (No 2)	8	10	—	—
2016–17	Finance (*carried over*)	—	—	10	—
2016–17	Finance (No 2)	2	2	1	1

Source: Votes and Proceedings of the House of Commons.

VIII. CERTIFICATION OF STATUTORY INSTRUMENTS

The Office of Speaker's Counsel provides advice to the Speaker each week, or more frequently when required, on the certifiability of statutory instruments requiring approval. A list of the certificates recorded in the Votes and Proceeding, usually on a Wednesday, is set out in Table 9.3. The painstaking effort to discern territorial application and corresponding devolved legislative competence in relation to each instrument is normally greatly assisted by the instrument's accompanying explanatory material which is prepared by departmental lawyers in accordance with Cabinet Office guidance. An instrument may be certified only if the whole of it covers matters of devolved legislative competence and relates exclusively to England, or to England and Wales (or, in the case of financial instruments, to England and Wales and Northern Ireland). Some instruments may paradoxically not qualify for certification because while they extend only to England and Wales, some provisions apply in England only while the instrument's other provisions apply in England and Wales. No more than a handful of statutory instruments subject to annulment (the negative or 'prayer' procedure) reach the floor of the House for decision in any Session, though several subjects of such 'prayers' for annulment may be referred for debate in a Delegated Legislation Committee. Prudence in the deployment of the scarce resource of expertise in the Speaker's Counsel means that only those 'negative' statutory instruments which are virtually certain to reach the floor of the House for decision are considered for certification.

Of the 67 certified statutory instruments in Sessions 2015–16 and 2016–17, six were the subject of Divisions in the House where a double majority was required. All of those instruments had been debated in a Delegated Legislation Committee before coming to the floor of the House for decision. The Official Opposition used an Opposition Day to force a vote on a motion to annul student support Regulations which were subject to the negative procedure. The other five certified statutory instruments voted upon were drafts subject to approval, three of which dealt with mayoral elections and were opposed by fewer than 10 Members on each occasion. Two of the approval motions took place as deferred Divisions, where Members' written votes are gathered on a Wednesday, following objections to the approval motion made in the Chamber after the normal time for opposed business on a previous day. A further four EVEL divisions took place at the end of debates on the floor of the House on police and local government finance reports to which the EVEL procedure applies, under Standing Order No 83R. The Government comfortably won all of the votes on certified statutory instruments in Sessions 2015–16 and 2016–17, with no discernible difference being made by the EVEL procedure. The SNP continued its previously established practice of refraining from voting on matters of no direct interest to Scotland such as the annual police grant reports for England and Wales and the annual local government finance reports for England.

It has been argued that a double majority requirement ought not to be required to annul a statutory instrument.[42] Instead, it is suggested, a 'negative' statutory instrument ought to be subject to a double jeopardy so that an annulment of a certified instrument would result if either the House or a majority or qualifying Members voted for its annulment.[43] The Government rejected this proposition in

---

[42] Kenny and Gover, 'Finding the Good in EVEL' (n 9).
[43] ibid, 32.

its March 2017 Technical Review, preferring to retain the default position applying to 'negative' statutory instruments.[44] Apart from those SIs subject to approval in draft, delegated or secondary legislation is rarely even debated and almost never overturned in Parliament.

The 'veto' aspect of EVEL was apparent in the fate of the draft Hunting Act 2004 (Exempt Hunting) (Amendment) Order 2015.[45] Although hunting wild mammals with dogs is not primarily a party matter, and has supporters and opponents on both sides of the House, it was clear to business managers that even if the Order was supported by a majority of Members with constituencies in England, it would not be supported by the House as a whole. It became apparent that SNP Members would vote against the Order, despite the fact that the proposed legislative changes would have applied only to England and were supposedly modelled on the legislation extant in Scotland.[46] No time was found to debate the draft Order, in either House, during the 2015–17 Parliament.

Table 9.3: EVEL certificates for Statutory Instruments in Sessions 2015–16 and 2016–17

Session	Title of Statutory Instrument	Certificate
2015–16	Draft Non-Domestic Rating (Levy and Safety Net) (Amendment) (No 2) Regulations 2015	E
2015–16	Draft Police and Criminal Evidence Act 1984 (Codes of Practice) (Revision of Code E) Order 2015	E&W
2015–16	Draft Legal Services Act 2007 (Claims Management Complaints) (Fees) (Amendment) Regulations 2016	E&W
2015–16	Draft Agricultural Holdings Act 1986 (Variation of Schedule 8) (England) Order 2015	E
2015–16	Education (Student Support) (Amendment) Regulations 2015 (SI 2015/1951)	E
2015–16	Draft Infrastructure Planning (Onshore Wind Generating Stations) Order 2016	E&W
2015–16	Draft Warrington (Electoral Changes) Order 2016	E
2015–16	Draft Tees Valley Combined Authority Order 2016	E
2015–16	Draft Crown Court (Recording) Order 2016	E&W

(continued)

[44] 'English Votes for English Laws Technical Review', March 2017, para 38.

[45] The House of Lords Secondary Legislation Committee summarised the Order in its Seventh Report of Session 2015–16, HL Paper 28, as follows: 'By amending existing exemptions to the ban on hunting with dogs of wild mammals which was introduced by the Hunting Act 2004, this Order proposes to increase the number of dogs that can be used to stalk or flush out wild mammals (the existing exemption allows only two dogs to be used); and also to allow the use of a dog below ground to flush out wild mammals, in order to prevent and reduce serious damage to livestock (the existing exemption allows such use in order to protect birds kept for shooting).'

[46] 'SNP will vote to keep English fox hunting legislation', BBC News online, 14 July 2015, www.bbc. com/news/uk-scotland-scotland-politics-33516713.

Table 9.3: (*Continued*)

Session	Title of Statutory Instrument	Certificate
2015–16	Draft Access to Justice Act 1999 (Destination of Appeals) (Family Proceedings) (Amendment) Order 2016	E&W
2015–16	Draft Energy Efficiency (Private Rented Property) (England and Wales) (Amendment) Regulations 2016	E&W
2015–16	Draft Licensing Act 2003 (Her Majesty the Queen's Birthday Licensing Hours) Order 2016	E&W
2015–16	Draft Pubs Code etc Regulations 2016	E&W
2015–16	Draft West Midlands Combined Authority Order 2016	E
2015–16	Draft Access to Justice Act (Destination of Appeals) Order 2016	E&W
2016–17	Draft West Midlands Combined Authority Order 2016	E
2016–17	Draft Access to Justice Act 1999 (Destination of Appeals) (Family Proceedings) (Amendment) Order 2016	E&W
2016–17	Draft Access to Justice Act (Destination of Appeals) Order 2016	E&W
2016–17	Draft Energy Efficiency (Private Rented Property) (England and Wales) (Amendment) Regulations 2016	E&W
2016–17	School Governance (Constitution and Federations) (England) (Amendment) Regulations 2016 (SI 2016/204)	E
2016–17	Town and Country Planning (General Permitted Development) (England) (Amendment) Order 2016 (SI 2016/332)	E
2016–17	Draft Rehabilitation of Offenders Act 1974 (Exceptions) Order 1975 (Amendment) (England and Wales) Order 2016	E&W
2016–17	Draft Telecommunications Restriction Orders (Custodial Institutions) (England and Wales) Regulations 2016	E&W
2016–17	Draft Water and Sewerage Undertakers (Exit from Non-household Retail Market) Regulations 2016	E
2016–17	Draft Halton, Knowsley, Liverpool, St Helens, Sefton and Wirral Combined Authority (Election of Mayor) Order 2016	E&W
2016–17	Draft Tees Valley Combined Authority (Election of Mayor) Order 2016	E&W
2016–17	Draft Criminal Justice Act 1988 (Offensive Weapons) (Amendment) Order 2016	E&W
2016–17	Draft Pubs Code etc. Regulations 2016	E&W
2016–17	Draft Pubs Code (Fees, Costs and Financial Penalties) Regulations 2016	E&W
2016–17	Draft Barnsley, Doncaster, Rotherham and Sheffield Combined Authority (Election of Mayor) Order 2016	E
2016–17	Draft Neighbourhood Planning (Referendums) (Amendment) Regulations 2016	E

(*continued*)

Table 9.3: (*Continued*)

Session	Title of Statutory Instrument	Certificate
2016–17	Draft West Midlands Combined Authority (Election of Mayor) Order 2016	E
2016–17	Draft Durham, Gateshead, Newcastle Upon Tyne, North Tyneside, Northumberland, South Tyneside and Sunderland Combined Authority (Election of Mayor) Order 2016	E
2016–17	Draft Self-build and Custom Housebuilding (Time for Compliance and Fees) Regulations 2016	E
2016–17	Civil Legal Aid (Merits Criteria) (Amendment) Regulations 2016 (SI 2016/781)	E&W
2016–17	Draft Coasting Schools (England) Regulations 2016	E
2016–17	Draft Housing and Planning Act 2016 (Compulsory Purchase) (Corresponding Amendments) Regulations 2016	E&W
2016–17	Local Government Pension Scheme (Management and Investment of Funds) Regulations 2016 (SI 2016/946)	E&W
2016–17	Draft Legal Services Act 2007 (Claims Management Complaints) (Fees) (Amendment) Regulations 2017	E&W
2016–17	Draft Greater Manchester Combined Authority (Functions and Amendment) Order 2016.	E
2016–17	Draft Non-Domestic Rating (Chargeable Amounts) (England) Regulations 2016	E
2016–17	Draft Police and Criminal Evidence Act 1984 (Codes of Practice) (Revision of Codes C, D and H) Order 2016	E&W
2016–17	Draft Combined Authorities (Mayoral Elections) Order 2017	E
2016–17	Draft Combined Authorities (Mayors) (Filling of Vacancies) Order 2017	E
2016–17	Draft Combined Authorities (Overview and Scrutiny Committees, Access to Information and Audit Committees) Order 2016	E
2016–17	Draft Housing And Planning Act 2016 (Permission In Principle Etc) (Miscellaneous Amendments) (England) Regulations 2017	E
2016–17	Draft National Health Service Commissioning Board (Additional Functions) Regulations 2017	E
2016–17	Draft West of England Combined Authority Order 2017	E
2016–17	Draft Cambridgeshire and Peterborough Combined Authority Order 2017	E
2016–17	Draft Tees Valley Combined Authority (Functions) Order 2017	E
2016–17	Draft Transport Levying Bodies (Amendment) Regulations 2017	E
2016–17	Draft Water Supply Licence and Sewerage Licence (Modification of Standard Conditions) Order 2017	E&W

(*continued*)

Table 9.3: (*Continued*)

Session	Title of Statutory Instrument	Certificate
2016–17	Draft Liverpool City Region Combined Authority (Functions and Amendment) Order 2017	E
2016–17	Draft Tees Valley Combined Authority (Functions and Amendment) Order 2017	E
2016–17	Draft Greater Manchester Combined Authority (Fire and Rescue Functions) Order 2017	E
2016–17	Draft Barnsley, Doncaster, Rotherham and Sheffield Combined Authority (Election of Mayor) (Amendment) Order 2017	E
2016–17	Draft Water Industry Designated Codes (Appeals to the Competition and Markets Authority) Regulations 2017	E&W
2016–17	Draft Non-Domestic Rating (Rates Retention) and (Levy and Safety Net) (Amendment) Regulations 2017	E
2016–17	Referendums Relating to Council Tax Increases (Alternative Notional Amounts) (England) Report 2017–18	E
2016–17	Draft Public Guardian (Fees, etc.) (Amendment) Regulations 2017	E&W
2016–17	Draft Public Sector Apprenticeship Targets Regulations 2017	E
2016–17	Draft Non-Contentious Probate Fees Order 2017	E&W
2016–17	Draft Local Authorities (Public Health Functions and Entry to Premises by Local Healthwatch Representatives) (Amendment) Regulations 2017	E
2016–17	Draft West Midlands Combined Authority (Functions and Amendment) Order 2017	E
2016–17	Draft Public Sector Apprenticeship Targets Regulations 2017	E
2016–17	Draft Combined Authorities (Finance) Order 2017	E
2016–17	Draft Greater Manchester Combined Authority (Functions and Amendment) Order 2017	E

Source: Votes and Proceedings of the House of Commons.

IX. CONCLUSION

From the introduction of EVEL in October 2015 to the May 2017 Dissolution of Parliament, there were no Divisions in any Legislative Grand Committee, out of a total of 23 consent motions agreed to, with little or no debate. As can be seen from Table 9.4, double-majority votes were required in the House on only 21 occasions: in addition to the 10 votes on secondary legislation mentioned above, there were eight double-majority votes on Lords Amendments to the Housing and Planning Bill and three double-majority votes on Lords Amendments to the Policing and Crime Bill. None of the outcomes of any of these votes was affected by the EVEL procedure.

Table 9.4: Double-majority Divisions in Sessions 2015–16 and 2016–17

Session	Date	Subject	Decision	House	EVEL (E/E&W)
2015–16	19 January 2016	Education (Student Support) (Amendment) Regulations 2015 (SI 2015/1951)	SI Prayer taken on Opposition Day forthwith after debate in DL Committee	292/303	203/291 (E)
2015–16	10 February 2016	Police Grant Report (England and Wales) for 2016–17 (HC 753)	SI approval SO No 83R	310/212	305/208 (E)
2015–16	10 February 2016	Local Government Finance Report (England) 2016–17 (HC 789)	SI approval SO No 83R	315/209	301/181 (E)
2015–16	3 May 2016	Housing and Planning Bill	Disagree Lords Amendment 9	287/182	279/158 (E)
2015–16	3 May 2016	Housing and Planning Bill	Disagree Lords Amendment 47	288/172	279/158 (E)
2015–16	3 May 2016	Housing and Planning Bill	Disagree Lords Amendment 54	286/171	278/157 (E)
2015–16	3 May 2016	Housing and Planning Bill	Disagree Lords Amendment 108	286/163	277/149 (E)
2015–16	3 May 2016	Housing and Planning Bill	Disagree Lords Amendment 110	285/164	285/161 (E)
2015–16	9 May 2016	Housing and Planning Bill	Disagree Lords Amendment 10B	289/206	273/176 (E)
2015–16	9 May 2016	Housing and Planning Bill	Insist disagreement Lords Amendment 110 and propose (a) in lieu	292/205	276/175 (E)
2015–16	11 May 2016	Housing and Planning Bill	Disagree Lords Amendment 47E	292/197	275/166 (E)
2016–17	15 June 2016	West Midlands Combined Authority Order 2016	SI Approval deferred Division after debate in DL Committee	278/4	260/3 (E)
2016–17	14 September 2016	Draft West Midlands Combined Authority (Election of Mayor) Order 2016	SI Approval after debate in DL Committee	290/3	271/3 (E)
2016–17	12 December 2016	draft Coasting Schools (England) Regulations 2016	SI Approval after debate in DL Committee	252/103	239/86 (E)

(continued)

Table 9.4: *(Continued)*

Session	Date	Subject	Decision	House	EVEL (E/E&W)
2016–17	10 January 2017	Policing and Crime Bill	Disagree Lords Amendment 24	299/196	296/190 (E&W)
2016–17	10 January 2017	Policing and Crime Bill	Disagree Lords Amendment 96	297/202	290/195 (E&W)
2016–17	10 January 2017	Policing and Crime Bill	Disagree Lords Amendment 136	298/198	289/193 (E&W)
2016–17	18 January 2017	Draft Combined Authorities (Mayoral Elections) Order 2017	SI Approval deferred Division after debate in DL Committee	299/6	280/6 (E)
2016–17	21 February 2017	Draft Housing and Planning Act 2016 (Permission in Principle etc) (Miscellaneous Amendments) (England) Regulations 2017	SI Approval after debate in DL Committee	273/107	260/84 (E)
2016–17	22 February 2017	Police Grant Report (England and Wales) for 2017–18 (HC 944)	SI approval SO No 83R	275/179	269/173 (E)
2016–17	22 February 2017	Report on Local Government Finance (England) 2017–18 (HC 985)	SI approval SO No 83R	269/158	253/141 (E)

Source: Votes and Proceedings of the House of Commons.

EVEL has nonetheless attracted considerable attention, not least from an array of Select Committees in both Houses. Fears of politicising the role of the Speaker, or of exposing the Speaker's assessment of devolved legislative competence to judicial scrutiny, have not been realised.

In the short 2015–17 Parliament, there was no vote on any EVEL-certified provision where the decision of the House as a whole differed from that of the Members for qualifying constituencies. For the minority Conservative Government taking office in 2017, however, EVEL may offer a lifeline. The minority Government is vulnerable to defeat in the House as a whole, but has stronger majorities in the other permutations: England, England and Wales, and England, Wales and Northern Ireland (see Table 9.5). Double majority votes could protect the Government from defeats on motions to annul statutory instruments or on motions relating to Lords Amendments in some circumstances. Consent Motions in Legislative Grand Committees might offer a route to overturning defeats in committee or on report, though at the expense of parliamentary time in bringing into play the reconciliation (or internal 'ping-pong') process prescribed by Standing Order No 83N.

It remains to be seen whether EVEL survives the 2017 general election. The Standing Orders may be discarded altogether if the minority Conservative Government is overborne by the collective will of the Opposition parties.[47]

Table 9.5: EVEL in the 2017 Parliament

	England	England and Wales	England, Wales and Northern Ireland	Whole House
Conservative	296	304	304	317
Labour	227	255	255	262
Scottish National	0	0	0	35
Liberal Democrat	8	8	8	12
Democratic Unionist	0	0	10	10
Plaid Cymru	0	4	4	4
Green	1	1	1	1
Independent	0	0	1	1
Speaker	1	1	1	1
TOTAL	**533**	**573**	**584**	**643**

Source: House of Commons Library. Note: the seven Sinn Féin MPs, who do not take their seats, are excluded from the totals. No account is taken of the three Deputy Speakers, two of whom will be drawn from the Opposition side of the House.

---

[47] In the final vote adopting the EVEL Standing Orders, 312 Conservatives defeated 270 Members from all other parties, including the DUP and Lady Hermon, the Independent Member for South Down, who has on more than one subsequent occasion expressed her objection to the EVEL procedure: see for example HC Deb 13 January 2016, cols 861–62.

Alternatively, EVEL may become such an entrenched part of parliamentary procedure that it might survive even a future change of Government.

It is hard to disagree with the House of Commons Public Administration and Constitutional Affairs Committee's conclusion of February 2016 that:

> the [EVEL] Standing Orders have attracted such hostility and can be removed on the basis of a simple majority must raise doubts as to whether they can ever be more than a temporary expedient, and currently they cannot be considered to be part of a stable constitutional settlement that will endure.[48]

---

[48] 'The Future of the Union, part one' (n 26) para 50.

Part 4

Rights, Justice and Scrutiny

10

Parliament and Human Rights

ALEXANDER HORNE AND MEGAN CONWAY[1]

I. INTRODUCTION

A T A TIME when concerns around Brexit and government proposals for reform of human rights laws predominate, it might surprise readers that the editors decided to consolidate two of the chapters on human rights and Parliament from the previous edition of *Parliament and the Law*[2] into this single examination. Yet the current authors do not have a crystal ball, and discussion on the consequences of Brexit on human rights (or of the likely chances of the Government publishing a consultation on a new Bill of Rights in the 2017 Parliament) were likely to be, at best, entirely speculative.

At the time of writing, it appeared clear that the UK would leave the EU. The Government served formal notice under Article 50 of the Treaty on European Union on 29 March 2017. One of the consequences of this, as noted by both the Joint Committee on Human Rights (JCHR) and the Lords EU Committee, is that as a result of Brexit, the UK will no longer be bound by the EU Charter of Fundamental Rights.[3] Both Committees acknowledged that the European Convention on Human Rights (ECHR) would provide continued protection for human rights. Nonetheless, they highlighted evidence that 'A lot of the rights that are derived from EU law are simply not replicated in other instruments' so there is potentially 'a real deficit'.[4] It may be that the loss of the EU Charter of Fundamental

---

[1] The authors would like to thank Dawn Oliver, Graham Gee, Hélène Tyrrell and Colm O'Cinneide for their advice and comments on an earlier draft of this chapter. Any errors or omissions are our own. The authors write in a purely personal capacity and their views do not represent those of either House.

[2] M Hunt, 'The Joint Committee on Human Rights' and A Horne and L Maer, 'From the Human Rights Act to a Bill of Rights?' both in A Horne, G Drewry and D Oliver (eds) *Parliament and the Law* (Oxford, Hart, 2013).

[3] House of Lords European Union Committee, 'Brexit: acquired rights', 10th Report of Session 2016–17, HL 82 and Joint Committee on Human Rights, 'The human rights implications of Brexit', 5th Report of Session 2016–17, HL 88, HC 695.

[4] See, eg, evidence of Professor Douglas Scott in House of Lords European Union Committee, 'Brexit: acquired rights', 10th Report of Session 2016–17, HL 82, para 100. These rights include free movement, certain social rights and also various workers' rights.

Rights has a significant impact on human rights issues.[5] However, the timing and full consequences cannot be understood fully whilst the UK is still negotiating the terms of its exit from the EU (particularly since the terms of the European Union (Withdrawal) Bill have not yet been debated fully).

It also remains unclear whether the minority Conservative Government will follow through with its previous commitment to bring forward proposals for a British Bill of Rights.[6] With the UK leaving the European Union, it would appear that the potential difficulties of introducing reforms have been exacerbated. Rather than repeating the earlier promises to introduce a new Bill of Rights, the 2017 Conservative Party Manifesto merely contained a commitment that:

> We will not repeal or replace the Human Rights Act while the process of Brexit is under-way but we will consider our human rights legal framework when the process of leaving the EU concludes. We will remain signatories to the European Convention on Human Rights for the duration of the next Parliament.[7]

Following the 2017 general election it is not clear whether there is a parliamentary majority in favour of reform.

In the light of these challenges, the authors determined that we would concentrate our efforts on providing an assessment of what Parliament currently does to monitor human rights compliance and also consider what it might do better. We concede at the outset that our emphasis is very much on the role of the Westminster Parliament and, in particular, the role of the JCHR.[8] Thus, following a short discussion of the question of political constitutionalism (and why it is important for politicians to take an interest in human rights), the first section of this chapter sets out the basic working methods of the JCHR. This is followed by an assessment of the effectiveness of the JCHR's approach to thematic inquiries and legislative scrutiny. Regarding legislative scrutiny, the first part of this assessment is essentially quantitative, but the study of legislative scrutiny is supplemented by four case studies from the 2015–17 Parliament. We end by considering whether there are any lessons to be learned and whether the JCHR could conduct any of its functions more effectively.

II. HUMAN RIGHTS AND POLITICAL CONSTITUTIONALISM

In the previous edition of this book, Murray Hunt (who was then the legal adviser to the JCHR) focused, in part, on the need to 'mainstream' human

---

[5] For example, issues around privacy and data protection. Leaving the jurisdiction of the CJEU might also impact on the vexed question of prisoner voting. Whereas it had been thought that develop-ments at the CJEU might make the issue of dealing with the outstanding judgment from the ECtHRs in *Hirst* rather more pressing, this appears no longer likely.

[6] See: www.gov.uk/government/speeches/queens-speech-2016.

[7] Conservative and Unionist Party Manifesto 2017, 'Forward Together, Our Plan for a Stronger Britain and a Prosperous Future', May 2017, 37.

[8] For information on scrutiny of rights in the Devolved Jurisdictions, see, eg, M Hunt, H Hooper and P Yowell, *Parliaments and Human Rights: Redressing the Democratic Deficit* (Oxford, Hart, 2015).

rights, particularly given the limited resources of a joint committee made up of just 12 members. He suggested that a concerted effort should be made by Parliamentary staff to identify more proactively and effectively any rule of law and human rights dimensions of any work that Parliament is carrying out. This, he argued, would make it more likely that Members would be informed of human rights standards and applicable international frameworks.[9] It is undoubtedly true that more could still be done in this area, particularly linking up the work of lawyers, Clerks and the information services of both Houses.

But this approach sidesteps one of the more problematic arguments about rights—namely their political legitimacy. Hunt himself acknowledges that 'too often "human rights" are perceived by parliamentarians as standards articulated and imposed on Parliament and government by outside actors, judges and lawyers in particular, who lack democratic legitimacy'.[10] And this is not a new concern. In 2000, when the Human Rights Act first came into force, Professor Costas Douzinas noted that law-making relating to human rights had been taken over by government representatives, diplomats, policy advisors, international civil servants and human rights experts and that 'this is a group with little legitimacy'.[11] Although there may be a general political consensus in favour of human rights, there is often considerable disagreement as to how they should be interpreted and applied (and by whom). While it might be easy to find support for measures against the most egregious breaches of human rights, popular consensus quickly breaks down when considering whether even basic rights should be enjoyed by, for example, terrorists, prisoners, or even those who do not behave 'responsibly'. The consequences of this can be profound: Marina Wheeler QC contended before the JCHR that:

> [P]ublic confidence in European supervision of human rights is already at a low ebb, and we can see that by virtue of the fact that it has been Conservative Government policy to repeal the Human Rights Act.[12]

The recent establishment of a Judicial Power Project at the think-tank Policy Exchange has highlighted a number of specific concerns about human rights judgments.[13] More generally, there is a more basic risk here: that if human rights laws are extended far beyond universally accepted boundaries and values, these concepts might be diluted so far as to render them meaningless. Moreover, to some observers (often on the political right), some developments are perceived to be efforts to entrench what are in effect liberal political and moral orthodoxies, rather than fundamental human rights.

The journalist Libby Purves highlighted the potential danger bluntly when she argued that human rights need to be kept 'tight, sharp and limited', because 'the

---

[9] Hunt, *Joint Committee* (n 2) 247.
[10] ibid.
[11] C Douzinas, *The End of Human Rights* (Oxford, Hart, 2000) 119.
[12] See: http://data.parliament.uk/writtenevidence/committeeevidence.svc/evidencedocument/human-rights-committee/what-are-the-human-rights-implications-of-brexit/oral/42410.pdf.
[13] See also ch 12.

woollier they get', the more endangered they become. She contended that 'whenever an opportunist … uses the phrase "human rights"—even unsuccessfully—the concept is tarnished and the weakest are that bit less protected in the future.'[14]

Whatever lawyers and academics might think about a more limited conception of human rights, we must all recognise that these are becoming political questions as much as legal ones. Lawyers might argue that it is too simplistic to crudely divide rights up into 'the basics'. Many rights that are assumed to be fundamental today, such as the right to privacy in one's sexual life, were once regarded as questionable extensions of core concepts. While some civil and political rights may have greater political endorsement and other rights (particularly economic and social rights) may be more contested, rights cannot be boiled down to a popularity contest if one accepts a need to protect unpopular minorities. Moreover, the protection of all rights will have some economic consequences.[15] Nonetheless, without sufficient political legitimacy, laws which do not enjoy popular support can be swept away under the UK constitution.

In 1978, John Griffith, gave a seminal lecture entitled 'The Political Constitution', which was subsequently published as an article in the *Modern Law Review*.[16] Griffith referenced an earlier, celebrated, speech in which Lord Hailsham had raised potential concerns about the risks of an 'elective dictatorship'. Lord Hailsham noted the alarming position when:

> [A] Government elected by a small minority of voters, and with a slight majority in the House, regards itself as entitled, and according to its more extreme supporters, bound to carry out every proposal in its election manifesto.

Hailsham assessed the types of safeguard which might be necessary to counter the dangers of centralised Government. He considered now well-worn issues, such as a Bill of Rights, a proportionately elected second chamber, a limit by law on the right of Parliament to legislate without restriction, and devolution to Scotland, Wales, Northern Ireland and the English regions in a federal structure.

Griffith was sceptical about the benefits that would be brought by any new Bill of Rights. He argued that 'political questions of much day-to day significance would, even more than at present, be left to decision by the judiciary'. He went on to claim that:

> The law is not and cannot be a substitute for politics. This is a hard truth, perhaps an unpleasant truth. For centuries political philosophers have sought that society in which government is by laws and not by men. It is an unattainable ideal. Written constitutions do not achieve it. Nor do Bills of Rights or any other devices. They merely pass political decisions out of the hands of politicians and into the hands of judges or other persons.

---

[14] 'No you don't have the right to demand a child' *Times* (24 October 2016).
[15] For example, the cost of policing of a political demonstration.
[16] JAG Griffith, 'The Political Constitution' (1979) 42 *Modern Law Review* 1.

To require a supreme court to make certain kinds of political decisions does not make those decisions any less political. I believe firmly that political decisions should be taken by politicians. In a society like ours, this means by people who are removable. It is an obvious corollary of this that the responsibility of our rulers should be real and not fictitious. And of course, our existing institutions, especially the House of Commons, need strengthening.

Since Griffith wrote those words, we have moved, at least to some extent, in Hailsham's direction. We may not have a consolidated written constitution or an elected Second Chamber. But we do live in a much more rights-orientated democracy, where power has been devolved to the constituent parts of the UK, and where the judges are much more confident in using procedures such as judicial review and proportionality review under the Human Rights Act 1998 to ensure that the Government does not exceed its legal powers. The late Lord Bingham made this plain in *A v Home Office*[17] when he concluded that the 1998 Act 'gives the courts a very specific, wholly democratic, mandate'. He quoted Professor Jeffrey Jowell, stating:

> The courts are charged by Parliament with delineating the boundaries of a rights-based democracy.[18]

In that case, Lord Bingham also addressed the question of whether the doctrine of deference precluded the courts from scrutinising the issues raised. He said:

> It is of course true that the judges in this country are not elected and are not answerable to Parliament. It is also of course true … that Parliament, the executive and the courts have different functions. But the function of independent judges charged to interpret and apply the law is universally recognised as a cardinal feature of the modern democratic state, a cornerstone of the rule of law itself. The Attorney General is fully entitled to insist on the proper limits of judicial authority, but he is wrong to stigmatise judicial decision-making as in some way undemocratic.[19]

This is a relatively recent development and the change in approach is a direct result of the Human Rights Act.[20]

In spite of these moves towards a rights-based democracy, Griffith's arguments still have resonance in the twenty-first century. And what is new is the traction that these arguments have acquired in recent years, even at a time when human rights law appeared to have become established as part of the standard repertoire of democratic constitutionalism across the globe.

---

[17] [2004] UKHL 56, para 42.

[18] ibid.

[19] ibid. See also Lord Neuberger in the case of *R (on the application of Evans) v Attorney General* [2015] UKSC 21, particularly at para 52 ff.

[20] It is all a far cry from the comments of Lord Hoffmann on 'deference' at para 62 of an earlier case on national security, *Secretary of State for the Home Department v Rehman* [2001] UKHL 47, delivered immediately after the events of 9/11.

III. THE JCHR

Without seeking to re-open the long-standing and seemingly endless debate between those who favour legal constitutionalism and those who prefer Griffith's arguments in favour of political control, it is worth considering the role of parliamentary select committees as *agents* of political constitutionalism. Taking forward Griffith's argument, one might start by considering the question of effectiveness; and whether the JCHR's processes are in need of some strengthening.

Professor Robert Hazell has previously written about the work of a number of Committees—most notably the House of Lords Select Committee on the Constitution, the Delegated Powers and Regulatory Reform Committee and the JCHR.[21] As Hazell put it, these three committees might represent 'three new pillars of the constitution'. Following on from this analysis, the JCHR might be seen as one of the guardians of legal values in the legislative process. So is this overstating the position; and how can one judge the impact of the JCHR?

House of Commons Standing Order No 152B makes plain that the JCHR's primary role is to consider:

(a) matters relating to human rights in the United Kingdom (but excluding consideration of individual cases);
(b) proposals for remedial orders, draft remedial orders and remedial orders made under Section 10 of and laid under Schedule 2 to the Human Rights Act 1998.

This seems a fairly wide-ranging definition and has been interpreted by the JCHR to mean that it should scrutinise Government Bills for their compatibility with human rights, (including the rights under the ECHR protected in UK law by the Human Rights Act 1998, common law fundamental rights and liberties, and the human rights contained in other international obligations of the UK). The JCHR also scrutinises the Government's response to court judgments concerning human rights, and the UK's compliance with its human rights obligations contained in a range of international treaties. It also conducts thematic inquiries, where it chooses its own subjects of inquiry and seeks evidence 'from a wide range of groups and individuals with relevant experience and interest'.[22]

So, essentially, one might say that it is the function of the JCHR to protect human rights and the rule of law in Parliament. However, at the outset and as already touched upon in the introduction to this chapter, it is worth acknowledging that these are heavily contested concepts, particularly in the political sphere.

---

[21] R Hazell, 'Who is the Guardian of Legal Values in the Legislative Process: Parliament or the Executive?' [2004] *Public Law* 495.
[22] See: www.parliament.uk/business/committees/committees-a-z/joint-select/human-rights-committee/role.

In relation to the protection of human rights, on one side of the debate, NGOs (and others committed to enhancing what they perceive as 'fundamental rights') may be disappointed by the compromises required to do business in a political environment. On the other side, some believe that a focus on rights is essentially an attempt to entrench political concepts as legal ones. As Vernon Bogadnor has put it:

> One of the dominant intellectual trends of our time is the transformation of political questions into legal questions, the transformation of questions in political thought, political philosophy and the historical questions of political philosophy into jurisprudential questions.[23]

One can quickly be drawn into a perilous discussion about the limits of parliamentary sovereignty, the role of the judiciary, and who should have the final say on important questions of public law and human rights.[24] From the outset it is therefore important to outline that we accept that reasonable people can (and do) disagree about the extent of rights, their justiciability and the proper bounds of the judicial role.

It is also relevant to raise here the discourse regarding the balance of rights. Over a decade on, the example given by the then Leader of the Opposition, David Cameron MP, of balancing freedom and security remains at the forefront of political debate, and increases with every terrorist attack in Western Europe.[25] This can be seen in the JCHR's recent focus on thematic inquiries looking at topics including the use of drones for targeted killing and counter-extremism. Consideration of the Government's counter-terrorism legislation has always formed a significant part of the JCHR's work. It is to be expected that the JCHR will sometimes disagree with the Government regarding the balance of these rights and indeed public opinion and views amongst parliamentarians are often divided. Ultimately, some decisions will always be determined by the courts (although Parliament has the final say).

Discussions about human rights usually lead to a debate about the rule of law. Often this takes one little further. The concept may be ancient—Lord Bingham notes that it may be traced it back to Aristotle;[26] although the foundation of our modern understanding can probably be attributed to Dicey. Bingham quotes Margaret Thatcher in an interview with Japanese television in 1988 where she observed that 'the freedom of peoples depends fundamentally on the rule of law'. Bingham's own conception of eight fundamental conditions which capture the essence of the rule

---

[23] V Bogdanor, 'Human Rights and the New British Constitution', JUSTICE Tom Sargant Memorial Lecture 2009, 14 October 2009.

[24] See, eg, R Ekins and G Gee, 'Making the Case Against Expansive Judicial Power', 19 November 2015, available at www.policyexchange.org.uk.

[25] D Cameron, 'Let's work together to make our country safer', speech to the International Institute for Strategic Studies, 22 November 2006.

[26] T Bingham, *The Rule of Law* (London, Allen Lane, 2010) 3.

of law[27] is widely admired by lawyers—but not necessarily accepted by government. Griffith appeared to take a more limited view of the term. He contended that:

> If the Rule of Law means that there should be proper and adequate machinery for dealing with criminal offences and for ensuring that public authorities do not exceed their legal powers, and for insisting that official penalties may not be inflicted save on those who have broken the law, then only an outlaw could dispute its desirability.[28]

Yet he suggested that when the concept is extended to mean more than that:

> [I]t is a fantasy invented by Liberals of the old school in the late nineteenth century and patented by the Tories to throw a protective sanctity around certain legal and political institutions which they wish to preserve at all costs.[29]

Today, one can see similar arguments deployed by those in favour of Brexit, or those who wish to repeal the Human Rights Act—a suspicion that those they perceive as 'elites' will use the concept of the rule of law as a brake on, or even to derail, what they see as radical but necessary political reform. Much like the term 'rights' the rule of law can and does mean different things to different people. Any discussion of the efficacy and effectiveness of the JCHR has to be viewed through this prism.

IV. THE JCHR AND LEGISLATIVE SCRUTINY

A. Introduction

There already exist a number of detailed accounts of the work of the JCHR since its inception in 2000.[30] Accordingly, this chapter does not seek to revisit these assessments, or provide a comprehensive account of the JCHR's past work. Rather, it aims to supplement the existing accounts, focusing in particular on the question of the JCHR's effectiveness.

Since its inception the JCHR has sought to increase the impact of its legislative scrutiny work. This led it to move away from comprehensive scrutiny of the human rights compatibility of every single Bill. Instead it has sought to focus on prioritising the most significant human rights issues; essentially trying to ensure that the human rights implications of proposed government action or inaction are identified as early as possible in the political process and the justifications highlighted and tested in a public and transparent way.

---

[27] ibid.

[28] Griffith, 'The Political Constitution' (n 16).

[29] ibid.

[30] See, eg, AP Lester and P Uccellari, 'Parliamentary Scrutiny of Human Rights' in AP Lester, D Pannick and JW Herberg (eds) *Human Rights Law and Practice*, 3rd edn (London, LexisNexis, 2009) 803–21; M Hunt, 'The Impact of the Human Rights Act on the Legislature: A Diminution of Democracy or a New Voice for Parliament?' (2010) *European Human Rights Law Review* 601; D Feldman, 'Can and Should Parliament Protect Human Rights?' (2004) 10 *European Public Law* 635; Hunt, *Joint Committee* (n 2); Hunt, Hooper and Yowell, *Parliaments and Human Rights* (n 8). The Committee's first meeting was held in January 2001.

At the beginning of every session of Parliament, immediately after the Queen's Speech, the JCHR is advised by its legal advisers[31] as to which measures announced in the Government's legislative programme are likely to raise significant human rights issues. The JCHR's Members consider this advice at their first meeting after the Queen's Speech. They then decide, in principle, which issues in which Bills the Committee should scrutinise. The JCHR issues a call for evidence in relation to those issues, announcing its likely legislative scrutiny priorities, and inviting submissions in relation to those Bills. Typically, this process leads to the Committee scrutinising aspects of about 20–30 per cent of the Government Bills in the legislative programme in any given session.

Unless a Government Bill has been published in draft the JCHR has no prior sight of it before its publication. As soon as possible after publication, the JCHR's legal advisers scrutinise the Bill and advise the JCHR as to whether the Bill raises any significant human rights issues. The Committee has published criteria by which it judges whether a human rights issue raised by a Bill is sufficiently significant to warrant scrutiny. They include considerations such as: 'how important is the right affected, how serious is the interference, how strong is the justification, and how vulnerable are the people likely to be affected by it'.[32] Time is at a premium once the Bill has been published, because the JCHR often aims to report on Bills before report stage in the first House, so that any amendments to the Bill recommended by the Committee can be moved at report stage. In reality, however, and as we discuss later, any amendments taken forward by the Committee are most likely to be in the House of Lords.

B. Meetings with Bill Teams

During the period following publication of a Bill identified as being a priority for scrutiny, there will often be a meeting between the department's Bill team and the JCHR staff. These meetings provide an opportunity for the Committee's legal advisers to identify to the Bill team the human rights issues that Members of the Committee are likely to raise, to identify any additional information which has not so far been provided by the department (but which might assist the JCHR in its scrutiny of the Bill), and to point out any relevant legal standards or other human rights material relevant to the subject matter of the Bill, but which does not appear so far to have featured in the department's human rights assessment (often contained in an ECHR memorandum). The meetings are intended both to facilitate scrutiny by the JCHR and to help the department. They are informal and

---

[31] In the 2015–17 Parliament the Committee had a permanent Legal Adviser and Deputy Legal Adviser. During the 2005–10 Parliament it had two Assistant Legal Advisers in addition to the Legal Adviser.

[32] See Joint Committee on Human Rights 23rd Report of Session 2005–06, HL 241, HC 1577, at [27]; see also F Klug 'Report on the Working Practices of the JCHR' in (Annex 1 to the 23rd Report).

off the record, and are conducted on the understanding that there will be formal, on the record correspondence between the Chair of the Committee and the minister. Certain contentious or 'political' issues are best left to that correspondence rather than being the subject of discussion at official level.

C. Information Provided to the Committee: Explanatory Notes and Human Rights Memoranda

Possibly the single most important factor which determines the JCHR's effectiveness in performing the task of scrutinising legislation for human rights compatibility is the quality of the information that is provided by the Government giving reasons for the Secretary of State's view that the provisions of a Bill are human rights compatible.

In the early days, the information provided on publication of a Bill was usually confined to the section of the Explanatory Notes accompanying the Bill that dealt with ECHR compatibility. The JCHR found that the information provided in those Explanatory Notes was often rather sparse and sometimes did not go much beyond a formulaic recitation of the relevant Convention test followed by an assertion that in the Government's view any interference with a Convention right was justified.[33] The variable quality of this analysis was, no doubt, due in part to the novelty of the task. And there was another constraint: the Explanatory Notes to Bills are drafted by the Government, but are published by the parliamentary authorities and must be approved by them before they are published. As Daniel Greenberg explained in his account of the legislative process, *Laying Down the Law*, the rules applied by the Public Bill Office prevent the inclusion of argumentative material.[34] This can be an issue for human rights scrutiny: often the human rights issue that requires assessment is whether a Bill's interference with a Convention right is justified in the sense of being 'necessary in a democratic society', and proportionate to the social need which the measure is seeking to address. Justifications of that sort can require arguments to be put forward which might fall foul of the strictly applied rules about the contents of a Bill's Explanatory Notes.

Other parliamentary committees that perform a technical scrutiny function are routinely provided by the Government with a detailed memorandum prepared for the purposes of that committee's particular scrutiny of the Bill. This now frequently happens with government assessments of human rights compliance. Since 2010 the Government has begun to publish regular free-standing ECHR memoranda in circumstances where a department believes a Bill raises significant human rights questions.

---

[33] See discussion in D Feldman 'Can and Should Parliament Protect Human Rights?' (2004) 10 *European Public Law* 635.

[34] D Greenberg, *Laying Down the Law: A Discussion of the Peoples, Processes and Problems that Shape Acts of Parliament* (London, Sweet & Maxwell, 2011) 97–103. See also ch 7.

There should be a direct correlation between the amount of detail contained in the information provided by the Government and the length of the letter sent by the JCHR to the Minister probing the assertions about human rights compatibility. Generally speaking, the more information that is offered by the department at the outset, the fewer questions that should be necessary. A free-standing human rights memorandum is also capable of being a more wide-ranging document, dealing not just with the Bill's compatibility with the ECHR, but also its compatibility with other relevant international human rights standards (eg, the UN Convention on the Rights of the Child). Hence a memorandum can be the repository for all the relevant information generated in the preparation of the Bill.[35]

Although good practice is not universal across government departments, a steady increase in the quality of the relevant information provided to Parliament has made possible more focused human rights scrutiny of legislation. In the previous edition, Murray Hunt observed that these 'are the informal means and processes by which human rights in the UK's unwritten constitutional arrangements become "entrenched" in a practical, rather than strictly legal sense: that is, embedded within the process of making policy and turning that policy into law'.[36] He also argued that laws which have been preceded by human rights scrutiny and informed deliberation are not only more likely to be proportionate but are also, for that reason, 'more likely to pass muster with the courts if their human rights compatibility is subsequently tested'[37], observing that:

> [T]he Government is increasingly aware of this psychological fact about adjudication and there are signs that this awareness is leading to a greater willingness on the part of the Government to encourage detailed debate in Parliament about the human rights implications of its legislative proposals.[38]

V. THEMATIC INQUIRIES, HUMAN RIGHTS TREATY MONITORING, AND THE SCRUTINY OF REMEDIAL ORDERS

A. Thematic Inquiries

The JCHR conducts thematic inquiries, in a similar fashion to the House of Commons departmental select committees and House of Lords select committees. The inquiries follow a pattern: deciding upon a line of inquiry, the gathering of written and oral evidence, and findings that are then reported to the two Houses and published. The evidence and final reports are public and available on the Committee's website (reports are also published in hard copy).

---

[35] See, eg, Joint Committee on Human Rights, 'Legislative Scrutiny: Welfare Reform Bill', 21st Report of Session 2010–12, HL 233, HC 1704.

[36] Hunt, *Joint Committee* (n 2) 232.

[37] See, eg, *Friend v United Kingdom* (2010) 50 EHRR SE6; *SH v Austria* (20011) 52 EHRR 6.

[38] Hunt, *Joint Committee* (n 2) 232–33.

The Committee's inquiries have been wide-ranging, but typically have investigated the UK Government's compliance with or implementation of an international human rights treaty or a new policy that is pertinent to the Committee's remit, whilst reflecting the interest and expertise of the Committee's membership at the time. Over the last five years, the Committee has typically published one to two thematic inquiry reports per session.[39]

The effectiveness of the Committee's thematic inquiries will be discussed in more detail in the next section. When the JCHR focuses less on the legal boundaries and starts to investigate the merits of Government policy on human rights grounds, or starts to look at the merits of whether (or to what extent) the UK should be bound by international conventions, finding political consensus on recommendations can be more difficult.

B. Human Rights Treaty Monitoring

Before the establishment of the JCHR, the regular cycle of monitoring the UK's compliance with its obligations by the UN treaty bodies passed Parliament by completely. Although legally binding on the state in international law, and of growing relevance even in domestic law, these norms and the treaty bodies' recommendations about their implementation, were rarely discussed in Parliament.

The Committee has attempted to change this in a number of ways. In the first few years of the Committee's existence it sought to engage Parliament with the main UN international human rights treaties by conducting major inquiries into the UK's record under each of those treaties. The UK's compliance with the UN Convention on the Rights of the Child, the UN Convention Against Torture, the International Covenant on Economic, Social and Cultural rights, and the Convention on the Elimination of Racial Discrimination were all the subject of such inquiries. These exercises highlighted the Government's approach to preparing the UK's compliance reports and for the first time brought about direct interaction between the Executive and Parliament about the UK's record of compliance with these obligations. However, such inquiries were very resource-intensive and, as was the case with its scrutiny of legislation, from about 2006 the Committee changed its approach, away from systematic monitoring and scrutiny of compliance with the UN treaties, towards a more selective approach, seeking to incorporate references to relevant recommendations into its general work programme. As a result, although the Committee has continued to refer to

---

[39] These have ranged from looking at the implementation of the right of disabled people to independent living, the human rights of unaccompanied migrant children and young people in the UK, the implications of access to justice of the Government's proposals to reform legal aid and judicial review, violence against women and girls, the UK's compliance with the UN Convention on the Rights of the Child, the Government's policy on the use of drones for targeted killing and most recently the human rights implications of Brexit and human rights and business.

recommendations of the treaty bodies, the Committee's engagement with those recommendations has become more sporadic and reactive in nature.

The Universal Periodic Review (UPR), the process by which the UK's human rights record is periodically reviewed by other states in the UN Human Rights Council, has also to date been unscrutinised by Parliament. The Committee has considered ways in which it can take a proactive approach to monitoring the Government's implementation of a selection of key recommendations from the UPR and the treaty bodies.[40] In the 2015–17 Parliament, the Committee had intended to commence such work and it announced an evidence session to consider the UK's human rights record in advance of the examination by the United Nations Human Rights Council in Geneva.[41] This session had to be cancelled following the Prime Minister's announcement of a general election in April 2017.[42]

In the 2005–10 Parliament, the Committee also pioneered the equivalent of a form of pre-and post-legislative scrutiny in relation to a major human rights treaty, the UN Convention on the Rights of Disabled People. For the first time it subjected such a treaty to rigorous parliamentary scrutiny before it was ratified by the Government, seeking to ensure that the process by which the Government proposed to enter reservations and interpretative declarations in respect of certain rights in the treaty was transparent, accountable and informed by the views of those who would be most directly affected.[43]

C. Scrutiny of Remedial Orders

The Committee's work includes scrutiny of remedial orders under the Human Rights Act (orders remedying incompatibilities with Convention rights which have been found by courts), which its standing orders require it to perform.[44] When the Committee was established it was envisaged that this might constitute

[40] See Note of the Conclusions of the Inter-Parliamentary Union/Commonwealth Secretariat conference, 'Strengthening the Role of Parliamentarians in the Implementation of Universal Periodic Review Recommendations', available at www.ipu.org.

[41] For details see: www.parliament.uk/business/committees/committees-a-z/joint-select/human-rights-committee/news-parliament-2015/uk-record-human-rights-evidence-16-17. At this session, the Committee would have taken evidence from both human rights actors at the national level (including the UK's three National Human Rights Institutions) as well as the Government.

[42] The Committee had also announced an inquiry into the UK's record on children's rights which had to be ended following the announcement of the election. The Committee had previously published a report on this subject at the end of the 2015 Parliament: Joint Committee on Human Rights, 'The UK's compliance with the UN Convention on the Rights of the Child', Eighth Report of Session 2014–15, HL 144, HC 1016.

[43] Joint Committee on Human Rights, 'The UN Convention on the Rights of Persons with Disabilitie's, First Report of Session 2008–09, HL 9, HC 93; Joint Committee on Human Rights, 'The UN Convention on the Rights of Persons with Disabilities: Reservations and Interpretative Declaration', 12th Report of Session 2008–09, April 2009, HL 70, HC 397.

[44] Standing Orders of the House of Commons (Public Business), 10 February 2016, Standing Order No 152B. See also: Joint Committee on Human Rights, The Making of Remedial Orders, Seventh Report of Session 2001–02, HL Paper 58, HC 473.

a significant proportion of its work. In the event, final declarations of incompatibility under the Human Rights Act have been relatively few and far between in the first 16 years of the Act's operation.[45] Although remedial orders can also be used to remedy an incompatibility found by the Strasbourg Court they have not often been used for this purpose.[46] In the 2010–15 Parliament there were three remedial orders, on each of which the Committee reported twice, as it is required to do.[47] On each occasion the Government agreed to amend the remedial order in the light of recommendations from the Committee. No remedial orders were published during the course of the 2015–17 Parliament, although the Government stated that it intended to bring forward a remedial order to address the incompatibility found in the case of *Z (A Child) (No 2)*.[48]

The Committee's scrutiny of a remedial order can sometimes take the heat out of a politically controversial issue. An example is that following the Supreme Court's judgment in *F*,[49] which declared section 82 of the Sexual Offences Act 2003 incompatible with Article 8 of the ECHR (to the extent that it provided for indefinite notification requirements on all who are sentenced to 30 months' imprisonment or more for a sexual offence without any opportunity for review). The Government expressed displeasure with the Supreme Court's judgment and the then Prime Minister said he would do 'the minimum necessary' to comply.[50] The remedial order which was first brought forward was so minimalist that, in the view of the Committee, it failed to comply with the judgment: it provided for a review of indefinite notification requirements by the police, not a court. The Committee reported that the remedial order was deficient because it failed to provide for independent review. Notwithstanding the political controversy which had greeted the original judgment, the Government accepted the Committee's recommendation and brought forward an amended remedial order which provided for access to an independent court to challenge the continued need for the notification requirements.

---

[45] In its Report to the Joint Committee on Human Rights on the Government's response to Human Rights judgments 2014–16 (Cm 9360, November 2016) the Ministry of Justice noted that since the Human Rights Act came into force in October 2000, until the end of July 2016, 34 declarations of incompatibility had been made. Eight were overturned on appeal, four were subject to appeal and 22 had become final. Of those 22, 13 had been remedied by primary or secondary legislation and only 3 had been remedied by remedial order.

[46] The Naval Discipline Act 1957 (Remedial) Order 2004 was used to address a judgment of the European Court of Human Rights in *Grieves v United Kingdom* [2003] All ER (D) 292 (Dec).

[47] See the following reports of the Joint Committee on Human Rights: 'The Terrorism Act 2000 (Remedial) Order 2011: Stop and Search without Reasonable Suspicion'; 'Draft Asylum and Immigration (Treatment of Claimants, etc) Act 2004 (Remedial) Order 2010'; and 'Draft Sexual Offences Act 2003 (Remedial) Order 2012'.

[48] [2016] EWHC 1191 (Fam). A declaration of incompatibility was sought on the basis that section 54 of the Human Fertilisation and Embryology Act 2008 was a discriminatory interference with a single person's rights to private and family life, and therefore incompatible with Articles 8 and 14 of the Convention.

[49] *R (on the application of F) v Secretary of State for the Home Department* [2010] UKSC 17.

[50] A Travis, 'David Cameron Condemns Supreme Court Ruling on Sex Offenders' *The Guardian* (16 February 2011).

VI. THE EFFECTIVENESS OF THE JCHR

A. How can Effectiveness be Measured?

It is well known that in the United Kingdom, the formal powers of the select committees are weak by comparison with certain other parliamentary committee systems.[51] Westminster select committees cannot officially amend, veto, or propose legislation of their own motion (although Members can, of course, act individually), nor are they able to block supply, which is supposed to be the weapon of last resort for Parliament against Government.[52]

Until the mid-2000s, there was little empirically based literature on the policy impact of committees. However, with somewhat of a resurgence of academic interest in the work of Parliament, a number of studies have now been conducted. One of the first papers to examine the topic was by Andrew Hindmoor, Phil Larkin and Andrew Kennon.[53] It considered the range of actors over whom select committees might be thought to have influence and identified four separate groups: the Government; Parliament; the media; and political parties. When focusing on the impact on government, Hindmoor *et al* took an empirical approach, by examining government responses to 1,022 recommendations contained within 40 reports published by the Education Committee between 1997 and 2005. They concluded, amongst other things, that:

> In comparing committee reports with government legislation there are certainly instances of correlation, but causation is much harder to establish. Where there was influence, this was more often a result of the committee's role as a mediating forum between the backbenches and government.[54]

In 2011, the Constitution Unit at UCL published a report by Professor Meg Russell and Meghan Benton entitled 'Selective Influence: The Policy Impact of House of Commons Select Committees'. This study examined the work of seven select committees over the period 1997–2010 and, amongst other things, considered the success rate of committee recommendations (and whether this was a good way of judging committee effectiveness). The report stated that general consensus was that adoption of committee recommendations is only one form of committee success, and perhaps not even the most important one. It argued that select committees influence the policy process in many other more subtle, and less measurable, ways, including: contributing to debate, drawing together evidence, spotlighting issues, brokering between actors in government, improving the quality of government decision-making through accountability, exposing failures, and perhaps most importantly 'generating fear'.

---

[51] For further details on select committee powers, see ch 5.
[52] For more on financial control of government, see ch 13.
[53] A Hindmoor, P Larkin and A Kennon, 'Assessing the Influence of Select Committees in the UK: The Education and Skills Committee, 1997–2005' (2009) 15 *The Journal of Legislative Studies* 71.
[54] ibid, 86.

Another way of examining impact is to look at the way that Committee reports are used in debates. Paul Yowell noted a 'dramatic increase' in the use of JCHR reports during debates in Parliament, indicating that in the 2005–10 Parliament 'reports were cited 1,006 times in total' and that the reports provoked 'robust, evidence-based deliberation'.[55] He concluded that although 'the work of the JCHR did not receive much notice in the first years of its operation' it was noticeable that 'attention to its reports increased dramatically beginning in 2005'—although about one-third of references to JCHR in Hansard in that period were by seven 'high frequency users'.[56]

Aileen Kavanagh has suggested that:

> The quantity and possibly also the quality of engagement with JCHR reports is far greater in the unelected House of Lords than in the democratically elected House of Commons. This may be because of the affinity between the scrutinising functions of the JCHR and the role of the House of Lords as a revising, scrutinising chamber, or it may be due to the expertise available in the House of Lords.[57]

A further reason for this may well be the less partisan nature of the House of Lords. As with many things, it is difficult to separate causation and result. If, as suggested above, the JCHR's reports are more likely to have an impact in the House of Lords, the Committee may, perhaps unconsciously, tailor its report for the House of Lords, focusing more on legal and technical aspects of Bills and recommending amendments that are far more likely to be given air time and gather a wider support in the Second Chamber.

Yet committees which conduct legislative scrutiny such as the JCHR can also have more directly identifiable impacts—by proposing amendments to government legislation. While there is no provision for amendments to be tabled directly by committees, individual Members of both Houses are able to table amendments to Bills. When supported by a legislative committee, Members who table such amendments will be assisted by the underlying research conducted by committee staff; the fact that they can often rely on an accompanying report by a specialist cross-party committee (which can be 'tagged' to the order paper or have an italic note in the business[58] and which will contain a clear rationale for the proposed amendment); and, the fact that the amendments are drafted by specialist lawyers. Some JCHR legislative scrutiny reports include the text of proposed amendments, so that it is plain that they have been endorsed by the entire Committee.[59]

---

[55] P Yowell, 'The Impact of the Joint Committee on Human Rights on Legislative Deliberation' in Hunt, Hooper and Yowell, *Parliaments and Human Rights* (n 8) 141–42.

[56] ibid, 162. As Lord Norton notes in ch 6, all bar one of these high frequency users were at that time Members of the JCHR.

[57] A Kavanagh, 'The Joint Committee on Human Rights: A Hybrid Breed of Constitutional Watchdog' in Hunt, Hooper and Yowell, *Parliaments and Human Rights* (n 8) 133.

[58] If a Committee Report is 'tagged' to the Commons Order Paper or an 'italic note' is put next to the entry in the House of Lords business, this means the Houses are given notice that a Committee Report on a Bill is available

[59] See, eg, Joint Committee on Human Rights, 'Legislative Scrutiny: Investigatory Powers Bill', First Report of Session 2016–17, HL 6, HC 104.

B. The Impact of Thematic JCHR Reports on Government Policy

The authors began by examining the JCHR's thematic inquiry reports. In previous Parliaments, these appeared to have less impact or traction than the Committee's legislative reports. However, whilst it is too early to highlight a permanent shift in approach, there were some indications in the 2015–17 Parliament that the Committee's focus may have moved towards linking the more typical evidence based investigative work with its other activities. Examples of this can be seen in its work on counter-extremism, Brexit and mental health in prisons (some of which are discussed in further detail below).

We have been conscious of previous criticisms of the sort of analysis which simply looks at select committee recommendations and then tracks the number that are immediately accepted by the Government (as noted by Christopher Johnson in chapter five). Accordingly, we have not attempted to judge the impact of thematic inquiry committee reports on this basis. Instead, we have focused on recent JCHR thematic inquiry reports and observed whether the key recommendations in the reports have had any impact in either House, or with the Government (actual or perceived); as well as any inherent limitations on impact from the political environment. We have also not concentrated on recent thematic inquiry reports from the 2015–17 Parliament, as it is well argued that the impact is not always immediate. Consequently, we have focused principally on thematic inquiry reports from 2013–15.

By contrast, in looking at legislative reports in the next section, we have taken a rather more straightforward approach in terms of recommendation impact and success. This is because the desired impact can be measured in the short term: put simply the Committee has made a recommendation to amend a piece of legislation and once that legislation becomes an Act, the Committee's scope for action is at an end (at least until secondary legislation under the Act is introduced, or the primary legislation is subject to post-legislative scrutiny or later Government review).

i. Thematic Inquiries between 2013 and 2015

Taking first two thematic inquiry reports into the implications for access to justice of the government's proposals on legal aid and judicial review in the 2013–14 session,[60] the Committee published two reports which looked at proposed changes being introduced under the Legal Aid, Sentencing and Punishment of Offenders Act 2012 (LASPO). On access to legal aid, the Committee made six specific recommendations on the introduction of a residence test for access to legal aid for civil matters. Its two main recommendations were for the Government to

---

[60] Joint Committee on Human Rights, 'The implications for access to justice of the Government's proposals to reform legal aid', Seventh Report of Session 2013–14, HL 100, HC 766 and 'The implications for access to justice of the Government's proposals to reform judicial review', Thirteenth Report of Session 2013–14, HL Paper 174, HC 868.

introduce the measure through primary rather than secondary legislation, and to exclude children from the residence test. Neither of these recommendations were accepted by the Government. The Government did accept one more minor recommendation, relating to the exclusion of asylum seekers or refugees resettled in the UK—for example under the Gateway Scheme).[61] The Government agreed that these individuals would not have to satisfy the residence test for 12 months upon submitting their claim for asylum or arriving in the UK for resettled refugees.

In the end, the Government never introduced the residence test, withdrawing the statutory instrument it had laid before Parliament. Whether the JCHR can take credit for this is doubtful; the Government must also have been mindful of a legal challenge launched by Public Law Project against the proposal,[62] as well as the likely recommendations of the Joint Committee on Statutory Instruments on the vires of the proposed regulations. In response to the Committee's work, the Government made small technical concessions: for example, allowing refugees resettled in the UK to be exempt from the residence test for 12 months or exempting certain protection of children cases, but it never publicly agreed with or was moved by the recommendations relating to the need for primary legislation or the exclusion of children. Moreover, the Government did not accept any recommendations the Committee made relating to prison law, nor the removal of exceptional funding for cases with borderline prospects of success.

The Government's response to the JCHR's report into unaccompanied migrant children showed little engagement with the Committee's conclusions. The Government partially accepted a recommendation relating to the collection of data of children whose age is disputed and either rejected or answered non-committally on the other 30-plus recommendations. But it did, for the first time, start a dialogue regarding the merits of incorporating the UNCRC into domestic law although at this time (June 2013) the Committee did not express a settled view either way.

The JCHR's report into violence against women and girls (VAWG) also had seemingly little impact immediately following its publication. Its main recommendation, for the UK to ratify the Istanbul Convention, was not accepted by the coalition Government despite repeated pressure from NGOs and the third sector. The Government did not bring forward the relevant legislation to ratify the Convention citing difficulties with extra-territorial jurisdiction. There was also little movement on several of the Committee's other recommendations, such as making sanctuary scheme properties exempt from the spare room subsidy, ending detention of asylum-seekers, compulsory training for the judiciary hearing domestic violence cases and making personal, social, health and economic education (PHSE) compulsory in schools.

---

[61] Government response to the Joint Committee on Human Rights, 'The implications for access to justice of the Government's proposals to reform legal aid' (2014) Cm 8821.

[62] *R (on the application of Public Law Project) v Secretary of State for Justice* [2014] EWHC 2365 (Admin).

Despite this limited impact, the Committee's report was used by numerous organisations to re-energise their calls for the ratification of the Convention. In 2017, a Private Members' Bill (the Preventing and Combating Violence Against Women and Domestic Violence (Ratification of Convention) Bill) was introduced and successfully passed by both Houses. This new Act requires the Government to set out its timetable and report annually to Parliament on the steps taken to enable the Government to ratify the Convention. Can the JCHR take any credit for this development? The Committee's report was referred to in passing during Report Stage in the House of Commons, and was raised by several peers in the Lords stages of the Bill. Therefore whilst the Committee cannot claim responsibility for the renewed activity, it is certainly possible that the report added to consistent pressure from an already growing lobby of external actors pushing for ratification of the Istanbul Convention (as well as raising the profile of the Convention within Parliament). Nonetheless it is likely that this movement may well have succeeded on its own steam.

The JCHR issued a report on the UK's compliance with the UNCRC before the 2010–15 Parliament dissolved.[63] The Government did not respond to this report, but it is mentioned here as it demonstrates the Committee's commitment to follow up on an issue persistently over a parliament—namely how well UK bodies are taking account of and complying with the principles of UNCRC and whether the UNCRC should be placed on a statutory basis. It also shows the Committee's long-standing interest in the role of the Children's Commissioner in their ability to uphold children's rights, a complementary overlap with the Education Committee's area of interest.

C. Pre-appointment Hearings

Whilst not a thematic inquiry, as such, the Committee traditionally had responsibility for conducting the pre-appointment hearing for the Chair of the Equality and Human Rights Commission. Following the creation of the Women and Equalities Committee, the JCHR held this hearing jointly with that committee in March 2016. Committee influence in this area was immediate, evident and direct. Both committees were concerned about whether the Government's preferred candidate, David Isaac, a partner at a law firm that conducted work on behalf of the Government, was subject to a potential conflict of interest. The committees' persistence on this issue, including raising concerns of the independence from Government required under the 'Paris Principles',[64] delayed the appointment of the Mr Isaac. Eventually, certain undertakings which satisfied both committees

---

[63] Joint Committee on Human Rights, 'The UK's compliance with the UNCRC', Eight Report of Session 2014–15, HL 144, HC 1016.

[64] Principles relating to the Status of National Institutions adopted by UN General Assembly resolution 48/134 of 20 December 1993.

were obtained from Mr Isaac prior to his appointment. In judging the question of impact on this occasion, it is likely that the presence of two high-profile chairs (representing both main political parties) may have swayed the Government approach to some extent.

D. Conclusions on the Thematic Work of the JCHR

This chapter cannot hope to provide a significant assessment of the full impact of the JCHR's thematic work. In any event, impact on both ministers and stakeholders is not always immediately measurable and may sometimes only become apparent as a form of indirect influence at a much later date. A former Government minister told us that JCHR inquiries did not necessarily generate a 'fear factor' in Government. Rather, a department might note that the JCHR was interested in a policy area. While this would likely result in a minister being called to give evidence, and might also result in a critical report, none of this would necessarily affect Government policy.

What might account for this? We consider that there are a number of factors that might be relevant. The first is that recommendations from the JCHR may often be 'cross-cutting': no one government department may be responsible for the policy. In such circumstances, the Government may not be well placed to react in the short timeframe that departments are given to respond to select committee reports. Moreover, where an issue is cross-cutting, Committee follow up with departments, may also be an issue. The departments concerned are likely to recognise this limitation and may well hope that the Committee's focus will soon shift to another policy area. Follow-up work does happen (see, for example, the Committee's work on Business and human rights in the 2015–17 Parliament). But it can take many years. The JCHR is, in this sense, significantly different from the seven Commons departmental select committees that were assessed as part of the Constitution Unit study.

On a related matter, recommendations which refer to potential treaty obligations may not immediately be within the Government's gift to accept. In relation to the VAWG inquiry, the Government indicated that some of the policy areas were the responsibility of the devolved administrations.

The JCHR, unlike other committees, undertakes a large amount of legislative scrutiny. The timing of such work is dictated by the Government's legislative timetable and so Committee attention is often drawn away from thematic inquiries to this area of work. This is not unique, but it places an additional burden on the Committee when it is trying to undertake thematic inquiries: any committee only has so many resources and Members can only take so many issues forward. Perhaps the JCHR's thematic inquiries suffer as a result of this additional responsibility.

Finally, there are the issues that impact on all committees: new members and their interests, changes in political landscape and a desire to continually look at new things means that detailed, systematic, effective follow up can be rare.

If thematic inquiry reports have limited impact, what is the purpose in the JCHR undertaking them? The answers given here are entirely open for debate, but it appears there are a number of positive arguments in favour of the Committee's work in this area. First, by virtue of the cross-departmental nature of the inquiry topics, the Government and civil servants in engaging with the inquiry and responding to a report, are forced to work together (potentially on a subject which was otherwise being treated in silos or ignored altogether).

The Committee's thematic inquiries also allow for relevant evidential points to be woven through the Committee's different reports. For example, the Committee's report on access to legal aid raised concerns regarding the evidence required for victims of domestic violence. The VAWG report commended the Government for bringing forward legislation to criminalise coercive behaviour, yet it could also flag, from its previous work, that the evidence threshold to prove such cases of domestic abuse would be difficult. In this sense, the Committee can benefit from its cross-departmental approach as it can sometimes see unintended consequences when Government policy has originated in different places.

Thematic reports also, potentially, help to raise awareness of international human rights treaties and conventions within Parliament. The UNCRC has gained considerable awareness in this way.

When the JCHR approaches an issue from a human rights perspective, this can also add weight to the work of other committees. Given its cross-cutting nature, it is unsurprising that many of the topics the JCHR has looked at were also of interest to departmental select committees. Although the VAWG report pre-dated the creation of the Women and Equalities Committee, the issue of PHSE in schools was subject to a parallel Education Committee inquiry (and compulsory PHSE has subsequently been the subject of recommendations by five Select Committee chairs in a joint letter to the Government.[65]) Other examples include the Home Affairs Committee which was also conducting an inquiry into FGM and honour-related crimes within the same Parliament. The JCHR inquiries into legal aid were complementary to a Justice Committee inquiry: the JCHR approached the same legislation and policy, but with a human rights lens. Whilst immediate impact may not be apparent, it is arguably helpful to all parliamentary committees if multiple committees are considering policy from different angles to add weight to the parliamentary debate and scrutiny of a Government policy.

E. The Impact of JCHR Reports on Government Legislation

Before we turn to look at the specific Committee recommendations to legislation, the following tables should provide helpful background. Table 10.1 shows the

---

[65] www.parliament.uk/business/committees/committees-a-z/commons-select/education-committee/news-parliament-2015/phse-sre-letter-published-16-17.

number of Government Bills the JCHR has reported on since the start of the 2010 Parliament, and the department that was responsible for the Bill:

Table 10.1: Legislative scrutiny by department

Number of Bills reported on	2010–12	2012–13	2013–14	2014–15	2015–16	2016–17	Total by dept
DCMS	0	0	1	0	0	1	2
DfE	1	0	1	0	0	1	3
DExEU	–	–	–	–	–	1	1
DECC	0	0	1	0	0	–	1
HMT	1	0	0	0	0	0	1
HO	4	1	2	3	0	2	13
CO	3	1	2	0	0	0	6
MoJ	1	2	2	2	0	0	6
MoD	1	0	0	1	0	0	2
DWP	1	0	0	0	0	0	1
BIS	0	0	0	0	1	–	1
DH	0	0	1	0	0	0	1
Total number of bills	**12***	**4****	**10*****	**6******	**1**	**5**[66]	

* Two Bills were reported on twice, thus the number of legislative reports in 2010–12 was 14.
** The Justice and Security Bill was a joint Cabinet Office and Ministry of Justice Bill, therefore is double counted.
*** Two Bills were reported on twice, thus the number of legislative reports in 2013–14 was 12.
**** One report in 2014–15 was on a Bill already reported on in 2013–14 thus skewing the MoJ statistic.

When assessing the data, above, it is worth noting that a number of factors may have skewed the statistics. Notably, in the 2015–16 session, the JCHR was established late (and thus some legislation was dealt with via correspondence, rather than in reports). Nonetheless, certain patterns can be observed: notably the Home Office was responsible for a substantial proportion of the Bills (approximately 35 per cent of the Bills considered by the Committee over the last seven years).

---

[66] The European Union (Notification of Withdrawal) Bill is included in this table, although the Committee's inquiry was undertaken prior to the publication of the Bill (and therefore constituted a pre-emptive recommendation).

We subsequently analysed the specific recommendations contained in these reports. We considered how successful the Committee was at securing debates on the issues raised or even amendments to the Bill; or whether the Committee was successful in more subtle ways (for example, the Government will more often accept a recommendation in debate and bring forward its own amendment).

A more detailed explanation of the methodology used for Table 10.2 below (and the underlying data) can be found on the Study of Parliament Group website.[67] In brief, Table 10.2 draws upon the Committee's legislative scrutiny reports and correspondence from the last three parliamentary sessions. The authors catalogued all conclusions and recommendations made by the Committee before assessing whether these sought to amend the Bill in question or not. The authors then tracked whether the recommendations were taken forward by any Members of Parliament (including, but not limited to, Committee Members), or were brought forward by the Government. Amendments that were won on division, or agreed to without debate or division were recorded. Where there is direct and public evidence of the Committee's recommendation being a driver (either as a result of being referenced in the debate, or correspondence, or the amendment being brought forward by a Committee Member) these are counted as a 'change'. Such a classification is evidently subject to a degree of interpretation. Equally, the data understandably cannot capture any unseen influence where changes were agreed behind the scenes. It may also, at times, be overly generous in attributing changes to the Committee in circumstances where the Government may have intended to bring forward amendments in any event.

Table 10.2: Immediate impact of legislative scrutiny recommendations

	2014–15[68]	2015–16	2016–17
Number of Government public Bills passed during the session	26	26	24
Number of Bills on which the JCHR wrote to the department	5	2	6[69]
Number of Bills to which amendments were proposed	4	1	5
Number of amendments proposed to all Bills	29	3	15
Number of amendments taken forward	20	1	15
Number which resulted in a change that can be attributed to the JCHR	6	1	1

[67] A more detailed table showing all report recommendations can be found on the Study of Parliament Group website. See: www.studyofparliament.org.uk/spgpubs.htm.

[68] The Criminal Justice and Courts Bill is excluded as this Report was a secondary Report on the Bill carried over from the previous session.

[69] Correspondence on the Counter-Extremism Bill is not included in this figure, as a Bill was never published.

If we first take the number of recommendations to amend a Bill over the last three years, 85 per cent have been in respect of a Home Office Bill, around four per cent to Department for Education, four per cent to Department for Culture Media and Sport, four per cent to Department for Exiting the European Union and around two per cent to the Ministry of Defence.

If we then turn to assess the number of amendments taken forward in the 2015–17 Parliament, Home Office Bills have been the subject of 10 amendments, and DFE, DEEU and DCMS were subject to two. In comparison to the 2014–15 session, when all 18 amendments that were taken forward were in the House of Lords, the amendments taken forward over 2015–17 were relatively evenly split across both Houses. The potential cause of this, in particular a more high-profile Chair, is discussed later in the chapter.

In the 2015–17 Parliament, all the JCHR's scrutiny work resulted in only two substantive changes which can be directly attributed to the Committee. Both were to Home Office Bills; both were in the House of Lords (and both were the result of concessions by the Government, which brought forward its own amendments to each Bill after debate).[70] If we look at these figures, was the JCHR's legislative scrutiny work worth it? The success rate certainly seems to pale in comparison with some of the Committee's work in the 2010–15 session (which had a big impact on Bills, such as the Justice and Security Bill).[71] The Committee's lack of obvious impact on the Investigatory Powers Bill is perhaps a significant example (discussed further below).

It remains an open question as to whether the Committee is best to focus on technical, legal matters which the Government can quietly accept in the House of Lords; or, whether it should be focusing its efforts on raising awareness within Parliament when Bills raise significant human rights issues (irrespective of the prospects of actually amending a Bill).

One notable example of the latter activity was the Committee's report on the human rights implications of Brexit. The report predated the publication of the Government's European Union (Notification of Withdrawal) Bill. One of the principal recommendation made in the report was that the Government should act immediately on the question of EU residence rights. The JCHR recommended that the Government do this by providing an undertaking to the effect that

---

[70] The two amendments secured in the 2015–17 Parliament, which can be directly attributed to the JCHR, were on the Policing and Crime Bill and the Immigration Bill. It is worth noting that amendments were made to the Trade Union Bill and the Investigatory Powers Bill (in line with Committee recommendations); however, it is not possible to say that the Committee was directly responsible for these amendments, a point discussed in the case studies below.

[71] In a previous study, Paul Yowell notes amendments to a number of Government Bills in the 2005–10 Parliamentary session, including the Charities Bill (to ensure that there was no discrimination between religious and non-religious charities), the Terrorism Bill 2005 (to remove terrorism against property from the offence of glorification of terrorism), the Police and Justice Bill (to ensure conformity with the UN Convention on the Rights of the Child) as well as the Education and Inspection Bill; the Safeguarding Vulnerable Groups Bill; the Digital Economy Bill and the Equality Bill; Yowell (n 56) 162.

all of those legally resident at a reasonable cut-off date would be guaranteed permanent residence rights. The Government refused to do this, arguing that any such commitment could damage its negotiating position with the EU. Unusually, the chair of the Committee, Harriet Harman MP, tabled a Committee drafted amendment to this effect in the House of Commons. The proposed new clause garnered significant cross-party support; before it was eventually voted down.[72] Nonetheless, it still gained considerable traction during the debate on the Bill. In the Lords, the response was even greater.[73] A vote on a similar Opposition-led amendment resulted in the highest turnout since 1999, and an initial Government defeat (which was eventually reversed in the Commons).[74] However, the JCHR cannot take full credit for this activity: it was supported by other parliamentary committees and senior parliamentarians.

As was the case with the thematic VAWG report, proving the JCHR's impact is virtually impossible. Would the clause have been proposed and debated anyway in the Lords? Almost certainly so. Would the focus of the debate in the House of Lords been as focused on the issue from a human rights perspective? Possibly. Are the answers the same for the House of Commons debates on the Bill? Perhaps not. At the very least, the JCHR highlighted the human rights questions that were raised by the Government's approach to Brexit.

The JCHR's report on a potential counter-extremism Bill in the 2015–17 Parliament is another example where proving the Committee's impact is difficult. A key conclusion of the Committee's report was that 'the Government had not demonstrated a need for new legislation'. Indeed the Committee said that there was 'a danger that any new legislation may prove counter-productive'. The Minister responsible for the policy suffered a torrid appearance before the Committee: she was asked to define 'counter-extremism' on multiple occasions and could not identify the sort of activities that were not covered by current counter-terrorism and public order offences. The Government never did bring forward legislation during the 2015–17 Parliament. Is this a success for the Committee? The media certainly though so, but again, this cannot be proved and it is likely that there were many other factors in play which prevented the Government from bringing forward a Bill.[75]

In examining the potential factors influencing the Committee's impact on legislation, we first return to the point made repeatedly by others relating to what has been described as the 'fear factor'. Does the JCHR elicit such a response with its recommended amendments to legislation? A former minister we spoke with indicated that it was likely this only happened in the Lords. A JCHR recommended

---

[72] New cl 57, see: HC Deb 6 February 2017, col 72 ff; HC Deb 8 February 2017, cols 556–57.

[73] See, eg, 'Britain's EU nationals are critical to every part of our public and private sector' *Financial Times* (21 February 2017).

[74] Unlike in the Commons, the lead amendment on EU residence rights voted on in the House of Lords was tabled by the official Opposition rather than a member of the JCHR.

[75] 'Theresa May's counter-terrorism bill close to "sinking without trace"' *The Guardian* (29 January 2017).

amendment, with cross-party support—or worse, apparently, with support from legal experts on the crossbenches—usually gave the Government some cause for concern. By contrast, party discipline in the Commons, combined with lack of time and less of an interest (and sometimes expertise) in detailed legal matters in the Commons, meant the Committee's reports had less impact in that House. As Janet Hiebert has previously observed:

> Although departments anticipate the JCHR's review, and where possible make adjustments to avoid a negative report, their primary focus is on whether the proposed legislation satisfied the government's legal advisers' assessment of compatibility in the complex pre-legislative review process that can include review by the Attorney General. Thus, the Government is unlikely to change its mind on the basis of a single but contrary parliamentary committee report.[76]

Secondly, the Committee makes many recommendations which are not explicitly about amending Bills. Over the last three sessions there were 62 'true recommendations'[77] within the Committee's legislative scrutiny reports, yet only 40 were specifically about amending the Bill itself. Others included recommendations such as considering the Bill for post-legislative scrutiny, or asking for additional memorandum to be published alongside secondary legislation arising from the Bill. The Committee's lack of follow-up on these recommendations could reduce its impact. For example, in relation to the issue of a new regulatory regime for social workers, the Committee's Report on the Children and Social Work Bill states: 'We recommend that the Government publish a full ECHR memorandum alongside the detailed regulations when they are laid so that they can be fully scrutinised for human rights compatibility'.[78] It does not appear that the Committee tends to follow up on such recommendations. This could mean the Committee is restricting its impact on legislative scrutiny solely to amending the Bill during its passage through both Houses.

As interesting as this analysis may be, it is also worth acknowledging Francesca Klug and Helen Wildbore's cautionary observation that:

> [I]t is very difficult to assess the extent to which JCHR reports have been directly responsible for amendments to Bills. Even where there is a connection between what the JCHR suggests and an amendment, it is not always possible to assess how crucial the Committee's proposals have been or whether there were other more significant sources or reasons for an amendment.[79]

---

[76] J Hiebert, 'Governing Like Judges?' in T Campbell, KD Ewing and A Tomkins (eds), *The Legal Protection of Human Rights: Sceptical Essays* (Oxford, Oxford University Press, 2011) 40.

[77] We have used the UCL Constitution Unit's definition of 'true recommendations': these refer to recommendations which the Government or Parliament had the power to enact, rather than conclusions or observing comments.

[78] At para 70.

[79] F Klug and H Wildbore, 'Breaking New Ground: The Joint Committee on Human Rights and the Role of Parliament in Human Rights Compliance' [2007] *European Human Rights Law Review* 231, 241.

Therefore, in addition to the quantitative analysis, provided above, it is also useful to examine, in some further detail, the type of legislative changes that might be attributed to committee scrutiny. The four short case studies below consider the Government's response to the JCHR's work on four Bills in the 2015 Parliament: the Trade Union Bill; the Immigration Bill; the Investigatory Powers Bill; and the Cultural Property (Armed Conflicts) Bill. Each of these Bills were subject to some degree of scrutiny and the different approaches taken by Government departments to the JCHR's recommendations (and proposed amendments) demonstrate some of the difficulties in assessing the policy impact of select committees more generally.

i. The Trade Union Bill

The JCHR wrote to the Secretary of State on the Trade Union Bill in November 2016, shortly after it was re-established. It was the Committee's first piece of legislative scrutiny for the Parliament (and by the time the JCHR appointed its chair on 29 October 2015, the Bill had already completed its Committee Stage in the House of Commons). In the event, the JCHR's letter posed four specific questions on issues relating to ballot thresholds, facility time, 'check-off,[80] and the International Labour Organisation (ILO) Conventions. Although the Committee did not suggest specific amendments, it did produce a short report, in December 2016, which was critical of some of the Government's proposals: specifically on the abovementioned issues.[81] By the time the JCHR commenced its scrutiny, the Government had already dropped some other potentially problematic proposals (such as a requirement for trade unions to consult with the police about certain social media use—on which it had consulted but which did not make it onto the face of the Bill).[82] The Government made a number of concessions on the matters identified by the JCHR during the passage of the Bill in the House of Lords. However, the precise impact of the Committee's work is far from clear. It is notable that the JCHR's report was raised in debate by both Lord Pannick QC (a cross-bench peer who endorsed the Committee's conclusion on Article 11 ECHR) and Baroness Wheeler, a senior Labour whip, who placed some reliance on the Committee's arguments in relation to the check-off provision.[83] Yet in spite of this, it is hard to know whether the Government's concessions were in any way attributable to the JCHR's involvement.

In a typically robust critique, Professor Keith Ewing (writing with John Hendy QC) argued that it is difficult to assess the extent to which the Government was constrained by human rights considerations at all, contending that it seemed unlikely

---

[80] This refers to the facility to deduct union subscriptions from wages in the public sector.

[81] Joint Committee on Human Rights, 'Legislative Scrutiny: Trade Union Bill', First Report of Session 2015–16, HL 92, HC 630.

[82] 'Trade Union Bill: Sajid Javid drops social media measures as part of Government climb down' *The Independent* (3 November 2016).

[83] See: HL Deb 8 February 2016, col 2007; HL Deb 25 February 2016, col 401 and HL Deb 25 February 2016, col 432.

that such arguments had 'a decisive impact' or even 'much traction'. Ewing and Hendy concluded that 'although the Government made a number of notable concessions, these were informed more by political than by legal considerations'.[84] Some of their criticisms, particularly of the JCHR, were less than measured. In particular, they said that by leaving open contested questions on the ILO the Committee had essentially confined its role to being a mere 'repository of correspondence'.[85] This complaint is misconceived. It ignores that fact that the Government's own analysis of the ILO Conventions was prompted by the intervention of the JCHR: without the Committee's intervention it is likely that no such information would have provided by the Government. While it is not always possible for a select committee to provide discreet analysis and conclusions on every matter of interest, it might be thought that one of the clear benefits of committee scrutiny is the extraction of both information and justification from Government departments so that this can be done by other interested stakeholders. Ewing and Hendy also suggested that the JCHR's critique of the Bill ought to have gone further, without perhaps having sufficient regard for the need for a parliamentary select committee to retain some consensus amongst its Members. This argument was also somewhat undermined by their acknowledgement that a successful legal challenge to the provisions which struck them as problematic was 'unlikely' as the European Court of Human Rights had been 'notably sympathetic to the British Government in Article 11 cases'.[86] It is perhaps naïve to imagine that a parliamentary committee would go further that the Strasbourg court in relation to such a potentially politically contentious issue.

ii. The Immigration Bill

Some direct and clear impact, albeit on a rather narrow point, can be seen in the Government's response to the JCHR's scrutiny of the Immigration Bill in the 2015–16 session. As the Committee had been established late, it did not have time to produce a report on the Bill. Instead it wrote to the Government on 20 January 2016 posing a series of discrete questions. The most notable of these was a concern (which the JCHR shared with the House of Lords Constitution Committee)[87] relating to a proposed power to allow the Home Secretary to vary or override a decision of the First Tier Tribunal on immigration bail. The JCHR argued that this was a 'rule of law issue' and quoted the relevant section of the judgment of Lord Neuberger in the case of *R (on the application of Evans) v Attorney General*:[88]

[A] statutory provision which entitles a member of the executive to overrule a decision of the judiciary merely because he or she does not agree with it would cut across

---

[84] KD Ewing and J Hendy, 'The Trade Union Act 2016 and the Failure of Human Rights' (2016) 45 *Industrial Law Journal* 391.

[85] ibid at 402.

[86] ibid at 391.

[87] For more on the House of Lords Constitution Committee, see: J Simson Caird and A Le Sueur, 'The House of Lords Select Committee on the Constitution' in Horne, Drewry and Oliver, *Parliament and the Law* (n 2).

[88] [2015] UKSC 21.

fundamental constitutional principles—most notably the fact that 'it is a basic principle that a decision of a court is binding as between the parties, and cannot be ignored or set aside by anyone including (indeed it may fairly be said, least of all) the executive.[89]

The JCHR also queried provisions relating to the freezing of bank accounts (without the right to compensation), the extension of an out-of-country appeals regime, and provisions relating to housing and support made available to migrants. The Government responded indicating that it had reflected on the reservations raised by both the House of Lords Constitution Committee and the JCHR and that it would table amendments to deal with the issue of immigration bail.[90] In the event, the Government was able to replace the objectionable provisions with a duty, on both the Secretary of State and the Tribunal, to impose an electronic monitoring condition when granting or varying bail to an individual being deported (without including a power to overrule decisions of the First Tier Tribunal). The Government remained unmoved by any of the other concerns raised by the JCHR.

iii. The Investigatory Powers Bill

The Investigatory Powers Bill was probably the most high-profile Bill considered by the JCHR in the early stages of the 2015 Parliament. A draft Bill had been subject to pre-legislative scrutiny by a Joint Committee, and the issue had also been considered extensively by the (then) Independent Reviewer of Terrorism Legislation, David Anderson QC. The draft Bill was also scrutinised by Parliament's Intelligence and Security Committee[91] and the Science and Technology Committee.

The Government's eventual Investigatory Powers Bill (which had already been dubbed a 'Snooper's charter' by opponents) was introduced in the 2015–16 session, subject to a carry-over motion. It clearly engaged a number of fundamental human rights: notably the right to privacy under Article 8 of the ECHR (and also Article 7 of the EU Charter of Fundamental Rights). It was the only Bill on which the JCHR took oral evidence during the 2015–16 Parliamentary session.

The JCHR published a report in June 2016 and recommended a series of amendments to the Bill on issues as diverse as thematic warrants, warrants for targeted interception, the interception of communications by members of Parliament, legal professional privilege and the confidentiality of journalist sources. The JCHR also recommended that the Government should publish a detailed operational case for bulk powers and that this should be reviewed by David Anderson QC. The Committee did not receive a Government response to its report (this is not

---

[89] www.parliament.uk/documents/joint-committees/human-rights/correspondence/JCHR_Immigration_Bill_Letter_200116.pdf.

[90] www.parliament.uk/documents/joint-committees/human-rights/Lord_Bates_re_Immigration_Bill_010316.pdf.

[91] For more on the work of this committee, see, eg, A Horne and C Walker, 'Parliament and National Security' in A Horne and A Le Sueur (eds) *Parliament: Legislation and Accountability* (Oxford, Hart, 2016).

unusual—unlike with thematic inquiries the Government does not consider that it is under an obligation to respond to all legislative scrutiny reports). It is likely that the JCHR's intervention had only limited impact. Shortly before the publication of the Committee's report, the Government agreed that David Anderson QC could review the case for bulk powers.[92] This was reported in the press as a concession to win the support of the opposition Labour Party. Further reported concessions on privacy were announced on the day the Committee's report was published, including a privacy clause that was supposedly designed to ensure that the new mass surveillance powers were not authorised 'in situations where less intrusive means could be used'.[93] None of the JCHR's proposed amendments were passed in the House of Commons.[94] The Bill was, however, subject to further amendment in the House of Lords, where a late concession was made by the Government to introduce additional safeguards for items subject to legal privilege.[95]

Whether any of these changes can be attributed directly to the work of the JCHR can only be the subject of speculation. Reacting to the Committee's recommendations is unlikely to have been central to the Government's thinking—but it is certainly likely to have been a consideration.[96] Other (probably weightier) factors include the political pressure brought to bear by Opposition Members, the Government's small majority in the House of Commons, and the fact that the Bill (and the earlier draft Bill) had been subject to extensive scrutiny by other Parliamentary committees and the Independent Reviewer of Terrorism Legislation—all of whom had expressed some concerns. Perhaps the most that can be said is that the work of the JCHR was cited in debate both by Members of the Committee and other Members of Parliament; and that many of the issues that it raised were subject to concessions by the Government. At the very least (as with the Trade Union Bill) the JCHR had identified matters of significant concern which were of interest to other parliamentarians.[97]

iv. The Cultural Property (Armed Conflicts) Bill

The Cultural Property (Armed Conflicts) Bill, was introduced early in the 2016–17 session and was designed to enable the United Kingdom to implement the Hague

---

[92] 'Theresa May agrees to review of snooper's charter powers' *The Guardian* (24 May 2016).

[93] 'Snooper's charter: Theresa May makes concessions' *The Guardian* (2 June 2016).

[94] HC Deb 7 June 2016, cols 1131–32.

[95] 'Legal privilege safeguard strengthened in snooping bill' *Law Society Gazette* (1 November 2016).

[96] See, eg, HL Deb 11 July 2016, col 77 where Earl Howe (Deputy Leader of the House of Lords and Minister of State for Defence) observed 'the Bill proceeds from the widely accepted position, endorsed by the Joint Committee on Human Rights, that, "review by a judge or other independent and impartial decision-making body", is the most significant safeguard required to protect the confidentiality of a journalist's source.'.

[97] See, eg, HL Deb 11 October 2016, cols 1797–98, HL Deb 19 July 2016, col 594; HL Deb 13 July 2016, col 245; HL Deb 13 July 2016, cols 231 and 232; HL Deb 11 July 2016, col 74; HL Deb 27 June 2016, cols 1407, 1434, 1447–48, 1454 and 1456.

Convention for the Protection of Cultural Property in the Event of Armed Conflict of 1954 and the Protocols to that Convention of 1954 and 1999. Initial interactions with the Department were constructive: it provided an ECHR memorandum and arranged a meeting between Committee staff and the Bill team. The JCHR then wrote to the Government on 29 June raising two issues of concern.[98] The first related to the maximum penalty for ancillary offences under the Bill. This had been set at 30 years which appeared potentially disproportionate. The second issue related to an immunity from seizure provision which was worded in such a way that it purported to give objects protected under it complete immunity from seizure under any other legislation or rule of law. On the latter point, the Committee pointed out that a similar provision in the Tribunals, Courts and Enforcement Act 2007 had used similar language but had been made subject to both other international law and EU obligations. This point was also raised in separate correspondence from the House of Lords Constitution Committee.

Following the Government's initial response to the JCHR on 8 July,[99] the Committee decided not to issue a report on the Bill; but instead proposed two amendments at Report Stage in the House of Lords. These were tabled by Lord Woolf (the former Lord Chief Justice of England and Wales), Baroness Hamwee (a Liberal Democrat Peer) and Lord Brown of Eaton-under-Heywood (a former Supreme Court judge who was not a Member of the JCHR). The amendments were considered on 6 September 2016 and were debated, but eventually withdrawn.[100] During the course of the debate, Lord Brown observed (in relation to the question of maximum sentences) that 'it is a pity that Parliament looks by this to be a little out of touch. The maximum penalties cease to have quite the same conviction if they lose perspective'. The JCHR eventually published a legislative scrutiny report which drew the attention of both Houses to the concerns that had been raised. It regretted 'the Government's reluctance to consider amendments to the Bill on these specific points notwithstanding the criticism that they attracted from a number of quarters during Report Stage in the House of Lords'.[101]

The Government's approach to the proposed amendments (including one which raised a clear rule of law issue) provides a useful contrast to its positive engagement on the rule of law issue raised in respect of the Immigration Bill. The Home Office clearly recognised a potential problem and acted accordingly.[102]

---

[98] Letter from Rt Hon Harriet Harman MP, Chair, to Baroness Neville-Rolfe DBE, CMG, Parliamentary Under Secretary of State, June 2016.

[99] Letter from Baroness Neville-Rolfe DBE, CMG, Parliamentary Under Secretary of State, to Chair, July 2016.

[100] HL Deb 6 September 2016, cols 948–52 and 954–57.

[101] Legislative Scrutiny: (1) Children and Social Work Bill; (2) Policing and Crime Bill; (3) Cultural Property (Armed Conflict) Bill, Third Report of Session 2016–17, HL 48, HC 739, para 92.

[102] A similar pragmatic approach by the Home Office can be seen in relation to the Committee's scrutiny of the Policing and Crime Bill where, in the light of a tabled amendment on the question of nationality documents, the Minister responded that while the Government's view was that 'this matter can properly be addressed through guidance ... in the light of the Joint Committee's recommendation, I am content to take this amendment away and consider it further in advance of Report'. HL Deb 9 November 2016, col 1259. This became ss 160 and 161 of the 2017 Act.

By contrast, the DCMS (which was, no doubt, rather less used to such legislative scrutiny) ignored the heavyweight legal objections from former judges and ploughed on regardless: perhaps taking the view that any future legal challenge was remote given that the powers conferred were unlikely to be used on a regular basis. One can only speculate about the difference in approach between the two departments, but perhaps the Home Office's more constructive tactics can be explained by the fact that it is responsible for a considerable amount of legislation (thus Home Office staff are more likely to be 'repeat players' and used to dealing with the JCHR—as evidenced by Table 10.1). In addition, Home Office Bills are frequently controversial and lengthy: portmanteau bills are not uncommon. In such circumstances, concessions in the House of Lords seem more likely.

F. Constraints on Impact

There are several factors which limit the Committee's effectiveness. Turning first to the reasons that are out of the Committee's control, one of the criticisms raised by the UCL Constitution Unit Report was 'a failure by some in government to take committees sufficiently seriously'.[103] This is particularly evident for the JCHR at the start of a Parliament: the Committee is not always set up expeditiously. In practice, this means that the Government's initial legislation is not adequately scrutinised. This happened in 2010 and 2015 (in the latter case, the Queen's Speech took place on 27 May 2015; but the Committee was not formally appointed until 29 October[104] and did not put out a call for evidence on its legislative priorities until 9 November.[105] By then, a significant Bill—the EU Referendum Bill—had completed its Commons Stages and had already entered Committee in the House of Lords). As a consequence of this delay, in the 2015–16 session, the JCHR only reported on one piece of legislation and only made inquiries to the Government about two Bills.

There have also been occasions where the whips have not ensured the membership of the Committee is maintained adequately. In the 2010–15 Parliament, there was a delay in appointing a new Conservative Member (after a Member had left to take up the position of Solicitor General). Eventually, a Conservative backbencher was appointed to the Committee; but he never appeared and later indicated that he had not agreed to be a Member of the Committee. Maintaining a quorum, on the House of Commons side, became difficult towards the end of the 2010–15 Parliament, and this impacted heavily on the Committee's work.

---

[103] M Russell and M Benton, 'Selective Influence: The Policy Impact of House of Commons Select Committees', UCL Constitution Unit, June 2011, 8.

[104] www.parliament.uk/documents/joint-committees/human-rights/2015-20-parliament/Formal_Minutes/Formal_Minutes_201516.pdf.

[105] www.parliament.uk/business/committees/committees-a-z/joint-select/human-rights-committee/news-parliament-2015/legislative-scrutiny-launch.

By nature of being a joint Committee, the intended audience and focus of the Committee's work is split. This means that debates on thematic reports are far less common, and amendments on legislative reports are usually intended to be taken up in one House only.

As mentioned throughout this chapter, the politics within which the human rights frameworks and standards are viewed (combined with a preference for unanimity in recommendations) leads to compromise, or reports which merely make conclusions and observations. The cross-party nature of the Committee does bring advantages but also constraints, particularly where views on the HRA and ECHR became more divided.

The Committee is also limited by time, both of the Committee's Members and also by staff resources. The scope of the Committee's work is potentially vast, routinely covering treaty monitoring, legislative scrutiny, thematic inquiries and following human rights judgments in the UK and Strasbourg. The Committee's broad remit means that its impact may be lessened. At present, the need to prioritise means that the fact there is no report or recommendation on any particular Bill does not mean that there is not a problem—merely that there may not have been sufficient time or resources to consider the issue in detail.

The Committee does not routinely scrutinise secondary legislation. Whilst acknowledging the previous point relating to Committee's lack of resources, this is again an area where the Committee's silence does not mean there is not an issue. Ignoring secondary legislation also, arguably, harms the Committee's effectiveness at legislative scrutiny. For example, many of the conclusions relating to the Trade Union Bill concerned the Government's reliance on introducing some of the measures through secondary legislation and therefore the Committee could usefully have scrutinised these once they were laid. This may prove more significant following the introduction of the European Union (Withdrawal) Bill in the 2017 Parliament, since it seems likely that much will be left to secondary legislation.

G. Room for Improvement?

Earlier sections of this chapter have given numerous examples of areas for improvement. This includes following up on recommendations in legislative scrutiny reports which go beyond amendments to the Bill, more systematic follow up to thematic inquiries (ensuring that inadequate Government responses are not ignored) and, crucially, tying in the thematic inquiry work to recommendations on and amendments to legislation.

The Committee has taken proactive steps to increase its engagement with a wider audience and hear less from 'the usual suspects' during its inquiries. The Committee's Twitter account has been a useful step towards instituting informal interaction with a wider community and the Committee has experimented with hearing directly from individuals affected by human rights issues (rather than the organisations representing their voices).[106] This is arguably a welcome move away from any work being conducted in a 'political echo-chamber'; yet if individuals put forward to speak to the Committee do not come directly, but are referred through NGOs and charities, true outreach can prove difficult. The sometimes complex nature of the Committee's work can make it very difficult for more authentic public interaction.

The Committee has also had successes in collaboration with other Committees, most notably the Women and Equalities Committee on the EHRC pre-appointment hearing. The Committee could do more to co-operate with other Select Committees. For example, the Committee's recommended amendment to the Armed Forces (Service complaints and Financial Assistance) Bill during the 2014–15 session was, in fact, attempting the same change to the Bill (the restriction on the length of time the ombudsman could serve) as recommended by the Defence Committee and taken forward by one of its members (Madeleine Moon MP). Better co-ordination between committee chairs could pay dividends.

VII. REFLECTIONS

At the outset of our consideration of the JCHR we posed a question: namely whether the Committee could be regarded as a 'guardian of legal values in the legislative process'. Whilst acknowledging the various difficulties inherent in the Committee's work, including the fact that reasonable people can (and do) disagree about rights, and that working in a political environment is unlikely to satisfy purists; this chapter has, nonetheless, identified a number of areas where it might be argued that the JCHR provides some added value.

First, the JCHR often identifies technical legal difficulties in legislation, which can sometimes be dealt with in an efficient and uncontentious fashion in the House of Lords. If the JCHR did not exist, it is unlikely that individual parliamentarians would have the time, or the resources, to conduct this work on their own behalf.

Second, the Committee can highlight high-profile human rights issues, providing actors and stakeholders with a parliamentary forum for debate. This does not always result in immediate change. The JCHR's most notable legislative success in this regard was probably its work on the Justice and Security Bill in the 2010–15 Parliament. Despite a profile raising debate on the European Union (Notification of Withdrawal) Bill, it saw more limited returns in 2015–17 Parliament.

However, whether there is an immediate impact or not, the Government is obliged to enter into a dialogue with the Committee. This often results in Ministers having to provide additional reasoning, elucidation and justification. The development of ECHR memoranda are a good example of an increasing focus on human rights concerns. Even if this does not result in change in Parliament, it

---

[106] Most recently, in the 2016–17 session, the Committee took evidence from four individuals who had suffered from mental health issues whilst in detention.

will frequently aid those considering whether to challenge a particular policy in the courts. Moreover, as Lord Norton and Lucinda Maer have noted in chapter six, it may be that this 'culture of justification', combined with the prospect of the JCHR raising human rights issues, deters the Government from introducing non-compliant legislation in the first place, or encourages the Government to find ways of achieving its objects without raising human rights problems. The prospect of scrutiny by the JCHR may encourage departmental lawyers (and ultimately the Attorney-General) to warn against including objectionable measures in Bills.[107]

More broadly, the JCHR can also act as an agent of political constitutionalism, essentially providing democratic legitimacy to human rights discourse (which would otherwise only take place amongst interested NGOs and stakeholders). Different human rights, such as the right to liberty and the right to life, are often in conflict with one another and sensible people can disagree about legitimate responses. It is important that debate is not conducted in a partisan political echo chamber, with NGOs merely speaking to those who are already engaged with their causes. It is also essential that parliamentarians from all parties feel invested in discussions about human rights. The human rights debate is one where it is very easy for parties to caricature their opponents, talk past one another, and engage in shallow arguments which fail to acknowledge rational concerns.

The 2015–17 Parliament may have been short, but the election of Harriet Harman, a high-profile Member of the House of Commons, as Chair of the Committee did result in changes. Most notably, there was an increased focus on thematic inquiries and regular evidence sessions. There was also a recognition that it is possible to combine thematic work with legislative amendments. The Brexit inquiry was a good example of how this could work in practice, with the thematic report reinforcing the JCHR legislative amendments. One could also see a similar approach in the Committee's work on prisons and counter-extremism. Further, dynamic, reform may be required in the future, particularly given the volume of legislation expected to be required to implement Brexit. There is also a tension as to whether the Committee's primary focus should be on improving the quality of legislation by revising it in the Upper House (whilst acknowledging that more significant changes might be overturned in the Commons), or whether it should focus its resources to seek to make an impact in the Commons (irrespective of the actual prospects of success).

There will clearly be many challenges going forward. Brexit, and any new proposals relating to the UK's human rights framework, may result in people having more limited legal avenues to pursue remedies for alleged breaches of human rights both domestically and in Europe. Thus, it is arguable that the role of the JCHR may become more important in the new Parliament: it will need to ensure that the Government continues to have adequate regard to human rights norms, while trying to make sure that the Government gets it right first time around.

---

[107] See also: Cabinet Office, 'Guide to Making Legislation', April 2017, particularly 113–22.

11

Parliamentary Accountability for the Administration of Justice

GAVIN DREWRY

The courts exist for the benefit of the public and provide, and should be seen to provide, a public service, as much as, say, the National Health Service. We would like to see a wider recognition of this fact. The customer in the law courts may not always be right but it is he or she, and not the judges or lawyers, for whom the service is provided.[1]

As an agency of state power, the judiciary as a body are, or ought to be, accountable for the general manner in which the court system serves the public at large. But methods of ensuring this form of accountability must not be such as to prejudice judicial independence.[2]

I. THE CONSTITUTIONAL TERRITORY OF ACCOUNTABILITY

We are all familiar with the vocabulary of 'territory' as it is normally used with reference to spatial entities like cities, regions, nation states and back gardens. By extension, the concept of territory—and the mindset of territoriality (protective or defensive feelings about bits of territory that we feel to be ours)—is sometimes used metaphorically in non-spatial senses to elucidate tricky ideas and concepts. Thus, in this chapter, which is concerned with the constitutionally important but sometimes contested frontier between a sovereign Parliament, with its (at least as far as the Commons is concerned) democratic mandate and its key role of holding policy-makers and the providers of public services to account for what they do and what they spend, and a judiciary that is fiercely protective of its independence from executive control and political interference, the concept of *constitutional* territory provides an apt starting point.

Like spatial territories, constitutional territories have their boundaries—boundaries that are patrolled, defended and policed. Squabbles about the location

---

[1] JUSTICE, *The Administration of the Courts* (London, JUSTICE, 1986), para 3.1.
[2] A Bradley, 'The New Constitutional Relationship Between the Judiciary, Government and Parliament', Appendix 4 of House of Lords Select Committee on the Constitution, 'Relations between the Executive, the Judiciary and Parliament', Sixth Report of the Session 2006–07, HL Paper 151, para 18.

of those boundaries can give rise to cross-border skirmishes and turf wars. Sometimes there may even be civil wars, within one of the institutional branches of the constitution—as with the intermittent disagreements that arise between Commons and Lords and between the Ministry of Justice and the Home Office, instances of which will be encountered later in this chapter.

Constitutional territories may of course also have some spatial aspects that can be interesting and significant—eg, the respective physical configurations of the two chambers of Parliament and the relocation in 2009 of the final appellate jurisdiction from the Palace of Westminster to a UK Supreme Court located in the Guildhall, on the other side of Parliament Square (noted below). But this chapter is concerned mainly with territory in its abstract, metaphorical sense.

We have traditionally tended to delineate the main areas of constitutional territory through the eighteenth-century language of 'separation of powers'—with its triangulation of 'executive', 'legislative' and 'judicial' branches; but the tendency for legislative bodies and legislative agendas to be controlled in many countries, to varying degrees, by executive government has rendered this vocabulary seriously out of date, at least insofar as the relationship between the executive and legislative branches are concerned. This is particularly the case in the UK, where (unlike the United States) members of the political executive are also members of one or other of the two Houses of Parliament—a 'fusion' rather than a 'separation' of powers. But the aspect of separation of powers that signals the distinctive role of the judiciary and its claims in democratic polities to constitutional independence from both the executive and the legislature remains as important and as relevant as ever, and is central to the theme of this chapter. Sensitivities and concerns surrounding judicial independence—some of which were, as we shall see, manifested in the litigation in the aftermath of the Brexit referendum in 2016—have long been an impediment to parliamentary scrutiny of the administration of justice though there have been important changes in the last decade or so that have gone some way to rectifying this. It is important to bear in mind that, as is persuasively argued in a recent study of judicial independence, that 'scrutiny' and 'accountability' are by no means antithetical to 'independence'—indeed, these concepts are mutually complementary.[3]

Another item of territorial vocabulary deserves a mention in the present context—the word 'arena'. In the 1970s the US political scientist, Nelson Polsby, distinguished between 'arena' legislatures which are the locus for public debate and legitimation of decisions taken elsewhere and 'transformative' legislatures that have a proactive role in law-making.[4] All legislative bodies in the real world fall somewhere between these two extremes, and other scholars have refined Polsby's

---

[3] G Gee, R Hazell, K Malleson and P O'Brian, *The Politics of Judicial Independence in the UK's Changing Constitution* (Cambridge, Cambridge University Press, 2015).

[4] N Polsby, 'Legislatures' in N Polsby and FI Greenstein (eds), *Handbook of Political Science* (Reading, MA, Addison Wesley, 1975).

typology to reflect this.[5] The UK Parliament is generally depicted as being located somewhere near the 'arena' end of the spectrum, spending much of its time debating and scrutinising business—including legislative business—brought before it by government ministers, and with backbenchers and Opposition frontbenchers (and crossbenchers in the Lords) doing what they can, through parliamentary questions, correspondence with ministers, debates and select committee enquiries, to hold the Government frontbench to account for its deeds and misdeeds.

The following account of parliamentary accountability for the administration of justice will consider some of the ways in which this role is played out in that context, and how the relevant mechanisms and procedures have adapted to changes in the culture of public administration, to efforts to procedural reform and to shifts in constitutional boundaries. But it will look also at the part played by Parliament as *an arena* for debating matters pertaining to the constitutional relationship between itself, as the legislature, and the judiciary. In the latter context, particular attention will be given to the enactment of the transformative Constitutional Reform Act 2005.

As we shall see, until quite recently the prevailing orthodoxy was that the judges and, by extension, the civil servants who administer the court system, were exempt from even the most routine and non-partisan forms of parliamentary scrutiny. This claim to immunity was founded upon a very literal interpretation of the principles of separation of powers and judicial independence. Lord Chancellors—themselves a living negation of separation of powers by virtue of their being members of the Cabinet and of the upper chamber of Parliament[6] while also exercising judicial functions—regarded themselves as links or 'buffers' between the judiciary and government/Parliament, and fiercely resisted any hint of parliamentary intrusion into judicial territory. Lord Chancellors always sat in the House of Lords and there had long been strong resistance by them and by the legal establishment to any suggestion of establishing a continental-style (or indeed any other 'style') ministry of justice, headed by a minister in the Commons.

That resistance was eventually overcome, with the establishment in 2007 of a Ministry of Justice, whose Secretary of State, sitting—as the most recent holders of the office have done—in the Commons, subsumes the office of Lord Chancellor. The responsibilities of the Ministry of Justice include those aspects of the administration of justice with which this chapter is principally concerned—the running of courts and tribunals, the working of the legal professions, legal education, law reform and the funding and delivery of legal services (including legal aid). However, it should be borne in mind (and this point will be discussed later) that the Ministry has other major responsibilities—in particular for prisons and

---

[5] eg, P Norton, 'Legislatures in perspective' in P Norton (ed), *Parliaments in Western Europe* (London, Frank Cass, 1990); P Norton, 'The legislative powers of parliament' in C Flinterman, AW Heringa and L Wadington, *The Evolving Role of Parliaments in Europe* (Antwerp, MAKLU Uitgevers NV, 1994); M Mezey, *Comparative Legislatures* (Durham NC, Duke University Press, 1979).

[6] And indeed was, until 2005, the presiding officer of the House of Lords.

the probation service—which account for much of its manpower and its budget. The House of Commons itself now has well-established machinery—including a departmentally related Justice Committee—to oversee justice-related matters. However, it is with the historic role of Lord Chancellors that this account begins.

II. A NEGATIVE TRADITION OF ACCOUNTABILITY—THE VIEW FROM THE LORD CHANCELLOR'S WINDOW

The office of Lord Chancellor can be traced back to Saxon times. In the nineteenth century, with the early development of cabinet government, it acquired some ministerial attributes, but they were of a peculiar and constitutionally incongruous kind, combined as they were with the speakership of the House of Lords and sitting regularly as presiding judge in the judicial House of Lords. A Lord Chancellor's Office was not created until 1885 and then on a very small scale—'an interesting little museum', as it has aptly been described by one twentieth century commentator[7]—its functions being almost wholly limited to judicial and ecclesiastical patronage. It was not until the early 1970s, when the Courts Act 1971 brought the County Courts Service under the wing of a greatly enlarged Lord Chancellor's Department that we saw the first move towards 'normalising' the bureaucratic infrastructure underpinning the administration of justice by embedding it in a major Whitehall spending department. Although it may not have appeared so at the time—and the very idea would probably have been viewed with horror by Lord Chancellors of this period—this prefigured a gradual, but ultimately irresistible, demand for greater public accountability for the administration and funding of the courts.

But why did the Lord Chancellor's 'little museum' last for so long? Why did it take until the 1970s for a small private 'Office' to metamorphose into a 'Department' and, eventually, in 2007, into the Ministry of Justice, with an annual gross expenditure (in 2014–15) of about £9.3 billion,[8] headed by a Secretary of State sitting in and accountable to the House of Commons?

The debate, insofar as there was something coherent enough to merit the title of 'a debate', about whether the United Kingdom should bring itself, at least terminologically, into line with much of the rest of the world by establishing something called a Ministry of Justice dates back to a report by the Committee on the Machinery of Government, set up under the auspices of the Ministry of Reconstruction at the end of the First World War under the chairmanship of Viscount Haldane.[9]

---

[7] RM Jackson, *The Machinery of Justice in England*, 7th edn (Cambridge, Cambridge University Press, 1977) 583.

[8] Of which about £3.8 billion relates to HM Prison and Probation Service; £1.9 billion to legal aid and £1.6 billion to the Courts and Tribunals Service. See 'A Short Guide to the Ministry of Justice', National Audit Office, June 2015.

[9] Cd 9230, 1918, ch X. For an account of the chequered history of the debate about a Ministry of Justice see G Drewry, 'Lord Haldane's Ministry of Justice—Stillborn or Strangled at Birth?' (1983) *Public Administration* 396; G Drewry, 'The Debate about a Ministry of Justice—A Joad's Eye View' (1987) *Public Law*, 502.

The Report recommended that the Home Office be redesignated as a Ministry of Justice, with the Lord Chancellor retaining his responsibility for judicial appointments and presiding over a new Imperial Court of Appeal. However, in the result, these and other recommendations in the Haldane Report came to nothing.

Other proposals for establishing a Ministry of Justice surfaced subsequently from time to time, but invariably foundered on fears that such a Ministry, with its minister sitting in the party-political hothouse of the Commons, would pose some kind of threat to judicial independence. Lord Chancellor Birkenhead, writing in the aftermath of the Haldane Report, also thought that the distractions of political life in the Commons might be inimical to the effective performance of the Lord Chancellor's functions:

> [T]he very fact that the Lord Chancellor is not a member of the House of Commons, is neither subjected to the daily pressure of the personal and political intimacies formed in that House, nor swayed by the necessity of conciliating any one at the critical stages of a critical Bill, enables him to take a broader view. It may be questioned whether the Minister of Justice will have the same freedom. Seeing the life of the House of Commons from day to day, his brain must constantly be preoccupied with the political considerations of the moment.[10]

It is only quite recently that countervailing arguments in favour of subjecting the Minister responsible for the administration of justice to accountability in the elected chamber began to gain significant traction. Meanwhile, the opposition to such proposals had often been characterised by serious conceptual and semantic confusion, giving rise to a lot of talk at cross-purposes about what form a Ministry of Justice might actually take in a UK context. Perhaps unsurprisingly, Lord Chancellors (and senior officials in the Lord Chancellor's Department), sensing a need to protect their territory against such threats—real or imagined—were often at the forefront of opposition, much of which was of the knee-jerk variety, couched in emotive language with sometimes a hint of Eurosceptical xenophobia— redolent perhaps of AV Dicey's notorious attacks on the French *droit administratif.* A faint echo of this kind of thinking resurfaced in a passing reference (uttered, no doubt, with tongue in cheek) by the Shadow Lord Chancellor, Lord Kingsland, on the day that the Ministry of Justice eventually came into existence, to the 'continentalisation of our justice system'.[11]

Of course, the circumstances surrounding the debate had changed significantly over the years. From the 1940s, with the establishment of the Appellate Committee of the House of Lords at the end of the Second World War, the frequency with which Lord Chancellors were able to sit judicially sharply diminished—and became all but extinct in the decade or so before the Lords' appellate jurisdiction was transferred to the Supreme Court in 2009.[12] We have already noted the great

---

[10] Viscount Birkenhead, *Points of View* (London, Hodder and Stoughton, 1922) Vol 1, 118–19.

[11] HL Deb 9 May 2007, col 1450.

[12] Although Lord Irvine did sit on rare occasions, and it is arguable that it was only due to the political sensitivities surrounding the Human Rights Act that he felt constrained from doing so thereafter: See BBC News report, 17 February 1999: http://news.bbc.co.uk/1/hi/uk_politics/281047.stm.

expansion of the manpower of the Lord Chancellor's Department following the Courts Act 1971. In 1981, Lord Hailsham—perhaps the last of the really 'traditionalist' Lord Chancellors in the fierceness of his resistance to any parliamentary scrutiny of judicial business and a declared opponent of any moves to establish a Ministry of Justice[13]—told the Home Affairs Select Committee, without any apparent ironic intent, that he regarded himself as the Minister of Justice.[14]

But the biggest circumstantial changes were yet to come, when, in the late 1980s the 'New Public Management'[15] reforms of the Thatcher years gradually began to have a substantial impact on the hitherto inviolate territory of Lord Chancellors and the administration of justice. The nature and significance of these changes are outlined below. But let us pause, briefly, to reflect on the nature and intensity of an entrenched culture that treated all things to do with justice and the judiciary to be completely outside the scope of legitimate parliamentary scrutiny.

A. Non-accountability in the 1980s

One could doubtless find plenty of illustrative examples of the deeply engrained presumption of judicial immunity from parliamentary accountability up to and during the Hailsham era, but let one instance suffice. In 1986, the well-regarded legal reform body, JUSTICE, set up a committee under the chairmanship of John Macdonald QC, to inquire into the machinery for dealing with public complaints about the administration of the courts. Its Report (a forward-looking document in many respects—see epigraph to this chapter) discussed, among other things, the role of the Parliamentary and Health Service Ombudsman (whose original statutory title is the Parliamentary Commissioner for Administration, PCA) an Officer of Parliament, who in 1984 had reached a 'concordat' with the Lord Chancellor's Department about the location of the boundary line between 'administrative' matters (deemed to lie within the remit of the Ombudsman) and 'judicial' matters (definitely excluded from the Ombudsman's jurisdiction). The 1984 agreement had subsequently broken down following the Lord Chancellor's Department's (LCD) obtaining counsel's opinion to the effect that court staff supplied by the LCD but working under the instructions of judges did not come within the purview of the Parliamentary Commissioner Act 1967: and the then Select Committee

---

[13] Subsequently, in a speech to the Bar Conference, Lord Hailsham said that a Ministry of Justice would be 'a menace to the independence of the courts and the judiciary' *The Times* (28 May 1986).

[14] Home Affairs Committee, 4th Report from Session 1980–81, HC 412-ii (Evidence and Appendices, q 996).

[15] 'New Public Management' was a much-discussed academic concept in the 1990s, and it generated a substantial UK and comparative literature, though the original inclusion of the adjective 'new' has inevitably faded with the passage of time. An essay by Laurence E Lynn, Jr, 'Public Management', in BG Peters and J Pierre (eds), *The Sage Handbook of Public Administration*, 2nd edn (London, Sage, 2012) 17–31, includes an excellent comparative bibliography. For an introductory account of public management in the UK see N Flynn, *Public Sector Management*, 7th edn. (London, Sage, 2016). See also O Hughes, *Public Management and Administration*, 3rd edn (Basingstoke, Palgrave Macmillan, 2003).

on the PCA took evidence on the subject from Lord Hailsham and later from Lord Mackay, who succeeded Hailsham as Lord Chancellor in October 1987.[16] The Lord Chancellor subsequently agreed to bring his Department within the remit of the PCA, a change that was effected by section 110 of the Courts and Legal Services Act 1990.

The JUSTICE Report also noted the rather startling fact that, in dealing with complaints by disgruntled litigants, the Lord Chancellor's Department's refusal to accept responsibility for administrative actions carried out on the instructions of a judge had meant that only five per cent of complaints were being accepted for consideration—observing, with some understatement, that it was not surprising if such a low take-up rate gives rise to 'some lack of confidence' in the system.[17]

In fact, the Committee became preoccupied with the issue of judicial independence, to a point where it virtually lost sight of any legitimate claims of public and parliamentary accountability. At one point it considered the objections that might be raised to extending the powers of the PCA to include investigations of judicial behaviour, a change apparently favoured by some members of the Committee. One objection, it said, 'is that, as the Ombudsman reports to the House of Commons, this would *encourage MPs to pry into the affairs of the judiciary*'[18] (italics supplied). But this objection was then promptly rejected on the grounds that the PCA is an independent officer who 'would only investigate a complaint if he were satisfied that it was serious', and, the Report continues, 'if a serious complaint is made, it would seem better that it should be investigated by an independent person of the standing of the Ombudsman than for it to become *the subject of ill-informed speculation in Parliament*'[19] (italics supplied).

While it is certainly true that the Ombudsman was and is an officer of Parliament, reporting to a Commons select committee, the use of this kind of language, by a committee representing a reformist organisation like JUSTICE, speaks volumes about the depth of the resistance, at least until the 1980s, to any notion of parliamentary accountability for the administration of justice.

B. Enter Lord Mackay—The Green Paper Furore

The picture began to change with a change of Lord Chancellor in 1987 and when the new public management reforms that had transformed the landscape of UK public administration in the 1980s began for the first time to have a major impact on the administration of justice. The justice system began to be seen less as a constitutionally ring-fenced special case and more as a big, important and public

---

[16] Select Committee on the Parliamentary Commissioner for Administration, Evidence of Lord Hailsham, 31 March 1987, 1986–87, HS 284-II; evidence of Lord Mackay, 26 January 1989, 1988–89, HC 159.

[17] JUSTICE Report (n 1), para 3.7.

[18] ibid, para 4.14.

[19] ibid, para.4.14.

service, much like health or education—with all that that entails in terms of public accountability. Judicial independence remained an important principle, but the efficiency and funding of the courts and legal aid were increasingly seen as legitimate areas of parliamentary concern.

In June 1987 Lord Hailsham stood down as Lord Chancellor, and was succeeded in the office briefly by Lord Havers and then by Lord Mackay of Clashfern. Lord Mackay was a Scottish lawyer and so not a member of the close-knit English legal establishment. He had held office as Lord Advocate in the early Thatcher years (1979–84) and had then been appointed a Lord of Appeal in Ordinary. As well as being very much in the 'Lord Chancellor as buffer' mould, Lord Hailsham had been quintessentially a party politician (he had once, after all, been a candidate for leadership of the Conservative Party): Lord Mackay was neither of these things; his disposition was that of a non-partisan judge.

Two years into his tenure, Mackay published three Green Papers, suggesting some major changes in the legal system. These 1989 Green Papers generated an extraordinary furore both inside and outside Parliament. Much of the fuss was directed at the one entitled 'The Work and Organisation of the Legal Profession',[20] which, among other things, proposed relaxing the barristers' long-established monopoly in respect of advocacy in the higher courts, and introducing a new system for licencing advocates. A lay-dominated advisory committee would advise the Lord Chancellor,

> on the education, qualifications and training of advocates appropriate for each of the various courts. The Lord Chancellor should be required to consult the judiciary before reaching decisions as a result of advice tendered by the Advisory Committee, although the final decision would be for him.[21]

Many leading members of the Bar, and senior judges, promptly went on record as saying, often in rather colourful language, that this posed a gross threat to judicial independence and the rule of law. In the Lords' debate on the Green Papers[22] the then Lord Chief Justice, Lord Lane, attacked the new advisory committee procedure as a movement towards executive control over the judiciary, adding for good measure that: 'Oppression does not stand on the doorstep with a toothbrush moustache and a swastika armband'.[23] Lord Donaldson, Master of the Rolls, said that, if necessary, he would tell the Government to, 'Get your tanks off my lawn'.[24] Former Lord Chancellor, Lord Hailsham, said that he was 'shocked' by the prospective threat posed to judicial independence by the proposal 'that a member of the executive, advised by an advisory committee which is staffed secretarially by his own department and composed of a majority of persons unqualified in the

---

[20] Cm 570, 1989.
[21] ibid, ch 5.
[22] HL Debs, 7 April 1989, cols 1307–1480.
[23] ibid, col 1331.
[24] ibid, col 1369.

law, shall be in command of the qualifications, the ethics and the statutory frame-work within which the right to practice is exercised'.[25]

In the event, when it came to the enactment of the Courts and Legal Services Act 1990, the Government managed to cool this over-heated controversy by watering down various aspects of its scheme in response to some of the objections raised. But the episode serves to remind us what a powerful lobby the legal profession can be when faced by what it perceived to be threats to its traditional professional interests. It also reminds us that, until quite recently—in the days before the Constitutional Reform Act 2005 and the establishment of the UK Supreme Court—the profession had a powerful voice within Parliament itself, through the presence of the Law Lords in the Second Chamber, all of whom had been practising barristers or Scottish advocates before becoming judges.

III. NEW PUBLIC MANAGEMENT AND THE ADMINISTRATION OF JUSTICE

Any discussion of parliamentary accountability for the administration of justice must take due note of the nature of the administrative arrangements for which those responsible are being held to account—and those arrangements have undergone transformative changes in the last two decades or so. Parliament has had a hand in debating the legislative changes that have underpinned some important aspects of the transformation but—as an 'arena' legislature—it has played little part in initiating them. And many such changes have been effected by executive fiat. The territory of justice is now subject to more parliamentary scrutiny than in the past, but Parliament has played only a peripheral part in redrawing the boundaries and setting the parameters of accountability.

Margaret Thatcher's term of office as prime minister from 1979 to 1990 marked the beginning of a revolution in the management and delivery of public services as 'new right' politicians began to embrace fashionable neo-liberal free market economic theories that condemned the inefficiency of traditional bureaucracies and lauded the virtues of management, markets and competition. Old-style public administration was displaced, at least in part, by a culture of 'new public management' (NPM),[26] which rejected traditional process-driven and hierarchical bureaucratic methods and structures in favour of market-based and business-like regimes of public service with a much stronger emphasis on target-setting and performance-measurement.

Many state-owned public service providers were privatised, and functions and services were extensively contracted out. One of the most significant NPM reforms of the Thatcher era was the 'Next Steps' programme, launched in February 1988, which transferred many of the executive functions of central government

---

[25] ibid, col 1333.
[26] Home Affairs Committee (n 14).

departments to semi-independent agencies, headed by chief executives employed on fixed-term contracts. The Prison Service, which became a Home Office agency in 1993 was one early example. It was subsequently combined, in 2004, with the Probation Service as the National Offender Management Service (NOMS), subsequently renamed HM Prison and Probation Service, which is now an agency of the Ministry of Justice—and accounts for a very large proportion of the MoJ budget.[27]

Meanwhile, John Major's Government continued where its predecessors had left off and the launch of the Citizen's Charter in 1991 promised to shift the emphasis of service delivery from the interests of the provider to those of the citizen-customer—a move that was particularly pertinent to the provision of legal services, much criticised over the years for a perceived tendency to put the convenience of judges before the interests of litigants. Courts charters were introduced during the 1990s, marking a sharp cultural shift and adding a further dimension to public accountability. The election of Tony Blair's Labour Government in 1997 did nothing to diminish the momentum of change.

Taken together, all these reforms had a huge impact on the machinery and the culture of public services in every sector and at every level. Or, at least, on *almost* every sector: the Thatcher Government, like its predecessors, was generally deferential towards judicial independence, and—at least until 1987 while Lord Hailsham remained on the Woolsack—initially seemed disinclined to expose the judicial process to the full rigour of the public management reforms that were being imposed on every other part of the public sector. However, even in the Hailsham era some new public management themes, such as the Financial Management Initiative (introducing new disciplines of financial accountability across Whitehall) had begun to impinge upon the Lord Chancellor's Department: in 1985 Hailsham himself instigated a major review of Civil Justice.[28]

As noted earlier, by the time Lord Mackay became Lord Chancellor in 1987, the winds of change were already beginning to blow. Lord Justice Nicolas (later Lord) Browne-Wilkinson, had already addressed some of the implications of public management reform in a public lecture delivered in 1987. In it he warned of threats to the continuing independence of the administration of justice that lay in the increasing application of strict value for money and financial management disciplines to the Lord Chancellor's Department:

> The requirements of judicial independence make the Lord Chancellor's Department wholly different from any other department of state. It is not for the executive alone to determine what should be the policy objectives of the courts. It is not for the executive alone to determine whether or not a particular judicial procedure provides 'value for money'. Justice is not capable of being measured out by an accountant's computer ...

---

[27] Jackson, *The Machinery of Justice in England* (n 7).
[28] The Review Body, which was chaired by Sir Maurice Hodgson, former chairman of ICI and British Home Stores, reported in June 1988, Cm 394.

[U]nder our constitution it is for the judge to determine what is just, and what is not just, subject always to legislation passed by Parliament. As a result of such policy being applied to the Lord Chancellor's Department, that department is being required to formulate policy and to make determinations as to 'value for money' according to financial yardsticks and without, for the most part, even consulting the judges.[29]

But the public management reforms had, inexorably, begun to catch up with the administration of justice. Far from being recognised as 'wholly different' from other government departments, the LCD moved increasingly into the mainstream of public administration. From 1 April 1992, responsibility for the funding and organisation of the Magistrates' Courts Service in England and Wales was transferred from the Home Office to the Lord Chancellor's Department, thus removing a long-standing anomaly in the distribution of ministerial responsibilities for the administration of justice. Partly because of the additional burdens arising from this, a Parliamentary junior minister to the Lord Chancellor was appointed to answer in the House of Commons for the administration of the courts; a second junior minister was appointed in the Commons in 1999, and another junior minister was appointed in the Lords in 2000 to take responsibility for commons and leasehold reforms.[30] Prior to these appointments, the only available Commons spokesman for the Lord Chancellor had been the Attorney-General—who had no ministerial responsibility for the LCD.

The former statutory requirement that the Permanent Secretary of the Department must have substantial legal qualifications and experience was repealed by the Supreme Court (Offices) Act 1997: Sir Hayden Phillips was the first non-lawyer appointed to the office. In January 2003 the Department appointed its first Director General of Finance to oversee the Department's multi-billion pound annual budget.

In 1995, much of the Department's work and staffing was concentrated in a large executive agency—the Courts Service, which in 2005 was converted into a unified Courts Agency, which absorbed the Magistrates' Courts Service. A major overhaul of the tribunals system, effected by the Tribunals, Courts and Enforcement Act 2007, led to the creation of another large agency, the Tribunals Service, which, in 2011, was amalgamated with the Courts Service to form an integrated Courts and Tribunals Service. The proliferation of executive agencies posed interesting challenges for parliamentary accountability, given that agency chief executives—including the heads of the Courts Service Agency and its successors—rather than ministers are responsible for day-to-day operational matters:[31] since the early 1990s, replies by chief executives to parliamentary questions referred to them by ministers have been printed in Hansard.[32]

---

[29] N Browne-Wilkinson, 'The Independence of the Judiciary in the 1980s' (1988) *Public Law* 44, 50.

[30] D Woodhouse, *The Office of Lord Chancellor* (Oxford, Hart Publishing, 2001), 169.

[31] ibid, 181–83.

[32] M Jack (ed), *Erskine May: Parliamentary Practice*, 24th edn (London, LexisNexis, 2011), 367.

IV. THE CONSTITUTIONAL REFORM ACT 2005—REDRAWING
THE BOUNDARIES

Having embarked on the task of modernising various aspects of the UK Constitution, the Blair Government turned its attention to the judiciary (already exercising
new functions under another recent constitutional innovation, the Human Rights
Act 1998), to the appellate functions of the House of Lords and to the antique
office of the Lord Chancellor. The Constitutional Reform Act 2005 (hereafter
referred to as the CRA) transferred the Lord Chancellor's judicial functions as
head of the UK judiciary[33] to a President of the Courts of England and Wales—the
Lord Chief Justice. It paved the way for the establishment of a new Supreme Court
to take over the appellate functions of the House of Lords (the Supreme Court
began work in October 2009) and set up an independent Judicial Appointments
Commission, to limit the extent of the Lord Chancellor's powers of patronage over
judicial appointments.

A significant aspect of the prehistory of this legislation, the statutory culmination of the continuing process of redefining the boundaries of judicial accountability as outlined above, was a bitter departmental turf war between the Home
Secretary, David Blunkett, and the Lord Chancellor, Lord Irvine, an opponent of
the reforms—culminating in a ministerial reshuffle in June 2003, in which Lord
Irvine, was sacked and replaced by Lord Falconer.[34] More unexpected—not least to
the Prime Minister's Cabinet colleagues and to the judiciary, and much more controversial was the announced intention of abolishing the office of Lord Chancellor
altogether—though this intention was later abandoned in the face of a Government defeat on the Constitutional Reform Bill in the Lords in Committee of the
whole House.[35] The office was retained and subsumed in the office of Secretary of
State for Constitutional Affairs, the LCD having been rebadged as the Department
for Constitutional Affairs in the 2003 reshuffle—a transitional arrangement that
prefigured the establishment of the Ministry of Justice, four years later. The Prime
Minister also announced the Government's plans to create a new Supreme Court
in place of the Appellate Committee of the House of Lords and to reform the
judicial appointments process in England and Wales.

Although the Prime Minister's announcement was followed by a public consultation exercise,[36] and was the subject of critical reports by the then Constitutional

---

[33] The Lord Chancellor's entitlement to sit judicially in the Appellate Committee of the House of
Lords and the Judicial Committee of the Privy Council, were also removed by the CRA.

[34] See A Le Sueur, 'From Appellate Committee to Supreme Court: A Narrative' in L Blom-Cooper,
B Dickson and G Drewry (eds), *The Judicial House of Lords 1876–2009* (Oxford, Oxford University
Press, 2009) 64–94, at 67–68.

[35] HL Deb 13 July 2004, col 1194.

[36] Department for Constitutional Affairs (DCA), 'Constitutional reform: a Supreme Court for
the United Kingdom' Consultation Paper CP 11/03; Department for Constitutional Affairs (DCA),
'Constitutional reform: a new way of appointing judges' Consultation Paper CP 10/03.

Affairs Select Committee,[37] the judges complained in the meantime that they had not been consulted about or even given advance notice of these major changes,[38] and the Government eventually agreed what became known as the 'concordat'[39] to meet their objections; a provision, embodying the basic principle of this agreement, was later added to the Constitutional Reform Bill, imposing a statutory duty on ministers to uphold the independence of the judiciary: later in this chapter we will encounter some Brexit-related controversies relating to this. The initial judicial protests were led by the then Lord Chief Justice, Lord Woolf, acting as spokesman for the judiciary, who was to become the new President of the Courts of England and Wales under the provisions of the CRA.

Meanwhile, the Constitutional Reform Bill had its second reading in the House of Lords on 8 March 2004, whereupon it was—very unusually—committed to a special select committee of the House[40] and was also subject to a carry-over motion, to enable parliamentary consideration of it to continue in the following session. Although nowadays a lot of government legislation is subject to some degree of pre-legislative consultation, once it reaches Parliament the normal pattern of legislative scrutiny gives little or no opportunity in either House for canvassing the views of outside experts and critics. It is a measure both of the constitutional significance of this Bill and of the widespread unease about the exiguous extent of pre-legislative consultation that prompted the use of a more pro-active and inquisitorial procedure in this case. The Select Committee's report was published on 2 July 2004.[41] The extent of evidence gathering undertaken by the Committee was described by its Chairman, Lord Richard, when the Bill came back to a Committee of the whole House in July 2004:

> [W]e met in public to take oral evidence from more than 32 witnesses. We received over 80 written submissions. We considered the views of 14 serving judges, seven retired judges, 14 academics, the lawyers' professional bodies in England, Wales, Scotland and Northern Ireland, as well as campaign groups, individual lawyers and members of the public.[42]

The Committee proposed more than 400 amendments to the Bill, which were later considered on the floor of the House. It was more or less evenly divided on two of the most contentious issues—abolition of the office of Lord Chancellor and

---

[37] www.publications.parliament.uk/pa/cm200304/cmselect/cmconst/48/48.pdf. The CASC also produced a report intended to 'inform the second reading debate', www.publications.parliament.uk/pa/cm200304/cmselect/cmconst/48/48.pdf. It recommended that: 'The consultation process has been too short and the legislative timetable is too restrictive to deal with changes which are so far reaching in their effects. The reason for haste seems to be primarily political. The Committee recommends that the Government proceed with the Bill as draft legislation to enable proper scrutiny of these fundamental changes'.

[38] See Gee et al, *Judicial Independence* (n 3) 37.

[39] Announced by the Lord Chancellor in January 2004, see Le Sueur, 'A Narrative' (n 34) 74.

[40] The background to the use of this unusual procedure is outlined in the report of the House of Lords Committee on the Constitutional Reform Bill, 2004–05, HL 125-I, paras 4–9 (see below).

[41] First Report, 2004–05, HL 125-I and II.

[42] HL Deb 13 July 2004, cols 1138–39.

establishment of the Supreme Court—but, in the interests of consensus, it avoided putting disputed matters to a vote.[43]

A. Some Implications for Parliamentary Accountability

Accounts of the unusual and politically contentious background to the June 2003 announcement and of the events leading up to the enactment of the 2005 Act have been written by others—notably by Andrew Le Sueur,[44] who has served as a specialist adviser and legal adviser to several parliamentary committees—and the following comments will deal only with those aspects that have a particular bearing upon the issue of parliamentary accountability.

One such aspect concerns the respective functions of the two Houses relating to the administration of justice. The House of Lords has tended in the past—by virtue of its appellate functions and the presence in the House of many Law Lords and eminent legal practitioners—to be regarded as a repository of top-quality legal expertise. Law reform Bills and measures dealing with matters of particularly complex legal technicality (sometimes characterised as 'lawyers' law' Bills) have tended to begin their parliamentary passage in the Lords rather than in the Commons. And matters to do with reform of the legal system or touching upon the prerogatives of the judiciary are perhaps best considered, in the first instance, by the less party-political of the two Houses. The Constitutional Reform Bill was not particularly technical, but because its subject matter was of such constitutional importance and bore directly on the appellate functions of the Lords and the role of the Lord Chancellor (who was then Speaker of the House) it was deemed appropriate to begin its passage in the Lords rather than the Commons.

Even though participation in Lords debates by serving judges had greatly diminished in the years leading up to the passage of the CRA and the setting up of the Supreme Court, there was always a sense that the Lord Chancellor, as both senior Cabinet minister and de facto head of the judiciary, was publicly engaged in a regular and expert dialogue with the top minds and voices of his profession in a forum that is and was for the most part non-party political. Moreover, the expertise of the judges could usefully be harnessed in appropriately non-partisan contexts to important aspects of parliamentary business: for instance, the Joint Committee on Delegated Legislation was always chaired by a Law Lord. In a Lords debate in March 2003 on the proposal to establish the Supreme Court, the former Lord of Appeal, Lord Brightman, pointed out that, in the preceding session,

---

[43] A good account of the parliamentary proceedings surrounding the passage of the Constitutional Reform Bill and the amendments proposed and carried can be found in A Le Sueur, 'From Appellate Committee' (n 34).

[44] A Le Sueur, 'New Labour's (Surprisingly) Quick Steps on the Road to Constitutional Reform' [2003] *Public Law*, 368; A Le Sueur, 'From Appellate Committee to Supreme Court' (n 34). See also, R Stevens, *The English Judges: Their Role in the Changing Constitution* (Oxford, Hart, 2005).

12 places on Lords committees had been occupied by Law Lords.[45] It is arguable that the departure of the then-serving Law Lords (though some have returned to the House on retirement from the Supreme Court and there are still a lot of other distinguished lawyers among the active membership of the House) and the relocation of the Lord Chancellor from the Lords to the Commons has significantly challenged any previous claims of the House to a near monopoly of parliamentary legal expertise and to being at the sharp end of parliamentary accountability for the administration of justice.

Giving evidence to the Constitutional Affairs Committee, soon to be rebadged as the Justice Committee, shortly after his appointment as Justice Secretary, Jack Straw said (responding to a question about his role in judicial appointments) that:

> I am very conscious of the fact that precisely because I am the first Lord Chancellor in the Commons and I am an elected politician, I have to be seen to be preserving the independence of the judiciary and ensuring an arm's length relationship with them, to a degree that was not necessary with the previous Lord Chancellors because they were in the unelected House and everybody knew what their position was.[46]

Although, as noted above, the Bill was introduced into the Lords, in the run-up to its introduction, the Commons Constitutional Affairs Committee instituted an enquiry into the proposals, took evidence from the main protagonists (including Lord Bingham, then the Senior Law Lord and Lord Woolf, then the Lord Chief Justice of England and Wales) and produced a highly critical report.[47] The Committee revisited the subject in the following session and produced a further report,[48] by which time the original proposals had been significantly amended—in particular, by the adoption of the concordat—in ways that met many of the Committee's original concerns.

This exercise illustrates an important point about the function and significance of select committees more generally, that whether or not their recommendations have little direct impact on the Government (and often they do not), their evidence sessions, conducted in public and on the record, bring into the public domain a mass of valuable material that would otherwise remain unrevealed. The evidence volumes of the reports just cited are a mine of useful information on this topic, offering a substantial contribution to the information base of public debate. The same general comment applies to the reports of the Commons Justice Committee (and to other select committees that have conducted enquiries in this subject area).[49] Extracting and making public high-quality information and expert critical comment goes to the very heart of what accountability is about.

[45] HL Deb 8 September 2003, cols 119–20.

[46] Select Committee on Constitutional Affairs, Minutes of Evidence, 24 July 2007, Q24.

[47] Constitutional Affairs Committee, 'Judicial appointments and a Supreme Court (court of final appeal)', First Report of Session 2003–04, HC 41-I and II.

[48] Constitutional Reform Committee, 'Constitutional Reform Bill [Lords]: the Government's Proposals', Third Report of Session 2004–05, HC275-I and II.

[49] The role of Select Committees is discussed in ch 5 and referred to in several of the other chapters of this volume.

One potentially important reference to parliamentary accountability appears in section 5 of the CRA, which reads as follows:

5 Representations to Parliament

This section has no associated Explanatory Notes

(1) The chief justice of any part of the United Kingdom[50] may lay before Parliament written representations on matters that appear to him to be matters of importance relating to the judiciary, or otherwise to the administration of justice, in that part of the United Kingdom.

(2) In relation to Scotland those matters do not include matters within the legislative competence of the Scottish Parliament, unless they are matters to which a Bill for an Act of Parliament relates.

(3) In relation to Northern Ireland those matters do not include transferred matters within the legislative competence of the Northern Ireland Assembly, unless they are matters to which a Bill for an Act of Parliament relates.

(4) In subsection (3) the reference to transferred matters has the meaning given by section 4(1) of the Northern Ireland Act 1998 (c. 47).

(5) In this section 'chief justice' means—

(a)   in relation to England and Wales or Northern Ireland, the Lord Chief Justice of that part of the United Kingdom;

(b)   in relation to Scotland, the Lord President of the Court of Session.

The implications of this provision were considered by the Lords Constitution Committee, in its 2007 Report, 'Relations between the Executive, the Judiciary and Parliament'.[51] The Committee accepted the view given in evidence by the Lord Chief Justice (and echoed by The Lord Chancellor, Lord Falconer) that this power was 'a nuclear option' to be used only where legislative proposals were so contrary to the rule of law that the judges felt compelled to step in and make plain their objections. Recognising that the section 5 power will, in practice, rarely be used,[52] the Committee went on to consider 'whether there need to be other more routine ways in which lesser concerns can be conveyed to Parliament'.[53] In his evidence to the Committee, the Lord Chief Justice of England and Wales had asked, 'might

---

[50] On 17 January 2012, the Lord President of the Court of Session (the Chief Justice in Scotland for the purpose of the Act) used this power to lay before both Houses written representations relating to the Scotland Bill. In the House of Lords, the laying of the written representations was accompanied by a written statement from the Chairman of Committees. (This was restricted to a comment that the statement had been made and that copies of it were available in the Printed Paper Office; see HL Deb 17 January 2012, col WS37).

[51] Sixth Report of Session 2006–07, HL Paper 151, paras 113–19.

[52] For a Scottish instance of the use of this provision, see n 44 above. The power had previously been used on 31 March 2008 by the Lord Chief Justice for England and Wales to lay a 'Review of the Administration of Justice in the Courts'.

[53] Sixth Report (n 51), para 120.

there not be a machinery, if there was a particular topic that I thought it desirable to ventilate, whereby I could let the appropriate [select] committee know that if they were interested in hearing about this I would be happy to discuss it?' The Committee agreed 'that select committees offer a suitable arena for the Lord Chief Justice, or other senior judges, to air concerns about the administration of justice and the impact of legislation and other policy proposals upon the courts and the judiciary'.

Considering more generally the issue of judicial accountability, the Committee went on to note that, 'since the Lord Chancellor is no longer head of the judiciary, and therefore cannot answer to Parliament on its behalf, Parliament must hold the judiciary accountable in other ways'.[54] It saw the select committees of both Houses as the key to achieving this—and this is something that we will return to in the next section of this chapter.

V. THE MINISTRY OF JUSTICE AND PARLIAMENT

The Department of Constitutional Affairs was in existence for nearly four years, until the establishment of the Ministry of Justice in May 2007. Meanwhile, the Lord Chancellor's Department had come under the purview of its own Commons select committee, which met for the first time on 4 February 2003, under the chairmanship of Sir Alan Beith. It was succeeded by a Constitutional Affairs Committee[55] in January 2003 and then, in 2007, by the Justice Committee. In the 2015–17 Parliament, the Conservative MP, Robert Neill, became chairman of the Justice Committee in succession to Beith, who had been elevated to the House of Lords.

For the first few weeks of the Ministry of Justice's existence the office of Secretary of State and Lord Chancellor was held by Lord Falconer, formerly Secretary for Constitutional Affairs, but in July the position passed to a legally qualified (though non-practising) senior Member of the House of Commons, Jack Straw, formerly Leader of the House. The obvious constitutional significance of this relocation was noted by Mr Straw himself, in the passage quoted above. The advent of the coalition Government in 2010 saw another prominent non-practising lawyer-MP, Kenneth Clarke, appointed to the office.

A huge constitutional step-change occurred in September 2012, when Clarke was succeeded by the Conservative MP, Chris Grayling—the first non-lawyer to hold the office of Lord Chancellor for more than four centuries. Grayling quickly became embroiled in various controversies to do, among other things, with his hard-line approach to the treatment of prisoners, with severe cutbacks in legal aid and with restrictions on access to judicial review—some of which earned him

---

[54] Sixth Report (n 51), para 123.
[55] For an overview of the work of this Committee see A Horne, 'Parliamentary Scrutiny: An Assessment of the Work of the Constitutional Affairs Select Committee' (2006) *JUSTICE Journal* 62.

highly critical comments from senior lawyers and members of the judiciary.[56] He, in turn, was succeeded in 2015 by another non-lawyer, Michael Gove—also a controversial figure though with a somewhat more emollient approach to some of the policies initiated by Grayling. When Theresa May became Prime Minister, after the Brexit referendum, she appointed Elizabeth Truss as the third non-lawyer Lord Chancellor, and the first woman to hold the office—another controversial minister who we will encounter again later in this chapter. Following the June 2017 general election, Ms Truss was replaced by yet another non-lawyer, David Lidington MP.

One important thing to bear in mind when discussing parliamentary account-ability in this context is that 'justice' does not only mean what happens in and around the courts. Historically, the Lord Chancellor was responsible for a lot of things that had very little to do with judges and courts, such as ecclesiastical patronage.[57] In the aftermath of devolution, the Department of Constitutional Affairs acquired responsibilities for some matters pertaining to Scotland and Wales. The responsibilities of the Ministry of Justice for courts, tribunals, legal aid, etc, sit alongside its responsibility for prisons—both functions administered by large executive agencies. An analysis of parliamentary questions to the Minis-try of Justice over a six-month period in 2013[58] revealed that while 20 per cent of the PQs related to prisons, only seven per cent were concerned with the court system—and nearly all of those were to do with the lower courts (inevitably so, given that the Lord Chancellor's previous responsibility for administration of the higher courts has now passed to the higher judiciary). Broadly defined, 'justice' also covers policing and prosecutions—which are the responsibility of the Home Office.

The present distribution of functions resembles in many respects the classi-cal Continental European dichotomy between Ministry of Justice and Ministry of the Interior—leaving plenty of scope for earnest debate (no doubt flavoured, as always, by Eurosceptical imaginings) about whether this disposition is the opti-mal one. It also offers scope for occasional cross-border skirmishes between these two big ministries—as illustrated by some bickering about human rights issues between the then Justice Secretary, Kenneth Clarke, and the then Home Secretary, Theresa May, in the early months of the coalition Government that came to power in 2010.

Dawn Oliver has noted, in chapter 12, the extraordinary attack on the judges by the Brexit-supporting tabloid press—in particular by *The Daily Mail*, with its lurid headline 'Enemies of the People', directed at the three judges who decided the *Miller* case in the Queen's Bench Divisional Court in November 2016. The widespread criticism of the then Lord Chancellor, Elizabeth Truss, for a belated and seemingly lukewarm defence of the judiciary—seen by many critics, including

---

[56] See Gee et al, *Judicial Independence* (n 3) 40.
[57] See: www.publications.parliament.uk/pa/cm200304/cmselect/cmconst/300/4012901.htm and www.publications.parliament.uk/pa/cm200304/cmselect/cmconst/300/300we01.htm.
[58] Gee et al, *Judicial Independence* (n 3) 99–100.

some of the judges, as an egregious dereliction of her statutory duty to defend judicial independence in accordance with section 3(6) of the Constitutional Reform Act—inevitably found its way onto the parliamentary agenda.

In the Lords, the Conservative peer, Lord Lexden, asked the Government 'what steps they are taking to ensure that the Lord Chancellor fulfills her duty to uphold the independence of the judiciary'.[59] A predictably bland reply (from the Advocate General for Scotland, Lord Keen) received scant support from the peers who took part in the ensuing exchanges. Three weeks later, Lord Beith (former Chair of the Commons Justice Select Committee) similarly asked what steps the Government was taking 'to promote public understanding of the rule of law and the independence of the judiciary'.[60] The reply (this time from a Government whip, Lord Henley) also elicited skeptical responses from most of the subsequent contributors. Meanwhile, the Lord Chancellor herself, for the time being secure in the relatively unthreatening environment of the House of Commons, had found little difficulty in blandly stonewalling a question by Labour MP, Liz McInnes, about what steps she was taking to fulfill her duty to uphold the independence of the judiciary'.[61] The widely recognised ritualistic shortcomings of Commons Question Time as an effective instrument of ministerial accountability hardly need to be repeated here.

Of greater interest was the remarkable rebuke to the Lord Chancellor, delivered by the Lord Chief Justice, in his evidence to the Lords Constitution Committee, as described below. It is to the role of committees that we now turn.

VI. THE ROLE OF SELECT COMMITTEES

As noted above, the Lords Select Committee on the Constitution, in its 2007 Report, saw select committees—in particular itself and the Commons Constitutional Affairs Committee (soon afterwards to become the Justice Committee)—as key instruments for holding the post-CRA judiciary accountable to Parliament for matters pertaining to the administration of justice, apart from issues to do with the rights and wrongs of decisions in particular cases:

> We believe that select committees can play a central part in enabling the role and proper concerns of the judiciary to be better understood by the public at large, and in helping the judiciary to remain accountable to the people via their representatives in Parliament. Not only should senior judges be questioned on the administration of the justice system, they might also be encouraged to discuss their views on key legal issues in the cause of transparency and better understanding of such issues amongst both parliamentarians and the public. However, under no circumstances must committees ask judges to comment on the pros and cons of individual judgments.[62]

---

[59] HL Deb 15 November 2016, vol 776, col 1293.
[60] HL Deb 7 December 2016, vol 777, col 729.
[61] HC Deb 6 December 2016, vol 618, col 107.
[62] Sixth Report of Session 2006–07 (n 51), para 126.

An interesting memorandum of guidance (reminiscent of the 'Osmotherly Rules' for civil service witnesses) has been prepared by the Office of the Judiciary for England and Wales (headed by the Lord Chief Justice) for judges appearing before or providing written evidence to parliamentary committees.[63]

This author of this chapter has, from the outset (see above), implicitly adopted a fairly narrow definition of 'the administration of the justice system', as having to do with the running of courts and tribunals and the delivery and funding of legal services; but, of course, the classical instruments of parliamentary account-ability—questions addressed to the Justice Secretary and his or her departmental ministerial colleagues, and enquiries undertaken by the select committees like the House of Lords Constitution Committee, and the House of Commons Constitu-tional Affairs Committee, which became the Justice Committee—cover a lot of other things too, particularly in the case of the Constitutional Affairs Committee. The time and resources available for committee scrutiny of Ministry of Justice matters are limited—and they are diluted by the breadth of the ministerial portfo-lio. We have already noted that in the subject distribution of parliamentary ques-tions addressed to the Ministry of Justice, crime, punishment and prisons tend to engage the interest of parliamentarians appreciably more than the nuts and bolts of the courts system (much of which, in any case has now become judicial rather than ministerial territory)—and this further compounds the dilution.

This becomes very apparent when we look at the subject matter of recent reports published by the two select committees just mentioned. In the (unusually long) parliamentary session 2010–12, the House of Lords Constitution Commit-tee published 25 Reports[64] of which only three concerned the administration of justice, narrowly defined (ie excluding issues like policing, constitutional change and prevention of terrorism). They were:

— 9th Report, 'Meetings with the Lord Chief Justice and the Lord Chancellor';[65]
— 21st Report, 'Part 1 of the Legal Aid, Sentencing and Punishment of Offenders Bill';[66]
— 25th Report, 'Judicial Appointments'.[67]

The latter report was based on a particularly illuminating and wide-ranging enquiry into the working of the reformed judicial appointments system estab-lished by the CRA—and took evidence from an array of senior judges, including the then Lord Chief Justice of England and Wales Lord Judge, the then Master of

---

[63] The Judicial Executive Board, 'Guidance to Judges on Appearances before Select Committees', October 2012. By way of complementing these guidelines, the Judicial Executive Board has also pub-lished 'Guidance to the judiciary on engagement with the Executive' (July 2016). Both documents can be accessed at www.judiciary.gov.uk.

[64] See www.parliament.uk/business/committees/committees-a-z/lords-select/constitution-committee/publications1/previous-sessions/Session-2010-12/.

[65] Constitution Committee, 9th Report of Session 2010–12, HL 89.

[66] Constitution Committee, 21st Report of Session 2010–12, HL 222.

[67] Constitution Committee, 5th Report of Session 2010–12, HL 272.

the Rolls Lord Neuberger, the then President of the Supreme Court Lord Phillips and the Supreme Court Justice Lady Hale as well as from the then Justice Secretary Ken Clarke MP and his immediate predecessors as Lord Chancellor. Among its recommendations, it firmly rejected any suggestion that the accountability functions of parliamentary committees might be extended to include pre- and post-appointment hearing of judges—seen as a step too far into the territory that is ring-fenced to protect judicial independence from any risk of political interference.

Among the more recent reports of the Constitution Committee, the subject matter of this chapter prompts special mention of its report, published in December, 2014 on 'The Office of Lord Chancellor'.[68]

As one might have predicted, given the departmental specificity of its remit, a much higher proportion of the 12 reports (excluding special reports) published by the Commons' Justice Committee in the 2010–12 session[69] dealt with administration of justice issues, as defined above. They included the following:

— 1st Report, 'Revised Sentencing Guidelines: Assault';[70]
— 2nd Report, 'Appointment of the Chair of the Judicial Appointments Commission';[71]
— 3rd Report, 'Government's Proposed Reform of Legal Aid';[72]
— 6th Report, 'Operation of the Family Courts';[73]
— 10th Report, 'The proposed abolition of the Youth Justice Service'.[74]

The Committee also held evidence sessions on various subjects including the following:

— the work of the Legal Services Commission;[75]
— the work of the Ministry of Justice and its resources.[76]

The committee reports listed above merely constitute a thumbnail snapshot of a much bigger picture. A different working definition of our subject matter and/or a choice of other parliamentary sessions might yield different pictures of the spread of accountability (though more recent sessions do in fact show a very similar pattern); but the 'dilution' point is an important one, and it applies in other subject areas too, given that select committees, however industrious and conscientious

---

[68] 6th Report of Session 2014–15, HC 75. See also House of Commons Library Briefing Paper, 'The Role of the Lord Chancellor,' SN02105. March 2015.

[69] See www.parliament.uk/business/committees/committees-a-z/commons-select/justice-committee/Publications/previous-sessions/Session-2010-12/.

[70] 1st Report of Session 2010–12, HC 637.

[71] 2nd Report of Session 2010–12, HC 770.

[72] 3rd Report of Session 2010–12, HC 681 (three volumes).

[73] 6th Report of Session 2010–12, HC 518 (two volumes).

[74] 10th Report of Session 2010–12, HC 1547 (two volumes).

[75] 2010–12, HC 649-i.

[76] 2010–12, HC 378-ii.

they may be, cannot—simply because of lack of time and manpower—match the span of responsibilities of a major Department of state.

The deeply engrained territoriality of Whitehall departments (the term 'silo mentality' is sometimes used, pejoratively, in this context) finds echoes in the select committee system. But committee scrutiny of the administration of justice is not confined to the two committees considered above. Other parliamentary committees have also looked from time to time at aspects of the administration of justice. To take a fairly recent example: the Public Accounts Committee has reported on the procurement of legal aid by the Legal Services Commission[77] and on the youth justice system[78]—both subjects, as noted above, having also been considered by the Justice Committee.

We have already noted that the 2007 report of the Lords Constitution Committee favoured the use of select committees as a conduit of communication between the judges and Parliament—and judges have indeed appeared quite frequently as witnesses before committees in recent years, though some of them have expressed misgivings about the practice.[79]

The Lord Chief Justice, as Head of the Judiciary, is empowered by section 5 of the CRA to issue reports, which are usually laid before Parliament,[80] and recent holders of the office have appeared regularly before the Constitution Committee. A particularly striking recent example was an evidence session with Lord Thomas of Cwmgiedd on 22 March 2017,[81] which included some very sharp comments— including some direct and pointed criticisms of the then Secretary of State (and Lord Chancellor) herself. He was critical of confusion that had been caused by an inaccurately premature ministerial announcement of new procedures for the pre-recording of evidence in criminal trials—which were in fact still being piloted and had not yet been introduced. But his fiercest comments, delivered at some length, were to take strong issue with the Lord Chancellor's failure to uphold judicial independence and support the judges who had come under media attack in the aftermath of *Miller*. He ended this passage of his evidence thus:

> I regret to have to criticize her as severely as I have, but to my mind she is completely and absolutely wrong about this, as I have said, and I am very disappointed. I understand what the pressures were in November, but she has taken a position that is constitutionally absolutely wrong.

Such unequivocal language from a top judge addressing a parliamentary committee in open session bears eloquent testimony to the extent to which the internal

---

[77] 9th Report of Session 2009-10, HC 322.

[78] 21st Report of Session 2010–11, HC 721.

[79] See for instance Lord Phillips of Worth Matravers, 'Judicial Independence', Commonwealth Law Conference 2007, Kenya, 12 September 2007; Sir Jack Beatson, 'Judicial Independence and Accountability: Pressures and Opportunities', Nottingham Trent University, 16 April 2008.

[80] See Gee et al, *Judicial Independence* (n 3) 100–01.

[81] http://data.parliament.uk/writtenevidence/committeeevidence.svc/evidencedocument/constitution-committee/lord-chief-justice/oral/32610.html.

borders of the constitutional territory inhabited by the executive, the judiciary and Parliament have been relocated in recent years.[82]

Oral and written judicial evidence is frequently presented to the Commons Justice Committee and a lot of other committees have taken judicial evidence from time to time. To cite just two instances among many, in May 2009, Sir Anthony Clarke, MR, and Lord Justice Rupert Jackson, appeared before the Culture, Media and Sport Committee, in its enquiry into Press standards, Privacy and Libel;[83] and Sir Nicholas Wall and Mr Justice Baker and Lord Neuberger and Mr Justice Tugendhat appeared in separate witness hearings before the Joint Committee on Privacy and Injunctions in November 2011.[84] There is fuller and more recent coverage of judges appearing as witnesses before committees—including accounts of how those appearances are managed, and what ground is covered by such judicial evidence—in a recent major study of judicial independence, already cited in this chapter.[85]

VII. CONCLUSIONS

This account began with the metaphor of constitutional territory. Until the 1980s the judges, fiercely protective of their independence, were accountable to no one but themselves. As head of the judiciary, the Lord Chancellor exercised some supervisory and disciplinary functions, but did so completely behind closed doors; in practice, he saw his main function as shielding the judges from parliamentary scrutiny and sometimes from attacks by other ministers rather than as being an accountable minister himself. Parliament was, by and large, complicit in this arrangement. Judges got on with their task of judging; parliamentarians looked nervously at a frontier guard-house marked 'judicial independence', occupied by the formidable figure of the Lord Chancellor, and kept their distance.

The picture began to change from the 1980s onwards as, gradually, the Lord Chancellor's Department—caught up in the rising tide of public management reform and constitutional modernisation—began to look more and more like an ordinary department of state, providing an important and expensive public service. The Constitutional Reform Act 2005—incorporating the concordat on judicial independence, refashioning the historic role of the Lord Chancellor, transferring the appellate functions of the Lords to the new Supreme Court and putting the chief justices of England and Wales and of Northern Ireland (and there is separate legislation, similarly empowering the Lord President of the Scottish

---

[82] Lord Thomas elaborated his views about the location of these borders in his Michael Ryle Memorial Lecture, delivered to the Study of Parliament Group in June 2017: www.judiciary.gov.uk/announcements/michael-ryle-memorial-lecture-by-the-lord-chief-justice-the-judiciary-within-the-state-the-relationship-between-the-branches-of-the-state.

[83] 2008–09, HC 275.

[84] Oral evidence, 1 November 2011, QQ 445–85; QQ 486–535.

[85] Gee et al, *Judicial Independence* (n 3) 101–12.

Court of Session[86]) in overall charge of the judiciary—was a path-breaking measure but, in truth, it was really no more than the statutory culmination of a whole raft of cumulatively radical reforms that had been unfolding over the previous two decades or more. The exorcising, two years later, of the old taboo about creating a Ministry of Justice, headed by a Secretary of State in the House of Commons, was an almost inevitable sequel—one with major, obvious and positive implications for parliamentary accountability.

So a major part of the story told in this chapter has been to do with the accountability consequences of normalising the administration of justice, and bringing it administratively into line with other important public services, and of harnessing parliamentary procedures to accommodate the new arrangements. But it also needs to be recognised that the moves to make those responsible for running and delivering the administration of justice—the Justice Secretary and the judges—more accountable to Parliament is not just about management reform and modernisation, it also has to do with the increasing political salience of the judicial role through the growth of judicial review[87] and, in particular, by the enactment of the Human Rights Act 1998.[88] Some judicial decisions in these areas have had significant political consequences and triggered strong reactions—particularly from ministers and, even more particularly, from Home Secretaries. The media began to sit up and take notice (often fuelled by Home Office briefings). It is not without significance that the ousting of Lord Irvine as Lord Chancellor in 2003—the beginning of the saga leading up to the enactment of the CRA and the establishment of the Ministry of Justice—is rumoured to have been triggered by complaints from Home Secretary David Blunkett, one of the most vociferous ministerial critics of what he and some of his colleagues saw as unwarranted judicial interference with the legitimate prerogatives of the elected Government.[89]

And once judicial decisions start attracting that kind of political and media attention—an extreme instance being the disgraceful *Miller* episode, triggered by the hyperbole and malice that has characterised some of the tabloid coverage of post-referendum Brexit-related issues—the pressure begins irresistibly to grow for enhanced opportunities for parliamentary scrutiny. That scrutiny does not extend to allowing parliamentary criticism of the merits of judicial decisions but, short of that, the replacement of the old, closely guarded frontier by something much more permeable and transparent has changed the whole constitutional landscape. Moreover, since the enactment of the Constiutional Reform Act 2005, the judges (headed in England and Wales by the Lord Chief Justice) have far more of a 'management role' that needs scrutinising independently from the administrative

---

[86] Judiciary and Courts (Scotland) Act 2008.

[87] See V Bondy and M Sunkin, *The Dynamics of Judicial Review Litigation* (London, Public Law Project, 2009) 2–3. Detailed statistics relating to judicial review can be found in the annual volumes of *Judicial Statistics*, published on the website of the Ministry of Justice.

[88] See ch 10.

[89] See S Pollard, *David Blunkett* (London, Hodder and Stoughton, 2005) 268–71; A Le Sueur, 'From Appellate Committee' (n 34) 70–71.

functions exercised by the Ministry of Justice. One wonders what old-style Lord Chancellors such as Lord Birkenhead and Lord Hailsham would have made of all this and whether, even in those pre-CRA days, they would have felt obliged to denounce headlines describing senior judges as 'enemies of the people'.

It remains for us to make some kind of qualitative assessment of the transformation, but here we must be cautious. There can be little doubt that transparency has been improved; the Constitution Committee and the Justice Committee, in particular, have done invaluable work, not least (as noted earlier) by bringing a lot of high-quality information and expert opinion into the public domain, to the benefit of informed debate on a lot of subjects that have, in the past, been shrouded in darkness. This has been very apparent in recent debates on justice-related legislation, notably on the cutting of legal aid funding, and the contentious parliamentary passage of the Legal Aid, Sentencing and Punishment of Offenders Act 2012, which was preceded by intensive committee scrutiny.[90] This, incidentally, is just one example of many recent and continuing financial cutbacks in the justice system, some of which have posed egregious threats to access to justice and presented interesting challenges for accountability. Some aspects of the Government's continuing preoccupation with cost-saving have also highlighted the tensions inherent in the fact that, as noted earlier, the MoJ spend on prisons dwarfs that on the courts.[91]

The debates on the Constitutional Reform Bill, drawing heavily on the work of committees in both Houses (see above), perhaps showed Parliament at its best—reminding us that even an 'arena' legislature can, when it puts its mind to it, play a crucial part in the fashioning of important public policies.

The work of these committees and the routine array of questions to justice ministers makes one realise how deficient the old system was and how groundless were the claims that judicial independence would be an inevitable casualty of such scrutiny. But we do have to remember that, notwithstanding welcome procedural reforms in recent years (in particular, the establishment of the departmentally related Commons select committees in the early 1980s)[92] Parliament is still, essentially an arena legislature, dominated (with occasional interesting exceptions) by the Executive. Most decisions happen inside government departments

---

[90] House of Lords Select Committee on the Constiution, 21st Report of Session 2010–12, *Part 1 of the Legal Aid, Sentencing and Punishment of Offenders Bill*, HL 222, November 2011; Joint Committee on Human Rights, 22nd Report of Session 2010–12, Legislative Scrutiny: *Legal Aid, Sentencing and Punishment of Offenders Bill*, HL 237, HC 1717, 2010–12, December 2011. See also, Justice Committee, *Government's Proposed Reform of Legal Aid*, 3rd Report of Session 2010–11, HC 681.

[91] One interesting illustration of this may be found in the Prisons and Courts Bill that fell at the end of the 2015–17 Parliament. The Bill would have provided, among other things, for the provision of online courts—an interesting proposal—albeit intended primarily, as with many other recent measures, such as legal aid cuts and court closures, not to improve the quality of justice but to save money.

[92] See G Drewry (ed), *The New Select Committees*, 2nd edn (Oxford, Clarendon Press, 1989). The role and effectiveness of select committees are also discussed elsewhere in this volume, particularly in ch 5.

and Parliament is often given little chance to influence them while they are still at a malleable stage. Criticisms of Parliament's weaknesses—the ritualistic nature of question time, the imbalance of resources between departments and Parliament, the uphill struggle faced by committees to get their recommendations taken seriously by Government[93]—have been a frequent lament of commentators. Yes, accountability for the administration of justice has greatly improved—but from a very low baseline and only to the extent of being brought up to the same unsatisfactory level as applies to other areas of government.

[93] Some interesting proposals for improving the effectiveness of select committees can be found in the report of the House of Commons Reform Committee (the Wright Committee), 'Rebuilding the House', First Report of Session 2008–09, HC 1117. See ch 5 of this volume.

12

Parliament and the Courts: A Pragmatic (or Principled) Defence of the Sovereignty of Parliament[1]

DAWN OLIVER[*]

I. THE DOCTRINE OF THE SOVEREIGNTY OF PARLIAMENT

THE TRADITIONAL AND orthodox view is that it is a fundamental principle of the UK Constitution that the courts will treat Acts of Parliament—that is, Acts passed by the two Houses of Parliament with the assent of the Monarch (or under the Parliament Acts 1911 and 1949, by the House of Commons with royal assent)—as the highest form of law.[2] This is known as the 'sovereignty', or 'legislative supremacy' of Parliament. The doctrine entails that the courts will give effect to provisions in Acts of Parliament, and that provisions in later Acts that are inconsistent with provisions in earlier Acts impliedly repeal the earlier provision.[3] The courts interpret Acts consistently with the UK's treaty obligations, and with fundamental rights[4] and, as the law develops, with principles of legality, constitutionalism and the rule of law; if Parliament intends to legislate

[*] Dawn Oliver is Emeritus Professor of Constitutional Law, University College London.

[1] The following friends and colleagues have given me comments and feedback on drafts of this chapter, for which I am very grateful: Andrew Blick, Carlo Fusaro, Conor Gearty, Alexander Horne, Murray Hunt, Jeff King, Stuart Lakin, Sir Stephen Laws, Colm O'Cinneide, Sir Stephen Sedley, Gijsbert ter Kuile. All weaknesses and errors are entirely my responsibility.

[2] AV Dicey, *Introduction to the Study of the Law of the Constitution*, 10th edn (London, Macmillan, 1959); J Goldsworthy, *The Sovereignty of Parliament* (Oxford, Clarendon Press, 1999) and *Parliamentary Sovereignty: Contemporary Debates* (Cambridge, Cambridge University Press, 2010); M Gordon, *Parliamentary Sovereignty in the UK Constitution* (Oxford, Hart, 2015); M Elliott, 'The Principle of Parliamentary Sovereignty in Legal, Constitutional and Political Perspective' in J Jowell, D Oliver and C O'Cinneidge (eds), *The Changing Constitution*, 8th edn (Oxford, Oxford University Press, 2015); *Edinburgh and Dalkeith Railway v Wauchope* (1842) 8 Cl 7 F 710; *Pickin v British Railways Board* [1974] AC 965; *Cheney v Conn* [1968] 1 All ER 799.

[3] *Ellen Street Estates v Minister of Health* [1934] 1 KB 590. For further discussion of the complex arguments around these issues see: Elliott (ibid); Goldsworthy, *Contemporary Debates* (ibid), ch 10.

[4] The Human Rights Act 1998 s 3 requires the courts so far as possible to interpret provisions compatibly with Convention rights.

in breach of these then it should use express and clear language, not general or ambiguous words.[5]

Another aspect of the relationship between Parliament and the courts arose in relation to the decisions of the UK Government as to leaving the European Union in the light of the referendum in June 2015. The vote was 52 per cent in favour of Brexit. The Government took the view that it had power under the royal prerogative on the conduct of foreign relations to notify the EU of the decision of the UK to leave without authority in an Act of Parliament. This was challenged in the case of *R (on the application of Miller and another) v Secretary of State for Exiting the European Union*. The Supreme Court held[6] that an Act of Parliament was required before the government could give notice under Article 50 of the Treaty on the European Union of its decision to leave, because the decision would adversely affect the rights of many citizens. The case was not, therefore, about whether the court could or should strike down a provision in an Act, the focus of this chapter. It was about interpretation of the European Communities Act 1972. The significant point for the purpose of this chapter is that the majority in the Supreme Court maintained—obiter in the circumstances—that 'Parliamentary sovereignty is a fundamental principle of the UK constitution'.[7] This entails the notion that laws of constitutional nature should be made or changed by Parliament and not, for instance, by the executive.

In this chapter I suggest that what I prefer to call the 'doctrine' of parliamentary sovereignty rather than a 'principle' is based, in part at least, on a pragmatic recognition by politicians and the courts that the functioning of the British system imposes responsibility for the constitution and the rule of law on every organ of state rather than placing that responsibility solely or primarily in the hands of a Supreme or Constitutional Court. While this approach leaves open the possibility that politicians or judges might make 'unconstitutional' laws, in practice the making of such laws is rare. A number of informal preventative procedures are in place to protect constitutionality and the rule of law. It may well be possible for these preventative mechanisms to be improved and this will be explored in section IV of the chapter. But overall, I suggest, it is preferable for the UK to retain the doctrine of parliamentary sovereignty and the pro-constitutional culture that goes with it than to move to a system of judicial review and quashing of laws for unconstitutionality, and thus to import negative cultures into the system, such as political irresponsibility and a process of politicisation of the judiciary which countries where the courts do have such powers may experience.

---

[5] See, for instance, *Anisminic v Foreign Compensation Commission* [1969] 2 AC 147; *R. v Secretary of State for the Home Department, ex p Simms* [2000] 2 AC 115, per Lord Hoffmann at p 131; and *R v Secretary of State for the Home Department, ex p Pierson* [1998] AC 539, per Lord Browne-Wilkinson at p 575, and per Lord Steyn at p 591; *AXA General Insurance Ltd and others v The Lord Advocate* [2011] UKSC 46; *Thoburn v Sunderland City Council* [2002] EWCA 195 (Admin).

[6] [2017] UKSC 5 (henceforth *Miller*). For elaboration of what has become the orthodox view of the reasoning of the majority (eight SCJs) and the minority (three SCJs) in this case see M Elliott 'The Supreme Court's Judgment in *Miller*: In Search of Constitutional Principle' 76 *Camb LJ* 257.

[7] *Miller* (n 6), 43. See also paras 42, 45, 61, 67 and 122.

It is worth bearing in mind that the UK is not alone in subscribing to doc-trines of parliamentary sovereignty and lacking US-style judicial review or judicial strike-down powers: other Northern European countries including the Netherlands[8] and Sweden[9] survive as well-functioning liberal democracies based on the rule of law without such arrangements, as does our close constitutional cousin New Zealand.[10]

At this point a brief explanation of the use of the phrase 'rule of law' in this discussion is needed. While the general concept is complex[11] and has a wide range of meanings, here I take it to mean that laws are relatively certain, that there is wide cultural acceptance of requirements to obey the law, whether it is found in Acts or other sources such as the common law, general respect for the content of the law and for judges (including their independence) and the judicial system, and widespread voluntary compliance with orders made by the courts by politicians, officials and the general public. There are of course many other matters that fall within most accounts of the rule of law, including that the rights of individuals should be respected. The relatively smooth operation of constitutional arrange-ments in the UK depends on these aspects of the rule of law. However, as will be mentioned in due course, politicians and lawyers may take different views as to when and whether judges and judicial decisions call for respect. Disagreement on this issue this may undermine respect for the rule of law as a constitutional principle.

In the rest of this introductory part of the chapter I shall explore two aspects of the doctrine of sovereignty. First, the assumption that it is of the essence of sover-eignty that Parliament may legislate on any matter on simple majorities of those present and voting:[12] I suggest that this view is erroneous. Nowadays the doctrine is commonly taken to be a democratic principle: but is it?[13]

---

[8]   On the Netherlands see CAJM Kortmann and PPT Bovend'Eert, *The Kingdom of the Netherlands: An Introduction to Dutch Constitutional Law* (Boston, Kluwer Law and Taxation Publishers, 1993); and WJM Voermans, 'The Netherlands' in X Contiades, *Engineering Constitutional Change: A Comparative Perspective on Europe, Canada and the USA* (Abingdon, Routledge, 2012).

[9]   On Sweden see L-G Malmburg, 'Sweden' in Contiades, *Engineering Constitutional Change* (n 8); I Cameron 'Protection of constitutional rights in Sweden' [1997] *Public* Law 488; T Bull, 'Judges without a Court: Judicial Preview in Sweden' in T Campbell, KD Ewing and A Tomkins, *The Legal Protection of Human Rights: Sceptical Essays* (Oxford, Oxford University Press, 2011); U Bernitz, 'Swedish Report' in J Schwarze (ed), *The Birth of a European Constitutional Order* (Baden-Baden, Nomos Verlagsgesellschaft, 2000).

[10]   On New Zealand see PA Joseph, *Constitutional and Administrative Law in New Zealand* (Wellington, Thomson Brookers, 2007) and G Palmer and A Butler, 'A Constitution for Aotearoa New Zealand' (2016).

[11]   For a classic lawyer's account see T Bingham, *The Rule of Law* (St Ives, Allen Lane, 2010).

[12]   But note the argument that it would be possible and consistent with the system in the UK for special majorities to be required for certain kinds of legislation: RFV Heuston, *Essays in Constitu-tional Law*, 2nd edn (London, Stevens and Sons, 1964); Goldsworthy, *Contemporary Debates* (n 3), chs 6 and 7.

[13]   Where European law applies the courts will accept its primacy: *R v Secretary of State for Transport ex p Factortame (No 2)* [1991] 1 AC 603. This may be regarded either as an exception to the doctrine of sovereignty, or as an example of its operation.

A. Sovereignty vs Privilege

The British doctrine of parliamentary sovereignty is linked with the fact that each of the two Houses of Parliament legislates on any matter on simple majorities of those present and voting at the various stages of a bill's progress through Parliament.[14] The basis of this majoritarian practice, I suggest, is not necessarily a 'democratic principle'—a concept which will be explored below—since the Constitutions of many countries prescribe absolute or special majorities or special procedures for constitutional amendment or changes to some 'fundamental' constitutional rules: it could not credibly be suggested that these countries are all, for that reason, not democracies.

The basis of the 'bare majority of those present and voting' doctrine is, I suggest, parliamentary privilege and the exclusive cognisance of its proceedings that each House enjoys;[15] the basis is not parliamentary sovereignty. The existence of exclusive cognisance and parliamentary privilege as they operate in the UK immunises Parliament from challenge to its proceedings by the courts: to that extent parliamentary privilege reinforces legislative supremacy. But a parliament lacking such privilege in relation to its own legislative procedures could nevertheless be 'sovereign' in the sense that its laws on whatever matter, *if duly passed*, were valid laws.[16]

Parliamentary privilege is based in the common law[17] and in Article 9 Bill of Rights 1689.[18] The courts may not go behind the formal document that is the 'Act' to determine whether the prescribed intra-parliamentary legislative procedures were complied with. The rationale for this doctrine is acceptance of the need for comity between the courts and Parliament: in the nineteenth century, in conflicts between the courts and Parliament over a wide range of issues including the validity of elections, publication of parliamentary papers and the swearing of the oath of allegiance to the monarch, it came to be recognised that, while the courts are entitled to determine whether a parliamentary privilege exists, it is for Parliament alone to deal with contempts and breaches of privilege. The lesson was sharply learned in the battles between the courts and Parliament in the *Stockdale v Hansard*[19] and *Case of the Sheriff of Middlesex*[20] saga which resulted in a stand-off in which the courts acknowledged the 'exclusive cognisance' and primacy of the Houses of Parliament in these matters.[21]

---

[14] But note the Parliament Acts 1911 and 1949 which permit Royal Assent to legislation without the consent of the House of Lords; and the Fixed-term Parliaments Act 2011 on super-majority votes—but not in the form of an Act of Parliament.

[15] See ch 1 above.

[16] See *Ranasinghe* case, discussed below.

[17] *Edinburgh and Dalkeith Railway v Wauchope* and *Pickin v BRB* (n 2).

[18] 'The freedom of speech and debates and proceedings in Parliament shall not be called in question in any court or place outside of Parliament.' See discussion of privilege in chs 1 and 2 above.

[19] (1839) 9 Ad & El 1.

[20] (1840) 11 A & E 273.

[21] See ch 2 above. And see Bradley, Ewing and Knight, *Constitutional and Administrative Law*, 16th edn (Harlow, Longmans, 2014) ch 11; M Elliott and R Thomas, *Public Law* (Oxford, Oxford University

Legislation could of course be passed to abolish or transfer responsibility for aspects of parliamentary privilege—'exclusive cognisance'—to a court, as has been done with contested elections which are now dealt with by an Election Court. If an Act were passed to enable a court to investigate whether the prescribed procedures for legislation had been followed during the legislative process in Parliament— including perhaps requirements for special majorities for the passage of certain laws—and to determine the validity of an Act or parts of an Act in the light of procedural defects, that would not of itself affect the sovereignty or legislative supremacy of the UK Parliament. The British practice according to which Parliament may legislate on any matter on simple majorities of those present and voting is not an essential element of sovereign Parliaments. It would be surprising if the legislatures of, for instance, Germany, the United States and many other countries were considered by the UK not to be 'sovereign' because they are bound to follow special procedures for certain kinds of legislation. In *Bribery Commissioners v Ranasinghe* the Constitution of Ceylon as it then was (now Sri Lanka) provided that two-thirds majorities in the Parliament and a Speaker's certificate were required for certain laws to be passed and to be valid. The Judicial Committee of the Privy Council held that this provision could be enforced by the courts. They held that legislation that had not complied with the requirement was invalid. Such a position was not, the Privy Council held, incompatible with the sovereignty of the Parliament.[22]

Given that requirements as to special procedures to be followed in the enactment of Acts of Parliament would not of themselves undermine the legislative supremacy of Parliament, there must be one or more other reasons or justifications for exclusive cognisance. I suggest that the pragmatic reason why the British Parliament will not legislate to permit the courts to examine the intra-parliamentary legislative process must be that this might lead to the courts disapplying provisions in Acts that had not been duly passed or clash with the courts' understanding of the rule of law when—unlike the position in *Ranasinghe*—there is no written Constitution giving them the power to strike down legislation; such a provision could result in major constitutional conflicts, loss of trust between institutions— notably between the courts on the one hand and the Houses of Parliament and the executive on the other; and ultimately it could lead to a loss of authority in the courts and thus a weakening of the rule of law itself: I consider these issues more fully below.

Press, 2017) ch 2; *Erskine May: Parliamentary Practice*, 24th edn (London, LexisNexis, 2011) ch 12. See also *R v Chaytor and others* [2010] UKSC 52: the claiming of expenses by MPs is not protected by parliamentary privilege; MPs may therefore be prosecuted for criminal offences committed in relation to expenses. See ch 2 above.

[22] [1965] AC 172 at p 198 (Privy Council). See G Marshall, *Constitutional Theory* (Oxford, Clarendon Press, 1971) 53–57. The decision was only possible because, unlike the position in the UK, the legislative procedures were laid down in the governing instrument (the Constitution). Hence parliamentary privilege Westminster-style did not apply in Ceylon. See also Goldsworthy, *Contemporary Debates* (n 3) 141–73 and 174–201 on manner/procedure and form.

B. The Special Position of European law

The doctrine that the courts will give effect to European law even if it conflicts with provisions in Acts of the UK Parliament was first elaborated by Lord Bridge in *Factortame (II)*[23] and it has been applied in many cases since then. It is based on a range of justifications—contractual in the sense that it was part of the terms of the UK's membership of the European Communities, now Union, that the UK would accept the primacy and direct effect of European law, since the doctrine had already been established in rulings by the European Court of Justice when the UK joined; and functional because the EU could not operate unless the courts of the members states give direct effect and primacy to EU law.[24] Another way of looking at it—and one which the European Union Act 2011 seeks to emphasise by its declaratory section 18[25]—is that British courts accept the express instructions that were given to them in the European Communities Act 1972 section 2(4) to give direct effect and primacy to European law: the courts are giving effect to their *duty in UK law* to obey legislation of the UK Parliament;[26] to that end these Acts have modified the doctrine of implied repeal.[27] However, in effect the rights conferred by European law in the UK have been 'entrenched' and as and when the UK leaves the EU it will be open to Parliament to change, even repeal, them in future without the legal and political inhibitions to which Parliament is subject by EU membership.

C. A Democratic Principle?

Moving away from parliamentary privilege and the basis for the effect of European law in the UK, the most widely offered rationale for the doctrine of parliamentary sovereignty or supremacy in relation to Acts of Parliament is that it is 'a democratic principle':[28] the courts should recognise and give effect to Acts as law and as the highest form of law because they are produced by a formal legislative procedure (and thus mere resolutions of Parliament are not law[29]) in which elected representatives determine the content of laws. (We should pause here to remind ourselves that the House of Lords is not elected.) On this approach it is the duty of elected representatives to exercise their powers in the interests of their

---

[23] [1991] 1 AC 603.

[24] Lord Bridge in *Factortame* (n 13), and P Craig 'Britain in the European Union' in Jowell, Oliver and O'Cinneide (n 2).

[25] The European Union Act 2011 s 18 provides that EU law 'falls to be recognised and available in law in the UK only by virtue of' the European Communities Act 1972 or any other Act.

[26] *Thoburn v Sunderland City Council* [2002] EWCA 195 (Admin).

[27] *Ellen Street Estates Ltd v Minister of Health* (n 3).

[28] The doctrine of parliamentary sovereignty began to develop in the seventeenth century, before democracy: the 'democratic' principle is therefore a post-rationalisation of parliamentary sovereignty.

[29] *Bowles v Bank of England* [1913] 1 Ch 57.

constituents and the general public.[30] It is possible, in the light of the referendum on UK membership of the EU in 2016 and the Government's acceptance of the result and consequent commitment to leaving the EU, that a moral or political— but not legally binding[31]—duty on government is developing to give effect to the will of a majority expressed in a referendum. This is not the place to explore the serious implications such a development would have for the system of representative democracy on which most of our constitutional arrangements are based.

It would be contrary to the—in my view foundational—public interest principle for the courts to refuse to give effect to laws enacted by Parliament, as they would be substituting their own concepts of where on balance the public interest lies for those that have been put in place in primary legislation by the representative and electorally accountable legislature and government.[32] The courts would also be changing an important constitutional principle unilaterally, informally and without following appropriate consultation and consent-giving procedures.[33] And, if the court's decision challenges the sovereignty of Parliament, it follows that it can only be reversed by a higher court or, if made in the Supreme Court, by that court in exercise of its power under the 1966 Practice Statement[34] to depart from a previous decision when it appeared right to do so. The court's decision could not be reversed by Act of Parliament. Thus the position after a judicial striking down of an Act in the UK would be even more rigid or entrenched than in many democracies with written Constitutions in which political processes are commonly available to override judicial determinations by constitutional amendment, eg by referendum (as in Ireland) or by parliamentary super-majorities (as in the USA, India and many European countries).

The 'democratic principle' basis for UK style parliamentary sovereignty raises a number of further issues. If we consider that democracy is a good thing, a positive value, then how do we deal with the possibility that a Parliament that is 'sovereign' (in the sense that the courts will give effect to its laws as the highest form of law) may pass laws that deny access to justice or discriminate against certain categories of people (children, foreigners, homosexuals, men,[35] Muslims, paedophiles, Roman Catholics, and women,[36] for example)? How can we justify Acts that

---

[30] E Burke, 'Speech to the Electors of Bristol' (1774). And see reports of the Committee of Privileges in the W J Brown Affair 1948, HC 118 (1946–47) and HC Deb 15 July 1947, col 284, and cases involving the National Union of Mineworkers and the National Union of Public Employees sponsorship of MPs: HC 50 (1971–72), HC 634 (1974–75), HC 512 (1976–77); and see Lord Hope in *AXA General Insurance Ltd and others v The Lord Advocate* [2011] UKSC 46, para 49.

[31] See *Miller* (n 6) at para 124.

[32] If, however, the courts have been tasked by Act of Parliament to decide where the balance between public and private interest lies, as under section 2 of the European Communities Act 1972 and section 4 of the Human Rights Act 1998, then it is their duty to do so.

[33] See House of Lords Constitution Committee, 'The Process of Constitutional Change', Fifteenth Report of Session 2010–12, HL 177.

[34] [1966] 3 All ER 77.

[35] Let us not forget that men are a minority in most populations.

[36] Women are a majority in most populations.

explicitly favour others (party funders, friends, relations and cronies, for example) over the general public? Such a position would be even more unacceptable if those laws could be passed by a simple majority of those present and voting when the law is passed.

It may be that giving effect in law to the will of the majority in Parliament is considered by supporters of parliamentary sovereignty as a democratic principle to justify or legitimate all laws; that concept of democracy, if it operates in a country, does not in my view make a democratic system 'good' or result in good government or good governance.[37] But 'good' or not, raw majoritarianism, is likely to result in long-term discrimination against sections of the population or favourable treatment for others, or the limitation of the franchise or indefinite postponement of elections. Such measures can lead to the alienation of large sections of the population, lack or loss of legitimacy of the system in the eyes of those who are discriminated against, and ultimately to disorder and even civil war. The Troubles in Northern Ireland provide an example of this, to the extent that they were caused by the majoritarian and discriminatory rule by unionists at Stormont from 1921 to 1972, which led to the imposition of direct rule from Westminster.[38]

So the 'democratic principle' rationale for the sovereignty of Parliament is weak, and the present position allows for the abuse of parliamentary sovereignty by passage of laws that are inconsistent with important constitutional principles, including the rule of law.

II. A CHOICE FOR THE UK: CONSTITUTIONAL SUPREMACY OR PARLIAMENTARY SOVEREIGNTY AND PRAGMATISM?

As is well known, since the 1960s courts in the UK, including the House of Lords and the Supreme Court, have developed important administrative law principles in cases in which the discretionary decisions of public bodies have been called in question.[39] A question is whether this line of cases opens up the possibility that the

---

[37] See R Dworkin, *Freedom's Law: The Moral Reading of the American Constitution* (Oxford, Oxford University Press, 1996) 15ff.

[38] See C McCrudden, 'Northern Ireland and the British Constitution' in J Jowell and D Oliver, *The Changing Constitution*, 6th edn (Oxford, OUP, 2007); P Dixon, *Northern Ireland: The politics of war and peace*, 2nd edn. (Basingstoke, Palgrave Macmillan, 2008); B O'Leary and J McGarry, *The Politics of Antagonism: Understanding Northern Ireland* (London and Atlantic Highlands, NJ, Athlone, 1996); J Whyte and G Fitzgerald, *Interpreting Northern Ireland* (Oxford, Clarendon Paperbacks, 1991); D Birrell and A Murie, *Policy and Government in Northern Ireland: Lessons of Devolution* (Dublin, Gill and Macmillan, 1980).

[39] The landmark cases have included *Associated Provincial Picture Houses v Wednesbury Corporation* [1948] 1 KB 223 (ultra vires rule); *Ridge v Baldwin* [1964] AC 40 (HL) (natural justice); *Padfield v Minister of Agriculture* [1968] AC 997 (HL) (relevant/irrelevant considerations); *Council of Civil Service Unions v Minister for the Civil Service* [1985] AC 374 (grounds of review are procedural propriety, legality and irrationality; justiciability issues). For brief summaries see Bradley, Ewing and Knight, *Constitutional and Administrative Law* (n 21) chs 30 and 31, and Elliott and Thomas, *Public Law* (n 21) ch 12.

courts may decide that they have the power at common law to disapply or strike down a statutory provision on the ground of its unconstitutionality or breach of the rule of law.

Since the mid-1990s the rhetoric of the courts in judicial review cases has changed so as to identify some principles as 'constitutional' or 'fundamental'[40] and not merely administrative. Lord Hoffmann famously indicated in *R v Secretary of State for the Home Department, ex parte Simms* '[The] courts of the United Kingdom, though acknowledging the sovereignty of Parliament [will] apply principles of constitutionality little different from those which exist in countries where the power of the legislature is expressly limited by a constitutional document'.[41] Reliance on 'constitutional' laws and principles formed important elements of the reasoning of the majority in *Miller*.[42]

A. Towards Judicial Striking Down of Statutory Provisions?

The application of 'constitutional' or 'fundamental' principles of interpretation and decision-making to the discretions exercisable by public bodies is very different from the striking down of provisions in Acts of Parliament on grounds of unconstitutionality or breach of the rule of law: although there is a substantial academic literature to the effect that the courts may, even should, properly do so, the courts have not as yet gone so far as to refuse explicitly[43] to give effect to a provision in an Act of Parliament.

---

[40] See, eg, *R v Secretary of State for the Home Department, ex p Leach (No 2)* [1994] QB 198 (prisoner's constitutional right to communicate in confidence with his lawyers); *R v Lord Chancellor, ex p Witham* [1998] QB 575, per Laws J (imposition of court fees on impecunious litigants denied a fundamental constitutional right of access to the courts); *R v Secretary of State for the Home Department, ex p Pierson* [1998] AC 539 (retrospective alteration of the minimum term of imprisonment to be served before release on parole was possibly a breach of the rule of law, a constitutional principle). In the *AXA* case (n 30) members of the Supreme Court referred to such principles as based in the common law, though taking care not to state that their existence gives rise to a power in the court to strike down provisions in Acts of the Westminster Parliament: see, for instance, Lord Hope at para 48 (but *cf* paras 50–51), Lord Reed at para 141.

[41] [2000] 2 AC 115.

[42] See paras 43, 50 and 67.

[43] However, in *Anisminic v Foreign Compensation Commission* [1969] 2 AC 147, the House of Lords gave very strained interpretation to the ouster clause in the Foreign Compensation Act 1950 and accepted jurisdiction to review a decision that appeared to be protected by it on the ground that it was invalid and therefore not a 'decision' within the meaning of the Act as it was ultra vires the Commission. See also critical commentary on *(R) Evans v Attorney General* [2015] UKSC 21 by the Policy Exchange Judicial Power Project and their report, '50 Problematic Cases' (2017) at http://judicialpowerproject.org.uk/50-problematic-cases. In that case the Supreme Court Justices held in carefully reasoned judgments that under the Freedom of Information Act 2000 the Attorney-General did not have reasonable grounds to exercise a power to veto the disclosure of correspondence between government departments and Prince Charles. Hence disclosure should take place. The Project claimed that the Supreme Court ignored 'the limits of judicial review by rewriting the Freedom of Information Act to effectively remove the power to prevent the publication of information that the UK Parliament had conferred on the Attorney General'.

However, in recent years some judges, in extra-judicial lectures and articles,[44] have suggested that the courts might be justified in refusing to give effect to a provision in an Act of Parliament which breaches what they consider to be fundamental principles to do with constitutionalism or the rule of law. These would be the kinds of provisions that could be struck down by Constitutional or Supreme Courts in countries such as the USA and Germany: in other words, they may not be regarded as 'polycentric' (and therefore unsuitable for judicial determination) but 'justiciable' in other systems.[45] A similar pro-constitutionalism message was given, obiter, by Lord Hope in *Jackson v Attorney General*: 'Parliamentary sovereignty is no longer absolute, if it ever was'. And '[t]he rule of law enforced by the courts is the ultimate controlling factor on which our constitution is based ... The courts have a part to play in defining the limits of Parliament's legislative sovereignty'.[46]

There is a growing academic literature to similar effect.[47] And another literature in defence of parliamentary sovereignty, including writings by judges.[48] Particularly significantly, Policy Exchange, a right-leaning think tank,[49] is conducting a Judicial Power Project[50] designed to substantiate the view that judges

---

[44] See Lord Woolf, 'Droit Public—English style' [1995] *Public Law* 57; Sir John Laws, 'Law and Democracy' [1995] *Public Law* 72; compare J Sumption QC (now Lord Sumption, a Justice of the Supreme Court) 'Judicial and Political Decision-Making: The Uncertain Boundary', FA Mann lecture (2011).

[45] See L Fuller, 'The forms and limits of adjudication' (1978) 92 *Harvard Law Review* 351.

[46] [2006] 1 AC 262, at paras 104–07. See also comments in the *AXA* case (n 30) in which some of the judges discussed the question of whether a common law jurisdiction existed to review the exercise of legislative powers by the Scottish Parliament. They were careful to distinguish the UK Parliament.

[47] See, for instance, TRS Allan, *Constitutional Justice: A Liberal Theory of the Rule of Law* (Oxford, Oxford University Press, 2001); DE Edlin, *Judges and Unjust Laws: Common Law Constitutionalism and the Foundations of Judicial Review* (Ann Arbor, University of Michigan Press, 2008); A Kavanagh, *Constitutional Review Under the UK Human Rights Act* (Cambridge, Cambridge University Press, 2009); S Lakin, 'Debunking the Idea of Parliamentary Sovereignty: The Controlling Factor of Legality in the British Constitution' (2008) *Oxford Journal of Legal Studies* 28, 709. The various positions are discussed by Goldsworthy, *Contemporary Debates* (n 3).

[48] See, for instance, JAG Griffith 'The Political Constitution' (1979) 42 *Modern Law Review* 1; J Waldron, *Law and Disagreement* (Oxford, Oxford University Press, 1999); and see Goldsworthy, *Contemporary Debates* (n 3) for a review and discussion of this literature; extra-judicial writings by judges defending parliamentary sovereignty include T Bingham, *The Rule of Law* (London, Penguin, 2010), 167; Lord Neuberger 'Who are the masters now? (Lord Alexander of Weedon lecture, 6 April 2011).

[49] Policy Exchange was set up in 2002 by a trio including Michael Gove as chair, and Francis Maude, both of whom later became Conservative cabinet ministers in the coalition Government of 2010–15. See also www.conservativehome.com/thinktankcentral/2009/11/profile-of-policy-exchange. html: 'PX's links with the Tories are particularly strong ... It is seen as the leading think tank of Tory modernisers'.

[50] See http://judicialpowerproject.org.uk/about. The project focuses on negatively critical evaluation of the judicial role. The project's publication, 'Judicial Power: 50 Problematic Cases' of May 2016 'collates some of the more flagrant and well-known occasions (as well as some less well-known occasions) where the courts ignored well-established and (as we see it) appropriate limits on their role'. The criteria are not, however, articulated in that report. Nor has the project published work on judicial decisions of which it approves, and on what criteria: see http://judicialpowerproject.org.uk/judicial-power-50-problematic-cases.

have been overreaching their powers in a number of cases and that this threatens the rule of law and democratic government. Their central idea is that 'the decisions of Parliament ought not to be called into question by the courts and that the executive ought to be free from undue judicial interference, which fails to respect political judgments and discretion'. Concerns relate primarily to judicial review of administrative discretion, a different matter entirely from the striking down of provisions in Acts of Parliament. However, they claim that provisions in Acts were struck down by the courts in the *Anisminic* and *Evans* cases noted elsewhere in this chapter. In both cases the courts' reasoning excluded any claim to a right to strike down legislation. The Project took a different view but without engaging with the judges' reasoning.

The work of the Project and its links with a political party highlight the fact that the relationships between the courts and politicians, and between varying understandings of the meaning of the rule of law, raise delicate issues about relations between state institutions, a matter discussed further below. It is not possible or necessary to summarise, analyse or critique either of those positions in the space available here, though my own view is that the Judicial Power Project lacks academically satisfactory theoretical underpinning and balance. My thesis is that the present doctrine is in reality (and whether you like it or not) a pragmatic and not necessarily a principled arrangement between the courts, Parliament and the executive, an arrangement that is unlikely to be terminated by either side and that works relatively well. I discuss this in the next section.

B. Parliamentary Sovereignty—A Doctrine, not a Democratic Constitutional Principle

I have tried to avoid until now referring to parliamentary sovereignty as a principle. Sovereignty is rather, I suggest, a tenet of the constitution, a proposition that serves as the foundation for a system of belief or behaviour (Shorter OED). But it is not, or at least not unarguably, based on a principle in a normative sense of morally correct behaviour and attitudes. It accepts that Parliament may pass and expect the courts to give effect to immoral laws or laws that are incompatible with international obligations or not consistent with important constitutional principles, such as the rule of law or respect for human rights.[51]

I suggest that the doctrine of parliamentary sovereignty is—like parliamentary privilege which I discussed briefly above—instead of or, depending on one's view, as well as—a constitutional principle, a pragmatic constitutional arrangement making for an effective, cooperative working relationship between the executive, Parliament, and the courts.

Let us consider what the implications would be if a court were to refuse to give effect to an Act of Parliament on grounds advocated by the judges and

---

[51] See Ungoed-Thomas J in *Cheney v Conn* [1968] 1 All ER 779.

commentators noted above—breach of the rule of law, for instance. If a court were to do so it would be changing an important, fundamental constitutional law—the sovereignty of Parliament—unilaterally, without formal process or prior consultation and without endorsement from the electorate.[52]

It would not be the first time that a constitutional rule has been changed unilaterally by the courts. The *CCSU* case is a strong example.[53] The Appellate Committee of the House of Lords decided that, contrary to what had been understood to be the legal position, exercises of royal prerogative power could, if the nature of the power was justiciable, be subjected to judicial review. However, that was not a case about the validity of an Act or part of an Act, it was a change in a common law rule and it was open to Parliament—as it always is under the doctrine of parliamentary sovereignty—to reverse the rule. Even if the sovereignty of Parliament is a common law creation—and I do not propose to engage in the debates about that[54]—there is a qualitative difference between changing a common law rule which it would be open to Parliament to reinstate, and changing the doctrine of Parliamentary sovereignty itself: it would not be open to Parliament to reinstate its sovereignty by recognised legal processes. It would need to resort to doing so in the political sphere: recriminations between the organs of state, the mobilisation of public opinion against the courts, the politicisation of judicial appointments, and eventual undermining of the authority of the courts and thus the rule of law.

i. A hypothetical

Imagine that Parliament has recently passed a provision authorising the indefinite detention without trial of suspected terrorists. The measure was passed during a public panic about terrorism. Public opinion and the press and parliamentarians of the party in government which promoted the legislation were strongly in favour of using such powers. The Home Secretary orders the detention under that provision of suspect A. A applies to the court for habeas corpus, and release on the ground that the provision in the Act is contrary to fundamental common law principles and the European Convention on Human Rights. The court finds that the Act is indeed defective in these ways, that the Home Secretary's order for detention was therefore unlawful and of no effect, and that compliance by state bodies with fundamental common law principles and the ECHR is a requirement of the rule of law (as it is understood by the courts), a constitutional principle which binds all bodies including Parliament and the executive. The court releases A.

---

[52] See 'The Process of Constitutional Change' (n 33).

[53] *Council of Civil Service Unions v Minister for the Civil Service* (n 39). In the earlier case of *R v Criminal Injuries Compensation Commission, ex p Lain* [1967] 2 QB 364 the Divisional Court reviewed the exercise of power that had been granted under royal prerogative powers to make Orders in Council.

[54] See, eg, Kavanagh, *Constitutional Review* (n 47); Lakin 'Debunking the Idea of Parliamentary Sovereignty' (n 47).

What would happen if the minister ordered the rearrest of A and refused to produce him to the court on his next application for habeas corpus? It would be easy to reply: 'The minister—and the prison governor—would be committed for contempt of court if he refused to release or order the release of the suspect, of course', implying that this is an obvious answer to an obviously stupid question. But the implications of such a finding for the relationships between politicians and the courts would need to be thought through before such an answer was accepted.

Our system, particularly because we lack a written constitution which is considered by the institutions of government and by the public to legitimate such activities of the courts, depends for its working in part upon mutual respect and comity between institutions, particularly between the courts on the one hand and Parliament and executive bodies on the other. Lord Carswell had this in mind in his speech in *Jackson v Attorney General*: referring to the principles of the sovereignty of Parliament and the conclusiveness of the parliament roll or the speaker's certificate, he noted that they are:

> [J]udicial products of that carefully observed mutual respect which has long existed between the legislature and the courts. As a judge I am very conscious of the proper reluctance of the courts to intervene in issues of the validity of Acts of Parliament. I should be most unwilling to decide this or any other case in a way which would endanger that tradition of mutual respect. I do not, and I have no doubt your Lordships do not, have any wish to expand the role of the judiciary at the expense of any other organ of the State or to seek to frustrate the properly expressed wish of Parliament as contained in legislation. The attribution in certain quarters of such a wish to the judiciary is misconceived and appears to be the product of lack of understanding of the judicial function and the sources of law which the courts are bound to apply.[55]

According to *M v Home Office*[56] a court might, having made an order which a minister disobeyed, just declare the minister to be in contempt. A mere declaration would not do the court's authority any good at all in this hypothetical situation. It is unlikely that the press or the members of the House of Commons would take the court's side and press the government to respond positively to the declaration. If the declaration were ignored, the lesson that the executive learned would be that it can get away with such responses to the courts. Would we want that?

Alternatively, the court could commit the Home Secretary to prison for contempt. The Minister of Justice (who is responsible for prisons) might then order the prison governor to release the Home Secretary on the basis that it was unconstitutional, anti-democratic and unlawful—a breach of the rule of law as understood by politicians which, according to the Judicial Power Project prioritises non-interference by the judiciary with discretionary executive decisions—for the court to refuse to give effect to an Act of Parliament. The prison governor might

---

[55] *Jackson v Attorney General* [2005] UKHL 56, para 168.
[56] [1994] 1 AC 377, HL.

obey the Minister of Justice and release the Home Secretary while continuing to detain A, and so himself be committed for contempt, along with the Minister of Justice.[57] The battle would continue, with press and public opinion probably behind the ministers.

So such a court order might turn out not to be practically enforceable if resisted by government on the ground that it was not legitimate for the courts to change the law unilaterally and (unless the Supreme Court were to change its mind) irreversibly—in such a way. Or, if it was enforced, the backlash might be that Parliament legislates to politicise the judicial appointment system, the courts could then be packed with judges sympathetic to the Government, the Court Service could come under ministerial directions as to the deployment of judges and the listing of cases so as to ensure that 'unreliable' judges did not sit on certain kinds of case. Ouster clauses could become commonplace. And so on. I think the courts would be defeated, and in the end the Supreme Court would exercise its power under the Practice Statement of 1966 to reverse its position and reinstate the doctrine of parliamentary supremacy. But by then untold damage would have been done to the respect in which the courts are held in government, in Parliament and by the general public and to good relations between those institutions. The rule of law itself would have been weakened.

The relationship between the executive and the courts in the UK, lacking as it does a written constitution which defines that relationship, depends upon reciprocity, trust, cooperation—the basic elements of human social interaction.[58] Any system of government involves such interaction. If those collapse then the very constitutional system itself might collapse into recurring conflicts between the courts and the executive, tit-for-tat battles, ostracism of the courts by ministers, and mistrust. It is by no means certain that the rule of law as understood by lawyers would win over politics and parliamentary supremacy in such a situation.

But, you will be thinking, surely this hypothetical is fanciful: normally ministers do obey court orders. Yes—and that is part of the culture of the rule of law. But if the courts were to challenge parliamentary supremacy, ministers would be able to invoke a whole lot of arguments in support of their refusal to obey the court—democracy, separation of powers, etc. Indeed, it is likely that there would be a great hue and cry against the courts not only from the Government, but from MPs, the press and the public. In my view, therefore, it could well be extremely unwise, damaging to the authority of the judiciary and the rule of law itself and to the stability of our constitutional arrangements, and counter-productive for

---

[57] For an account of a damaging conflict between the courts and the executive resulting in contempt proceedings in Ireland in 1921 see KD Ewing and C Gearty *The Struggle for Civil Liberties* (Oxford, Oxford University Press, 2001) 365–69, and the case out of which it arose, *Egan v Macready* [1921] 1 IR 265.

[58] See, for instance, S Blackburn, *Ruling Passions: A Theory of Practical Reasoning* (Oxford, Clarendon Press, 1998); H Gommer, *A Biological Theory of Law: Natural Law Theory Revisited* (Seattle, Create Space/Amazon, 2011); and N Barber, *The Constitutional State* (Oxford, Oxford University Press, 2010), which recognises the state as a social organisation.

the courts, to strike down a provision in an Act, however much it is contrary to some of the elements of the rule of law and other constitutional doctrines and 'principles'. Bear in mind that the duties of judges are not limited to upholding individuals' rights. They include ensuring the practical working of constitutional arrangements, for instance relationships with the EU and between the UK and devolved bodies, which in turn facilitate the rule of law. There are in other words respectable consequentialist reasons for judges in the UK accepting parliamentary sovereignty and holding back from making judgments that might be impossible to enforce against the executive in such a nuclear option situation, especially when we take into account the important influence of the non-legal environment in which government and Parliament operate in the UK and which upholds constitutional principles—the subject of the next section of this chapter.

So in my view a 'principle' that the rule of law is *the* controlling principle and might entitle courts to disapply statutory provisions—as Lord Hope indicated in *Jackson*—would come up against the typical, pragmatic and wise English response: the principle is all very well in theory, but what about the practice? The practice of striking down legislation in our unwritten constitution and constitutional culture would not work. Griffith was right in 'The Political Constitution'[59] that many parts of our constitution (not all) are the outcome of conflicts. The restoration of parliamentary sovereignty would be the outcome of a conflict between the courts and the executive, but the courts would have lost authority and face in the course of that conflict.

III. CONFLICT, COMITY AND CULTURE IN RELATIONS BETWEEN THE COURTS, PARLIAMENT AND THE EXECUTIVE

I suggest that an important rationale for the British courts' recognition of Acts of Parliament as the highest form of law besides the 'democratic principle' and 'parliamentary privilege'—neither of which is convincing when seen in a comparative perspective—is based in a culture of comity between institutions and workability: pragmatic principles established over centuries that the courts will uphold Parliament's role and refrain from questioning the legal validity of Acts passed by the UK Parliament, and that members of the two Houses of Parliament will respect the courts and their decisions and will not seek to undermine them and the rule of law. I suspect therefore that the dominant though seldom articulated reason why courts in the UK accept parliamentary sovereignty is that it represents a way of avoiding a conflict between the courts and the executive which the courts could not win. It might be different if the UK had a written Constitution which mandated the courts to refuse to give effect to 'unconstitutional' laws—a matter discussed below. But that is not the current position.

---

[59] Griffith, 'The Political Constitution' (n 48).

This is not something that British judges, or others as far as I know, have discussed publicly. But Lord Justice Stephen Sedley had the following to say in his review of Vernon Bogdanor's book *The New British Constitution* (2009).

[W]hat would happen in real life if the higher courts treated ... a withdrawal of their jurisdiction [by a provision in an Act which ousted judicial review of a tribunal's decisions on asylum claims] as unconstitutional, ignored it and allowed an asylum seeker's appeal? The home secretary, not recognising their jurisdiction, would proceed with deportation, and the court would arraign him for contempt. How would it end? We do not know, and most of us would prefer not to find out.[60]

Interestingly, since the position in the UK resembles that in New Zealand, Matthew Palmer has recently written that:

Institutionally, over the long term and particularly in New Zealand, the independence of the judiciary depends on the forbearance of the political branches of government. Cabinet and Parliament have the formal tools available in New Zealand's constitution to undermine the independence of the judiciary if they wished: through appointments, dismissals, under-resourcing or restructuring various benches.[61]

Palmer suggests that the approach of parliamentarians is based in part on the high standing of the judiciary in public opinion; that standing could be damaged by a series of negative public reactions to judicial decisions and 'whether consciously or unconsciously, the judiciary, especially at the level of Heads of Bench and the Supreme Court, understands and should understand the importance of public opinion, according to a medium and long-term perspective, for the sustenance of its branch of government'.[62] Elliott suggests that relations between politicians and the courts in the UK and New Zealand are part of the 'the mystery of the unwritten constitution' which entails 'voluntary exhibition of mutual respect'.[63] These phenomena may be difficult to explain rationally, but they work.

[60] S Sedley, 'On the Move' *London Review of Books*, 8 October 2009 at www.lrb.co.uk/v31/n19/print/sed101_.html. See also Sir Stephen Sedley in *Ashes and Sparks* (Cambridge, Cambridge University Press, 2011) at 130, commenting on what would have happened if the ouster clause in the Immigration and Asylum (Treatment of Claimants) Bill had been passed, if the courts had refused to give effect to it, and the Home Secretary is found to be in contempt for disobeying their order: 'And then? There would be no winner, no famous victory even, in such a confrontation. Even so ... It was not necessarily a bad thing that [the proposed ouster clause] had gone as far as it had: the government had realised that there were limits to what it could properly ask Parliament to do; constitutional lawyers had realised that the limits were less secure) than they had thought, and the sky still seemed to be in place'.

[61] M Palmer, 'Open the Doors and Where are the People?: Constitutional Dialogue in the Shadow of the People' in C Charters and DR Knight (eds), *We, The Peoples: Participation in Governance* (Wellington, Victoria University Press, 2011) 71, available at http://works.bepress.com/matthew_palmer/33.

[62] ibid. For further discussion of the importance of culture in the working of the New Zealand constitution see M Palmer, 'New Zealand Constitutional Culture' (2007) 22 *NZ L Rev* 565, available at http://works.bepress.com/matthew_palmer/26.

[63] M Elliott, 'Interpretive Bills of Rights and the Mystery of the Unwritten Constitution' (2011) *NZ L Rev* 591, 591 and 622.

IV. DETERRENTS AGAINST ABUSE OF PARLIAMENTARY SOVEREIGNTY

Assuming that the doctrine of parliamentary sovereignty is here to stay, let us focus on the measures that are currently in place which operate to deter Parliament from passing 'unconstitutional' legislation, and to deter the Government from promoting or proposing such legislation.[64] I shall consider in section V whether any further arrangements need to be put in place to strengthen the protection of constitutionalism and constitutionality.

A. Political Cultural Capital

The UK possesses valuable cultural capital, including respect among politicians, civil servants and lawyers for the international[65] and national rule of law. This is exemplified in section 1 of the Constitutional Reform Act 2005 which states that the Act does not affect the rule of law and retains the role of the Lord Chancellor in relation to it.[66] The rule of law culture is coupled with strong attachment to the doctrine of parliamentary sovereignty. These might seem to be contradictory cultural tendencies, but the two are brought together by the existence of constitutional conventions and many soft law documents which regulate political processes (codes, manuals and others, discussed below); they articulate the importance of respect for constitutional principles and the rule of law in the context of continuing legal sovereignty, and of practical political realities: for instance, the fact that ministers proposing 'unconstitutional' legislation (or refusing to secure the enactment of legislation to comply with the international rule of law) know that they will be advised against them by the Treasury Solicitor, their departmental lawyers, parliamentary counsel and the Law Officers, and criticised by parliamentary committees charged with scrutiny of bills against broadly constitutional criteria.[67] The British system relies very heavily on its politicians to take responsibility for the international reputation of the country and for internal compliance with constitutional principles. This approach is shared by the Netherlands, Sweden and New Zealand. Broadly these political responsibilities are taken seriously.

If the courts were to assume responsibility for respecting and upholding the rule of law by the development of judicial review of Acts for constitutionality, the political culture might change. In American terms we would have moved from a

---

[64] I am particularly indebted to Sir Stephen Laws for information and advice on ss IV and V of this chapter.

[65] But note discussion of *Hirst v UK*, below.

[66] See ch 11.

[67] These are discussed below in this section.

system of parliamentary sovereignty to one of judicial supremacy.[68] Politicians may become less concerned about their responsibilities in these matters and content to leave them to the courts: the implications for the independence of the judiciary and its status and legitimacy and thus for the rule of law would be very negative if the courts found themselves driven to making controversial decisions because politicians had neglected their responsibilities as to the constitutionality of the laws they pass. This would be even more serious if it led to pressure for politicisation of judicial appointments.

B. International and European Standards

The British Government and Parliament, like most others in democratic countries, operate under the shadow of international law—the European Convention of Human Rights, International Covenant on Civil and Political Rights and many other instruments. The Human Rights Act 1998 provides a strong example not only of a statutory commitment to compliance with international obligations, including the section 4 power of higher courts to make declarations of incompatibility, but also of political commitment to compliance with the ECHR: the requirement under section 19 of the Human Rights Act that a minister in charge of a Bill must make a statement of its compatibility with Convention rights or a statement that the Government wishes to proceed with the Bill even if it is not compatible places responsibility for compliance clearly on ministers and the Government. Such 'possible non-compliance' statements had only been made on two Bills as of summer 2017.[69] The Government was concerned that the Communications Bill 2002 (which became the Communications Act 2003) might breach Article 10 (freedom of speech) because of its provisions for restrictions on political advertising on television: in due course the House of Lords decided that the provision in the Act was not incompatible with Article 10: *R (Animal Defenders' International) v Culture, Media and Sport Secretary*.[70] The Explanatory Notes to the House of Lords Reform Bill 2012[71] included a 'possible non-compliance' statement because no prisoners would be entitled to vote in elections to the second chamber, contrary to the European Court of Human Rights decision in *Hirst v UK (No 2)*,[72] which found that the blanket denial of the right to vote in parliamentary elections to all prisoners in the UK was incompatible with Article 3 of Protocol 1 of the European Convention on Human Rights. That bill was withdrawn in September 2012 after a vote against the proposed programme motion.

---

[68] See *Brown v Board of Education* 347 US 483 (1954): '[T]he federal judiciary is supreme in the exposition of the law of the Constitution'; M Tushnet, *The Constitution of the United States of America* (Oxford, Hart Publishing, 2009) 138–40.

[69] See also M Hunt, 'The Joint Committee on Human Rights' in A Horne, G Drewry and D Oliver, *Parliament and the Law* (Oxford, Hart, 2013).

[70] [2008] UKHL 15.

[71] See www.publications.parliament.uk/pa/bills/cbill/2012-2013/0052/en/13052en.htm.

[72] (2006) 42 EHRR 41. See below for further discussion of this case.

The UK has, until recently, had a good record of compliance with decisions of the European Court of Justice, and with the decisions of the European Court of Human Rights, despite the fact that, unlike the Netherlands—another country with a sovereign Parliament—it is a dualist country. However, it has not implemented the ECtHR decision in *Hirst*, referred to above.[73] The culture of compliance with the UK's international obligations among politicians is not watertight.

C. The Roles of Civil Servants and Government Lawyers

Politicians may not have much idea what the rule of law is and what it requires and, as with the Government's and the House of Commons response to the *Hirst* case on prisoners' votes, may not realise how serious breaches of the rule of law can be for the UK's reputation and for the rule of law itself. This was demonstrated in the slowness of the response by the Lord Chancellor, Liz Truss, to the *Daily Mail*'s front-page condemnation of judges who decided the *Miller* case in the Administrative Court, labelling them 'Enemies of the People'.[74] However, the rule of law cultures exists, and strongly, among many public officials who are engaged in the legislative and general governmental processes.[75] This culture is reflected in many of the informal codes and guidance documents which regulate governmental activity—for instance, the 'Guide to Making Legislation' (henceforth GML),[76] the Ministerial Code,[77] the Cabinet Manual,[78] the Civil Service Code,[79] 'Working with Parliamentary Counsel'[80] and others: they impose duties of good government, in accordance with law and with the Seven Principles of Public Life, ie selflessness, integrity, objectivity, accountability, openness, honesty and leadership.[81]

All civil servants are bound by the Civil Service Code, which requires them to conduct themselves with honesty, integrity, impartiality and objectivity. The Treasury Solicitor, departmental lawyers and parliamentary counsel are bound

---

[73] For discussion of the position see A Horne and H Tyrrell, 'Sovereignty, Privilege and the European Convention on Human Rights' in A Horne and A Le Sueur (eds), *Parliament, Legislation and Accountability* (Oxford, Hart, 2016) 271–78 and 282–84; see also Ministry of Justice, 'Responding to Human Rights Judgments: 2014 to 2016' 37–38, at www.gov.uk/government/publications/responding-to-human-rights-judgments-2014-to-2016; and A Horne in ch 10 in this volume.

[74] *Daily Mail* (4 November 2016). See ch 13.

[75] See TC Daintith and A Page, *The Executive in the Constitution: Structure, Autonomy and Internal Control* (Oxford, Oxford University Press, 1999).

[76] See 'Guide to Making Legislation' (GML), Cabinet Office (2013), updated from time to time.

[77] Cabinet Office (May 2010), updated from time to time.

[78] Cabinet Office (2011).

[79] 2015, first presented to Parliament in November 2010 in accordance with the Constitutional Reform and Governance Act 2010, s 5.

[80] www.cabinetoffice.gov.uk/sites/default/files/resources/WWPC_6_Dec_2011.pdf.

[81] Formulated by the Committee on Standards in Public Life in their First Report, Cm 2850, 1995 and updated in Committee on Standards in Public Life, 'Standards Matter: A Review of Best Practice in Promoting Good Behaviour in Public Life', Fourteenth Report, Cm 8519 (January 2013). These standards have been adopted and incorporated in the above documents and in the Standing Orders of both Houses of Parliament.

in addition by their professional ethics to uphold the law. In the course of the discussion and development of proposals for legislation, the Treasury Solicitor and departmental lawyers, mindful perhaps of section 1 of the Constitutional Reform Act ('This Act does not adversely affect ... the existing constitutional principle of the rule of law') and the importance of the rule of law, will recognise any constitutional and rule of law pitfalls that arise and may advise ministers to drop them or to find other, constitutionally unobjectionable ways of achieving their ends.[82] Discussions may take place at staff level between Bill teams and the legal advisers to Parliament's Joint Committee on Human Rights (discussed below). Parliamentary counsel are in many ways constitutional watchdogs—guardians of legality, though they are not regulators of government—and they may raise issue with the minister when receiving instructions on the drafting of Bills.[83]

If, notwithstanding the concerns of government lawyers and parliamentary counsel, a minister is adamant that an 'unconstitutional' provision be included in a draft Bill, then parliamentary counsel may not refuse to do the drafting. They owe professional duties to do their best by their client, the Government. Ultimately all civil servants are accountable to their ministers and not to Parliament and they are not in a position to veto the inclusion of 'unconstitutional' provisions in Bills. However, there may come a time when an issue has to be referred to the Attorney-General, who will be in a strong position to advise against pursuing legislative proposals that would be considered unconstitutional or in breach of the UK's international obligations and would run into trouble in one or other or both Houses of Parliament.[84] Parliamentary counsel are expected to contribute to the brief for the Law Officers for the meetings of the Parliamentary Business and Legislation Committee of the Cabinet when it considers a Bill or amendments.[85] (However the source or contents of the legal advice received by the Government is not disclosed to Parliament, although Explanatory Notes to Bills dealing with section 19 statements of compatibility will outline any governmental doubts about compatibility.[86]) Thus concerns of a constitutional nature may be brought up in these discussions. And ministers do not welcome the uncertainty[87] that goes with constitutionally controversial proposals for legislation.

---

[82] Daintith and Page, *The Executive in the Constitution* (n 75) 248.

[83] ibid, 254–56.

[84] ibid, 256–58, 297–315. See also GML (n 76) ch 13, 'Legal Issues' and 20, 'Handling Strategies in the Lords and the Commons'; Cabinet Manual, para 3.46 and ch 6 on Ministers' overarching duty to comply with the law and the seven principles of public life, and to consult the Law Officers if departmental lawyer advise that there are doubts of a legal nature about proposals in a Bill. For guidance on some of the categories of issues in which the Law Officers may be interested, see 'Working with Parliamentary Counsel' (n 80), paras 55–56, 230 and 281; these include the rule of law, retrospectivity and matters involving fundamental rights and freedoms, delegated powers, And see D Oliver 'Constitutional scrutiny of executive bills' (2004) 4 *Macquarie Law Journal* 33.

[85] See *Working with Parliamentary Counsel* (n 80) paras 275–84.

[86] For discussion of the rules about disclosure of legal advice, see debate on the Identity Documents Bill 2010 at www.publications.parliament.uk/pa/ld201011/ldhansrd/text/101221-0002.htm, cols 1030–33.

[87] See discussion of uncertainty below.

All of those involved in the later stages of preparation of the bill for Parliament will also be in a position to predict whether proposals in a bill or draft bill are likely to attract criticism there. GML requires[88] the development of a strategy for handling bills in Parliament, particularly in the House of Lords: the Government will normally not have a majority in this House; constitutional arguments will attract special attention from the Joint Committee on Human Rights,[89] the House of Lords Constitution Committee[90] and its Delegated Powers and Regulatory Reform Committee or the European Union Committee and its sub-committees. House of Commons Committees,[91] too, may decide to scrutinise Bills for constitutional issues and raise questions about them—in particular, the Justice Committee, and the Public Administration and Constitutional Affairs Committee. Ministers, the Bill team and parliamentary counsel will be concerned that the courts may choose to interpret provisions so as to be compatible with the rule of law or constitutional principles, and that this may mean that such provisions will not have the desired practical effect, or that it may provoke the courts into more interventionist interpretation, thus 'debasing the coinage of communication between Parliament and the courts'.[92]

D. The Houses of Parliament: The Roles of Select Committees

I have already referred to the fact that a number of Select Committees[93] in the two Houses have in their remit the scrutiny of Bills and draft Bills and of executive action and policy against broadly constitutional and rule of law criteria. Many of these committees are assisted by officials of the two Houses with legal expertise and by independent legal advisers.[94] They include the Joint Committee on Human Rights. The House of Commons' Public Administration and Constitutional Affairs, Justice, and Home Affairs Select Committees may also concern themselves with constitutional matters including the scrutiny of bills and draft bills, although formal scrutiny of bills is done by public Bill committees. The House of Lords Constitution Committee, Delegated Powers and Regulatory Reform Committee, and European Union Committee and its six sub-committees have specifically constitution-related remits. And from time to time ad hoc select committees are established to scrutinise bills and draft bills—for instance, the Joint Committee on the Draft House of Lords Reform Bill 2011–12.[95] Many of these committees

---

[88] Chapter 20.
[89] ibid, ch 10.
[90] See A Le Sueur and J Simson Caird, 'House of Cords Constitution Committee' in 1st edition.
[91] ch 7.
[92] I am grateful to Sir Stephen Laws for the information in this sentence, and for this phrase.
[93] See also ch 5 in this volume.
[94] See ch 7 in this volume.
[95] See Joint Committee on the Draft House of Lords Reform Bill, 'Draft House of Lords Reform Bill' Report of Session 2010–12, HL Paper 284, HC 1313, 23 April 2012.

have produced highly critical and independent reports on bills and draft bills and on constitutional issues. The Government is expected to respond to select committee reports within two months of publication. These responses and other correspondence between the committees and government are published. The prospect of these committees scrutinising and reporting on constitutional issues that arise in Bills and draft Bills in non-party political and non-partisan ways and the requirement for the Government to respond have effects upstream in government departments when policies are developed and instructions to parliamentary counsel are drawn up.

The House of Lords Committees are particularly significant when it comes to consideration of the constitutionality of bills. These Committees, like those in the House of Commons, are separate from and independent of the Government; however, the members of Lords committees, being for the most part appointed to the House rather than elected and subject to being re-elected, are less party political than House of Commons MPs. They conduct preventative and abstract review of Bills and draft Bills against broadly constitutional criteria; they are served by expert or legal advisers; their membership includes cross-bench, independent members; and they work in a non-partisan way.

In their reports on Bills and in reports on inquiries—for instance into *The Process of Constitutional Change*[96]—the House of Lords Constitution Committee articulates objective constitutional standards and criteria against which Bills and draft Bills may be evaluated.[97] The committee is a skilful interrogator of government on these issues. It makes recommendations as to how constitutional standards can be upheld, and it engages in dialogue and correspondence with relevant ministers about its concerns. It is highly regarded. It is the authoritative—because of its membership and its position in the Upper Chamber—articulator of widely accepted, but often previously unarticulated, constitutional standards.

The fact that the Constitution Committee and other constitutionally focused committees such as the Delegated Powers and Regulatory Reform Committee are in the second chamber is of great significance, both as regards the importance of non-partisan approaches to constitutional issues in the House of Lords and—perhaps counter-intuitively—because of its lack of electoral legitimacy, from which duties on its members to refrain from party politics in relation to the Constitution may be inferred.[98] Whether this would remain true of these

---

[96] n 33.

[97] These standards have been identified and brought together as a 'code' by J Simson Caird, R Hazell and D Oliver in *The Constitutional Standards of the House of Lords Select Committee on the Constitution*, 2nd edn (London, The Constitution Unit and The Constitution Society, 2015). See also D Oliver, 'Improving the Scrutiny of Bills: The case for standards and checklists' (2006) *Public Law* 219 for a taxonomy of the principles elaborated by the Constitution Committee in the 2001–05 Parliament, and J Simson Caird, 'Parliamentary Constitutional Review: Ten Years of the House of Lords Select Committee on the Constitution' (2012) *Public Law* 4–11.

[98] The House of Lords delaying power and its veto under the Parliament Acts over the extension of the life of a Parliament beyond five years also serve to deter the passing of such legislation for party political purposes.

Committees if the House of Lords were elected is an open question. Members of an elected second chamber would be more politically partisan, enjoying electoral legitimacy they would not experience inhibitions from politically motivated activity, and they would not include the range of expertise in law, politics and other constitution-related disciplines of the present House and its constitutional committees.

E. Some Reflections

It would be mistaken to assume that, lacking ex post facto constitutional review of statutes, the UK has no protections against abuses of parliamentary sovereignty. There are in existence elaborate organic systems of intra-governmental and intra-parliamentary constitutional preview.

Many of the measures that protect constitutionality that have been discussed in this part of the chapter protect the selfish interests of politicians, and they are obeyed for that reason: we are not in the field of pure public spirited political altruism here. Breaches of international standards bring international opprobrium, loss of reputation, and uncertainty in government as to the international sanctions that will be used against them. Breaches of conventions and codes or confrontations with parliamentary select committees charged with constitutional protection may—and again, governments do not enjoy uncertainty—generate not only public and political criticism but also withdrawal of cooperation, tit-for-tat behaviour on the part of other political actors and governmental bodies and loss of trust from the electorate.[99] These all reflect the cultures in which government operates and the realities of practical politics. The incentives to self-restraint and compromise on constitutional and rule of law issues by governments also include the avoidance of a conflict with the courts which the Government fears that it might lose, and the risk of erosion of the effectiveness of their legislation over policy outcomes which narrow 'constitutional' interpretation by the courts could lead to.

V. WHAT MORE IS TO BE DONE ABOUT PARLIAMENTARY SOVEREIGNTY?

What more, if anything, needs to be done to prevent abuse by politicians of parliamentary sovereignty? The UK is definitely at risk of Parliament passing laws which would, in most civilised Western democracies, be considered 'unconstitutional' or incompatible with broadly accepted principles of constitutionalism and the rule of law,[100] including the international rule of law. It is also at risk of

---

[99] See D Oliver, 'Psychological Constitutionalism' (2010) 69 *Cambridge Law Journal* 639.
[100] In *AXA* (n 30), Lord Hope specifically considered the possibility that the Scottish Parliament in which the Government enjoyed a large majority might seek to abolish judicial review and stated (obiter) that 'The rule of law requires that the judges must retain the power to insist that legislation

attracting international calumny if legislation is not passed to implement judgments of the European Court of Human Rights, for instance in relation to prisoner votes, noted above. An example of a near miss was the ouster clause in the Immigration and Asylum (Treatment of Claimants) Bill 2003: while the Bill would establish an independent and impartial tribunal charged with dealing with asylum claims and related issues, and would thus not be in breach of Article 6 of the ECHR, it contained a drastic ouster clause which was designed to prevent that tribunal's decisions being subjected to judicial review on any grounds, including illegality, excess of jurisdiction, and breach of procedural propriety. It is unlikely that the courts would have been able to interpret the clause in such a way as to allow judicial review of the tribunal's decisions.[101] The bill passed in the House of Commons, despite the criticisms of the ouster clause from the House of Commons Constitutional Affairs Committee in which it cited the views of judges and leading counsel given to them in evidence to the effect that the clause would be contrary to important constitutional principles.[102] The Government was ready to pursue it in the House of Lords. It was only stopped because it was known that the previous Lord Chancellor, Lord Irvine, was planning to make an excoriating attack on the clause in debate in the House; this led the then Lord Chancellor, Lord Falconer, to withdraw the clause.[103]

A. Written Constitution?

One answer to the question how can constitutionalism be protected against parliamentary sovereignty is that we should follow the examples of many Western democracies and adopt an entrenched written constitution which would limit Parliament's power either absolutely in 'eternity clauses' or by imposing special procedures on its amendment and granting the courts, or the Supreme or Constitutional Court, the power to disapply or invalidate provisions in Acts and other laws which are incompatible with the Constitution. Such a provision in a written constitution—assuming that the Constitution enjoyed broad public

---

of that extreme kind is not law which the courts would recognise' (at para 51). Scotland has a written constitution in the Scotland Act 1998 and that Act does not include the statutory power to do such things; Lord Brown in *AXA* indicated that if a devolved legislature enacted a completely arbitrary measure, eg, discriminating against red-haired people, it would be capable of challenge as offending against fundamental rights or the rule of law, at the very core of which are principles of equality of treatment. (para 97).

[101] By contrast, in *Anisminic v Foreign Compensation Commission* [1969] 2 AC 147 the House of Lords interpreted an ouster clause in such a way as not to protect a 'determination', ie a decision which was outside the jurisdiction of the Commission and was thus not a legally valid determination; the House of Lords did not admit to refusing to give effect to the clause on the basis that it was contrary to the rule of law or constitutional principles. See also *Evans* (n 43).

[102] Constitutional Affairs Committee, 'Asylum and Immigration Appeals', 2nd Report of Session 2003–04, HC 211, paras 50–71.

[103] See Sir Stephen Sedley in *Ashes and Sparks* (n 60) 128–30; Oliver 'Constitutional scrutiny' (n 84).

support—could provide the courts with the legitimacy for overriding a statutory provision which they lack under current arrangements.

It will have become clear from what has gone before that I would not favour this. I am confident that other techniques can provide reasonably good protection without bringing about the negative consequences for judicial appointments and working relationships between the courts, government and Parliament that would flow from such a move. However, my prediction is that adoption of a written constitution is quite simply not going to happen. There is a lack of consensus about what such a constitution should contain: president or monarch; established Church or not; federal state or not; second chamber elected, appointed or a mixture; regionally or nationally based—or no second chamber at all; proportional representation or first past the post; a British Bill of Rights? I see no chance of reaching broad consensus unless we reach a 'constitutional moment'[104]—unless one is precipitated by Scottish independence, which I do not expect to happen for some time, if at all.[105]

B. Stronger Parliamentary Committees

I have already noted the role of parliamentary committees in the scrutiny of bills and draft bills and reporting on concerns about matters such as the process of constitutional change. These committees could develop their roles so as to increase the pressures upstream in government against 'unconstitutional' legislation.

It is open to the House of Lords Constitution Committee to formalise its scrutiny standards, drawing them from its past reports, so that government lawyers and the Cabinet could take them on board when preparing legislation. It could, in other words, formally endorse the approach recommended by Simson Caird, Hazell and Oliver in their Report, 'The Constitutional Standards of the House of Lords Select Committee on the Constitution', referred to above. Responses by government to that Committee's concerns about breach of such standards could lead to their incorporation in the GML. And the Cabinet Manual could also incorporate guidance on complying with the standards. Such steps would strengthen

---

[104] See B Ackerman, 'The Living Constitution' (2007) 7 *Harvard Law Review* 1738.

[105] For discussion of the written constitution issue see A Blick, *Beyond Magna Carta. A Constitution for the United Kingdom* (Oxford, Bloomsbury, 2015); V Bogdanor, *The New British Constitution* (Oxford, Hart Publishing, 2009); R Gordon, *Repairing British Politics: A Blueprint for Constitutional Change* (Oxford, Hart Publishing, 2010); D Oliver, 'Review of *Repairing British Politics*' (2010) 6 *International Journal of Law in Context* 399; N Barber 'Against a written constitution' (2008) *Public Law* 11; V Bogdanor, 'Enacting a British Constitution. Some Problems' (2008) *Public Law* 38; R Brazier, *Constitutional Reform* (Oxford, Oxford University Press, 2008); D Oliver, 'Written Constitutions. Principles and Problems' (1992) 45 *Parliamentary Affairs* 135; IPPR *Written Constitution for the UK* (London, Institute of Public Policy Research, 1991); D Oliver, 'Towards a written constiution' in C Bryant (ed), *Towards a new constitutional settlement* (no place of publication, Smith Institute, 2007); see also ibid, from p 153, a formulation of the present UK constitution; KC Wheare, *Modern Constitutions*, 2nd edn (London, Oxford University Press, 1971).

the culture in favour of constitutionality in government and in Parliament. The Constitution Committee could press government to provide constitutional impact statements with bills, just as it provides environmental and regulatory statements, when a bill is lodged in the vote office. The knowledge in government that the Committee will press on this and examine those statements should, again, have effect upstream when bills are being drafted.

If such reforms were to take place and be effective the institutional arrangements in the two Houses for dealing with constitutional and human rights issues would need to be strengthened. More joint committees may need to be formed, committees would need more staffing, the clerks and officials of committees would need to cooperate and avoid unnecessary duplication of effort or missing of issues, and a proactive well-staffed legal service might be required.[106] There may need to be established lines of contact between clerks and officials serving 'constitutional' committees and parliamentary counsel and departmental lawyers.

C. A Greater Role for the Courts?

The courts could develop ways of signalling their concerns about the constitutionality or rule of law aspects of Acts, for instance by non-statutory, common law 'indications of inconsistency' with constitutional principles on the lines of section 4 of the Human Rights Act 1998, or by outlining what is wrong with a government decision and then indicating why they refuse a discretionary remedy. This technique has been adopted by the New Zealand Supreme Court in the making of 'declarations of inconsistency' under the New Zealand Bill of Rights Act 1990.[107] The making of declarations of, in effect, 'unconstitutionality' without statutory authority would no doubt generate hostile political, press and public opinion, with politicians attacking judges for interventionist and Ivory Tower approaches.[108] Such declarations would not give rise to the Human Rights Act section 10 power to remove incompatibility in remedial orders or imply that the country was in breach of its international obligations. Declarations of unconstitutionality might thus well be ignored by the executive. These points underline the precarious position of judges in the UK and may be taken to illustrate the virtues of the pragmatic justification for parliamentary sovereignty.

---

[106] See A Kennan, 'Legal Advice to Parliament', in 1st edition (cited above).

[107] See *Attorney General v Taylor* [2017] NZHC 215 in which the NZ Court of Appeal issued a formal declaration that a statutory provision depriving prisoners of the right to vote 'is inconsistent with the right to vote' under the NZBORA: for discussion of the case, see A Geddis, 'Declarations of Inconsistency under the New Zealand Bill of Rights Act 1990' on the *UK Const L* blog at https://ukconstitutionallaw.org. See also *Moonen v Board of Film and Literature Review* [2000] NZLR 9 (NZCA) and *R v Hansen* [2007] 3 NZLR 1 (NZSC), discussed by P Rishworth, 'New Zealand' in D Oliver and C Fusaro (eds), *How Constitutions Change* (Oxford, Hart Publishing, 2011) 255; and see Palmer, 'New Zealand Constitutional Culture' (n 62).

[108] See blog by Geddis (n 107) for discussion of the political reaction in New Zealand to the declaration in *Taylor*.

D. Towards an Independent Scrutiny Commission?

Looking ahead, the roles of the Constitution Committee and of other watchdog committees such as the JCHR and the Delegated Powers and Regulatory Reform Committee as guardians of the constitution and the rule of law might be less effective if the Second Chamber comes to be entirely or substantially elected. If an elected second chamber were to be established I suggest that we should consider a different approach to securing the proper scrutiny of bills on non-political constitutional related grounds: regulation of the executive's role in the legislative process. This could be done, for instance, by a Scrutiny Commission,[109] which would be a rough equivalent to the Swedish Law Council[110] or the Netherlands Council of State.[111]

My proposal is that, if the Second Chamber became less effective in constitutional scrutiny, the executive should be required by statute to submit its bills before and after each stage in the parliamentary process to scrutiny by an independent, appointed body—a Scrutiny Commission—consisting of experts on the range of government policies, and lawyers. This Commission would subject bills and draft bills to 'technocratic' scrutiny according to statutory standards[112] or criteria, for instance:

— What is the evidence base for the policy?
— Have appropriate constitutional, environmental, equality and regulatory impact assessments and risk assessments been made?
— What consultations took place before the bills was presented to Parliament?
— Is the drafting legally workable?
— Does the bill affect recognised principles of a constitutional kind—for instance, legal certainty, non-retroactivity, respect for the independence of the judiciary?
— Does the bill comply with the UK's international obligations and standards, eg as to human rights protection?

The Commission would be required to report to Parliament and to the Government on these matters and on the constitutional, legal and workability aspects of each bill within a given time of its publication. The Commission would be entitled to propose amendments. The Government would be required to publish its response to the Commission's report within a given time before it could take the

---

[109] See D Oliver, 'The Parliament Acts, the Constitution, the Rule of Law and the Second Chamber' (2012) 33 *Statute Law Review* 1.

[110] See sources in n 9.

[111] On the Netherlands, see n 8. For a proposal for an independent Law Council with fewer powers than those outlined in this section, see W Dale, *Legislative Drafting: A New Approach. A comparative study of methods in France, Germany, Sweden and the United Kingdom* (London, Butterworths, 1977) 336–37.

[112] For discussion of scrutiny standards see Simson Caird, Hazell and Oliver, *Constitutional Standards* (n 97) and Oliver, 'Improving the Scrutiny of Bills' (n 97) above.

bill to the next stage in the parliamentary process. The Commission would report again each time the bill is amended whether on the initiative of the Government or of backbench MPs. This would happen as the bill progresses through both Houses. It would be for consideration whether, in cases of grave concern about a bill, the Scrutiny Commission could impose additional delay on the progress of the legislation through Parliament. There would obviously have to be special provisions for emergency legislation.

The fact of the reporting and responding requirements placed on the government and the Scrutiny Commission at each stage in each House would introduce delay and, in particular, uncertainty as to the progress of the bill, which the Government would not welcome. This should mean that 'upstream' the bill was carefully drafted in order to avoid objections from the Scrutiny Commission. If a government is in a hurry it must do its best to avoid breaching the statutory scrutiny standards. The opposition—and government—parties in each House would be expected to draw on the Scrutiny Commission reports and government responses in their debates during the legislative process.

Such arrangements should secure that bills and draft bills are carefully considered in government before being introduced into Parliament, that they are efficiently scrutinised by the Commission against non-partisan, non-party political, constitutional standards, and that each House conducts its own scrutiny against a better information base. A Scrutiny Commission would ensure that the Government is under pressure to respond positively to scrutiny because of the delay at its disposal.

An alternative—and weaker—model for regulating the executive's role in the legislative process would be less formal: the New Zealand Legislation Design and Advisory Committee could be a model. It is appointed by the Attorney-General and its role is to enable departments to address certain standards as quality law-making through obtaining advice from that Committee. It has adopted and is currently revising a lengthy document, 'Guidelines on the Process and Content of Legislation', which sets out the standards.[113] Since such a body in the UK would have no statutory delaying or amending power, its effectiveness in protecting constitutional principles and promoting good-quality laws would depend upon the respect in which it was held, and this in turn would depend upon the quality of its appointees, their method of appointment and security of tenure and the state of the constitutional and rule of law culture in government and Parliament. A Legislation Design and Advisory Committee, if highly regarded, could be influential but, lacking statutory delaying or amending powers, less so that a Scrutiny Commission.

---

[113] See also Joseph, *Constitutional and Administrative Law* (n 10) 22.3.6 on the previous Legislation Advisory Committee.

VI. SUMMARY AND CONCLUSIONS

I have explored the ways in which the British doctrine of parliamentary sovereignty affects relationships between the courts, Parliament and the executive, and the rationales for the doctrine. The rationale most commonly cited is the democratic principle. But this explanation is unconvincing for a range of reasons: it allows for the passing of legislation that undermines the representative principle on which democracy is built, and of discriminatory laws.

It is often assumed or asserted that the UK Supreme Court should follow the American example and take upon itself to refuse to give effect to provisions in Acts of Parliament, which in their view are incompatible with the rule of law or other constitutional principles. However, importing American-style judicial review into the UK without the authority of a written constitution would bring with it severe disadvantages including conflict between the courts and Parliament, freeing politicians from their primary responsibilities in relation to constitutional matters, and the probable politicisation of the judiciary

Other countries besides the UK, including New Zealand and some of our Northern European neighbours, have developed alternative processes to judicial disapplication or striking down of statutes, and these are effective to uphold constitutional principles and the rule of law in those countries. They include the participation of independent expert bodies with responsibility for constitutional scrutiny of Bills, as in the Netherlands and Sweden, and/or careful intra-parliamentary scrutiny of Bills. The characteristics which those countries and the UK share—long-term constitutional continuity without revolution; parliamentarianism; and a pro-constitutional and pro-rule of law culture among politicians and public officials which does not treat constitutional arrangements in a partisan manner as being assets to be exploited by the government of the day—help to explain why the UK system works quite well without judicial review—if not perfectly.

I have suggested that there is a pragmatic rationale for the doctrine of parliamentary sovereignty in the UK: given the absence of a formal written constitution which enjoys public support and legitimacy, the courts know that a challenge by them to the legal validity of a provision in an Act of Parliament may itself be challenged and disobeyed by government, that in such a conflict the courts could well find themselves unable to enforce their orders, and that this may result in damage to the effectiveness of the rule of law and thus to the very constitutional foundations of the system of government in the UK. This is a reason, *both pragmatic and principled*, for the courts to refrain from disapplying or striking down statutory provisions.

In practice, parliamentary sovereignty is seldom abused by the Executive and Parliament in the UK. I have considered how temptations to do so are currently counteracted: by respect for international standards; the role of parliamentary select committees especially in the House of Lords; and internal arrangements in government and among government lawyers which promote respect for the rule of law and constitutionalism. Bearing in mind how our cousins in other jurisdictions without judicial review manage nevertheless to function relatively well as liberal democracies, there are lessons to be learned about the importance of maintaining a pro-constitutional culture in government, including among civil servants and government lawyers, and of not undermining the functions of Parliament, especially the House of Lords and its range of watchdog committees in upholding constitutional principles. Given that the UK is unlikely to adopt a written Constitution which grants the Supreme Court the right to review provisions in Acts for constitutionality, further development of the current system of constitutional preview along the lines of the arrangements in New Zealand and our northern European neighbours should take place in order to strengthen protections of constitutional principles and the rule of law.

The relationship between Parliament and the courts in the light of the doctrine of parliamentary sovereignty works relatively well and broadly in the public interest because the doctrine is a typically British pragmatic way of avoiding damaging conflict between the courts and our political bodies. Indeed, the importance of pragmatism in UK constitutional arrangements was recognised by the majority in the Supreme Court in *Miller*: they noted that 'Our constitutional arrangements have developed over time in a pragmatic as much as a principled way, through a combination of statutes, events, conventions, academic writings and judicial decisions'.[114] The doctrine works largely because other arrangements are in place to constrain government, but not by law: law is not everything. And law without a supporting culture that values the rule of law and constitutionalism is very little. The British system works for reasons of tradition and culture. We share many of these with other countries which lack judicial review of legislation. We in the UK may be tempted by siren calls from elsewhere to follow what looks like a global trend towards ex post, concrete, judicial 'control' of 'unconstitutional' laws. But unlike those other countries, the UK lacks an entrenched written constitution. In my view, it is unlikely to acquire one in the foreseeable future. Meanwhile, the UK is in a strong position to survive without court-invented ex post, concrete constitutional review, and to build on its own home-grown cultural capital in a continuous process of incremental reform.

In summary, in the absence of an entrenched written constitution establishing a constitutional court with constitutional review powers, parliamentary sovereignty can be just as, if not more, effective in preserving good government, good governance and compliance with widely accepted constitutional principles. It can avoid the negative unintended consequences of judicial review that have been experienced in other countries, as long as the culture is right and includes non-legal mechanisms that uphold constitutionality

---

[114] *Miller* (n 6) at para 40.

13

Financial Control and Scrutiny

COLIN LEE AND PHIL LARKIN[1]

I. INTRODUCTION

THERE ARE FEW areas of public policy where the formal control exercised by Parliament over the actions and decisions of the executive is greater than in relation to public money. Taxes cannot be raised without the consent of Parliament. Both the levels and purposes of most public expenditure are subject to detailed legislative control. How that money is spent is then the subject of thorough audit and wider examination in relation to value for money by independent organs established by and reporting directly to Parliament. And yet there is a vast gulf between the formal position of Parliament in relation to financial matters and the political reality. The most important decisions on public money—about the overall fiscal judgement regarding taxation, spending and borrowing and about the spending allocations for departments which endure for much of an electoral cycle—are made within government with little reference to Parliament. Financial scrutiny within Parliament has improved, and continues to develop, but faces limitations in seeking to close this gulf. This chapter describes the role of Parliament in relation to public money, explores the gap between the formal role and the political processes at the heart of fiscal decision-making and examines how far reform might reduce this gap.

Section II of this chapter seeks to draw out three distinct elements of financial control, including the legislation most relevant in relation to each of those elements. Section III focuses on formal arrangements for control and scrutiny of taxation and for approval of public expenditure subject to annual control. Section IV looks at the scrutiny functions of select committees, including the Committee of Public Accounts (PAC). Part V considers approaches to reform.

[1] The authors are grateful to the editors, Professor David Heald, Professor John McEldowney, Dr Henry Midgely, Larry Honeysett and Adam Wales for comments on a draft of this chapter.

II. THE THREE DIMENSIONS OF FINANCIAL CONTROL

A. The Constitutional Foundations of Control

i. Taxation

The 1688 Bill of Rights states 'That levying Money for or to the Use of the Crowne by pretence of Prerogative without Grant of Parlyament for longer time or in other manner then the same is or shall be granted is Illegall'.[2] This provision was a direct response to the concern that Charles II and then James II had established such a reliable revenue from taxes not subject to such control, principally Customs duties, that they did not need to have recourse to Parliament for financial support, reviving memories of Charles I's use of extra-parliamentary revenue-raising in the 1620s and 1630s. From the outset of the reign of William and Mary, Customs duties were time-limited and the rapid growth of expenditure in two decades of almost continuous war from 1689 onwards ensured that annual recourse would be required to Parliament to approve new or recurring taxes to finance the needs of the State.

Until at least the early years of the twentieth century, the greatest intrusion of the state into the everyday lives of most British subjects in peacetime came in the form of tax collection, whether through direct taxes such as the land tax and the income tax, or indirect taxes such as the Excise. This was held to justify, and continues to justify, more specific parliamentary control of taxation than many other types of law and public administration. The Bill of Rights serves as the basis for a constitutional principle which has endured—that taxation must be determined by statute law, reflecting a clear decision of Parliament. It is an area which is barely subject to administrative discretion, as asserted in a 1921 judgment of the Court of Appeal:

> If an officer of the executive seeks to justify a charge on the subject made for the use of the Crown (which includes all the purposes of the public revenue), he must show, in clear terms that Parliament has authorised the particular charge. The intention of the Legislature is to be inferred from the language used, and the grant of powers may, though not expressed, have to be implied as necessarily arising from the words of the statute.[3]

The extent of parliamentary control over taxation is further reinforced by the fact that certain taxes are limited to a single tax year, with authorisation being granted afresh in each year's Finance Act to the charging of income tax and corporation tax.[4]

---

[2] Bill of Rights 1688, c 2, Art IV.

[3] Court of Appeal's judgment in *Attorney-General v Wilts United Dairies Ltd* (1921) *TLR* 884, cited in Select Committee on Statutory Instruments, Twenty-sixth Report of Session 2016–17, HC 93–xxvi, para 1.12.

[4] Finance Act 2016, ss 2(1) and 45. The taxes with this annual character have varied over time, being formerly tea duty and sugar duty: see J Jaconelli, 'Continuity and Change in Constitutional Conventions' in M Qvortrup (ed) *The British Constitution: Continuity and Change* (Oxford, Hart, 2013) 131, fn 26.

Parliament has, however, increasingly ceded direct control over a range of taxes to devolved legislatures in Scotland, Wales and Northern Ireland.[5]

ii. The Voting of Supplies

The same principle of parliamentary control is largely replicated in relation to government expenditure subject to annual control by means of parliamentary authorisation through Supply procedure. According to Sir Thomas Erskine May, 'No constitutional change has been more important in securing popular control over the executive government than the voting of supplies by the House of Commons'.[6]

For most of the eighteenth century, taxes were rather haphazardly prescribed for particular types of military and naval expenditure, and most civil expenditure was exempt from the requirement for statutory authorisation. In 1787, William Pitt the Younger created the Consolidated Fund as one single fund 'into which should flow every stream of the public revenue, and from which should issue the supply of every public service'.[7] Although Estimates had been presented since the early eighteenth century, the creation of the Consolidated Fund paved the way for Parliament systematically to approve expenditure distinct from the approval of taxation, establishing greater control over expenditure by Parliament. The requirement for specific authorisation for expenditure was reaffirmed by the Privy Council in a seminal judgment of 1923:

> [I]t has been a principle of the British Constitution now for more than two centuries ... that no money can be taken out of the Consolidated Fund into which the revenues of the State have been paid, excepting under a distinct authorization from Parliament itself. The days are long gone by in which the Crown, or its servants, apart from Parliament, could give such an authorization or ratify an improper payment.[8]

The courts have continued to affirm the primacy of Parliament over expenditure and limited the role for the courts on spending matters.[9] It remains the case that some expenditure is paid from the Consolidated Fund without the requirement for annual authorisation by Parliament, most notably payments of interest on the National Debt, the salaries of judges and certain independent officers such as the Speaker where it would be invidious for their remuneration to be the subject of recurring parliamentary debate, and contributions to international organisations, including those arising from obligations as a member of the European Union.[10]

---

[5]   HM Treasury, 'Statement of funding policy: funding the Scottish Parliament, National Assembly for Wales and Northern Ireland Assembly', November 2015, chs 8 to 10; Northern Ireland (Corporation Tax) Act 2015; Scotland Act 2016, ss 13 to 19; Wales Act 2017, s 17.

[6]   T Erskine May, *Constitutional History of England* (London, Longmans, 1912) vol I, 155–56.

[7]   JED Binney, *British Public Finance and Administration 1774–92* (Oxford, OUP, 1958) 109.

[8]   *Auckland Harbour Board v The King* [1924] AC 318, 326–27.

[9]   J McEldowney, 'Public expenditure and the control of public finance' in J Jowell, D Oliver and C O'Cinneide (eds), *The Changing Constitution*, 8th edn (Oxford, OUP, 2015) 350–77, at 363–65.

[10]   European Communities Act 1972, s 2(3).

However, the overwhelming majority of central government expenditure is subject to authorisation in part through legislation arising from Supply proceedings. All such expenditure is authorised only for use in relation to a specified and single financial year and must 'be applied towards the service of that year'.[11] The block grants for the devolved administrations in Scotland, Wales and Northern Ireland are formally authorised in this way, although decisions on the allocation of those grants are for the devolved legislatures.[12]

iii. Appropriation

The third foundation of constitutional financial control through Parliament is provided through the process of appropriation, whereby money authorised to be released from the Consolidated Fund is authorised for spending only on specified purposes. According to Sir William Anson, 'It is not the need of supply, but of the appropriation of supply … which makes it legally necessary for Parliament to sit every year'.[13] As well as giving statutory authorisation for the release of sums from the Consolidated Fund and the associated use of resources, Parliament must also specify the purposes to which that expenditure is to be assigned.[14] There is a limited exception to this principle in the form of the Contingencies Fund, whose use is subject to Treasury rather than parliamentary control in relation to its purposes, albeit subject to statutory restrictions on the duration and scale of such funding.[15]

iv. Audit

The final foundation of the constitutional system is that of audit. The controls exercised through annual supply and appropriation would serve little purpose without Parliament having an independent assurance that expenditure was used in accordance with statute. The circle of control was first completed by William Gladstone through the passage of the Exchequer and Audit Departments Act 1866 after which, he felt, it 'could fairly be said that the office of the House [of Commons], as the real authoritative steward of public monies, had been discharged'.[16] Under the successor legislation, the Government Resources and Accounts Act 2000, each government department must prepare an account of its expenditure which is then subject to audit by the National Audit Office (NAO) under the leadership of the Comptroller and Auditor General (C&AG), who must be satisfied that the

---

[11] Government Resources and Accounts Act 2000, s 1(1). The financial year in question is from 1 April to 31 March.
[12] HM Treasury, 'Statement of funding policy, (n 5) chs 1 to 3.
[13] W Anson, *The Law and Custom of the Constitution*: Part I—Parliament (Oxford, Clarendon Press, 1897) 288.
[14] On the development and effect of appropriation, see House of Commons Procedure Committee, 'Estimates and Appropriation Procedure', First Report of 2003–04, HC 393 43, 53–55.
[15] McEldowney, 'Public expenditure' (n 9) 361–62.
[16] Parl Deb, 1 March 1866, col 1373.

accounts represent 'a true and fair view' and that 'money provided by Parliament has been expended for the purposes intended by Parliament'.[17]

B. The Procedural Rules for Financial Business

i. Introduction

Parliamentary control over finance is ultimately expressed through statute law, but the methods by which the necessary primary legislation is passed differ from those in respect of other legislation. In part, this reflects the different responsibilities of the Crown and of the two Houses in relation to financial business summed up in Erskine May's classic formulation that 'the Crown demands money, the Commons grant it, and the Lords assent to the grant'.[18] But those methods also differ as a result of specific procedures and rules of the two Houses—in some cases reinforced by statute—for certain proceedings relating to public money. In the Commons, distinct procedures emerged in the eighteenth century for the authorisation of taxation and duties ('Ways and Means') and for the authorisation of expenditure subject to annual control ('Supply'). This section explores common rules which apply to both types of proceedings.

ii. The Crown Initiative

The Crown and its ministerial representatives exercise an effective monopoly on proposals for taxation and expenditure placed before Parliament for formal consideration. Only a minister may move a Supply or Ways and Means Motion, which starts the process of legislating for authorisation (see section iv). The request from the Crown embodied in such motions establishes the upper limit on the level and duration of a tax and on the amount of a spending proposal, so that amendments which seek to increase a tax rate or extend its duration, or increase a spending total are inadmissible.[19] These limitations had their origins at a time when the amounts voted for taxation and for spending were required to be balanced within each parliamentary session, but in modern circumstances can be said to reflect the need for the Executive to retain overall control on so-called fiscal aggregates; in other words, the key overall totals for spending and taxation.[20] Governments can be defeated on individual tax and spending proposals, principally through amendments to reduce tax rates, but these were generally not matters of confidence even before the passage of the Fixed-term Parliaments Act

---

[17] Government Resources and Accounts Act 2000, s 6(1).

[18] T Erskine May, *A Treatise upon the Law, Privileges, Proceedings and Usage of Parliament* (London, Charles Knight, 1844) 324.

[19] *Erskine May: Parliamentary Practice*, 24th edn (London, LexisNexis, 2011) 782–83, 738.

[20] See Memorandum by the Clerk Assistant to the Procedure Committee for inquiry into Scrutiny of the Government's Supply Estimates, April 2016, paras 45–48.

2011, provided that the overall ability of the Government to secure authorisation for its broad approach to taxation and spending is not called into question.[21]

iii. The Primacy of the House of Commons

As the elected and representative House, the House of Commons has primacy in matters relating to financial business. This was recognised from at least the 1390s, and attempts by the Lords in the Tudor period to amend tax measures were invariably rejected by the Commons.[22] Disputes in the 1670s led to the assertion by the House of Commons in 1678:

> That all aids and supplies, and aids to his Majesty in Parliament, are the sole gift of the Commons; and all bills for the granting of any such aids and supplies ought to begin with the Commons; and that it is the undoubted and sole right of the Commons to direct, limit, and appoint in such bills the ends, purposes, considerations, conditions, limitations, and qualifications of such grants, which ought not to be changed or altered by the House of Lords.[23]

While the Lords did not substantively contest the question of its power to amend such bills thereafter, it retained the power to reject such bills outright. In 1860, the Paper Duty Repeal Bill was so rejected, leading to the establishment of the general practice maintained to this day of enshrining almost all tax proposals in a single annual Bill, now termed the Finance Bill. In 1909, such a Bill was rejected by the House of Lords, leading to the eventual passage of the Parliament Act 1911. Under that Act, a Bill certified as a Money Bill by the Speaker would be enacted a month after being sent to the Lords even if not passed by that House without amendment.[24] This provision has never been required, and many modern Finance Bills contain provisions which mean they are not certified as Money Bills. However, the House of Lords respects the primacy in respect of all bills of aids and supplies—including all Finance Bills and Supply Bills—in its procedures, usually now by-passing committee stage, and rejection is inconceivable.

iv. Preliminary Resolutions and Sessionality

All Bills of aids and supplies must be founded upon resolutions of the House of Commons, themselves based on motions moved by a minister (see section ii). The content of the Bills follows directly from those resolutions, and the scope for amendment is limited by them. From the late seventeenth century onwards, it was felt that the burden on the people implied by such legislation justified a

---

[21] Jaconelli, 'Constitutional Conventions' (n 4) 130–35; Memorandum by the Clerk Assistant, paras 49–50.

[22] J Loach, *Parliament under the Tudors* (Oxford, Clarendon Press, 1991) 2; J Hatsell, *Precedents of Proceedings in the House of Commons* III.111–20.

[23] *Commons Journal, 1667–87*, 418–23.

[24] Parliament Act 1911, s 1.

multi-stage approach to avoid over-hasty decisions. Until 1967, the resolutions had to be agreed first by a Committee of the whole House—generally either a Committee of Ways and Means or a Committee of Supply—and then again by the House before legislation could be introduced. Prior to a legal judgment of 1912 on a case initiated by a former MP, Thomas Gibson Bowles, it was understood that such preliminary resolutions constituted an initial authority for the collection of taxes, pending subsequent enactment of legislation. When the High Court ruled that an Act of Parliament alone could enshrine the consent of Parliament, the Provisional Collection of Taxes Act 1913 was passed enabling such resolutions to have provisional effect pending the passage of such legislation within a specified period, initially four months.[25] This legislation was updated in 1968 to reflect the abolition of the Committee of Ways and Means.

Until recently, the requirement for preliminary resolutions was linked to a rule of sessionality, whereby the legislation giving effect to the resolutions had to be passed in the same Session of Parliament as those resolutions. This was disapplied in respect of Ways and Means and Supply resolutions at a time when the Budget was in the Spring and Parliament moved in 2012 from autumn-to-autumn to spring-to-spring Sessions, with provisions in Standing Orders and in statute enabling resolutions passed in one Session to have continuing effect in the next Session of the same Parliament.[26]

C. The Politics of Fiscal Control

i. Budget-making, Monetary Policy and Spending Reviews

If there are few if any Parliaments with more complex and well-established systems of formal control over spending and taxation decisions than that of the United Kingdom, there are also not many in the developed world with less influence over the fundamental fiscal policy decisions about taxation, spending and borrowing. The powers of budget-making are concentrated on the Executive, and even within the Executive concentrated at the Treasury. By tradition, Budget preparations are veiled in secrecy, with Hugh Dalton resigning as Chancellor of the Exchequer in November 1947 after inadvertently leaking his own Budget in what one of his successors termed 'one of the most bizarre episodes in modern British politics'.[27] More recently, the concept of 'purdah' has been abandoned, with governments accused of leaking their own Budgets extensively, so that the 2012 Budget was described as having 'all the leak-free qualities of a teabag in a sieve'.[28] An element

---

[25] J Jaconelli, 'The "Bowles Act"—Cornerstone of the Fiscal Constitution' (2010) 69 *Cambridge Law Journal* 582.

[26] House of Commons Standing Order No 80B; Finance Act 2011, s 88; HC Deb 14 December 2011, col 832.

[27] R Jenkins, *The Chancellors* (London, Macmillan, 1998) 457.

[28] HC Deb 22 March 2012, col 932.

of Budget secrecy is warranted by the need to prevent possible tax measures being the subject of forestalling activities prior to introduction, thus reducing the revenue that can be gathered, but it extends in effect to many wider Budget decisions, minimising the influence of traditional methods of collective Cabinet agreement and of public and parliamentary consultation.

The formal parliamentary system was devised to secure a balance within a parliamentary session of the expenditure totals subject to annual control through Supply and the totals of revenue raised—the 'Ways and Means' of funding that Supply. In reality, there have been few sustained periods since 1689 when there has not been a shortfall of revenue to meet spending demands—the annual deficit. In 2016–17, this deficit (as measured by public sector net borrowing) was £48.7 billion, having reached a post-war peak of £151.7 billion in 2009–10.[29] Subject to certain broad fiscal rules considered below, the deficit is not subject to direct parliamentary control. The accumulated past deficits in the form of the National Debt are largely financed through borrowing, and payments of interest on the National Debt are paid directly from the Consolidated Fund as standing charges, not subject to annual parliamentary control through the Supply Estimates.[30] In 2015–16, the cost of debt servicing funded directly from the Consolidated Fund was £42.75 billion.[31]

Prior to 1997, the overall budgetary judgement related in considerable measure to the balance between the use of fiscal policy instruments—taxation, spending and borrowing—and monetary policy instruments, principally short-term interest rates. Much parliamentary scrutiny, most notably by the House of Commons Treasury Committee, focused on the so-called fiscal/monetary balance. In May 1997, monetary policy was largely ceded by the new Labour Government to the Bank of England. This change was given statutory effect in the Bank of England Act 1998, which set objectives for the Bank to maintain price stability and, subject to that, support the economic policy of the Government, including its objectives for growth and employment. The Government retained a power to define price stability and explain its own economic policy, but the formulation of monetary policy was wholly devolved to the Bank of England's Monetary Policy Committee (MPC), subject to reserve powers in exceptional circumstances, which have not been exercised.[32] Parliamentary accountability of the Bank's monetary policy functions takes two principal forms, both exercised largely through the House of Commons Treasury Committee. The first is scrutiny of proposed appointments of Governors and Deputy Governors, and other members of the MPC. Adverse findings by the Treasury Committee can lead to appointments not going ahead, as was seen most recently in March 2017 in the almost immediate resignation of Charlotte Hogg as a Deputy Governor following publication of a report highly

---

[29] Office for Budget Responsibility, Public Finances Databank, May 2017 (accessed 26 June 2017).
[30] National Loans Act 1968, ss 8(1), 13(1), 15(1).
[31] 'National Loan Funds Account 2015–16', HC 476, July 2016, 19.
[32] Bank of England Act 1998, ss 10 to 13, 19.

critical of her failure to declare possible conflicts of interest.[33] The second form of accountability is through regular hearings on the Bank of England's quarterly inflation reports with members of the MPC, which secure greater transparency and accountability about the positions of individual members reflecting the principle of one person, one vote within the MPC.[34]

Alongside the delegation of monetary policy to the Bank of England, there has been a less marked but still profound change in the planning of public expenditure for coming years. From 1982 until 1997, annual public expenditure plans for the ensuing financial year were announced in an Autumn Statement.[35] Public expenditure plans for departments were generally published from the 1970s onwards for the next three financial years, but the totals for years two and three were understood to be provisional and subject to subsequent revision, especially in periods of high inflation. From 1998, the incoming Labour Government switched to multi-year Spending Reviews, with spending for up to three future years largely settled in a single spending round, with the results generally announced in July. Additional spending was sometimes announced in Spring Budgets and Autumn Pre-Budget Reports (the successor to Autumn Statements), but the overall departmental totals were not revisited on an annual basis. This pattern was broadly retained by the ensuing coalition and then Conservative Governments. Although the Pre-Budget Report was renamed the Autumn Statement from 2010, this did not constitute a return to yearly spending rounds. The 2015 Spending Review, which was announced alongside the Autumn Statement in November of that year, set out spending plans up to 2019–20 for all departments, matching the duration of the Parliament expected at the time. Despite the centrality of multi-year spending plans to fiscal decision-making, Spending Reviews are not subject to parliamentary control, and have not been the subject of systematic parliamentary scrutiny. They are not always the subject of debates in the House of Commons. The timing of the Reviews has often been inimical to select committee scrutiny, with publication often shortly before the Summer recess and major commitments made early in a Parliament before new select committees have got into their stride.

ii. Fiscal rules and the Office for Budget Responsibility

The fiscal decisions at the heart of Budget-making have in recent years been made subject to rules, but these rules have been devised by successive Governments themselves with limited parliamentary involvement. In 1998, the new Labour Government put in place a Code for Fiscal Stability which required the

---

[33] Treasury Committee, 'Appointment of Charlotte Hogg as Deputy Governor of the Bank of England: Second Report', Twelfth Report of Session 2016–17, HC 1092.

[34] Bank of England, 'Transparency and the Bank of England's Monetary Policy Committee Review by Kevin Warsh', December 2014, 39.

[35] A Robinson, 'The House of Commons and Public Money' in M Ryle and PG Richards (eds), *The Commons under Scrutiny* (London, Routledge, 1988) 141–56, 144.

Government to state the rules through which fiscal policy would be operated.[36] The main rule for the period to 2008 was the so-called 'golden rule'—that, over the economic cycle, the Government will borrow only to invest and not to fund current spending. Any beneficial impact of this rule was greatly vitiated by the lack of parliamentary involvement in the development of the rules, the difficulties in measuring the start and end points of the economic cycle to which it related, and by over-optimism about revenue forecasts.[37] Since 2011, fiscal rules have arisen from the Charter for Budget Responsibility, as part of which the Government is required to set objectives relating to fiscal policy and explain how those fiscal objectives will be achieved. The Charter requires approval by a resolution of the House of Commons, but the House has no power to amend the contents.[38] The fiscal objectives and the associated fiscal rules have generally set targets expressed as financial years for public finances to be brought into balance, with each revision setting a later year for this to be achieved. The House of Commons has thus been asked to approve changes to the targets so that the targets themselves can never actually be missed,

The most significant shift in the politics of fiscal control away from the Treasury has not been to Parliament, but to a new body, the Office for Budget Responsibility (OBR), which has only limited links to Parliament. The OBR was created in May 2010, and given statutory foundations in the Budget Responsibility and National Audit Act 2011. In essence, it assumed the economic and fiscal forecasting role previously undertaken within the Treasury. The OBR provides an independent element to a process of policy formulation and associated forecasting which was previously undertaken wholly within Government, but it carries out this central role within the sphere of Budget confidentiality. As such, its role does not change the role of Parliament, although the OBR is accountable to Parliament, and to the Treasury Committee in particular, and the Treasury Committee has a unique veto over the appointment or dismissal of the Chair of the OBR and the other two members of the Budget Responsibility Committee.[39]

iii. Budgetary Cycles

The UK's budgetary cycles represent an outlier when viewed in relation to other OECD countries and when compared with the practices of the devolved administrations and legislatures of the UK. The financial year begins on 1 April, and the tax year almost a week later on 6 April, but formal statutory authorisation of both spending and taxation proposals does not usually take place until three or four months into the financial year. Ultimately, this derives from the formal control exercised by Parliament on both a sessional and annual basis. Prior to

---

[36] McEldowney, 'Public expenditure' (n 9) 354.
[37] See Treasury Committee, 'The 2007 Budget' Fifth Report of Session 2006–07, HC 389–I, paras 28–31, 22.
[38] Budget Responsibility and National Audit Act 2011, s 1.
[39] Budget Responsibility and National Audit Act 2011, Sch 1, paras 1(1) and 6(3).

the twentieth century, sessions of Parliament generally began early in the new year, with financial proceedings beginning around February and ending in the summer. Even when sessions began in autumn, the pattern of spring proposals and summer approvals was firmly entrenched. The budgetary cycle was not altered by the switch to spring-to-spring parliamentary sessions, with the requirement for sessionality being modified to allow for measures in one session to receive their statutory form in the subsequent session.

From 1993 to 1997, this pattern was modified significantly by the introduction of an Autumn Budget. This enabled tax measures to be introduced well in advance of the tax year, and to receive statutory authorisation soon after its start. From 1997, there was a reversion to a Spring Budget, and the introduction of a second major fiscal event in the calendar in the form of the Pre-Budget Report (PBR). Although the PBR was introduced primarily to allow for consultation on tax measures in advance of the Budget, it became an event of considerable political importance, with major spending and other policy announcements. From 2010, the PBR was replaced by the Autumn Statement, but with a similar mix of spending and other policy announcements to the PBR.[40] In the 2016 Autumn Statement, the Chancellor of the Exchequer, Philip Hammond, announced that he proposed to return to an Autumn Budget from 2017, 'announcing tax changes well in advance of the start of the tax year', with a Spring Statement to meet the statutory requirement for two annual fiscal and economic forecasts, but with the Spring Statement not intended as the occasion for 'significant changes … just for the sake of it'.[41] The House of Commons Procedure Committee has identified the potential for formal approval of spending to take place at an earlier juncture following the return to an Autumn Budget, remedying some of the weaknesses that flow from Estimates published after the start of the financial year to which they relate.[42]

III. FORMAL AUTHORISATION OF TAXATION AND SPENDING

A. The Budget Statement and Ways and Means Resolutions

Whether in the Spring or the Autumn, the Budget Statement remains pre-eminent in the financial business of Parliament both as political theatre and in terms of its impact on the wider political atmosphere within Westminster and beyond. The Chairman of Ways and Means (the senior Deputy Speaker) takes the chair, reflecting the former practice of the Budget statement being made in

---

[40] Chartered Institute of Taxation, Institute for Fiscal Studies and Institute for Government, Jill Rutter and others, 'Better Budgets: Making Tax Policy Better' (2017) 11.

[41] HC Deb 23 November 2016, col 910.

[42] Procedure Committee, 'Authorising Government expenditure: steps to more effective scrutiny', Fifth Report of Session 2016–17, HC 190, paras 53–62.

the Committee of Ways and Means. The Chancellor of the Exchequer usually speaks for an hour or so, without interruption, setting out economic and fiscal forecasts from the OBR, and tax proposals. As soon as the Chancellor of the Exchequer sits down, the question is usually put without debate on a motion giving provisional effect in law to tax changes having immediate effect, such as changes in alcohol and tobacco duties.[43] This can come into force by virtue of section 5 of the Provisional Collection of Taxes Act 1968, subject to requirements relating to the passage of the relevant provision of the ensuing Finance Bill.[44] This is followed by debate for the remainder of Budget day and three subsequent days on the Budget measures and fiscal and economic policy more generally. The timing of this debate can limit the opportunities for detailed scrutiny of individual fiscal measures, although debate on the second and subsequent days usually draws upon immediate analysis of the proposals and can sharpen focus on controversial measures. In March 2017, a Budget measure relating to National Insurance contribution rates was withdrawn within a week of the Budget, and a day after the conclusion of the Budget debate.[45]

The debate on the Budget generally takes place on a Motion for the Amendment of the Law, which provides general authorisation for the contents of the Finance Bill—'It is expedient to amend the law with respect to the National Debt and the public revenue and to make further provision in connection with finance'— while also limiting the scope for provision about VAT, principally by preventing zero-rating or exemptions. This motion is amendable, and has been amended on occasions, most notably in December 1994 when the Government was defeated on a proposal to increase VAT on fuel to the main rate.[46] More recently, in March 2016, the House agreed without a vote to two amendments to the motion, one to prevent a rise on VAT on solar panels and one to remove VAT at 5 per cent on women's sanitary products, the so-called 'tampon tax'.[47] The remaining resolutions are decided immediately at the end of the Budget debate without the possibility of amendment.[48] These resolutions serve as the basis for the Finance Bill which is formally introduced immediately thereafter. Some of the resolutions contain detailed provision for tax measures akin to legislation and have effect under section 1 of the Provisional Collection of Taxes Act 1968 after their passage and prior to the coming into force of the Finance Act. Some resolutions are cast in more general terms, allowing for tax measures to be contained in the Finance Bill which do not come into effect prior to enactment. Finally, some (so-called procedure) resolutions permit the Finance Bill to include measures which go beyond specific tax provisions, relating, for example, to the administration of the tax system.

---

[43] HC Deb 8 March 2017, col 822.
[44] Provisional Collection of Taxes Act 1968, s 5(2).
[45] HC Deb 15 March 2017, cols 420–21.
[46] HC Deb 6 December 1994, cols 247, 280–81.
[47] HC Deb 22 March 2016, col 1481.
[48] House of Commons Standing Order No 51(3).

B. The Finance Bill and Scrutiny of Tax Measures

The Finance Bill was formerly viewed as a centrepiece of the legislative year. In 1963, the Procedure Committee of the House of Commons noted that in recent years the House of Commons had spent about 16 days a session considering the Budget and the subsequent Finance Bill, representing 10 per cent of its business days, which the Committee concluded did not seem 'to be an undue proportion of time to spend on the most important legislation of the Parliamentary year, one by which every person in the country is affected and in which a large number of Members is interested'.[49] The 1964 Finance Bill was debated in the House for more than 20 days.[50] Now, far less time on the floor of the House is devoted to scrutiny of the Finance Bill, and far fewer Members are engaged.[51] After a second reading debate which provides an opportunity for another broad debate on the overall Budget judgement and fiscal policy generally, scrutiny is generally very low key compared with the scrutiny process for major Government programme legislation. Until the late 1960s, the Finance Bill's committee stage took place exclusively in Committee of the whole House. Since then, the Bill has usually been subject to a 'split committal', with some provisions in Committee of the whole House and the remainder considered in a Public Bill Committee, albeit a larger Committee than for other Government Bills. In recent years, two days have been set aside for the Committee of the whole House stage. Since 2011, these have generally been programmed, to provide debates on measures chosen by Opposition parties. The report stage lasts two days, longer than for most Government Bills, but a long way from the time when extended debates on report stage, with many late nights, dominated the business of the House of Commons for much of the Summer.

Scrutiny of the Finance Bill is widely seen as weak, both in comparison with that of other legislation and compared with the expectations of those with a close interest in tax and fiscal policy. The Chartered Institute of Taxation, the Institute for Fiscal Studies and the Institute for Government have recently argued that 'Parliament needs to do a better job at scrutinising Finance Bills and tax policy'.[52] There have been six main reasons ascribed for the relative weakness of scrutiny of the Finance Bill compared with other legislation. First, the legislation was subject to unusual time constraints: for almost a century from the first Provisional Collection of Taxes Act, the Finance Bill arising from a Budget in March or April had to receive the Royal Assent by the Summer Recess, limiting the time available for the legislative stages. However, as part of the switch to spring-to-spring Sessions from 2012, the law was amended to require resolutions having

---

[49] Select Committee on Procedure, 'Expediting the Finance Bill', Second Report of Session 1962–63, HC 190, para 3.

[50] J McEldowney and C Lee, 'Parliament and Public Money' in P Giddings (ed), *The Future of Parliament: Issues for a New Century* (London, Palgrave Macmillan, 2005) 78–87, at 79.

[51] W McKay and C W Johnson, *Parliament and Congress: Representation and Scrutiny in the Twenty-First Century* (Oxford, OUP, 2010), 257.

[52] 'Better Budgets' (n 40) 5.

provisional statutory effect to be passed only within seven months of the Budget in question.[53] This means that Finance Bills arising from future Autumn Budgets will have the period from around Christmas until shortly before the Summer Recess for parliamentary scrutiny.

The second factor is the lack of involvement of the House of Lords. It has been demonstrated that effective legislative scrutiny of much legislation arises from the combined efforts of the Commons and the Lords.[54] For Bills starting in the Commons, amendments tabled and debated in the Commons can pave the way for further amendments in the Lords, either in the form of Government concessions or Government defeats, followed in turn by further concessions during the stages of 'ping-pong' between the two Houses. In the case of the Finance Bill, this synergy between the two Houses is not possible. The entire weight of responsibility for amending the Bill, and for legislative scrutiny in the form of amendments, lies with the Commons.

The third factor arises from the nature of the Budget and the presumption of secrecy concerning tax measures. As a result of this, the Finance Bill often contains measures which have not been the subject of consultation and wider public discussion comparable to that seen on other elements of the Government's legislative programme. This contrast can be overstated, however. Much tax legislation is published in draft each year, well in advance of the Budget and the eventual incorporation of those provisions in the Finance Bill. Some of these proposals have been the subject of consideration by the Economic Affairs Committee of the House of Lords, which has often established a sub-committee to examine some of the provisions of the Bill published in draft, most recently considering those relating to Making Tax Digital.[55] The Treasury Committee also undertakes some work arising from draft clauses for the Finance Bill. It remains the case, however, that pre-legislative scrutiny is less systematic and less impactful in relation to the Finance Bill than for individual Bills published in draft and considered by departmental select committees or ad hoc joint committees.

The fourth constraint arises from the particular procedural rules governing proceedings on the Finance Bill described earlier, most notably the limitations on the scope for debate in the case of a Bill whose scope is pre-determined by resolutions agreed prior to its introduction and the restrictions arising from the rule of the Crown initiative. In consequence of these rules, propositions for change to the Finance Bill cannot take the form of amendments proposing a new tax or an increased rate of a current tax. This generally means that the debates on the Bills do not provide an opportunity for Opposition parties to advance alternative approaches to taxation. The procedures effectively require them to concentrate

---

[53] Provisional Collection of Taxes Act 1968, s 1(3), as inserted by Finance Act 2011, s 88.

[54] eg, M Russell and P Cowley 'The Policy Process and the Westminster Parliament: The "Parliamentary State" and the Empirical Evidence' (2015) 29 *Governance* 121.

[55] Economic Affairs Committee, 'Draft Finance Bill 2017: Making Tax Digital for Business', Third Report from Session 2016–17, HL 137.

their fire on the tax increases that are proposed, or to seek tax reductions. This disincentivises Opposition parties from making the Committee and report stages of the Finance Bill a forum for the adumbration of an alternative fiscal approach. The overwhelming majority of amendments tabled to Finance Bills are technical and drafting changes tabled by the Government. This is not to say that amendments cannot be made. In 2016, a Labour backbencher, Caroline Flint, had an amendment accepted by the Government and incorporated in the ensuing Finance Act which required large multinational corporations with significant operations in the United Kingdom to report on their profits and tax on a country-by-country basis. This arose from the work undertaken by the PAC on apparent low levels of corporation tax collected from a number of prominent multinational companies.[56]

The fifth factor is the increasing length and complexity of tax legislation. To some degree this reflects the view that tax legislation should not be unduly reliant on delegated legislation to express provisions with a concrete effect on the burdens on individuals and companies, so that the balance between primary and secondary legislation differs for tax legislation from other spheres. Also, the Treasury and HMRC are keen to include detailed and prescriptive provisions to reduce the extent to which their revenue-raising capacity is subject to the interpretative decisions of the courts. Finally, the activities which the Government are seeking to tax are themselves increasingly complex. As has been noted, many provisions 'close tax loopholes of terrifying complexity by provisions even more Byzantine'.[57] This complexity means that Finance Bills are hard to read and individual Members of the Commons, including Opposition spokespersons, find it hard to identify amendments which give rise to focused debates on the key provisions.

The final factor arises from the politics of fiscal control referred to earlier. A Finance Bill is generally seen as giving effect to a central plank of Government policy. Fiscal policy is generally so close to the heart of the conflict between the parties that cross-party alliances are less likely develop on the Bill's provisions. There have been some exceptions, including the amendment passed in 2016, especially on matters relating to tax evasion and tax avoidance. A notable amendment was also agreed to a Finance Bill during a period of minority Government in the late 1970s on the basis of a Government backbench rebellion, leading to the so-called Rooker-Wise amendment about the indexation of personal allowances.[58]

C. The Estimates and Supply Procedure

The formal activities of the House of Commons to consider and approve the Estimates have long been recognised as some of the least satisfactory of parliamentary

---

[56] HC Deb 5 September 2016, cols 132–6, 146–7; Finance Act 2016, Sch 19, para 17(6).
[57] McKay and Johnson, *Parliament and Congress* (n 51) 257.
[58] Hansard Society, 'A Numbers Game: Parliament and Minority Government', June 2017, 22.

proceedings. This partly reflects the timing and contents of the Estimates, which serve as the Government's request for approval for spending. The Main Estimates— setting out the spending totals for each Government department subject to annual parliamentary control, and divided into four categories—are usually published in April, after the financial year to which they relate has begun. They are usually approved by the House of Commons in June or early July. Any in-year adjustments are reflected in Supplementary Estimates published in February and approved in March. At the same time, the House approves preliminary outline totals for the coming financial year in the form of Votes on Account, a down payment for the coming financial year to ensure the financing of departments until the approval of the Main Estimates. The Estimates documents have been criticised for many years for their complexity and for the apparent disconnect between their content and the underlying policies and spending commitments of each Government department. Although Governments have made efforts in recent years to improve the read-across between the annual Estimates and the multi-year Spending Reviews from which they are largely derived, the documents contain little narrative and there are few concessions to the reader, with no graphical representation of the financial information.

The vast majority of the Estimates are approved without the possibility of debate in the House of Commons. There is a single roll-up motion which covers all Estimates other than those separately debated on Estimates days to approve the Estimates and then later the Supplementary Estimates. As is noted later in this chapter, debates on the three Estimates days each Session are chosen by the Liaison Committee and are on subjects usually derived from select committee reports. Although many debates, especially in recent years, have had an element relating to spending, the debate is rarely about the Estimates themselves. The approval motions are very rarely the subject of amendment, not least because the rule of the Crown initiative means that any amendment must be expressed as a proposal to reduce the approved total, and so cannot propose an increase in expenditure or a redistribution of expenditure.

The roll-up motions and the Estimates day motions are almost invariably approved without a division. They then give rise to an Appropriation Bill, which serves as the basis for the statutory authorisation of the spending totals and of their appropriation to specified purposes directly reflecting the Estimates. That Bill receives its second and third reading in the House of Commons without debate, and is similarly not debated in the House of Lords. Thus, formal authorisation of expenditure of annual spending by Parliament gives rise to only three days of debate, often on subjects only tangentially connected to spending, if at all. During the authorisation process, amendments are rarely tabled and votes are exceptionally rare, and Government defeats unknown in the modern era.[59] The process has been likened by one Member to 'rubber-stamping tablets of stone handed down by the Executive of the day'.[60]

---

[59] See HC 190 (n 42) and Memorandum from the Clerk Assistant cited in fn 17.
[60] Andrew Mackinlay MP, HC Deb 3 December 2002, col 87.

IV. SELECT COMMITTEE SCRUTINY

A. Introduction

Westminster-style democracies have been characterised by a greater emphasis on *ex post* scrutiny of Government policy and its effect and less on its *ex ante* authorisation.[61] This is evidently the case with expenditure.[62] Whilst the authorisation of expenditure is characterised by executive dominance and limited scrutiny,[63] there is considerable specialist machinery dedicated to the after the fact audit and scrutiny of public expenditure. The select committee system of the House of Commons is the primary part of this machinery with both the individual departmental select committees and the PAC playing roles in financial scrutiny.

B. The Public Accounts Committee

The PAC is Parliament's primary vehicle for scrutinising government spending. It was established in 1861, following a long struggle by Parliament to gain a greater oversight of what government money was being actually used for and the model has been widely adopted in other jurisdictions, including those without a direct Westminster lineage.[64] The PAC is appointed for the duration of each Parliament 'for the examination of the accounts showing the appropriation of the sums granted by Parliament to meet the public expenditure, and of such other accounts laid before Parliament as the committee may think fit'.[65] It shares the power of the other select committees to 'send for persons, papers and records' and,[66] like other scrutiny committees, its membership is elected (the chair by the membership of the whole House, the other members within their Parliamentary parties). But, where the chairs of other select committees are distributed between the parties in proportion to their relative strength in the House of Commons, the PAC is always chaired by an MP from the Official Opposition.[67]

The other major difference between PAC and the departmental select committees relates to resources. Where the departmental select committees are typically staffed by small teams of less than 10, PAC is supported by the NAO,

---

[61] eg, A Lijphart, *Democracies: Patterns of Majoritarian and Consensus Government in Twenty-One Countries* (New Haven, Yale University Press, 1984).

[62] A Brazier and V Ram, *The Fiscal Maze: Parliament, Government and Public Money* (London, Hansard Society, 2006) 35.

[63] eg, A Schick 'Can National Legislatures Regain an Effective Voice in Budgeting' (2002) 1 *OECD Journal on Budgeting* 19; J Wehnher 'Principles and Patterns of Financial Scrutiny: Public Accounts Committees in the Commonwealth' (2003) 41 *Commonwealth and Comparative Politics* 24.

[64] R Stapenhurst, K Jacobs and R Pelizzo, *Following the Money: Comparing Parliamentary Public Accounts Committees* (London, Commonwealth Parliamentary Association, 2014) 24.

[65] House of Commons Standing Order No 148.

[66] House of Commons Standing Order No 135(1).

[67] House of Commons Standing Order No 122B(8)(f).

so that it can draw upon the NAO's staff of around 800.[68] The NAO itself both audits the accounts of the government departments and agencies as well as conducting Value for Money (VfM) investigations on programmes or policy areas. Rather than the narrow focus on accounts that PAC's name would suggest, it is these VfM reports provide the basis of its subsequent inquiries.

The PAC is

> principally concerned with whether policy is carried out efficiently, effectively and economically, rather than with the merits of government policy. Its main functions are to see that public moneys are applied for the purposes prescribed by Parliament, that extravagance and waste are minimised and that sound financial practices are encouraged in estimating and contracting, and in administration generally.[69]

The NAO too is expected to focus on implementation rather than policy. Reflecting this distinction between policy and administration, the PAC typically interrogates civil servants, as those responsible for routine administration rather than the direction of policy, in evidence hearings. However, policy design and implementation can be hard to unravel and it is a distinction that is not always easy to maintain. As a minister in the Cabinet Office, Francis Maude MP, said:

> Sometimes … a bit of an artificial distinction is made between policy on the one hand and delivery on the other, as if they're wholly separate things and, of course, that's not the case. For a start, officials are intimately involved. On the suggestion that Ministers do policy and officials bear away the policy and execute it, first, officials are intimately involved in the development of policy—crucial to it, central to it—and, secondly, there isn't a separation; there's a continuum between policy and delivery, and there should be a whole sort of iterative process, where the two feed off each other, and you should not have a process where there's no pushback on policy if the effect of a policy is that it's very, very difficult or expensive and risky to implement it.[70]

Maude made the comments in an 'unprecedented' ministerial appearance before the PAC. In practice, both NAO and PAC have appeared willing to push the boundaries of their remits at times.

The C&AG is an officer of Parliament and, like the NAO staff, accountable to Parliament rather than the Government. However, both have their own remit; neither the NAO nor PAC could be regarded as addendum to the other.[71] This, recent evidence suggests, can make the relationship an uneasy one on occasion. In particular, PAC's staff is smaller than most other select committees. An attempt by the then-chair of the PAC to overcome this and to broaden the sources of advice available to the Committee through the appointment of Special Advisers (as the departmental select committees are free to do) was successfully opposed by the C&AG.[72]

---

[68] Though not all 800 are involved in the VfM reports on which PAC focuses.

[69] *Erskine May* (n 19) 849–50.

[70] PAC, 'Accountability for Public Money', 28th Report of Session 2010–12, HC 740, Ev 1–2.

[71] National Audit Act 1983; Exchequer and Audit Departments Act 1866; House of Commons Standing Order No 148(1).

[72] M Hodge, *Called to Account* (London, Little Brown, 2016) 33–34.

C. Other Select Committees

Whilst the PAC focuses on the *ex post* scrutiny of public spending, the departmental select committees' remits are rather broader: 'to examine the expenditure, administration and policy' of the Government department they shadow and its associated agencies.[73] To try to ensure greater consistency in the work of the select committees, the Liaison Committee—the select committee comprising the chairs of the other select committees and which deals with cross-committee issues—set out core tasks that they should seek to fulfil. Included in these core tasks is the examination of the expenditure plans, outturn and performance of the department and its arm's length bodies, and the relationships between spending and delivery of outcome.[74] To this end, the departmental select committees have both an *ex ante* and *ex post* scrutiny role. They would typically hold a hearing *ex post* on the Annual Report and Accounts in the autumn as well as considering the Main and Supplementary Estimates and the accompanying Explanatory Memorandum provided by their departments *ex ante*. In doing this, the Committee secretariats can draw on analysis provided by the small team of public accounts experts in the House of Commons Scrutiny Unit as well as on material provided by the NAO.

The departmental select committees do not have the nominal constraint over commenting on policy that the NAO and PAC do and, as such, are better placed to tie financial scrutiny to the scrutiny of government more generally. With their focus on individual departments, continuity of membership through the Parliament and dedicated staff, they can bring to bear a degree of accumulated knowledge about the way their departments operate. They also have the advantage of being able to return to topics. Whilst PAC can do this, in practice it has limited capacity to do so: because the NAO publishes around 60 VfM reports annually and the PAC will hold hearings on most of them, it has usually moved swiftly onto the next topic after completing the previous one.

However, in spite of the widespread praise for their role in scrutinising government policy more generally, there has been concern that financial scrutiny rarely has as high a prominence as the other aspects of their remit. In its report on the scrutiny of Estimates, the Procedure Committee noted that 'In practice, there is a broad variation in how this task is approached'.[75] The committees retain autonomy over their agendas but this was, critics have said, leading to inconsistency between them. In particular, it was felt that their financial scrutiny role was frequently being ignored. A Hansard Society Commission considering Government accountability to Parliament asked a committee chair why financial scrutiny had not been a more prominent part of committee activity: 'he mournfully replied that it was impossible

[73] House of Commons Standing Order No 152.
[74] House of Commons Library, 'Select Committees—Core Tasks', Standard Note SN/PC/03161 (2013) (2017 para 104).
[75] HC 190 (n 42) para 64.

to get MPs to turn up at meetings which were discussing finance because "They're simply not interested".[76] The introduction of the core tasks was in part an attempt to get the committees to address the full range of their roles and, in particular, financial scrutiny.[77] Reviewing the financial scrutiny activities of the departmental select committees suggests that this has only been partially successful. Most, though not all, committees take oral evidence on the Annual Report and Accounts: a report into the Parliament's scrutiny of government spending by the Public Administration and Constitutional Affairs Committee (PACAC) reported that 13 of the 17 main departmental Report and Accounts were the basis for hearings. The PACAC report criticised these hearings for lacking sufficient focus on financial scrutiny. They involved few questions specifically relating to the accounts and tended to wander onto matters of broader policy.[78]

The Main and Supplementary Estimates are typically dealt with by the public accounts specialists in the Scrutiny Unit—a small team providing specialist support to select committees—with scrutiny limited to the summary they provide to the committees. Any issues that they might flag would be dealt with through correspondence. Neither the scrutiny of the Annual Report and Accounts nor of the Estimates takes place as part of a full inquiry and no report is usually produced nor any recommendations made. The publication schedule for the Main Estimates and, in particular, the Supplementary Estimates, leaves little time for detailed scrutiny or a full inquiry, even if the committees were inclined to do so.[79] Committees have sometimes considered the financial aspects of a major programme or policy as part of a broader inquiry, but this is not always the case and is not usually part of a more systematic scrutiny of the expenditure of the department more generally.

Select committees' scrutiny of Estimates also provides the basis for the three Estimates Days. These are nominally an opportunity for specific Estimates to be debated by the House. In practice, however, the Estimates Days provide one of the few opportunities for select committees to have their reports debated more widely. The choice of Estimates to be debated falls to the Liaison Committee, which makes its decision on the basis of bids made by individual select committees. It is unsurprising, then, to find that the topics chosen reflect the priorities of the select committees themselves. The Procedure Committee noted that this means that they tend to focus on policy and frequently have only a cursory relevance to the Estimates.[80] In its report on the scrutiny of Estimates, the Procedure Committee described them as 'neither fish nor fowl. They are an unsatisfactory way of ensuring debates on matters of policy chosen by select committees ... and they

---

[76] Commission on Parliamentary Scrutiny, *The Challenge for Parliament: Making Government Accountable—Report of the Hansard Society Commission on Parliamentary Scrutiny* (London, Vacher Dod, 2001) para 3.11.

[77] Liaison Committee, 'Select Committees: Modernisation Proposals' Second Report of Session 2001–02, HC 590, paras 10–13.

[78] PACAC, 'Accounting for Democracy', Fourteenth Report of Session 2016–17, HC 95, para 105.

[79] HC 190 (n 42) Q 130.

[80] ibid, para 74.

are an ineffective way of allowing all Members of the House an opportunity to voice their views on aspects of the Government's spending plans'.[81] The desire to increase the attention given to select committee reports seems stronger than that to increase financial scrutiny: a recommendation by the Liaison Committee that the number of Estimates Days be increased was motivated by a desire to increase the time available to debate select committee reports rather than the Estimates themselves.[82]

V. CONCLUSIONS

The control of taxation and of public expenditure lies at the heart of Parliament's formal powers and authority. With foundations deep in the constitutional statute of the Bill of Rights, in constitutional conventions of very long-standing, backed both by court rulings and modern statute, it appears an impressive edifice. And yet it is in many ways an empty shell. Executive dominance at times is such that Parliament seems to have responsibility without power.

The seeming hollowness of formal control exercised *ex ante* is partially offset by the growing effectiveness of *ex post* scrutiny. The PAC has grown in assertiveness, drawing more creatively on the value for money work of the NAO and creating a distinct and high-profile role for itself in relation to the tax system. Departmental select committees have undertaken some valuable work of financial scrutiny, but progress is patchy at best and in increasing contrast to the wider advances of the select committee system in relation to policy, administration and public appointments. Financial scrutiny is an area where the system of departmental select committees in particular seems to be punching below its weight.

More than a decade ago, it was suggested that 'for at least the last forty years the financial procedures of the House of Commons have seemed ripe for reform'.[83] More recently, McKay and Johnson have referred to 'a series of fundamental flaws' in a set of procedures that 'has not yet been subject to really thorough overhaul'.[84] The lack of far-reaching reform seems even more stark when set against the achievements of the select committee system and the creation of the Backbench Business Committee. There has been no shortage of reform proposals; many have emerged in recent years. These can be broadly characterised as procedural, institutional and behavioural.

Much discussion of procedural change has related to the continuing value of the Crown initiative, considered by numerous select committees over the years, with others also concerned that its operation represents an inhibition on prospects for progress. Proposals have been advanced to reform Estimates days to re-establish

---

[81] ibid, para 76.
[82] ibid, para 75.
[83] McEldowney and Lee, 'Parliament and Public Money' (n 50) 78.
[84] *Parliament and Congress* (n 51) 305.

the House's focus on the substance of financial business, most recently through the suggestion of the Procedure Committee that responsibility for choosing topics be transferred from the Liaison Committee to the Backbench Business Committee.[85] There have also been suggestions that debates on Estimates should be recast to allow for more direct questioning of Ministers on the detail of individual Estimates.[86] Recent ideas for reform of proceedings on the Finance Bill have focused on the opportunities for enhancing scrutiny of the Bill during its passage, principally by using evidence-taking sessions before the Public Bill Committee begins its line-by-line work, and through more systematic and better resourced select committee scrutiny of Finance Bill proposals.[87]

The second focus of reform has been institutional. In 2006, the Hansard Society proposed enhancing the role of departmental select committee through the establishment of sub-committees to focus on finance and audit matters. These would lead on the scrutiny of the spending of their respective department and agencies, and follow up on relevant NAO or PAC recommendations.[88] It has been noted that the UK is one of the few comparable legislatures without a dedicated budget or appropriations committee that might become the *ex ante* counterpart to the PAC's *ex post* scrutiny function.[89] In 2012, two senior MPs commissioned by the then Chancellor of the Exchequer to examine ways to improve financial scrutiny, Sir Edward Leigh and Dr John Pugh, proposed the creation of such a Budget Committee to examine spending plans and propose debates for Estimates days.[90] In 2014, Professor David Heald similarly proposed the creation of a Spending and Tax Committee of the House of Commons, to facilitate greater focus on what is otherwise part of the disparate remit of the Treasury Committee.[91]

Another aspect of proposals for institutional reform has been suggestions to create more support within Parliament for financial scrutiny. Since 2002, the Scrutiny Unit within the House of Commons Service has offered increasingly thorough analysis for Members of that House, and for select committees in particular.[92] Sir Edward Leigh and Dr John Pugh in 2012 proposed the appointment of a Parliamentary Budget Officer, with a status akin to the C&AG, backed by

---

[85] HC 190 (n 42), paras 83–84.

[86] House of Commons Liaison Committee, 'Financial Scrutiny: Parliamentary Control over Government Budgets', Second Report of Session 2008–09, 3–4; HC Deb 3 July 2014, col 1080.

[87] 'Better Budgets' (n 40) 35–37.

[88] Brazier and Ram, *The Fiscal Maze* (n 62) 32.

[89] P Posner and C-K Park, 'Role of the Legislature in the Budget Process: Recent Trends and Innovations' (2007) 7 *OECD Journal on Budgeting* 12.

[90] HM Treasury, 'Options to Improve Parliamentary Scrutiny of Government Expenditure: A Report to the Chancellor' (2012) 18–19.

[91] Written and oral evidence by Professor David Heald to House of Commons Political and Constitutional Reform Committee for inquiry on Fixed-Term parliaments (2013–14) HC 976.

[92] HC 190 (n 42), para 66.

a Parliamentary Budget Office. Such an Office, modelled on the Congressional Budget Office and Parliamentary Budget Offices in other Commonwealth countries such as Australia and Canada, could build on and enhance the existing expertise in the House of Commons Scrutiny Unit, providing higher profile support for scrutiny, including of cross-cutting themes.[93]

The third approach to reform has been behavioural, stressing the need for MPs to change their attitudes to the task. A 2006 Hansard Society study characterised Parliament as an 'interested and acquiescent bystander'.[94] A 2011 report by the Association of Certified and Chartered Accountants noted that 'There remains a lack of interest among UK MPs in scrutinising government expenditure'.[95] Professor John McEldowney has argued that the 'systemic weakness at the heart of public expenditure control' is that 'gaps left by parliamentary inertia are readily filled by executive controls driven by Treasury influence'.[96] Margaret Hodge, the former chair of PAC, recently suggested that:

> Members of Parliament prefer to dissect new policy proposals rather than current budgets. The departmental select committees spend their time exploring the challenges for the future. They rarely use the reports on past and present departmental expenditure produced by the National Audit Office for the basis of an inquiry.[97]

Another recent account argued that 'the power lies within the hands of select committees, if the will is there'.[98]

However, the limited engagement by MPs individually and through select committees with financial business is a rational response to the profound mismatch between the financial decisions that matter—about multi-year spending allocations between departments and the medium-term balance between spending, taxation and borrowing—and the financial decisions that the House of Commons is asked to reach as part of its formal proceedings. The complexity of procedures, and the baffling array of distinct characteristics of financial business, provide a further barrier. At root, what really matters in the sphere of public money is not controlled by Parliament and what is controlled by Parliament does not feel as if it matters.

The financial procedures of the House of Commons and its established practice encourage a focus on retrospective examination and plans for the current financial year, reflected in the Estimates and the Finance Bill. As the Liaison Committee observed in 2009, 'existing procedures are closely geared towards examination by

---

[93] 'Options to Improve Parliamentary Scrutiny' (n 90) 20.

[94] *The Fiscal Maze* (n 62) 9.

[95] ACCA, *Parliamentary Financial Scrutiny in Hard Times*, December 2011: www.accaglobal.com/content/dam/acca/global/PDF-technical/public-sector/tech-tp-pfs.pdf.

[96] McEldowney, 'Public expenditure' (n 9) 376.

[97] Hodge, *Called to Account* (n 72) 199.

[98] R Rogers and R Walters, *How Parliament Works*, 7th edn (London, Taylor & Francis, 2015) 251.

the House of the current year's spending plans' when 'it is generally too late to have any effect'.[99] The same can be said of procedures in relation to taxation and wider planning, with procedures on the Budget and Finance Bill focused principally on the current financial year. The switch from a Spring to an Autumn Budget means that there is an opportunity for decisions to be taken further in advance of a financial year, but this would not involve a move away from the concentration of the House's formal processes on a single financial year. As Professor David Heald has argued, 'The problem we have is that we do not have a process at all for the spending review, and then we have a formal process for the Estimates'.[100] Reform efforts should be centred less on changes relating to a single financial year than on developing parallel structures that give Parliament a greater role in planning and medium-term fiscal developments. This could take the form of procedures designed to allow for debate on the OBR's medium and longer term fiscal analysis, and associated decisions on priorities for the overall pattern of taxation and the distribution of spending on a multi-year basis, with requirements on the Government to respond to those decisions in their more formal proposals for individual financial years. The absence of a Government majority in the House of Commons means that the House itself should have more chance to reshape the role of Parliament in relation to public money before the reins of Executive control are pulled tight once again.

---

[99] Liaison Committee, 'Financial Scrutiny: Parliamentary Control over Government Budgets', Second Report of Session 2008–09, HC 804, 3.

[100] HC 190 (n 42), para 27.

14

Parliamentary Scrutiny of Delegated Legislation

I. INTRODUCTION

THERE ARE TWO aspects of Parliament's place in the contemporary constitution which are, superficially at least, sometimes thought of as surprising. First, Parliament is not just a legislator; it fulfils several non-legislative functions, perhaps the most notable of which is that of scrutinising and holding to account the Government.[1] Secondly, Parliament is not even the only legislator; rule-making authority is widely distributed in the United Kingdom's contemporary 'multi-layered' constitution.[2] The issue that this chapter examines is at the intersection of these two features of Parliament's contemporary role, namely the scrutiny in Parliament of the exercise of legislative power by government. I focus in particular on just one type of law-making by the executive—delegated legislation—but much of what I say is nonetheless intended to be applicable, in modified form, to other kinds of non-Parliamentary law-making.[3]

---

* I am indebted to Jeff King and to Peter Cumper for discussions as my thinking on this topic (slowly) developed. And I am grateful to Mike Gordon, Alexander Horne and Gavin Drewry for helpful comments on earlier drafts of this chapter.

[1] For a recent statement of the range of Parliament's responsibilities, and discussion of its significance, see M Gordon, 'Brexit: The Relationship Between the UK Parliament and the UK Government' in M Dougan (ed), *The UK after Brexit: Legal and Policy Challenges* (Cambridge, Intersentia, 2017) 17: 'Parliament has a number of overlapping responsibilities: it is the sovereign legislative body, with constitutionally ultimate (and legally unlimited) power to make law in the UK; it is the forum from which a Government is established, and sustained, by virtue of possession of the continuing confidence of the House of Commons; it scrutinises official conduct, and holds the Government and its Ministers to account for their activity; and it represents the electorate, who elect constituency MPs to the House of Commons'.

[2] On the multi-layeredness of the contemporary constitution see in particular N Bamforth and Pr Leyland (eds), *Public law in a multi-layered constitution* (Oxford, Hart, 2003).

[3] For example, primary legislation by the Government under the prerogative suffers analogous legitimacy concerns to those which afflict delegated legislation (as discussed below, in particular in section III B). In contrast, one way in which legislation by the devolved legislatures can be distinguished from executive legislation is its success in meeting those same concerns, see A McHarg, 'What is delegated legislation?' [2006] *Public Law* 539.

Unlike so many other aspects of the constitution, the place of delegated legislation has not been substantially reformed in recent years, So, in some senses at least, the constitutional position of delegated legislation as described here is relatively stable: the constitutional framework under which it is enacted and scrutinised, the justifications for the practice, the reasons for caution, and even its relative significance as a mode of governance are all broadly the same now as they have been for (at least) several decades. It is important to stress, though, that this stability in the position of delegated legislation is no reason for complacency about its constitutional role. There are two reasons for concern. First, the constitutional position of delegated legislation might not be unsettled, but it is unsettling; the legitimacy of the use of delegated legislation is persistently precarious. Secondly, and of more immediacy, we are at a critical juncture where this period of stability risks coming to an end. On the one hand, it is widely accepted that withdrawal from the European Union will involve an explosion in the use of delegated legislation. The European Union (Withdrawal) Bill creates an extremely broad power to use delegated legislation to 'prevent, remedy and mitigate' what it refers to as 'deficiencies' in domestic law relating to the EU following withdrawal.[4] The White Paper preceding the publication of the Bill (at that time referred to as the Great Repeal Bill) presented this power as intended to simply to ensure that the statute book remains 'workable' and estimated that 'between 800 and 1000' statutory instruments would need to be passed under the provision. Even those reforms will involve the exercise of extensive judgment by the Government as to what counts as deficient, and what reform is needed to ensure continued workability. Furthermore, that estimate is noticeably constrained as 'workability' or 'deficiency' concerns cover only a small proportion of the likely increase in delegated legislation as a result of withdrawal from the EU. These 800 to 1000 instruments will probably be outnumbered by more *substantive* delegations to the executive as the withdrawal process unfolds, and the UK thereby reacquires competence over a range of policy areas, in the years following withdrawal. On the other hand, this imminent and dramatic expansion in the significance of delegated legislation must be understood alongside an important increase in government hostility to scrutiny of their legislative activity. It is only natural for governments to resist constraints on their power, but in recent years governments have repeatedly mischaracterised the nature and level of scrutiny, and proposed—and pledged to keep under ongoing review—reforms to reduce its effectiveness.[5]

---

[4] European Union (Withdrawal Bill) cl 7. Clause 7(2) gives an extensive (but not exhaustive) list of workability concerns, including law which is made redundant by withdrawal, laws conferring functions on EU entities which no longer have any function in domestic law and laws which make arrangements including interaction with the EU.

[5] I discuss one such mischaracterisation below (text accompanying n 43). There are further examples in the Great Repeal Bill White Paper (above, n 4), which mischaracterises the nature of delegated legislation (para 3.8) and the intensity of parliamentary scrutiny (para 3.21). The proposals to reduce the effectiveness of scrutiny were made in the Strathclyde Review (see below, text accompanying n 58). In 2016 the Government decided against implementing Lord Strathclyde's recommendations, but cautioned that it would 'have to reflect on that decision' should the House of Lords' 'discipline and self-regulation ... break down' in future. HL Deb. 17 November 2016, col 1539.

In this context, clarity about the reality of the practice of delegated legislation, realism about the constitution's potential to control it, and vigilance in protecting—at the very least—the current safeguards are more important now than at any time in recent history. With those objectives in mind, this chapter unfolds as follows. Section II explains the nature and significance of delegated legislation in the contemporary constitution. Section III develops the argument, grounded in constitutional principle, that parliamentary scrutiny is essential to the legitimacy of delegated legislation. Section IV examines and evaluates the current procedures for parliamentary scrutiny of delegated legislation and their ramifications and suggests directions in which reforms might profitably be made.

II. THE NATURE AND SIGNIFICANCE OF DELEGATED LEGISLATION

Delegated legislation is legislation made by the executive, under the authority of an empowering piece of primary legislation, commonly referred to as a 'Parent Act'. Consider this recent, haphazardly chosen, example. Section 48 of the Finance Act 2014 empowers the Treasury as follows:

> Where a major sporting event is to be held in the United Kingdom, the Treasury may make regulations providing for exemption from income tax and corporation tax in relation to the event.

And, in exercise of this power, the Treasury made the Major Sporting Events (Income Tax Exemption) Regulations 2017, which relieved from liability for income tax a range of people (players, officials, UEFA delegates and so on) involved with the UEFA Champions League Final, held in June 2017 at the National Stadium of Wales. In this example, the 2014 Act (which empowers the Treasury to legislate) is the parent Act, and the 2017 Regulations (by which the Treasury legislated) are the Delegated Legislation. The crucial feature of this arrangement is that prior to 2014, tax exemptions for sporting events could only be granted by Parliament, in primary legislation, but since 2014 the Government has a discretionary power to grant such relief itself.[6] So the Government has the power to decide which events are subject to tax relief, who in particular benefits from that relief, its duration and form, and so on. The making of delegated legislation, then, is a way of exercising discretionary executive power.

There is no formal overarching constitutional framework for delegated legislative power. Rather, the boundaries of each delegation are individually set in each Parent Act. This means that whilst each delegation follows the same basic structure as this example, the details can vary widely from one delegation to the next: the

---

[6] The exercise of the delegated power is, of course, conditioned by pressure from sports governing bodies, but this is a non-legal constraint on the discretion. For an example that pre-dates the delegation of the power, the equivalent exemption for the 2012 Champions League Final was granted by Parliament in the Finance Act 2012.

holder or holders of the power, its breadth or scope, any restrictions on its exercise, its duration, any restrictions on the purposes for which it can (or cannot) be exercised, and so on are potentially different and individually specified each time Parliament makes a delegation.

Certain forms of parliamentary scrutiny tend to be required in parent Acts.[7] The most common forms of delegated legislation involve either (what are usually called) the *affirmative* or *negative* procedures. Under affirmative procedures, statutory instruments take effect only if they are approved by one or both Houses. Under negative procedures, instruments take effect unless they are voted down by one or both Houses.[8] Different procedures are, on occasion, specified—the European Communities Act 1972, for example enacts a hybrid procedure where instruments are vulnerable to annulment unless the Government seeks prior approval. Variants on these procedures seem to have become more common in recent years.[9] In particular, some statutes require so-called *strengthened* procedures, intended to be more rigorous than the conventional approaches. For example, some delegated legislation under the Legislative and Regulatory Reform Act 2006 is subject to a *super-affirmative* procedure, laid down in section 18 of that Act, which involves a 60-day consultation period and enhanced power (in both Houses) for Committees to prevent the passage of instruments.[10]

The importance of this way of structuring legislative power in the contemporary constitution can hardly be overstated. Delegated legislation is not merely a common practice; in some senses it is fair to say that it is the standard form of law-making. A vastly greater volume of delegated than primary legislation is passed each year. Legislation is notoriously difficult to meaningfully quantify, and delegated legislation is especially difficult to count but—even taking these difficulties into account—the volume of delegated legislation speaks for itself. Since 1980, the Government's output of delegated legislation has never fallen below 1,000 statutory instruments in any given calendar year. In some years, the coalition Government (which held office 2010–15) issued more than 3,000 statutory instruments. In comparison, even the unusually active Parliaments of 1991 and 1997 passed just

---

[7] The core approaches are canvassed in more detail in R Kelly, 'Statutory Instruments', House of Commons Library Briefing Paper Number 06509, 15 December 2016, 7–11.

[8] Scrutiny in the House of Commons alone tends to be restricted to instruments about financial matters, whereas other instruments tend to be subject to the scrutiny of both houses. But there are no firm rules—for example, the Tax Credits (Income Thresholds and Determination of Rates) (Amendment) Regulations 2015 (Tax Credits (Income Thresholds and Determination of Rates) (Amendment) Regulations 2015, discussed below, Part IV) required the approval of the House of Lords.

[9] Ruth Fox and Joel Blackwell counted 16 variations of scrutiny procedure: R Fox and J Blackwell, 'The Devil is in the Detail: Parliament and Delegated Legislation' (Hansard Society, 2014).

[10] This procedure is very onerous, and—perhaps as a result—is rarely used. Instruments made under the 2006 Act are known as *legislative reform orders*. The Delegated Powers and Regulatory Reform Committee catalogued these various enhanced scrutiny procedures (they counted 11) and the differences between them in a 2012 report: House of Lords Delegated Powers and Regulatory Reform Committee, 'Special Report: Strengthened Statutory Procedures for the Scrutiny of Delegated Powers' HL 2012–13, 19.

69 Acts of Parliament. In one year, 2012, there were just 23 Acts of Parliament. An annual output of 30 to 35 Acts would count as fairly typical.

More importantly (and more interestingly) delegated legislation is often the way in which decisions of fundamental national importance are made and statutory instruments now touch every area of national life. Consider the following examples of policies which have been enacted by delegated legislation.

A. The 'Bedroom Tax'

Possibly the most controversial social policy of recent years, the measure which is variously known (by its opponents) as the 'Bedroom Tax' or (by its proponents) as the 'removal of the spare room subsidy' was introduced by delegated legislation. Housing Benefit awards are partly determined by what is known as the *appropriate maximum housing benefit* (AMHB), which effectively acts as a ceiling on the amount any applicant can receive, before being subject to a variety of possible deductions.

Primary legislation provides that this ceiling is set by the Secretary of State in delegated legislation and that this power can be exercised so that the method for setting the AMHB is not necessarily tied to applicants' actual housing costs. So, at any given time, the Housing Benefit scheme in force is determined by the Government's exercise of these delegated powers. In the Housing Benefit (Amendment) Regulations 2012, the Secretary of State introduced provisions which make the AMHB conditional on the number of bedrooms to which the claimant is entitled, and set down the formula according to which that entitlement is calculated.

In summary: Parliament, in primary legislation, decided that there would be Housing Benefit, and that it would calculated by counting back from a certain ceiling. The Government, in delegated legislation, set the method by which that ceiling would be calculated, including the decision that it would depend on an entitlement to a certain number of bedrooms, and deciding how that entitlement would be set.

B. 'Workfare'

The schemes collectively known as Employment, Skills and Enterprise Schemes, were introduced by delegated legislation.

Entitlement to Jobseeker's Allowance has—since the allowance's creation in 1995—been conditional on actively searching for work. Since 2011, this condition has been supplemented by a further requirement, according to which some claimants of Jobseeker's Allowance an also be mandated to participate in schemes designed to assist them to succeed in their search for employment. There are several such schemes; for example, the Sector-based Work Academy Scheme provides up to six weeks of pre-employment training and work experience followed by a job interview for a genuine vacancy, and the Community Action Programme involves long-term (up to six months) unpaid near full-time work placements.[11]

The legal foundations of these schemes are the Jobseeker's Act 1995, The Welfare Reform Act 2009 and the Jobseeker's Allowance (Employment, Skills and Enterprise Scheme) Regulations 2011. The effective division of labour between Parliament and the Government in those enactments is as follows: Parliament, in primary legislation, decided that there would be a Jobseeker's Allowance, that it could be backed by compulsory schemes to assist employment searches, and that failure to participate in such schemes could be sanctioned. The Government, in delegated legislation, decided what those schemes would involve, who would administer them, how they would be arranged, the circumstances in which they would be provided, the duration for which they would run, which jobseekers could be compelled to participate, what form the compulsion would take, the criteria for the application of sanctions, and the level of those sanctions.

C. The Scope of Legal Aid

That reform of the Civil Legal Aid system in the Legal Aid, Sentencing and Punishment of Offenders Act 2012 (LASPO) was intensely controversial. One way in which it constituted a rupture with the previous legal aid regime was that it reversed the way in which the range of legal services eligible for legal aid—the scope of legal aid—is determined. Previously (under the Access to Justice Act 1999), legal services were eligible for legal aid *unless* they featured on a list of excluded services (in Schedule 2 of the Act). There was, then, something like a presumption of eligibility. Now, however, under LASPO, legal services are *only* eligible for legal aid if they feature on a list of included services (in Schedule 1 of the Act). There is now something like a presumption of ineligibility. But there is an important underlying continuity: under both Acts, the scope of legal aid depends on a legally authoritative list of services. Moreover, both regimes made the content of that list subject to the exercise of delegated legislative power—each Act delegates (and delegates in almost precisely the same terms) to the Lord Chancellor the power to 'vary, omit, or add' services to the list.[12] Under the Access to Justice Act, the (then Labour) Government used this power to widen the range of claims for personal injury which were ineligible for legal aid, and to remove representation at asylum interviews from the scope of Legal Aid.[13] More recently, under LASPO the (then

---

[11] Significant parts of these arrangements were found to be unlawful, for reasons which are beyond the scope of this chapter, in *Reilly v Secretary of State for Work and Pensions* [2013] UKSC 68. They were (retrospectively) validated by the Jobseekers (Back to Work Schemes) Act 2013.

[12] Access to Justice Act 1999, ss 6 and 25; Legal Aid, Sentencing and Punishment of Offenders Act 2012, s 9.

[13] In the Community Legal Service (Scope) Regulations 2005 and Community Legal Service (Scope) Regulations 2004 respectively.

coalition) Government used their equivalent power to bring legal appeals relating to Council Tax reduction schemes into the scope of legal aid and to expand the definition of domestic violence (some family legal services are only in scope for legal aid insofar as there has been or there is a risk of domestic violence) to include patterns of incidents and coercive and controlling behaviour.[14]

The division of labour in determining the scope of legal aid is thus well established. Parliament decided that there would be legal aid, that its availability would depend (amongst other things) on a list distinguishing those legal services which are and are not in scope, and the initial content of that list. The executive has ongoing authority over the entries on the list and hence over the substance of the law on the scope of legal aid.

D. Banking Failures in the Financial Crisis

State intervention in the banking sector is one of the enduring images (and indeed was one of the defining features) of the global financial crisis of 2008. In particular, the nationalisation of Northern Rock is emblematic of that crisis. And the legislation effecting that nationalisation was delegated legislation, made by the Treasury pursuant to powers in the Banking (Special Provisions) Act 2008. This Act empowered the Treasury, for a period of 12 months, to break up or to nationalise troubled financial institutions in order to prevent serious instability in the financial system and/or to protect the public interest where public financial assistance had been given. The Treasure duly exercised (some of) these powers by (immediately) nationalising the Bank in the Northern Rock plc Transfer Order 2008.

In this instance, the emergency nature of the legislation (once the Government had decided to nationalise Northern Rock, it effectively needed legislation immediately) exposed sensitivities towards using delegated, rather than primary legislation for the nationalisation. In the House of Commons, the Conservatives opposed the nationalisation *on principle*, and explicitly criticised the Chancellor for going further than necessary by proposing 'unprecedented, sweeping, draconian powers that will let him nationalise any other bank or deposit-taking institution in Britain by ministerial fiat' rather than 'a specific Northern Rock Bill: a narrowly focused, substantive measure specific to the case'.[15] The Chancellor argued that procedural barriers ruled out such a specific bill (it would have had to be a hybrid bill, and thus impossible to pass quickly) but reassured the House that despite the Parent Act's potential application to 'a range of financial institutions', the Government had 'no intention at present to use it to bring any institution other than Northern Rock into temporary public ownership'. Nevertheless, the delegated

---

[14] Both in the Legal Aid, Sentencing and Punishment of Offenders Act 2012 (Amendment of Schedule 1) Order 2013.

[15] HC Deb 18 February 2008, col 24 (George Osborne) and HC Deb 19 February, col 160 (Philip Hammond).

powers in the 2008 Act were used a further three times in the months that followed its enactment—to nationalise Bradford and Bingley, and to transfer (some of) the retail deposit liabilities in Heritable Bank and Kaupthing to ING.[16]

The 2008 Act was a temporary measure, but the decision-making structure it set up, whereby the Government has the power to break up and nationalise banks and building societies by delegated legislation, has nevertheless been enshrined in permanent legislation. The Banking Act 2009 gives the Bank of England sweeping powers (as the 'resolution authority' for the UK banking sector) to prevent financial crises. It also transposes, the same delegated powers that were initially created in the 2008 Act. Their use should now be less likely, but the 2009 Act still makes permanent the underlying executive power to nationalise financial institutions.[17] Parliament has decided that, in certain circumstances, state intervention including possible nationalisation is an appropriate response to instability in the financial sector. But it has delegated to the executive the authority to decide when those circumstances obtain, which institutions' crises to intervene in, the level of that intervention and so on.

E. Sunset Clauses in Anti-Terror Legislation

Since the House of Lords in the *Belmarsh* case declared the detention without trial of terror suspects incompatible with Convention Rights, the policy of detaining suspects has been replaced by an executive power to impose (stringent) conditions on their daily lives.[18] Initially, under the Prevention of Terrorism Act 2005, these measures were known as control orders. They were replaced in modified form with TPIM notices by the Terrorism Prevention and Investigation Measures Act 2011. Both are, broadly speaking, the same kind of power. The House of Lords Select Committee on the Constitution characterised them together as 'extraordinary schemes of executive power which, despite the gravity of the measures at stake, stand outside of and are largely independent of the criminal justice system'.[19] But these measures have something in common beyond this substantive similarity: Control orders were—and TPIM notices are—the subject of so-called sunset clauses, under which these extraordinary powers lapse if not reviewed and renewed on a regular basis. The power to make control orders needed renewing every 12 months; the power to make their replacements, TPIM notices, needs renewing every five years.

---

[16] In the Bradford & Bingley plc Transfer of Securities and Property etc Order 2008, Heritable Bank plc Transfer of Certain Rights and Liabilities Order 2008 and Kaupthing Singer & Friedlander Limited Transfer of Certain Rights and Liabilities Order 2008.

[17] Under section 9 of the 2009 Act, the power remains exercisable under the same two conditions as in 2008. But this is accompanied by measures aimed at making it less likely that either condition will materialise.

[18] *A and others v Secretary of State for the Home Department* [2004] UKHL 56.

[19] House of Lords Select Committee on the Constitution, 'Terrorism Prevention and Investigation Measures Bill Report', HL 2010–12, 198.

Importantly—and contrary to many characterisations of these safeguards—this power to review and renew is a delegated power, exercisable by the executive. It was the Government which was obliged to review, and empowered to renew the control orders regime every 12 months, a power which it duly exercised by making delegated legislation to renew the existence of the powers every year from 2006 to 2011.[20] And it is the Government which is required to review, and empowered to renew, the TPIM notices regime every five years, a power which it duly exercised by making delegated legislation to renew the scheme in 2016.[21]

So Parliament created these broadly similar schemes of executive power in primary legislation. But beyond the initial period set by Parliament for their existence (one year for control orders; five years for TPIM notices) it is the Executive, through delegated legislation, which determines the continued existence of these schemes. This division of labour is particularly important because this reviewability has been a crucial component of the cases in favour of the introduction of each scheme: the insertion of the sunset clause in the 2005 Act was a key concession securing its passage through Parliament, and the Government was forced in Parliament to amend the 2011 Act, whose original draft did not include a sunset clause. It is, though, an often overlooked feature of these sunset clauses that the review and renewal they mandate is ultimately the responsibility of (and hence empowers) the Executive.[22]

F. New Criminal Offences

Remarkably, delegated legislation even has a dominant role in the development of the criminal law. Consider, for example, the Animal Welfare Act 2006, section 12 of which (in England) empowers the Secretary of State to make regulations as he or she 'thinks fit for the purpose of promoting the welfare of animals for which a person is responsible', including the power to create new criminal offences punishable by fines up to level 5 on the standard scale or imprisonment for up to 51 weeks. In exercise of this power, The Secretary of State in 2015 made regulations for the compulsory microchipping of dogs, including the creation of a number of new offences of unauthorised implantation of microchips in dogs, failing to register a change of ownership of a microchipped dog, failing to report the failure of or an adverse reaction to a dog microchip, and so on, all punishable by fines.

---

[20] The sunset (parent) clause is s 13 of the 2005 Act. The powers were renewed in the Prevention of Terrorism Act 2005 (Continuance in Force of Sections 1 to 9) Orders 2006, 2007, 2008, 2009, 2010 and 2011.

[21] The sunset (parent) clause is in s 21 of the 2011 Act. The powers were (first) renewed in the Terrorism Prevention and Investigation Measures Act 2011 (Continuation) Order 2016.

[22] The exercise of this power and, in particular, the way in which the Government was (politically) constrained to exercise it each year is discussed in A Horne and C Walker, 'Lessons learned from political constitutionalism? Comparing the enactment of control orders and terrorism prevention and investigation measures by the UK Parliament' [2014] *Public Law* 273, 275–76.

This may seem like an obscure example, but it is important to stress that these are genuine new criminal offences and that they were created by the executive. Furthermore, whilst its subject matter might seem obscure, this is certainly not an isolated example. The creation of criminal offences in delegated legislation is an increasingly significant feature of the modern criminal law. The Law Commission considers that 'there is little room for doubt that the granting of powers to create criminal offences through secondary legislation has been an important factor in the growth of the criminal law'. And James Chalmers, in an assessment of the growth of the criminal law, cautions against an excess of attention on primary legislation on the grounds that 'the vast majority of offences ... are created by secondary legislation'.[23] The Animal Welfare Act of 2006 illustrates the standard framework by which delegated legislation can create new criminal offences: Parliament identifies an areas where regulation by criminalisation might be appropriate, and empowers the executive to create new offences. The executive exercises its discretionary power to create those offences.

This is just a superficial survey, and by no means a systematic account of the uses of delegated legislation. Still (and this is the reason I have dwelt on each one) each of these examples is valuable on its own terms: it is individually significant that the bedroom tax, workfare schemes, the scope of legal aid, bank nationalisation, sunset clauses in anti-terror legislation and the growth of the criminal law are all determined essentially by the exercise of executive power in delegated legislation. But (and this is the reason I have canvassed a disparate variety of examples), their accumulation is important as well. They illustrate the range of fundamental areas of national life which are governed by delegated legislation. Individually and collectively these examples show the depth and breadth of the significance of delegated legislation in the contemporary constitution.

Furthermore, this law-making technique is now firmly embedded in our constitutional culture. Nearly all new Acts of Parliament delegate some degree of legislative power to the executive. For example, of the 25 Acts passed in 2016, 22 include provisions delegating to the executive a power to make Regulations. Some of are essentially trivial, like provisions empowering the Government to choose the date on which enactments come into force.[24] Others, though, have genuine substance. The Investigatory Powers Act 2016 establishes the Investigatory Powers Commissioner to oversee surveillance law, but also delegates to the Secretary of State (in section 239) the power to modify the Commissioner's functions. The Charities (Protection and Social Investment) Act 2016 creates a list of specified offences which disqualify offenders from acting as a charity trustee, but also delegates

---

[23] J Chalmers, '"Frenzied Law Making": Overcriminalization by Numbers' (2014) 67 *Current Legal Problems* 483, 489.

[24] eg, Riot Compensation Act 2016, s 12(1). They are trivial on the face of it at least; even these provisions can become problematic as failing to exercise this kind of power renders primary legislation dead letter. For a famous example of this problem, see *R v Secretary of State for the Home Department ex parte Fire Brigades Union* [1995] 2 AC 513.

to the Minister (in section 9) the power to add to or remove from that list. Others go further still. The Childcare Act 2016 is essentially a skeleton statute, which gives effect to the Government's policy of 30 hours per week of free childcare for working parents by delegating to the Secretary of State a broad power to legislate a scheme to achieve that aim. And 2016 is not atypical; in any given year, nearly all statutes delegate some legislative power; many delegate important substantive legislative power; and some are simply skeleton Acts delegating almost plenary power to the executive over some policy area or other.

We are now in a position to draw together these various observations about the quantity and quality of delegated legislation into this rough assessment of the significance of the practice: delegated legislation is the dominant rule-making technique in the contemporary constitution across most areas of national life and we are thus substantially governed by the exercise of discretionary executive powers to legislate. This has two important consequences for constitutional analysis. First (and beyond the scope of this chapter), any evaluation of the legitimacy of legislation in the contemporary constitution must take into account the centrality of delegated legislation. Secondly (and directly relevant for the project in this chapter), any evaluation of the constitutional position of delegated legislation must take it seriously, not as a peripheral curiosity, but as a—and perhaps even *the*—central form of legislation in the contemporary constitution. With that in mind, the next section sets out the argument that Parliamentary scrutiny of delegated legislation is essential to its legitimacy.

III. THE CASE FOR PARLIAMENTARY SCRUTINY OF DELEGATED LEGISLATION

In the classic contemporary analysis of delegated legislation (which is, remarkably, as relevant in its entirety today as it was when it was published 20 years ago), Gabriele Ganz famously concluded that 'delegated legislation is a necessary evil'.[25] But this, I think, understates the extent to which delegated legislation is not just necessary, and not just an evil, but also a potentially valuable and important part of political life. This is underscored by Ian Loveland, who suggests, rightly, that 'it is not possible to govern a highly interventionist unitary state solely through primary legislation'.[26] In other words, the scale and type of intervention which we expect the modern state to engage in is only possible through the use of delegated legislation.

It is of course true that Parliament does not have the time, resources, or institutional competence to (for example), articulate precisely how to give effect to

---

[25] G Ganz, 'Delegated Legislation: A Necessary Evil or a Constitutional Outrage?' in P Leyland and T Woods (eds), *Administrative Law Facing the Future: Old Constraints and New Horizons* (Oxford, Oxford University Press, 1997) 80.

[26] I Loveland, *Constitutional law, administrative law, and human rights: a critical introduction*, 7th edn (Oxford, Oxford University Press, 2015) 140.

government policy linking housing benefit with the number of bedrooms, or the detailed scope and force of compulsory schemes to help jobseekers back into work, or to distinguish between those services which should and those which should not be eligible for legal aid, or to select which financial institutions need public support in a crisis and what support they need, or to assess the continued desirability of the scheme for controlling terror suspects currently in force, or to satisfactorily determine what new criminal offences will most effectively improve animal welfare, and so on. But this is only half the story; the other, more important half, is that each of these things (or at least things like them) are precisely the kind of thing that the modern state needs to be able to do. Delegated legislation is 'necessary' not (merely) in the sense that it is unavoidable, but also in the richer sense that substantial reliance on executive rule-making is the only way to build the kind of political community we aspire to build. In other words, as Loveland observed, 'to reject altogether the process of delegated legislation … is to reject the substance of social democratic government'.[27] Nick Barber and Alison Young are right when they refer to 'a deep-seated antipathy towards delegated legislation in general'.[28] But the appropriate attitude to delegated legislation is something more nuanced than antipathy. Rather than understanding delegated legislation, with Ganz, as a necessary evil in need of constraining, we should understand it as a potentially dangerous but valuable practice whose risks need containing. Some ways of containing those risks will stem not from the fact that it is a form of legislation, but rather from the fact that it is a power exercised by the executive—and here, our concerns about the legitimate exercise of delegated legislative power will merge with more general concerns about executive power itself. But some ways of containing that risk stem precisely from the fact that it is a form of *legislative* power. These latter type of risks, and the way in which they should be contained, are the focus of this section.

At the level of constitutional principle, delegated legislation poses two risks in particular. First, but only in specific and narrow circumstances, it threatens parliamentary sovereignty. Secondly, and persistently, it violates the separation of powers.

A. Parliamentary Sovereignty

It is only natural to worry that delegated legislation interferes in some way with parliamentary sovereignty. Lord Judge pursued this line of argument in an important recent lecture, arguing that it 'is the exclusive responsibility of Parliament to make, or amend or repeal, the laws which govern' and that 'every vague skeleton bill, is a blow to the sovereignty of Parliament'. However, this argument relies on an

---

[27] ibid.
[28] NW Barber and AL Young, 'The rise of prospective Henry VIII clauses and their implications for sovereignty' [2003] *Public Law* 112, 118.

excessively broad understanding of parliamentary sovereignty. In Dicey's famous, almost canonical, formulation the doctrine insists that:

> Parliament ... has, under the English constitution, the right to make or unmake any law whatever; and, further ... no person or body is recognised by the law of England as having a right to override or set aside the legislation of Parliament.[29]

Its positive aspect is that once an Act of Parliament is properly passed it becomes law, regardless of its content or effects and however undesirable they may be. This is reinforced by its negative aspect, which asserts that no institution is competent to override the requirements of an Act of Parliament. Neither of these two limbs of parliamentary sovereignty are threatened even by expansive resort to delegated legislation. The doctrine of parliamentary sovereignty is a doctrine about supremacy, or who has the last word, and, generally speaking, delegated legislation does not impinge on Parliament's authority to have this last word. Mark Elliott has suggested that, with this in mind, we approach Lord Judge's argument more charitably, as a broad appeal to 'the spirit of parliamentary sovereignty'.[30] But even this goes too far: parliamentary sovereignty has no such spirit because concerns about who has the last word are in no way necessarily related to concerns about who speaks the loudest, or the most. All else being equal, a reticent, cautious Parliament is, in principle, just as sovereign as an activist or dominant one—in the same way that, all else being equal, a reticent and cautious individual can be just as authoritative as an overbearing and dominant one. Generally speaking, the practice of delegated legislation is entirely consistent with the demands of parliamentary sovereignty.

There is, however, one important set of delegated powers where this consistency breaks down and which were, in fact, the true focus of Lord Judge's argument. Henry VIII clauses, which are now commonplace in the UK constitution, are an important category of parent clause. They give the executive the authority to override the requirements of primary legislation and thereby directly violate the principle of parliamentary sovereignty. This tension between Henry VIII clauses and parliamentary sovereignty probably, at least partly, explains why they have always been treated with particular hostility. The Donoughmore Committee recommended in 1932 that their use be restricted to 'exceptional circumstances' and that they be subject to 12-month time limits.[31] This recommendation has not been followed; Henry VIII clauses are now a constitutional commonplace.[32] Particularly striking are those which create the power to amend statutes passed even

[29] AV Dicey, *Introduction to the Study of the Law of the Constitution*, 10th edn (Macmillan, London, 1959) 39–40.

[30] M Elliott, 'Lord Judge on Henry VIII Powers and Parliamentary Sovereignty' (14 April 2016) https://publiclawforeveryone.com/2016/04/14/lord-judge-on-henry-viii-powers-and-parliamentary-sovereignty accessed 11 July 2017.

[31] 'Committee on Ministers' Powers Report' Cmnd 4060, 1932; See Ganz, 'Delegated Legislation (n 28) 64.

[32] Henry VIII clauses are not only or necessarily found in statutes of particular constitutional interest. But for a particularly prominent recent example see cl 7 of the European Union (Withdrawal) Bill, discussed above (text accompanying n 4), which extends to the amendment of primary legislation.

after the empowering statute, *prospective* Henry VIII clauses. It is at least plausible to see retrospective Henry VIII clauses as technically compatible with parliamentary sovereignty by casting the empowering statute as the instrument overriding the previous legislation, rather than any executive legislation made under it. But this is not possible with prospective Henry VIII clauses, which straightforwardly empower the executive to override the legislature. As Barber and Young observe, a Parliament which enacts a prospective Henry VIII clause creates 'a mechanism that may be used to fetter its future incarnations'.[33] Prominent prospective Henry VIII clauses include section 2(2) of the European Communities Act 1972 and section 10 of the Human Rights Act 1998.[34] Their validity was open to doubt until relatively recently; *Thoburn* was argued partly on the basis that 'a Henry VIII clause could only be deployed to amend legislation already on the statute book at the time of the clause's enactment' and shortly afterwards, Geoffrey Marshall described the failure of this argument as 'surprising'.[35] In any event, even prospective Henry VIII clauses are now an accepted (and growing) part of the contemporary constitutional landscape. The growth of Henry VIII clauses in general, and prospective Henry VIII clauses in particular, brings with it a standing challenge to parliamentary sovereignty. So these kinds of delegated legislation—which are by no means peripheral instances of the practice— bring it into conflict with the most fundamental principle of our constitution.

B. The Separation of Powers

More generally, the practice of delegated legislation persistently violates the require- ments of another important constitutional principle: the separation of powers. As Edith Henderson noted, observance of the separation of powers is 'a necessary condition for the rule of law ... and therefore for democratic government itself'.[36] In its peculiarly British variant, the principle of the separation powers was best captured by ECS Wade, who identified three dimensions to the principle:

(a)   That the same persons should not form part of more than one of the three branches of the state ...;

(b)   That one branch of the state should not control or intervene in the work of another ...;

(c)   That one branch should not exercise the functions of another ...[37]

These demands (and in particular the first of them) are often violated in the British constitution, a fact which leads some commentators to doubt whether it counts as

---

[33] Barber and Young, 'The rise of prospective Henry VIII clauses' (n 33), 112.

[34] There are other, narrower examples too: s 20 of the Civil Contingencies Act 2004; s 1 of the Legislative and Regulatory Reform Act 2006.

[35] *Thoburn v Sunderland City Council* [2002] EWHC 195 (Admin), [2003] QB 151 [41], [49]. G Marshall, 'Metric measures and martyrdom by Henry VIII clause' [2002] *Law Quarterly Review* 493, 496.

[36] EG Henderson, *Foundations of english administrative law* (Getzville, N Y, William S Hein & Company, 1963) 5.

[37] This text is now adopted in AW Bradley, KD Ewing, and C Knight, *Constitutional and administra- tive law*, 16th edn (Harlow, Pearson, 2014) 92. It originates with Professor Wade—see, eg, ECS Wade and G Godfrey Phillips, *Constitutional Law*, 3rd edn (London, Longman, 1946) 18.

a principle of the constitution at all. But its centrepiece is its final part, the demand that functions be distributed appropriately between the legislature, the executive and the judiciary, and that formulation has undoubted normative and explanatory force in the UK constitutional tradition. There is something especially constitutionally worrying about branches of the state exercising functions which ought properly be exercised by another branch. In particular, the legislature lends a legitimacy to the law it makes which executive-made law can never achieve. Of course (most) statutory instruments and (most) statutes are all, in the final analysis, initiated and drafted within the executive branch.[38] But in order to become Acts of Parliament, Bills are subject, in public, to a sustained and systematic examination by a large institution whose composition is representative of and thus reflects society as a whole. This examination is wide-ranging, from high-level debate of the policy objectives underlying a Bill to line-by-line technical examination of its detail. The Government must explain and defend its proposals, which are vulnerable to amendment and to ongoing negotiation. Parliament is obviously deficient in each of these dimensions, but its legislative procedures are—however imperfectly—arranged around them and its Acts are the most legitimate form of law recognised by the constitution. In contrast, the executive does not share these law-making virtues.[39]

This points to the best way to understand Ganz's characterisation of delegated legislation as an 'evil', and to give principled foundations to the kind of concerns expressed by Lord Judge (above) which manifest themselves in the 'antipathy' identified by Barber and Young. Hermann Pünder recently commented that:

> Constitutional purists may complain about the shift of lawmaking authority from the legislative to the executive branch. It is at odds with the idea of the separation of powers[40]

But concern about the threat to the separation of powers posed by the practice of delegated legislation should certainly not be confined to constitutional purists. Legislation by the executive, a straightforward and potentially dangerous violation of the separation of powers, is one of the dominant rule making techniques in the contemporary constitution. This should be of concern to us all.

C. The Need for Scrutiny

What emerges from all this is that delegated legislation is, on the one hand, essential to social democracy but, on the other hand, a threat to constitutional principle. All delegated legislation violates the principle of the separation of powers.

---

[38] On which see S Laws, 'What is the Parliamentary Scrutiny of Legislation for?' in A Horne and AP Le Sueur (eds), *Parliament: legislation and accountability* (Oxford, Hart Publishing, 2016).

[39] My account of the relative virtues of Parliament and the executive as law-makers is influenced by NW Barber, 'Prelude to the Separation of Powers' (2001) 60 *Camb Law J* 59–88. Barber's account neglects the importance of the democratic virtues of Parliament, and the contrast in that dimension with the executive.

[40] H Pünder, 'Democratic Legitimation of Delegated Legislation—A Comparative View on the American, British and German Law' (2009) 58 *Int Comp Law Q* 353, 354.

A significant subset of delegated legislation—that which amends primary legislation under Henry VIII clauses—violates parliamentary sovereignty. And a part of that subset—that which amends primary legislation enacted after the empowering legislation under prospective Henry VIII clauses—violates parliamentary sovereignty in a particularly striking way.

These are the risks which the constitution must successfully manage. Some ways of managing these risks are beyond the scope of this chapter: it is essential that Parliament responsibly exercise its power to delegated legislative authority, that its exercises of that power are properly reasoned and justified, that the powers it delegates are appropriately constrained, that the selection of scrutiny procedure is rationally made and that delegated legislation—which is, after all, just another kind of discretionary executive power—is vulnerable to being struck down following judicial review.

But measures like these cannot ever amount to a satisfactory mitigation of the risks inherent in delegated legislation. And this is why: even the scrupulously lawful exercise of a power sensibly delegated by Parliament still has the constitutional flaws identified above; scrupulously lawful and sensibly constrained it may be, but it is still a violation of the separation of powers and (in the event of modifications to primary legislation) an affront to the sovereignty of Parliament.

We can now see that the core of the problem with delegated legislation is that its legitimacy is attenuated even when it is well made. So even though the practice of delegated legislation, including Henry VIII clauses (even prospective ones), is valuable and important, Barber and Young are mistaken when they warn against overstating the normative problems with delegated legislation by arguing that 'secondary legislation need not be second rate'. In terms of legitimacy, and because of the challenges it poses to fundamental constitutional principle, legislation made by the executive is *by its very nature* second rate. If the 'wrong' political actors and institutions are, albeit for good reasons, to be endowed with legislative power, it is crucial that the constitution manage that power by embedding it in processes designed to ensure that it is well exercised. The risks it poses can only be managed by scrutiny aimed at boosting its legitimacy, that is by scrutiny aimed at maximising its merits. Some degree of parliamentary scrutiny of delegated legislation is essential, because Parliament is the only institution with the law-making virtues necessary for the making of legitimate legislation.

Here, then, we run up against something of a paradox. On the one hand, the only institution competent to scrutinise the exercise of delegated legislation in order to increase its legitimacy is Parliament. But on the other hand, delegated legislation exists precisely because, and ideally is made when, Parliament cannot fulfil that function. This paradox is essentially conceptual: delegated legislation subject to the full rigours of parliamentary scrutiny would cease to be delegated legislation at all.[41] But it has important practical ramifications too. Whilst constitutional

---

[41] This problem is illustrated by the rarity of legislative reform orders (see above, n 9), which are so onerous that the procedure is rarely used because, as Fox and Blackwell (above n 9) observe, it is better for the Government to use primary legislation.

principle demands that delegated legislation be subject to Parliamentary scrutiny, the paradox alerts us to the need to moderate our expectations of that scrutiny. The best the constitution can offer will still mean that delegated legislation is a compromise with attenuated legitimacy; the challenge the constitution faces is making sure that it arrives at the best compromise it can.

What, then, would count as a good compromise? How, and how much, should delegated legislation be subject to parliamentary scrutiny? The answer is that, within the institutional limitations of Parliament brought to our attention by the paradox outlined above, the merits of delegated legislation must be subject to at least a minimal level of meaningful scrutiny in Parliament. Meaningful scrutiny has two components: public justification; and vulnerability to defeat. So procedures must be put in place which require the Government to publicly defend the merits of its delegated legislative proposals, and run a genuine, even if only small, risk of them being voted down. However, as a result of the paradox discussed above, it is not realistic to demand that *all* exercises of delegated legislative power are publicly debated and voted on. Rather, the best we can demand is that *some* delegated legislation be scrutinised in this way.

Meeting these conditions is the best we can do towards mitigating the constitutional risks of delegated legislation. They ensure that the scrutiny that does take place is meaningful. Two important consequences flow from meeting the conditions. First, Parliament would be doing all that it can, in light of available resources, to manage the risk of delegated legislation. Second, even though all delegated legislation would not be scrutinised, it would all be made in circumstances where its authors were alive to a real possibility of having to publicly justify their proposals in circumstances where they might even be voted down.

IV. THE ADEQUACY OF PARLIAMENTARY SCRUTINY OF DELEGATED LEGISLATION

Naturally the scrutiny of delegated legislation is not Parliament's highest priority. It is not glamourous work and it is (rightly) seen as subordinate to, for example, the scrutiny of primary legislation. The House of Lords Constitution Committee recently noted that there is 'little incentive for Members of either House … to spend their precious time debating' delegated legislation.[42] And Andrew Bennett MP, who served on the Joint Committee for Statutory Instruments during four decades, described it (in comments which are hardly unrepresentative) as 'one of the most boring committees I have ever sat on'.[43] Still, the parliamentary resources dedicated to this part of its role are substantial. This section outlines the intensity of those arrangements and measures them against the criteria outlined in the previous section.

---

[42] Report on Great Repeal Bill [78].
[43] AF Bennett, 'Uses and Abuses of Delegated Power' (1990) 11 *Stat LR* 23, 23.

It is important to note that although the level of scrutiny applicable to each delegated power is determined in its primary, parent, legislation, its intensity and therefore effectiveness always ultimately depends on the internal rules and arrangements of the Houses which give effect to those requirements. Here, the House of Commons and House of Lords act not as legislators but as supervisors, charged with scrutinising an exercise of law-making power by the executive, and the level of supervision they thereby impose depends on what they make of their role as supervisors. As the Delegated Powers and Regulatory Reform Committee put the point in a recent report (referring to the House of Lords, but it is true of both Houses):

> The existence of these scrutiny procedures in legislation does not in itself ensure that the House exercises its … scrutiny role. Effective scrutiny in all cases relies on the House putting in place mechanisms (for example, nominating a committee) to undertake scrutiny and report its conclusions.[44]

The bulk of this work is carried out in committee and, as ordinary parliamentary committees naturally tend to focus the bulk, indeed usually all, of their attention on primary legislation, the committees involved tend to specialise in delegated legislation. The Joint Committee on Statutory Instruments is convened in order to consider essentially every piece of delegated legislation which comes before Parliament.[45] But, importantly, its terms of reference preclude it from engaging with the policy merits of delegated legislation. Instead, it performs what is sometimes characterised as *technical* scrutiny, assessing statutory instruments against a number of specified grounds (whether or not charges are imposed, any purported retrospective effect, doubts about vires, etc) or 'any other ground which does not impinge on its merits or on the policy behind it'.[46]

---

[44] House of Lords Delegated Powers and Regulatory Reform Committee, 'Special Report: Strengthened Statutory Procedures for the Scrutiny of Delegated Powers' HL 2012–13, 19 [27]. For a good example, consider the Public Bodies Act, s 11, which creates a new type of delegated legislation, subject to enhanced scrutiny, and presupposes that there will be committees charged with reporting on draft orders (that is scrutinising and reporting *at a specific and novel stage* in the process). The Merits Committee was given this responsibility.

[45] House of Commons Standing Order No 151, House of Lords Standing Order No 73. The qualifier 'essentially' is necessary because some small but significant categories of statutory instrument are excluded from its remit in favour of other committees. In particular, House of Commons-only instruments are scrutinised by the Commons-only variant of the JCSI, Legislative Reform Orders are scrutinised by the Regulatory Reform Committee and the Delegated Powers and Regulatory Reform Committee (each of which engage in what I call 'technical scrutiny' in the text) and Remedial Orders made under section 10 of the Human Rights Act 1998 are scrutinised by the Joint Committee on Human Rights (which scrutinises for conformity with human rights).

[46] The full list is as follows:

    (i)   that it imposes a charge on the public revenues or contains provisions requiring payments to be made to the Exchequer or any government department or to any local or public authority in consideration of any licence or consent or of any services to be rendered, or prescribes the amount of any such charge or payment;

    (ii)   that it is made in pursuance of any enactment containing specific provisions excluding it from challenge in the courts, either at all times or after the expiration of a specific period;

In the House of Commons, scrutiny is the responsibility of delegated legislation committees, convened on an ad hoc basis whenever an instrument is referred to committee. The appointment of the members of these committees by the Committee of Selection is opaque, beyond the fact that their party composition reflects the composition of the House as a whole.[47] Their sessions are ordinarily capped at 90 minutes.[48] Whilst these committees might be ad hoc, they are also very frequently convened. In the 2014–15 session 216 Committee meetings considered 315 statutory instruments, and in the 2015–16 session 98 Committee meetings considered 103 statutory instruments.[49] It is important to note that many of these Committees do not engage even in any pretence of scrutiny and meet only to pass a motion that they have met—Ruth Fox and Joel Blackwell report, for example, that the meeting to scrutinise the Draft Contracting Out (Local Authorities Social Services Functions) (England) Order in March 2014 lasted just 22 seconds.[50]

Their functional equivalent in the House of Lords is the, more permanent, Secondary Legislation Scrutiny Committee. In 2014–15 this Committee reported meeting 28 times, issuing 33 reports on 1153 statutory instruments, and in 2015–16 it reported meeting 37 times, issuing 35 reports on 712 instruments. These figures make clear that, like in the House of Commons, much of this scrutiny is illusory. But these two approaches to scrutiny do have another important commonality: whilst they do not always engage in any scrutiny at all, when they do, the

   (iii)   that it purports to have retrospective effect where the parent statute confers no express authority so to provide;

   (iv)   that there appears to have been unjustifiable delay in the publication or in the laying of it before Parliament;

   (v)   that there appears to have been unjustifiable delay in sending a notification under the proviso to section 4(1) of the Statutory Instruments Act 1946, where an instrument has come into operation before it has been laid before Parliament;

   (vi)   that there appears to be a doubt whether it is intra vires or that it appears to make some unusual or unexpected use of the powers conferred by the statute under which it is made;

   (vii)   that for any special reason its form or purport calls for elucidation;

   (viii)   that its drafting appears to be defective;

[47] The allocation of members to these Committees was at one point recorded, albeit vaguely, in the Sessional Returns—see, eg, between 2009–10 and 2014–15, a practice which has now apparently ceased. It is at least clear from the attendees revealed by the minutes of these Committees that some effort is made to match Members with scrutiny within their areas of interest or expertise. There is a rare, but brief, discussion of the issue in evidence to the House of Commons Political and Constitutional Reform Committee's inquiry 'Revisiting the Wright Inquiry' in 2013: Dr Sarah Woollaston MP endorsed reforms which had aimed to match Select Committee membership with 'genuine interest and expertise' and expressed the hope that this practice (which she called 'the principle of improved scrutiny') would be extended to appointments to Delegated Legislation Committees. Her suggestion, as far as I am aware, has not been formally pursued.

[48] The qualifier 'ordinarily' is necessary because sessions scrutinising instruments relating exclusively to Northern Ireland can last an extra hour: House of Commons Standing Order No 118(5).

[49] These numbers are published each year in the Sessional Returns; they are a little imprecise, but not materially so, due to the occasional inclusion of peripheral measures which do not truly count as delegated legislation such as Church of England Measures and Appointments to the Electoral Commission.

[50] Fox and Blackwell, 'The Devil is in the Detail' (n 9).

scrutiny they engage in is scrutiny of the merits of the delegated legislation before them. In the House of Commons, proceedings in DLCs are recorded in Hansard and where there is debate, which there often is, it is generally straightforwardly partisan. Particularly controversial sittings are even attended by MPs who are not members of the committee, who can (and do) contribute to the debate but are not entitled to vote.[51] And in the House of Lords, the Secondary Legislation Scrutiny Committee expressly conceives of its own role as that of 'examin[ing] the policy merits of ... secondary legislation'.[52]

Still, none of these committees have the power to vote down instruments. They cannot even recommend that either House vote anything down. The Joint Committee on Statutory Instruments and the Secondary Legislation Scrutiny Committee can only 'draw to the special attention of the House' (which is not, to be clear, code for recommending a rejection). And when they divide (which is relatively rarely) Commons Delegated Legislation Committees vote not on a substantive motion, but only on a motion 'that the Committee has considered' the instrument before it.[53] Opposition members do sometimes persist beyond the debate and vote against even that motion, but these moves are a purely symbolic way of expressing dissent; they are not just (strictly speaking) false, as divisions always come after some kind of consideration, but they are doomed to defeat in any event as the composition of DLCs ensures the Government a majority.

In any event, the House of Commons never votes against delegated legislation.[54] In fact, outside committee, it barely scrutinises delegated legislation at all and votes only when absolutely necessary—on affirmative measures as a vote is required for the instrument to come into force, and on negative measures when the Opposition use their time allocation to force a prayer to be heard. So prayers to annul instruments subject to negative procedures almost never make it to a

---

[51] House of Commons Standing Order No 118(2).

[52] From the description of the committee on its own website: www.parliament.uk/business/committees/committees-a-z/lords-select/secondary-legislation-scrutiny-committee/role accessed 11 July 2017.

[53] The form of the motion is prescribed in House of Commons Standing Order No 118(5). In 2015–16, only 13 DLC meetings went to a division.

[54] Two apparent counterexamples are sometimes cited. In October 1979, the House of Commons annulled the Paraffin (Maximum Retail Prices) (Revocation) Order 1979. But the circumstances of this annulment are bizarre. The Deputy Speaker put the question twice in succession, during the discussion of a point of order. Hansard records (at least the second time the question was put) both 'ayes' and 'noes' but the Deputy Speaker gave it to the 'ayes' and refused to call a division despite a government protest. David Owen MP conceded for the opposition that they were the beneficiaries of 'an error' but argued—successfully—that the rules of the House required the decision to stand. HC Deb 24 October 1979, cols 586–88. And in in November 1969, the House of Commons' refused to affirm the draft Parliamentary Constituencies (England) Order 1969, the draft Parliamentary Constituencies (Wales) Order 1969, the Parliamentary Constituencies (Scotland) Order 1969 and the Parliamentary Constituencies (Northern Ireland) Order 1969. But here, the Government was required by the House of Commons (Redistribution of Seats) Act 1949 to lay before Parliament a draft Order giving effect to a Boundary Commission Report with which it disagreed. The Government duly laid the Order, recommended its defeat and voted against it. HC Deb 12 November 1969, cols 428–555. I am unaware of any modern example of a *genuine* government defeat on a delegated legislative proposal in the House of Commons.

debate (even the Opposition generally have higher priorities for their limited time), let alone a vote, and votes to affirm instruments are routinely taken without debate. And this situation is often either misrepresented or misunderstood by its participants. As Leader of the House, Chris Grayling MP once responded to complaints from the opposition about the absence of an opportunity to debate an instrument about fracking by asserting (absurdly, but without being contradicted) that their concerns were misplaced as 'Every single statutory instrument that comes before Parliament is voted on by this House and this will be no exception'.[55] More recently, and from the other side of the House, Valerie Vaz MP pursued a debate by appealing (again, absurdly, and without being contradicted) to a 'convention … that there is a debate when a statutory instrument is prayed against'.[56]

The House of Lords never votes to annul negative instruments and, in fact, rarely finds time even to debate them.[57] It can refuse, but does so only very rarely as discussed below, to affirm instruments subject to the affirmative procedure, and hence exercise an effective veto over their coming into force.

The structure of these scrutiny arrangements is complex; the committee arrangements in particular can seem impenetrable. Nevertheless, it is possible to measure their success against the criteria of meaningful scrutiny set out in the previous section: the requirements that the Government publicly defend the merits of its delegated legislative proposals, and run a genuine, even if only small, risk of them being voted down.

First, the existing scrutiny procedures are marked by a surprising aversion to merits-based scrutiny of delegated legislation. The primary and best-publicised form of scrutiny, performed by the flagship specialist committee, the JCSI, as well as (in some senses in its stead) the Regulatory Reform Committee in the Commons and the Delegated Powers and Regulatory Reform Committee in the Lords, avoids engagement with merits in favour of technical scrutiny. To be fair, this requires substantial resources and these committees do important work; vigilance that a delegate stays within the four corners of the power delegated to them is an essential form of scrutiny in itself. Still, in the current arrangements, merits-based scrutiny is secondary to this technical scrutiny. In the Commons, it is performed essentially only in committee so its public component is badly attenuated as it takes place largely out of the public eye. The delegated legislation committees are each ad hoc, usually coming into existence only to scrutinise a single piece of legislation, and therefore ephemeral. This means they—necessarily—each have a low public profile. And even within Parliament this is a low-priority and low-profile activity. The merits-based scrutiny that does occur takes place in small committee rooms, not just away from public and press attention, but also in small groups of typically

---

[55] HC Deb 5 November 2015, col 1134.

[56] HC Deb 23 March 2017, col 951.

[57] There is one unusual exception: the Lords voted to annul the Greater London Authority Elections Rules 2000 (HL Deb 22 February 2000, col 184). The measures, in the same form, were subsequently passed.

fewer than 20 attendees—all of whom know that nothing is authentically at stake. In the Lords, the Secondary Legislation Scrutiny Committee does not suffer these handicaps; it has sufficient stability to have built a certain profile. But it operates decidedly in the shadow of the JCSI. Its terms of reference are—like those of the JCSI—a list of criteria against which it should measure proposals. They are more substance-focused than those of the JCSI, and thereby make merits-based scrutiny possible, and the Committee's own self-summary of their effect is that it enacts merits-based scrutiny, but it is worth stressing they do not themselves mention or explicitly mandate scrutiny of merits. If anything, there is still a certain pressure *away* from merits-based scrutiny. The committee was, until recently, known as the Merits of Statutory Instruments Committee (or Merits Committee for short). The motivation for its name change was not a decision to move away from merits-based scrutiny; rather it was a response to the changing demands placed on the committee by the advent of Regulatory Reform Orders, a particular type of delegated legislation. But there is no doubt that it had the important consequence of diluting the connection between the committee and the practice of merits-based scrutiny.

This aversion to merits-based scrutiny has deep historical roots. The Donoughmore Committee recommended in 1932 that committee-based scrutiny followed the pattern of reporting on specified matters rather than considering the merits of any given proposal. And in the 1944 House of Commons debate on setting up the committee which was the precursor to today's arrangements, the (then) Home Secretary Herbert Morrison outlined his ambitions as follows:

> If numbers are large it will inevitably tend to become a debating assembly and it will not be easy for it to maintain that high judicial spirit which everybody has urged it should endeavour to do. It is a question of building up a tradition. If the tradition behind this Commitee is all right, then, after two or three years, we need not worry further about the committee going astray[58]

It is clear from the rest of that debate that the 'high judicial spirit' to which Morrison referred equates broadly to what is today known as technical scrutiny. The tradition that he hoped to build was essentially a tradition of aversion to merits-based scrutiny. And that ambition was amply realised and continues to dominate the nature of parliamentary scrutiny of delegated legislation today. Unfortunately, it is a tradition which rules out precisely the kind of scrutiny which constitutional principle demands.

Secondly, it is a consequence of existing practice that delegated legislation is also almost always invulnerable to defeat. Instruments are almost never rejected. Here, the House of Commons essentially plays no role. For (obvious) political reasons, it acts purely as a rubber-stamping chamber, if at all. Furthermore, the House of Lords never exercises its power to annul instruments made under

---

[58] HC Deb 17 May 1944, cols 202–99.

negative procedures. So any power to make delegated legislation subject only to scrutiny in the Commons, and any power to make delegated legislation under a negative procedure (whether one or both Houses are empowered to annul) are therefore effectively powers for the executive to legislate free from all risk of defeat. In fact, the only form of delegated legislation subject to any risk of defeat at all is that subject to a positive procedure requiring the assent of the House of Lords. But, even here, the House of Lords is very restrained in its use of its power to decline to pass a motion authorising instruments made under the positive procedure. In fact, not only is this power rarely exercised, but the House of Lords is innovative in creating ways to avoid its exercise. In the event of resistance to an instrument, it is very common for the Lords to settle on a compromise whereby the Government's proposal is affirmed but that affirmation is accompanied by a complementary *motion of regret* expressing the House's disagreement with part, or even all, of the very measure just affirmed. These 'non-fatal' motions allow the House of Lords to record (and more prominently than, for example, any debate in a Commons Delegated Legislation Committee) its opposition to government policy without entering direct conflict. Even the recent, high profile, controversy over the Tax Credits (Income Thresholds and Determination of Rates) (Amendment) Regulations 2015 turned on a non-fatal motion. The House of Lords did not formally vote down a motion to affirm the measure but instead passed a novel, conditional, motion declining to pass the measure until certain changes were made. This consistent practice of restraint even encourages the Government to claim that there is a convention preventing the House of Lords from defeating delegated legislation at all. But there is no such convention: The House of Lords passed a motion denying its existence in 1994, The Report of the Leader's Group on Working Practices concluded that there was 'never a House-wide convention', The Joint Committee on Conventions rejected its existence and the Companion to the Standing Orders and Guide to the Proceedings of the House of Lords does not even entertain the possibility.[59] And both the Constitution Committee and the Secondary Legislation Committee found that the practice did not amount to a convention in their recent responses to the Strathclyde Review.[60] This government advocacy for the existence of a convention, which will likely emerge again in future, is best understood as a (just-about) plausible sounding claim which puts political pressure on the Lords to approach their scrutinising functions with caution. There are good reasons (of political legitimacy, of deference to Parliament's decision to delegate and so on) and regrettable reasons (the realities of time pressure, perhaps

[59] HL Deb 20 October 1994, cols 356–83; Leader's Group on Working Practices, Report, HL 2010–12, 136, [148]; Joint Committee on Conventions, 'Report of Session 2005-06', HL 2005–06, 265-I; HC 2005-05, 1212-I, [228].

[60] House of Lords Constitution Committee, 'Delegated Legislation and Parliament: A response to the Strathclyde Review', HL 2015–16, 116 [26]; House of Lords Delegated Scrutiny Committee, 'Response to the Strathclyde Review: Effective parliamentary scrutiny of secondary legislation', HL 2015–16, 128 [118].

a failure to react to the ever growing importance of delegated legislation) for this caution. But it is important to notice that if caution were amplified into a convention requiring inaction, that would eliminate the only juncture at which delegated legislation faces possible defeat, and would thus be an important step towards freeing executive law-making from all effective scrutiny.

V. CONCLUSION

These observations about merits-based scrutiny and vulnerability to defeat lead us to a disappointing conclusion: despite the parliamentary resources directed towards the scrutiny of delegated legislation, that scrutiny is inadequate and fails to meet the demands of constitutional principle. There is not enough scrutiny of the merits of delegated legislation and proposals are not sufficiently vulnerable to defeat. We are, then, at the edge of a legitimacy precipice.

This is why the proposals of the recent Strathclyde Review were so potentially constitutionally damaging. In response to its (near) defeat over the Tax Credits (Income Thresholds and Determination of Rates) (Amendment) Regulations 2015, the Government commissioned Lord Strathclyde to undertake a review examining how to protect the ability of governments to secure their business in Parliament. Strathclyde expressly framed his task as that of securing the 'primacy of the House of Commons' and—without acknowledging the nature of delegated legislation or the constitutional risks it poses—set out three ways to neutralise the House of Lords' role in scrutinising legislation.[61] But this was wholly misconceived. For the reasons set out above, the status quo is already—at best—the bare minimum that the constitution can reasonably provide. Any reduction in the intensity of scrutiny would be constitutionally unacceptable. These proposals, quite rightly, were uniformly resisted by the Parliamentary Committees which examined them.[62]

As this illustrates, my conclusion has at least one surprising and unusual element; it means that, in our current predicament, constitutional principle demands that we support and buttress the House of Lords' power to scrutinise and even to reject delegated legislation. This conclusion also has ramifications for the appropriate shape of constitutional reform in this area. Constitutional principle demands a dual move towards increased merits scrutiny and greater willingness

---

[61] The three options were: (i) to remove the House of Lords from the scrutiny of delegated legislation altogether; (ii) for the House of Lords to set out for itself, in a 'clear and unambiguous way' that its veto would never be used; and (iii) to create a new statutory procedure where the House of Lords would lose its veto but could ask the Commons to think again. Strathclyde favoured the third option. Strathclyde Review: Secondary legislation and the primacy of the House of Commons (Cmnd 9177, 2015). HL Deb 17 November 2016, col 1539.

[62] House of Lords Constitution Committee, 'Delegated Legislation and Parliament: A response to the Strathclyde Review',(n 65); House of Lords Delegated Powers and Regulatory Reform Committee, 'Special Report: Response to the Strathclyde Review', HL 2015–16, 119; House of Lords Delegated Scrutiny Committee, 'Response to the Strathclyde Review: Effective parliamentary scrutiny of secondary legislation', (n 65).

to vote down delegated legislation. Either House could conceivably provide the former, either by shifting the emphasis of existing procedures away from technical- and towards merits-scrutiny or by creating new fora for merits-based scrutiny. Realistically, under current constitutional arrangements, only the House of Lords could be expected to provide the latter, and demonstrate a greater willingness to resist delegated legislation, even if only rarely, or cautiously.

The likely increase in delegated legislation which will accompany withdrawal from the European Union makes such reform more pressing, but also more possible. It makes it more pressing because it heralds a surge in the quantity and significance of delegated legislation in the coming years, which will exacerbate the constitutional problems inherent in the existing scrutiny arrangements. It makes it more possible for (at least) two reasons. First, it is likely to free up some parliamentary resources. Competition for those resources will be fierce, but some (for example, those currently directed towards the scrutiny of incoming European Law) could be redirected to deepen scrutiny of delegated legislation. Secondly, we are entering a constitutional moment which, by necessity, will be accommodating of innovation.[63] Whilst concrete proposals for such innovation are beyond the scope of this chapter, it has at least pointed towards their shape: the House of Lords ought to consider reworking its institutional arrangements to underwrite greater assertiveness in considering the use of (even if not actually using) its power to vote down delegated legislation, and focus more attention on merits- rather than technical-scrutiny; and the House of Commons ought to consider greater systematisation of its existing mechanisms for merits-scrutiny so that the existing efforts both of Opposition MP's in arguing against delegated legislation *and* Government ministers in publicly articulating the justification for their choices can have a greater legitimating impact on the practice of delegated legislation.

Delegated legislation dominates the contemporary constitutional landscape and, under the current arrangements, it poses a pressing challenge to the legitimacy of our constitutional order. That challenge can be met, but achieving (and then maintaining) the legitimacy of the practice of delegated legislation will require not just an appreciation of its value, but also honesty about the dangers it poses and imagination about the ways in which it can be managed. Parliament will necessarily be at the heart of the response to this challenge in the coming years.

---

[63] The term 'constitutional moment' is becoming something of a term of art, albeit inconsistently. For Bruce Ackerman, it refers to a period of intense public interest in (certain aspects) of the constitution, resulting in constitutional change. BA Ackerman, *We the People, volume 1: Foundations* (Cambridge, Mass, Belknap Press, 1993). In the UK tradition, Dawn Oliver uses the same term slightly differently, to capture a period of pressure for constitutional change: D Oliver, 'Politics, Law and Constitutional Moments in the UK' in David Feldman (ed), *Law in Politics, Politics in Law* (Oxford, Hart Publishing, 2013). The coming years may well be a constitutional moment in both of these senses, but I do not mean to use it as a term of art here. I mean simply a period of time where the constitution is open to reform—regardless of public interest or pressure.

Index

Introductory Note

References such as '178–79' indicate (not necessarily continuous) discussion of a topic across a range of pages. Wherever possible in the case of topics with many references, these have either been divided into sub-topics or only the most significant discussions of the topic are listed. Because the entire work is about 'Parliament', the use of this term (and certain others which occur constantly throughout the book) as an entry point has been restricted. Information will be found under the corresponding detailed topics.